Political Econor
Early Modern N

Against the backdrop of England's emergence as a major economic power, the development of early modern capitalism in general and the transformation of the Mediterranean, Maria Fusaro presents a new perspective on the onset of Venetian decline. Examining the significant commercial relationship between these two European empires during the period 1450–1700, Fusaro demonstrates how Venice's social, political and economic circumstances shaped the English mercantile community in unique ways. By focusing on the commercial interaction between Venice and England, she also re-establishes the analysis of the maritime political economy as an essential constituent of the Venetian state political economy. This challenging interpretation of some classic issues of early modern history will be of profound interest to economic, social and legal historians and provides a stimulating addition to current debates in imperial history, especially on the economic relationship between different empires, and the socio-economic interaction between 'rulers and ruled'.

Maria Fusaro is Associate Professor (Reader) in Early Modern European History and directs the Centre for Maritime Historical Studies at the University of Exeter. She has published extensively in English and Italian, and is co-editor of Trade and Cultural Exchange in the Early Modern Mediterranean: Braudel's Maritime Legacy and Maritime History as Global History.

Political Economies of Empire in the Early Modern Mediterranean

The Decline of Venice and the Rise of England, 1450–1700

Maria Fusaro

University of Exeter

CAMBRIDGE
UNIVERSITY PRESS

CAMBRIDGE
UNIVERSITY PRESS

University Printing House, Cambridge CB2 8BS, United Kingdom

One Liberty Plaza, 20th Floor, New York, NY 10006, USA

477 Williamstown Road, Port Melbourne, VIC 3207, Australia

4843/24, 2nd Floor, Ansari Road, Daryaganj, Delhi - 110002, India

79 Anson Road, #06-04/06, Singapore 079906

Cambridge University Press is part of the University of Cambridge.

It furthers the University's mission by disseminating knowledge in the pursuit of education, learning and research at the highest international levels of excellence.

www.cambridge.org
Information on this title: www.cambridge.org/9781107630383

First published 2015
First paperback edition 2017

A catalogue record for this publication is available from the British Library

Library of Congress Cataloging in Publication data
Fusaro, Maria.
Political economies of empire in the early modern Mediterranean : the decline of Venice and the rise of England, 1450–1700 / Maria Fusaro.
   pages   cm
Includes bibliographical references and index.
ISBN 978-1-107-06052-4 (hardback)
1. Mediterranean Region – Commerce – History.   2. Venice – Commerce – History.   3. Great Britain – Commerce – History.   4. Venice – Foreign relations – Great Britain.   5. Great Britain – Foreign relations – Venice.
6. Mediterranean Region – History – 1517–1789.   I. Title.
HF3495.F87   2015
382.09182´2–dc23

2014042938

ISBN 978-1-107-06052-4 Hardback
ISBN 978-1-107-63038-3 Paperback

Contents

Figures, maps and graphs

Preface

It is a well-known fact that Venice has always held a special place in the English imagination: in the early modern period it was the favourite foreign setting of Shakespearian plays, later it became the preferred Italian destination of the Grand Tour and today it is a firm favourite for short-break holidays.

But Venice played a far bigger role in English history, especially in the evolution of its economy and politics. The extremely active Venetian propaganda machine found in early modern England the most receptive audience for its self-fashioned narrative of the Republic as the living embodiment of the Aristotelian/Polybian ideal form of state: the perfect mix of popular, aristocratic and monarchic elements. This long-standing interest and attraction towards the Venetian experience started during the Tudor period, was strengthened in the Stuart era and remained powerful throughout the civil wars up until the end of the seventeenth century. After the Restoration the so-called 'myth of Venice' started to be supplanted by the 'anti-myth', which saw in Venice the embodiment of a decadent state, oozing moral corruption and sexual scandal, an image of decay reinforced in the public imagination by its long decline throughout the course of the eighteenth century. After the fall of the Republic in 1797, this negative image was reinforced by nineteenth-century writers, from Byron onwards. Still, this critical attitude towards the Republic and its history did not seem to touch the reputation of Venice's past maritime and commercial glories, which continued to be admired in Britain and quoted as an example of what could be achieved through the proper administration and defence of a strong maritime empire. In the middle of the nineteenth century, John Ruskin opened his *Stones of Venice* with remarks that openly acknowledge the debt which the British empire owed the Venetian, and the lessons it should learn from its example:

Since first the dominion of men was asserted over the ocean, three thrones, of mark beyond all others, have been set upon its sands: the thrones of Tyre, Venice, and England. Of the First of these great powers only the memory remains; of the

Second the ruin; the Third which inherits their greatness, if it forget their example, may be led through prouder eminence to less pitied destruction.[1]

In commenting on Ruskin's passage and its influence on British Victorian culture, Andrew Lambert underlined how, after many centuries in close contact, 'not infrequently squabbling over trade, the British were already heirs to much of the Venetian naval legacy, of its ideas and ambitions, with England/Britain finding much to admire in the older sea power'.[2]

In an age marked by concerns about the effects of maturing globalisation on European politics and economy, it is thus topical to analyse the interaction of the Republic of Venice and the kingdom of England during the sixteenth and seventeenth centuries, the period of their closest direct interplay. The crisis of Venice and the rise of England can be seen as two early examples of the opposite consequences that the beginning of European expansion and the onset of proto-globalisation had on the old continent.

Expansion set into motion a series of events that very quickly undercut Venice's hegemony as the middleman between Europe and Asia. This is something of which contemporaries were fully aware, as the Portuguese Tomè Pires wrote in 1515 with a most evocative image: 'whoever is lord of Malacca has his hand on the throat of Venice'.[3] After the loss of Negroponte in 1470, the sixteenth century had started with more territorial losses at the hands of the Ottomans, swiftly followed by the news of the successful Portuguese voyages to India, which triggered panic amongst commercial operators as it seemed to herald the beginning of the end of Venice's role as the arch intermediary between Europe, the Levant and Asia. In 1509 a large alliance of Italian and European powers swept through the Italian mainland and seemed to threaten the Republic's very existence. Throughout the rest of the century, whilst these crises receded – the Italian mainland recovered by 1516,[4] and the Levant trade was recovering by then also – Venice underwent a profound restructuring of its economy, which was accompanied by dramatic changes of attitude in both its economic and foreign policy.

If Venice's overseas empire was shrinking and its economy suffering, the situation for England was rather different. In 1485 the end of the War of the Roses had provided a new political settlement under the Tudor dynasty. Even taking into account revisionist interpretations, during the

---

[1] J. Ruskin, *The Stones of Venice: The Foundations*, London, 1851, 1.

[2] A. Lambert, 'Now is come a darker day': Britain, Venice and the Meaning of Sea Power', in M. Taylor ed., *The Victorian Empire and Britain's Maritime World, 1837–1901: The Sea and Global History*, London, 2013, 19–42, 34.

[3] A. Cortesão ed., *The Suma Oriental of Tomè Pires*, 2 vols, London, 1944, ii: 287.

[4] Its recovery was sanctioned by the Treaty of Bologna in 1529–30.

sixteenth century England's internal stability improved and its population
and economy started a period of long-term growth, fostering new ambitions to play a bigger role on the global scale.[5] England's merchants and
entrepreneurs widened their range of actions, first in continental Europe,
beyond their traditional links with the Baltic and North Sea, and then,
helped by a series of maritime exploits, reaching out to the rest of the
globe. Although its first attempts at establishing colonial outposts
encountered mixed success, England was well set on its path towards
global assertion. It certainly behaved as a rising power, whilst Venice was
starting to suffer from fears about its own role and future.

The rise of England and the crisis of Venice are always mentioned in the
same breath by historians;[6] as Richard Rapp put it, 'it was the invasion of
the Mediterranean, not the exploitation of the Atlantic, that produced the
Golden Ages of Amsterdam and London'.[7] Before that, Venice dominated the Mediterranean and was rightly considered an international
trading power to be reckoned with. Afterwards the situation in the
Mediterranean changed drastically, and Venice's influence had to be
profoundly re-evaluated. The study of how this occurred touches upon
some of the most debated questions regarding the commercial expansion
of England in the sixteenth and seventeenth centuries, and it forces us to
reconsider the ways in which Venice dealt with this altered situation and
the fundamental reasons which led to its ultimate defeat.

The following pages focus on the socio-economic relations between
Venice and England during this time of transition, positing that the long
history of Venetian engagement with the Levant had a direct influence on
the development of English commercial and imperial development. The
book's main ambition is to introduce Venice into current historiographical

---

[5] For a recent reappraisal of these issues see S. Gunn, 'Politic History, New Monarchy and
State Formation: Henry VII in European Perspective', *Historical Research*, 82 (2009):
380–392, and the bibliography there cited.

[6] Just to mention a few: L. Beutin, 'La décadence économique de Venise considérée du
point de vue nord-européen', in *Aspetti e cause della decadenza economica*, 87–108;
R. Davis, 'Influences de l'Angleterre sur le déclin de Venise au XVIIème siècle', in
Aspetti e cause della decadenza economica, 185–235; D. Sella, *Commerci e industrie a
Venezia nel secolo XVII*, Venice and Rome, 1961; D. Sella, 'Crisis and Transformation
in Venetian Trade', in B. Pullan ed., *Crisis and Change in the Venetian Economy in the
Sixteenth and Seventeenth Centuries*, London, 1968, 88–105; R. H. Tawney, *Business and
Politics under James I: Lionel Cranfield as Merchant and Minister*, Cambridge, 1958, 14–30;
P. Jeannin, 'The Sea-Borne and the Overland Trade Routes of Northern Europe in the
XVIth and XVIIth centuries', *Journal of European Economic History*, 11 (1982): 5–61;
R. Brenner, *Merchants and Revolution: Commercial Change, Political Conflict, and London's
Overseas Traders, 1550–1653*, Cambridge, 1993, 1–91.

[7] R. T. Rapp, 'The Unmaking of the Mediterranean Trade Hegemony: International Trade
Rivalry and the Commercial Revolution', *Journal of Economic History*, 35 (1975): 499–
525, 501.

debates about the nature of empires and the role of emulation in these developments,[8] and in this way also foster new reflections on the long-standing debate on the nature and causes of 'decline', although I have some sympathy for David Landes' argument that 'decline' is perhaps not the most useful term to describe what ultimately is just a recurrent historical phenomenon: loss of leadership.[9]

In order to gain a fuller picture of the reversal of balance between Venice and England, it is necessary to investigate in detail their mutual economic relationship and to put it into the context of the wider Mediterranean stage. English and Venetian merchants fought in its waters a long and weary commercial war for control of the same markets. They shared interests in the same commodities, both for their own internal consumption and for distribution to the rest of continental Europe. Through the analysis of this interaction, I shall demonstrate how Venice's social, political and economic circumstances managed to shape the English mercantile community based there into a unique structure, different from all other English mercantile communities, and into an entity that was also different from other foreign communities active in Venice in the same period. I shall focus on the activities of the English merchants active in Venice and its Levant dominions and on the way direct trade between the two countries was organised – both in theory and in practice. In short, this volume focuses on the ways in which high politics was reflected in everyday economic activities. The goal is to show how formal policies and informal strategies shaped the economic relationship of the two countries, and how these long-term interactions played a role in shaping English Mediterranean policy in the following centuries.

The concluding part of this study will discuss the complexity of the Venetian empire and how its 'commercial' nature shaped both Venetian and English experience in the region. To properly understand these issues it is essential to connect them with the history of Anglo-Venetian trade in the *longue durée*, and with the everyday activities of the English mercantile communities active in Venice and its dominions. The existing bibliography on English commercial expansion in the early modern period has bypassed its Venetian side. Whilst there are several works on English trade and relations with the Ottoman empire,[10] and

---

[8] S. A. Reinert, *Translating Empire: Emulation and the Origins of Political Economy*, Cambridge (Mass.), 2011.

[9] D. Landes, *The Wealth and Poverty of Nations: why some are so rich and some are so poor*, London, 1998, especially the chapter on 'Loss of Leadership', 442–464, on the Venetian case 445–446.

[10] Amongst many: R. Davis, *Aleppo and Devonshire Square: English Traders in the Levant in the Eighteenth Century*, London, 1967; D. Goffman, *Britons in the Ottoman Empire*

the English presence in the rest of the Italian peninsula has been touched upon,[11] scholarship has so far underplayed how commercial relations between Venice and England were structurally different from those of England with the rest of Italy, as the Republic of Venice was the only part of Italy covered by a trade monopoly under the Levant Company. My analysis will also elaborate on the differences between English merchants active in the Ottoman territories and those in the Venetian territories, regarding both their business strategies and their economic and social status, even though these merchants all worked under the monopoly of one company.[12] Through the detailed analysis of day-to-day workings of Levant Company agents, rather than the better-known activities of merchant members in London, the book will show how the company based its success on allowing diverse strategies to coexist within its area of monopoly.[13] From the English perspective, the methodological novelty of this approach is to propose a revision of some of the classic issues of English economic and imperial history through the utilisation of non-English documentary evidence. From the Venetian perspective it is instead to show how its own self-perception and its role within European politics clashed with its economic goals, and how political and economic strategies failed to find an appropriate reconciliation between the two. This kind of approach will allow me to go beyond traditional economic history, moving towards a 'social history of commerce', overcoming the shortcomings of a purely quantitative approach that cannot give fully satisfactory results in the Venetian context.

The introduction discusses the underlying theme of 'political economies of empires' and provides the general interpretative frame of the volume. The book is then divided in four sections: the first introduces the background of the English arrival in the Mediterranean through four chapters which will analyse Anglo-Italian commercial and trade links during the Middle Ages; their developments under the Tudors, here introducing the currant trade – the long-term staple between the two countries, which will then be a 'red thread' running through the entirety of the volume; the beginning of English trade in the Ottoman Levant; and

---

(1642–1660), Washington, 1998; A. Games, *The Web of Empire: English Cosmopolitans in an Age of Expansion, 1560–1660*, Oxford, 2008.

[11] G. Pagano De Divitiis, *English Merchants in Seventeenth Century Italy*, Cambridge, 1997.

[12] M. Fusaro, 'Les Anglais et les Grecs: un réseau de coopération commerciale en Méditerranée vénitienne', *Annales. Histoire, Sciences Sociales*, 58 (2003): 605–625.

[13] For a 'London-based' analysis of the Company's activities see M. Epstein, *The Early History of the Levant Company*, London, 1908; A. C. Wood, *A History of the Levant Company*, Oxford, 1935; Brenner, *Merchants and Revolution*; R. Grassby, *The Business Community of Seventeenth Century England*, Cambridge, 1995.

the different roles played by Venice, Genoa and Livorno in these developments.

The second section concentrates on the political economy of Anglo-Venetian trade between the 1580s and the 1670s through three chapters which focus on the diplomatic relations between the two countries; the interplay of diplomatic, commercial and religious factors in their evolution; and on how political considerations on both sides shaped the foreign mercantile presence in Venice and its empire.

The third section reconstructs the English community in Venice and its relationships with other foreign mercantile communities, and analyses the major goods of the Anglo-Venetian trade beyond currants.

The fourth and final section concentrates on the 'colonial' Anglo-Venetian interaction and how the imperial nature of Venice, and its self-perception in this regard, was an essential element in facilitating English commercial penetration and later colonial presence in the Mediterranean.

Acknowledgements

Any book that takes many years to be written accrues a long list of debts, and it is a joy to finally be able to thank all those who helped and supported it since its inception.

As this volume is a direct descendant of my doctoral dissertation, it is therefore fitting that I start by acknowledging the financial assistance received from many institutions during the time of my Ph.D.: the Master and Fellows of St John's College, Cambridge, awarded me a most generous Benefactors' Scholarship that took financial worries out of my mind. The Ellen McArthur Fund and the Cambridge European Trust generously contributed in funding my research expeditions. Since then, I have been able to continue my archival trips thanks to the generosity of the Universities of Chicago and Exeter.

I would like to thank the Director and the whole personnel of the *Archivio di Stato* in Venice for their constant help over many years; I owe a particular debt of gratitude to everyone in *distribuzione* for their efforts at helping researchers. Amongst the archivists, I am particularly grateful to Franco Rossi for invaluable help and generosity with his time in allowing me to explore the *Notarile-Testamenti* section, which has not yet been fully indexed; to Claudia Salmini (now Director of the Trieste State Archive) for being absolutely indispensable in gaining access the *Giudice del Forestier* (I would also like to acknowledge the cooperative work done with Piera Zanon and Francesca Sardi, who were preparing the index of this magistrate in 1998–1999 when I started working on it); I am most grateful to Paola Benussi, Michela Dal Borgo, Andrea Pellizza and Sandra Sambo for useful indications and unfailing good humour. Maria Francesca Tiepolo has been such a stalwart support for generations of Venetian scholars that it is difficult to find words to thank her appropriately; I owe her much more than I can acknowledge here.

In London, a warm thank-you is due to the personnel of the British Library Rare Books Reading Room, which has become almost a second home.

The original idea for this project was developed during some long conversations with Sybille Backmann, and kept alive in its infancy to a great extent because of the enthusiasm of Vittorio Mandelli, who – with characteristic good humour and generosity – always reported any 'sightings' of English merchants; without his advice, tackling the notarial sources in Venice would have been far more difficult, time consuming and less rewarding than it has been. Over the years, I have met many colleagues and made many friends in the Venetian archives: Dimitris Arvanitakis, Vicky Avery, Ersie Burke, Isabella Cecchini, Jean-François Chauvard, Blake De Maria, Filippo de Vivo, Maartje van Gelder, Katerina Konstantinidou, Emma Jones, Mary Laven, Antonio Mazzucco, Anna Pizzati, Federica Ruspio and James Shaw have been extremely generous with their findings and suggestions, and for this I thank them deeply.

In Greece I would like to thank all the personnel of the ΑΡΧΕΙΑ ΝΟΜΟΥ ΚΕΦΑΛΛΗΝΙΑΣ and the personnel of the Gennadius Library in Athens. A particular thank-you is owed to Nicholas Cosmetatos, Maria Georgopoulou, Gelina Harlaftis, Marianna Kolivà, Anna Venezis Cosmetatos and Stamatoula Zapandi, all of whom, in different ways, made my research trips to Greece intellectually stimulating and humanly delightful.

At different times, and in different ways, my students at Chicago and Exeter, and several colleagues and friends across the world have provided healthy criticism of and support to this project. I owe a particular debt of gratitude to the late Edoardo Grendi, who was a supportive critic and a generous provider of intellectual stimuli at the very beginning of this project. In Cambridge I was privileged in having Peter Burke as my doctoral supervisor, and I thank him and Maria Lúcia Garcia Pallares-Burke for their unfailing support ever since.

Amongst the many who have helped me over the years it took to complete this project – far too many to list, I'm afraid – I would particularly like to mention David Abulafia, Julia Crick, Cornell Fleischer, Henry French, Tamar Herzog, Jonathan Israel, Wolfgang Kaiser, Isabella Lazzarini, Giovanni Levi, Peter Linehan, Luca Molà, Anthony Molho, Reinhold Mueller, Lucio Pezzolo, Steve Pincus, Richard Smith, Anastasia Stouraiti, Simon Szrater, Andrew Thorpe and Francesca Trivellato.

A special thank-you is due to the generosity of those who read the complete manuscript at various stages of its development: Patricia Allerston, Vicky Avery, Perry Gauci and Michael Knapton. Ruth McKay has been a wonderful eagle-eyed copy-editor. At Cambridge University Press, I wish to thank Elizabeth Friend-Smith, who has been following the text since the beginning, and Elizabeth Davey, Sara Peacock and Rosalyn Scott, who have been taking care of its production. The comments and criticism of the Cambridge anonymous reviewers have helped improve the final product.

My mother's good humour has always been a powerful help, especially since Hector and Agnes have done their very best to drag me away from my desk. This work is published at last mostly thanks to Rex Maudsley's unique mix of generous rock-solid support, patience tempered by caustic humour, and gentle persisting bullying – which he calls 'encouragement' ... This work is dedicated to him.

Note on documentary sources

To support the multifaceted nature of this analysis, it has been necessary to utilise lesser-known archival evidence. Venice is, unfortunately, unique in its scarcity of quantitative primary evidence available for the period before the mid-eighteenth century. Whatever figures were available for long-distance trade have been put to excellent use by previous generations, and are easily accessible through the works of Gino Luzzatto, Frederic Lane, Alberto Tenenti, Ugo Tucci and Domenico Sella. In general, given the nature of the archival evidence, it is not really possible to provide any solid and consistent figures on the real contribution of foreign capital to any of the pre-modern Italian economies. This situation is particularly evident in the Venetian state, where so many quantitative sources for the period have been lost or eliminated. I have already published specific quantitative data about the currant trade;[1] my hope to find additional quantitative material was not fulfilled, which I regret, as I fully subscribe to the analysis of Anglo-Italian commercial relations by Ralph Davis more than fifty years ago: 'Though of less importance to English economic development in the seventeenth century than the Turkish trade or the expansion of shipping operations in the Mediterranean, Anglo-Italian trade showed changes which were even more striking, involving in important respects a complete reversal of the economic role of England and Italy.'[2]

Histories of English commercial expansion are usually written starting from companies' records, or, in any case, with a clear London/England-based perspective. As Ralph Davis again perceptively observed, 'Company records only provide a very general view of the nature and methods of trade (however detailed a picture of Company organization may emerge from them), and pamphlets are polemical and often

---

[1] M. Fusaro, *Uva passa: una guerra commerciale tra Venezia e l'Inghilterra (1540–1640)*, Venice, 1997, 104, 121, 132–135, 145, 154, 156, 159, 161.
[2] R. Davis, 'England and the Mediterranean, 1570–1670', in F. J. Fisher ed., *Essays in the Economic and Social History of Tudor and Stuart England*, Cambridge, 1961, 117–137. 133.

ill-informed.'[3] The solution to these problems has been to investigate the private records of individuals engaged in this trade; Davis used this approach in his influential *Aleppo and Devonshire Square*.[4] But no such body of evidence seems to have survived for merchants engaged in Anglo-Venetian trade in the years I am analysing, and therefore alternative archival strategies had to be found. No business correspondence for Englishmen in Venice appears to have survived, and indeed these are extremely rare also for the Ottoman side before the eighteenth century. This forced me to use a wider variety of primary evidence, and the notarial archives have been particularly generous.

The vastness of notarial archives for medieval and early modern Italy is evidence of the authorities' long-standing concern with legalising transactions and guaranteeing property rights in a way that was easy and relatively cheap for all parties.[5] The fact that notarised documents had the value of 'fede pubblica' and acquired strength of evidence usable in court made them crucial elements in the development of Italian commercial culture.[6] Even so, and probably because of their richness, those archives have been said to provide a fragmented image of trade. In Italy this had led to a debate on the nature of notarial evidence and methodology of usage, especially in the study of economic history, with Federigo Melis, Edoardo Grendi and Steven Epstein amongst its major contributors.[7] Within this debate, one of the critiques has been that using notarial evidence would lead to an overestimation of foreign as opposed to local trade. Even assuming this to be the case, given the focus of this volume on international trade, here it cannot be considered a problem. I would additionally contend that notarial documents remain the most useful corrective to the use of normative and judicial evidence.

Notarial documents are a privileged source for the study of the foreign presence in Italy, and this is even more valid for mercantile

---

[3] R. Davis, *The Rise of the English Shipping Industry in the Seventeenth and Eighteenth Centuries*, London, 1972 (2nd edn), vii.

[4] Davis, *Aleppo and Devonshire Square*. An excellent recent example of this approach, which shows the full potential of using this kind of material, is F. Trivellato, *The Familiarity of Strangers: The Sephardic Diaspora, Livorno, and Cross-Cultural Trade in the Early Modern Period*, New Haven and London, 2009.

[5] R. Ago, *Economia barocca: mercato e istituzioni nella Roma del Seicento*, Rome, 1998, 122.

[6] M. Amelotti and G. Costamagna, *Alle origini del notariato italiano*, Rome, 1975, 209.

[7] Debate is summarised in Fusaro, 'Gli uomini d'affari stranieri in Italia', in *Il Rinascimento Italiano e l'Europa*, 12 vols, vol. iv: *L'Italia e l'economia europea nel Rinascimento*, F. Franceschi, R. A. Goldthwaite and R. C. Mueller eds., Treviso, 2007, 369–395, 379–380, and bibliography therein.

communities.[8] Merchants left a remarkable trail of contracts and deeds behind them in the expanses of notarial archives. The transformation of the office of the notary in the twelfth century was a crucial factor in the revival of Italian commerce in the same period. In earlier times, notarial acts had derived their validity from the testimony of witnesses, but during the twelfth century the notary emerged as a fully public official whose acts, authenticated by his *signum* and signature alone, were recognised as binding and valid in any court at any time.[9] Documents produced by a notary became 'written testimony of a fact or an action of juridical nature, which had such characteristic as to acquire public value and strength of proof'.[10] This gave trade a powerful tool of expansion, and makes notarial documentation the most important instrument for the study of everyday affairs.

In the Venetian state archives I explored both the *Notarile Atti* and the *Notarile Testamenti*. It would be impossible here to give a full list of the material consulted in building my database of more than 1,200 deeds. Some notaries were seen completely, covering the whole chronological period of the investigation, whereas other material has been more randomly accessed, having been brought to my attention by scholars during the past few years. In the footnotes, the name of the notary who registered the act follows in brackets the number of the *busta*.

In Venice there were plenty of notaries: the reform of 1514 decreed that there had to be sixty-six in total, one for each parish. Notaries did not need a degree, but they had to belong to the *cittadini* rank. Various factors came into play when choosing a notary: merchants tended to have a trusted notary with whom they worked most of the time. But in the case of wills – especially those written on the deathbed – geographical proximity was the most important factor; and in other circumstances, such as the power of attorney, it was common to employ the notaries, or their young trainees, who hung around the various magistrates' offices or circulated in the market area. In the case of foreigners, specialisation was even more marked. Knowledge of a foreign language was certainly an advantage in gaining a clientele, even if deeds had to be drawn up in Italian or Latin.[11]

The second pillar of my research in Venice has been the *Giudici del Forestier*, a magistracy which had been completely ignored by historians.

---

[8] G. Petti Balbi, 'Presenze straniere a Genova nei secoli XII–XIV: letteratura, fonti, temi di ricerca', in G. Rossetti ed., *Dentro la città: stranieri e realtà urbane nell'Europa dei secoli XII–XVI*, Naples, 1989, 121–135, 122.

[9] J. K. Hyde, *Padua in the Age of Dante*, Manchester and New York, 1966, 154.

[10] Amelotti and Costamagna, *Alle origini del notariato*, 209.

[11] M. P. Pedani Fabris, *'Veneta auctoritate notarius': storia del notariato veneziano (1514–1797)*, Milan, 1996, 11, 3, 127, 141–142.

Apart from two short articles concerned with its origin,[12] and based on normative material, its corpus of documents has laid untouched for centuries: of the ninety-nine files which survive up to the end of the seventeenth century, only one had been opened and examined – the others all still bore the official seals of the Republic. Moreover, to judge from the physical state of the *registri*, it seems very likely that these had not even been consulted for an equivalent length of time.[13] When I started working on this material in 1998, Dr Claudia Salmini, then of the *Archivio di Stato* of Venice, asked me to cooperate with the *Anagrafe* project, which now has been completed and provides up-to-date mapping of the series of documents in the repositories. For this reason I was allowed to freely consult documentary pieces from the *Forestier* archive. In a time when access to other material was made almost impossible by serious institutional problems, this allowed me to continue my research and immensely helped my work, something for which I wish to thank her here again.

Some series have been consulted in their entirety for the period up to 1700:

> *Esposizioni Principi*
> *Senato, dispacci, Rettori, Cefalonia* (ASV, *SDR*, Cefalonia)
> *Senato, dispacci, Rettori, Zante* (ASV, *SDR*, Zante)
> *Collegio, Risposte di dentro* (ASV, *Collegio, Rdd*)
> *Collegio, Risposte di fuori* (ASV, *Collegio, Rdf*)
> *Cinque Savi alla Mercanzia, Risposte.*

Other series were consulted as needed; prominent amongst these are *Senato Mar, registri*, which contain the deliberations of the Senate concerning the 'maritime' state, and the corresponding *filze* (which contain the extremely rich material used by the Senate as a preparation for the legislative process itself).

The following series in Venice have also been examined:

> *Avogaria di Comun, Miscellanea, Civile* – (ASV, *AdC*, Civile) *buste* 27, 29, 48, 152, 198, 245, 273, 276.
> *Avogaria di Comun, Miscellanea, Penale* – (ASV, *AdC*, Penale) *buste* 140, 146, 217, 285, 353, 378, 427.

---

[12] R. Cessi, 'Un patto fra Venezia e Padova e la Curia "Forinsecorum" al principio del secolo XIII', *Atti e memorie della Regia Accademia di scienze, lettere ed arti di Padova*, 30 (1914): 263–275; and 'La "Curia Forinsecorum" e la sua prima costituzione', *Nuovo Archivio Veneto*, 28 (1914): 202–207.

[13] An analytical description of the jurisdiction of the *Forestier* is in M. Fusaro, 'Politics of Justice, Politics of Trade: Foreign Merchants and the Administration of Justice from the Records of Venice's *Giudici del Forestier*', *Mélanges de l'École française de Rome*, 126/1 (2014).

Cinque Savi alla Mercanzia, new series, *buste* 3, 21, 22, 23, 24, 25,
   34, 44, 45, 49, 51, 54, 60, 75, 81, 92, 93, 103, 105, 116, 134,
   135, 164, 182, 188, 191, 197.

Collegio, relazioni, buste 61, 62, 63, 83, 87.

Compilazione delle leggi, buste 12, 19, 61, 76, 134, 138, 139, 140,
   141, 150, 155, 157, 175, 210, 231, 238, 240, 244, 277, 278,
   297, 299, 378.

Provveditori da Terra e da Mar – (ASV, *PTM*) *buste* 876, 862, 863,
   863bis, 930, 1079, 1082, 1151, 1191.

Quarantia criminale, buste 103, 114.

Senato, deliberazioni, Rettori, filze 50, 59, 64, 67, 72, 76, 81, 213.

Senato, Secreta, Ordini di Cefalonia (this file is not in any index; I
   wish to thank Alessandra Sambo for bringing it to my
   attention).

Sindici Inquisitori in Terraferma e Levante, buste 67 and 68.

The following sources were consulted in England:

The National Archives, London (TNA):

State Papers – (TNA, *SP*) 99 (Venice), from 1 to 57.

State Papers 105 – (TNA, *SP*) (Levant Company), 109, 110, 111,
   112, 143, 147, 148, 149.

British Library (BL):

Additional Mss, 18639, 22546.

Egerton Mss, 760, 2542.

Harleian Mss, 943, 6210.

Landsdowne Mss, 34, 38, 90, 93.

Sloane Mss, 682, 867, 2752, 1709, 2902, 3494.

Stowe Mss, 135, 219.

***London Metropolitan Archives* – *LMA* (material formerly
in the Guildhall Library):**

Court Minutes of Trinity House: CLC/526/MS30004/003.

The Trinity House Cash Book (1661–85): CLC/526/MS30032/
   002.

The Transactions of Trinity House (1609–25) CLC/526/
   MS30045/001/002/003/004.

Also on Trinity House, the 'Chaplin Papers' CLC/526/
   MS30323/001/002/003/004.

The 'Pepys Papers' that relate to Trinity House, especially CLC/
   526/MS30337.

The 'Corsini Papers': CLC/B/062/MS21317, CLC/B/062/
   MS21318, CLC/B/062/MS21319, CLC/B/062/MS21320,
   CLC/B/062/MS21322, CLC/B/062/MS21323, CLC/B/062/
   MS21324, CLC/B/062/MS21325, CLC/B/062/MS21326,

CLC/B/062/MS22274, CLC/B/062/MS22275, CLC/B/062/
MS22276, CLC/B/062/MS22277, CLC/B/062/MS22280,
CLC/B/062/MS22281, CLC/B/062/MS22282, CLC/B/062/
MS22283.

Papers of the Worshipful Company of Glass Sellers: CLC/270/
MS00366, CLC/239/MS03384, CLC/L/GC/D/001/MS05536,
CLC/L/GC/B/001/MS05538, CLC/GC/C/006/MS05542,
CLC/L/GC/E/001MS05556.

In Cephalonia (Greece) the following documents have been examined
in the General Public Records of the State – Archives of the District of
Cephalonia (ΓΑΚ-ΑΝΚ): in total more than 130 *buste* of the notarial
archive, the only source that survives for the period under investigation,
were consulted. They were chosen if notaries worked in areas where
foreign merchants were likely to be found – that is to say in areas of
currant production, or in towns with a harbour, or in the administrative
centre of Castle St George (Kastro). The fire of 1597 destroyed all papers
prior to that date, and various subsequent earthquakes and fires have
taken their toll on the documentation. The Archive of Zante was
completely destroyed in a fire following the earthquake of 1953.

In Athens (Greece) I have examined the Miscellaneous Mss regarding
the Ionian islands after the fall of Venice, which are preserved in the
Gennadius Library at the American School of Classical Studies at Athens.

All translations into English of documentary material written in
languages other than English are by the author unless otherwise
specified, and I thank Catherine Keen whose advice on these has been
invaluable.

Note on dates and spelling

The goal which has oriented all my choices in these fields has been to facilitate access to the documentary material, which is large and varied. All dates have been kept as in the original documents, and where they have been modernised this is clearly stated in the text. This was the only available option, considering all the different systems used in the areas under investigation. Additionally it was the only way to easily find documents that frequently do not have a *carta/folio* number and are ordered only by their dates. It is important to remember that during this period there was considerable variance in dating systems across European states. The Gregorian calendar promulgated by pope Gregory XIII in 1582 had been quickly adopted by Venice, where the year started on 1 March. For Venetian dates between 1 January and the end of February, the formula *mv* (*more Veneto*), has been added to show that it is a date following the Venetian-style calendar, and therefore it is necessary to add a unit to the figure of the year. If this abbreviation is absent, the date quoted in the text is to be considered critical.

Style in England was the Julian calendar – old style – according to which the days of the month were ten days behind those of the Gregorian calendar, and the legal year started on 25 March.

Spelling was not uniform in England during this period. Adding to this the creative translations of contemporary Venetian and Greek hands, the results can be quite far-fetched, and identification frequently is a guessing game. Where it has been possible to establish an acknowledged spelling of a particular name, this appears throughout the text; otherwise the names of English merchants are quoted in the text with the most frequent variant of the way in which they were written in the documents. The same applies to Greek names.

Abbreviations

AdC	*Avogaria di Comun*
ASG	Archivio di Stato di Genova
ASV	Archivio di Stato di Venezia
BL	British Library
CSPVe	*Calendar of State Papers, Venetian*
DBI	*Dizionario Biografico degli Italiani*, available on line at: www.treccani.it/biografie
DNB	*Oxford Dictionary of National Biography*, available on line at: www.oxforddnb.com
GdF	*Giudici del Forestier*
LMA	London Metropolitan Archive
NT	*Notarile, Testamenti*
PTM	*Provveditori da Terra e da Mar*
Rdd	*Risposte di dentro*
Rdf	*Risposte di fuori*
SDR, Cefalonia	*Senato, dispacci, Rettori, Cefalonia*
SDR, Zante	*Senato, dispacci, Rettori, Zante*
SP	*State Papers*
TNA	The National Archives
ΓΑΚ-ΑΝΚ	General Public Records of the State, Archives of the District of Cephalonia
b.	*busta*
bb.	*buste*
c.	*carta*
cc.	*carte*
cc.n.n.	*carte* not numbered
f.	*filza*
reg.	*registro*
fasc.	*fascicolo*
n.s.	new series.

Unless specified otherwise, all 'ducats' mentioned are those of 'account', each of these was made up of 'lire 6, soldi 4'.

Map 1. Western Europe, the Eastern Mediterranean and the Venetian empire

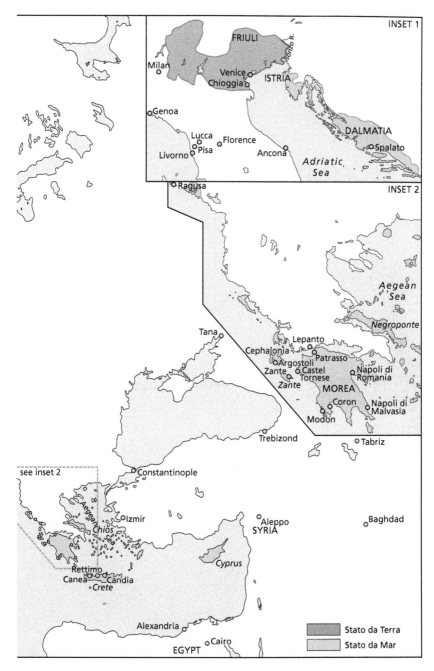

INSET 1

FRIULI

Milan

Venice
Chioggia

ISTRIA

Genoa

Lucca
Pisa

Florence

Livorno

Ancona

DALMATIA

Spalato

*Adriatic
Sea*

Ragusa

INSET 2

*Aegean
Sea*

Tana

Lepanto

Cephalonia

Patrasso

Argostoli

Castel
Tornese

Napoli di
Romania

Zante

Zante

Negroponte

MOREA

Coron

Napoli di
Malvasia

Modon

Trebizond

Tabriz

see inset 2

Constantinople

Aegean

Izmir

Aleppo

SYRIA

Baghdad

Chios

Rettimo

Canea

Candia

Cyprus

Crete

Alexandria

Cairo

EGYPT

Stato da Terra

Stato da Mar

Map 1. (cont.)

Introduction
Political economies of empire

The commerce of the world was to pass through Venice; other nations paying for their goods with great additional costs and duties. The Ionians could sell their oil, their staple production, only at Venice. Such a system, ruinous to the general interests, was also a great encouragement to smugglers, amongst whom the English appear to have taken the lead, and thus to have drawn upon themselves the especial [sic] anger of the Venetians. The proveditors of Zante and of other Islands complained, in 1596, that the revenue was defrauded by the skill and audacity of English seamen. Similar complaints were made in 1601. It appeared as if the then mistress of the sea was beginning, with prophetic instinct, to dread her future successor.[1]

It is difficult to improve on the power of synthesis of a mid-ranking British colonial officer, serving the British crown in the Ionian islands at the apogee of the empire. The pages that follow will provide some background and elaborate on his comments, trying to explain how and why the English managed first to penetrate and then to exploit the Venetian Mediterranean during the early modern period. Ultimately my analysis will connect this to British commercial and political global expansion at large, through the lens of the long-term connection between the English and the Venetian economies from the fifteenth century to the collapse of the Republic of Venice in 1797 and beyond.

But this book is more than the analysis of an important commercial relationship. It also has the ambition of tracing some of the roots of a relationship that was political, cultural and artistic, but which had also in the economy and in imperial governance one of its strongest and longest-lasting features. My additional goal is to provide an economic and social explanation for the onset of the Venetian crisis, moving away

---

[1] Viscount Kirkwall ed. [George William Hamilton Fitzmaurice, Earl of Orkney, Viscount Kirkwall, Captain 71st Highlanders], *Four Years in the Ionian Islands Their Political and Social Condition. With a History of the British Protectorate*, 2 vols, London, 1864, i: 37–38.

from the traditional Anglo-American approach that has been primarily concerned with the history of Venice as a 'city' or a 'republic' and, more recently, as one of the early modern Italian territorial states.[2] My intention is instead to focus on 'Venice as an empire' and to break free from the 'myth of Venice' in its political incarnation as the fundamental tool of historical interpretation.[3] The story that I will tell concerns the emergence of early modern capitalism in general and the transformation of the Mediterranean, explored through a comparative perspective which sets Venice and England in the European context. A consequence of this is that the Ionian islands will feature prominently, as for centuries they were the loci of frequent contact and interaction between Venice and England, and their long-term historical development is a privileged window from which to analyse together Venice and England under the rubric of imperial governance.

By focusing on the history of Venice as an empire, it is not my intention to deny that the story of Anglo-Venetian relations is also a story about two cities, and the entanglement between the economic development of cities and that of states is relevant for both, even given the peculiarities of the Venetian city-state.[4] In Fernand Braudel's oft-quoted evocative analysis of the pivotal role of certain cities at different stages of European economic development, Venice's apogee is situated in the fourteenth and fifteenth centuries, when it shared this dominant role with Bruges, in his words acting as 'northern and southern poles'.[5] In this scheme London's period of predominance started only in the eighteenth century, with the golden ages of Antwerp, Genoa and Amsterdam standing between Venice and London. The seventeenth century was a transitional time for both cities and states, and their reciprocal commercial and political interactions shed new light on their shifting statuses. Though Venice was a city-state, attention to its urban dimension should not make us forget that it controlled a Mediterranean empire, based on the control of sea lanes for the furtherance of trade, and that England – *mutatis mutandis* – was on its

---

[2] For excellent examples of these approaches see the works of Frederick Lane, William Bouwsma, Elisabeth Crouzet-Pavan, Michael Knapton and James Grubb.

[3] On this see the bibliographical essays J. Grubb, 'When Myths Lose Power: Four Decades of Venetian Historiography', *Journal of Modern History*, 58 (1986): 43–94; and F. de Vivo, 'The Diversity of Venice and Her Myths in Recent Historiography', *The Historical Journal*, 47 (2004): 169–177.

[4] C. Tilly, 'Entanglements of European Cities and States', in C. Tilly and W. P. Blockmans eds., *Cities and the Rise of States in Europe, AD 1000–1800*, Boulder, 1994, 1–27; recently discussed also in D. Ormrod, *The Rise of Commercial Empires: England and the Netherlands in the Age of Mercantilism, 1650–1770*, Cambridge, 2003.

[5] F. Braudel, *Civilization and Capitalism: 1400–1700*, vol. iii: *The Perspective of the World*, Berkeley, 1992, 96–98.

path to developing its own empire along rather similar lines. This book
will highlight how a long-standing concern about maritime trade – its
sustenance and expansion – was common to both states. From this
descends another striking common element between them, namely how
much of their state policy was directed by the interests of commerce and
the furtherance of international trade. Foreign trade was considered by
early modern states as the fundamental sector of the economy, regardless
of the existence or not of open 'mercantilist' policies; this had been
especially true for Venice since its beginnings, but for England this was
a new development, successfully employed to further its economic growth
whilst it acquired its own empire.

Venice as empire

Discussing Venice under the category of 'empire' is a contested issue.
Popular writers on Venice are not at all afraid of frequently using this
term; amongst the most prominent I am thinking of Jan Morris, Alvise
Zorzi and Garry Wills.[6] And empire appears in countless references in
fiction, journalism and assorted media when commenting on or illustrating Venice's past.

   The rightly famous and evocative image by Giambattista Tiepolo of
Neptune offering his gifts to a regal and serene Venice graces the cover of
a recent volume, *Political Economy of Empire in the Modern World*, yet
Venice appears in the volume only tangentially in a sophisticated essay
by Sophus Reinert dedicated to emulation between empires.[7] Its absence
is not really surprising, as for a long time academic specialists of Venice
have been shy in evoking 'empire' directly, generally preferring *Stato da
Mar* (or *Stato da Terra*) and *dominii* – which are the most common
expressions used in the sources to refer to Venetian possessions in the
Levant and the Italian mainland. Recently, though, there have been
some welcome signs of change, and a new attitude is emerging. The
introduction to *Venice Reconsidered* – a volume which presented the state
of the art in Venetian research on the occasion of the two-hundredth

---

[6] J. Morris, *The Venetian Empire: A Sea Voyage*, Harmondsworth, 1980; A. Zorzi, *Una città,
una repubblica, un impero, Venezia: 697–1797*, Milan, 1980; G. Wills, *Venice, Lion City, the
Religion of Empire*, London and New York, 2001.

[7] S. A. Reinert, 'The Empire of Emulation: A Quantitative Analysis of Economic Translations
in the European World, 1500–1849', in S. A. Reinert and P. Røge eds., *Political Economy of
Empire in the Modern World*, Basingstoke and New York, 2013, 105–128. Worth noting that
Patrick O'Brien regrets the absence of the Venetian case from a volume he co-edited on
these issues: P. O'Brien, 'Final Considerations', in P. O'Brien and B. Yun Casalilla eds.,
*European Aristocracies and Colonial Elites: Patrimonial Management Strategies and Economic
Development, 15–18 Centuries*, Aldershot, 2005, 247–263, 253.

anniversary of its demise – defined the Venetian state thus: 'its empire reached from the Alps, through the cities, towns and villages of north-eastern Italy, across the Adriatic to Istria, Dalmatia, Corfu, Crete and Cyprus'. And the editors concluded by saying 'Venice's organic history was most easily read through its imperial and economic fortunes'; however, both aspects were missing amongst the volume's contributions. Still, the term empire was introduced, and it is probably not a coincidence that subsequent Venetian scholarship has revived it as an analytical category.[8]

Interesting stimuli also are coming from recent Greek scholarship on Venice, which is becoming seriously engaged with issues of governance and identities, especially how these were reflected in the language describing – then as now – what has come to be known in Greek history and historiography as the Venetokratia (βενετοκρατία).[9] Monique O'Connell's book *Men of Empire* focuses on the *Dominio da Mar* as a stage where political careers were made (or destroyed), and its prosopographical approach draws readers' attention once more towards Venice's internal civic power mechanisms; even so, her analysis overcomes the traditional reticence in using the dreaded 'e' word.[10] A similar approach is visible in Natalie Rothman's analysis of trans-imperial subjects, people whose lives were at the frontiers between Venice and the Ottoman empire, and whose activities and self-representations 'straddled linguistic, religious, and political boundaries'.[11] Benjamin Arbel's essay 'Venice's Maritime Empire in the Early Modern Period' openly discusses empire in an 'operational' fashion, but does not attempt to define what exactly was meant by 'empire' within the Venetian context beyond *imperium* in its early modern sense of 'sovereignty'.[12] This can be a problem, as 'empire' is not only an important (and currently fashionable) concept, but also a

---

[8] J. Martin and D. Romano eds., *Venice Reconsidered: The History and Civilization of an Italian City-State, 1297–1797*, Baltimore, 2000.

[9] See the considerations of Chryssa Maltezou in 'La vénétocratie en Méditerranée orientale: tendances historiographiques et état actuel des études', in S. G. Franchini, G. Ortalli and G. Toscano eds., *Venise et la Méditerranée*, Venice, 2011, 161–180, 163–165 and bibliography quoted therein; also her 'Dove va la storia della venetocrazia in Grecia? Stato della ricerca e orientamento', in C. Maltezou, A. Tzavara and D. Vlassi eds., *I Greci durante la venetocrazia: uomini, spazio, idee (XIII–XVIII sec.)*, Venice, 2009, 21–38; also her 'The Greek Version of the Fourth Crusade: From Niketas Choniates to the History of the Greek Nation', in A. Laiou ed., *Urbs Capta: The Fourth Crusade and its Consequences*, Paris, 2005, 152–159.

[10] M. O'Connell, *Men of Empire: Power and Negotiation in Venice's Maritime State*, Baltimore, 2009.

[11] E. N. Rothman. *Brokering Empire: Trans-Imperial Subjects between Venice and Istanbul*, Ithaca, 2012, 11.

[12] B. Arbel, 'Venice's Maritime Empire in the Early Modern Period', in E. Dursteler ed., *A Companion to Venetian History, 1400–1797*, Leiden and Boston, 2013, 125–253.

lemma belonging to the select club of words whose meaning is so slippery and protean that they can be understood as an analytical category only within the same text, and unfortunately not always even in such a limited context. For the purposes of this volume I shall slightly modify Kenneth Pomeranz's wording and define empire as 'a polity in which leaders of one society also rule directly or indirectly over at least one other society, using instruments different from (though not always more authoritarian than) those used to rule at home'.[13] This was certainly the case for both the *Stato da Mar* and the *Terraferma*, the Italian mainland, where the hierarchy of government was very clear, as all these disparate territories were ultimately ruled by the same governing body, the *Senato*,[14] which, amongst the multiple republican institutions, had in this period the largest share of state governance. And the ultimate authority of Venice was unquestioned in three fundamental political spheres: foreign and defence policy; state finance, on which defence is utterly dependent; and the administration of justice.[15]

Behind the avoidance of the term empire in the Venetian context I believe stand three main reasons, all of them individually important and connected to each other. The first is chronological, as the 'imperial age' of Venice is traditionally posited between the end of the centuries-long war with Genoa (1380) and the 1571 loss of Cyprus – the 'royal crown' amongst Venetian possessions in the Levant.[16] This precocity of the Venetian imperial experience puts it out of synch with other European cases, thus making practical comparisons more complex. The second reason concerns issues of both 'size' and 'function' as, even when the

---

Conversely Maurice Aymard, in a very recent essay, is still most cautious about wording defining the *Stato da Mar* as 'a system of markets and "colonies" [...] which was a real empire of islands and ports to support its commercial activities and the naval support required to protect these', in his 'L'Europe, Venise et la Méditerranée', in Franchini, Ortalli and Toscano eds., *Venise et la Méditerranée*, 3–11, 5.

[13] K. Pomeranz, 'Social History and World History: From Daily Life to Patterns of Change', *Journal of World History*, 18 (2007): 69–98, 87.

[14] Freddy Thiriet went one step further, calling the territories in the Levant 'colonial': F. Thiriet, *La Romanie vénitienne su moyen âge: le développement et exploitation du domaine colonial vénitienne (XII–XV siècles)*, Paris, 1959; an analytical synthesis of these issues is in S. McKee, *Uncommon Dominion: Venetian Crete and the Myth of Ethnic Purity*, Philadelphia, 2000, 1–18.

[15] J.-C. Hocquet, 'Fiscalité et pouvoir colonial: Venise et le sel dalmate aux XVe et XVIe siècles', in M. Balard ed., *État et colonisation au Moyen Âge et à la Renaissance*, Lyon, 1989, 277–315, 279; G. Cozzi, 'La politica del diritto nella Repubblica di Venezia', in G. Cozzi ed., *Stato, società e giustizia nella Repubblica Veneta (sec. XV–XVIII)*, Rome, 1980, 15–152.

[16] See, amongst many, the classic: D. Chambers, *The Imperial Age of Venice, 1380–1580*, London, 1970.

existence of an empire is acknowledged, its relatively small size and lack of oceanic dimension compare it unfavourably with early modern examples such as Spain, Portugal, England and France. Regarding function, the Venetian one is usually (rightly) defined as a 'commercial' empire, and this appears to automatically slot it into a different, and somewhat inferior, category of analysis. Last, but by all means not least, is the lack of self-reflection on the concept of 'empire' embedded in the Venetian primary evidence. In the next few pages I shall confront directly these intertwined issues and present some introductory considerations on how these obstacles need to be overcome. Finally, I point out issues which are ripe for further development by future scholarship. My aim is to show how Venice's political economy was the result of *functional* imperial concerns, and it is only when this is fully appreciated and accounted for that the full picture becomes clear. These preliminary considerations will also provide further evidence on the importance of the Anglo-Venetian commercial interaction which is the main focus of analysis of this volume.

Regarding chronology

From its very beginnings Venice grew under the shadow of Byzantium, and – *pace* the 'myth' of primitive freedom – the subordinate status of Venice in the early centuries of its life has been conclusively accepted. Extremely helpful in tracing the development of the relationship between Byzantium and Venice has been the linguistic analysis of bilateral treaties, from an early language of gracious concessions from Byzantium to the *Commune Veneciarum*, to a later stage (from 1187) in which the pacts start to look like treaties between two separate sovereign states.[17]

The Fourth Crusade forced historians to engage with empire and how this affected and was affected by Venetian peculiarities. There are two separate analytical issues connected with this: first, the position of Venice 'within' the Latin empire during its short life (1204–1261); secondly – and far more crucially – the position of Venice towards its own *Stato da Mar* from 1204 until the end of the Republic in 1797.[18] The events following the conquest of Byzantine empire in 1204 forced Venice to

---

[17] M. Pozza and G. Ravegnani, *I trattati con Bisanzio, 992–1285*, 2 vols, Venice, 1993–1996, i: 80. See also D. M. Nicol, *Byzantium and Venice: A Study in Diplomatic and Cultural Relations*, Cambridge, 1988. On Byzantine trade concessions to Venice: P. Frankopan, 'Byzantine Trade Privileges to Venice in the Eleventh Century: The Chrysobull of 1092', *Journal of Medieval History*, 30 (2004): 135–160.

[18] Interesting elements on the supraregional, maritime and Mediterranean vocation of Venetian politics until its very end can be found in F. M. Paladini, *'Un caos che spaventa': poteri, territori e religioni di frontiera nella Dalmazia della tarda età veneta*, Venice, 2002.

negotiate its way and *modus operandi* with European crowns, and to formally deal with the entrance of feudal structures within the Venetian state. In the words of David Jacoby, the establishment of the Latin empire, and the solutions adopted in the choice of a Latin Emperor, 'entailed Venice's subordination to a feudal leader in the empire's framework. It also led to the integration of the Venetian state and its dependants within a feudal institutional network totally alien to Venice's own social structure, political system and mentality'.[19] In this hybrid situation, it is interesting to see how the position of Venice vis-à-vis the Latin emperor was exceedingly flexible, subordinate in certain things, and equivalent in others. In Jacoby's analysis, the role and activities of the Venetian *podestà* in Constantinople and his use of the title *dominator* suggest 'a formal affirmation of parity or quasi-parity directed towards the holder of the Imperial office in the Latin Empire, rather than an expression of authority with respect to the Doge'.[20]

It is not my intention here to enter into the debate on the existence of an overarching strategy supporting the supposed imperial ambitions of Venice, even given the elevation of the Doge to the title of 'quartae partis et dimidiae totius imperii Romaniae dominator'.[21] The events of the following two centuries will show clearly that the actual formation of the Venetian maritime empire was a gradual, and in many cases circumstantial, affair.[22] What I would like instead to argue is that, *however established*, the end result of the Fourth Crusade was to start a process of substantial territorial acquisition in the Eastern Mediterranean which was a true empire. When the Latin empire collapsed in 1261, what

---

[19] D. Jacoby, 'The Venetian Presence in the Latin Empire of Constantinople (1204–1261): The Challenge of Feudalism and the Byzantine Inheritance', in his *Latin Romania and the Mediterranean*, Aldershot, 2001, II: 141–201, 142.

[20] Jacoby, 'The Venetian Presence in the Latin Empire', 147; see also T. F. Madden, *Enrico Dandolo and the Rise of Venice*, Baltimore and London, 2003; A. Carile, 'Partitio terrarum imperii Romanie', *Studi Veneziani*, 7 (1965–1966): 125–305; M. Balard, *Les Latins en Orient, XIe–XVe siècle*, Paris, 2006, 217–218.

[21] A. Pertusi, '*Quaedam regalia insignia*: ricerche sulle insegne del potere ducale a Venezia durante il medioevo', *Studi Veneziani*, 7 (1965): 2–124; Laiou ed., *Urbs Capta*.

[22] See also M. Angold, 'The Anglo-Saxon Historiography of the Fourth Crusade: A Crime against Humanity or just an Accident?', in G. Ortalli, G. Ravegnani and P. Schreiner eds., *Quarta Crociata: Venezia, Bisanzio, Impero Latino*, Venice, 2006, 301–316. It is worth mentioning that a debate on the nature of England's imperial trajectory and on the possible existence of structurally different phases in its history is still a lively element in the historiography of the British empire. For a recent analytical synthesis see S. Pincus, 'Rethinking Mercantilism: Political Economy, the British Empire and the Atlantic World in the Seventeenth and Eighteenth Centuries', *William and Mary Quarterly*, 69 (2012): 3–34, especially 31–32 and the bibliography quoted therein.

remained of these territories (and those acquired in the intervening time) became in various ways subject to the ultimate authority of the Venetian government, and the same destiny befell those lands added until the eighteenth century, whether through conquest, exchange, purchase or self-devolution. Gaining territorial possessions in the Levant (and later on the Italian mainland) forced Venice to exercise its traditional pragmatism and flexibility in coming up with solutions to formalise the acquisition and political relationship and to govern these territories. Their political settlement and organisation and, increasingly, their defence, became a primary preoccupation of the Venetian ruling class, and would remain so until the self-dissolution of the Republic. This is what a *functional* empire looks like, regardless of what it was called by contemporaries.

Venetians themselves did not really discuss the nature of their possessions, whether in the Levant or, increasingly from the fifteenth century, on the *Terraferma*, nor did they usually refer to them as an 'empire'.[23] Behind this are two separate issues: on the one hand an important role was certainly played by the traditional Venetian disdain for abstract conceptualisation, which in some ways was a defining factor of the Republic's identity and self-perception.[24] On the other hand, Venice was both a 'republic' and a 'city-state', and the imperial city-state's ambiguous identity played an important role in Venetian self-perception and self-representation which still awaits precise definition and proper conceptualisation by scholars.[25] However, Venice's political economy shaped its strategy and policies in a way that made it *act* like an empire. Although this happened in both the *Stato da Terra* and *da Mar*, my analysis here will focus only on the latter, and I will argue that Venetian activities in the Levant – Venetian or Ottoman – is where there is plenty of common ground for introducing Venice into the debates on the comparative history of early modern empires. Another important element behind the lack of conceptualisation and reflection on Venice as an empire is that its commercial hegemony and heyday of imperial incarnation both substantially pre-date the eighteenth-century fascination with the

---

[23] On the meanings and usage of the terms *dominium* and *imperium* in fifteenth- and sixteenth-century Venice see M. Knapton and J. Law, *Marin Sanudo e la Terraferma*, in M. Sanudo, *Itinerario per la Terraferma veneziana*, G. M. Varanini ed., Rome, 2014, 9–80, 40–45 and bibliography quoted therein.

[24] On this cultural and political reticence see M. Knapton, 'The *Terraferma* State', in Dursteler, *A Companion to Venetian History*, 85–124, 91–93.

[25] Anastasia Stouraiti is currently working on these issues through her project *Rethinking Metropolitan Culture and Empire in Early Modern Venice*, which investigates the political culture of empire in Venice (Leverhulme Trust, 2014). Some initial considerations on these issues are in her 'Talk, Script and Print: The Making of Island Books in Early Modern Venice', *Historical Research*, 86 (2013): 207–229, esp. 224–229.

'science of commerce' and its connection with government.[26] By the time intellectual debates about the relationship between political action and economic supremacy came to dominate the European intellectual scene, Venice was a spent force, and the rise of fiscal-military and then nation-states with global empires (or aspirations thereof) made its example useful only as a moral cautionary tale, but (understandably) neglected for the purposes of comparative governance. In a sense this volume, and the research behind it, was born out of the desire to understand if something could be learned from this early example.[27]

The interlacing of these three issues – republican city-state, chronology and function – has hindered scholarly reflection on empire; here I would like to contend instead that it would be most stimulating to start a proper discussion on these questions in the realm of political economy. Introducing a comparative element should help to foster a debate which cannot have a strict nominalist approach: Venetians did not talk of 'empire', hence historians will not either. However, this is not just a semantic argument, as I would like to argue that the absence of Venice from the comparative history of empires derives in great part exactly from semantics: with empire scholars reasoning that, as historians of Venice mostly do not use the word (and they are the experts), this must mean that Venice was not an empire, and therefore not worth engaging with in a comparative fashion. My approach will be entirely *functionalist*, along the lines suggested by Robert Bartlett when, in his masterful treatment of medieval Europe's early colonisation patterns, he commented how

the pattern of the Italian colonial empires has some similarities to that of the British Empire of the year 1900 – a series of islands and headlands dotted along the main commercial pathways, linking the metropolis to distant markets. It has, indeed, been pointed out that the travelling times involved for those saltwater powers were closely comparable: 'one month from Venice to Canea [in Crete], just as one month was needed for the voyage from London to Bombay; seven to eight weeks from Venice to Constantinople, as from London to Hong Kong; nearly three months to link Venice and Trebizond and Tana, as London and New Zealand.' The scale of the age of the steamship was vaster than that of the age of the galleys but the peculiar elongated cape-and-island geography of a maritime empire was still the same.[28]

---

[26] I. Hont, *Jealousy of Trade: International Competition and the Nation-State in Historical Perspective*, Cambridge (Mass.), 2005; P. B. Cheney, *Revolutionary Commerce: Globalization and the French Monarchy*, Cambridge (Mass.), 2010.

[27] The relationship between the Venetian and the English commercial empires, when mentioned, is usually articulated not in terms of 'learning', but in terms of 'inheritance', see P. M. Kennedy, *The Rise and Fall of British Naval Mastery*, London, 2004, 30.

[28] R. Bartlett, *The Making of Europe: Conquest, Colonization and Cultural Change, 950–1350*, Princeton, 1993, 188–189; Paul Kennedy discussed a similar pattern for the 'tropical' regions of the nineteenth-century British empire (*The Rise and Fall*, 154).

There are, indeed, even more points of contact between the two imperial narratives. Both Venice and England controlled empires based on control of the sea and sea lanes. The interconnectedness of the maritime and naval element, and the way this offered possible comparisons between them, was frequently pointed out, starting in the sixteenth century. Just to give one example, the quotation at the beginning of this chapter by Viscount Kirkwall, commenting on commercial competition in the late sixteenth-century Eastern Mediterranean, is a classic formulation of these issues, phrased in terms of *exempla*: 'it appeared as if the then mistress of the sea was beginning, with prophetic instinct, to dread her future successor'.[29]

Empire and self-perception: dominion and jurisdiction

The aversion to theoretical conceptualisation is reflected in the utmost pragmatism with which the Republic approached issues concerning 'dominion' especially in the *Stato da Mar*. Its sensitivity and particularly its foreign-policy implications were very clear to the Venetian government, and Alberto Tenenti was extremely careful in arguing that the Venetian government never confused 'effective possession with a legitimate title'.[30] Such arguments were part of the self-fashioning of the Republic which we have come to know as the myth of Venice.[31] As much as the myth posited the 'eternal' – as in a-temporal – nature of the Venetian polity, unruffled by external events – hence the title of *Serenissima* – it is possible to detect clear lines of evolution in the political discourse employed by Venice on the issue of sovereignty. The centuries-long controversy on Adriatic jurisdiction is a case in point. The Republic had claimed jurisdiction of the Adriatic Sea, which was then known as the *Golfo*, and this was originally justified through a mythical tale about the role played by Venice in mediating the reconciliation between the pope and emperor which preceded the Peace of Venice (1177). The ceremony

[29] Kirkwall, *Four Years in the Ionian Islands*, 38. An analysis of several of these instances is in Lambert, 'Now is come'.
[30] Discussing the Venetian control of Dalmatia and parts of the Croatian coast: A. Tenenti, 'La politica veneziana e l'Ungheria all'epoca di Sigismondo', in T. Klaniczay ed., *Rapporti Veneto-ungheresi all'epoca del Rinascimento*, Budapest, 1975, 219–229, 222.
[31] Such as the representation of dominion through artistic production, where the imagery of dominion was particularly well developed and nuanced: Chambers, *Imperial Age*; P. Fortini-Brown, *Venice and Antiquity: The Venetian Sense of the Past*, New Haven and London, 1996; D. Howard, *Venice & the East: The Impact of the Islamic World on Venetian Architecture, 1100–1500*, New Haven and London, 2000; D. Rosand, *Myths of Venice: The Figuration of a State*, Chapel Hill, 2001.

of the marriage of the sea on the occasion of Ascension Day (*Sensa*) was for centuries the official commemoration of this event. This was not an empty claim, and policing the Adriatic was openly declared a Venetian responsibility in the articles of the 1573 peace with the Ottomans. This proved to be a serious problem in practical terms, as in the following decades it became increasingly difficult to effectively patrol it, especially given the growing violence of Uskok pirates, damaging for both Venetian and Ottoman interests.[32] As a result, Venice's claim came to be seriously contested, and a flurry of pamphlets and legal opinions were produced in the early seventeenth century. Filippo de Vivo has traced the development of these arguments, convincingly arguing how during this period Venetian justifications of its rights evolved from a mythical narrative into a pragmatic argument based on military might.[33]

When faced with the choice between 'republic' and 'empire' scholars of political thought resolutely have chosen to focus on the 'republic', whose traditional connection with 'freedom' makes it an uneasy companion to 'empire'. Interestingly this does not seem to be a concern for scholars of the commonwealth, who are more at ease with the concept that empire can coexist with a form of republican government.[34] This is, again, further evidence of the power of the myth, probably the most successful historical example of political spin – certainly one of the most long-lived.[35] But even the myth had to bow to Nicolò Machiavelli, whose long shadow still informs contemporary scholarship on the history of political thought in ways which one cannot help but think would have delighted him. Machiavelli challenged head-on the dichotomy between 'republic' and 'empire' in Venice, concluding his analysis by slotting

---

[32] W. Panciera, '"Tagliare i confini": la linea di frontiera Soranzo-Ferhat in Dalmazia (1576)', in A. Giuffrida, F. D'Avenia and D. Palermo eds., *Studi storici dedicati a Orazio Cancila*, Palermo, 2011, 237–272, 257; see also C. W. Bracewell, *The Uskoks of Senj: Piracy, Banditry, and Holy War in the Sixteenth-Century Adriatic*, Ithaca and London, 1992; E. Ivetic, 'Gli uscocchi fra mito e storiografia', in M. Gaddi and A. Zannini eds., *'Venezia non è da guerra': l'isontino, la società friulana e la Serenissima nella guerra di Gradisca (1615–1617)*, Udine, 2008, 389–397.

[33] F. de Vivo, 'Historical Justifications of Venetian Power in the Adriatic', *Journal of the History of Ideas*, 64 (2003): 159–176, 172–173 and bibliography quoted therein.

[34] Jonathan Scott talks of the commonwealth as 'a republic and empire fully apprised of its mercantile and naval interests and potential' in his *When the Waves Ruled Britannia: Geography and Political Identities, 1500–1800*, Cambridge, 2011, 72.

[35] On this topic the bibliography is simply massive. Classic starting points are W. J. Bouwsma, *Venice and the Defense of Republican Liberty: Renaissance Values in the Age of the Counter Reformation*, Berkeley and Los Angeles, 1968; J. G. A. Pocock, *The Machiavellian Moment: Florentine Political Thought and the Atlantic Republican Tradition*, Princeton, 1975; E. O. G. Haitsma Mulier, *The Myth of Venice and Dutch Republican Thought in the Seventeenth Century*, Assen, 1980.

'Venice' within those republics 'intent on peace' and therefore not determined enough for that territorial expansion which he deemed the mark
of true empires.[36] Machiavelli's comments on Venice have had a dispro-
portionate influence throughout the centuries, and fixed political scien-
tists' and intellectual historians' agenda as to what was the relationship
between republic and empire.[37] Machiavelli was a genius, there's no
doubt about that, but he was writing with a specific Florentine political
agenda at a very difficult time for Venice regarding its relationship with
other Italian states in the decade following its defeat at Agnadello (1509),
when Venice had faced alone the military aggression of a large alliance
of Italian and European states determined to curb its ambitions. The
Venetian acquisition of the *Terraferma* during the previous century
had been argued in terms of promoting Venetian trade and economic
interests; unsurprisingly the wealth and military successes of Venice had
rattled other Italian states.

It is not my intention to enter into a discussion of the nature of the
Venetian state: peaceful or bellicose? But, even assuming Machiavelli's
analysis was dispassionate, and corresponding to Venice's attitude
during the 1510s, and therefore taking it at face value, what he could
not know is how from the sixteenth century all territorial acquisitions in
the Levant – and there were several – depended on military action,
which is rather at odds with the myth of a peaceful republic.[38] In reality,
as perceptively stated by Ugo Tucci more than forty years ago, wars
are a very effective way to periodise Venetian historical development,
and I would claim even more so in analysing the fluctuation of
its economic fortunes.[39] *Pace* Machiavelli and his argument that the
non-acquisitive nature of the Venetian Republic prevented its being a
true empire, the connection between military events and economic

[36] N. Machiavelli, *Discorsi sopra la prima deca di Tito Livio*, F. Bausi ed., Rome, 2001, book I,
chapters 5–6, 37–49.

[37] This is an interpretative angle which has encountered particular success in studies of
Anglo-Venetian political and cultural thought: D. Wootton, 'Ulysses Bound? Venice
and the Idea of Liberty from Howell to Hume', in D. Wootton ed., *Republicanism,
Liberty, and Commercial Society, 1649–1776*, Stanford, 1994; M. Peltonen, *Classical
Humanism and Republicanism in English Political Thought, 1570–1640*, Cambridge,
1995; J. Eglin, *Venice Transfigured: The Myth of Venice in British Culture, 1660–1797*,
New York, 2001; V. B. Sullivan, *Machiavelli, Hobbes, and the Formation of a Liberal
Republicanism in England*, Cambridge, 2004. See also M. van Gelderen, and Q. Skinner
eds., *Republicanism: A Shared European Heritage*, 2 vols, Cambridge, 2005.

[38] Arbel, 'Venice's Maritime Empire', 142. See also B. Doumerc, 'An Exemplary Maritime
Republic: Venice at the End of the Middle Ages', in J. Hattendorf and R. W. Unger eds.,
War at Sea in the Middle Ages and in the Renaissance, Woodbridge, 2003, 151–165, 152,
where a direct connection is made between defence of economic interests and territorial
expansion.

[39] U. Tucci, *Mercanti, navi e monete nel Cinquecento veneziano*, Bologna, 1981, 47.

performance is a point well worth reflecting on, as Venetians themselves most certainly did.[40]

The relationship between Venice and its subject lands in the *Terraferma* and *Stato da Mar* was a nuanced one, where similarities in the overarching administrative structure coexisted with important differences. Dominion across the sea was different from that on the mainland, but the language binding them together was one, and was most pragmatic. In a recent synthesis on the relationship between Venice and the *Terraferma*, Michael Knapton argues how

> claims for the legitimacy of annexation and dominion were often generically framed: God's favour towards the Republic, its rights to self-defence, its commitment to freedom and peace, its altruism towards *Terraferma* communities earlier crushed by tyranny. And the most significant specific source of *de iure* sovereignty lay in subjects' spontaneous acceptance of Venetian rule; formulated in language which came to prefer the binding term *deditio*.[41]

The traditional discourse of peace emerges again strongly, the tale of the 'accidental' empire reinforced by the benevolent attitude of Venice towards its subjects. This kind of narrative is not exclusive to the *Terraferma*, as it emerges also from the language used by Greek subjects in the Levant. Towards these possessions, the need for vigilant peace was even more evident due to the proximity of the advancing Ottoman power, and fears associated with its 'tyranny' were unashamedly used by both Venice and its Greek subjects as a bargaining tool. The strong rhetoric of the contract binding the *Serenissima* with all its subjects is an essential constituent of the Venetian imperial experience and was at the basis of the communication between 'rulers and ruled' which underpinned both their political and economic dialogue.[42] The *Senato* might have been the overlord, but governance on the ground was influenced by local elites both in the *Terraferma* and in the Levant.[43] Venice's pragmatic approach to rule was generally implemented through the substantial preservation of local legislation and the

---

[40] On the costs of defending the *Stato da Mar*, see L. Pezzolo, 'La finanza pubblica', in G. Cozzi and P. Prodi eds., *Storia di Venezia*, vol. iv: *Dal Rinascimento al Barocco*, Rome, 1994, 713–773; especially 713–716, 743; for a less pessimistic tone see Arbel, 'Venice's Maritime Empire', 225–235.

[41] M. Knapton, 'Venice and the *Terraferma*', in A. Gamberini and I. Lazzarini eds., *The Italian Renaissance State*, Cambridge, 2012, 132–155, 146.

[42] On the historiography of political thought, in relation to the *Terraferma*, interesting considerations are in M. Casini, 'Fra città-stato e Stato regionale: riflessioni politiche sulla Repubblica di Venezia in età moderna', *Studi veneziani*, 44 (2002): 15–36.

[43] The most recent syntheses: Knapton, 'Venice and the *Terraferma*'; Arbel, 'Venice's Maritime Empire'.

insertion of Venetian magistrates at the top of existing hierarchies.[44] Especially in the Levant, where linguistic and religious differences were more prominent, local elites always played an important mediating role between Venice and the population. Since the beginning of Venetian domination these elites provided military service for the Republic in exchange for the enjoyment of land tenure and income, and their active engagement in the navy was evidenced by some roles – such as that of *sopracomito* on the galleys – which became their exclusive domain. Especially in the Ionian islands, engagement of the local elites slowly increased until the end of the Republic,[45] a development which created major problems for the British when the islands became their Protectorate in 1815.[46]

Venice did not actively attempt to export its own laws, even if in the prologue of Tiepolo's Statutes it was declared that 'volumus ut omnes nostrae jurisdictioni suppositi ipsis statutis utantur'.[47] However it is worth noting that their publication (1229–1232) followed the challenges created by early thirteenth-century external expansion. Notwithstanding this, a concern for the rule of law was embedded throughout Venetian territories, as the Statutes were included in the hierarchy of legal sources to act as an auxiliary source of law in all its subject territories.[48] All judicial appeals were sent to Venice, as the administration of justice was considered by the Republic the highest sign of *imperium*.[49]

There was not a single recipe for rule and administration in the *Stato da Mar*; in fact, there was a dazzling display of variety, frequently overlooked by scholars, to the point of creating interpretative problems.[50] Only considering the major territories which, at some point, were part of it,

---

[44] A. Ventura, *Nobiltà e popolo nella società veneta del Quattrocento e Cinquecento*, Milan, 1993 (1964).

[45] A. Viggiano, *Governanti e governati: legittimità del potere ed esercizio dell'autorità nello stato veneto della prima età moderna*, Treviso, 1993; M. Folin, 'Spunti per una ricerca su amministrazione veneziana e società ionia nella seconda metà del Settecento', in *Studi veneti offerti a Gaetano Cozzi*, Venice, 1992, 333–347.

[46] These issues are analysed at length in M. Fusaro, 'Representation in Practice: The Myth of Venice and the British Protectorate in the Ionian Islands (1801–1864)', in M. Calaresu, F. de Vivo and J.-P. Rubiés eds., *Exploring Cultural History: Essays in Honour of Peter Burke*, Aldershot, 2010, 309–325.

[47] 'We want these statutes to be used throughout our jurisdictions.'

[48] For an example of this interaction see M. Kolyva, '"Obbedir et esseguir tutti l'infrascritti Capitoli": i Capitoli dell'isola di Zante durante il dominio veneziano (fine XV–fine XII sec.)', in Maltezou, Tzavara, Vlassi eds., *I Greci durante la venetocrazia*, 483–495.

[49] Cozzi ed., *Stato, società e giustizia*.

[50] McKee, *Uncommon Dominion*, 7. A sample of these expressions is in Arbel, 'Venice's Maritime Empire', 125–253, 125 footnote 2. A proper analysis of this terminology would be a very welcome addition to scholarship.

we can see many different solutions employed to implement Venice's authority.[51] From the thirteenth to the eighteenth century there were possessions administered through a proper feudal structure, like Negroponte (1209–1470) and the Archipelago (1207–1566).[52] Crete (1211–1669) was probably the closest example of a settlers' colony.[53] From the point of view of successful administration and governance it is worth highlighting how, notwithstanding a notoriously rebellious local ruling class, the island remained Venetian for more than 450 years. In Sally McKee's evocative words: 'the Venetian commune kept possession of the largest Mediterranean island after Sicily for nearly five centuries, longer than the English held India, Spain held Mexico, or France held Québec'.[54] Cyprus (1489–1571) was a kingdom, but should also be seen as a plantation colony, whose sugar production technology provided the blueprint for those in the New World.[55] The Ionian islands (Corfu 1386–1797, the others 1485–1797) had a hybrid nature, in a sense a variety of settlers' colony, but the settlers were *stradioti*, ethnic Greek and Albanian soldiers coming from the rest of the Greek Levant.[56] The Morea (1684–1718) was again a kingdom.[57] This variety of institutional arrangements was devised by paying close attention to local realities and to what was considered in each case to be the most expedient way to administer and rule these distant territories. This system of rule lasted for centuries, and the government of the Republic constantly elaborated new administrative solutions. Venice's ruling bodies throughout its history remained engaged in a continuous dialogue on these matters, and its subject populations were always involved in local administration. This communication between the *Dominante* and its subjects made Venetians well aware that enactment *in situ* of the ideology and decisions of the metropolis was a complex exercise in negotiation; as Angelo Basadonna, former Rector of Cephalonia, put it in 1603: 'The laws are passed in Venice, but it is

---

[51] An exhaustive list is in Arbel, 'Venice's Maritime Empire', 132–136.

[52] Jacoby, 'The Venetian Presence in the Latin Empire', 197, 157.

[53] Chambers, *Imperial Age*, 53.

[54] McKee, *Uncommon Dominion*, 2.

[55] M.-L. von Wartburg, 'Production de sucre de canne à Chypre: un chapitre de technologie médiévale', in M. Balard and A. Ducellier eds., *Coloniser au Moyen Âge*, Paris, 1995, 126–131, and bibliography quoted therein on the extant archaeological evidence; see also E. Skoufari, *Cipro veneziana, 1473–1571: istituzioni e culture nel regno della Serenissima*, Rome, 2011.

[56] For an economic analysis of Zante and Cephalonia within the Venetian state see Fusaro, *Uva passa*.

[57] A. Stouraiti and M. Infelise eds., *Venezia e la Guerra di Morea: guerra, politica e cultura alla fine del Seicento*, Milan, 2005.

in the Levant that they have to be implemented'.[58] This flexible recipe for colonial government created a nuanced social and political landscape, crucially based on a constant dialogue with local elites, another reason to introduce Venice into the debate on the nature of empire. The British comparison again comes in handy, an empire governed with a massive dose of pragmatism and a large range of internal structures: colonies, dependencies, dominions, protectorates.[59]

Commercial empires . . .

The 'commercial' nature of the Venetian empire attracted the attention of England from this early modern period, and contemporaries saw parallels with the budding English experience. There is a general historiographical consensus that British colonial policy during the seventeenth and eighteenth centuries was based on the needs of commerce, and a similar consensus had existed for Venice since the beginning of its empire.[60] However, continuing engagement with Machiavelli's analytical categories led to a conceptual opposition between an empire based on territorial acquisitions and one striving towards maximising trade income, as if an unbridgeable opposition existed between the two. A similar attitude is also sometimes present when England is being discussed. David Armitage argued in this regard that 'the attachment to commerce – and the means by which commerce connected the various parts of the empire to one another – made the British empire different from its predecessors or its rivals, most of which (it was believed) had been integrated by force'.[61] Apart from the omission of the Venetian precedent, what perplexes me in this passage, just one example of a common attitude, is the direct link posited between the 'nature' of empire and the 'manner' of its acquisition, as if the latter was an absolute determinant in the successive manner of governance and economic exploitation. I could not agree more with Sophus Reinert in his unpacking of the recurrent 'historical judgment that sets in opposition conquest and commerce'.[62]

Where instead there is an acknowledged, seemingly inexorable, link is between commercial empire and naval hegemony – again a shared

---

[58] ASV, *Cinque Savi alla Mercanzia*, b. 836b, file I, cc.n.n. (25 May 1603). This argument is further developed in Fusaro, 'Representation in Practice'.

[59] T. O. Lloyd, *The British Empire, 1558–1995*, Oxford, 1996 (1984), ix.

[60] P. J. Marshall, 'The First British Empire', in R. W. Winks ed., *The Oxford History of the British Empire*, vol. v: *Historiography*, Oxford, 1999, 43–53, 47.

[61] D. Armitage, *The Ideological Origins of the British Empire*, Cambridge, 2000, 8.

[62] S. A. Reinert, 'Lessons on the Rise and Fall of Great Powers: Conquest, Commerce, and Decline in Enlightenment Italy', *American Historical Review*, 115 (2010): 1395–1425, 1397.

Anglo-Venetian concern – and for that reason alone the Levant territories represent an excellent case study.

Commercial empires lead to the creation of dependent markets where the ruling power can sell its wares – usually manufactures – and take advantage of natural resources, whose distribution is centrally controlled and whose taxation benefits the imperial centre at the expense of the periphery. Benjamin Arbel, one of the leading scholars in this field, argued that Venetian 'colonialism' assigned a tripartite function to possessions in the Levant: essential bases for the logistic and military support of shipping, centres of collection and redistribution, and sources of natural and human resources.[63] The famed freedom of Venice was in practice financed also by the economic exploitation of its territories. Following their acquisition, the rich agricultural lands of the *Terraferma*, along with the products manufactured there, played an increasingly central role in the economy of the Venetian state. The same happened in the *Stato da Mar*, which was a lot more than a series of commercial bases. For example, the production of salt had been one of the constituents of many colonial economies since the Middle Ages, and the monumental work of Jean-Claude Hocquet on the role of salt within the Venetian world openly discusses it in terms of 'colonial economy'.[64] Other Levantine colonial goods were also crucial in the early modern period: sugar, wine, currants and olive oil were all produced, taxed and commercialised under (theoretical) strict Venetian central control, as shall be discussed at length throughout this book. In this transfer of wealth from the periphery to the centre, the city-state's interests fully coincided with those of any other 'imperial capital' in acquiring income through monopolies of trade and rights of sovereignty.[65] The economic role of the *Stato da Mar* during the early modern period is another area now benefitting from new investigations and interpretations. The easiest way to trace these developments over the past twenty years is to compare two essays written by Arbel. In the mid-1990s, surveying the Venetian Levantine colonies over the *longue durée*, the bibliography he quoted showed a wealth of contributions for the period up to the fifteenth century and a relative lack of studies for the subsequent period.[66] Conversely, in a

---

[63] B. Arbel, 'Colonie d'oltremare', in A. Tenenti and U. Tucci eds., *Storia di Venezia*, vol. v: *Il Rinascimento: Società ed economia*, Rome, 1996, 947–985, 978.

[64] J.-C. Hocquet, *Le sel et la fortune de Venise*, Lille, 1978; for a discussion of the 'colonial' element see his: 'L'économie colonial et les sels grecs à la fin du Moyen Âge', in Maltezou, Tzavara, Vlassi eds., *I Greci durante la venetocrazia*, 65–81.

[65] Hocquet, 'Fiscalité et pouvoir colonial', 279.

[66] Arbel, 'Colonie d'oltremare'.

similar essay published in 2013, the bibliography contained instead many studies reflecting new attention to the socio-economic development of the early modern Venetian Levant.[67] There are many solid reasons for the late development of in-depth studies of the *Dominio da Mar*. The rather complex mix of languages (Italian, Greek, Turkish, Slovenian, Croat, Serb, Albanian), long-standing clashing political interests, and the diverging propaganda needs of the various states controlling these territories were all factors that impeded research. Considering just the Greek case, it is a relatively new development that Greek historians are addressing the period of foreign control of their territory in a less politicised way,[68] moving away from the relatively safe waters of the history of cultural relations – supported by a long and great tradition of Greek-Venetian studies[69] – into the hitherto uncharted territories of identities, social unrest, and mutual social and economic interaction.[70] And it seems rather banal to recall how works published in Italy before the Second World War were heavily influenced by a very politicised view of the *Mare nostrum*, just as much of nineteenth-century Greek scholarship was part of the propaganda exercise for the creation of the Greek state.[71]

---

[67] Arbel, 'Venice's Maritime Empire'.

[68] See N. Panayotakis, 'Premessa', in G. Ortalli ed., *Venezia e Creta*, Venice, 1998, 1–8, 1.

[69] On the cultural relations between Venice and the Greek world see H. G. Beck, M. Manoussakas and A. Pertusi eds., *Venezia, centro di mediazione tra Oriente e Occidente (secoli XV–XVI): aspetti e problemi*, 2 vols., Florence, 1977; D. J. Geanakoplos, *Greek Scholars in Venice: Studies in the Dissemination of Greek Learning from Byzantium to Western Europe*, Cambridge (Mass.), 1962; and the proceedings of the conferences: *Venezia ed il Levante fino al secolo XV*, 2 vols, Florence, 1973–1974; *Venezia e l'Oriente tra tardo Medioevo e Rinascimento*, Florence, 1966.

[70] D. Arvanitakis, *Το ρεμπελιό των ποπολάρων (1628): κοινωνικές αντιθέσεις στην πόλη της Ζακύνθου (The Revolt of the Popolari (1628): Social Contrasts in the City of Zante)*, Athens, 2001; K. Konstantinidou, *Το κακό οδεύει έρποντας ... Οι λοιμοί της πανώλης στα Ιόνια Νησιά (17ος–18ος αι.) (The Disaster Creeps Crawling ... The Plague Epidemics of the Ionian Islands (17th–18th Centuries))*, Venice, 2007; G. D. Pagratis, *Κοινωνία και οικονομία στο βενετικό «Κράτος της Θάλασσας». Οι ναυτιλιακές επιχειρήσεις της Κέρκυρας (1496–1538) (Society and Economy in the Venetian Stato da Mar: The Maritime Enterprises of Corfu (1496–1538))*, Athens, 2013.

[71] E. Lunzi, *Della condizione politica delle Isole Ionie sotto il Dominio Veneto*, Venice, 1858; D. d'Istria, 'Les Iles-Ioniennes sous la Domination de Venise et le protectorat britannique: origines et tendances actuelles des partis indigènes', *Revue des deux mondes*, 16 (1858): 381–422; D. De Mordo, *Saggio di una descrizione geografico-statistica delle isole Ionie (Eptanesia) proposto ad uso della gioventù studiosa*, Corfu, 1865; M. and N. Pignatorre, *Memorie storiche e critiche dell'isola di Cefalonia dai tempi eroici alla caduta della Repubblica veneta*, 2 vols, Corfu, 1889. Classic examples of the Italian approach are G. Damerini, *Le isole Ionie nel sistema Adriatico dal dominio veneziano a Buonaparte*, Milan, 1943; B. Dudan, *Il dominio veneziano di Levante*, Bologna, 1938. An analysis of these issues is in F. M. Paladini, 'Velleità e capitolazione della propaganda talassocratica veneziana', *Venetica*, 17 (2002): 147–172.

The importance of the period between the fall of Cyprus (1571) and the war of Candia (1669) had always been acknowledged. However, very little was done to try to define its general impact, not only for the Venetian economy and state structure but also for the shifting attitudes and balance of power in the greater Mediterranean.[72] The roads opened in the 1960s by seminal texts like *Crisis and Change in the Venetian Economy* and the proceedings of the conference on *Aspetti e cause della decadenza economica veneziana nel secolo XVII*, which took a multifaceted approach to the Venetian state economy, were not well trodden after such auspicious beginnings.[73] But even though these publications laid out most of the crucial issues of Venetian political and economic administration in the Levant, they were interested in the transition between the sixteenth and seventeenth centuries, above all in its 'trade crisis' facet, and did not analyse the problems and challenges faced by the Venetian government structure and production organisation in the territories themselves. The classic topics of 'woollens' and 'spices' were for a long time the dominant parameters of analysis, virtually suffocating any other point of view. What was lacking, and what is now starting to happen, was a view of the *Dominio da Mar* as an integral part of the Venetian system, an effort to see it as more than just an issue of trade routes, defence and the decadence of the Venetian mercantile fleet. By thus changing the focus to the system as a whole, it is possible to see the *Dominio da Mar* as the great 'lost opportunity' of Venice in the early modern period. It is absolutely essential to have a clear view of the situation and events in the Venetian territories in the Levant to appreciate the crucial impact of the English penetration of the Venetian commercial – and political – space. Only against this background is it possible to fully understand in what ways the English presence was a catalyst for economic and social change in the islands themselves and in the Eastern Mediterranean at large. The Ionian islands were the stage where it can indeed be argued that the interests of the 'commercial' empire clashed with those of the 'territorial' empire, with

---

[72] There were, of course, some exceptions. See the catalogue of the exhibition *Venezia e la difesa del Levante: da Lepanto a Candia 1570–1670*, Venice, 1986; M. Costantini ed., *Il Mediterraneo centro-orientale tra vecchie e nuove egemonie: trasformazioni economiche, sociali ed istituzionali nelle Isole Ionie dal declino della Serenissima all'avvento delle potenze atlantiche (sec. XVII–XVIII)*, Rome, 1998. Nonetheless, it is extremely telling that even in the excellent volume dedicated to Crete and Venice (Ortalli ed., *Venezia e Creta*), the issue of the economic crisis was almost ignored, and the greatest part of the attention was primarily focused on the period up to the sixteenth century.

[73] *Aspetti a cause della decadenza economica veneziana nel secolo XVII*, Venice and Rome, 1961; B. Pullan ed., *Crisis and Change in the Venetian Economy in the Sixteenth and Seventeenth Centuries*, London, 1968.

dramatic long-term repercussions for the Venetian state as a whole and for the balance of power in the area.

... and mercantile networks

Within the 'economic realm' Venice *acted* and *thought* as an empire. From 1204 to 1797, its ruling class took advantage of colonial products, whether produced in the *Terraferma* or the Levant, introduced land taxes and tried to fully centralise in Venice the collection and redistribution of colonial income. The high profile of Venice and its commercial might for many years also benefitted its subjects. Whilst they did not have any chance of meaningful political activity beyond the local level, Greek subjects especially found in the economic sphere possibilities to improve their status both within their communities and vis-à-vis the state at large. For its subjects the imperial nature of Venice was a comfortable identity to use, especially abroad, to support and enhance their chances of economic success; their link to Venice gave them visibility and the opportunity to take advantage of practical privileges they otherwise would have not been able to access. For a long time the relationship between rulers and ruled was mutually beneficial also in underpinning the economy of the Venetian *Stato da Mar*. I have argued elsewhere how financial analysis allows us to follow the structural changes of Venetian and subjects' trading networks in the first half of the seventeenth century.[74] This allows us to see clearly how between the loss of Cyprus and that of Candia – again war periodisation – the Venetian government developed a veritable obsession with the needs of defence, and consequently the need to defend its maritime empire became more important than its effective management. The result of this was that Venice did not manage to control and direct the new mercantile networks emerging within its empire, and this failure had important repercussions in managing it. The real failure of Venice was in not making its subjects, who increasingly articulated their economic activities through such networks, into real stakeholders of the empire. These developments in the *Stato da Mar* appear to mirror those in the *Terraferma*, whose population was also cut off from political action at the highest level, but with the added burden that its wealth was increasingly spent to support the defence of the maritime empire.

The main body of the book will flesh out how, during those decades, English merchants belonging to the Levant Company, and Greek

---

[74] M. Fusaro, 'Cooperating Mercantile Networks in the Early Modern Mediterranean', *The Economic History Review*, 65 (2012): 701–718.

merchants who were subjects of the Republic, developed a fruitful economic partnership that lasted for more than two centuries and laid the groundwork for the establishment of a British Protectorate on the Ionian islands after the fall of the Venetian Republic. The establishment and strengthening of this relationship was a direct consequence of the Venetian inability to conceive and implement a coherent economic policy for its dominions in the Levant, as issues of defence engulfed everything else. The result was that the economic interests of its Greek subjects ended up being better taken care of by an alliance with the English. The erstwhile 'mistress of the sea' failed to fully appreciate the co-dependency of commercial empires and merchant networks, and how the interplay of trade, finance and shipping can fundamentally affect the basic structure of empire.[75]

This leads us neatly to the vexed issue of decline, the 'elephant' peeking from the pages of all analyses of Venice in the early modern period. The topic of maritime decadence became a veritable obsession for Venetians themselves, and later a commonplace of Venetian history, economic or otherwise. In a classic contribution, Gino Luzzatto dated the onset of the Venetian decline to around 1620 when for the first time the Venetian customs authority defined as 'merci ponentine' ('western goods') the oriental spices imported to the Mediterranean by Dutch ships.[76] It was indeed a moment of profound symbolic value; the reclassification of 'spices' – once the mainstay of Venetian European trade supremacy – into a product from Western Europe cannot have failed to have an impact. Sophus Reinert recently commented how the decline debate

[was] embedded in the political economy of Enlightenment Italy, which was almost certainly the most advanced debate on decline in the history of the West. Why? Because, uniquely, Italy had twice declined from a hegemonic position: once through conquest, with the barbarian invasions that toppled Rome's Western Empire; and once through commerce, with the economic competition from territorial monarchies that signalled the end of the Italian Renaissance.[77]

Venice was at the centre of this process, and its direct interaction with England – the rising star of those times – can elucidate substantive differences and similarities between states and empires.

---

[75] On the role of informal merchants' networks activities within empires see Catia Antunes' ERC project *Fighting Monopolies, Defying Empires 1500–1750: A Comparative Overview of Free Agents and Informal Empires in Western Europe and the Ottoman Empire.*

[76] G. Luzzatto, 'La decadenza di Venezia dopo le scoperte geografiche nella tradizione e nella realtà', *Archivio veneto*, 84 (1954): 162–181; see also his 'Introduzione', in *Aspetti e cause della decadenza economica veneziana nel secolo XVII*, Venice and Rome, 1961, 9–20, 19–20.

[77] Reinert, 'Lessons on the Rise and Fall', 1395.

Towards an organic vision of Venice

It is time to bring empire back into the history of Venice. John Martin and Dennis Romano listed four main ways in which Venice has been interpreted: as a great city, an enduring republic, an expansive empire and a regional state.[78] In the middle of the twentieth century, the historiographical perception of Venice was skewed towards the *Stato da Mar*, and the *Terraferma* was barely taken into account. In the last fifty years the *Terraferma* has become a strong and almost independent field of enquiry.[79] This has been a welcome development, but it is time to start considering the Venetian state in its entirety – *terra* and *mar* – blending together different historiographical strands and traditions, aiming at a holistic approach to the topic of statecraft and political economy. In doing this it will be necessary to arrive at an analytical definition of the totality of the Venetian state. In the last few decades we have started to conceptualise it mostly as a peculiar variety amongst the Italian 'regional states', which has not made it easy to include the *Stato da Mar*. This volume aims at contributing to this effort by reintegrating the history of the *Stato da Mar* within the larger Venetian state and empire. Venice's history has always been categorised as 'unique' – from its peculiar setting on water, which was such a strong determinant of its nature and development,[80] to the distinctive pattern of its economic evolution.[81] It was the longest-lived and most stable republic and was also the only one of all the Italian regional states to hold possessions outside of Italy for centuries. This uniqueness has been an element of strength, and made the study of its history an almost independent field of scholarship; it should not become a weakness by making that study too self-referential and averse to a comparative approach. Now that full agreement has been achieved that one of the intrinsic characteristics of early modern European states was their composite nature, it is time to start reflecting on how to integrate into this vision the Venetian state with its geographically distant territories.[82]

---

[78] Martin and Romano, *Venice Reconsidered*, 1.

[79] For a recent reassessment of the economic contribution of the mainland see the contributions in P. Lanaro ed., *At the Centre of the Old World: Trade and Manufacturing in Venice and the Venetian Mainland, 1400–1800*, Toronto, 2006, and bibliography quoted therein.

[80] For these issues see especially the work of Elisabeth Crouzet-Pavan: *Sopra le acque salse: espaces, pouvoirs et société à Venise à la fin du Moyen Âge*, Rome, 1992 and *Venice Triumphant: The Horizons of a Myth*, Baltimore and London, 2002.

[81] F. C. Lane, *Venice: A Maritime Republic*, Baltimore, 1973.

[82] H. G. Koenigsberger, 'Dominium Regale or Dominium Politicum et Regale', in his *Politicians and Virtuosi: Essays in Early Modern History*, London, 1986, 1–26; J. H. Elliott, 'A Europe of Composite Monarchies', *Past and Present*, 137 (1992): 48–71. A discussion of these issues within the Venetian *Terraferma* is in I. Pederzani,

Gasparo Contarini, the 'handmaiden' of the myth, did not discuss the economy in his famous treatise on the government of Venice. His aim was the glorification of the political and intellectual legitimacy of the Republic; the focus of his attention was the political genealogy of the Venetian political structure, not the income which built and supported it.[83] However, the economy was the source of Venice's success and wealth, praised as the primary activity of all its people: patricians, citizens, *popolani* and subjects. Throughout the long history of Venice, economic considerations were essential in building and maintaining its empire, and this was valid for the expansion in the Italian *Terraferma* as much as for its possessions in the Levant.

Acquiring, managing and defending empire were defining experiences in the development of the Venetian state. An analysis of the social and political implications of colonisation and empire-building, as well as those of administration and the loss of empire, is thus long overdue. The ultimate goal of the Venetian government was commercial hegemony through long-distance trade and the administration of its possessions. The sad irony is that one of the main reasons why Venice lost its role of commercial broker between Europe and the Levant lies precisely in the imperial nature of the Venetian state. The need to defend the *Stato da Mar* forced Venice to choose between aggressive commercialism and appeasement of a neighbour whose might and scale of resources were incomparable.

Venezia e lo 'Stado de Terraferma': il governo delle comunità nel territorio bergamasco (secc-XV–XVIII), Milan, 1992.

[83] G. Contarini, *The Commonwealth and Gouernment of Venice*, trans. Lewes Lewkenor, London, 1599 (1543). On Contarini's life and work, see *DBI* s.v.

1   The medieval background

The economic connection between the Italian peninsula and England had been a strong one since the Middle Ages. First as agents of the papacy, then as financial backers of the crown and as importers of Mediterranean products and exporters of English raw wool and woollen cloths, Italian merchants and financiers had been active in England since the thirteenth century.

Particularly involved in the financial administration of the kingdom were the Tuscans; in 1275 merchants from Lucca were allocated the farm of the New Customs of England, and in the same period Florentines were in charge of tax collection in Ireland.[1] Tuscan financial operators played indeed a multifaceted role in the English medieval economy, and the impact of the insolvency of Edward III in the 1340s was an important contributing factor in the famous bankruptcies of the Bardi and Peruzzi.[2] Like the Bardi and Peruzzi, several Tuscan companies also acted as agents of the papacy in the collection of dues and their transmission back to Rome. Closely tied to this activity was that of wool buyers, as English wools were deemed of excellent quality and essential to the production of luxury textiles in Tuscany, as in Flanders.[3]

---

[1] E. Carson, *The Ancient and Rightful Custom: History of the English Custom System*, London, 1972, 17.

[2] The traditional interpretation is in E. Russell, 'The Societies of the Bardi and the Peruzzi and Their Dealings with Edward III', in G. Unwin ed., *Finance and Trade under Edward III: The London Lay Subsidy of 1332*, London, 1918, 93–135; A. Sapori, *La crisi delle compagnie mercantili dei Bardi e dei Peruzzi*, Florence, 1926; R. de Roover, *The Rise and Decline of the Medici Bank 1397–1494*, Cambridge (Mass.), 1963, 2–3. Michael Postan (*Medieval Trade and Finance*, Cambridge, 2002 (1973), 209, 335–341) sees in the reign of Edward III the moment of highest influence of Italians within the English economy, with the Bardi and Peruzzi bankruptcies heralding the beginning of the rise of locals both in trade and finance. For a more recent, and revisionist, view see: E. S. Hunt, 'A New Look at the Dealings of the Bardi and Peruzzi with Edward III', *The Journal of Economic History*, 50 (1990): 149–162, and his *The Medieval Super-Companies: A Study of the Peruzzi Company of Florence*, New York, 1994.

[3] Hunt, 'A New Look at the Dealings of the Bardi and Peruzzi', 151.

In the Middle Ages, international trade and exchange at this level were possible only with strong political – that is to say, in most cases, 'royal' – support, and in fact the activities of the Tuscans and the tight interconnection of their business with political patronage, such as the tax farm, are a clear example of this. The eternal problem of any medieval monarch – cash flow – which was especially crucial in times of military engagement, could be easily solved by borrowing from merchants, and foreign merchants were particularly desirable targets of this policy as their activities were almost totally dependent on the crown's favour, which usually made them more receptive to opening credit lines.[4] The importance of foreign trade in financing the crown was particularly true for England throughout the Middle Ages and the early modern period; in the mid-fifteenth century half of royal income came from the duties on foreign trade.[5]

The important financial role played by the Italians – sometimes referred to as Lombards – in the economy of England facilitated the growth of trade links. However, notwithstanding these long-standing connections with England, the various Italian economic operators active in England rarely enjoyed special treatment or commercial privileges. In the fourteenth century, the Peruzzi did indeed receive some advantages in the export of wool from England,[6] but these kind of deals were always *ad hoc* – personally bestowed by the monarch on specific individuals – and never amounted to the kind of substantial and consistent privileges that other groups of foreigners, especially the Hanseatic merchants, enjoyed in England in those centuries.

Beginnings of maritime trade

Direct maritime trade between Italy and England began towards the end of the thirteenth century. As Roberto Lopez convincingly argued, behind this late start lay considerations of costs and markets; during the thirteenth century the important and substantial trade between Italy and Flanders was efficiently run through land routes, with the fairs of Champagne providing an obvious and convenient financial and commercial hub, whilst England was less important for Italian merchants

---

[4] A dated, but still rather good synthesis of the issues at play is in A. Beardwood, 'Alien Merchants and the English Crown in the Later Fourteenth Century', *The Economic History Review*, 2 (1930): 229–260.

[5] E. B. Fryde, 'The English Cloth Industry and the Trade with the Mediterranean', in his *Studies in Medieval Trade and Finance*, London, 1983, XV: 343–363, 348, quoting J. L. Kirby's figures ('The Issues of the Lancastrian Exchequer and Lord Cromwell's Estimates of 1433', *Bulletin of the Institute of Historical Research*, 24 (1951), 133).

[6] Hunt, 'A New Look at the Dealings of the Bardi and Peruzzi', 158.

as it 'had few valuable goods that Mediterranean merchants desired, and it was a poor consumer of the more valuable Mediterranean and Eastern goods'.[7] It was only towards the end of the thirteenth century that English wool started to find a growing market in Florence, and this helped to boost trade between Italy and England.[8] Tuscans played an important role for the burgeoning English woollen and textile industry; exports were not exclusively directed towards Florence, whose cloth industry relied on several sources of supply, and some of the English wool they traded was also destined for the textile industries of Flanders and Brabant, in the Low Countries.[9] During this period both the Italians and their English commercial partners were fully aware of the Italians' superiority, both commercially and financially: thirteenth-century England was still an underdeveloped country, which exported raw materials and imported luxury and manufactured goods, and the trade between the two countries – whether sea or land based – was unquestionably run by the Italians.[10]

This first phase of Anglo-Italian direct trade came to an end in the 1340s with the demise of the Bardi and Peruzzi companies. Their bankruptcies (1343–1345) correspond to a period for which extremely scant economic documentary evidence survives in England, and it is therefore most difficult to follow trade flows in any detail until the last quarter of the fourteenth century.[11] What we know for sure is that Italian mercantile colonies were present in various port cities of the southern coast of England, Southampton having the largest one throughout the Middle Ages. This was the favourite destination of Italian shipping and merchants not only because of its excellent harbour, but also because it acted as the wool and cloth commercial centre for the southwest of

[7] R. S. Lopez, 'Majorcans and Genoese on the North Sea Route in the Thirteenth Century', *Revue belge de philologie et d'histoire*, 29 (1951): 1163–1179, 1164, 1166.

[8] Lopez, 'Majorcans and Genoese on the North Sea Route', 1168.

[9] E. B. Fryde, 'Italian Maritime Trade with Medieval England (c.1270–c.1530)', in his *Studies in Medieval Trade*, XIV: 291–337, 295–296. See some interesting consideration on the interconnectedness of these trades in M. Arnoux and J. Bottin, 'La Manche: frontière, marché ou espace de production? Fonctions économiques et évolution d'un espace maritime (XIVe–XVIIe siècles)', in S. Cavaciocchi ed., *Ricchezza del mare, ricchezza dal mare, secc. XIII–XVIII*, 2 vols, Florence, 2006, ii: 875–906.

[10] On this see C. Dyer, *An Age of Transition? Economy and Society in England in the later Middle Ages*, Oxford, 2005, 8–13. A comparative overview of the economic sectors is in R. H. Britnell, 'England and Northern Italy in the Early Fourteenth Century: The Economic Contrasts', *Transactions of the Royal Historical Society*, 39 (1989): 167–183, 167–172; and K. G. Persson, 'Was there a Productivity Gap between Fourteenth Century Italy and England?', *Economic History Review*, 46 (1993): 105–114.

[11] Fryde, 'Italian Maritime Trade', 302–304, and his 'The English Cloth Industry'; E. M. Carus-Wilson, *Medieval Merchant Venturers*, London, 1954, 259.

England and was relatively close to London. In fact Southampton, during the fourteenth and fifteenth centuries, became the centre of direct trade between England and the Mediterranean in general, with Italian, Balearic and Spanish products arriving there on Italian bottoms.[12] Thanks to the growth of its role in international trade, the town also became a regional commercial entrepôt and acquired a growing role within the kingdom at large.[13] As much as the Italians were criticised by local merchants, it is clear that in this period 'through the Italians, and in particular through the use of Genoese shipping, the English cloth producers gained access to new markets which otherwise would have remained much longer out of their effective reach'.[14]

The Genoese had been the first Italians to sail directly to England. Roberto Lopez dated at 1278 their first ship arriving in England, and from 1298 regular stops on the route to Flanders were organised, originally under the auspices of Benedetto Zaccaria, the leading alum monopolist.[15] Alum was the chief commodity of the Anglo-Genoese trade in the Middle Ages; indispensable to the textile proto-industry for fixing colours, it was needed throughout Europe, and the Genoese, who had an abundance of it from their Anatolian colony of Phocea, for centuries enjoyed a near-monopoly of its European trade.[16]

The expansion of Genoese trade with the Iberian peninsula, especially with Castile, at the end of the thirteenth century fostered the increase of direct maritime links with the North of Europe, and trade with England benefitted from this. By the following century, Genoese trade with England was well established and branched out from alum to other chemicals (especially dyes such as woad and madder)[17] which were indispensable for the textile industry. In exchange for these they exported wool which they redistributed in Flanders and in Italy – mostly in Florence and Tuscany. By 1378, Southampton had become so important for the Genoese trading system that the Genoese toyed with the idea of establishing there a general staple which would coordinate the entirety of

[12] A. A. Ruddock, *Italian Merchants and Shipping in Southampton, 1270–1600*, Southampton, 1951, 76–77; see also Fryde, 'Italian Maritime Trade', 313.

[13] D. Abulafia, 'Cittadino e "denizen": mercanti mediterranei a Southampton e a Londra', in M. Del Treppo ed., *Sistema di rapporti ed elites economiche in Europa (sec. XII–XVII)*, Naples, 1994, 273–291, 274–276.

[14] Fryde, 'The English Cloth Industry', 348.

[15] Lopez, 'Majorcans and Genoese on the North Sea Route', 1176–1177.

[16] On the Genoese alum trade and Phocea see R. S. Lopez, *Genova marinara nel Duecento: Benedetto Zaccaria ammiraglio e mercante*, Milan, 1933; details on the alum trade with England are in J. Heers, *Gênes au XVe siècle: civilisation méditerranéenne, grand capitalism, et capitalism populaire*, Paris, 1971, 286–290.

[17] Woad is a blue dyestuff prepared from the leaves of the plant *Isatis tinctoria*; madder is a reddish-purple dyestuff from the the the root of the plant *Rubia tinctorum*.

their woollen trade with the North of Europe. The project collapsed due to the political entanglements of the Hundred Years War and conflicting interests amongst the Genoese merchants, at that time divided between supporters of trade with France and supporters of trade with England.[18]

In 1381 the long conflict between Venice and Genoa ended with a hard-earned and costly victory for Venice, which established its naval pre-eminence in the Eastern Mediterranean and hegemony over Levantine trade. In practice, even though Genoa kept the important island of Chios until 1566, the end of this war was also the end of Genoese ambitions in the Levant. From being mediators between eastern and western markets, thus following a rather similar development to their arch competitor Venice, Genoese merchants turned decisively westward and started to shift their interests from trade to finance.

Venice was the last of the Italian states to establish direct contacts with England. Only from the 1390s did the Flanders galleys – as the northern branch of the state galleys was known – start to stop regularly in Southampton on their way to Bruges.

Around the same time as when Venice was finally establishing direct commercial links with England, Florentine merchants based in London seemed to have recovered after the mid-century bankruptcies, and, as evidenced by the Datini papers, between 1391 and 1410 on average more than eight ships per year were active between England and the Mediterranean to cater to the needs of Florence.[19] This resurgence was helped in the 1460s by the discovery of the alum mines at Tolfa, in the Papal States, something that weakened Genoese hegemony in this trade and allowed the Florentines to penetrate the circuit through the strong links between the papacy and Florence.[20] A consequence of this was that for a short period Florence found it profitable to send its own galleys to England:

the Florentine galleys for England and Flanders relied very much for their north bound cargoes on goods picked up in Provence and Spain. Florence itself as we have seen had little to offer but the luxury wool and silk cloths for which she was famous, and for these there was a limited market in the north, particularly in England where there was a tendency to restrict the import of such cloths.[21]

---

[18] Abulafia, 'Cittadino e "denizen"', 277.

[19] F. Melis, 'Sulla "nazionalità" del commercio marittimo Inghilterra-Mediterraneo negli anni intorno al 1400', in his *I trasporti e le comunicazioni nel Medioevo*, Florence, 1984, 81–101, 84–85; see also G. A. Holmes, 'Florentine Merchants in England, 1346–1436', *Economic History Review*, 13 (1960): 193–208.

[20] J. Delumeau, *L'alun de Rome XVe–XIXe siècles*, Paris, 1962.

[21] M. E. Mallett, *The Florentine Galleys in the Fifteenth Century. With the Diary of Luca di Maso degli Albizzi. Captain of the Galleys, 1429–30*, Oxford, 1967, 133.

Collaboration amongst Italians in England

Italian commercial operators active in England throughout the Middle Ages tried to avoid getting involved in local politics, and maintained a close level of collaboration which went above and beyond the relationships amongst their home states back in Italy. Political confrontations aside, from the early fourteenth century, it is possible to speak of an 'Italian economic system', and evidence of the interdependence of the major Italian cities – Venice, Genoa, Milan and Florence – is 'implied by the parities of their gold currencies'.[22] This economic interdependence, and the frequent instances of collaboration between Italian merchants, becomes visible when analysing their activities abroad. When in 1340 Edward III approached the Venetian Doge trying to secure his naval support against France, which at that time was backed by Genoa, Venice declined, citing the Ottoman naval threat as the main reason, notwithstanding the offer of a very privileged tax regime for Venetians active in the kingdom.[23] Venice might have been fighting a tough commercial war with Genoa in home waters, but when outside of Italy or the Mediterranean, the overall interests of supporting trade seem always to have come first, and neutrality was the preferred default option.

Collaboration was stronger between Venetians and Florentines; indeed, up to the mid-fifteenth century, Venetians frequently employed Florentine merchants as their agents in Southampton.[24] At the end of that century Florentine merchants would resist the temptation to accept the privileges offered them by the English crown to get them on their side against the Venetians during the malmsey commerce war, which shall be discussed in some detail later.[25] In the same period the Venetians chose a Genoese merchant as their consul in Southampton; as much as this has been seen as a sign of the declining Venetian presence, it is also a clear sign of cooperation between Italians.[26]

The importance of Italian shipping and commerce in England reached its climax in the period 1390–1460. In those decades Genoese, Venetians and Florentines were all increasing the volume and value of their trade by

---

[22] R. H. Britnell, 'The Towns of England and Northern Italy in the Early Fourteenth Century', *Economic History Review*, 44 (1991): 21–35, 22.

[23] S. Romanin, *Storia documentata di Venezia*, 10 vols, Venice, 1855–1861, iii: 142–143; J. C. Buzzati, 'Relations diplomatiques entre l'Angleterre et Venise au XIV siecle', *Revue de droit international et de legislation comparée*, 16 (1884): 589–597, 592–594; also Ruddock, *Italian Merchants and Shipping in Southampton*, 39.

[24] Ruddock, *Italian Merchants and Shipping in Southampton*, 123.

[25] Ruddock, *Italian Merchants and Shipping in Southampton*, 223.

[26] Abulafia, 'Cittadino e "denizen"', 282.

cornering different areas of the English market; there was certainly an element of competition in these activities, but overall there was also a high level of collaboration and synergies, especially evident in the provision of shipping services.[27] In fact cooperation in the transport sector was strong exactly because there was no direct competition, either in their import or export goods. An interesting example of this collaboration, and a splendid case of the so-called 'International republic of money',[28] is the role played in the 1430s by the Borromei bank – with agencies in Milan, Venice, Florence, Bruges and London – in financing several Italian merchants who were based in London or had economic interests there. The survival of the bank's London agency ledger for the period 1436–1439 allows us to see in detail the interconnections, both financial and commercial, between the multifarious activities of Italian merchants in England and in Northern Europe.[29]

The dependency of Tuscan merchants on Genoese shipping, with the exception of the central decades of the fifteenth century when Florence organised its own galley service,[30] consolidated the links between the two groups, whilst the growing reliance of Venetian merchants on their own shipping – whether through state galleys or private shipping – made them more self-reliant. Together with the Venetians' specialisation in the luxury trade, this contributed to the formation of their separate identity in English eyes.

The continued centrality of alum to Anglo-Genoese commercial relations is exemplified well by the misadventures of Robert Sturmy. He was a Bristol merchant who in 1457–1458 organised what is considered to be the first proper English commercial enterprise in the Mediterranean. With the help of powerful backers from both Bristol and London, he obtained a licence to export tin, lead, wool and cloth worth some £37,000. The return voyage turned into a disaster as the Bristol ships were attacked off Malta by the infamous Genoese pirate Giuliano Gattilusio. Sturmy died in the attack, though his partner survived and managed to come back to London. There he accused the Genoese

---

[27] Fryde, 'Italian Maritime Trade', 311.

[28] A. De Maddalena and H. Kellenbenz eds., *La repubblica internazionale del denaro tra XV e XVII secolo*, Bologna, 1986.

[29] Fryde, 'Italian Maritime Trade', 322–325; F. C. Lane, *Andrea Barbarigo, Merchant of Venice, 1418–1449*, Baltimore, 1944; G. Biscaro, 'Il banco Filippo Borromei e compagni di Londra (1436–1439)', *Archivio Storico Lombardo*, series iv, 19 (1913): 37–126, 283–386. The ledger of the London branch for the years 1436–1439 is now available on line (calendared and translated) thanks to the Borromei Bank Research Project, which was completed under Jim Bolton and Francesco Guidi Bruscoli: see www.queenmary historicalresearch.org/roundhouse/default.aspx (accessed 21 July 2011).

[30] Mallett, *The Florentine Galleys*.

merchants in England of being behind this attack, and a tense diplomatic standoff ensued between Genoa and England. After a long trial in England, the Genoese were condemned to pay a large fine to Sturmy's investors. Although the Genoese government denied any involvement in this episode, events of this kind had negative repercussions on Italian business interests not only in England but also in Bruges, given the level of interconnectedness of Italian interests in Northern Europe. It took a few years for things to return to normal.[31]

Italian reputation in England

Since the beginning of direct commercial links between England and the Italian peninsula, Italians had to fight against prejudice and unpopularity. It is difficult to pinpoint a principal reason for this, although it can be hypothesised that their earlier involvement in the tax farm certainly did not help to win friends amongst the English populace.[32] Later on, when their numbers in England increased, their superior proficiency in finance and trade made them the object of envy on the part of the indigenous mercantile group.[33] Already in the early fourteenth century there had started to be demonstrations of ill feelings towards them, and in Southampton, which we have seen was the English port they most frequented, 'there is evidence of particular animosity against all Italian merchants, irrespective of their precise nationality or state'.[34]

As financiers, tax farmers and importers of luxury goods, it is undeniable that Italians in general were not overtly popular and their commercial superiority was deeply resented. It is also important to underline how this anti-Italian feeling was connected with issues related to the internal political economy of the English kingdom as, unsurprisingly, these feelings were particularly vivid amongst English wool traders. The superior credit facilities available to the Italians, thanks to their financial savvy and more developed credit instruments, put them in a privileged position to take advantage of the volatility of the expanding English wool market – due

---

[31] J. Heers, 'Les Génois en Angleterre, la crise de 1458–1466', in *Studi in onore di Armando Sapori*, 2 vols, Milan, 1957, ii: 807–832, 811–812; see also G. Petti Balbi, *Mercanti e nationes nelle Fiandre: i genovesi in età bassomedievale*, Pisa, 1996.

[32] Ruddock, *Italian Merchants and Shipping in Southampton*, 24; E. B. Fryde, 'Italian Merchants in Medieval England, c.1270-c.1500', in *Aspetti della vita economica medievale*, Florence, 1985, 215–242.

[33] L. Hunt Yungblut, 'Straungers and Aliaunts: The "Un-English" among the English in Elizabethan England', in S. McKee ed., *Crossing Boundaries: Issues of Cultural and Individual Identity in the Middle Ages and the Renaissance*, Turnhout, 1999, 263–276, 265.

[34] Ruddock, *Italian Merchants and Shipping in Southampton*, 25.

mostly to the fluctuating yearly supply – and allowed the Italians excellent opportunities to reap better profits.[35]

So far we have talked of 'Italy' and 'Italians', and indeed 'in English documents from the fourteenth, fifteenth and sixteenth centuries, the terms "Italian" and "Italians" are commonplace'.[36] I have discussed elsewhere how the perception of Italy as having a common culture and being one 'economic system' is evident from the late medieval period.[37] However, as Fryde has noted, it is also true that the diverse economic interests of Venetians, Genoese and Florentines did have an important bearing on nuancing the reputation of each group within the kingdom. In his words, 'the author of the *Libelle of Englyshe Polycye* (ca 1436–8) disliked them all, but the Genoese were the one species of Italians to whom he was willing to accord a grudging acceptance thanks to the usefulness of their imports for the textile industry. By the reign of Henry IV woollen cloth had become a far more substantial export good for the Italians than wool. This cloth did not necessarily reach the peninsula, parts of it were again sold along the return journey to Italy, and part was destined to the Spanish and Muslim markets'.[38] If the Genoese trade was begrudgingly accepted, only insults were reserved for Florentines and Venetians, who were accused of importing 'fripperies' of great cost and little practical use, amongst which the author of the *Libelle* delights in mentioning 'long-tailed marmusets'.[39] This critical attitude towards the import of luxury and superfluous goods – be they jewellery, glass or indeed 'marmusets' – was frequently employed against Italian merchants, especially by bullionist pamphleteers. Nearly one century after the *Libelle*, Clement Armstrong penned his *How to reform the Realme*, where he strongly condemned what his fellow countrymen were spending, especially on 'wines and silks, which every year end up, the first pissed against the walls, the second, reduced to rags'. He concluded his argument by

[35] Fryde, 'Italian Maritime Trade', 328; Heers, *Les Génois en Angleterre*.
[36] Hunt Yungblut, 'Straungers and Aliaunts', 264
[37] Fusaro, 'Gli uomini d'affari stranieri', 371–374, and bibliography quoted therein.
[38] Fryde, 'Italian Maritime Trade', 317–318.
[39] Marmosets (which at that time was the generic name for 'small monkeys') had a good market in England, being a favourite pet of the upper classes in the late medieval and early modern period; on this see J. Summit, *Memory's Library: Medieval Books in Early Modern England*, Chicago, 2008, 76–77; J. S. Block, 'Political Corruption in Henrician England', in C. Carlton *et al.* eds., *States, Sovereigns and Society in Early Modern England: Essays in Honour of A. J. Slavin*, New York, 1998, 45–57; 50. On the criticism of Florentine goods see Mallett, *The Florentine Galleys*. On the *Libelle* see G. A. Holmes, 'The *Libel of English Policy*', *The English Historical Review*, 76 (1961): 193–216; on its criticism of Italian business practices see *The Libelle of Englyshe Policie: a poem on the use of sea power, 1436*, D. Warner ed., Oxford, 1926, xxvi–xxvii, 17–21; R. A. Ladd, *Antimercantilism in Late Medieval English Literature*, New York, 2010, 112–119.

wishing that the English kingdom were instead well furnished with abundant gold and silver, not with merchants and merchandise, especially
foreign.[40] Around the same time, Sir Thomas Smith was another strong
critic of the import of luxuries such as glass, perfumes, paper, ribbons,
gloves and toothpicks. In his analysis a strong moral negative value is
imparted to such expenditures, which should either be avoided or produced more readily in England.[41] Smith takes the argument beyond
simple criticism and towards the encouragement of learning from the
strategy used by Venice – 'that most florishinge citie at these dayes of all
Europe' – of attracting capable merchants and entrepreneurs to enrich the
coffers of the state whilst providing the goods coveted by the market.[42] In
Smith's analysis we start to see a shift in attitude towards Venice, earlier
considered as the provider of inessential and expensive goods, now still
criticised for that but also seen as an example to imitate, at least as far as
commercial strategy was concerned. What emerges clearly, even from
such a brief sketch, is how the real delicate issue was already that of the
balance of trade. Another important element is the permanence of such
discourse across the centuries. In the eighteenth century English political
economists will not tire to highlight that England in the fifteenth century
had an unfavourable balance with Venice and Florence and a positive one
with Genoa – and thus trade with the latter was praised, and the former
condemned.[43]

Spurred by a commercial depression that engulfed the whole kingdom,
but which was felt more strongly in the capital, in 1456 and 1457 there
were serious anti-alien riots in London, with violent demonstrations
against foreigners' property. At the same time several petitions were
brought before Parliament to limit the activities of foreign merchants.

---

[40] Clement Armstrong, *Howe to Reforme the Realme* [1535?], quoted by J. H. Munro,
'Bullionism and the Bill of Exchange in England 1272–1663: A Study in Monetary
Management and Popular Prejudice', in R. S. Lopez and J. Le Goff eds., *The Dawn of
Modern Banking*, New Haven, 1979, 169–240. On the author see S. T. Bindoff, 'Clement
Armstrong and His Treatises of the Commonweal', *Economic History Review*, 14 (1944):
64–73.

[41] J. Thirsk, *Economic Policy and Projects. The Development of a Consumer Society in Early
Modern England*, Oxford, 1978, 13–15.

[42] [Sir Thomas Smith], *A Discourse of the Common Weal of this Realm of England* [1549],
E. Lamond ed., Cambridge, 1929, 128.

[43] A. Anderson, *An Historical and Chronological Deduction of the Origin of Commerce From the
Earliest Accounts to the Present Time containing An History of the great Commercial Interests of
the British Empire . . .*, 2 vols, London, 1764, i: 259; G. Holmes, 'Anglo-Florentine Trade
in 1451', *English Historical Review*, 108 (1993): 371–386, which gives a glimpse of the
potential of the still largely untapped Salviati archive in Pisa for studying medieval trade
between Italy and the North of Europe.

Italians were the prime targets of these riots and were also the main victims of the king and Parliament's response to this crisis, which was to subject them to far higher tax rates than other alien residents; until then all aliens – irrespective of origin – had enjoyed the same tax rate. It was a difficult situation indeed, and merchants from different Italian states active in England joined together to try to find a solution for the smooth continuation of their commercial and financial activities.[44] At the beginning they threatened to leave London *en masse* and establish their base somewhere else, the obvious choice being Southampton, but this plan was abandoned when riots broke out there as well. Still, feelings seem to have been stronger in London than on the south coast, and, as a consequence, some reorganisation of trade did take place: for a few years Venetian and Florentine shipping avoided London altogether and made Southampton their local base.[45]

After the riots of the late 1450s, episodes of xenophobia continued throughout the Tudor period, including the reign of Elizabeth. In the period following the Protestant Reformation on the continent, large numbers of religious refugees had arrived on English shores.[46] On the one hand they were frequently welcomed by the authorities for the skills they brought with them – one just needs think of the massive importance the arrival of the Huguenots had on English cloth production and trade – but on the other they were generally vilified by the populace, which perceived them as an economic threat to their chances of employment. In regard to the Italians, this increase in xenophobia compounded a long-term animosity towards their wealth. During the same period, Italians were very popular at court and in educated circles; both Henry VIII and Elizabeth hosted Italian intellectuals, and Elizabeth frequently openly acknowledged her admiration for the Italian culture and language.[47] It was not an issue of quantity, as the Italians in England were never a large number. By the 1570s the Italian community in London was around 150 individuals (as opposed to more than 3,000 Dutch); but even if their numbers were small, still they were perceived to have an unduly large influence and, as such, they were an easy target for popular displeasure.[48]

---

[44] Heers, *Les Génois en Angleterre*, 811–812; see also Biscaro, 'Il banco Filippo Borromei', 283–386.

[45] Ruddock, *Italian Merchants and Shipping in Southampton*, especially 66–67, 162–186.

[46] Hunt Yungblut, 'Straungers and Aliaunts'.

[47] M. Wyatt, *The Italian Encounter with Tudor England: A Cultural Politics of Translation*, Cambridge, 2005, 137. On the different attitude towards the Huguenot see I. Scouloudi ed., *Huguenots in Britain and their French Background, 1550–1800*, London, 1987.

[48] Wyatt, *The Italian Encounter with Tudor England*, 138.

Venetians in England

The principal reason for Venice's late arrival in England in the 1390s was the weakness of its demand for English wool, and the marginal involvement of the Republic in provisioning the Italian peninsula with Northern European cloth. Pairing this with the weak demand for luxury goods and spices in England, it is no surprise that trade with England was for Venice, for a long time, just a small appendage of its trade with Flanders.[49]

Since at least 1409 Venetian merchants in London were organised under a vice-consul,[50] and by the 1430s the Venetian colony in London had increased to around forty merchants, some of whom were also active in trade with Bruges.[51] For both Venetians and Florentines the London–Bruges link was very strong, both commercially and financially, and most Florentine merchants active in the two cities belonged to different branches of the same companies, with the London one frequently being a subsidiary of Bruges.[52]

The arrival of the Tudor dynasty did not seem to challenge the position of Italian merchants. In 1488 Henry VII granted a three-year abatement for tonnage and poundage to merchants from Genoa, Venice, Florence and Lucca who had lobbied for it.[53] From the beginning of the following century the Italian presence started to concentrate in London, mirroring the growing importance of the city as the economic heart of the kingdom. The Venetians pioneered this move amongst Italians, as their main imports were the kind of luxury goods that were in demand in the capital.[54] London had become 'the chief market and distributing centre for Mediterranean imports, the site of the largest Italian colony and the chief cloth market in the kingdom'.[55]

The Venetian relationship with England was substantially different from that of the Tuscans, as from the beginning it was based on commerce and not on finance. From the early fourteenth century the bulk of

---

[49] Ruddock, *Italian Merchants and Shipping in Southampton*, 26; for an analytical synthesis of European trade flows in the fourteenth and fifteenth century see B. Dini, 'Produzioni e mercati nell'occidente europeo', in S. Gensini ed., *Europa e Mediterraneo tra medioevo e prima età moderna: l'osservatorio italiano*, Pisa, 1992, 99–124.

[50] Ruddock, *Italian Merchants and Shipping in Southampton*, 136–138.

[51] Lane, *Andrea Barbarigo, Merchant of Venice*, 123.

[52] Mallett, *The Florentine Galleys*, 132.

[53] See for example the interpretation given by D. Macpherson, *Annals of Commerce, manufactures, fisheries, and navigation, with brief notices of the arts and sciences connected with them. Containing the Commercial transactions of the British empire and other countries, from the earliest account to the meeting of the union Parliament in January 1801; and comprehending the most valuable part of the late Mr. Anderson History of commerce, viz. from the year 1492 to the end of the reign of King George II*, 4 vols, London, 1805, i: 711.

[54] Ruddock, *Italian Merchants and Shipping in Southampton*, 51.

[55] Ruddock, *Italian Merchants and Shipping in Southampton*, 55.

trade between Venice and England had travelled by sea on Venetian bottoms. The history of the Republic of Venice in its late medieval centuries of great economic success is inextricably tied to that of the famed galley convoys that transported spices and luxury items from the Levant to Venice, and from there redistributed them to the rest of Europe. Because of the strong symbolic political value of public shipping for Venetian history, and in the wake of Frederick Lane's magisterial studies, the classic literature has generally tended to overestimate its relative importance in Venetian economic performance. Even with this caveat, though, for a century and a half – between the last quarter of the fourteenth century and 1533 – the state galleys were the most constant element in the trade between the Venetian Republic and Northern Europe. During the fifteenth century four or five state galleys travelled to England and Flanders, two of these normally wintered in London and in the spring they all returned together to Venice.

As Claire Judde de Larivière has recently shown, the 'state galley system' was a complex economic structure with a very high level of interdependence between its different branches, with punctuality and regularity as the essential tools for its economic efficiency and success.[56] In following this state-organised trade the care and attention which the Republic bestowed on the political and diplomatic side of this trade becomes immediately evident. Given its peculiar organisation, with its heavy dependence (including financial) on the *Senato*, the galley trade is indeed over-represented in the extant documentation, exactly because the Venetian government – as a stakeholder – followed particularly closely each journey and intervened frequently when problems arose.[57] Still, it needs to be remembered that Venetian long-distance maritime trade in general always relied mainly on private 'round ships', which carried more cargo than merchant galleys on all of the Republic's routes even in the fifteenth century, at the apogee of the state galley system.[58]

The variety of goods imported by Venetians into England listed by Bartolomeo Paxi leaves no doubt that luxury merchandise dominated. He starts the list in a rather subdued manner with cotton thread (*gotoni*

---

[56] C. Judde de Larivière, *Naviguer, commercer, gouverner: économie maritime et pouvoirs à Venise (XVe–XVIe siècles)*, Leiden, 2008.

[57] G. Luzzatto, 'Navigazione di linea e navigazione libera nelle grandi città marinare del Medio evo', in his *Studi di storia economica veneziana*, Padua, 1954, 53–57.

[58] F. C. Lane, 'Wages and Recruitment of Venetian *Galeotti*, 1470–1580', in his *Studies in Venetian Social and Economic History*, B. G. Kohl and R. C. Mueller eds., London, 1987, X: 15–43, 17.

filadi), but then follows with various kinds of gold threads and cloths, several varieties of silk brocades, various types of camlets,[59] many different kinds of silk threads and cloth in several colours, fustians from Northern Italy and raw silks from Calabria and Sicily. The list of textiles is followed by that of spices, and just about all the spices which the Venetians imported from the East are present there. Amongst the other items there are currants from Patras (Ionian production was still very small at that time), sugar, different types of corals from Sicily, and Candia wine. Such a luxurious list of Venetian imports into England contrasts starkly with the list of exports, which comprised various kinds of woollen cloths (both white and coloured), tin and lead.[60] Amongst the woollen cloth, pride of place was given to so-called 'bastard cloth', whose exact composition is unclear but which was probably made of two different types of wool yarn, one for the warp and the other for the weft. This particular composition would make these textiles a forerunner of those lighter draperies which the English would export with so much success to the Ottoman lands in the late sixteenth and seventeenth centuries, and it is interesting to note that these cloths were then re-exported by Venetians to Constantinople.[61] English wool was instead generally destined for Venetian textile makers.[62] Trade with England was thus showing the same features that characterised the general organisation of Venetian maritime trade: high-value goods (spices, silks, brocades, fine textiles) travelled on the state galleys; more bulky merchandise (cotton, wines, sugar) sailed instead on privately owned vessels.[63]

As early as the fifteenth century sweet wines from Candia were finding a growing market in England. The attention of economic historians of Venice has focused on trade from the metropolis; however, it is important to mention that there was also direct traffic between Venetian Crete and

---

[59] These were luxury textiles made with a mix of camel's (or Angora goat) hair and silk.

[60] [Bartolomeo Paxi] *Tariffa de pesi et mesure correspondenti dal Levante al Ponente: da una terra a l'altra: e a tutte le parte del mondo: con la noticia delle robe che se trazeno da una Paese per laltro* [sic], Venice, 1521, 204v–205v.

[61] F. C. Lane, *Venice and History: The Collected Papers of Frederic C. Lane*, Baltimore, 1966, 119, 123; and E. B. Fryde, 'Anglo-Italian Commerce in the Fifteenth Century: Some Evidence About Profits and the Balance of Trade', in his *Studies in Medieval Trade*, XV: 345–355, 352.

[62] For the activities of Vincenzo Priuli we have the diary he kept whilst in London between 1503 and 1506, see F. Ortalli, 'Introduzione', in F. Ortalli ed., *Lettere di Vincenzo Priuli capitano delle galee di Fiandra, 1521–1523*, Venice, 2005, v–xlviii, v; also R. C. Mueller, *The Venetian Money Market: Banks, Panics and the Public Debt, 1200–1550*, Baltimore, 1997, 345–348.

[63] Fryde, 'Italian Maritime Trade', 321.

England and this played a considerable role for Anglo-Venetian relations in establishing a pattern in the bilateral trade which would continue for centuries.

In the decades after the Venetians' defeat at Agnadello (1509), political concerns arose regarding the state galley system, not only because of Venice's fears about its own safety but also because the Republic was exceedingly careful to avoid any involvement with the momentous events in the North of Europe. The *Senato* was wary of the long conflict between France and the Habsburgs, and later its worries shifted to the political fallout of the Protestant Reformation. In short, Anglo-Venetian trade, which had always been beset by reciprocal protectionism, from the times of Henry VIII entered into a new phase in which the new and delicate European balance of power made commercial relations a complex and sometimes fraught business. After 1509 the link that had regularly connected Venice with England started to become erratic – there were trips in 1516, 1517, 1519 and 1520 – then just two last trips in 1530 and 1533. The demise of the Venetian state galleys was strongly influenced by two sets of different but inter-related structural changes. On the one hand the galley system was extremely dependent for its success on the punctuality of arrivals and departures, as these journeys were connected to many other economic activities in Venice. The reality is that the sixteenth-century Mediterranean was becoming a very crowded sea, and the rules underpinning the galley system were too rigid for the new market conditions. Therefore the regularity of their schedule – which had been a factor of efficiency when the Venetians had an effective monopoly and was extremely beneficial to the internal economy of the Republic – became a hindrance when other commercial operators entered the market. To beat this new competition it was essential to be able to sail swiftly to take advantage of the increasingly volatile economic conjuncture.[64]

By the last decades of the fifteenth century Florentines and Genoese just about abandoned shipping to England, and the Venetians thus became the primary carriers of Mediterranean goods, with an interesting mix of state galleys and private shipping.[65] When the galleys stopped in 1533, the space was left open for new operators to keep these maritime routes open. Venetian Greek subjects first, and later the English would fill this gap.

---

[64] Judde de Larivière, *Naviguer, commercer*, 179–235.
[65] Fryde, 'Italian Maritime Trade', 332–333.

2   The reversal of the balance

Even though the last voyage of the state galleys took place in 1533, the maritime route between Venice and England was kept active by private shipping. However, for the following decades, the majority of trade seemed to have shifted onto the land routes which crossed the continent. Italian and Venetian merchants in England continued to thrive through the connection with Antwerp, which in this period functioned as a communal entrepôt for Italian trade with the North of Europe. Particularly prosperous for the Italians were the 1540s, when their custom tariffs were equivalent to those paid by native merchants.[1] The situation started to deteriorate from 1552, when the Company of Merchant Adventurers was formed and quickly gained crown support. The English merchants' lobbying paid handsome returns, and in 1558 a new tariff was published which strongly penalised foreigners. Their response was to appeal both to the crown and to the exchequer, but to no avail. From this date onwards the number of Italian merchants in England began to contract, and their shrinking numbers were not compensated for by an increase in their per capita imports.[2]

Throughout the 1560s Italians in England found themselves the target of continuous accusations of misdemeanours – from customs evasion to illegal purchase of housing in the City – most brought forward by members and associates of the increasingly powerful Merchant Adventurers, who were determined to expand their activities and increase their control over foreign trade, especially with the Low Countries.[3] Part of this strategy involved passing legislation which redirected English exports to the Low Countries from Antwerp to Bergen-op-Zoom. This measure was

---

[1] Pagano De Divitiis, *English Merchants*, 5; also Munro, 'Bullionism and the Bill of Exchange'.
[2] G. D. Ramsay, 'The Undoing of the Italian Mercantile Colony in Sixteenth Century London', in N. B. Harte and K. G. Ponting eds., *Textile History and Economic History: Essays in Honour of Miss Julia de Lacy Mann*, Manchester, 1973, 22–49, 39.
[3] Ramsay, 'The Undoing of the Italian Mercantile Colony', 31; Hunt Yungblut, 'Straungers and Aliaunts'.

particularly punishing for Italian merchants based in Antwerp, where they had all the facilities for finishing, re-packaging and dispatching English cloth.[4] By the end of the 1560s, with the political situation in Antwerp deteriorating due to the impending conflict between Spain and the Low Countries, the land route which connected England and Italy through Antwerp was getting narrower. In 1569 the Duke of Alba ordered the arrest of all English merchants in the Netherlands and the sequestration of their goods. So this road was closed. Amongst the Italians, the Venetians found themselves in a particularly delicate position. With heavy military engagement against the Turks in the Mediterranean, private maritime trade to the North of Europe seemed to have vanished altogether, whilst the interruption of the land-based trade with Antwerp virtually isolated them from the English market. As a result, the beginning of the 1570s saw a series of bankruptcies amongsts Venetians active in London.[5] Trade routes between the Venetian Mediterranean and England were indeed difficult in the central decades of the century, but what was the real state of maritime trade after the 1530s? To provide an answer to this question we need to backtrack in time.

English in the Mediterranean: Candia wines

In Crete, under Venetian rule since 1211, a consistent share of agricultural output was destined for export. From the fourteenth century, taking advantage of the decline of Syrian and Egyptian production, sugar had been produced, but cotton and wine also were widely exported from the island.[6] Towards the middle of the fifteenth century the sweet wines produced in Candia started to become very popular in England. There were several varieties of this wine, which in England was generally known as malmsey (which seems to correspond to both *malvasie* and *moscati*).[7]

---

[4] W. Brulez, 'L'exportation des Pays-Bas vers l'Italie par voie de terre au milieu du XVIe siècle', *Annales*, 14 (1959): 461–491; Ramsay, 'The Undoing of the Italian Mercantile Colony', 28–29; see also P. Subacchi, 'Italians in Antwerp in the Second Half of the Sixteenth Century', in H. Soly and A. K. L. Thijs eds., *Minorities in Western European Cities (Sixteenth-Twentieth Centuries)*, Brussels, 1995, 73–90.

[5] Ramsay, 'The Undoing of the Italian Mercantile Colony', 37.

[6] E. Ashtor, 'Levantine Sugar Industry in the Late Middle Ages: A Case of Technological Decline', in A. L. Udovitch ed., *The Islamic Middle East, 700–1900: Studies in Economic and Social History*, Princeton, 1981, 91–132; D. Jacoby, 'La production du sucre en Crète vénitienne: l'échec d'une entreprise économique', in *Rodonia: time ston M.I. Manousaka*, Rethimno, 1994, 167–180; U. Tucci, 'Le commerce venitien du vin de Crete', in K. Friedland ed., *Maritime Food Transport*, Cologne, 1994, 199–211, 199; and his 'Il commercio del vino nell'economia cretese', in G. Ortalli ed., *Venezia e Creta*, Venice, 1998, 183–206.

[7] On the shift beween *malvasie* and *moscati* see Tucci, 'Il commercio del vino'.

The growth of its trade stimulated private shipping between the Eastern Mediterranean and England, as wine rarely travelled on state galleys. The value of merchandise was the crucial factor determining the galleys' cargo; those sailing to England and Flanders had to first load all the spices available on the Venetian market before they could load other merchandise (such as wine). Quite apart from the issue of space, the galleys' high freight charges discouraged the shipping of heavy and bulky loads such as wine.[8] Thus wine normally travelled to England on private ships, usually 'the biggest and therefore the most defensible of the Venetian cogs, ships of about 400 tons', capable of carrying large quantities of wine but also of defending themselves in the frequently dangerous Channel waters.[9] It was indeed a risky route: in 1431 Pietro Querini was sailing from Crete to Bruges when his ship was blown off course, and, with a couple of his crewmates, he ended up in the Lofoten islands, in Norway.[10] But in reality we do not have a lot of evidence – especially quantitative – which would allow us to properly discuss the volume, value or 'nationality' of this trade. Private shipping was an essential element of the Venetian economy, but its activities are very difficult to reconstruct. State galleys left behind a magnificent trail of evidence; private trade did not, though its protagonists were roughly the same. Venetian patrician merchants made use of both public and private shipping; the main difference was that *cittadini* and Venetian subjects – under-represented in the state galleys trade – were very active in private shipping. However, their lower social profile makes their activities far harder to follow.

English ships entering the Mediterranean seem to have been few and far between, and again we have very patchy evidence to precisely reconstruct their activities. Stuart Jenks has recently argued that Robert Sturmy's 1457 expedition was an attempt at breaking the Genoese monopoly on the alum trade by going directly to the Ottomans for its supply.[11] Sturmy's exploit is indeed famous, but the rarity of expeditions of this kind is probably the reason for its fame. What can be said with confidence is that in the first half of the fifteenth century wine travelled exclusively on Venetian bottoms, whilst from the reign of Henry

---

[8] Ruddock, *Italian Merchants and Shipping*, 73, 80.
[9] Lane, *Andrea Barbarigo, Merchant of Venice*, 50, 55–56.
[10] A. Tenenti, 'Proiezioni patrizie quattrocentesche alle soglie dell'ignoto', in *Studi veneti offerti a Gaetano Cozzi*, Venice, 1992, 109–120; Querini's narrative is in G. B. Ramusio, *Navigazioni e viaggi*, M. Milanesi ed., 6 vols, Turin, 1978–1980, iv: 51–98; P. Querini et al., *Il naufragio della Querina*, P. Nelli ed., Venice, 2007.
[11] S. Jenks, *Robert Sturmy's Commercial Expedition to the Mediterranean (1457/8)*, Bristol, 2006; *DNB*, s.v. (accessed 16 August 2011); Heers, 'Les Génois en Angleterre'; on Sturmy's role in Bristol's trade with the Mediterranean see also Carus-Wilson, *Medieval Merchant Venturers*, 64–73.

VII we have some evidence that some English ships were starting to be active on the Candia–England route.

Legislation forbidding loading Cretan wine on foreign ships had been issued by the local Venetian government in 1441 and 1451, including provisions prohibiting the freighting of foreign vessels to transport the wines westward.[12] However, clearly these measures had not been effective, an early sign that enforcing legislation on customs tariffs for foreigners within its own empire was problematic for Venetian authorities.[13] The existence of such legislation, which mentions 'foreigners' without providing further details on who these might have been, can also be seen as an indirect sign of the appearance of the English in the area. What we know for sure is that by 1488 the English presence in Candia was the basis of the first tariff war between the Republic and England, as in that year the Venetian *Senato* imposed a tax of four ducats on every barrel of malmsey wine loaded in Candia on 'foreign' ships (i.e. non-Venetian) and directed to Western Europe.[14] The English response was relatively fast, and in 1491 Henry VII imposed an additional duty of eighteen shillings on each butt of malmsey imported into England on foreign vessels. The new imposition was to be in force until the Venetians removed their extra charge in Candia and it amounted to roughly the same sum, so as to leave little doubt that this was a 'tit for tat' measure.[15]

The pattern of development of this small commercial war was indeed a taste of things to come. More worryingly for the Venetians, it can also be seen as an early signal of a new policy by the English crown: to wager on the continuing growth of the English economy and supporting local merchants.[16] The high tariffs did not stop this trade or, indeed, deter the English; in fact, for the years 1504–1509 we have evidence of an increase in malmsey traffic in English hands.[17] Behind this was probably the extreme profitabilty of the trade, as Cretan wine was extremely well

---

[12] Tucci, 'Il commercio del vino', 187. A copy of this *parte* is in ASV, *Compilazione Leggi*, b. 27, cc.549r–550r (25-7-1441). This legislation was reiterated and reinforced in 1488: ASV, *Senato Mar*, reg. 12, cc.156r–157v (18-11-1488).

[13] D. Jacoby, 'Creta e Venezia nel contesto economico del Mediterraneo Orientale sino alla metà del Quattrocento', in Ortalli ed., *Venezia e Creta*, 73–106.

[14] Ruddock, *Italian Merchants and Shipping in Southampton*, 221–223. For the Venetian perspective see ASV, *Senato Mar*, reg. 12, cc.156r–157v; M. Sanudo, *I diarii*, R. Fulin *et al.* ed., 58 vols, Venice 1879–1903, i: column 934; ii: column 870.

[15] Anderson, *An Historical and Chronological Deduction*, i: 312; see also Macpherson, *Annals of Commerce*, i: 716.

[16] J. B. Williamson, *Maritime Enterprise 1485–1558*, Oxford, 1913, 228–240; also Fusaro, *Uva passa*, 13.

[17] U. Tucci, 'Costi e ricavi di una galera veneziana ai primi del Cinquecento', in his *Mercanti, navi, monete*, 161–230, 176.

appreciated in England, something reflected in its high price.[18] During the reign of Henry VIII wine exports to England had increased to such an extent that a consul was appointed in Candia to take care of this specific trade.[19] In those years English ships also appeared in Ragusa (present-day Dubrovnik), where their presence was duly reported by Venetian sources, but it was occasional enough not to warrant any action by the government.[20]

English return to the Mediterranean: Ionian currants

In 1564 William Cecil wrote a memorandum highlighting the disadvantages to England of its dependence on the Antwerp staple market. His argument was that the proximity of Antwerp, and the excellence of its trading and financial infrastructure, had acted as a deterrent for the development in England of new commercial ventures, and – in a sense – had contributed to the lack of growth of long-distance English shipping.[21] He was indeed right; if the proximity of the pan-European emporium of Antwerp to English shores could be considered to have stunted English long-distance shipping, it can definitely be argued that the demise of Antwerp spurred its development.

Precisely when the English withdrew from the Mediterranean, in the central decades of the sixteenth century, has been subject of a long debate.[22] But though the date of the withdrawal is still a matter of controversy, the date on which the English returned is agreed upon to

[18] E. Basso and P. F. Simbula, 'Il commercio del vino nelle pratiche di mercatura italiane del basso medioevo', in *I Symposion de la Associación Internacional de Historia de la Civilización de la Vid y del Vino (18–20 March 1999)*, Cadiz, 2002, 393–402.

[19] C. Maltezou, 'The Historical and Social Context', in D. Holton ed., *Literature and Society in Renaissance Crete*, Cambridge, 1991, 17–47, 29–32.

[20] L. Villari, *The Republic of Ragusa*, London, 1904, 264; S. Anselmi, *Venezia, Ragusa, Ancona fra Cinque e Seicento*, Ancona, 1969, 9.

[21] R. H. Tawney and E. E. Power eds., *Tudor Economic Documents*, 3 vols, London, 1924, ii: 45–47 (also in K. N. Chaudhuri, *The English East India Company. The Study of an Early Joint-Stock Company, 1600–1640*, London, 1965, 6–7).

[22] An informative bibliography on the subject is: T. S. Willan, 'Some Aspects of English Trade with the Levant in the Sixteenth Century', *English Historical Review*, 70 (1955): 399–410; J. I. Israel, 'The Phases of the Dutch *Straatvaart* 1590–1713: A Chapter in the Economic History of the Mediterranean', in his *Empires and Entrepôts: The Dutch, the Spanish Monarchy and the Jews, 1585–1713*, London, 1990, 133–162; S. A. Skilliter, *William Harborne and the Trade with Turkey, 1578–1582: A Documentary Study of the First Anglo-Ottoman Relations*, Oxford, 1977; J. Parry, 'Transport and Trade Routes', in E. E. Rich and C. H. Wilson eds., *Cambridge Economic History of Europe*, vol. iv: *The Economy of Expanding Europe in the Sixteenth and Seventeenth Century*, Cambridge, 1967, 155–219; F. Braudel, *The Mediterranean and the Mediterranean World in the Age of Philip II*, 2 vols, London, 1972, i: 614–621; R. Hakluyt, *The Principall Navigations, Voyages,*

be 1573.[23] And the last quarter of the sixteenth century was when the English presence became pervasive throughout the Mediterranean.

We have already seen how English ships had been reaching Candia in the fifteenth century and, if we trust Williamson, in 1513 there was an English consul in the island of Chios, and in 1522 a small commercial colony in Candia.[24] Epstein dates to 1533 the beginning of the direct trade in currants between the Ionian islands and England.[25] If Williamson did not support with any reference his statement on the topic, which Epstein then picked up, there is additional indirect evidence which supports this period (if not this specific date) as the beginning of the currant trade. From the 1540s, the steady increase in the cultivation of currants in Zante and Cephalonia attracted the attention of the local *Rettore*, who highlighted it in his final *Relazione*: '[currants] which recently have started to be cultivated in good quantity'.[26] Given the delay with which events in the islands were fully appreciated in Venice it is probably not too much of a stretch to think that the process had been going on for a decade. An increase in the production of a product destined for export needs to correspond with a growth in its demand somewhere else; however, we have no evidence that this was happening in Venice, which was the primary market for its own colonial goods and whence their redistribution was, at least formally, tightly controlled.

In the Ionian islands, things were changing fast. In 1545, for the first time, there was some alarm regarding customs evasion, as the local authorities were concerned that unspecified 'foreign merchants' were exporting out of the islands with the support and cover of locals.[27] No more details are given in the final *Relazioni* of the *Rettori*, which are the only serial evidence we have for this period. Although it is legitimate to venture the hypothesis that, given the events of the following years, the market where demand was expanding was the English one, we simply do

Traffiques & Discoveries of the English Nation: Made by Sea of Over-Land to the Remote and Farthest Distant Quarters of the Earth at any time within the compasse of these 1600 Yeeres, London 1589–1600 (reprint McLehose, Glasgow 1903–1905); Pagano De Divitiis, *English Merchants*, 4–7. My argument is fully developed in Fusaro, *Uva passa*, 17–19, 155.

[23] F. Braudel and R. Romano, *Navires et marchandises à l'entrée du Port de Livourne (1547–1611)*, Paris, 1951, 49–50.

[24] Williamson, *Maritime Enterprise*, 228–239. Williamson claims that regular English trips to the Mediterranean date from the end of the fifteenth century, at least towards Candia, Chios and other 'Venetian dependancies'.

[25] Epstein, *The Early History*, 6 quoting J. B. Williamson, *The Foreign Commerce of England under the Tudors*, London, 1883, 20.

[26] ASV, *Collegio, Relazioni*, b. 61, II tomo, cc. 33r/v.

[27] ASV, *Senato Mar*, reg. 28, cc. 26r–27v.

not have any solid extant evidence that can give us certainty about this, or indeed about how much of their traffic travelled on foreign bottoms. On 12 November 1564 Marco Basadonna presented his *Relazione* at the end of his period as *Rettore* of Zante. There he reiterated, more strongly, the arguments already put forth by his predecessors. He complained of constant 'damage' by foreign ships, which he defined as 'maxime Ponentine' – for the most part 'Westerners' – and he added how this caused losses for the Republic's customs duties, as the ships which should have discharged their merchandise in Zante, from where it should have been redistributed in the Ottoman Morea, instead were discharging their cargo directly in Ottoman territories.[28]

So in the central decades of the sixteenth century in the waters surrounding the Ionian islands there was an increase of foreign ships, whose trading activities were not limited to Venetian lands but extended also to the adjacent Ottoman territories. For Zante – and therefore for Venice – these activites also meant the loss of 'transit custom', an important source of income for the local exchequers. What is particularly interesting is that these ships were defined as *Ponentine*, the term used in Venice for both merchants and ships coming from the Low Countries and England. For this period it is difficult to argue the case of an increase in the Flemish presence; the classic interpretation brought forward by Fernand Braudel and Jonathan Israel that the Dutch arrived in the Mediterranean with the great famine of 1590 has been confirmed, if not strengthened, by recent studies.[29] Goods from the Levant by then had been arriving in Amsterdam on Dutch bottoms for some time, but this trade was based in Venice, as it was still in the hands of Venetian merchants. In short, Israel agrees that these 'northerners' whose presence in the Levant so worried Venetian authorities were actually English.[30] The only merchandise which could be bought in the Ionian islands was currants, and there is no evidence of Flemish (or indeed Dutch) merchants active in this trade before 1592.[31] Until well into the

---

[28] ASV, *Collegio, Relazioni*, b. 61, II tomo, cc. 47v–55r.

[29] P. C. van Royen, 'The First Phase of the Dutch *Straatvaart* (1591–1605): Fact and Fiction', *International Journal of Maritime History*, 2 (1990): 69–102; M. van Gelder, 'Supplying the *Serenissima*: The Role of Flemish Merchants in the Venetian Grain Trade during the First Phase of the *Straatvaart*', *International Journal of Maritime History*, 16 (2004): 39–60; and her *Trading Places: The Netherlandish Merchants in Early Modern Venice*, Leiden and Boston, 2009.

[30] Israel, 'The Phases of the Dutch *Straatvaart*', 139–140; see also his *Dutch Primacy in World Trade 1585–1740*, Oxford, 1991, 54.

[31] Based on a comprehensive analysis of Notarial deeds in Venetian archives in W. Brulez and G. Devos, *Marchands flamands à Venise, 1568–1605*, 2 vols, Brussels and Rome, 1965–1986.

seventeenth century, Low Countries merchants and shipping played only a small role in this part of Mediterranean trade, something confirmed by the collapse of their numbers in good harvest years.[32]

Already by 1550 Andrea Priuli felt the need to try and stop the proliferation of currant plantations, which he deemed potentially dangerous for Zante's grain production; we shall see how right he was in his forecast, and how ineffective he and his successors were in trying to stop this phenomenon.[33] By the mid-1560s similar voices of alarm were raised in Cephalonia, and on both islands a new breed of speculator was accused of making a lot of money by sending currants directly abroad, and not to Venice, as they should have done.[34]

Two questions arise at this juncture: what did 'abroad' mean, and who were these 'speculators'? We have seen how in the Ionian islands from the 1540s there had been an increase in production of currants; at the same time the presence of foreign – *Ponentini* – merchants was also highlighted. By the 1560s there was talk of speculators hoarding the currant crop and selling it directly abroad. Lack of evidence on both the English and the Venetian side of the documentation does not make the answer easy. For the sixteenth century we do not have dispatches from the islands' *Rettori*, and the matter had not yet reached such a level of importance in Venetian eyes to warrant the central government's attention. We also have very little data in England regarding imports. London Port Books between the 1550s and the 1570s do not show imports from the Levant registered to English merchants, but for these periods records are very patchy and therefore cannot really be considered a reliable source.[35] Also important to keep in mind is that whilst currants arrived just about in their entirety at London from 1580 (when the Levant Company monopoly took over their trade), in the previous period these might also have arrived at Margate and Southampton, although since the early fourteenth century Venetians

---

[32] Israel, 'The Phases of the Dutch *Straatvaart*', 133–138, 143–144.

[33] ASV, *Collegio, Relazioni*, b. 87, cc.n.n., in a *terminazione* enclosed with Andrea Priuli's *Relazione* (7-9-1552).

[34] ASV, *Collegio, Relazioni*, b. 62, cc.151r–153r (17-8-1564).

[35] Many of the sixteenth-century London Port Books got lost or are so damaged as to make them unusable; see Willan, 'Some Aspects', 400; see also the unpublished typescript by A. M. Millard, *Lists of Goods Imported into the Port of London by English and Alien and Denizens Merchants for Certain Years between 1560 and 1640: Compiled from London Port Books and Other Sources*, typescript, 1955 (available at both BL and TNA). Millard gives data only for 1558 and 1565 and then jumps to 1599; an additional problem is that whilst later Port Books specify whether goods had been imported by Englishmen or aliens, for those two years data is provided collectively. We can learn that in 1558 a total value of £3,000 of currants was imported, but currants are not even mentioned in 1565.

had tended to trade with London and less with Southampton, which was instead favoured by the Genoese and Catalans.[36]

Susan Skilliter argued that English navigation in the Levant can be considered to have ceased by 1553; she arrived at this date by contraposing Hakluyt, who 'attributes the first English withdrawal to the increasing Turkish influence in the Mediterranean, culminating in the seizure of Chios in 1566 and of Cyprus in 1571', with Braudel's conviction that 'the English had left long before 1566 and reappeared soon after 1571', putting this withdrawal in relation to the mid-century crisis of the English economy.[37]

What is known is that between the 1560s and 1570s there is a contraction of both volume and value in the trade of Venetian merchants active in London, and that the Merchant Adventurers were successful in eliminating foreign competition in their commercial area of interest.[38] The break between England and Antwerp was reflected by a diminution in the quantity of Mediterranean imports, with a consequent increase of their price in London. However if their prices spiked in 1572–1573, they had already returned to normal in 1574, so if there was in interruption in trade it must have been short-lived.[39]

On the basis of the evidence discussed above I believe that the 'interruption' of direct maritime traffic between England and the Mediterranean can be dated to the period 1566–1573, a rather shorter period than the one traditionally accepted by modern scholars (1550–1573), and more in line with the dates proposed by Hakluyt. It is more difficult to evaluate the nationality of the ships involved in Anglo-Venetian traffic in these decades. What we can say is that after the demise of the state galleys in 1533, Venetian private ships were active between Venice and its Greek dominions up to the middle of the century, and there were also some English ships on these routes, as lamented in the *Provveditori* reports mentioned above. To summarise: English merchants

---

[36] E. Ashtor, *Levant Trade in the Later Middle Ages*, Princeton, 1983, 107–108; and Ruddock, *Italian Merchants and Shipping in Southampton*, 84. On Port Books see G. N. Clark, *Guide to English Commercial Statistics 1696–1782*, London, 1938.

[37] Skilliter, *William Harborne and the Trade with Turkey*, 11; J. H. Parry ('Transport and Trade Routes', 187–188) also agrees with Skilliter's dating, and attributes this withdrawal more to English domestic economic crisis than to troubles in Mediterranean navigation. See F. Braudel, *The Mediterranean and the Mediterranean World*, i: 615; Hakluyt, *The Principall Navigations*; see also Pagano De Divitiis, *English Merchants*, 4.

[38] Brenner, *Merchants and Revolution*, 8.

[39] J. E. T. Rogers ed., *A History of Agricolture and Prices in England*, 7 vols, Oxford, 1963 (1856–1902), iii: 666–668; see also Ramsay, 'The Undoing of the Italian Mercantile Colony', 46.

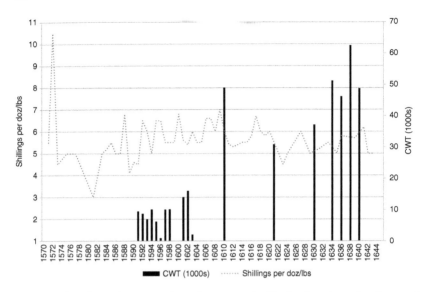

Graph 1. Average price of currants in England and total volume of currants imported to London 1570–1643

were already active in the Mediterranean, even if on a limited scale;[40] they seem to have appeared in the Ionian islands around the 1530s, they disappeared in the critical years of the Veneto–Turk crisis (1566–1573) and the speed with which they came to dominate the islands' trade immediately after this period points to the existence of previous strong links with the local Greeks. So they were most likely the 'foreigners' and *Ponentini* whose activities started to worry local authorities in the 1550s.

The reorganisation of the currant trade: Velutelli, Venice and Levant Companies

In 1573 English ships re-entered the Mediterranean, and Venice and Livorno were their most common destinations. Little direct traffic existed at this stage between England and the Ottoman empire, and the little that there was was under French protection. Very shortly afterwards a protégé

---

[40] Mentioned also in C. G. A. Clay, *Economic Expansion and Social Change: England 1500–1700*, 2 vols, Cambridge, 1984, ii: 107; Clay supports the end of English presence in the Mediterranean from the 1550s, in his view compensated for by traffic taking the land route.

of the Earl of Leicester, a merchant from Lucca resident in England named Acerbo Velutelli – Mr Asharbo in the English sources – obtained from Queen Elizabeth a ten-year exclusive monopoly for the trade in currants and olive oil. At this date Velutelli was considered to be the richest Italian merchant in England; under his name or as an intermediary he imported annually goods to the value of £30,000.[41]

The news of Velutelli's monopoly was not well received in England and Venice. In London several local merchants felt damaged in their fledgling attempts to penetrate Levantine markets and reacted accordingly. In Venice, instructions were sent to the Venetian ambassador in Paris to contact his English colleague there and make sure that the queen was made aware of the Venetian displeasure at this move. In January 1576 Giovanni Francesco Morosini, the Venetian ambassador in Paris, reassured the *Senato* that the English ambassador there would be delighted to intercede with his queen for the revocation of Velutelli's monopoly if direct diplomatic links were re-established between the Republic and England.[42] The lack of direct diplomatic links between the two countries put Venice in a very disadvantaged negotiating position. The absence of an ambassador was, however, just one of many reasons behind the sluggish Anglo-Venetian negotiations concerning Velutelli's monopoly. Whilst the issue was debated, he did manage to make some money thanks to his privilege, but this just provided English merchants with evidence that trade with the Mediterranean could indeed be very profitable and therefore worth fighting for. The lobbying against Velutelli in London increased, with local merchants complaining to the queen especially about the fact that he was allowed – through the terms of his privilege – to levy 'licence money' on English merchants if they wanted to import currants and olive oil into the kingdom. The fact that a foreigner could 'tax' English merchants in their own country

---

[41] Ramsay, 'The Undoing of the Italian Mercantile Colony', 39–47. Amongst the Italians still active in London, Ramsay mentions others coming from Lucca such as the Buonvisi, and Filippo Burlamacchi – the latter was also involved in trying to facilitate the restablishment of diplomatic links between Elizabeth and Venice. Other important Italians in London were Benedetto Spinola, considered to be a good friend of the queen, and Orazio Pallavicino, of whom we shall have occasion to talk more. On these see also: L. Stone, *An Elizabethan: Sir Horatio Pallavicino*, Oxford, 1956; Pagano De Divitiis, *English Merchants*, 20; M. E. Bratchel, 'Italian Merchant Organization and Business Relationships in Early Tudor London', *Journal of European Economic History*, 7 (1978): 5–32; and his 'Regulation and Group Consciousness in the Later History of London's Merchant Colonies', *Journal of European Economic History*, 9 (1980): 585–610.

[42] ASV, *Senato, Dispacci, Ambasciatori, Francia*, f. 9, cc.n.n. (13-1-1575mv); *CSPVe*, vol. vii, n. 645, 542. See: www.british-history.ac.uk/report.aspx?compid=95093 (accessed 14 February 2014).

was deemed particularly unacceptable.[43] The queen agreed and limited his exacting 'licence money' only from non-English merchants, which in practice meant that Venetians (citizens and subject) would have to pay for trading goods produced in their own colonial territories: again unacceptable. The government of Venice retaliated by dramatically increasing taxation on currant exports through the *Nuova Imposta*. Velutelli's position became untenable, and in 1582 Elizabeth withdrew his privilege. The following year the same concession was granted instead to a group of English merchants.

These merchants were united in the Venice Company, and their area of monopoly extended to Venice and its dominions. Velutelli tried for years to fight them and at least recover some of the money he had invested in his venture and lost. His main line of argument was that English merchants had colluded against him and that the Venetian customs increase was a consequence of lobbying by Greek subjects of the Republic. His complaints fell on deaf ears, but his insistence in pursuing redress once again provides evidence of the profitability of trading with Venice.[44]

The Venice Company started its life with an acrimonious dispute with another recently founded company, the Turkey Company (1580). Their areas of monopoly were adjacent, and part of their trade routes and merchandise effectively overlapped. The Venice Company felt aggrieved by the extra duties the Venetian government had put on its major commodity – currants – and the Turkey merchants complained about the high cost of maintaining the English embassy at the Ottoman court.[45] At some point at the beginning of the 1590s, the solution proved to be to merge the companies into one, which was chartered in 1592 with the name Levant Company.[46] The 1592 charter was supposed to last for twelve years and the original members were fifty-three, but the charter also specified that 'twenty others were also named who were to form fresh blood. Two of these should be admitted for the mere asking and the others on payment of an entrance fee of £130' – a hefty figure, again evidence of the potential of the trade. 'In addition to these, the members

---

[43] Ramsay, 'The Undoing of the Italian Mercantile Colony', 47; Epstein, *The Early History*, 21.
[44] TNA, *SP* 99/1, *passim*.
[45] Epstein, *The Early History*, 27.
[46] It is not possible to be precise about the exact date of the Levant Company creation. Brenner dates it to 1592, when Elizabeth granted the charter; Epstein, on the basis of some of the charges of its members, talks instead of 1589 as the date when merchants of the two companies started to operate jointly: see Brenner, *Merchants and Revolution*, 18–21; Epstein, *The Early History*, 25–36. Unfortunately we have no surviving records for the Turkey Company, and the archive of the Levant starts only in 1599, see Skilliter, *William Harborne and the Trade with Turkey*, 186.

of the Company were empowered to admit their servants, factors and agents according as they or the most of them shall think requisite'; the area of activity of the company was defined as comprising the Dominions of the Grand Seigneur and of the Signory of Venice, including Zante, Cephalonia and Candia, as well as the East Indies 'lately discovered'.[47] It was not by chance that the East India Company would be dominated by Levant Company members for quite some time after its creation in 1600. This first phase of English commercial expansion was characterised by great permeability between different areas of commerce, both within Europe and beyond; specialisation would follow.[48] We shall have occasion to discuss the peculiarites of the internal organisation of the Levant Company, and how this resulted from the double exposure – Ottoman and Venetian – of its trade. What is important to note for the moment is that the Levant, since its beginning, counted amongst its members some of the principal English merchants of the time, who frequently also enjoyed powerful support at court.[49]

The Levant Company inherited from the Venice Company all the privileges included in Velutelli's original patent, but there was also a specific clause that gave the company the right of granting licences to English merchants upon payment of a fee. It was forbidden to any other 'foreigner' to import currants, with the theoretical exceptions of Venetians and their subjects, but this last clause was connected to the abolition of the *Nuova Imposta* by the Venetian government and the re-establishment of direct diplomatic links between the two countries.[50] The former never happened; the latter, only in 1603.

The *Nuova Imposta* and its aftermath

On 22 December 1578 the Venetian merchant Zuan Domenego de Lazarini handed in a most intriguing memorandum to the *Serenissima*

---

[47] Epstein, *The Early History*, 37–38.

[48] Clay, *Economic Expansion*, ii: 129–130; on this see also Epstein, *The Early History*, 40–41; both, and also Robert Brenner (*Merchants and Revolution*, 12–23), dealt extensively with the connection between the capital invested in the Muscovy Company and the creation of the Levant, also analysing how, later on, Levant Company capital was essential in the creation of the East India Company. A good synthesis is in A. H. De Groot, 'The Organization of Western European Trade in the Levant 1500–1800', in L. Blussè and F. Gaastra eds., *Companies and Trade*, Leiden, 1981, 231–241; also Games, *Web of Empire*.

[49] As an example, Thomas Cordell, one of the pioneers of the Turkey traffic, had been a Spanish Company member, and was a member also of the Mercers', the Venice, the Levant and the East India Companies, and in all of these he enjoyed positions of power and responsability; see Skilliter, *William Harborne and the Trade with Turkey*, 11–13; on this in general see also Brenner, *Merchants and Revolution*, passim.

[50] Epstein, *The Early History*, 39.

Signoria. In it he detailed some 'interesting discoveries', the principal of which was the rise in the production of currants on the islands of Zante and Cephalonia – 'a product so necessary and esteemed everywhere that it is almost as popular and famed as pepper'. But there was more to it, as he described how in the early autumn months many ships came from different countries to collect the currant crop from the islands to take it directly abroad. In this way Venice suffered triple damages: to the state's coffers, to its subjects' commercial interests and to her own shipping. Clearly knowledgeable about the Venetian customs system – both in the city and empire – Lazarini highlighted that the loss of income was particularly important, as previously currants were taxed twice: first upon exiting the islands and then on being re-exported out of Venice. He was also at pains to highlight how, in previous times, four to six large Venetian ships had brought currants to England each year, whilst now this traffic was slipping away. This was another powerful argument, given the traditional concerns of the Venetian government, which Lazarini did not fail to elaborate by detailing at length how it could potentially have wide-ranging and long-term effects on the seaworthiness of the Republic's commercial fleet.

His final argument was, if possible, even stronger, as he claimed that these English ships were also starting to stop on the coasts of the Peloponnese and Anatolia, establishing direct trading links with the Ottomans, something which – if left unchecked – would have had terrible consequences for the Venetian role of mediator between the Levant and Europe. He concluded by suggesting the levying of a new customs tax on all foreign ships that loaded in the Ionian islands and in Candia, and humbly petitioned (in traditional fashion) for a pension for him to be carved out of this new state income.[51]

The *Cinque Savi alla Mercanzia* – the Venetian Board of Trade – took quite some time to prepare a response to Lazarini's *scrittura*, as their reply is dated August 1580. This was an uncommon delay, as usually this was done in a matter of weeks, not years. An essential part of their work was to thoroughly research the topic under examination and then provide the *Collegio* with an appropriate reply, which would become part of the Republic's legislative record.[52] One of the possible reasons for this delay is that the issues raised by Lazarini were indeed very serious, interconnected and directly touched the Republic's main concerns at that time. Overall the *Savi* agreed with Lazarini's analysis of Anglo-Venetian

---

[51] ASV, *Cinque Savi alla Mercanzia*, b. 836b, I fasc., doc n. 1.
[52] A sketch of the magistrate organization and functioning is in M. Borgherini-Scarabellin, *Il Magistrato dei Cinque Savi alla Mercanzia dalla istituzione alla caduta della Repubblica*, Venice, 1925.

commercial relations and on the negative impact of the absence of direct diplomatic relations between the two states. Still, in line with their remit, their analysis was primarily concerned with the economic situation, and therefore they concentrated most of their comments on the bilateral trade between the two countries and on trade with the Levant in general.

Amongst their principal concerns was the way in which currants were purchased. First, they focused on how foreigners in the islands paid the same customs duties as citizens and subjects, which was not deemed appropriate, especially in light of the exceedingly higher duties that Venetians were subjected to in England. However, more worrying for the *Savi* was how these purchases were taking place on credit thanks to the presence in England of 'subjects of Your Serenity' who organised these deals in advance, arranging for payment once the currants had been sold, so that in practice the English merchants involved in the currant trade 'could profit without capital'.[53]

The idea of establishing a new customs duty payable by all foreigners was judged to be an appropriate measure and, with a direct reference to the customs war of the previous century in Candia, they advised trying to avoid the escalation which had characterised that particular confrontation. To achieve this end the *Savi* recommended that the duty not be openly directly at the English 'as, being by nature a haughty Nation', were they to feel specifically targeted their reaction might worsen the situation. Their suggestion was to establish a new duty aimed generically at all 'non-subjects', which hopefully would discourage 'them' to come directly to the islands to load currants. Moreover, the *Savi* also recommended that this duty be set up as a transitory measure, set to automatically lapse if 'foreign princes' abolished the extra duties to which Venetians were subject in their lands. It was a solution which was linguistically and formally general but which could not – and did not – fail to be felt by the English as directed against them. The real challenge for the Venetian authorities, as the *Savi* could not but underline, was how to make sure that the 'subjects' – that is to say, the Greek merchants – were kept under close surveillance so as to avoid deals between them and the English aimed at shirking payment of the new customs.[54] Legislation against these sorts of deals was already in place, but implementing it properly had always proven difficult. We shall have ample occasion to see exactly *how* difficult this would prove.

[53] ASV, *Cinque Savi alla Mercanzia, Risposte*, reg. 137, cc.18r–19r.

[54] ASV, *Cinque Savi alla Mercanzia, Risposte*, reg. 137, cc.18r–19r. On forbidding private commercial deals between Venetian citizens and subjects see the *Senato* decrees of 19-4-1524 and 9-5-1525, printed copies of which are enclosed also in ASV, *Cinque Savi alla Mercanzia*, b. 836b, pieces not indexed after piece n. 10.

Suddenly the English presence in the Ionian islands had become a big
headache for the Venetian authorities. Lazarini had been the first to raise
the issue directly with the *Collegio*, but many voices were now clamouring
for the problem to be confronted. As we already saw, concerns about the
increase in currant production in Zante and Cephalonia dated from
the middle of the century, but by 1580 the 'foreigners' whose presence
in the islands had been bemoaned suddenly got a name: the English. In
that same year, both returning *Rettori* from Zante and Cephalonia –
Gabriele Emo and Alvise Lando – highlighted the increased English
presence in the islands, and both recommended that an additional levy
be raised to offset their encroachment on local trade.[55] Emo detailed how
'in the last four years four or five English ships of good load' had been
coming to Zante to take currants. Interestingly, the number of English
ships mirrors that given by Lazarini of Venetian ships previously going
to England with the same cargo. Not only did they both suggest an
additional levy, and express worry about the growing collusion between
local Greek subjects and English merchants, but they also both stressed
how English ships were also trading with the Ottoman territories and how
this could have profoundly negative consequences for Venetian control of
local commercial sea routes. Zante's harbour seemed to have suddenly
become 'the major port in the Levant'.[56]

The *Nuova Imposta* was established by the *Senato* with a decree (*parte*)
dated 26 January 1580mv.[57] It was a hefty and rather articulated piece
of legislation, prefaced – as was traditional – by an analysis of why it
was needed. The central part of the decree described the new imposition
of 10 ducats on every thousandweight of currants exported by foreign
merchants out of the Ionian islands 'for every place in the West beyond

---

[55] Emo suggested a relatively low additional duty of 1 ducat per thousandweight of currants,
to be paid when exporting out of the city of Zante directly to foreign lands; in his
calculations this would have provided the island with an additional yearly income of
more than 3,000 ducats per year ('alle uve passe che si contrazeno da quella città, per
condurle in terre aliene, se gli facesse pagar di datio un ducato di più per ogni migliaro,
che questo solo veria a render da tre mille ducati et più all'anno'): see ASV, *Collegio,
Relazioni*, b. 62, cc.nn.n. (Gabriel Emo, 1580). Lando also suggested an additional levy,
but of comparable weight to the additional one to which Venetians were subjected in
England, see ASV, *Cinque Savi alla Mercanzia*, b. 836b, I fasc., n. 3; this document
discussing the levy is also enclosed in his final *relazione* in ASV, *Collegio, Relazioni*, b. 62,
reg. 2, cc.116v–119v.
[56] ASV, *Collegio, Relazioni*, b. 62, cc.nn.n. (Gabriel Emo); also in ASV, *Cinque Savi alla
Mercanzia*, b. 836b, I fasc., piece n. 2.
[57] ASV, *Senato Mar*, reg. 44, cc.238v–240r; another full copy in ASV, *Cinque Savi alla
Mercanzia*, b. 836b, I fasc., piece n. 5. (mv means *more Veneto*, with the year starting on 1
March, so in the Gregorian calendar the date would have been 26 January 1581).

the Strait of Gibraltar' on foreign ships.[58] Another duty of 6 ducats per barrel (*botte*) was also levied on Candia wines exported in the same way. Similar taxation was also put onto the import into the islands of typical English export goods – such as kerseys, woollen cloth, wool and tin. Existing legislation aimed at re-routing all imports into the Venetian state and dominions through Venice itself – a long-standing pillar of the Republic's political economy – was also reiterated, specifically mentioning the goods of this particular branch of trade. Every infraction of these rules was to be considered contraband and had to be dealt with accordingly; once again, the previous legislation on this topic was republished.[59]

Particularly detailed dispositions were also put into place to quash commercial partnerships between Venetian subjects and foreigners; these were already forbidden by law, and rightly perceived to be one of the most serious issues behind the growing success of the English. First, the existing legislation on this issue was reiterated,[60] and then instructions were given for all subjects who had entered into such partenerships to notify the *Avogadori di Comun* within one month of the decree's publication if based in Venice and within two months if based in the Ionian islands, where they would notify the local *Rettori*. In any case such partnerships should be wound down within six months. After this date, non-compliers would be referred to the *Avogadori* or to the *Rettori*.[61]

Spurred into action by Lazarini's *scrittura*, whose analysis was supported by the recent reports of the *Rettori*, the Venetian legislative machine had started moving, and the establishment of the *Nuova Imposta* was just the beginning. Later in the book we shall see how this affected political and diplomatic relations between the two states; for the moment let us

---

[58] 'Per qual si voglia sorte di forestieri, et per ogni luoco di Ponente oltra il stretto di Zibilterra, con navilij forestieri.'

[59] Especially the *Senato* decrees of 20-7-1568, 15-2-1568mv and 21-4-1572, which established in detail the modalities of denunciation, judicial procedure for such trials, and benefits for whoever denounced to the authorities the existence of such practices.

[60] Specifically mentioned here are the *Senato* decrees of 19-4-1524 (ASV, *Senato Mar*, reg. 20, cc.97v–98r), of 26-2-1536mv (ASV, *Senato Mar*, reg. 23, cc.191r/v), and of 27-7-1543 (ASV, *Senato Mar*, reg. 27, cc.49r/v).

[61] ASV, *Senato Mar*, reg. 44, c.239v; another complete copy is in ASV, *Cinque Savi alla Mercanzia*, b. 836b, I fasc., piece n. 5. The decree then ended with a thankful acknowledgment for Lazarini's original *scrittura*, which had set into motion the legislative machine. In practice Lazarini would have to wait until 1584 to receive his recompense: then he was assigned 1½ per cent (and not 3 per cent as he had asked) of the *Nuova Imposta* income for the rest of his life, in case of his death before twenty years had expired; this income would have been reversible to his heirs until the twentieth year (see ASV, *Cinque Savi alla Mercanzia*, b. 188 ns, cc.n.n. (6-6-1584).

concentrate on the effect that Lazarini's *scrittura* had on the activities of the *Cinque Savi*. The years following the establishment of the new levy were characterised by a multifaceted and articulated debate on how to respond to the English arrival in the Eastern Mediterranean. It was very clear to all participants in this debate that the latest war with the Ottomans (1570–1573) had represented a crucial watershed for Venetian hegemony in the region. Before, they had dominated maritime trade in the Eastern Mediterranean, and now they were losing their grip.

The collection of information on the real state of Anglo-Venetian trade continued well beyond the promulgation of the *Nuova Imposta*. The *Savi* solicited former *Rettori*, former and present tax farmers, and merchants with specific local expertise, to provide them with data on reciprocal customs between the two countries, and on the general state of trade both with the North of Europe and in the Eastern Mediterranean. Many reports (*scritture*) were also voluntarily submitted by various parties, some of whom did so anonymously. What is immediately evident in reading the documentation is the interconnection between the two trade regions, and how the recent conflict with the Ottomans had been a catalyst for important structural transformations of the Republic's maritime trade. What emerged was a truly worrying picture.

All parties in this debate attributed the interruption of direct maritime trade with England to the recent English legislation which had dramatically increased customs duties for foreigners, and substantially limited the freedom of foreign merchants to operate in England. An anonymous merchant complained vociferously about the unfair obligation for foreign merchants to sell all import goods exclusively to London merchants, without the possibility of selling to merchants from other parts of the country, a very interesting comment considering that legislation of this kind was also in place in Venice itself![62] The arrival of the English in the Mediterranean was connected with the stoppage of Venetian shipping to Northern Europe, on this again they all agreed; on the possible solutions, however, there was a wide variety of opinions. There was general concern about the situation in Zante and Cephalonia, but far larger loomed the danger of the English taking over the position of intermediaries between the Ottomans and Western Europe.

Another understandable concern of the Venetian authorities was the damage to its fiscal income in the Ionian islands and in Venice inflicted by the arrival of the English and by their evident collusion with Venetian

---

[62] See ASV, *Cinque Savi alla Mercanzia*, b. 836b, II fasc., cc.nn.n. 'scrittura di persona secreta' (27-6-1583).

subjects, usually aimed at avoiding customs duties.[63] Both the Ionian subjects of the Republic and the English merchants started separate lobbying campaigns with the same objective: the abolition of the *Nuova Imposta*. The *Savi*'s answers to the abundance of opinions and memorandums they received with the passing of time revealed a certain hardening of their position. Not only were the *Savi* confronting a commercial crisis, which was exactly what they had been created to deal with, but they also found themselves enmeshed in the foreign policy of the Republic, and its attitude to England. Two issues clearly emerge from these exchanges in the years immediately after 1580: first, the *Savi* wanted to see what kind of income the *Nuova Imposta* would have provided before deciding its future; second, the political and diplomatic impasse was playing an increasingly important role in how the debate was evolving.[64] The previous century's Candia wine customs war seemed to be repeating itself, with two substantial differences worsening the situation: Venetian shipping in general was incomparably weaker, and currants enjoyed a substantially smaller market than Candia wines, as their demand was increasingly concentrated in England.[65]

Greeks in England

In their original reply to Lazarini's *scrittura*, the *Savi* had mentioned the presence in England of 'subjects of Your Serenity', but we have seen how Venetian merchants in England had been decimated by a wave of bankruptcies in 1570s. Who were these 'subjects'? After the collapse of the northern branch of the Venetian state galley system, merchants and shipowners from the Ionian islands and Crete tried to continue the sea route to the North of Europe, which was already one of their main export markets. In the late fifteenth century, in the aftermath of the first Anglo-Venetian tariff war, a series of measures had been implemented in Candia to improve the economic situation of the local population and maintain their loyalty to Venice.[66] These had some positive effects on local shipowners, and enabled the emergence of Greek maritime operators of international stature who enlarged the scope of their trades beyond traditional routes in the Eastern Mediterranean and towards Venice. But, unfortunately, the problems of the Venetian merchant marine were structural and could not be solved by occasional legislation,

---

[63] For two typical examples of these see ASV, *Cinque Savi alla Mercanzia*, b. 836b, I fasc., pieces n. 4 and 5.

[64] For a detailed analysis of this debate see Fusaro, *Uva passa*, 33–44.

[65] ASV, *Cinque Savi alla Mercanzia, Risposte*, reg. 137, cc.132r–133v (12-11-1584).

[66] Maltezou, 'The Historical and Social Context', 29–32.

mostly concerned with tax rebates for people willing to build galleons.[67] However, in both Crete and the Ionian islands, products that were coveted in international markets clearly were a stimulus for entrepreneurship. It was for these reasons that the majority of Venetians present in England in the last quarter of the sixteenth century were Greek subjects of the Republic. In that network are to be found the roots of the Anglo-Greek alliance that was to become so crucial for English penetration in the Mediterranean.[68]

The major players in these trades were the Sumacchi and Seguro families of Zante – who kept their own agent in London, Zuanne da Riviera[69] – and a few Cretan merchants and shipowners, amongst whom the most important was Thodorin Lombardo. In addition, two Venetians *cittadini* – the brothers Giacomo and Placido Ragazzoni – were also heavily involved.[70] In London these Venetians enjoyed a fruitful commercial and financial relationship not only with their English counterparts but also with the principal Florentine merchants and financiers resident in the City, headed by Filippo and Bartolomeo Corsini.[71] Through them they were connected with the Florentine Northern European commercial

---

[67] M. Costantini, 'I galeoni di Candia nella congiuntura marittima veneziana cinque-seicentesca', in Ortalli ed., *Venezia e Creta*, 207–231; F. Baroutsos, 'Sovention per fabricar galeoni: Ο Βενετικός μερκαντιλισμός και οι αντανακλάσεις του στην Κρητική κοινωνία του υστέρου 16ου αιώνα' ('Financing Galleons: Venetian Mercantilism and Its Consequences on Late Sixteenth Century Cretan Society'), *Thesaurismata*, 29 (1999): 187–223.

[68] For a detailed analysis of these activites see Fusaro, 'Les Anglais et les Grecs'.

[69] Giovanni da Riviera (also known as Zuanne Darevera) was still active in London in 1592: see ASV, *Cinque Savi alla Mercanzia, Risposte*, reg. 138, c. 166v; see also U. Tucci, 'The Psychology of the Venetian Merchant', in J. R. Hale ed., *Renaissance Venice*, London, 1973, 346–378, 348.

[70] Giacomo Regazzoni is a classic case of Venetian merchant-entrepreneur, extremely representative of a new kind of non-noble Venetian merchant, who managed to acquire a large fortune with an intelligent diversification of investments. Equally interested in landed investments in the Venetian *Terraferma* and in commercial enterprises all around Europe (when still very young he set up a company with Giacomo Foscarini for trading between Venice and England), he was also active in the insurance business and in the Venetian financial market. A sketch of the activities of both Ragazzoni brothers is in L. Pezzolo, 'Sistema di valori ed attività economica a Venezia, 1530–1630', in S. Cavaciocchi ed., *L'impresa, l'industria, commercio, banca, secoli XII–XVIII*, Florence, 1991, 981–988, 986–987; see also B. De Maria, *Becoming Venetians: Immigrants and the Arts in Early Modern Venice*, Princeton, 2010, 38–39.

[71] Filippo was born in Florence in 1538 and came to London in 1559; within ten years he was the largest importer in England of European goods besides being a substantial exporter. In 1579 his younger brother Bartholomew joined him, and by 1584 the name of the business was Bartholomew Corsini & co. The brothers operated their import-export business out of their house in Gracechurch Street. Filippo was also an agent for the Medici bank in England: see Wyatt, *The Italian Encounter with Tudor England*, 131.

networks. The Ragazzoni brothers, Da Riviera and Corsini were the links between the English and the Greek-Venetians, and they were all connected in a tight network which operated within the triangle: Venice–Zante, Cephalonia and Crete–London.

Giorgio Sumacchi and his son Michele divided their interests between the Ionian islands and Venice, but they also traded with Crete, whence they exported wines to England.[72] In their dealings in Cretan wines to the North of Europe they were frequently associated with the powerful Cretan merchant Thodorin Lombardo.[73] The Sumacchi also acted as intermediaries for other Venetian merchants in trading to the Ionian islands,[74] where they were powerful members of the local elite. They were especially involved in the currant trade with England, and they were well-known figures in London commercial circles as powerful intermediaries.[75] Their influential position in the islands was well known in England, so much so that when Acerbo Velutelli lost his monopoly on currant imports into England, he accused the 'Italian' merchants Nicolò de Gozzi Pange and Innocenzo Locatelli of having colluded with the Sumacchi in pushing for new customs duties for foreigners in the islands. Nikola Gucetić – in the Venetian documentation known as Nicolò de Gozzi Pange – was in fact not 'Italian', but the most prominent member of the Ragusan mercantile community in Southampton in the last quarter of the sixteenth century. He was an important trader in Mediterranean commodities and an intermediary between Greeks and English merchants.[76] It is interesting to

---

[72] For example see ASV, *Notarile Atti*, b. 7867 (Gerolamo Luran), cc.657v–658v (19-5-1590).

[73] For typical contracts between them see ASV, *Notarile Atti*, b. 7857 (Gerolamo Luran), cc.134v–135r (13-6-1586); and b. 7866 (Gerolamo Luran), cc.127r/v (11-2-1590). The latter regards a particularly complex shipment of Rethimo Muscat wines destined for Danzig.

[74] See, for example, ASV, *Notarile Atti*, b. 6529 (Luca and Giulio Gabrieli), cc.110v–111r (1-4-1583). They also rented Flemish ships jointly with the Seguro: see Brulez and Devos, *Marchands Flamands*, ii, n. 3803, 670 (12-11-1618); n. 3805, 671–672 (17-11-1618); n. 3808, 672–673 (22-11-1618). Michele was also active in the insurance business: see A. Tenenti, *Naufrages, corsaires et assurances maritimes à Venise 1592–1609*, Paris, 1959, *passim*.

[75] For a deal of this kind, see ASV, *Notarile Atti*, b. 7847 (Gerolamo Luran), cc.166r–167r (18-9-1580); in this case, Sumacchi was supposed to procure a large quantity of currants for Henry Ferenton, agent of the Levant Company member William Garway. On their crucial role as 'facilitators' see also the comments of Alfonso Strozzi to Bartolomeo Corsini, in *LMA*, CLC/B/062/MS21317, n. 239 (16-6-1581).

[76] Acerbo Velutelli's supplication to the queen after the loss of his monopoly in TNA, *SP* 99/1, 16r (1583–4). Locatelli and the Sumacchi had been doing business together in Northern Europe since the early 1570s; for a typical deal between them, see ASV, *Notarile Atti*, b. 11886 (Gerolamo Savina), cc.201v–202v (27-1-1576), in this case their business had been in Antwerp; for an example of their joint business interests in London see *LMA*, CLC/B/062/MS21317, n. 193 (14-8 and 22-8-1579). Nicolò de Gozzi was one of the

note that the Seguro and Sumacchi prominence was clearly acknowledged even by important Venetian merchants – such as the Ragazzoni brothers and the patrician Corner family – for whom they acted in England.[77]

Other important members of this Greek-Venetian network were the brothers Agesilao and Marco Seguro of Zante,[78] active as merchants and as shipowners; vessels belonging to them regularly reached England well into the late 1580s carrying currants and oil, not only for themselves but also for other merchants from Venice and her dominions.[79] Like all the other Venetian merchants mentioned above, the Seguro owned ships that regularly travelled to England and, again like all the others, they frequently employed English pilots. Employing an English pilot, and sometime even a whole English crew, was an *escamotage* that guaranteed some measure of security in the dangerous northern seas, where Venetian crews were no longer used to navigating.[80] This is in itself an admission of the depths of the seamanship (*marinarezza*) crisis of Venice. Furthermore, the Seguros used some Venetian-built ships, although they also bought and commissioned some to be built abroad, a classic way in which Venetian and Greek merchants and shipowners responded to the crisis.[81] The ships were then naturalised and could be used, taking full advantage of the benefits in place for Venetian ships. It was, of course, a policy open to abuse and one which certainly did not help to overcome the

leading merchants in England at the time, and probably one of the wealthiest foreigners along with Sir Oratio Pallavicino; on him see Abulafia, 'Cittadino e "denizen"', 286–287.

[77] On the Ragazzoni using Greek ships to collect currants from the Ionian islands and the Morea, see ASV, *Capi del Consiglio dei Dieci, Lettere di Rettori ed altre cariche*, b. 297, fasc. ii, n. 64 (16-12-1574); LMA, CLC/B/062/MS22274, n. 439 (9-3-1582) and *passim* throughout this file. For Giacomo Ragazzoni loaning a ship from the Seguro see *LMA*, CLC/B/062/MS22274, n. 104 (10-3-1590). The Ragazzoni brothers were also active in the trade from Crete: see ASV, *Notarile Atti*, b. 8166 (Vettor Maffei), cc.91r–92v (30-1-1571).

[78] The Seguro family had been for a long time one of the most powerful of the island of Zante. Already in 1542 the then *Rettore* had written of them: 'Sonno li primi in questo luoco, sonno conivuti in consanguinità con tutti li altri cittadini, hanno la mittà di questa Isola in sua mano', in ASV, *Capi del Consiglio dei Dieci, Lettere di Rettori e altre cariche*, b. 296 (Zante 1506–1749), fasc. i, cc.n.n. (25-8-1542).

[79] *LMA*, CLC/B/062/MS22274, n. 1394 (8-3-1591). Not all their ventures were successful. In 1587 they were to lose a cargo of currants in a shipwreck in Gibraltar: see ASV, *Notarile Atti*, b. 6534 (Luca and Giulio Gabrieli), cc.34r/v (6-2-1587).

[80] Interesting documents regarding a complex series of 'loans' and 'swaps' of English crews amongst the above-mentioned merchants are in ASV, *Notarile Atti*, b. 7850 (Gerolamo Luran), cc.394r/v and 395r/v (23-4-1582); b. 7849 (Gerolamo Luran), cc.77r/v (24-4-1582). Notwithstanding these precautions, shipwreck in the dangerous northern seas was a distinct possibility: Thodorin Lombardo would lose one of his galleons in 1582 on the coast of Brittany on his way to England; see ASV, *Notarile Atti*, b. 6529 (Luca and Giulio Gabrieli), cc.54r/v (29-1-1583); see also b. 6536 (Luca and Giulio Gabrieli), c.38r (30-1-1589).

[81] For example in Danzig: ASV, *Collegio, Rdd*, f. 7, cc.n.n. (27-5-1581 and 29-7-1581).

shipbuilding crisis. From the last quarter of the sixteenth century the *Senato* had authorised the buying of foreign ships, but still in 1627 legislation was being put into place to properly regulate these issues.[82] Quite apart from the negative impact on the Venetian shipbuilding industry, a further negative corollary of purchasing vessels in Northern Europe was to push shipowners towards the employment of foreign crews, more used to the technology involved in handling these kinds of vessels, and this had a further negative impact on the employment of local seafarers.[83]

These Greeks were serious players on the international stage. In Venice they also provided crucial links between northern traders and the Jewish commercial web. The English took advantage of the Jewish Mediterranean trade network extremely rarely, and it can be argued that the Greek network played the mediating role traditionally associated with the Jews. The Seguro and the Sumacchi also traded in partnership with Portuguese Jews based in Venice, and through them sometimes English merchants participated in those trades. Trading in association with English merchants was certainly financially convenient at a time when Anglo-Spanish hostilities were at their height, but it could also lead to problems with the Spanish authorities, as the following episodes amply demonstrate. In 1588 the ship *Sumacchia* was stopped in Palermo because local authorities believed it to be carrying merchandise belonging to English subjects; instead, it was carrying goods belonging to the Portuguese Jews Gerardo Malines and Garzia Pimentel.[84] The following year it was the turn of the *Segura* to be stopped in Cadiz, also wrongly suspected of carrying English

[82] ASV, *Senato Mar*, reg. 44, cc.149r/v (23-8-1579), see also ASV, *Senato Mar*, f. 260, cc.n.n. (22-12-1627).

[83] On these issues see R. W. Unger, 'The Technology and Teaching of Shipbuilding 1300–1800', in M. Prak and J. Luiten van Zanden eds., *Technology, Skills and the Pre-Modern Economy in the East and the West*, Leiden, 2013, 161–204.

[84] On the ship there were also goods belonging to Flemish traders based in London, such as Thomas Coteels, and this led local authorities to believe that the ship was English and acting under a cover name: on this see Brulez and Devos, *Marchands Flamands*, i: n. 195, 69. This episode can be also followed in *CSPVe*, vol. viii (1581–1591), London, 1894, n. 624, 336, see: www.british-history.ac.uk/report.aspx?compid=95256; n. 647, 347–348, see: www.british-history.ac.uk/report.aspx?compid=95258; n. 664, 357, see: www.british-history.ac.uk/report.aspx?compid=95259; n. 676, 362, see: www.british-history.ac.uk/report.aspx?compid=95260; n. 769, 409 and n. 774, 412, see: www.british-history.ac.uk/report.aspx?compid=95265; n. 821, 430–432, see: www.british-history.ac.uk/report.aspx?compid=95268; n. 854, 455, see: www.british-history.ac.uk/report.aspx?compid=95272 (accessed 3 March 2014). On the relations between the Sumacchi and the Portuguese Jews based in Venice see F. Ruspio, *La nazione portoghese: ebrei ponentini e nuovi cristiani a Venezia*, Turin, 2007, 280 and footnote. On the contacts between Michele Sumacchi and the Ribeira family of Portuguese Jews, see also: ASV, *Notarile Atti*, b. 7847 (Gerolamo Luran), cc.74r/v (20-5-1580) and b. 7849 (Gerolamo Luran), cc.115v–166v (7-6-1582); their contacts are also mentioned in

goods.[05] Another similar episode took place in 1592, when the *Sumacchia* was itself thought to be English and was captured by the Spanish, who suspected secret dealings between the Republic and England. This ended up being a complicated diplomatic case, as on this occasion part of the cargo did actually belong to English merchants.[86]

When the *Cinque Savi* in 1584 asked some of the principal Venetian merchants about trade with England, the replies all highlighted how the recent increase in customs duty in England had made it unprofitable for foreigners to import goods into the country. Therefore, they said, direct trade had entirely stopped.[87] But from the 'Corsini papers' kept in the London Metropolitan Archives a different picture emerges which supports the notarial documents found in Venice. Traffic diminished substantially, but it was not interrupted, and a small group of Greek merchants were fully involved in international trade both as merchants and as shipowners. They enjoyed fruitful business contacts with Venetian merchants and throughout the Mediterranean basin, but they were also very active in trade with England, where they were able to send their ships both earlier and for longer periods of time than previously thought. Their trading was characterised by extreme flexibility in their choice of carriers and by an interesting mix of shipowners and crews.[88]

This complex series of connected contracts shows a strong willingness to keep the trade in Venetian hands as much as possible in the face of

G. V. Scammell, 'Shipowning in the Economy and Politics of Early Modern England', *The Historical Journal*, 15 (1972): 385–407, 396. There he wrongly called Michele Sumacchi 'nominal owner of the *Santa Maria*', following a line of interpretation in which English merchants kept the trade open in markets otherwise closed to them, such as the Spanish one.

[85] The *Segura* was going from Crete to Lisbon, and probably afterwards to London. After being freed it remained in the harbour of Cadiz to avoid the English corsairs who were raiding the area, on this episode see *CSPVe*, viii (1581–1591), *passim*.

[86] On this see *CSPVe*, viii (1581–1591), *passim*. On the ship there were also goods belonging to Hamburg and Cologne merchants. On the episode see: *CSPVe*, ix (1592–1603), London, 1897, *passim*.

[87] ASV, *Cinque Savi alla Mercanzia*, b. 836b, fasc. ii (3-11-1584) and (27-10-1584); the latter is signed by all the 'parcenevoli di navi per Inghiltera': 'Hieronimo Corner *quondam* Andrea, Todorin Lombardo, Raphael Sumachi, Jacomo et Placido Regazzoni, Domenego da Gagliano, Paolo Tabiò, Alvise Balanzer, Vincenzo Costantini, Piero Grataruol, Domenego et Piero Innocenti; Zuanne Muscorno, Marin Tressa, Zeb.no [sic] Balbianij'. For a comparative overview of custom duties paid in England, and the debate on the traffic, see Fusaro, *Uva passa*, 27–44.

[88] For contracts that confirm this interpretation, see ASV, *Notarile Atti*, reg. 11920 (Andrea Spinelli), cc.42r/v (16-1-1599); reg. 3371 (Gio Andrea Catti), c.121v (29-3-1600); reg. 11923 (Andrea Spinelli), cc.73v–74r (28-1-1602); reg. 11925 (Andrea Spinelli), cc. 569r/v (11-8-1604); reg. 7868 (Gerolamo Luran), cc.351v–352v (17-5-1591).

ever-mounting difficulties. Ultimately, this strategy was not successful. The Anglo-Greek alliance was a crucial element in the beginning of English trade in the Mediterranean, and we shall see how it remained essential for the English for centuries, well beyond the life span of the Republic of Venice.

3   The Ottoman Levant

Since the first Crusade, the growth of Western European trade and ship-ping in the Eastern Mediterranean had had massive social and economic implications not only for the Levant, but for Western Europe as well. The beginning of the Venetian *Stato da Mar* between the twelfth and thirteenth century was just a particularly successful example of a more general phenomenon that involved many of the crusader countries, as the increase of trade and shipping encouraged Latin migration and settlement in the area.[1] Both Venice and Genoa made the best of these opportunities and, throughout the Middle Ages, used their Eastern Mediterranean outposts in ways which were perfectly integrated with the political economy of the two *Dominanti* and, in fact, became important elements in shaping these. Unlike Genoa, though, Venice pursued a more focused campaign of conquest, in the process of which she developed a tight yet flexible govern-ance structure of her overseas territories. This multiplicity of structures compounded the peculiarities and uniqueness of the Venetian state, which has made it difficult to attempt a comparative analysis of Venice's colonial experience.[2]

The century-long fight with Genoa ended with the peace of Turin in 1381. This conflict was, in its ambitions and goals, fought for the Levant far more than for predominance on the Italian peninsula, and the costly victory left Venice as the sole Western European power with important territorial holdings in the region and a hegemonic economic presence. On this near-monopoly Venice built its economic fortunes and established herself as the arch-mediator between the East and Western Europe, a position maintained until the beginning of the sixteenth century, when the Portuguese establishment of a direct maritime route to Asia dramati-cally transformed the structures of Eurasian trade.[3] In the following

---

[1] D. Jacoby, *Latins, Greeks and Muslims: Encounters in the Eastern Mediterranean 10th–15th Centuries*, Farnham, 2009, ix.

[2] On the desirability of a comparative take see also Arbel, 'Venice's Maritime Empire', 239.

[3] E. Ashtor, 'The Venetian Supremacy in Levantine Trade: Monopoly or Pre-Colonialism?', *Journal of European Economic History*, 3 (1974): 5–53.

century Venice managed to regain some control over the spice trade, but by the last quarter of the sixteenth century too many other players were entering the long-distance trade game, and its position was severely diminished.[4]

Thus when discussing 'Levant' within the Venetian context, one must be aware of its double meaning: it was used to indicate all the Republic's territorial possessions beyond the Otranto strait – the *Stato da Mar* – which I shall also call the 'Venetian Levant', but it also meant the entirety of the Eastern Mediterranean where her influence was active, politically, militarily and commercially – and most of this area, by the sixteenth century, can be called the 'Ottoman Levant'.

Venetian–Ottoman confrontations

Amidst all Venice's economic success, the middle of the fifteenth century was also a period of distress and turmoil for the city and its state. The first half of the century had seen quick expansion of the Venetian state into the Italian mainland – the *Terraferma*. In these decades for the first time Venice got seriously involved in the delicate and complex military and diplomatic game being played by the Italian states, which entailed a substantive reorganisation of the Republic's political and economic strategies. Particularly hard had been the conflict with the Duchy of Milan, which ended with the Peace of Lodi in 1454; this proposed an agreement on the control of trade routes in northeastern Italy, which were coveted by both states.[5] The negotiations also included a non-aggression pact between various Italian states, which lasted until 1494, when Charles VIII of France invaded the peninsula, starting another long period of uncertainty.

In the Eastern Mediterranean things were moving equally fast. The Ottoman conquest of Constantinople in 1453 was just one episode – although symbolically the strongest – of the long and seemingly unstoppable Ottoman advance. In the following decades many European outposts in the area were quickly eroded by the military might supporting the Porte, the Ottoman court. Particularly worrying for Venice was that Ottoman troops in 1472 arrived in the Italian peninsula, raiding the mouth of the river Isonzo, and in the following years they appeared also in the Friuli region.[6] In the Aegean Sea Negroponte had been the first major Venetian territorial loss in 1470, and others followed in the

---

[4] F. C. Lane, 'The Mediterranean Spice Trade: Further Evidence of Its Revival in the Sixteenth Century', *American Historical Review*, 45 (1940): 581–590.

[5] I. Lazzarini, *L'Italia degli Stati territoriali: secoli XIII–XV*, Bari, 2003, 69–74.

[6] A. Tenenti, 'Il senso dello spazio e del tempo nel mondo veneziano dei secoli XV e XVI', in *Credenze, ideologie, libertinismi tra Medioevo ed età moderna*, Bologna, 1978, 75–118, 92.

following decades – with the Venetian Aegean islands and the strongholds of Modon and Coron in the Peloponnese all conquered during the so-called second Venetian–Ottoman war (1499–1503). These losses were offset by the acquisition of the Ionian islands of Zante, Cephalonia, Theaki (present-day Ithaca) and Santa Maura (Lefcada), which entered into the Venetian empire between 1482 and 1502. The loss of Negroponte had been somewhat compensated by the acquisition of the kingdom of Cyprus, which happened in a peculiar way as the Cornaro family left it to the Republic as a legacy. From a practical point of view, since the fourteenth century Cyprus had already been fully embedded into the Venetian economic space. But formal acquisition of the 'crown' of Cyprus represented an important tessera in the Venetian imperial strategy, and its loss in 1571 was a major structural change not only in Venetian but in Mediterranean history.[7]

Eliyahu Ashtor has calculated that during this complex century, the zenith of Venetian economic expansion, profits of Levantine trade oscillated between 35 and 50 per cent of the capital invested, with higher returns for some specific items such as cloves, nutmeg, gum-lac and raw cotton.[8] Therefore it is most interesting to note how in that century the Republic of Venice faced war on two fronts – the Italian peninsula and the Levant – with the corollary growth of military expenditure, which was possible thanks to the wealth of the Republic but which also was consumed as soon as it was created.[9] Up to the fifteenth century, the bulk of the wealth of the Venetian state and of its citizens was indeed created though trade; a far smaller percentage was due to financial activities. However, recent studies have highlighted how manufacturing was increasing its share of wealth-creation in the city of Venice itself, a phenomenon which would boom in the sixteenth century.[10]

---

[7] G. Cozzi, 'Venezia Regina', *Studi Veneziani*, 17 (1989): 15–25; G. Denores, *A Discourse on the Island of Cyprus and on the Reasons for the True Succession in that Kingdom*, P. Kitromilides ed., Venice, 2006; V. Costantini, *Il sultano e l'isola contesa: Cipro tra eredità veneziana e potere ottomano*, Turin, 2009.

[8] E. Ashtor, 'Profits from Trade with the Levant in the Fifteenth Century', *Bulletin of the School of Oriental and African Studies*, 38 (1975): 250–275, 268.

[9] For a quick summary of the financial implications of these wars see L. Pezzolo, 'Stato, guerra e finanza nella Repubblica di Venezia fra medioevo e prima età moderna', in R. Cancila ed., *Mediterraneo in armi (sec. XV–XVIII)*, Palermo, 2007, 67–112.

[10] L. Molà, *La comunità dei lucchesi a Venezia: immigrazione e industria della seta nel tardo Medioevo*, Venice, 1994, and his *The Silk Industry of Renaissance Venice*, Baltimore, 2000; A. Mozzato, 'The Production of Woollens in Fifteenth- and Sixteenth-Century Venice', in Lanaro ed., *At the Center of the Old World*, 73–107; and his 'Scelte produttive e di mercato di drappieri veneziani in area adriatica e levantina nel XV secolo', in D. Andreozzi, L. Panariti and C. Zaccaria eds., *Acque, terre e spazi dei mercanti. Istituzioni, gerarchie, conflitti e pratiche dello scambio nel Mediterraneo dall' età antica alla modernità*,

On the Italian mainland, the new territorial acquisitions soon started to pay dividends, at least economically. The conquest of the *Terraferma*, which had started as a defensive manoeuvre to guarantee the safety of the lagoons, quickly engendered a substantial transformation of the Venetian state and economy. In the analysis of Gino Luzzatto, 'that rapid conquest determined a decisive turn in the history of Venice, transforming it from a purely maritime – almost insular – power, into a maritime and continental power, something that created a whole new set of problems, to begin with political but after, directly or indirectly, economic'.[11] Over the next two centuries, the compounded effects of the continuing Ottoman success in the Levant and, especially after the 1510s, the need to establish their presence in the newly regained *Terraferma*, made the 'turn to land' the only logical economic choice to pursue, especially as income from the maritime empire was starting to decrease. Income from the mainland came through investment but particularly through taxation. Through this phenomenon we can appreciate one of the contradictions innate to the Republic's strategy and policy, the fact that the *Terraferma* was always considered an 'accessory' to Venetian power, and was treated as such even when its economic importance overtook that of the *Stato da Mar* and that of the city itself.

The sixteenth century started for Venice on a difficult note also in the Levant. A consequence of the worsening economic climate on the eve of the latest war with the Ottomans had been a substantial weakening of Venice's banking system, with many private banks being hit by a wave of bankruptcies between 1495 and 1499.[12] In 1504, notwithstanding the peace signed the previous year with the Ottomans, maritime trade in the Eastern Mediterranean was still extremely difficult. In February the Alexandria galleys had come back to Venice without spices, as very few had been available there, and these only at exorbitant prices, something which had never happened before. In March this happened again with the Syrian galleys. This compounded the fears generated by news of the Portuguese reaching Calicut. Reaction to these events was quick, and as early as the autumn of that year we see a realignment of Levant traffic from import to export based, as the galleys for Alexandria left with 'not a ducat of cash' but loaded with textiles.[13] The following spring, the dangers associated with the interconnectivity within the galley system became very evident, as the paucity and high prices of spices in the markets of

Trieste, 2009, 303–332; F. Trivellato, 'Murano Glass, Continuity and Transformation (1400–1800)', in Lanaro ed., *At the Center of the Old World*, 143–184.
[11] G. Luzzatto, *Storia economica di Venezia dall'XI al XVI secolo*, Venice, 1961, 161.
[12] Mueller, *The Venetian Money Market*, 230–251.
[13] Tucci, 'Costi e ricavi di una galera', 165–167.

Egypt and Syria created problems in the subsequent loading of the galleys destined for England and Flanders. For Venetian merchants who had shifted their business from the purchase of spices to the export of textiles it must have been weirdly reassuring to hear, in a letter from London in January 1504, that spices from Lisbon were arriving on the London market, and this resulted in a depression of their price.[14] If reassuring from a personal perspective, this was prime evidence that the entire structure of the Eurasian spice trade was changing fast. A few months later, in May, the *Senato* was delighted to hear that the galleys had completely filled their loads in London, so much so that it voted against the Venetian consul's request to send the remaining wool to Venice via private ships, instructing him instead to wait for the next galleys to load the cargo in London.[15] But in the following decades the galley system unravelled, with private trade taking over some of the commercial routes.

The sixteenth century was a period of economic and demographic crisis in the *Dominio da Mar*, primarily because of constant Ottoman military pressure.[16] Venice's well-oiled commercial and financial machine was being sorely tested by a rather unfriendly conjuncture. Between 1479 and 1571 Venice pursued a more defensive stance in foreign policy in the Levant. This becomes particularly evident from the late 1530s, when we see a two-pronged strategy, providing, on the one hand, increasing investments to the fleet, especially to reinforce naval patrols in Eastern Mediterranean waters, and, on the other, an ambitious policy of refortification of all Venetian-controlled territories in the area, especially after experiencing further losses in the Aegean and Morea during a further war with the Ottomans (1537–1540).[17] No expense was spared on this last point. The sustained and costly military engineering programme lasted more than half a century, beginning in 1538 when the famous architect Michele Sanmicheli redesigned the fortifications in Candia, Canea and Rethymnon as well as several strongholds in Dalmatia.[18] By the end of the century these military interventions had made a massive impact on the urbanistic fabric of the Venetian Levant, now dotted by state-of-the-art fortifications.

[14] Tucci, 'Costi e ricavi di una galera', 167.
[15] Tucci, 'Costi e ricavi di una galera', 170.
[16] Tenenti, 'Il senso dello spazio e del tempo', 99–100.
[17] A. Tenenti, 'La congiuntura veneto-ungherese tra la fine del Quattrocento e gli inizi del Cinquecento', in V. Branca ed., *Venezia e Ungheria nel Rinascimento*, Florence, 1973, 135–143, 143; see also Arbel, 'Venice's Maritime Empire', 206–213.
[18] M. Georgopoulou, *Venice's Mediterranean Colonies: Architecture and Urbanism*, Cambridge, 2001, 22.

Faced with new challenges, the Republic also reassessed its commercial strategic interests, and from the middle of the sixteenth century a neglect of so-called Ponentine navigation – *navigazione di Ponente* – is evident.[19] This does not mean that there were no Venetian ships employed in those routes, at least until the beginning of the seventeenth century (as we have seen in the previous chapter), but that government policy was now more concerned to preserve and enhance its share of maritime trade in the Mediterranean, especially towards its eastern shores.[20] During the sixteenth and seventeenth centuries, support for the army and the fleet engaged around 40 per cent of the Venetian state budget in time of peace, increasing to more than 60 per cent in wartime. This last figure is comparable to those of other European states in the same period; what is peculiar to Venice is how much was spent on the military even in times of peace, and how especially the navy had become a weighty and necessary expense for the protection of maritime trade.[21] The Venetian *Armata* remained, indeed, a bastion of strength, and throughout their centuries of conflict Venetian naval superiority resisted Ottoman challenges well, notwithstanding the impressive naval development of the Ottoman navy in the sixteenth and seventeenth centuries. Even during the war of Candia most Ottoman victories over Venice took place on land and not on sea.[22]

The loss of Cyprus was the more serious setback of the 1570–1573 Venetian–Ottoman war, when Venetian naval superiority – this time supported by other Western countries, as at the battle of Lepanto – was unable to counter the overwhelming Ottoman strength on land. The period between 1573 and the beginning of the Candia war in 1646 was, at least formally, a rare moment of pacific coexistence between Venice and the Ottoman empire. Many diplomatic sources underline how more collaboration between authorities – and between merchants of both sides – became visible on the ground, especially in frontier areas such as Dalmatia.[23] In the middle of the sixteenth century, the redrawing of the

---

[19] A. Tenenti, 'La navigazione veneziana nel Seicento', in *Storia di Venezia dalle origini alla caduta della Serenissima*, vol. vii: *La Venezia barocca*, G. Benzoni and G. Cozzi eds., Rome, 1997, 533–567.

[20] Tenenti, 'La navigazione veneziana nel Seicento', 534.

[21] L. Pezzolo, 'Sistema di potere e politica finanziaria nella Repubblica di Venezia (secoli XV–XVII)', in G. Chittolini, A. Molho and P. Schiera eds., *Origini dello Stato: processi di formazione statale in Italia fra medioevo ed età moderna*, Bologna, 1994, 303–327, 313.

[22] A. Tenenti, 'Profilo di un conflitto secolare', in *Venezia e i Turchi: scontri e confronti di due civiltà*, Milan, 1985, 9–37; P. Brummett, *Ottoman Seapower and Levantine Diplomacy in the Age of Discovery*, New York, 1994; G. Candiani, *I vascelli della Serenissima: guerra, politica e costruzioni navali a Venezia in età moderna, 1650–1720*, Venice, 2009.

[23] Panciera, '"Tagliare i confini"', 268.

Dalmatian borders between the Republic and the Ottoman empire reduced Venetian economic hegemony in the area, but towards the end of the century things were looking better for Venice. The most notable example of Venetian–Ottoman collaboration was the development between the late 1570s and 1590 of the so-called *Scala di Spalato* (present-day Split) – a project involving Jewish merchants, first and foremost Daniel Rodriga, the originator of the project – some based in Venice and others in the Ottoman empire.[24] Based around a series of privileged tariffs devised to stimulate trade between Venice and the Balkans under Ottoman control, this project developed Spalato into a preferred commercial hub in the region, the aim being to weaken the recently established links between Ragusa and Ancona. Since the latter's proper incorporation into the Papal States in 1532, serious investments had been made there to strengthen its harbour to make it a competitive centre for exchanges with the Balkans.[25] On this occasion Venice and the Sultan did indeed find reason to collaborate against a common enemy: the pope.

England and the Levant

In some ways it can be argued that the pope played a role in the first direct contacts between England and the Ottoman empire. The publication by Pius V of the *Regnans in Excelsis* bull in 1570, which excommunicated Queen Elizabeth and all her subjects, is widely reputed to have acted as a stimulus for the establishment of formal diplomatic and commercial relations between England and the Ottoman empire. Informal maritime trade between them started immediately in the early 1570s, at first under French protection. Whether the French actually had the formal right to act as intermediaries for foreign traders under the terms of their 1569 capitulations is still matter for debate, but what is certain is that in practice they did so and profited by collecting fees from all foreign traders – with the exception of the Venetians and Ragusans, who had their own trading concessions in the empire.[26] However, in 1597 French consular representatives were still arguing that everyone who was trading

---

[24] R. Paci, *La 'Scala' di Spalato ed il commercio veneziano nei Balcani fra Cinque e Seicento*, Venice, 1971.

[25] On this see Fusaro, 'Gli uomini d'affari stranieri' and bibliography quoted therein.

[26] Susan Skilliter argued the French did not enjoy this privilege (*William Harborne and the Trade with Turkey*, 1–3). Domenico Sella argued instead that the treaty of 1569 allowed France to 'loan' its own flag to ships and merchants of other states (in his *Commercio e industrie a Venezia*, 6, with reference to J. Billioud, 'Histoire du commerce de Marseille: de 1515 à 1599', in *Histoire du commerce de Marseille*, G. Rambert ed., 6 vols., Paris, 1959, iii: 197).

with the empire, with the exception of Venetians and now the English, had to do so under the French banner.[27]

The so-called 'Walsingham Memorandum', conclusively dated by Susan Skilliter to 1578,[28] clearly spelled out English ambitions in the area and the best strategy to achieve these:

> The fyrst thinge that is to be done [...] is to make choice of some apte man to be sent with her Majestes letters unto the Turke to procure an ample safe conducte, who is alwayies to remaine there at the charge of the merchantes, as Agent [...], whose repaire thither is to be handled with grett secrecie, and his voyage to be perfourmed rather by lande than by sea, for that otherwise the Italians that are here will seeke under hande that he may be disgraced.[29]

Secrecy was indeed deemed to be crucial for ensuring the success of the operation, and the 'Italians' – which in practice meant 'Venetians' – were singled out as objecting to these manoeuvres; interestingly, less attention was paid to the French.[30] The central issue was that the latter were rightly considered to be newcomers to the area, whilst Italians not only had been successfully trading there for a long time, but were also still involved in the sale of spices and Levantine goods to Northern Europe, something the French never did or even attempted to do. And there is no doubt in the memorandum that the goal was not just the establishment of direct trading relations between England and the Ottoman empire, but also to take up Venice's role as intermediary between the empire and Europe:

> You shall furnishe not onlie this Realme but also the most parte of Ewrope with such Commodyties as are transported owt of the said Turkes dominions, to the great enriching of this realme.[31]

The fact that this manoeuvre was conceived as an opportunity to commercially cut off the Venetians is also evident by another point made in the text, this time discussing possible expansion of English Mediterranean commercial shipping in more general terms:

> Whether the said shippes shall all goe to Constantinople or whether som of theme shall not goe to Alexandria and to Tripoly where it is likely they shall have

---

[27] See the letter of John Sanderson to Richard Staper, in J. Sanderson, *The Travels of John Sanderson in the Levant 1584–1602*, Sir W. Foster ed., London, 1931, 165–166, 166.

[28] Skilliter, *William Harborne and the Trade with Turkey*, 27–32.

[29] F. Walsingham, 'A Consideration of the Trade into Turkey [1578]', in Skilliter, *William Harborne and the Trade with Turkey*, 28–33, 29; see also Epstein, *The Early History*, 245–251.

[30] On Walsingham's wide network of spies: J. Cooper, *The Queen's Agent: Francis Walsingham at the Court of Elizabeth I*, London, 2011.

[31] Walsingham, 'A Consideration of the Trade into Turkey', 28.

good vent, for that both those two portes do serve well for Aleppo beinge the staple Towne for those Carsies that are dispersed into Persia, as also at Alexandria they shalbe best furnished of spices and other Commodities fitte for these places.[32]

The need to have large and powerful ships capable of establishing, maintaining and defending this new trade route was also highlighted, especially in terms of the beneficial effect this would have on English shipbuilding and shipping in general. To keep this operation secret, it was also suggested that a good strategy for avoiding Italian galleys would be to sail during the winter on both legs of the journey. Venetian patrols in the Eastern Mediterranean normally did not sail during the winter months to avoid bad weather, and this was well known to the English. Walsingham's advice became a general pattern for the Levant trade in its early decades, as in this way it was also possible to avoid the Spanish galleons which patrolled the Straits in good weather.[33]

When diplomatic correspondence started in earnest in 1580, the tone of the exchanges between Queen Elizabeth and Sultan Murad provides us with clear evidence that she had been thoroughly briefed and knew well how to exact the maximum amount of good will and concessions from him. She knew how to play her hand well, fully aware that her position outside of Catholicism and her growing confrontation with the Ottoman arch-enemy, Spain, made England an obvious choice of European partner – if not a proper ally – for the Ottomans. A 'heretic' queen could indeed be the perfect interlocutor for the 'infidel' Sultan: politically this connection would have strengthened her hand in Europe, and economically the potential profits of the intrinsic commercial exchange would not only be mutually beneficial but also would help satisfy the small but powerful commercial group which had been lobbying for such links to be established. Tin and lead, together with woollen cloth, were the traditional English export goods in the Mediterranean, and the Ottomans were now in dire need of these strategic goods as the war with Persia required large amounts of munitions.[34] Venice previously had been the major supplier of metals into the area, much of it from England; already from the reign of Richard II the Venetian galleys had been the largest single

---

[32] Walsingham, 'A Consideration of the Trade into Turkey', 30.

[33] Sella, *Commerci e industrie a Venezia*, 10.

[34] A lively summary of these issues in L. Jardine, 'Gloriana Rules the Waves: Or, the Advantage of Being Excommunicated (and a Woman)', *Transactions of the Royal Historical Society*, 14 (2004): 209–222.

carriers of tin to the Mediterranean.[35] This trade was famed for its high profits; Eliyahu Ashtor calculated that in the 1420s Venetian merchants achieved net profits of 100 per cent on lead and up to 300 per cent on iron, profits similar to those of the most valuable of spices such as camphor and rhubarb.[36]

In this first phase of English commercial expansion, characterised by great permeability between different areas of commerce, merchants involved in the Turkey Company were connected with the Muscovy Company, which was then trying to expand its trade southwards towards the Mediterranean, and a number of them also had been leading operators in the Iberian peninsula, whose trade was now closed to Englishmen due to the Anglo-Spanish conflict. Deprived of the Oriental goods they had accessed through Venice and Lisbon, it made perfect sense to try and get them directly from the Ottoman empire.[37]

Success followed relatively swiftly, and exactly along the lines argued by Walsingham. Nicolò Contarini, writing his *Historiae* in the early 1620s, discussing the entrance of the first English ambassador into Constantinople, sadly commented:

> thus, whilst beforehand Venetian ships went to England and brought back to Venice the goods we then redistributed in the East, [...] the Queen having burdened foreigners with unbearably heavy duties, Venetians were all but excluded from that country, and now Englishmen were the most expert and knowledgeable on the seas. On this side of the Ocean, in every place they denied Venetians traffic in Western merchandise and, what's even more odious, they themselves were now sailing in these seas.[38]

Intra-European competition and success

The reasons for England's success in quickly dominating the Ottoman Levant trade are as complex as the accompanying reasons for the failure of the Venetians and, to a lesser extent, the French. The Ottoman Levant trade was a long-distance trade, rarely carried out by a single individual or firm, as too many specialised functions were involved. From the producer to the consumer, goods passed through many hands, including freight agents, transporters and wholesalers.[39] The traditional argument has

---

[35] Ruddock, *Italian Merchants and Shipping*, 90–91.
[36] Ashtor, 'Profits from Trade with the Levant', 271–272.
[37] Brenner, *Merchants and Revolution*, 17; see also Games, *Web of Empire*.
[38] N. Contarini, *Historiae*, ii, book vi, cc.368–373, quoted in G. Cozzi, *Il Doge Nicolò Contarini*, Venice, 1958, 363.
[39] P. D. Curtin, *Cross-Cultural Trade in World History*, Cambridge, 1984, 53.

been that its many parts would function better under the superstructure provided by a trading company. Ralph Davis was convinced that

large-scale trade with the Levant was only made possible, in the beginning, by the foundation of the Levant Company. Turkish governments were not unwilling to allow foreigners to trade within the Sultan's dominions; but the Ottoman culture, institutions and methods of government were completely alien to those of Western Europe. English, French, Italians, and Dutch were reluctant to put themselves or their goods under the physical control of officials of the Ottoman Empire unless they were assured that they would have some special protection, and would in important respects be governed on essentially western rather than Turkish terms. The Levant Company was founded to provide a permanent machinery for securing the observance of such terms, which had just been negotiated with the Ottoman court by a group of merchants.[40]

The capitulations were not 'a treaty between the Sultan on the one hand, and on the other the Levant Company acting as commercial and diplomatic agent for the English Crown', as Davis has argued, but rather, in line with Ottoman legal structure, more akin to a gracious concession of the Sultan to the English sovereign and her subjects.[41] Along those lines they specified customs duties on imported and exported goods and guaranteed that no other taxes would be imposed on the English. Crucially, they established that judgement of disputes amongst English merchants would be handled by their own consuls rather than by Turkish officials, and controversies between Englishmen and Ottoman subjects would be handled in the capital city and not in provincial courts.

However, other Europeans were trading or would soon be trading with the Ottoman Turks, and none did so under the organisation of a trading company. The French had been the first to challenge the Venetian monopoly, signing a treaty with Sultan Suleiman in 1536 which had both an anti-Habsburg political motivation and the commercial goal of freeing France of intermediaries (read Venice) in Levantine trade.[42] The French, though, were mostly interested in providing for their domestic market, so their trade had not been as damaging to the Republic as had been feared in Venice. The Dutch also began trading in the area at around the same time as the English, and their enterprise met, at the beginning, with moderate success. Like the English, they had no particular experience of the Levant; however, it was possible for them to combine the

---

[40] Davis, *Aleppo and Devonshire Square*, 44–45.

[41] On the legal nature and development of the capitulations see M. H. van den Boogert, *The Capitulations and the Ottoman Legal System: Qadis, Consuls and Beraths in the 18th Century*, Leiden and Boston, 2005.

[42] Sella, *Commerci e industrie a Venezia*, 5. Susan Skilliter (*William Harborne and the Trade with Turkey*, 2–3) declared instead that trade started in 1569.

Venetian pattern with their own previous experiences, developed under different conditions.[43] In Amsterdam long discussions ensued on the subject of whether there was the need for a trading company organised along the lines of the English model, but since the Dutch could never agree on this need, the main purpose of the 'Directors of Commerce in the Levant' was not to operate as a trading company but merely to organise convoys to protect ships sailing in the dangerous Mediterranean.[44] Even without this structure, their trade prospered throughout the seventeenth century, weakening Davis's argument about the necessity of a structured company.

Considering that England was a newcomer in a commercially crowded area like the Mediterranean, and that trade through companies was the default mechanism of this phase of English commercial expansion, the choice of establishing the Levant Company seems a rational one. And it becomes even more so once the total cost of the envisaged enterprise is taken into account. The Walsingham memorandum was quite ambitious, pointing towards a completely new role for English merchants as inter-mediaries between the Levant and Europe. The point made about this trade requiring substantial investment in new shipping – with the plan of building and engaging twenty large and well-armed ships – implied enterprise on such a large scale as to create concern about how to raise the appropriate capital. The memorandum itself ended on an open note in this regard:

Divers other Cautions may be added here unto upon conference with skillfull merchants & other acqwainted with the midland seas.[45]

Under such circumstances the kind of political support and control which could have been exercised through a chartered company was probably the best choice for the English, especially considering their long-term ambitions about becoming a commercial power in the area, an ambition never shared by the Dutch. This trade was clearly potentially lucrative, but also costly to set up and likely to encounter a substantial amount of political and military opposition from its established protagonists. Although primarily 'economic', a direct trade link with the Ottoman empire was for the English more than a commercial choice; it was conceived from the start as part of a general strategy to give England a larger role in European politics and economy. The tight connection between economic and

---

[43] N. Steensgaard, 'Consuls and Nations in the Levant from 1570 to 1650', *Scandinavian Economic History Review*, 15 (1967): 13–55, 14.

[44] M. C. Engels, *Merchants, Interlopers, Seamen and Corsairs: The 'Flemish' Community in Livorno and Genoa (1615–1635)*, Leiden, 1997, 59–60.

[45] Walsingham, 'A Consideration of the Trade into Turkey', 30.

political interests was exemplified by the peculiar status of the English ambassador at the Porte. Returning from his embassy in England in 1611, Marcantonio Correr was careful in describing the relations between England and the Ottomans: 'with the Turk [they have] more than a friendship, they have a commercial relationship, the ambassador in Constantinople being paid by the Company of the Levant merchants even though he enjoys official patents from the king'.[46]

Venice ended up being the major victim of the English presence. The textile trade in the Ottoman empire is a good example of the multifaceted challenges posed by the arrival of the English. For Venice the problem had been not so much what to take from the Ottoman empire but rather what to ship to it. Since the fourteenth century, Venetian woollen manufacturing had diversified its production, and part of the cloth destined for sale in the Levant was of mediocre to low quality, specifically designed to appeal to a mass public.[47] From 1445 the *Senato* had even incentivised the import into Venice of English cloth of medium to low quality specifically destined for re-export in Ottoman territories.[48] This proved to be a lucrative business; Ashtor described how 'Victor Andrea in 1482 exported to Syria 22 pieces of cloth of Southampton. They had been bought for 1,100 ducats and were sold for 1,540.63. So he had gross proceeds of 40 per cent'. Frequently these cheap woollens were dyed in Italy before being re-exported to the Levant, and the volume of this trade expanded in the second quarter of the fifteenth century.[49] This strategy of importing low- to mid-quality English textiles, finishing them in Venice and the Veneto and then re-exporting them to the Ottoman empire had negative consequences for the production of similar low-quality textiles in Venice and the Veneto. Needless to say, when the English arrived in the Ottoman empire bringing their own textiles, this strategy became uneconomical and had to be abandoned. A substantial amount of the woollen textiles shipped by Venetians to the Ottoman empire were of the more expensive variety produced either in Venice itself or on the Italian mainland, and this line of trade was also severely hit by the phenomenal success of English textiles.

By the 1590s around twenty English ships 'were going every year to Turkey, Venice and the Greek islands', proving right – once again – the

---

[46] Marcantonio Correr, 'Relazione d'Inghilterra (1611)', in L. Firpo ed., *Relazioni di ambasciatori veneti al Senato*, vol. i: *Inghilterra*, Turin, 1965, 565–617, 607.

[47] Mozzato, 'Scelte produttive e di mercato di drappieri', 304.

[48] Mozzato, 'Scelte produttive e di mercato di drappieri', 305.

[49] Ashtor, 'Profits from Trade with the Levant', 269; and his *Levant Trade*, 155–156, 205–206, 326–327.

estimate given by Walsingham.[50] At the very beginning of their trade with the Ottoman empire, English merchants had been unsure which kind of goods to export beyond lead and tin, which they had in abundance and the Ottomans badly needed. The sale of strategic goods with military ends was always forbidden by the pope, and Catholic countries for the most part complied with this. The position of England after the 1570 excommunication made these exports an obvious choice. The question was: what else? At the beginning it proved challenging to select which kind of woollen cloth – the bread and butter of English exports – would find the best market there. In short, this kind of uncertainty supports Robert Brenner's argument that entrance in the Levant trade was motivated primarily by a desire to go to the direct source of imports, the search for suitable exports being for English merchants a constant work in progress.[51] The importance of the new Levant trade for the English derived also from the fact that, in marked contrast to the other established London trades, it ended up – in this, rather similarly to their fledging colonial operations – stimulating investment in commodity production at home, not merely in commodity exchange.[52]

The reputation of the Italian medieval textile industry was based on the quality of its high-end textiles, although these were by no means the only kind which the Venetians sold in Ottoman lands. The English, in the first phases of penetration into the Ottoman market, produced counterfeits of Venetian textile products, and these proved very successful, much to the Venetians' horror. This was a sophisticated strategy to penetrate a market, but by no means a novel one; in fact, at the end of the fourteenth and the beginning of the fifteenth centuries, the Venetians themselves had used a similar technique to increase the volume of their exports to Ottoman lands. Counterfeiting as such was forbidden everywhere in Italy, but 'imitation'– as long as 'precise marks' of provenance were employed – was not, and the Venetian woollen industry had developed a series of products heavily 'inspired' by Tuscan and northern Italian textiles, and successfully marketed them in the Eastern Mediterranean.[53] The difference was that the English did not imitate but instead produced

---

[50] Davis, *The Rise of the English Shipping Industry*, 4.

[51] Brenner, *Merchants and Revolution*, 25–33.

[52] R. Brenner, 'The Social Basis of English Commercial Expansion, 1550–1650', *Journal of Economic History*, 32 (1972): 361–384, 377.

[53] Mozzato, 'Scelte produttive e di mercato di drappieri', 306–308. On the general practice of imitation in the medieval Italian textile industry see H. Hoshino, *L'arte della lana in Firenze nel basso medioevo: il commercio della lana ed il mercato dei panni fiorentini nei secoli XIII–XIV*, Florence, 1980.

real counterfeits, down to replicating Venetian marks and 'making borders after the Venetian manner'. In short, they were producing what came to be called 'anti-Venetian cloth'.[54]

With the approach of the seventeenth century, other textiles were developed in England specifically for the Ottoman market: 'the first broadcloths sent to the Levant, around 1600, had been expensive Suffolk qualities. By the 1620s however, cheaper broadcloths from Gloucestershire and Wiltshire were beginning to figure amongst the exports, and they grew rapidly in popularity until by 1670 they had completely supplanted the Suffolk variety'.[55] Barry Supple, in his classic analysis of English early modern economic development, describes these strategies as a fundamental shift for the English textile industry, as 'this keener perception of the competitive environment was, from one point of view, a fundamental departure in economic thought'.[56] To these two strategies – counterfeiting Venetian products and introducing cheaper ones – we need to add price dumping as another of the means employed by the English to penetrate this new market. Benjamin Braude has argued that the price of English broadcloth in Constantinople by the 1620s was up to 30 per cent cheaper than in London.[57] This policy paid off splendidly and provided another blow to the Venetian woollen cloth industry by pricing it out of one of its largest and heretofore most profitable markets.[58] Richard Grassby has argued that 'earlier in the [seventeenth] century, the profit of the Spanish and Levant trades came principally from imports, which fuelled London's growth. From mid-century, however, re-exports changed this situation and the terms of trade with Turkey moved in favour of exports.'[59]

Regarding exports from the Ottoman lands, Venice had its own source of raw silk in Italy, and its silk industry concentrated on luxury fabrics,

---

[54] Rapp, 'The Unmaking of the Mediterranean', 511. Counterfeiting was not limited to textiles: at the same time English-produced fake Venetian luxury soap was also flooding the Mediterranean, Rapp, 'The Unmaking of the Mediterranean', 508–510.

[55] Davis, *Aleppo and Devonshire Square*, 97–98.

[56] B. Supple, *Commercial Crisis and Change in England, 1600–1642*, Cambridge, 1964, 148.

[57] B. Braude, 'International Competition and Domestic Cloth in the Ottoman Empire, 1500–1650: A Study in Underdevelopment', *Review*, 2 (1979): 437–451, 445.

[58] On the problems which confronted the Venetian production see D. Sella, 'The Rise and Fall of the Venetian Woollen Industry', in Pullan ed., *Crisis and Change*, 106–126. On the aftermath of these events see W. Panciera, *L'arte matrice: i lanifici della Repubblica di Venezia nei secoli XVII e XVIII*, Treviso, 1996. A long-term analysis of Italian woollen production and trade in the Mediterranean is in J. H. Munro, 'I panni di lana', in *Il Rinascimento Italiano e l'Europa*, vol. iv: *L'Italia e l'economia europea nel Rinascimento*, F. Franceschi, R. A. Goldthwaite and R. C. Mueller eds., Treviso, 2007, 105–141.

[59] R. B. Grassby, *The English Gentleman in Trade: The Life and Works of Sir Dudley North*, Oxford, 1994, 99 footnote, where he also contested Braude's trade figures; see footnote 57.

which could not really utilise the cheaper, but generally poor quality, Middle Eastern silk. Therefore Venice did not need to compete as much for Iranian raw silk as did England. Raw silk became the most important single commodity imported from outside Europe into England, and this was to remain the case for the whole of the seventeenth century.[60] The result of this 'perfect storm' was that, by the beginning of the seventeenth century, the total volume of Venetian trade with the Ottoman empire shrank, as there were far fewer commodities with which to barter, and the Venetians refused to pay with specie, unlike the English, who used this means to penetrate a new market and only later reverted to bartering. By the 1620s in Ottoman lands, the Venetian share of traffic was down to 25 per cent, on par with the French and substantially below the English, who by then controlled 40 per cent. By the following decade, in Ralph Davis' words, 'the Levant trade, then, fulfilled all the dreams of the mercantilist; balanced, offering raw material in exchange for English manufactures, employing large ships on a distant voyage, handled throughout by English merchants'.[61]

Aleppo, due to its central position – almost equidistant from Constantinople, Cairo, Baghdad and Tabriz – was the key to trade with Persia and beyond, and thus is a perfect observatory to gauge the Venetian position within the Ottoman commercial world. Until the war of Cyprus the Venetians in Aleppo controlled the largest share of its market, but one century afterwards trade there had dwindled to such an extent that the Venetian government abolished the position of Venetian consul in the city.[62]

From the strictly economic perspective, powerful market forces were pushing Venetian merchandise aside. Higher production costs of its textiles, as has been extensively argued by the relevant literature, could not but price Venice out of the mass Ottoman market, especially when its English competitors were entering the game with aggressive strategies based on blatant counterfeits and price dumping.

The dual organisation of English Levant trade

To appreciate the behaviour of the English merchants, it is important to appreciate how the Levant Company was structured and the repercussions this had on the organisation of trade in its areas of monopoly. As

---

[60] B. Masters, *The Origin of Western Economic Dominance in the Middle East: Mercantilism and the Islamic Economy in Aleppo, 1600–1750*, New York, 1988, 25.

[61] Davis, 'England and the Mediterranean', 125.

[62] Tucci, *Mercanti, navi e monete*, 111, 98; Masters, *The Origin of Western Economic*, 14.

discussed in the previous chapter, the Levant Company was created in 1592 from the fusion of the Turkey Company (1580–1581) with the Venice Company (1583). Before their merger, the two companies had been embroiled in a debate with the English government centred principally on the overlapping of their reciprocal areas of monopolies. Other points of contention were the challenges the Venice Company faced because of the high duties on currants, whilst the Turkey Company was burdened with the expenses of the Constantinople embassy. Merging the two companies was considered a way to solve some of these issues and facilitate trade.[63] Still, even after the creation of the Levant Company, division between the two areas – Ottoman and Venetian – survived, and taking this into account is fundamental to the correct understanding of the modalities and characteristics of the English presence in the Mediterranean. We can certainly assume that this division originated in the way the traffic was originally set up; however, there are other considerations. First we need to take into account the organisation of the Levant Company, 'which was not in itself a trading organisation: its members traded individually, as independent merchants, subjecting themselves to such restrictions as they might impose in their corporate capacity as the Levant Company'.[64] The everyday running of business was left to the men on the ground, who could organise the trade in practically any way they saw fit. Instructions sent from London were in fact rather generic and mostly concerned quantities of imports, allowing great scope for differentiating the internal organisation of the different areas of trade, and leaving merchant members and their agents extraordinary freedom. This meant that, under the formal institutional structure provided by the company, there was ample opportunity for informal arrangements amongst merchants themselves and between merchants and other local economic operators. The ways in which the Levant Company's agents organised the everyday running of their trade could therefore be studied also from the perspective of the relations between social groups and institutions relating to the organisation of economic life. The wealth of surviving documentary evidence on the everyday running of trade in Venice and in the Ionian islands will allow us, in later chapters, to further

---

[63] On the debate about the fusion of the two companies see Epstein, *The Early History*, 25–39; Wood, *A History*, 18–20; Brenner, *Merchants and Revolution*, 64–65.

[64] Davis, *Aleppo and Devonshire Square*, 43. Although the Company started as a joint stock, it quickly became a regulated company and it remained such for all its life (with some exceptions for short periods). In Wood's interpretation, to which I subscribe, '[this] seem to prove that it suited better the circumstances of the trade', in Wood, *A History*, 22–23; Brenner, *Merchants and Revolution*, 66–67.

investigate the informal networks of merchants active within a formal institution.

There also were structural differences in the organisation of trade in the two areas, especially in the relationship between political and economic activities. These opposing attitudes towards the political sphere were a crucial factor in shaping the differences between the two sides of the Levant Company trade. In Venice there was an almost total separation between the commercial and diplomatic sides of the English presence. In Constantinople the two aspects were intertwined: the ambassador was a royal representative – commissioned by the sovereign and employed in diplomatic duties – whilst, at the same time, he was a commercial agent paid by a company of merchants, pledged to safeguard and promote their business interests.

A consequence of this was that, for a young and ambitious English merchant, being involved in the Turkish trade was also a way to be introduced into political circles. This connection between trade and diplomacy created a background context to trading which was highly desirable for merchants of higher social status – mostly offspring of the gentry – whose social and political aspirations could be pursued at the same time as their business careers.[65] A successful mercantile career in the Ottoman territories seemed often to have resulted in a successful homecoming. On the contrary, on the Venetian side, where there was an almost total lack of contact between diplomacy and trade, doing business afforded far fewer opportunities which would be useful back in England, and the field was therefore left open for people of lower social status and more modest ambitions. Another interesting consequence was that in Venice there were effectively two English communities – one revolving around the embassy, and another made up exclusively of merchants – and contact between the two was rather infrequent.

The practical organisation of the trade was also different: in the Ottoman territories, the legal position of the English merchants was strictly defined by the privileges and immunities granted to the English with the Capitulations. The nature of Ottoman state organisation was such that involvement of the ambassador and of the company's consuls was necessary to conduct any sort of business, another argument in favour of the establishment of the Levant Company to run the trade. In Venice, on the contrary, there was no such need. Being subject to less control in

---

[65] On the Levant Company's popularity amongst gentry's offspring see Grassby, *The Business Community*, 68; see also R. G. Lang, 'Social Origins and Social Aspirations of Jacobean London Merchants', *Economic History Review*, 27 (1974): 28–47.

the Venetian territories than in Ottoman lands, English merchants there enjoyed a far broader degree of freedom in their everyday life. This resulted in closer contact with the local population – both Venetian and subject – which led to more frequent informal links, commercial dealings and business partnerships. Second, but no less importantly, the nature of the trade was intrinsically different. Once the English were established in the Ottoman empire, from the 1620s their trade there can be described as an exchange heavily relying on textiles, roughly definable as the barter of wool for silk and spices, whilst on the Venetian side, bilateral commerce was based on the purchase of a few commodities in exchange mostly for ready cash.

The above-mentioned differences between the two areas of trade can be exemplified by a quick analysis of the two principal goods that the English exported out of the Mediterranean: silk and currants. The trade in silk with the Ottoman territories, like many others, was based on the English need to procure a peculiar commodity with two defining characteristics: it should have a constant and reliable quality and should correspond to the needs of fashion in England. This created the preoccupation of having to successfully manage a large supply market with instructions partially sent from home and partially improvised on the spot. This kind of trade required a highly sophisticated degree of knowledge of both the intrinsic qualities of the purchased goods and of the English market.[66] The purchase of silk epitomised these problems. Once again in Davis' words: 'a great demand was made on his [the factor's] skill as a buyer and a thorough understanding of the commodity; for silk from any particular source could vary, to an extent that materially affected the price, from "very good", which was extraordinary, through "mercantile" or good quality to "ordinary", which was poor stuff, and "inferior", a rubbish rarely bought by Europeans. It had to be judged and bought in a dirty state, and given the best appearance possible after cleaning.'[67] This need for quality checks on the spot, whilst keeping a constant eye on what was coveted in London, made the job of the factors in the Ottoman territories more difficult than in other areas of trade, where commodities were less influenced by fashion. One had to acquire skills which went far beyond the ability to judge the intrinsic quality of a commodity, such as knowledge of

---

[66] Davis, *Aleppo and Devonshire Square*, 144. On the Venetian experience of the importance of knowledge of current fashions for textile produced for exports, some interesting considerations in Mozzato, 'Scelte produttive e di mercato di drappieri', 317–318; see also U. Rublack, *Dressing Up: Cultural Identity in Renaissance Europe*, Oxford, 2010, especially chapter 6.

[67] Davis, *Aleppo and Devonshire Square*, 144.

the latest fashions on both sides of the transaction, the kind of knowledge which is also a function of one's social status and lifestyle. The trade with Venetian Greek dependencies, instead, based as it was on currants as the staple commodity, in practice required knowledge only of the intrinsic quality of the product, and except for the quantities required, there was no need for a constant stream of updates from London. Once organised, this trade ran like a well-oiled machine, needing only fuel – that is to say, cash – to work. A trade uninfluenced by fashion is one that can better withstand frequent interruptions to the information flow, a classic weakness of medieval and early modern trade, and also can be performed very effectively by people who are less conversant with the vagaries of London fashion.[68]

The economic and political entanglements of Venice

Even though recent interpretations of the economic crisis of Venice in the early modern period have shown a strong revisionist tendency, arguing in favour of a relative – and not absolute – decline, it is difficult to support this when faced with the swiftness of the diminution of the Venetian share of the Ottoman market. In just fifty years, between 1570 and 1620, this share collapsed from more than 40 per cent to 25 per cent, mirroring exactly the rise of the English in the same area. This reversal of fortune did not result only from purely economic factors, as has been argued by the classic literature. Rather, it was an outcome of the political and social underpinnings of the political economy of the two countries, which can be elucidated by analysing the Anglo-Venetian interaction at this particular junction.

The swiftness of the 'invasion of the northerners' was first highlighted by Fernand Braudel, and more recently subjected to two important revisionist interpretations.[69] Molly Greene has argued in favour of a reappraisal of its overall importance for Mediterranean maritime trade structures which, as she properly stresses, remained unchanged in their general patterns – with cabotage and seasonal coastal shipping remaining the unchallenged great protagonists of commercial exchanges.[70] Colin

---

[68] On the currant trade needing less-qualified personnel, see also Brenner, *Merchants and Revolution*, 87. There are interesting considerations on the information flow in G. Doria, 'Conoscenza del mercato e sistema informativo: il know-how dei mercanti-finanzieri genovesi nei secoli XVI e XVII', in De Maddalena and Kellenbenz eds., *La repubblica internazionale*, 57–122.

[69] Braudel, *The Mediterranean*, i: 621–631, and the bibliography at page vi.

[70] M. Greene, 'Beyond the Northern Invasion: The Mediterranean in the Seventeenth Century', *Past and Present*, 174 (2003): 42–71.

Heywood, meanwhile, has taken issue with the 'northern invasion' as one of the 'grander narratives of the past' and successfully provided a reassessment of its daily realities – far grittier and less triumphalist than described by Braudel, who, as he rightly argues, based his narrative on 'Hakluyt's own unashamedly triumphalist and patriotic stance'.[71] I agree with the major points made by both scholars; however, I also believe it is necessary to underline that their arguments consider the Mediterranean as a trading region in its entirety, and that two important caveats needs to be added. First, if the arrival of the northerners did not substantially change the underlying structure of Mediterranean cabotage, it is true that the English and Dutch from the beginning of the seventeenth century started to penetrate short-distance inter-Mediterranean trade, replacing its traditional operators, and, in this way, contributed to its change over the long term. Second, although the 'northern invasion' was indeed, in its day-to-day activities, no swashbuckling adventure, involving instead slow and humdrum activities, it also proved to be a powerful agent of social and economic change. It embodied the reality of an economic system infiltrating and then dominating new markets and, in a second stage, helping to transform this economic supremacy into a political one. This is true especially for the English, as the penetration of their commercial shipping in the Mediterranean was swiftly followed by that of their navy.[72]

Once one moves the scale of analysis from that of Mediterranean trade in its entirety to a tighter Venetian perspective, the consequences of the 'northern invasion' become more pervasive and its effects far more immediately pernicious. With an extremely evocative image, Braudel described the Dutch as swarming 'into the Mediterranean like so many heavy insects crashing against the window panes – for their entry was neither gentle nor discreet'.[73] But the 'swarm' image works a lot better with the English, as their entrance was swiftly followed by their establishment in the crucial commercial nodes of the Mediterranean, in this way dramatically accelerating the demise of the traditional strong commercial leader of the past – Venice. English trading on sea routes that for centuries had been hers accelerated an existing maritime crisis and ended up

---

[71] C. J. Heywood, 'The English in the Mediterranean, 1600–1630: A Post-Braudelian perspective on the "Northern Invasion"', in M. Fusaro, C. J. Heywood and M.-S. Omri eds., *Trade and Cultural Exchange in the Early Modern Mediterranean: Braudel's Maritime Legacy*, London, 2010, 23–44, 27.

[72] On these issues, and related ones such as on the peculiarly Mediterranean problem in separating cabotage from long-distance shipping, see M. Fusaro, 'After Braudel: A Reassessment of Mediterranean History Between the Northern Invasion and the Caravane Maritime', in Fusaro, Heywood and Omri eds., *Trade and Cultural Exchange*, 1–22, 11–14.

[73] Braudel, *The Mediterranean*, i: 634.

downgrading Venice's commerce – and therefore her economy – to the level of a regional player. Seen from Venice's vantage point, the northerners were indeed invaders, and it was due not only to the economic conjuncture, but also to political considerations, that Venetians proved unable to defend themselves.

The analysis of Venetian trade with the Ottoman territories provides us with a very clear example of the interconnectedness of economic and political issues in the pursuance of commercial profit in the Mediterranean.

The Venetian government had developed a fairly complex and bureaucratic structure of supports for its own merchants. Daniel Goffman has defined this structure as 'centralized and mired in bureaucratic and diplomatic tradition', and he partially blames its intrinsic rigidity for the increasing difficulties encountered by Venetian merchants within the empire in the early modern period. In his analysis, such a system 'provided neither incentive, time, nor money for a Venetian consul to explore innovations in the trade'.[74] I agree with him that the more flexible internal organisation of the Levant Company on the ground afforded the English a valuable advantage in coping with the vagaries and uncertainties of local politics – in Anatolia, as he argues, as much as in the Venetian Ionian islands.[75] However, I fear he overplayed his argument when considering the comparative fortunes of the Venetians and the English within the Ottoman empire at large. A fundamental and substantive difference between the two was the whilst the former were local colonial powers, and as such had to take into account strategic and political considerations above and beyond the pursuit of profit, the English at this stage could concentrate exclusively on the economic element of their relationship with the Ottomans. A constructive political engagement was an essential part of commercial success, as we have seen, but the bilateral relationship was primarily an economic one, evidenced by the fact that the English ambassador at the Porte was paid by the Levant Company itself.

For the Venetians, the harsh reality was that political and economic issues were far more complex and inextricably entangled in the region, and the existence of a long, direct 'frontier' between the two states put them – politically and militarily – on a direct collision course, a fight the Venetians were destined to lose if nothing else for reasons of scale. When Venetian consular authorities in Izmir were trying to sort out local

---

[74] D. Goffman, *Izmir and the Levantine World 1550–1650*, Seattle and London, 1990, 94; see also E. R. Dursteler, *Venetians in Constantinople: Nation, Identity and Coexistence in the Early Modern Mediterranean*, Baltimore, 2006.

[75] Fusaro, 'Les Anglais et les Grecs'.

problems by appealing to the central authorities in Constantinople, they were doing this not 'wrongly assuming that Ottoman provincial authorities conformed promptly to Istanbul's will',[76] as Goffman has argued, but because at its heart, the relationship between the two states was primarily political, and problems at Izmir were not for the Venetians a local disturbance which could be dealt with by judicious negotiations with local authorities, maybe helped by a few bribes here and there. 'Problems' at Izmir (as in every other Ottoman commercial centre) could be – and frequently were seen as – symptomatic of larger problems between Venice and the Porte and, as such, they needed to be dealt with through appeal to the central authorities. What was needed was not a quick local fix, but renegotiation – or simply respect for the reciprocal agreement already in place between the two states.[77] The Venetian–Ottoman centuries-long economic relationship was built on careful and delicate continuous political negotiation, where the existence of Venetian dominions contiguous to Ottoman lands, and therefore in danger of direct military attack, was always at the forefront of both players' minds. Both governments – in Venice and in Constantinople – were fully aware of this dimension, and for this reason the Ottoman central authorities tended to respond favourably to Venetian complaints. If the positive response from the central authority was not implemented at the regional level, this points to the growing weakness of the Porte in controlling some of its regional administrations (something which it shared with Venice), especially in areas where trade was expanding and local officers could make an awful lot of money by getting involved with the new players.

The centuries-long fight between Venice and the Ottoman empire – beyond the propaganda statements and the spin supporting it on both sides – was never a religious conflict but rather a straightforward direct confrontation for territorial control and naval superiority. However, it can also be defined as a conflict between two 'imperialisms'. Indirect evidence of this is provided by the excellent relationship that the Republic maintained with Mamluk Egypt and Persia – both Muslim states. Even the economic relationship between Venice and the Ottoman empire worked – above and beyond the direct military confrontations – as the Ottomans

---

[76] Goffman, *Izmir and the Levantine World*, 118.

[77] A telling example of the potential reach of commercial incidents in the running of political and diplomatic relationships between Venice and the Ottoman empire was the case of the ship *Girarda*; see B. Arbel, 'Maritime Trade and International Relations in the Sixteenth Century Mediterranean: The Case of the Ship *Girarda* (1575–1581)', in V. Costantini and M. Koller eds., *Living in the Ottoman Ecumenical Community: Essays in Honour of Suraiya Faroqhi*, Leiden, 2008, 391–408, especially 400–408.

were never interested in achieving the kind of international commercial supremacy craved by the Venetians. Recent scholarship has shed new light on the trade activities of Ottoman subjects and shown that many groups played an important role within the Ottoman economic sphere; the days when it was assumed that trade within the empire was run by foreigners with the support of Jews, Greeks and Armenians are long gone.[78] Within the economic sphere, though, the major concern of Ottoman authorities was not the achievement of commercial hegemony but, rather, guaranteeing the flow of commodities within the empire's lands, what Mehmet Genç synthetically defined as 'provisionism, fiscalism and traditionalism'.[79]

With the exception of the Spaniards, who were never really involved in the Eastern Mediterranean, all the other early modern European players in the area were interested exclusively in commercial penetration and trade superiority. Therefore their policies were as 'commercial' as possible, *not* political and *not* even religious – even given all the so-called crusading expeditions and the propaganda which occasionally flared up. We shall have ample occasion to see how overwhelming the issue of defence of the Levant became for Venice in the period between the loss of Cyprus and that of Candia. Alberto Tenenti antedated this by a full century, and underlined the 'clear subordination of economic interests to those of defence' already in the period between the loss of Negroponte (1470) and that of Modon (1500), which he saw as the toughest for the Republic, who found herself alone at sea against the Ottoman advance.[80] It is certainly true that Venice was alone at that juncture; the Spanish empire with its allies would enter the frame only at a later stage, and the Knights of St John were at that time more concerned with the defence of their own base in Rhodes.

Comparing Venice with other Western European countries active in the Eastern Mediterranean, without taking into account the substantive structural differences of Venice's colonial presence, becomes therefore a rather sterile exercise. Venice had settled in the Levant, with barely hidden imperial ambitions, since 1204, and throughout the following centuries

---

[78] S. Faroqhi, 'Crisis and Change', *1590–1699*, in H. İnalcik, S. Faroqhi, B. MacGowan, D. Quataert and S. Pamuk, *An Economic and Social History of the Ottoman Empire*, 2 vols, Cambridge, 1997, ii: 413–636, 474–530; E. Eldem, 'Capitulations and Western Trade', in S. Faroqhi ed., *The Cambridge History of Turkey*, 4 vols, Cambridge, 2013, iii: 283–335.

[79] As quoted by Murat Çizakça in his 'The Ottoman Government and Economic Life: Taxation, Public Finance and Trade Controls', in Faroqhi ed., *The Cambridge History of Turkey*, ii: 241–275, 258.

[80] Tenenti, 'Il senso dello spazio e del tempo', 90–91; also his 'Profilo di un conflitto secolare'.

had doggedly fought to strengthen, if not positively expand, its territorial holdings and naval power in the region. The Venetian empire in the thirteenth and fourteenth centuries developed as a varied collection of territories which can be defined as a patchwork but which was ultimately designed to be the expression of a clear political and military – to be more precise, naval – hegemonic design, an essential element to defend and protect the commercial and economic goals of the Venetian ruling class, who at that stage corresponded with its economic elite. Ugo Tucci called this collection of territories a 'commercial' empire more than a 'colonial' empire, a state which had its territorial base not on land but on the sea – a 'regnum aquosum'.[81] For Venice, therefore, the Levant was always a political problem, and its vocation for commerce was tightly and inextricably connected with its political action. From the thirteenth to the sixteenth centuries, the Republic had been run by merchants who developed an empire suited to the ambitions of its ruling class, which were as 'imperial' as they were 'commercial'. The Venetian patriciate might have been in the process of abandoning its leading role in trading during the sixteenth century, when increasingly its income started to come from its possessions in the *Terraferma*, but the underlying principle of thinking of Venice as a maritime Republic and empire continued beyond the time when it actually made financial sense for Venice to keep overseas possessions at all.

The government of the Republic remained firmly settled in these policies until its demise in 1797. Venice always looked east.

---

[81] U. Tucci, 'La Grecia e l'economia veneziana', in G. Benzoni ed., *L'eredità greca e l'ellenismo veneziano*, Florence, 2002, 139–156, 142.

4 Genoa, Venice and Livorno (a tale of three cities)

When Dutch and English ships started to regularly sail and trade within the Straits in the last quarter of the sixteenth century, a new era began in Mediterranean history; for the first time its waters witnessed the presence and influence of maritime powers not based on its shores. The onset of Venice's maritime crisis, which halted its direct sea trade bringing Oriental and Mediterranean products to England and Flanders, together with the crisis of the entrepôt of Antwerp, had prompted the northerners' arrival, a process facilitated by the absence of a hegemonic power capable of claiming Mediterranean waters. As I have argued elsewhere, although I agree that their arrival did not immediately result in their dominance of all maritime trade in the area, it is undeniable that it had important repercussions on long-distance maritime trade, which they quickly came to dominate.[1]

The analysis of the 'invasion of the northerners' and its effect on the Italian economic system is tightly linked to long-standing debates on the crisis which enveloped the peninsula in the sixteenth and seventeenth centuries. Traditional interpretations saw this crisis as all-encompassing: political, social, economic and cultural. Seen under the lens of *Risorgimento* ideology, starting at the beginning of the sixteenth century – when foreign powers fought for pre-eminence in the peninsula – Italian states quickly lost their political freedom and economic primacy, a decline which was then sealed by the Counter-Reformation, which put the final nail in the coffin of the Italian Renaissance.[2]

Since the 1980s this interpretation has been revised and nuanced in all its facets; from the economic perspective the chronological boundaries of

---

[1] Fusaro, 'After Braudel', 10–11; Greene, 'Beyond the Northern Invasion'.
[2] C. M. Cipolla, 'The Decline of Italy: The Case of a Fully Matured Economy', *Economic History Review*, 5 (1952): 178–187; for a sharp recent analysis of the Anglo-Italian nexus concerned with crisis (especially of manufactures) and its connection with political disunity in the eighteenth century see S. A. Reinert, 'Blaming the Medici: Footnotes, Falsification, and the Fate of the "English Model" in Eighteenth-Century Italy', *History of European Ideas*, 32 (2006): 430–455.

the crisis itself have been redrawn, and many studies have helped to reassess the impact of the general European crisis on the Italian economic system.[3] But however revisionist one might strive to be, it is undeniable that the centre of the European economy had indeed shifted away from Italy towards the North of Europe, though it is interesting to note how this revisionist approach has primarily focused on manufactures, neglecting commerce,[4] as the former could be argued to have undergone a restructuring, whilst Italian primacy in long-distance trade was indeed gone forever.

Temporarily leaving aside Venice, the pages that follow will briefly discuss two Italian cities – also used as shorthand for the states they belonged to – which are frequently discussed in the literature on the northern invasion: Genoa and Livorno. My goal is to highlight the structural reasons behind their relative importance in relation to the growing English role in the Mediterranean, and to argue that comparisons between them and Venice – frequently raised by the secondary literature – make little sense given the fundamental structural differences of their economic specialisation.

Genoa: from trade to finance

In an earlier chapter we saw how Genoese ships had been the first to regularly reach English shores in the thirteenth century. By the mid-fifteenth century the Genoese commercial networks distributed English woollens in Spain, North Africa and Asia Minor, orienting their purchases in England towards medium- to high-quality woollen cloths to meet the requirements of the Spanish markets.[5] The expansion of Florentine suppliers of wool, paired with the increased reluctance of the Florentine government to subsidise their state galleys, brought about their demise in 1480. The diminished Florentine demand for English wool also negatively affected Genoese shipping to England. The Genoese presence in England collapsed in the last decades of the fifteenth century, a disappearance usually attributed to political upheavals in Genoa and the subsequent restructuring of its trading patterns, but also probably due to

---

[3] For an analysis of the reasons why the various Italian states' economies can be seen as a single system in this period may I refer to my own 'Gli uomini d'affari stranieri', esp. 372–374, and bibliography quoted therein.

[4] Amongst these studies: D. Sella, *Crisis and Continuity: The Economy of Spanish Lombardy in the Seventeenth Century*, Cambridge (Mass.), 1979; Panciera, *L'arte matrice*; Molà, *The Silk Industry*; P. Malanima, *La fine del primato: crisi e riconversione nell'Italia del Seicento*, Milan, 1998; F. Trivellato, *Fondamenta dei vetrai: lavoro, tecnologia e mercato a Venezia tra Sei e Settecento*, Rome, 2000; Lanaro ed., *At the Centre of the Old World*.

[5] Fryde, 'Anglo-Italian Commerce', 352.

their loss of primacy in the alum business, whose trade we have seen
playing a fundamental role in their cargoes to England.[6] As a consequence of this the Genoese community in Southampton quickly shrank,
though its erstwhile most prominent member – Benedetto Spinola –
decided to remain there and apply for naturalisation.[7]

A century later, the alum trade was again the basis of the economic
success of probably the most successful Italian in Elizabethan England:
the Genoese Orazio Pallavicino, later naturalised and knighted by the
queen, becoming Sir Horatio Palavicino.[8] Horatio was indeed an exceptional individual, especially in the range of his financial success and how
he managed to acquire political and social clout in England. His life
trajectory, from birth in a family of prominent Genoese financiers, to
his early career in Antwerp, where he took part in the management of the
papal alum monopoly (since 1566 handled by the Pallavicino family) is a
textbook example of the behaviour of the top echelons of Genoese financiers of that time, those active in what has been called the 'international
republic of money'.[9] Far less bound to their city than Venetians usually
were, and by the sixteenth century in actual command of European high
finance, they displayed a high level of geographical mobility, and also a
tendency to easily integrate in the societies hosting them.

By the beginning of the sixteenth century the Genoese economy had by
and large completed its shift to finance, and was tying its political and
economic destiny to that of Spain and its empire. Still, this reconversion
to finance saw Genoese bankers also lending their services to England,
sometimes in connection with the needs of the Roman Curia.[10] In this
new phase of its history, Genoa actually increased its overall importance
and, through the effective control of European high finance and a dominant role in the redistribution of the silver pouring into Europe from
Spanish American possessions, played a crucial role in this era of proto-
globalisation – so much that the period between 1557 and 1627 has been
defined by Fernand Braudel as the 'century of the Genoese'.[11] The
English crown took advantage of Genoese financiers far less than its

---

[6] Fryde, 'Italian Maritime Trade', 331–332; see also Mallett, *The Florentine Galleys*.
[7] Abulafia, 'Cittadino e "denizen"', 280.
[8] Stone, *An Elizabethan*; see also the *DNB*, s.v.
[9] De Maddalena and Kellenbenz eds., *La repubblica internazionale*.
[10] For the involvement of Genoese bankers and financiers in the finances of England see
    G. Ramsay, 'Thomas More, Joint Keeper of the Exchange: A Forgotten Episode in the
    History of Exchange Control in England', *Historical Research*, 84 (2011): 586–600.
[11] Braudel, *The Perspective of the World*, 157–170; and his *The Mediterranean*, i: 500–504; see
    also F. Ruiz Martín, 'La banca genovesa en España durante el siglo XVII', in D. Puncuh
    and G. Felloni eds., *Banchi pubblici, banchi privati e monti di pietà nell'Europa*

European counterparts; Henry VIII between 1544 and 1574 borrowed from Antwerp bankers, but the vast majority of the crown's financial needs were taken care of by his willingness to debase the coinage and sell crown lands, the latter thanks to the holdings acquired through the dissolution of monasteries.[12]

This is not the place to discuss in detail the deep historiographical schizophrenia regarding Genoa, on the one hand hailed as the cradle of global financial capitalism, and on the other described as a 'failed state'.[13] However, it is very difficult not to at least mention the debate on the nature of the Genoese state, traditionally considered weak and constantly having to negotiate with the informal power groups which were the result of the financial and social links underpinning the Genoese elite.[14] The supposed weakness of Genoese institutions becomes even more evident when compared to the traditional view – albeit highly mythologised – of the strength of the Venetian state and government.[15] In short, roughly comparing the two maritime republics, the main difference boils down to the fact that the Genoese polity, with a fragmented and geographically dispersed economic elite which enjoyed tight networks for the exchange of information, lent itself better to act as financial linchpin to the Iberian crown empire than to the sustenance of a commercial empire of its own.[16] Seen in this light, the effective Genoese retreat from the top tier of European commercial players and its conversion to high finance made perfect sense – achieving the goal of being 'a free Republic in the Imperial system' in Arturo Pacini's words.[17]

preindustriale: amministrazione, tecniche operative e ruoli economici, 2 vols., Genoa, 1991, i: 265–274.

[12] Clay, *Economic Expansion*, ii: 251–281, 262–263, 269.

[13] On this see the very perceptive analysis of Arturo Pacini and the bibliography quoted therein: A. Pacini, 'Genoa and Charles V', in W. Blockmans and N. Mout eds., *The World of Emperor Charles V*, Amsterdam, 2004, 161–199; for an interpretation of how Genoese state institutions influenced its economic growth in the Middle Ages see A. Greif, *Institutions and the Path to the Modern Economy: Lessons from Medieval Trade*, Cambridge, 2006, 170–177.

[14] E. Grendi, *I Balbi: una famiglia genovese fra Spagna e Impero*, Turin, 1997; O. Raggio, *Faide e parentele: lo stato genovese visto dalla Fontanabuona*, Turin, 1990.

[15] Interesting to note how this opposition between Venice and Genoa was a *topos* even in Byzantine political thought since the Middle Ages: see V. Syros, 'Between Chimera and Charybdis: Byzantine and Post-Byzantine Views on the Political Organization of the Italian City-States', *Journal of Early Modern History*, 14 (2010): 451–504, especially 456–460, 465–467.

[16] Doria, 'Conoscenza del mercato e sistema informativo'; for a detailed case study of this operational structure see C. Álvarez Nogal, L. Lo Basso and C. Marsilio, 'La rete finanziaria della famiglia Spinola: Spagna, Genova e le fiere dei cambi (1610–1656)', *Quaderni Storici*, 124 (2007): 97–110.

[17] Pacini, 'Genoa and Charles V', 186–190.

This shift to finance did not mean that trade with the North of Europe, and therefore with England, came to a complete stop, but the volume of direct traffic substantially diminished, especially if compared with the steadily increasing volume of its closest competitor: Livorno. Between 1573 and 1583 a total of forty-seven northern ships reached Genoa, whilst eighty-four arrived in Livorno, seventy-one of which were English. Genoa no longer possessed a large commercial fleet of its own, a situation similar to that of Venice, but the availability of silver on its market maintained its attraction for foreign shipping.[18]

Genoa's vocation as an international port was by the end of the six-teenth century mostly embodied by its growing trade in cereals (especially wheat) for its own needs and as a regional and international redistribution centre. Starting in 1591, when Southern Europe was in the grip of an unprecedented grain famine, the Genoese government established, sup-ported and encouraged grain trade through the establishment of a very favourable tax regime, with low customs duties for wheat, a sort of limited *portofranco*.[19] Apart from the periods of severe shortage, such as the 1590s, when prices skyrocketed and there were plenty of opportunities for speculation, customs rebates were necessary to attract a steady flow of Northern European grain to the south. High prices, or competitively low customs duties, were essential to make long-distance transport worthwhile.[20] Albeit in smaller numbers than their Flemish and Hamburg counterparts, English ships carrying grains arrived in Genoa fairly regularly during the last two decades of the sixteenth century, and this drew the attention of the Spanish authorities, to the point that in 1589 the king of Spain himself complained to the Genoese government about the presence of English ships in the city's harbour.[21]

Anglo-Genoese trade

We have rather scant details about Anglo-Genoese traffic in the early decades of the seventeenth century. What we know is that until the 1630s

---

[18] Engels, *Merchants, Interlopers*, 109–110.
[19] T. Kirk, 'Genoa and Livorno: Sixteenth- and Seventeenth-Century Commercial Rivalry as a Stimulus to Policy Development', *History*, 86 (2001): 3–17; see also his *Genoa and the Sea: Policy and Power in an Early Modern Maritime Republic, 1559–1684*, Baltimore and London, 2005, 151–185.
[20] M. C. Engels, 'Dutch Traders in Livorno at the Beginning of the Seventeenth Century: The Company of Joris Jansen and Bernard van den Broecke', in C. Lesger and L. Noordegraaf eds., *Entrepreneurs and Entrepreneurship in Early Modern Times: Merchants and Industrialists within the Orbit of the Dutch Staple Market*, The Hague, 1995, 63–75, 69.
[21] E. Grendi, 'Gli inglesi a Genova (sec. XVII–XVIII)', *Quaderni Storici*, 39 (2004): 241–278, 242.

no English and very few Flemish merchants seem to have been permanently based in the city.[22] Resistance to allowing Protestants to settle in
town was certainly partly to blame for this late date, but the relatively low
level of direct trade was undoubtedly the strongest reason. The needs of
English ship-captains were satisfied by the services of a joint consul shared
with the Dutch up to 1616. And it is remarkable that the English consul
remained a Genoese citizen up to 1658.[23]

With a clear break from previous policies, which had aimed at protecting the redistribution role played by local merchants, in 1654 legislation
was issued in Genoa openly encouraging foreign merchants to settle
there, and this certainly helped to increase the flow of ships and goods
into the city.[24] But throughout these decades the Genoese authorities
remained focused more on European financial markets than on the
development of a comprehensive commercial strategy, which went
beyond trying to increase the flow of maritime traffic into the port by
granting low tariffs, especially on the grain trade. Finance and (maritime)
commerce had slowly grown apart in Genoa.

Once established in the second half of the seventeenth century, the
English community in Genoa was, like every other foreign 'nation', at the
junction between two experiences: a socio-economic one focused on
the definition and control of the group, and a diplomatic one focused
on the relationship between the two states. There was some permeability
between these two worlds and, free from the constraints of a company's
monopoly, the English presence in Genoa was, albeit small, rather diverse
in its socio-economic makeup. It mostly comprised merchants and shipowners, but there were also tailors, sock-makers and financiers. This is a
more varied group than the one in Venice, which is interesting given that
the Genoan community was numerically far smaller. Once again exact
figures are hard to come by, but insofar as it is possible to rely on the
official lists of ship-captains/masters (*patroni*), in the decades between the
sixteenth and seventeenth centuries, even the Flemish were more numerous than the English; in both cases, though, figures were already lower
than those of Livorno. Numbers grew from the 1630s and remained at
around fifty for the rest of the century, with some oscillation due to naval
engagements in the Mediterranean.[25] Still, these figures relate to seamen,
and not to merchants or artisans, so they cannot provide a proper image of

[22] On the English: E. Grendi, 'I nordici e il traffico del porto di Genova: 1590–1666', *Rivista Storica Italiana*, 83 (1971), 23–63, 25, 47; see also his 'Gli inglesi a Genova'; on the Flemish Engels, *Merchants, Interlopers*, 120–123.

[23] Grendi, 'Gli inglesi a Genova', 249–250.

[24] Kirk, *Genoa and the Sea*, 179–180.

[25] Grendi, 'Gli inglesi a Genova', 246.

the English presence in town. Settled merchants seem to remain in single digits for the rest of the century, a number substantially smaller than either in Livorno or Venice.[26]

In 1655 the Genoese government tried to persuade the English to transfer the centre of their Mediterranean operations from Livorno. This was envisaged through the establishment of a bilateral agreement between the two states in which Genoese financial liquidity and ability was used as an enticement. Nothing would come out of these negotiations, however, and the Venetian representative in London was rather sceptical about the Genoese chances of overcoming Livorno's primacy as an English base in the Tyrrhenian Sea.[27] This slow and partial opening towards the northerners seems to support Kirk's argument, which sees Genoa slowly shifting from proximity to Spain to some sort of neutrality in the period between the mid-sixteenth century and the end of the seventeenth century, in response to the growing crisis of the Iberian crown. But the episodic nature of such overtures signals also that the English connection was not a high priority for Genoese authorities.[28]

Throughout the early modern period Genoa and Venice were similar in being centres dealing with the redistribution of goods and active ports, though Venice had developed into a far more important production centre whilst Genoa had become a financial centre.[29] With the exception of the years 1590–1593, when the Southern European grain famine made it a very attractive port for northern shipping, the presence of English ships (and merchants) in Genoa was rather limited before the 1630s, something which can also be attributed in part to the strong links between Genoa and Spain. However, quite apart from political considerations, another issue was England's difficulty in acquiring return cargoes from Genoa, a problem quickly surmounted in Livorno and never present in Venice.[30] Crucially, the Levant Company was never interested in Genoa,[31] and Venice was the only area of the Italian peninsula on which it exercised a monopoly. From the English perspective the rest of Italy was open for all traders, and we shall see how Livorno became the hub of English activities in the Mediterranean.

---

[26] Grendi, 'Gli inglesi a Genova', 247–249.
[27] Grendi, 'Gli inglesi a Genova', 243–244.
[28] Kirk, *Genoa and the Sea*.
[29] G. Rossetti, 'Introduzione', in Rossetti ed., *Dentro la città*, i–xxxiii, xviii.
[30] Grendi, 'I nordici ed il traffico'; Davis, *The Rise of the English Shipping Industry*, 244.
[31] Grendi, 'Gli inglesi a Genova', 244.

Livorno and Tuscany

Florence never aspired to become an entrepôt along the lines of Genoa and Venice, and its economic and commercial interests had always been dominated by its industrial vocation, as a major centre of textile production.[32] It is therefore not surprising that the fortunes of its merchants on the international stage mirrored that of its cloth production. Between the 1520s and the end of the century Florentine merchants practically disappeared from long-distance trade, paralleling the decline in cloth exports.[33] Still, throughout the Tudor period, Florentine merchants and especially bankers continued to maintain a relatively high profile in London, where we have already seen how Filippo and Bartolomeo Corsini were active both as merchants and bankers, and were involved in financing the Venetian Greeks discussed in a previous chapter.

The small Florentine community also was rather successful in navigating the religious changes which took place starting with Henry VIII's break with Rome. Merchant bankers such as Giovanni Cavalcanti were also involved as art brokers in England, as the history of the unfinished tomb for Henry VIII and his then wife Catherine proves.[34] This relatively strong connection, even given the diminished commercial links, lasted throughout the Tudor dynasty, as on the occasions of the coronations of successive English sovereigns (Mary, Elizabeth and James), Tuscans always contributed to the erection of temporary triumphant arches in different areas of London, thus displaying their embeddedness in the political and social fabric of the kingdom (and the city).[35]

Relations between the two states were not always smooth, though. Tensions ran understandably high at the time of the Ridolfi plot in 1570–1571 to assassinate Elizabeth – let's not forget that Ridolfi was a Florentine banker active in London – especially as the role of the Medici in that conspiracy had been rather ambiguous. However, with the accession of Ferdinand as Grand Duke relations improved dramatically.

---

[32] Mallett, *The Florentine Galleys*, 9–10.

[33] R. Goldthwaite, *The Economy of Renaissance Florence*, Baltimore, 2009, 129–132.

[34] C. M. Sicca, 'Pawns of International Finance and Politics: Florentine Sculptors at the Court of Henry VIII', *Renaissance Studies*, 20 (2006): 1–34. It is interesting to note that the main structure of this monument, stripped of most of its original decoration, was recycled and now forms the basis of the monumental tomb of Admiral Horatio Nelson in St Paul's Cathedral. On these links see also her 'Consumption and Trade of Art between Italy and England in the First Half of the Sixteenth Century: The London House of the Bardi and Cavalcanti Company', *Renaissance Studies*, 16 (2002): 163–201.

[35] Wyatt, *The Italian Encounter with Tudor England*, 103, 124.

It certainly helped that 'after 1589, indeed, the Grand Duke assumed the difficult and important role of secret informer to Elizabeth on the movements of the Spanish fleet'.[36]

Unlike other major Italian commercial centres, which hosted groups of non-Italian merchants, Florence never had sizeable foreign mercantile communities. Notwithstanding efforts to make Pisa the centre of the English wool trade in the Italian peninsula, only occasionally is it possible to glimpse the presence of English merchants in fifteenth-century Tuscany.[37] Florentine bankers remained involved in financing the Anglo-Florentine wool trade throughout the fifteenth century and, to a minor extent, the crown itself, but by the end of that century their role was substantially diminished.[38] Regarding Europe at large, in the course of the following century they proved unable to withstand the competition first of Southern Germans and then of Genoese bankers. Severely affected by the crises first of Bruges and then of Antwerp, they mostly retreated from large-scale activities in the North of Europe, whilst their Genoese competitors successfully limited Florentine financial involvement with the Spanish crown and eventually came to control it.[39]

With the creation of the Grand Duchy (1569), Florence finally lost its absolute centrality in the region, and investment in the development of Livorno was one of the ways – the most successful one – in which the Tuscan state was restructured from a 'city-state' into a 'regional' one. Livorno was developed to compensate for silting in the Pisa harbour, until then the main one in the region. The site of the town had been purchased by the Medici from Genoa in 1421, but its development started in earnest only after the establishment of the Grand Duchy as part of a wider strategy aimed at strengthening the commercial and maritime sector within a state which never before had had a strong presence on the seas.[40]

[36] A. Contini, 'Aspects of Mediceans Diplomacy in the Sixteenth Century', in D. Frigo ed., *Politics and Diplomacy in Early Modern Italy: The Structures of Diplomatic Practice, 1450–1800*, Cambridge, 2000, 49–94, 91.
[37] M. Mallett, 'Anglo-Florentine Commercial Relations, 1465–1491', *Economic History Review*, 15 (1962): 250–265, 253, 261–264.
[38] The very messy final decades (1460–1480) of the Medici bank London branch are described in detail in De Roover, *The Rise and Decline*, 326–338.
[39] For a comprehensive analysis of these events see Goldthwaite, *The Economy of Renaissance Florence*.
[40] With the exception of the Florentine trade galleys active in the central decades of the fifteenth century and mentioned in an earlier chapter, see Mallett, 'Anglo-Florentine'; and his *The Florentine Galleys*.

How to create a maritime hub

The whole conception and practical implementation of the Livorno project was a most innovative social and economic experiment, with far-reaching global consequences. It showed how to successfully create *ex novo* a commercial hub through a policy of tax and customs reduction, and the elimination of customs duties for merchandise in transit – the creation of a free port, the *portofranco*, was a powerful innovation indeed.

Crucial for Livorno's rapid success was its strategic position, which allowed it to act as a maritime hinge between the eastern and western Mediterranean, taking full advantage of the new commercial routes which crossed the sea.[41] Equally important proved to be the excellence of the city project drawn by Bernardo Buontalenti, one of the leading architects and military engineers of the time. It was designed to be an embodiment of the Renaissance rational city, and particular attention was lavished on harbour infrastructures, which provided both cutting-edge military defences and plenty of convenient and well-organised spaces for stocking and handling merchandise of the most diverse varieties. Installations for ship repairs were also put into place, and particular attention was given to ensuring that the local food market could care for the victualling needs of ships.[42]

Livorno's site was rather insalubrious, and malaria was rife in the marshy plains surrounding the town. Therefore, the first stages of the settlement saw massive drainage to make it suitable for a large human settlement. Authorities gave special attention to issues of sanitation, which led to the excellent provisions of the local *Sanità*, which was put in charge of controlling health issues relating to shipping. By 1599 new and old legislation on these issues was brought together and streamlined.[43] Quarantine was particularly well taken care of, with three successive *lazzaretti* (quarantine stations) built between 1580 and 1643 to address the need for spaces sufficiently large to host high numbers of men and large quantities of goods.[44]

One corollary of Livorno's rise from semi-deserted malaria-ridden swamps was that it did not really have an indigenous population, even

---

[41] H. van der Wee, 'Structural Changes in European Long-Distance Trade, and Particularly in the Re-Export Trade from South to North, 1350–1750', in J. D. Tracy ed., *The Rise of Merchant Empires: Long-Distance Trade in the Early Modern World, 1350–1750*, Cambridge, 1990, 14–33, 21.

[42] L. Frattarelli-Fischer, 'Merci e mercanti nella Livorno secentesca', in S. Balbi de Caro ed., *Merci e monete a Livorno in età granducale*, Milan, 1997, 65–104, 66.

[43] C. Ciano, *La Sanità marittima nell'età medicea*, Pisa, 1976, 29–33.

[44] C. M. Cipolla, *Il burocrate e il marinaio: la 'Sanità' toscana e le tribolazioni degli inglesi a Livorno nel XVII secolo*, Bologna, 1992, 35–39.

less a local group of merchants and shipowners to kick-start the new project. The absence of a local commercial elite with entrenched economic and political interests was pivotal for both the establishment and the future development of the city, as it gave the Grand Dukes a lot of leeway in making strategic decisions quickly and without the need to negotiate with local stakeholders. To populate this new city, exceedingly generous conditions were granted to people willing to move there with their skills. Everyone could easily become a citizen; however, this did not entail any political power, as this remained firmly into the hands of the Grand Dukes and their local representatives. This was a unique experiment in early modern Europe: a city populated with foreigners and designed to cater to the interest of foreigners.

These freedoms were greatly enhanced when the famous 'Livornine' were issued in 1591 (and expanded in 1593) by Ferdinand I, granting extremely generous tax exemptions, amnesty from many crimes and religious freedom to merchants and entrepreneurs willing to establish themselves in the new city.[45] Quickly the city experienced dramatic demographic growth and it also became the favourite destination of religious dissenters of all varieties, who enjoyed there a freedom of religious practice which was unconceivable in the rest of Italy, and most rare in Europe. Particularly targeted by this legislation were merchants belonging to the Jewish diaspora, whose strong links with the Iberian and Ottoman empires made them coveted by several Italian states as a possible solution to the impending economic crisis of the peninsula.[46] Livorno was exceptionally successful in attracting Jews from Europe and the Levant, and already in the decades 1600–1620 the bulk of the overseas trade of the Grand Duchy was controlled by the Portuguese Jews based in Livorno.[47] This peculiar makeup of the city's inhabitants, with the corollary need to keep a close political eye on it, put Livorno under the direct control of the Grand Duke, and this

---

[45] A. Mangiarotti, 'Il porto franco, 1565–1676', in Balbi de Caro ed., *Merci e monete*, 17–35. A critical edition of the two 'Livornine' is in R. Toaff, *La nazione ebrea a Livorno e a Pisa (1591–1700)*, Florence, 1990, 419–435.

[46] A sharp and synthetic narrative of this phenomenon is in B. Ravid, 'A Tale of Three Cities and their "Raison d'Etat": Ancona, Venice, Livorno and the Competition for Jewish Merchants in the Sixteenth Century', in A. Meyuhas Ginio ed., *Jews, Christians and Muslims in the Mediterranean World after 1492*, London, 1992, 138–161. On the growing role of the Jewish diaspora in long-distance trade see J. I. Israel, *Diasporas within a Diaspora: Jews, Crypto-Jews and the World Maritime Empires (1540–1740)*, Leiden, 2002, 1–39; an excellent debate on its variety is in the 'Discussione coordinata da Girolamo Arnaldi', in G. Cozzi ed., *Gli ebrei a Venezia*, Milan, 1987, 89–94.

[47] J. I. Israel, *European Jewry in the Age of Mercantilism 1550–1750*, Oxford, 1985, 61.

centralisation increased after the promulgation of the "Livornine". In 1595 the governor of the city was also granted wide jurisdiction over the administration of justice, with instructions to report back directly to the Grand Duke or his secretary.

In the long term English merchants both contributed to and benefitted from Livorno's creation and success at least as much as the Jewish merchants who settled there. England as a state was not a priority for the Grand Dukes' foreign or commercial policy; distant were the times when Florentine finance supported the kingdom and English wool was needed for the local textile industry. But if England was not a priority, the English were: both merchants and corsairs, the latter coveted for the superiority of their ships and the contribution they could – and did – give to the Tuscan fleet and especially to the Knights of St Stephen, the local religious and military order founded in 1561 to protect the state and its shipping from Barbary corsairs' attacks and free Christian captives.

Corsairs, pirates and merchants

Amongst the many reasons which made Livorno a desirable base for corsairs and pirates, and which will make it also a hub for naval fleets, needs to be mentioned the local freedom in the arms' trade. All types or arms and munitions were available in the city, a quite exceptional situation which provided local dealers with a large income and, for this reason, the authorities were rather happy to support it.[48]

At the end of the Anglo-Spanish conflict in 1604 many English captains and crews who had been roaming the Mediterranean engaged in corsairing activities against Spanish shipping found themselves out of business. Given the fierceness and length of that conflict, and the rather fragile borders between corsairing and piratical activities, for some of them going back home was not really an option, as they were afraid that their questionable behaviour could catch up with them. Some of them joined the anti-Spanish activities of the Barbary Coast fleets, and in some cases converted to Islam in the process; others found alternative employment in Christian navies.[49]

Both Ferdinando I and later his son, Cosimo II, granted safe conducts to English corsairs and privateers, some of whom found employment in the Tuscan navy or collaborated with the Order of St Stephen as military

---

[48] J. P. Filippini, *Il porto di Livorno e la Toscana*, 3 vols, Naples, 1988, ii: 220.

[49] B. and L. Bennassar, *Les chrétiens d'Allah: l'histoire extraordinaire des renégats XVIe–XVIIe siècles*, Paris, 1989; S. Bono, *I corsari barbareschi*, Turin, 1964 and his *Corsari nel Mediterraneo: cristiani e musulmani fra guerra, schiavitù e commercio*, Milan, 1993.

and naval consultants.[50] Thanks also to their influx, the English presence in town continued to grow, and it is significant to evaluate the balance of power between shipping and trade; until the 1620s the English consul was chosen by ship-captains and accredited by Trinity House, not by local resident merchants, as would happen later.[51] By that date the close connections between the local English mercantile community and captains with piratical connections was becoming counterproductive, and in 1621 King James I supported the election of Richard Allen to the post of consul.[52] This election is interesting for two reasons: first, it was supported by the Levant Company – whose area of monopoly did not include Livorno or Tuscany but whose local interests were growing rapidly – and, second, in supporting Allen, King James contested the choice of Trinity House, which had supported Robert Thornton, a captain with a strong reputation as a pirate in the Mediterranean.

Livorno, with its fast-growing international trading community, and by now with a very streamlined customs organisation as a result of its status as a *portofranco*, also had become an excellent place to get rid of merchandise of uncertain origin – in other words, ill-gotten or gained through piracy.[53] English merchants resident in Livorno had previously tried to distance themselves from such activities, as on several occasions English pirates had acted directly against their interests.[54] As usual in such circumstances, the nature of the evidence makes it difficult to assess the effective links between *bona fide* merchants and piratical activities. It might very well be that for young factors the temptation of earning

[50] M. G. Biagi, 'Da Ferdinando I a Ferdinando II: congiunture internazionali e "politica corsara"', *Bollettino Storico Pisano*, 62 (1993): 1–23; C. Ciano, 'Corsari inglesi a servizio di Ferdinando I', in *Atti del Convegno di Studi 'Gli inglesi a Livorno e all'isola d'Elba (sec. XVII–XIX)'*, Livorno, 1980, 77–82.

[51] S. Villani, '"Una piccola epitome di Inghilterra". La comunità inglese di Livorno negli anni di Ferdinando II: questioni religiose e politiche', in S. Villani, S. Tutino and C. Franceschini eds., *Questioni di storia inglese tra Cinque e Seicento: cultura, politica e religione*, Pisa, 2003, 179–208, 180. Trinity House's main function was to protect the interests of masters and mariners of the Thames; its competencies also included the erection of beacons, the laying of buoys, the granting of certificates to pilots, and the examination and recommendation of masters for the Navy. There were also Trinity Houses in Hull, Dover and the Cinque Ports, and Newcastle, see R. Blakemore, 'Laws and Customs of the Sea: The Legal World of English Sailors, c. 1575–1729', in M. Fusaro, B. Allaire, R. Blakemore and T. Vanneste eds., *Law, Labour, and Empire: Comparative Perspectives on Seafarers, c. 1500–1800*, London, 2015, 100–120, and bibliography quoted therein.

[52] P. Castignoli, 'La Nazione Inglese', in *Livorno: progetto e storia di una città tra il 1500 e il 1600*, Pisa, 1980, 231.

[53] Engels, *Merchants, Interlopers*, 44.

[54] Pagano De Divitiis, *English Merchants*, 28–29; TNA, *SP*, 99, 2, c.243r; R. H. Tawney, *Business and Politics*, 14–15; A. Tenenti, 'Aspetti della vita mediterranea intorno al Seicento', in *Bollettino dell'Istituto di storia della società e dello stato veneziano*, ii (1960): 3–17, 4.

some easy money on the side must have been a strong one indeed, and so it may be that they had a far more articulated (albeit hidden) role within the local economy than can be ascertained by analysing official documents. But the consul election of 1621 represented a turning point in the fortunes of the English factory in Livorno, as this public rejection of piratical activities, which had been criticised by all England's commercial partners in the area for decades, greatly favoured the English and helped them to increase their share of local traffic.

Trade and neutrality

Livorno displayed many of the characteristics of a 'frontier town' in its first few decades of life. A fast-growing harbour, the intermingling of maritime and naval activities, the lack of a local established group of native citizens, and a large number of transients brought to the fore the violent and quasi-legal sides of maritime life. If the social life of the city was turbulent, the political strategy of the Grand Dukes was instead cautious and most shrewd. Ferdinand I charted a delicate political course during his long reign (1587–1609), with a constant balancing act between Spain and France. He was successful in his plan to equip Tuscany with a strong naval force, and was also an active supporter of the Christian corsairing activities of the Knights of St Stephen, 'who kept Livorno well stocked with plunder from Turkish merchantmen' even if this 'lost what careful diplomacy at Constantinople had almost won for it: a part in the current revival of the Levant trade'.[55] In fact, it can be argued that the presence of the Knights made Livorno – and the Grand Duchy – officially hostile to the Ottoman empire, and 'deeply implicated in the corsairing economy that developed in the seventeenth century Mediterranean'.[56] It was not only goods plundered from Muslim corsairing ships which were sold in town, but also merchandise originally plundered from Christian shipping which found its way there, sometimes even from North Africa.[57] Booty from these expeditions could easily be sold, as long as a percentage of the profits was duly paid in the grand-ducal coffers. This policy extended also to human merchandise, as Livorno became the largest slave market on the northern shores of the Mediterranean.[58]

---

[55] E. Cochrane, *Florence in the Forgotten Centuries, 1527–1800: A History of Florence and the Florentines in the Age of the Grand Dukes*, Chicago, 1973, 113.

[56] Cochrane, *Florence in the Forgotten Centuries*, 113.

[57] M. Greene, *Catholic Pirates and Greek Merchants: A Maritime History of the Mediterranean*, Princeton, 2010, 82.

[58] Frattarelli-Fischer, 'Merci e mercanti', 69.

If hostility towards the Ottomans became an integral part of the Grand
Duchy's political stance, on the other hand a policy of neutrality towards
European states was more and more strictly enforced as traffic grew in the
harbour. This policy was embodied in the rather long and detailed list of
forbidden activities and rules which users of the port were supposed to
follow. Amongst the principals: any act of war and violence was forbidden
in the harbour and on the docks; armed vessels of any kind – whether navy
ships or privateers – could not exit the harbour when the arrival of a ship
had been announced; and an interval of twenty-four hours was strictly
enforced between the departures from the harbour of ships belonging to
hostile states.[59]

Sometimes neutrality was endangered by factors unrelated to Grand
Duchy politics. The local English mercantile community openly
divided along political lines during the civil wars, to the point that in
1644 the local governor wrote to the Grand Duke expressing his concerns that public peace in town could easily be broken by fighting
between English crews of different political allegiance. It was feared
that King Charles' instructions to attack ships loyal to Parliament could
have had a rather damaging impact on port neutrality. The situation
within the English community appears to have been relatively tense, as
since 1634 Morgan Read – Catholic and loyalist – had been consul in
Livorno. Amongst merchants, things turned out to be smoother than
expected, though, even when a parliamentary agent arrived in 1651 to
work at his side.[60]

The government of Genoa was particularly worried about Livorno's
success in the grain trade, especially as since the middle of the sixteenth
century a series of fiscal exemptions had been implemented aimed at
increasing its availability in Genoa, a policy which can be described as a
type of limited *portofranco*.[61] Venice also quickly grew rather worried
about Livorno's success as an entrepôt throughout the seventeenth
century. The primary reason for Venice's concern was that Livorno,
thanks to its exceedingly low tariffs, was increasing its share in the
redistribution trade of northern and colonial goods in Central and
Northern Italy, usurping a role which Venice had dominated for centuries.
Venice's governmental bodies debated at length on how to confront this
challenge, but in practice nothing was done about it. The *Cinque Savi*
frequently supported giving foreign merchants privileges similar to those

---

[59] Filippini, *Il porto di Livorno*, ii: 220.
[60] Villani, 'Una piccola epitome di Inghilterra', 187–188.
[61] Kirk, 'Genoa and Livorno'; see also his *Genoa and the Sea*, 151–185.

available in Livorno, but such a policy was too alien to the strong Venetian tradition of protectionism and defence of its own ruling mercantile class, and therefore these suggestions were not actually implemented.[62]

The Levant Company and Mediterranean trade

Unlike Venice and its territories, Livorno was not subject to the monopoly of the Levant Company and therefore all sorts of English merchants did business there freely.[63]

Livorno quickly became the preferred entrance into the Italian market for many colonial goods coming from the Atlantic, but also for the classic English exports: lead, tin and dry fish (*salumi*). These developments were originally challenged by the Company as damaging to its original ambitions to channel through Venice all English trade to the peninsula. This ambiguous situation on the ground makes it difficult to disentangle English 'free trade' from 'Company trade' there, and in fact in everyday practice the two were frequently mixing. It is a testament to the flexibility of the Company as a trading institution that this situation could exist and flourish, but it is also probably evidence of the fact that Levant Company members in London had, by the 1620s, come to the realisation that Livorno provided them with a most useful operational base in the central Mediterranean. Evidence of this is that from the 1630s Livorno became the common stopover for company ships on the way to Ottoman lands.[64] At the same time, the freedom of trade in Livorno helped to lower the pressure waged in England by merchants from the outports, ill represented in the London-based major trading companies such as the Levant, and therefore frequently complaining about their monopolies. The London mercantile elite had been rather successful in freezing out other ports from the chartered companies, and this had been particularly damaging for Bristol, where there was a strong tradition of direct trading with the Mediterranean.[65] The argument behind this exclusion centred on the nature of local merchants' trade and their almost inevitable connections with retail. In the words of Richard Grassby, 'in the

---

[62] Ravid, 'A Tale of Three Cities', 149.

[63] Epstein, *The Early History*, 37, 58, 64–65; Wood, *A History*, 20, 40. G. Pagano De Divitiis, 'Il Mediterraneo nel XVII secolo: l'espansione commerciale inglese e l'Italia', *Studi Storici*, 27 (1986): 109–148, 132–133.

[64] G. Pagano De Divitiis, 'Il porto di Livorno fra l'Inghilterra e l'Oriente', *Nuovi Studi Livornesi*, 1 (1993): 43–87, 43.

[65] Grassby, *The Business Community*, 61; J. Vanes ed., *Documents Illustrating the Overseas Trade of Bristol in the Sixteenth Century*, Bristol, 1979, 21–25.

provincial ports, the volume of foreign trade was often insufficient to support a whole business, and, despite strenuous efforts in ports like Bristol to exclude retailers and artisans, it was inevitable that overseas merchants would engage in the domestic trade and vice versa'.[66] For merchants from outports, therefore, Livorno provided excellent opportunities to continue to pursue their trades without infringing the monopolies of the London-based companies. Therefore it is arguable that from the Company's perspective it was probably worth turning a blind eye to possible losses caused by interlopers. Bristol merchants, though, did not stop lobbying for a share of Levant trade, and in 1618 one of their petitions to the Privy Council was successful, which resulted in the local Merchant Venturers being granted leave to import yearly 200 tons of currants from Zante and Cephalonia in exchange for a small fee to be paid to the Levant Company. The latter did not really appreciate this concession, and tensions between the two companies flared occasionally throughout the century.[67]

Livorno's share of Anglo-Italian trade continued to grow unabated throughout the seventeenth century. By the late 1660s around nine-tenths of England's Italian imports came from there. So the Venetians were indeed right to worry about how much of her own exports towards England took that road, as by then it was cheaper to move goods overland from Venice and the *Terraferma* to Livorno than to do so via the sea route.[68]

Trade and the *portofranco*, some conclusions

Livorno is famous for being the blueprint for a 'free port' – *portofranco*. Compared to all other ports at that time, Livorno enjoyed exceedingly low customs tariffs and costs, which were further lowered in a first reform of the port legislation in 1629, and then just about fully abolished in 1676.[69] This customs regime favoured the growth in town of a diversified trade, whose volume increased steadily until the end of the seventeenth century. Grain was imported in large quantities, both for the use of the Tuscan

---

[66] Grassby, *The Business Community*, 62–63.
[67] J. Latimer, *The History of the Society of Merchant Venturers of the City of Bristol: With Some Account of the Anterior Merchant Guilds*, Bristol, 1903, 137–138; P. McGrath, *The Merchant Venturers of Bristol: A History of the Society of Merchant Venturers of Bristol from Its Origin to the Present Day*, Bristol, 1975, 55–56; P. McGrath ed., *Records Relating to the Society of Merchant Venturers of the City of Bristol in the Seventeenth Century*, Bristol, 1951, 213–221, 248–249.
[68] H. Roseveare ed., *Markets and Merchants of the Late Seventeenth Century: The Marescoe-David Letters 1668–1680*, Oxford, 1987, 100.
[69] Mangiarotti, 'Il porto franco'.

state and for re-export both to Italy and to the rest of the Mediterranean. From the Low Countries came dried and salted fish; from the Iberian peninsula wool and cochineal; from England lead, tin and iron, many varieties of salted fish which was re-exported throughout Italy, where it enjoyed a growing market, and some textiles; other goods arriving in Livorno were pepper, spices and sugar. From North Africa leather, wool and wax were common along with, as mentioned above, slaves; in Livorno it was also possible for Protestants to acquire the alum from Tolfa, in the Papal States, which the pope refused to sell to them directly.[70]

The absence of a local ruling class, paired with the tight control exercised on urban government directly by the Grand Duke, allowed Livorno to develop its institutions in a rather different way from its competitors. Economic policy is the area in which these differences are most evident and, unsurprisingly, the comparison with Venice – where instead the ruling class had always (and would always, until 1797) considered the economy its own main area of action – bring these differences to the fore.

Livorno became a centre for storage and redistribution, not a real commercial entrepôt. Most of the merchandise discharged on its docks could be kept in its warehouses without paying any additional transit or storage duty, and was then re-exported to other Italian states or to different areas of the Mediterranean. But this kind of trade was utterly dependent on the presence and activities of foreign merchants, and therefore on their interests and speculation opportunities. Many merchants from other parts of Italy traded in Livorno, but their role was always shaped by other operators, and they ended up mostly acting as middlemen at the mercy of market conditions set by foreign operators.

Unlike Venice or Genoa, which were also capital cities and therefore had a very different role to play within their states, Livorno could thus function and thrive in relative isolation from its host state. The extremely generous concessions to religious and ethnic minorities which were at the basis of their success could not – and, indeed, should not – be extended beyond the town boundaries. The Grand Dukes could not have successfully implemented them had they not, at the same time, severely limited the geographical extension of this kind of jurisdiction. By the late 1640s, when the *portofranco* regime was finding its proper settlement, Livorno was more and more an extraneous body within the Tuscan state. Directly

---

[70] Frattarelli-Fischer, 'Merci e mercanti', 71.

answering to the Grand Duke, the local government was dominated by the maritime commercial interests of foreign states. With the exception of the *Sanità*, the central government in Florence was less involved in it, and when in 1646 a regime of full neutrality was established, the fact of being an island of peace in a militarised sea allowed the harbour to experience a veritable boom.[71]

For all the reasons mentioned above, it is unfair, and makes little sense, to compare the situations of Venice and Livorno, as has frequently been done. From the very beginning Livorno was created as a staple and as a centre designed to attract foreign merchants. In Engels' words:

Livorno became an interesting place for strangers, since, as a 'new' city, it could be easily dominated by settlers. Forming a financially powerful and therefore influential group, the foreigners were able to safeguard or even augment the privileges granted to them. In 'old' cities foreign merchants had to cope with a strong and protective local hierarchy.[72]

It has been argued that Venice and Genoa, with strong ruling classes actively involved in economic and financial activities, strong artisanal guilds and well-rooted proto-industries, were not places where this kind of innovative approach could practically be enforced.[73] The policy of facilitating settlements of foreign merchants – rightly considered necessary to catalyse a commercial hub – made Livorno much more attractive than both Genoa – its main rival, if nothing else for geographical reasons – and Venice. In Livorno a merchant needed only to register – without any discrimination – in the 'book of foreigners' to be allowed to compete for official positions within the city. In this way, the Tuscan Grand Dukes created a new kind of commercial emporium, totally different from its predecessors and from traditional ways of trading.[74] Venice was also known as a city full of foreigners, thanks to a well-known and often quoted passage in Philippe de Commynes' *Mémoires* which mentioned how 'La pluspart de leur people est etranger'.[75] However, attitudes towards foreigners were very different in these three cities and, especially in Venice,

---

[71] C. Ciano, 'Uno sguardo al traffico fra Livorno e l'Europa del Nord verso la metà dei Seicento', in *Atti del Convegno Livorno e il Mediterraneo nell'età Medicea*, Livorno, 1978, 149–168, 151.

[72] Engels, *Merchants, Interlopers*, 39.

[73] E. Stumpo, 'Livorno in età granducale: la città ideale e la patria di tutti', in Balbi de Caro ed., *Merci e monete*, 105–137, 109.

[74] Grendi, 'Gli inglesi a Genova', 242. On the peculiarities of the Livorno's *portofranco*, and the substantive differences with other Mediterranean *portifranchi* which followed, see Fusaro, 'After Braudel', 21–22.

[75] Philippe de Commynes, *Mémoires*, J. Blanchard ed., Paris, 2001, 557.

the paradox consisted in being a cosmopolitan centre, whilst at the same time adopting a protectionist economic policy which privileged its own citizens and subjects above foreign operators.

Frequently the issue of 'mentality' is raised in this context, implying that what was lacking in Genoa and Venice was a 'modern' outlook, and the right mentality to modify economic strategy and policy to accommodate the new economic players active in the Mediterranean. However, it appears to me that there were far deeper reasons behind this; Genoa was part of the Spanish system and increasingly embedded in Euro-Atlantic financial networks, whilst Venice was the centre of its own empire, whose commercial nature remained essential to its policies. These factors were not based on supposed 'mentality' but on hard institutional and structural realities connected with ruling and administering complex economic systems. In short, Venice and Genoa had concerns which were totally absent in Livorno.

In the prologue to the 'Livornine', Ferdinando de' Medici invited foreign merchants to settle in Livorno, openly declaring his ambition 'that the whole of Italy benefit from this'.[76] But, in effect, Livorno always remained excluded from the productive part of the 'Italian economic system', and it is unclear how much – if at all – it benefitted even the Tuscan economy beyond the city boundaries.[77] Livorno seems to have been a solution more for the economic needs of the Grand Duke than for those of the Grand Duchy, a flash of entrepreneurial genius worthy of his Medici ancestors. Without doubt the city, directly dependent on the Grand Duke,[78] soon became his major source of income thanks especially to its success as a grain entrepôt, the trade in cereals being one of the major business interests of the dynasty.[79] However, Livorno was not a solution to the economic crisis of early modern Italy. Its success was strictly

---

[76] Toaff, *La nazione ebrea a Livorno*, 419–420.

[77] Engels, *Merchants, Interlopers*, 34–46; see also C. Ciano, *Navi, mercanti e marina nella vita Mediterranea del Cinque Seicento*, Livorno, 1991, 118. There are some cases of proto-industrial activities moving in town, but these are rare: see L. Frattarelli-Fischer, 'Livorno città nuova 1574–1609', *Società e storia*, 46 (1989): 872–893, 891. Rita Mazzei uncovered some economic links between Livorno and Pisa: R. Mazzei, 'L'economia pisana e la dinamica del commercio internazionale dell'età moderna', in M. Tangheroni ed., *Pisa e il Mediterraneo: uomini, merci, idee dagli Etruschi ai Medici*, Milan, 2003, 293–297.

[78] A synthetic and precise description of this is in P. Castignoli, 'Il governo', in *Livorno: progetto e storia di una città tra il 1500 e il 1600*, Pisa, 1980, 217–218.

[79] A. Mangiarotti, 'La politica economica di Ferdinando I de Medici', in Balbi de Caro ed., *Merci e monete*, 37–64. An analysis of Italian eighteenth-century political economists' criticism of the Medici progenitors of Ferdinand, and the ideological bias regarding the economic policy of textile production, is in Reinert, 'Blaming the Medici', 442–444.

localised, and favoured the foreigners who had been so quick to answer Ferdinand's call. Once again we must agree with Fernand Braudel, who considered Livorno's success the litmus test of the Italian exit from European economic global expansion.[80]

---

[80] F. Braudel, 'L'Italia fuori d'Italia: due secoli tre Italie', in *Storia d'Italia: dalla caduta dell'Impero romano al secolo XVIII*, ii, Turin, 1974, 2092–2247, 2227; this opinion is shared also by the bibliography which followed, amongst many see Pagano De Divitiis, 'Il porto di Livorno', 75; Grendi, 'Gli inglesi a Genova', 242.

5   Trade, violence and diplomacy

Venice's defeat by the French at Agnadello (1509) constituted a real watershed, and this was immediately evident in the Republic's foreign policy. In the following decades Venice was extremely careful in conserving a diplomatic balance towards the major European powers, avoiding involvement in the momentous events surrounding the Protestant Reformation and the long-drawn-out conflict between the Holy Roman empire and France, given that some imperial advisors, notably Mercurino di Gattinara, were rather wary of the Republic, considering it to be leaning towards France. This cautious attitude was deemed necessary to preserve trading links with as many markets as possible, something important in those years of conflict and turmoil, with all the corollary disruption of trade. To this we need to add the fears generated by the reports of Da Gama's expedition and their impact on the spice trade. Given the objective limitations of the Republic's strategic and military ambitions, and the greedy eyes of the major continental powers towards the Italian peninsula, Venetian foreign policy became more geared towards a strategy of guarded neutrality to best support its own commercial and trading aims. Keeping out of trouble in the Italian peninsula was also considered a good strategy given the aggressive Ottoman stance which threatened her maritime empire.

These early decades of the sixteenth century saw the demise of the system of the state galleys, and I have sketched the political and economic reasons behind its decline. However, further consideration is needed of its role in the trade with England and its involvement with high politics. Its peculiar and unique organisation made it a favourite subject for historians, skewing the analysis of its economic role and most probably contributing to an overestimation of its importance within the overall trade of the Republic. Another factor behind this bias is the high political visibility of state galleys as, given that the Venetian state was itself a stakeholder, all problems which arose in their travels ended up leaving a documentary trail, and frequently long diplomatic negotiations were carried out to solve them. A case in point is that of the Flanders galleys which remained 'captives' in Southampton for two years (1521–1523) and whose mis-adventures can be followed in harrowing details in the letters of Captain Vincenzo Priuli to the Doge, an episode which perfectly embodies the political and diplomatic complexities of protecting a state-sponsored commercial enterprise in times of political uncertainty.[1]

Private Venetian trade did not attract this kind of institutional attention from the Republic's magistrates, because there was less direct economic interest of the state, and private shipowners were far less likely to ask for government help unless the problems were indeed very serious. Private shipping therefore left a far lighter documentary trail, and this has led to an underestimation of its volume and value. A further corollary of the high visibility of state shipping is that, on its demise, scholars have generally tended to assume that overland trade took its place, which was not always the case. As discussed in an earlier chapter, the entrepôt of Antwerp played an important role in Anglo-Italian trade, but this was limited to the more expensive goods, such as spices. There was indeed some resilience towards the usage of land routes for certain other types of merchandise; for example, in 1556 some Italian merchants declared that English kerseys were unsuited to sea travel due to the length of the trip (a three-month journey was considered excellent in the early six-teenth century),[2] the dangers of pirates and storms and the negative effect of humidity on the fabric itself.[3] Fernand Braudel noticed a relative resurgence of the land-based trading routes between Venice and the North of Europe only at the very end of the sixteenth century. Behind this shift he saw the increasing dangers of Mediterranean corsairs – the Uskoks roaming the Adriatic and the English 'privateers' involved in the Anglo-Spanish conflict – which were causing a general rise of insurance costs for maritime trade throughout the Mediterranean.[4] This increased importance of land routes only marginally affected Anglo-Venetian trade, as *direct* maritime private trade between the two countries remained strong. As has been discussed before, this trade was already in part shared by the English and the Greek subjects of the Republic (the latter frequently employing English crews). This mix of nationalities amongst the crews helped these ships escape the negative effects of the Anglo-Spanish conflict, and be well enough armed to cope with Uskoks. Also, the bulky nature of the merchandise – lead, tin and dried fish from

[1] Ortalli ed., *Lettere di Vincenzo Priuli.*
[2] Tucci, *Mercanti, navi e monete*, 172–173.
[3] W. Brulez, 'Les routes commerciales d'Angleterre en Italie au XVIe siècle', in *Studi in onore di Amintore Fanfani*, 6 vols, Milan, 1962, iv: 123–184, 126.
[4] Braudel, *The Mediterranean*, i: 284–293.

England in exchange mostly for wine and currants, but also rice, alum and tartar – still made the sea route cheaper.[5]

With this complex and shifting background, it is necessary to keep in mind that Anglo-Venetian diplomatic relations, especially throughout the sixteenth century, were heavily influenced by general European political and economic issues, and their development should always be analysed and judged within this wider context. There are also some specific bilateral issues to consider: first, aggressive commercial competition in the Levantine markets, which we have seen was openly expressed by Walsingham in his memorandum, was a major concern for both parties. To this needs to be added the peculiar English interest in the currants produced in the *Stato da Mar*, a bilateral trade which grew beyond all parties' expectations and which had profound long-term political consequences for centuries to come. Thus the end of direct diplomatic links during the reign of Elizabeth was a far more complex matter than just a moment of uncharacteristic compliance by Venice to the wishes of the Holy See.

Diplomacy and trade

The Republic of Venice and the kingdom of England had a relatively long tradition of contact. Luigi Firpo dated to 1496 the establishment of permanent diplomatic relations, as in that year two Venetian merchants based in London – Luca Valaresso and Pietro Contarini, the latter consul since 1490 – were entrusted by the *Senato* with the mission of involving Henry VII in the Holy League.[6] The complex negotiations behind these dealings clearly show that the Tudor king had a perceptive understanding of Italian politics, and that his desire to stop the French in the peninsula was one of several factors behind his foreign policy choices. Henry VII's keen interest in and knowledge of Italian affairs were connected to the growing cultural and economic contacts between Italy and England in the fifteenth century.[7] The following year, Andrea Trevisan was sent to negotiate a reduction of the duty on wine, which had soured the relationship between the two countries.[8] Towards the end of Henry's reign, when

---

[5] Brulez, 'Les routes commerciales d'Angleterre', 128.

[6] *CSPVe*, vol. i, n. 675, see: www.british-history.ac.uk/report.aspx?compid=94101 (date accessed: 16 February 2014); see also Firpo ed., *Relazioni di ambasciatori veneti*, ix.

[7] J. M. Currin, 'Henry VII, France and the Holy League of Venice: The Diplomacy of Balance', *Historical Research*, 82 (2009): 526–546, 529–530.

[8] Firpo ed., *Relazioni di ambasciatori veneti*, x; N. Barozzi and G. Berchet eds., *Le relazioni degli stati europei lette al Senato dagli ambasciatori veneziani nel secolo decimosettimo*, 9 vols., Venice, 1863, iii.

the king appeared to have lost interest in Italian affairs, he still clearly deemed Venice a potentially important ally, as he offered diplomatic assistance to an isolated Venice facing the League of Cambray.[9]

In subsequent years, England's interest in Italian affairs waned temporarily, with the notable exception of the relation with the Papal States, which took centre stage in the decades leading to Henry VIII's divorce. Gregorio Casali, an Italian nobleman who built a diplomatic career on the basis of his family links with the Papal Curia, was from 1525 resident ambassador for England in Rome and held responsibilities covering most of the Italian peninsula.[10] Later the same year it appears that his brother was appointed English ambassador in Venice, where he remained until 1528.[11] The commercial element resurfaced in the following decades. In 1531 Carlo Cappello arrived in London and successfully arranged that Venetian galleys could take out up to 1,600 sacks of English wool, but on the other leg of the journey – which was going to be the penultimate one of state galleys to England – the quantity of spices which arrived in England was inferior to the expectations of local merchants, who duly complained. The Venetians' answer to these complaints is very telling as it blamed this 'on a changed world, as now spices which used to come to Venice arrive in Portugal'.[12] Licence to trade was denied to Venetians the following year (1532), and behind this move Cappello saw the desire of Henry to punish the *Senato*, which had just forbidden a team of professors from the University of Padua from defending his decision to divorce Catherine before the pope.[13] Trade and politics were mixing again.

Henry's divorce marked a turning point in the history of English diplomacy. One of the political side-effects of the break between England and Rome was the severing of diplomatic ties with Italian and continental powers. Before the Reformation, itinerant papal representatives and mediators had a crucial role in maintaining links between England and the continent. In the words of Michael Wyatt, 'it was the rupturing of these bonds following the divorce [of Henry and Catherine] that simultaneously isolated the country and created the space within which

[9] Currin, 'Henry VII, France and the Holy League of Venice', 545; see also his 'England's International Relations 1485–1509: Continuities amidst Change', in S. Doran and G. Richardson eds., *Tudor England and Its Neighbours*, Basingstoke, 2005, 14–43, 27.

[10] C. Fletcher, *Our Man in Rome: Henry VIII and His Italian Ambassador*, London, 2012, 7.

[11] C. Fletcher, 'War, Diplomacy and Social Mobility: The Casali Family in the Service of Henry VIII', *Journal of Early Modern History*, 14 (2010): 559–578, 570.

[12] 'Venice: November 1531', *CSPVe* vol. iv, see: www.british-history.ac.uk/report.aspx? compid= 94624&str (date accessed: 3 August 2012).

[13] 'Venice: January 1532', *CSPVe* vol. iv, see: www.british-history.ac.uk/report.aspx? compid= 94626 (date accessed: 3 August 2012).

its singularly Protestant culture could develop'.[14] After Henry's Act of
Supremacy (1534), the *Senato* chose to keep a low profile by sending
residents to London recruited from the secretarial body – the *cittadini
originari*, the upper echelon of Venetian citizenship from which the higher
ranks of state bureaucracy were filled – as opposed to proper ambassadors
elected from the patriciate. This contrivance gave a less prominent profile
to the legation but changed little in practice, as the residents' practical
functions were equivalent to those of an ambassador.[15] Conversely,
English embassies arrived in Venice on occasion, but no resident ambassador settled there until the reign of James I.[16]

Venice interrupted these lesser diplomatic contacts at the time of the
marriage of Queen Mary and Philip II, as the *Senato* reasoned that a single
ambassador – based in Spain – could efficiently cover both countries.[17]
Giovanni Michiel was followed for a few months by Michiel Surian, but
the latter was never replaced. This decision was taken against the advice
of Michiel who, writing the customary final relation after his embassy to
Queen Mary in May 1557, having left England to follow Philip II to
Madrid, had been most keen to underline the potential advantages of
maintaining direct diplomatic links between the two countries. Michiel
was convinced that the presence of Venetian merchants in England
needed official support, without which Venetians would abandon that
country 'to the prejudice and damage of this city [Venice] (which
supports itself principally through trade)'.[18] The issue of trade was still
centre stage, but the situation both in England and in Rome was rather
delicate, so the matter rested. When Elizabeth ascended the throne in
1559, the *Senato* actively debated whether to send an ambassador, but a
decision on this matter was postponed.

Throughout the reign of Elizabeth the Venetian embassies in Madrid and
Paris relayed information about England, with Paris especially playing a

---

[14] Wyatt, *The Italian Encounter with Tudor England*, 53.

[15] A. Zannini, 'Economic and Social Aspects of the Crisis of Venetian Diplomacy in the
Seventeenth and Eighteenth Centuries', in Frigo ed., *Politics and Diplomacy*, 109–146,
111–112.

[16] Edmund Harvel enjoyed the status of envoy in Venice in the early 1540s, but was never
granted the status of ambassador, see *DNB*, s.v. and H. F. Brown, 'The Marriage Contract,
Inventory, and Funeral Expenses of Edmund Harvel', *English Historical Review*, 20 (1905):
70–77. Peter Vannes (Vanni) was appointed ambassador to Venice in 1550, but his position
appears to have been itinerant around Italy, see *DNB*, s.v.; G. M. Bell, *A Handlist of British
Diplomatic Representatives, 1509–1688*, London, 1990, 289; K. R. Bartlett, *The English in
Italy, 1525–1558: A Study in Culture and Politics*, Geneva, 1991.

[17] Barozzi and Berchet eds., *Le relazioni degli stati europei*, vi.

[18] Giovanni Micheli [sic], 'Relazione d'Inghilterra' (1557), in E. Albèri ed., *Relazioni degli
ambasciatori veneti al senato*, serie 1, vol. ii, Florence, 1840, 289–381, 357.

part in the indirect dialogue between the two governments. It was thanks to currants that the issue of sending an ambassador to England was raised again in the *Senato*, as the licence granted by Elizabeth to Acerbo Velutelli in 1575 triggered a lobbying campaign by Venetian merchants, most of them keen for their government to defend them at court.

Within the small Venetian community still active in London in the second half of the sixteenth century, requests to their government to re-establish diplomatic links had never really stopped. With their calls for representation going unheeded, and in the absence of a consul to at least take care of the operational issues surrounding trade, the Venetians in London selected one of their own as consul to liaise with the local authorities.[19] At the end of 1560 they chose Placido Ragazzoni, with no official sanction by the Venetian government. His confirmation was hotly debated by the *Senato*, which finally let him continue in this capacity only until 1562, stating that 'from now it shall be prohibited to elect consuls or vice-consuls without the direct licence of our *Collegio*'.[20] The following year Giovanni da Cà da Pesaro was officially elected as Venetian consul in London, where he resided until June 1570.[21] After that date Ragazzoni informally resumed the position of consul, playing a quasi-political role which was severely limited by his lack of political endorsement. When he returned to Venice in the early 1580s, the only remaining 'Venetian' based in London was Giovanni da Riviera,[22] who inherited Ragazzoni's position and helped to build a lasting commercial alliance between his countrymen and the founding members of the Levant Company.[23] In 1591 his efforts to keep this trade alive were acknowledged by the Venetian government, and he was officially granted the role of consul.[24]

---

[19] On these issues see *CSPVe*, vol. vii (1559–1580), *passim*.

[20] ASV, *Senato terra*, f. 38, cc.n.n.; the *Collegio* reprimand of the Venetian merchants based in London is dated 15-1-1561mv, but is enclosed in a *parte* dated 6-3-1563. The election of Ragazzoni to the consulship had been confirmed until 25-4-1562.

[21] From 'Preface', *CSPVe*, vol. vii: see www.british-history.ac.uk/report.aspx?compid= 94934&amp (date accessed: 7 August 2012).

[22] Da Riviera was a native of Zante and agent for two Veneto-Greek commercial firms: the Seguro and Sumacchi, see ASV, *Quarantia Criminale*, b. 103, fasc. 73, cc.77v–80r.

[23] Da Riviera's actions came also to the attention of the Venetian ambassador in Paris in 1586 (Giovanni Dolfin), who kept on receiving requests of information about him and his role, which he duly reported to the *Collegio*. *CSPVe*, vol. viii (1581–1591), n. 350, 163: see www.british-history.ac.uk/report.aspx?compid=95235 (date accessed: 16 February 2014).

[24] On his efforts to keep the trade alive, which ultimately obtained him the title of consul, see ASV, *Cinque Savi alla Mercanzia, Risposte*, reg. 138, c.166v; another copy is in *Cinque Savi alla Mercanzia*, b. 34 n.s., fasc. v, cc.n.n. (27-2-1591mv). His name escaped Rawdon Brown's list of Venetian consular representatives in London: see 'Venetian Consuls in England', *CSPVe*, vol. i; see www.british-history.ac.uk/report.aspx?compid= 94079 (date accessed: 19 July 2011). The regulations for the election of consul had been

Still, even with official sanction, given the objective limits of his consular role, and his own relatively low social status, he could not be particularly effective handling such delicate political and commercial problems.

Throughout his embassy in Paris in the mid-1570s, Giovanni Francesco Morosini found himself acting as a sort of unofficial envoy in England. His position allowed him to provide the *Senato* with intelligence coming from London regarding the Velutelli privilege and to keep it abreast of the complex negotiations to secure its repeal. Throughout these dealings he forcefully lobbied for the re-establishment of the London embassy, to the point that Rawdon Brown saw in him a supporter of the 'commercial party' which he saw acting in opposition to the 'papal party', which he argued had for years maintained control of the *Senato*.[25] Morosini found himself at the centre of a frantic correspondence with the *Senato* on the one hand and the small Veneto-Greek community still resident in London on the other.[26] After long conversations with the English ambassador in Paris – Dr Valentine Dale – Morosini was convinced that Velutelli's privilege would have been revoked immediately if an official representative of the Republic had been sent to England. He was not shy in advising *Senato* and *Signoria* that this should be done as a matter of urgency for both economic and political reasons.[27]

Pressure to re-establish direct links was coming also from other directions. Venetian ambassadors in France and Germany were both conveying Elizabeth's desire for a representative from Venice, and Venetian patricians travelling there reported the same. Though the nature of their trip to England was private, at the end of their journey Giovanni Faliero,

published in 1586: see ASV, *Cinque Savi alla Mercanzia*, b. 34 n.s., fasc v, cc.n.n. (7-3-1586). On Da Riviera's role see Fusaro, *Uva passa*, 25, 109–110.

[25] *CSPVe*, vol. vii, 'Preface': see www.british-history.ac.uk/report.aspx?compid= 94934 (date accessed: 16 February 2014). This internal division within the Venetian patriciate is also known as that of *vecchi* (old) vs. *giovani* (young), and is a debated issue within Venetian historiography; a short synthesis is in G. Cozzi, 'La Spagna, la Francia e la Repubblica di Venezia (1573–1598)', in G. Cozzi, M. Knapton and G. Scarabello, *La Repubblica di Venezia nell'età moderna*, 2 vols., Turin, 1986–92, vi: 60–67, 61–63; see also Bouwsma, *Venice and the Defense*; Grubb, 'When Myths Lose Power', 53–56; M. Lowry, 'The Reform of the Council of X, 1582–3: An Unsettled Problem?', *Studi veneziani*, 13 (1971): 275–310.

[26] ASV, *Senato, Dispacci, Ambasciatori, Francia*, f. 9 cc.n.n. (13-1-1575mv); (6-2-1575mv); (22-2-1575mv); (20-3-1576); (17-4-1576); (19-6-1576); (26-8-1576); (19-12-1576); and also f. 10, cc.n.n. (16-7-1578).

[27] *CSPVe*, vol. vii, n. 658, 550–551 (19-6-1576): see www.british-history.ac.uk/report.aspx? compid=95098 (date accessed: 16 February 2014); vol. vii, n. 661, 551–552 (26-8-1576): see www.british-history.ac.uk/report.aspx?compid=95100 (date accessed: 16 February 2014); vol. vii, n. 664, 552–553 (19-12-1576): see www.british-history.ac.uk/report. aspx?compid=95102 (date accessed: 16 February 2014).

Marc'Antonio and Zuanne Mocenigo (travelling with Alvise Foscari) delivered a memorandum to the *Senato* discussing diplomacy with England. Again the *Senato* vote was negative – with 131 against and only 44 positive. Three years later, the papacy weighed in as the Venetian ambassador in Rome reported back to the *Senato*.[28] A formal protest was sent by the pope through the nuncio in Venice at the end of 1578; the *Senato* was quick to rebuff the Holy See's demands, by defending its liberties in its usual style, but the vote was once again negative, and still no ambassador was sent to the queen.[29]

Elizabeth's keenness on establishing direct links with Venice was a constant of her long reign, and one cannot but have the distinct impression that her feeling was genuine, and possibly driven by some of the leading political figures of her kingdom who had connections with the Republic. During Queen Mary's reign, many high-profile English Protestant exiles had found a haven in Venice, and it has been argued that 'this exile community [. . .] was to have the greatest influence on the political complexion of the next reign' as, 'besides contributing a number of leading courtiers, the expatriates in Venice sent the largest representation by far of all the groups of refugees on the continent to the Elizabethan House of Commons'.[30] Culturally the link was equally strong, as not only was she knowledgeable of Italian culture, but, amongst the several languages she spoke, Elizabeth's Italian was apparently flawless, and throughout her reign she showed ample favour both to Italian culture and to Italian individuals at court.[31] And this was within a general English context in which, as in earlier centuries, Italian culture was well received in the upper classes, especially at court, but resented down the social ladder. This was particularly true of Venice, which represented for the English the apex of a fascination towards exoticism – made up of both 'fascination and contempt'.[32]

She also had solid realpolitik diplomatic reasons, such as her desire to combat the sense of isolation she felt due to the loosening of ties with continental Europe as a consequence of her father's break with Rome, confirmed by the shaky beginnings of her reign and the 1570

---

[28] Barozzi and Berchet eds., *Le relazioni degli stati europei*, vii–viii.
[29] ASV, *Collegio, Esposizioni principi*, reg. 4, cc.55r/v; ASV, *Senato, Deliberazioni Secreta*, reg. 80, cc.82r/v.
[30] K. R. Bartlett, 'The English Exile Community in Italy and the Political Opposition to Queen Mary I', *Albion: A Quarterly Journal Concerned with British Studies*, 13 (1981): 223–241, 224; see this also for a comprehensive bibliography on the topic.
[31] Wyatt, *The Italian Encounter with Tudor England*, 125.
[32] L. Bovilsky, *Barbarous Play: Race on the English Renaissance Stage*, Minneapolis, 2008, 108, and in general for an analysis of the ways in which the Italian identity was played on the stage see 103–133.

excommunication. It is curious therefore that during the reign of Elizabeth an important contradiction was daily played: elite English culture was intensely interested and engaged in keeping contacts with the rest of Europe, and the link with Italian culture remained especially strong, whilst – at the same time – the country was rather isolated from continental Europe.[33]

Piracy and trade

Venice had long experience of confronting piracy at sea starting in the fourteenth century, when Genoese and Catalans waged a corsairs' campaign for Mediterranean maritime hegemony.[34] The majority of these costs had been supported by Venice itself, but the Eastern Mediterranean dominions frequently contributed manpower. However, the violence at sea between the 1570s and the end of the seventeenth century, thanks first to the English and then to the Barbary corsairs, represented a true game change, which for Venice had devastating consequences. Alberto Tenenti talked of 'piracy as a mass phenomenon' in this period.[35] Since the 1560s, when Elizabeth got involved on the Protestant side in the French civil wars, in the words of Nicholas Rodger, 'the established connection between Protestantism and piracy grew stronger'.[36] In the following decades the worsening of Anglo-Spanish relations contributed to an increase in such activities, first in the Atlantic and then in the Mediterranean, and it was in the latter that these became more indiscriminate. The Ionian islands were a privileged place whence to gauge this behaviour, because of the presence of English sailors and merchants in their harbour and because their centrality made them popular victualling stops for many commercial routes.

In 1584, Antonio Veniero, in his final *Relazione* at the end of his rectorship of Zante, remarked on the growing insecurity of Levantine waters because of the deterioration of Anglo-Spanish relations and the increasing illegal behaviour of English ships and men, whom he said should be called 'corsairs and thieves rather than merchants'.[37] By 1590 the situation had

---

[33] Wyatt, *The Italian Encounter with Tudor England*, 117.

[34] A. Tenenti, 'Venezia e la pirateria nel Levante: 1300 circa–1460 circa', in A. Pertusi ed., *Venezia e il Levante fino al secolo XV*, Florence, 1973, 705–771; I. B. Katele, 'Piracy and the Venetian State: The Dilemma of Maritime Defense in the Fourteenth Century', *Speculum*, 63 (1988): 865–889.

[35] Tenenti, 'Aspetti della vita Mediterranea', 12.

[36] N. A. M. Rodger, *The Safeguard of the Sea*, vol. i: *A Naval History of Britain (660–1649)*, London, 1997, 199.

[37] ASV, *Collegio, Relazioni*, b. 87, cc.n.n. (Antonio Veniero, 1584).

worsened, and Anzolo Basadonna told the *Collegio* that 'Venetian seas and islands in the Levant are full of English ships', noting how these were becoming dominant also in Syrian and Ottoman ports. His considerations were first directed to trade, as he was worried about the English bypassing Venice and bringing English merchandise – mostly tin and kerseys – directly to the islands instead of to Venice, whence these goods should have been redistributed in the Levant. But his uppermost concern was the rise in violence and the effect this was having on Venetian and local shipping. The trade in currants had just been the beginning, he said, and now all sorts of other goods were being handled by the English, in many cases through contraband, openly flouting Venetian laws.[38] Most of these violent actions were attributed to English so-called 'privateers', a useful but somewhat confusing and anachronistic name if used for this period, as Nicholas Rodger has convincingly argued. Whatever the legal subtleties, in practice – quite apart from the crown itself – many English authorities issued letters of reprisals of dubious legality and 'English Lords Admiral were notoriously ready to turn a blind eye towards any activity from which they were entitled to ten per cent of the proceeds'.[39] Still, this kind of behaviour was clearly becoming politically damaging, and in 1590 Elizabeth issued a proclamation forbidding her subjects, under heavy penalties, to damage in any way ships or subjects belonging to 'friendly states' – amongst which special mention was made of Venice and Tuscany, both currently involved in complex legal suits in England for these very reasons.[40] Other similar proclamations followed in 1599, 1600 and 1602, all to no practical avail.[41]

Privateering might have been piracy for the neutral nations whose shipping got hit, but it was an essential element of England's very expensive domestic and foreign policies, marked by rebellions at home and by war with the wealthy Spanish empire abroad. It was a useful instrument of naval warfare because it effectively undermined an opponent's trade whilst providing a much-needed inflow of resources. The potential profits associated with it – huge in the case of Spanish silver cargoes, and usually fairly rich also in the Mediterranean – were for decades an effective enticement for the maritime community to support state policy, whilst overcoming the glaring deficiencies of the fledging English navy. Embedded into this policy was an extremely coy attitude by state

---

[38] ASV, *Collegio, Relazioni*, b. 83, cc.n.n. (Anzolo Basadonna, 1590).
[39] Rodger, *The Safeguard of the Sea*, 200.
[40] TNA, *SP* 99/1, 106r/v (3-2-1590).
[41] K. R. Andrews, 'Sir Robert Cecil and Mediterranean Plunder', *English Historical Review*, 87 (1972): 513–532, 514.

authorities, which allowed them to deny any official involvement when things got out of hand.

The fight with Spain was both military and economic, and 'plunder was a commercialized business' as much as it was a military strategy.[42] Given the growing complexity of maritime trade, especially concerning difficulties in defining the nationality of ships and cargoes – essential for selecting legitimate targets, namely Spanish goods and interests – deniability became a crucial strategy in the long undeclared Anglo-Spanish conflict. Piratical actions, with or without official endorsement, were political actions, not only against their military target – Spain – but also against England's commercial competitors – which in the Mediterranean meant Venice. That is how they were interpreted by all parties at the time.[43]

It has been estimated that in the last two decades of the sixteenth century the scale of the assault on Spanish shipping and goods in all theatres of operations was such 'that annually it brought in goods worth about ten or fifteen per cent of [England's] total imports by value'.[44] As these actions against Spain were deemed an appropriate strategy, a useful and cheap instrument of naval warfare both undermining the opponent's trade and providing profit, it is evident that a similar strategy was pursued towards Venice, which the English rightfully considered the main obstacle in their bid to penetrate the Levant. It is true that there was no official military conflict with Venice (although war with Spain was never declared either), but the advantages to England of further weakening the Republic's maritime strength could not have been lost on English merchants and on their political backers at home.[45]

The tensions between Venice and England were substantially worsened by the absence of direct diplomatic links, as negotiations were forced to laboriously unfold via alternative means, such as the diplomatic channels of the English and Venetian ambassadors in Paris. With attacks increasing – at least twelve Venetian ships were plundered by English pirates in 1603 alone[46] – Giovanni Carlo Scaramelli was sent as an envoy to London to try to sort out a situation which had become untenable. The behaviour of English privateers in the Mediterranean was truly scandalous, and there was a growing awareness of this even in English

---

[42] K. R. Andrews, *Trade, Plunder, and Settlement: Maritime Enterprise and the Genesis of the British Empire, 1480–1630*, Cambridge, 1984, 18.

[43] Andrews, 'Sir Robert Cecil'.

[44] Clay, *Economic Expansion*, ii: 135.

[45] On the connection between the profitability of trade and privateering activity, see an interesting analysis concerning the 'long' eighteenth century in H. Hillmann and C. Gathmann, 'Overseas Trade and the Decline of Privateering', *The Journal of Economic History*, 71 (2011): 730–761.

[46] Tenenti, *Piracy and the Decline of Venice*, London, 1967, 69.

governmental and court circles. The London mercantile community was wary of the loss of reputation these activities were causing them throughout Europe and in the recently opened Levant markets, and the Levant Company needed proper political support in Venice, especially an official channel which would allow more effective and efficient communication with the Republic's government. It was only after this level of pressure had built up that the 'old friendship' was, at least formally, renewed.[47]

How to defend Venetian navigation

The results of the English freely and violently roaming the Ionian Sea are particularly evident in the currant trade, which the English had quickly come to dominate. In 1589 Gerolamo Contarini, the captain of the state galleys convoy on the Ionian route, was forced to admit that the majority of currants exported out of Zante and Cephalonia belonged to Englishmen, something of a turning point.[48] The debate regarding currants became a debate on Venetian trade and foreign policy in general. Currants had become an *exemplum* which embodied the crisis of Venetian commercial navigation – 'the foundation of trade in this city' – whose dire state badly called for strong support and protection, at present lacking with extremely negative consequences.[49] Ten years from the promulgation of the *Nuova Imposta* it was possible to fully appreciate that whatever additional income it might have brought into state coffers, it had not helped to solve the underlying problems of navigation.

Francesco Malipiero, one of the *Cinque Savi*, summarised in an extensive report all these issues and produced an extremely detailed memorandum in twenty-four chapters which analysed the reasons behind the maritime crisis of the Republic, and proposed some solutions. He saw the arrival of English ships in the 1570s as the moment when all sorts of structural problems brewing in the background had come to the fore. He considered loss of control over seagoing traffic to the North of Europe as the first important mistake made by Venetians. He simply mentioned the demise of the state galleys, but he had more to say on the subsequent weakening of private shipping, the cause of which he attributed to increased English customs on currants and wine following the Velutelli licence. Malipiero concurred with the many analyses provided to the *Savi* in 1580, when all Venetian merchants questioned on the state of Anglo-Venetian trade had

---

[47] Tawney, *Business and Politics*, 14–15.
[48] Tenenti, *Piracy and the Decline*, 61.
[49] ASV, *Cinque Savi alla Mercanzia, Risposte*, reg. 140, cc.27v–29r; see also cc.31v–33r.

replied that the reason for Venetians abandoning it was the impossibility of competing from such a disadvantageous position.[50] To counteract this he suggested doubling customs for all merchandise coming into the Ionian islands and Crete from beyond the Straits, which at least would have improved fiscal income there; conversely, he suggested lowering customs for all exports from Venice itself. Malipiero also deemed it absolutely necessary to provide more generous state loans for local ship-building, both to curb the trend of purchasing ships abroad and to provide jobs for local shipbuilders. Amongst his other proposals was the halving of the *Nuova Imposta* in Venice (where it had also started to be levied in 1598) and doubling it in the Ionian islands, a four-fold increase in the cost of anchorage for foreigners in Zante and Cephalonia to further discourage foreign shipping there, and the establishment of a strict procedure for checking the cargo of foreign ships in these harbours. Most crucially, and evidence that the English role in intra-Mediterranean trade was already deemed dangerous, he was keen for the *Senato* to legislate that all English ships loading in Venice should be forced to take the entirety of their cargo only to destinations beyond the Straits.[51]

Thanks to the 'currant connection', the violence unleashed by English pirates was a real threat to Venetian navigation in Levantine waters, and the most obvious solution was to strengthen the commercial fleet. There was a total agreement on this; the issue became how to go about it. Over the sixteenth century the most common type of Venetian ship for short-range navigation – in the Adriatic and down to the upper Ionian Sea – had become the *marciliana*. Small, manoeuvrable and with a small crew, it was cheap but also relatively fragile and most certainly not defensible. Many suggested that *bertoni* and galleons should instead be used, vessels with a larger crew and cargo capability which made them far more defensible.[52] *Bertoni* were indeed already used, but we have seen how they were purchased abroad and therefore not really helping to counteract the shipbuilding crisis; if anything, buying them abroad contributed to the local industry's loss of business and skills. Other strategies were also tried. In 1600 Domenico Valaresso – formerly *Savio alla mercanzia* – proposed

---

[50] Further details (also quantitative) on the disparities in customs in England can be found in Fusaro, *Uva passa*, 39–44.

[51] ASV, *Cinque Savi alla Mercanzia, Risposte*, reg. 140, cc.91r–96r. The idea of establishing compulsory spot-searches on foreign vessels is further developed in ASV, *Cinque Savi alla Mercanzia, Risposte*, reg. 141, cc.2r–8r. On the advantages of buying or loaning foreign vessels see F. Braudel, P. Jeannin, J. Meuvret and R. Romano, 'Le déclin de Venise au XVIIe siècle', in *Aspetti e cause della decadenza economica*, 23–86.

[52] Details on the cost or arming a galleon for these purposes are in ASV, *Cinque Savi alla Mercanzia, Risposte*, reg. 136, cc.47v–48v (12-2-1574mv).

increasing state financial incentives to build galleons in Candia. This policy had started in 1576 in the aftermath of the loss of Cyprus; it was aimed both at strengthening local commercial navigation, in this way pleasing Cretan merchants, and at creating a sort of naval quick response unit in the Eastern Mediterranean which would help local defence in case of an Ottoman attack.[53] In 1602 financial incentives were indeed raised, but the positive results hoped for did not materialise.[54] The problem remained the same: Venetian shipping in the Levant was carried either on foreign-built ships, sometimes also with foreign crews, or on vessels which were small, not defensible and frequently overloaded and over-insured, with all the predictable results of shipwrecks and fraud. The *Rettore* of Zante, Piero Bondumier, could rant against the English – 'that foul nation of the English, who, whenever it is profitable, spare neither friend nor foe' – and recount in horror the tale of the ship *Veniera*, which had been robbed twice in a few days. Trying to mount a local defence force, he searched high and low for captains and ships to supplement the naval contingent in the area, all to no avail. Bondumier concluded by commenting that there was little he could do, given that the strength of the English vessels, the security that travelling on them provided as they were immune from attacks, had quickly made them the favourite carriers for all travellers, notwithstanding the fact that they charged passengers twice the going rate and treated them badly to boot.[55] It might just be a coincidence, but it is worth noting that the previous month the Venetian *Bailo* himself had used a Genoese ship (crewed by Englishmen) for the Constantinople–Zante leg of his journey back home.[56]

The issue of how to make navigation safer continued to be a principal concern at all levels of the Republic's government and administration, and all extant documentation discussed the role played by the English presence and its connection with the currant trade. Problems of this kind

[53] ASV, *Cinque Savi alla Mercanzia, Risposte*, reg. 140, cc.101r–103r. *Bertoni* usually had a burden of between 500 and 1,000 tons, against the 70/80 of *marciliane*, and an average crew of 60: see C. A. Levi, *Navi venete da codici marini e dipinti*, Venice, 1983 (1892), 180. Lane describes also rather larger *marciliane*, of up to 240 tons, in F. C. Lane, *Venetian Ships and Shipbuilders in the Renaissance*, Baltimore, 1934, 53.

[54] On the complex reasons for the effective failures of the Candia galleons see Baroutsos, 'Sovention per fabricar galeoni'; and M. Costantini, *Una repubblica nata sul mare: navigazione e commercio a Venezia*, Venice, 2006, 41–64.

[55] ASV, *SDR*, Zante, b. 1, cc.n.n. Piero Bondumier (15-1-1602mv); the story of the *Veniera* is also in Tenenti, *Piracy and the Decline*, 68.

[56] ASV, *SDR*, Zante, b. 1, cc.n.n. Piero Bondumier (23-12-1602). *Bailo* is the term used for the Venetian ambassador to the Porte.

did not cease with the Treaty of London, which ended the Anglo-Spanish conflict in 1604. Three years later, in 1607, the *Capitano Generale da Mar*, Zuanne Bembo, wrote a detailed memorandum of navigation in the Levant, again aiming at improving its safety.[57] He advised that trips be short and preferably taken during summer, and to sail in convoy if possible, ideally under an armed escort.[58] A week before, Filippo Pasqualigo, *Provveditore Generale da Mar*, Agustino da Canal and Piero Bondumier, *Provveditor dell'Armata*, had produced another memorandum on the same issues. Their suggestions were slightly different, as they deemed galleons to be a suitable escort only for very valuable cargoes, and also not very useful against pirates as they were not agile enough to manoeuvre out of trouble. They were also sceptical about the strategy of establishing consistent controls over dubious ships in wintertime, deeming it too uncomfortable for crews – both of sailing vessels and of galleys. However, it was in the winter months that the currant trade was at its height, and therefore that would have been the appropriate time for patrols.[59] The issue seemed unsolvable. Still, the needs of trade were pressing: just a month earlier, the *Cinque Savi* had confirmed their opposition to *marciliane* travelling beyond Zante whilst at the same time giving a positive response to a request to employ a *marciliana* to sail to Crete – 'due to the scarcity of other vessels'.[60] The ambitions of state policy were conflicting badly with the situation on the ground – and on the sea.

In the Ionian islands

The islands – due to their strategic position – had always had their fair share of corsairs and pirates, and the population had frequently petitioned Venice for protection.[61] In the years between the end of the sixteenth and the early seventeenth centuries the situation was particularly difficult as the Adriatic was under the influence of the infamous Uskoks – corsairs strategically positioned on the Venetian–Habsburg–Ottoman border – who, being under the protection of the Habsburgs, happily plundered the Venetian fleet and many others. Venice waged a proper war on them

---

[57] The *Capitano Generale da Mar* was elected only in wartime; the highest naval position during peacetime was the *Provveditore Generale da Mar*: he remained in service for three years and was also known as the *Provveditore Generale in Levante*: see M. Nani Mocenigo, *Storia della marina veneta da Lepanto alla caduta della Repubblica*, Rome, 1935, 19–22.

[58] ASV, *Materie Miste Notabili*, f. 67, cc.n.n., (3-9-1607). He also appears to have been *Procuratore di San Marco*.

[59] ASV, *Materie Miste Notabili*, f. 67, c.3v (25-8-1607).

[60] ASV, *Cinque Savi alla Mercanzia, Risposte*, reg. 142, cc.21r–22r (28-7-1607) and c.22v (2-8-1607).

[61] See for example: ASV, *Compilazioni leggi*, Zante, b. 378, cc.36r–42r (1515).

and managed to bring them under control by the late 1610s, helped by the neighbouring populations who were frequent victims of their attacks.[62]

English piracy, though, was rather different, and it quickly became another area in which the Anglo-Greek alliance prospered; the English needed help in getting rid of ill-gotten goods, and piracy frequently merged with contraband, where both groups were extremely active. 'Plundering' is by its very nature a collective enterprise and needs solidarity between pirates and local coastal populations in order to survive.[63] The particular geography of the Ionian islands, with a rugged coast full of convenient moorings and sparse population, made them a favourite haven for ships engaged in illegal activities and looking for a quiet stopover. This was a serious problem in fighting contraband. In 1620 the *Rettore* of Zante described how the length and articulation of the coastline made it really difficult for authorities to effectively patrol it.[64] The coastline of Cephalonia also provided plenty of opportunities for safe morrings away from the prying eyes of authorities, as can be appreciated in Figure 1.

Thus for the population of the Ionian islands English piracy became an additional business opportunity. The English only attacked ships and, unlike traditional corsairs such as the Uskoks and the North Africans, were not interested in plundering coastal villages. On the contrary, they needed the support of the local population. Water, victualling, information and manpower were all vital necessities and were all easily obtainable through the local inhabitants. But above all, coastal people provided pirates with a market to dispose of their booty, or at least a place to find contacts to help sell it.[65] Maffio Michiel, *Rettore* of Zante at the height of English piracy in the Mediterranean (1602–1604), fully appreciated all these issues and lamented the fact that whilst Ottoman authorities complained about English pirates, they also gained from the trade and protected pirate vessels in their harbours, leaving the Venetians to face the problem almost alone.[66] In truth, by 1603 Ottoman authorities were helping Venetians to reclaim their looted ships and cargoes when these appeared in their own harbours,

---

[62] M. Knapton, 'Tra Dominante e Dominio (1517–1630)', in G. Cozzi, M. Knapton and G. Scarabello, *La Repubblica di Venezia nell'età moderna*, 2 vols., Turin, 1986–92, ii: 203–325, 331; Lane, *Venice: A Maritime Republic*, 398–400.

[63] Bracewell, *The Uskoks of Senj*, 175–177.

[64] ASV, *SDR*, Zante, b. 7, cc.n.n. (1-10-1620).

[65] On this and on the worries of the Venetian *Provveditore all'Armata* about connivances between pirates in populations in all the *Dominio da Mar*, but particularly in Crete, see Knapton, 'Tra Dominante e Dominio', 229.

[66] ASV, *SDR*, Zante, b. 1, cc.n.n. (9-6-1603).

Figure 1. The island of Cephalonia (© Archivio di Stato di Venezia)

and the French ambassador at the Porte was also officially supporting Venetian complaints on this topic.[67]

The end of the war with Spain was not the end of English piracy in the Mediterranean. Heavily armed and unpredictable, these English ships remained a concern for the Venetian authorities. The *Inquisitore e Commissario in Levante*, Antonio Civran, breathed a loud sigh of relief when an English pirate fleet left the harbour of Zante in June 1628:

> The night between Tuesday 6th and Wednesday 7th the corsairing English *bertoni*, already notified to Your Serenity, left the harbour of Zante sailing for the Levant, although it is unknown where exactly they are heading. I must confess that I am delighted at their departure, especially for the public's interests.[68]

Zante and Cephalonia indeed provided the perfect harbours to find shelter, hide from enemies and dispose of merchandise, and they also represented the ideal place to find buyers. The only complete surviving trial transcript about piracy in the islands dates from 1589, and it is extremely revealing about the relationship between trade and plunder. The case started with the Venetian authorities intercepting an intriguing

[67] *CSPVe*, vol. x (1603–1607), *passim*.
[68] ASV, *PTM*, b. 863bis (1-6-1628 and 11-6-1628).

letter directed to Thomas Norden, an English merchant resident in the *Marina* of Zante. The letter was duly translated:

Mr. Norden, I captured the ship: but the birds have flown. If You want to buy it at cost, I shall sell it to You at cost, but I beg you to write to me in Patras whilst I have it, as here there is neither money nor goods, and I regret taking the ship as I am not profiting from her. I look forward to hear from you soon, in haste I remain your good friend.[69]

The letter was written by the captain of an English ship, the same ship Norden had recently welcomed full of grain and had reloaded with currants in the name of his Levant Company's principals, Thomas Cordell and Co. of London. When the letter was shown to him, Norden did not lose his composure, replying that the captain could write whatever he wanted, and he denied any knowledge of the letter's meaning. 'I have nothing to do with the ship, apart from receiving the cargo sent to me, and loading it up following the instructions I have been given'.[70] The second person to be interrogated was a young mariner – Gioan Stron – who was waiting for a passage home, Stron was one of the exceedingly few Englishman in the area who did not speak Italian, and his interpreter was Thomas Trent, another English merchant resident in Zante. After giving details of the cargo brought by the English ship (mostly grain, but also tin, lead and kerseys), Stron reported that in the days before the ship's departure, her master had the following exchange with the master of a Neapolitan ship, also present in the harbour of Zante:

He answered: the master of the Neapolitan ship discoursed with the master of the English ship and lamented that he had understood the English wanted to capture his ship. He said that the Neapolitans were good for fighting the English on land, sword to sword: but at sea would succumb, as they had no artillery. Asked what the English master replied, he answered that they were in the land of the Venetians and could not do these things.[71]

The story was confirmed by several witnesses, and the *Rettore* decided to arrest Norden and Stron and send two other English merchants to speak with the shipmaster, anchored fifteen miles away near Castel Tornese. The merchants recounted how the master, informed of these events, told them

that having taken the ship around three leagues outside the harbour, on her he found nothing of value, neither money nor things, and then he added that those detained [Norden and Stron] were in no way culpable, as what he had done he did

---

[69] ASV, *Quarantia Criminale*, b. 103, fasc. 71, c.4r.
[70] ASV, *Quarantia Criminale*, b. 103, fasc. 71, c.9v.
[71] ASV, *Quarantia Criminale*, b. 103, fasc. 71, cc.n.n.

on his own, because of the many insults which he [and his crew] had received from the Spaniards whilst in harbour, challenging them to fight every day and exposing their privy parts to shame them, shouting that our Queen is a public Whore ...[72]

He then handed over the captured ship to the Venetian authorities, and she was brought into the harbour of Zante. What can we say? The queen had been insulted and there was a state of war between the two countries... Still, this ship was not sailing for England with official letter-patents to authorise military action against enemy vessels. These ambiguities were the stuff of everyday life.

With such a complicit relationship between English piracy and trade in the Mediterranean, it is not surprising that the standard line of defence adopted by English merchants was to deny all involvement, even in the face of overwhelming evidence.[73] Alerted to some shifty dealings in the harbour in March 1603, Maffio Michiel summoned Ruberto Brachia, captain of the *bertone Thomaso Guelmo Buona Speranza*, who, on his way from Livorno to Chios, had captured near the Sicilian coast a French vessel loaded with Sicilian wheat. Summoned to justify his actions in front of the *Rettore*, Brachia declared:

As per instructions of our Queen, we took the wheat belonging to the Spaniards, who are our enemies, as if it was our own, we then brought it here and sold it, and then we let the vessel go after paying freight to the master, as [the French] are our friends.

His deposition was fully underwritten by the French captain, who added that not only had the English paid full freight, but they had treated him and the crew very well, so much so that he had no intention of denouncing them.[74]

It is difficult to separate contraband and piracy, and from the Venetian perspective the two phenomena were tightly interlinked. Especially in the waters around the Ionian islands, where currants contraband was rife, especially between 1602 and 1607, when the Venetian government forbade their export to any other destination but Venice,[75] it is clear that ships with something to hide – such as contraband

---

[72] ASV, *Quarantia Criminale*, b. 103, fasc. 71, cc.n.n.

[73] On the effect of English piracy on Zante and Cephalonia see Fusaro, *Uva passa*, 65–78 and *passim*.

[74] ASV, *SDR*, Zante, b. 1, cc.n.n., Maffio Michiel (29-3-1603).

[75] The *parte* instituting this is in ASV, *Senato, Mar*, reg. 62, cc.79v–80r. On the effect of this legislation, especially concerning the rise of contraband which ultimately led to its repeal, see Fusaro, *Uva passa*, 117–123.

currants – were more likely to act aggressively, therefore ending up being labelled as 'pirates'.

A typical example of this involved the ship *Livriera*. Whilst she was in the harbour, the *Rettore* heard news that she carried currants, loaded in violation of the prohibition of their freighting on the islands. He ordered an inspection whilst the captain was not on board, and his suspicions were proven true. Immediately the *Rettore*'s men were violently thrown off the ship, which then sailed out of the harbour – but still in sight of the town – where she remained for six days displaying the 'war flag'.[76]

This trick of displaying the 'war flag' seemed to be a favourite one, which continued well into the seventeenth century. In January 1631 Nicolò Erizzo, *Rettore* of Cephalonia, having received a written denunciation that Captain William Drevir was hiding four hundred barrels of smuggled olive oil – whose export was downright forbidden – aboard the *Pietro Bonaventura* alongside some smuggled currants, narrated the events which followed:

The captain arrived with his small boat at the moorings of the *Sanità* where, after many questions, having been asked to show the ship's bill of lading and warned that customs officers would inspect the ship, he immediately sheered off, and in spite of the threats and calls of the officers, he quickly reached ship. Once there, impudently and without any respect for the fact that he was in a harbour belonging to Your Serenity, which, albeit an open space, should always be respected and revered, he hoisted the war flag, threatening that place and also defying the armed boats in the canal . . .[77]

In this case, the smuggling had been discovered but nothing could be done about it because the ship immediately left harbour. The merchants on land always had some ready excuse to disassociate themselves from such events. And in such a situation, where the ship had arrived already laden with smuggled cargo, there was little that could be done to prove that the local resident merchants were directly involved. On other occasions, there were no problems during the inspections but, after having left the harbour, ships remained in the area, and Greek merchants would transfer the currants from the warehouses at the *Marina* to the ship, usually under the cover of night.[78] In these cases there was again little

---

[76] ASV, *SDR*, Zante, b. 2, cc.n.n. (6-3-1604). The Venetian ambassador in London presented the case in a memorandum and asked for severe punishment of such incidents: see PRO, *SP* 99, 2 cc.214r/v. Intimidating techniques to discourage inspections also happened in Venice, albeit on a more infrequent basis: see ASV, *Cinque Savi alla Mercanzia, Risposte*, reg. 142, cc.61r–62r.

[77] ASV, *SDR*, Cefalonia, b. 5, cc.n.n. (20-1-1631mv). It appears from this dispatch that Drevir had already been banned from Livorno for similar behaviour.

[78] ASV, *SDR*, Zante, b. 2, cc.n.n. (10-3-1604).

that could be done, especially as legislation on these kinds of international incidents was still in the making, and there were large areas of jurisdictional ambiguity. A peculiar incident of this kind in 1609 involved the ship *Coastley* (also known as *Corsaletta*), property of the foremost Levant company merchant Thomas Cordell. She was actually caught at sea by the Venetians, an extremely rare event, and smuggled cargo was discovered on board. The final argument used by the English in their defence memorandum is extremely interesting:

> It is undoubtedly clear that the currants were brought on board by Zantiot Greeks with their own boats, and were sold to our men on board, and although it was unlawful for the Greeks to sell these [currants], nevertheless they were fairly bought by us; therefore you [the Venetians] need to carry out the law against the Greeks, who are your own subjects, and not against us foreigners, who are not forbidden by your laws to buy this merchandise. Third, and most important, the ship was not taken in the harbour of Zante, but rather in Ottoman waters, on her way to England, and this is not allowed, as all jurists agree; and as for the cargo being contraband, under Civil Law and customary law, and also in Venetian lands, if one does not pay customs and is not caught within the harbour, one cannot be touched.

Unfailing logic; after long negotiations the Venetians admitted the ship had been unjustly seized and paid damages.[79]

We have seen how Maffio Michiel, *Rettore* of Zante during the worst years of English attacks, dedicated his best energies and resources to fighting the spread of piracy. Fully aware of the fuzzy borders between merchants and pirates, after the umpteenth attack at the beginning of 1604 – this time against a Greek ship full of grain, belonging to the Seguro family – he summoned all the principal English merchants resident in town to complain about the situation. Their response was marvellously in line with that of Elizabeth. They answered, he reported, that 'these are corsairs, crooks, banned in disgrace by our queen and the whole of the nation, we have nothing to do with them, nor it is in our power to compensate for the damages they inflict [on the Venetians]'. Michiel retorted that if these pirates truly were banned by their Queen, it was their duty as loyal subjects to capture them with their own ships and make sure they were sent to England to receive justice. Vague protestations followed, so to force their hand he locked the merchants overnight in the castle's prison and released them the following day after a bond of 4,000 *cechini* had been

---

[79] TNA, *SP* 99/5, 320r/v (no date; most probably September 1609); the developments can be followed in cc.336r–337r, 342r; TNA, *SP* 99/6, 61r–64v. The long affair was finally solved only in October 1613; the issue can be followed in some detail in *CSPVe*, vols. xi–xiii, *passim*.

deposited. In this case, especially considering the excellent contacts between English merchants and the Seguro family, it might really have been a case in which the Englishmen were not involved, and Michiel's subsequent enquiries came to nothing.[80] His next move was to prohibit any English vessel from leaving the harbour without posting a bond that the ship would not have attacked any Venetian ships. And he actually managed to implement this policy with commendable continuity, securing a substantial drop in the number of attacks. This bond was asked of everyone, even the well-known captain Gugliemo Brann, of the *Salamandra*, who regularly traded wheat between the Archipelago, the Ionian islands and the Morea. Gasparo Rols, one of the English merchants based in Zante, without any difficulty came up with the 10,000 ducats required, which gives a clear idea of the kind of ready cash available to English merchants.[81]

Maffio Michiel in his final *Relazione* spared no criticism for the 1602 decision to allow currant exports only through Venice, which in his analysis just increased 'robberies and depredations'. He suggested that armed, regular and frequent naval patrols between the Ionian islands and Crete were the only way to ensure the safety of navigation. He also strongly advised compulsory inspections of English cargoes before their departure.[82] Last but not least, he elaborated on the proposal of his predecessor Francesco Loredan to cease new buildings in the harbour of Zante, which he said would have been impossible to control even with one hundred men. The towns of Argostoli and Zante were becoming permanent building sites, with prime value being given to the *Marina*, the area closest to the sea (Figure 2). All sorts of private homes and warehouses were going up, most with direct sea access for easier smuggling. The area closest to the sea became so crowded with construction that the roads were impassable for the *Rettore*'s (small) cavalry troops. This was something that could have created serious problems in case of

---

[80] ASV, *SDR*, Zante, b. 1, cc.n.n. (22–2-1603mv).
[81] ASV, *SDR*, Zante, b. 1, cc.n.n., Maffio Michiel (23-5-1603); Gasparo Rol guaranteed for Captain Guglielmo Brann of the *Salamandra*; Rizzardon Person for Captain Thomas Gronson of the *Livriera*; Thomaso Fernelle for Capitan Joane Pontes of the *Manto*; Gugliemo Guerdiner for Capitan Guglielmo Abrnal of the galleon *Constantia*, in ASV, *SDR*, Zante, b. 1, cc.n.n. (20 and 23-5-1603). The idea of asking all English vessels to provide a bond that they would not attack Venetian shipping had been aired already in 1600 (ASV, *Cinque Savi alla Mercanzia, Risposte*, reg. 140, cc.98r–101r). In 1608, well after the signing of peace with Spain, English vessels still had to pay 1,000 ducats bond not to attack Venetian ships: see ASV, *Cinque Savi alla Mercanzia, Risposte*, reg. 142, cc.61r–62r (20-3-1608).
[82] ASV, *Collegio, Relazioni*, b. 87, cc.n.n., Maffio Michiel (25-5-1605).

Figure 2. The *Marina* of Zante (© Archivio di Stato di Venezia)

direct attack, and it also rendered the area completely impossible to patrol by the *Rettore*'s officers trying to deter illegal practices. The situation was absolutely ideal for smuggling.[83]

Maffio Michiel paid personally for his fight against piracy. He became notorious amongst Englishmen as the 'hanging governor', having caught and executed some English pirates. On the eve of his return to Venice he loaded his goods on the *bertone Moresina*, a safe and well-armed ship with a reputation for safety and, incidentally, an English captain. The ship was ambushed by pirates just outside Zante, and Michiel's goods were viciously plundered and vandalised, with testimonies reporting how the pirate crew clearly greatly relished it, falling on them 'like mad dogs though they left the other merchandize of value alone', smashing with glee his china and majolica, and killing (which Michiel thought the greatest proof of their cruelty) the doves the ladies of his family were sending to Venice. The English ambassador in Venice Sir Henry Wotton, apologised profusely for the behaviour of the pirates, which the sources described as 'all young and beardless, and most of them English'.[84]

Cephalonia was not faring much better; indeed, the problems caused by English pirates were particularly evident in its wide and most safe harbour of Argostoli, where ships could find ample shelter (Figure 3) and which, as Nicolò Bragadin lamented in the fateful year 1603,

has become a shelter for all vessels of evil doers, especially Englishmen who, once they have their booty, come here to share the spoils and probably (although this is impossible to know for sure) sell them.

When he sent his guards to the harbour, they were shot at. The impudence of the English was such, he said, that

not only when there are seven, eight or ten vessels, as it has happened many times, but even when there only two of them, they become masters of the harbour, and they even dare to tow other vessels outside the harbour then to rob them, so no one can be safe. To this needs to be added the support they get from the local population, as they have no self-control and decency and do business with all these vessels in spite of the law.[85]

---

[83] On unlawful buildings and the problems this created for the islands' *Reggimenti*, see Fusaro, *Uva passa*, 61–65.

[84] L. Pearsall Smith, *The Life and Letters of Sir Henry Wotton*, 2 vols, Oxford, 1907, i: 322; *CSPVe*, vol. x, nn. 302 and 303, 196–197: see www.british-history.ac.uk/report.aspx?compid=95620 (date accessed: 16 February 2014); vol. x, nn. 336 and 339, 216: see www.british-history.ac.uk/report.aspx?compid=95622 (date accessed: 16 February 2014).

[85] ASV, *Collegio, Relazioni*, b. 83, cc.n.n. Nicolò Bragadin (20-5-1603).

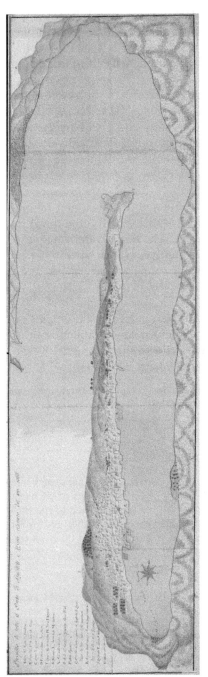

Figure 3. The bay of Argostoli in Cephalonia (© Archivio di Stato di Venezia)

The loss of control of sea lanes was extending onto land, and it was becoming difficult for Venetian authorities to govern the harbour of one of their main colonies. We shall have plenty of occasions to see what this meant for Venice in the following decades.

A difficult restart

Many reasons lay behind the Venetian commercial fleet halving in size between 1560 and 1600.[86] Defence was one of the most relevant. From the middle of the sixteenth century, Venice had implemented stringent policies to preserve the Republic's forests for the naval needs of the *Arsenale* (the state-owned shipbuilding factory), which ended up penalising private shipyards building commercial vessels. The financial and logistic effort of maintaining a permanent fleet to confront the Ottoman threat was clearly damaging commercial navigation.[87] Also connected with defence was English violence towards Venetian shipping, which inflicted great damage on an already shrinking fleet. Notwithstanding official protestations, it is difficult not to see these activities as aiming to hit the Republic's commercial interests. Alberto Tenenti linked English piratical actions to the steep rise in insurance costs for Venetian shipping, something which directly harmed trade by increasing transaction costs, but which also had a negative effect on the local insurance market.[88] In the second half of the sixteenth century insurances had became a privileged sector for private investment, with the *Cinque Savi* tightly regulating it to avoid frauds, given the increasingly frequent habit of insuring cargoes for sums superior to their real value.[89] The rising level of violence in the last quarter of the century afforded many opportunities for speculation and fraud and made these a desirable form of aggressive investment.

When secretary Scaramelli met Elizabeth and formally presented the Venetian complaints about English piracy at sea, the old and fragile queen – she would die a few weeks afterwards – swiftly retorted: 'I do hope, Mr Secretary, that you do not imagine my kingdoms so void of

---

[86] Sella, 'Crisis and Transformation', 92.

[87] M. Knapton, 'Lo stato veneziano fra la battaglia di Lepanto e la guerra di Candia', in *Venezia e la difesa del Levante da Lepanto a Candia (1570–1670)*, Venice, 1986, 233–241; L. Pezzolo, *L'oro dello stato: società, finanza e fisco nella Repubblica veneta del secondo '500*, Venice, 1990, 12; on the policies of forestry conservation enacted by the Republic see K. Appuhn, *A Forest on the Sea: Environmental Expertise in Renaissance Venice*, Baltimore, 2009.

[88] Tenenti, *Piracy and the Decline*, 100–103.

[89] Tucci, *Mercanti, navi e monete*, 145–160, 147–148.

people not to contain also some wicked individuals disregarding the laws and my will?'[90] The policy of 'deniability' was still going strong.

Whilst there is still some historiographical debate concerning the foreign policy change that accompanied the change of dynasty from the Tudors to the Stuarts, there is also growing agreement that peace with Spain had been a hot topic of discussion in political circles during Elizabeth's last decade in power. Debate had grown stronger especially after 1598, when England was invited to take part in the negotiations that preceded the Peace of Vervins between Spain and France. Seen in this light it can be argued that the Treaty of London was really the work of Cecil and his team and, in a sense, the last act of Elizabethan foreign policy.[91] Conversely, the shift in the crown's attitude towards privateering and piracy between the reigns of Elizabeth and James was sudden, at least formally, and it can be followed through the literature produced at that time.[92] Peace with Spain took away any legal justification for privateering, but retreating from a violent and financially rewarding activity proved less feasible than anticipated: privateering – in practice state-sanctioned piracy – had been easy to unleash and proved difficult to rein in. Therefore it is not surprising that whilst many moved back from piracy to lawful trading, many others just moved on from state-sponsored privateering under Elizabeth to straight piracy under James. The new king quickly issued a proclamation declaring all letters of marque issued by Elizabeth null and void, but this proved hardly effective, something indirectly proven by the fact that in the first decade of his reign proclamations against piracy in English waters or by Englishmen anywhere were issued almost annually.[93] Local authorities, happy in the past to support such activities, were indeed engaged in containing the actions of former privateers turned pirates on the British coast, but abroad it was a different matter.[94]

The attribution of such acts to deceitful and outcast subjects remained a common answer under her successor. When in 1603 the

[90] Contarini's *Historiae*, ii, book vii, c. 373, in Cozzi, *Il Doge Nicolò Contarini*, 375.
[91] P. Croft, 'Rex Pacificus, Robert Cecil, and the 1604 Peace with Spain', in G. Burgess, R. Wymer and J. Lawrences eds., *The Accession of James I: Historical and Cultural Consequences*, Basingstoke, 2006, 140–154, 151; A. Gajda, 'Debating War and Peace in Late Elizabethan England', *Historical Journal*, 52 (2009): 851–878; see also *DNB*, s.v. 'Robert Cecil'.
[92] See C. Jowitt, 'Piracy and Politics in Heywood and Rowley's *Fortune by Land and Sea* (1607–9)', *Renaissance Studies*, 16 (2002): 217–233.
[93] For a sample of such proclamations see J. F. Larkin and P. L. Hughes eds., *Stuart Royal Proclamations*, 2 vols, Oxford, 1973, i: 15, 28, 46, 50, 53, 93, 97.
[94] Rodger, *The Safeguard of the Sea*, 349.

Venetian ambassador complained that the Lord High Admiral was abetting piracy, James exclaimed 'By God I'll hang the pirates with my own hands, and my Lord Admiral as well'.[95] The same defence line was also employed by English merchants when confronted with the violent activities of their countrymen, as happened in Tuscany in 1601, when the notorious Richard Gifford was finally arrested and the local English merchants – whether affiliated with the Levant Company or not – all agreed to condemn his actions as nefarious for the peaceful running of their business.[96] Gifford's expedition had been partially financed by Cecil and other powerful men at court, something which – albeit supposed to remain secret – was probably behind his quick release from prison in Livorno.[97] It is indeed difficult to shake the impression that the attribution of piratical acts to criminal individuals was nothing more than a rhetorical move to cover what had become a national embarrassment. How else can we explain Cecil's own coyness towards his financial involvement in fitting out such expeditions, if not with the uncomfortable truth that the direct involvement of a statesman in what were formally fully legal ventures had also to be squared with the looseness of the behaviour of its protagonists at sea?[98] Although some of these pirates had a chequered history with justice, especially after peace with Spain made their activities truly illegal,[99] the scale of these activities, the calibre of their backers in England, and the general infamous reputation they gained allow one to think that these excuses were just a cover-up.

In Levantine waters, the English pirates' greatest allies were Ottoman provincial authorities, whose harbours and infrastructures they took advantage of in their expeditions. Politically this made perfect sense, as England and the Ottoman empire had a common enemy in Spain, and economically it allowed them some excellent extra income.[100] Also particularly active in providing support were the Barbary states – no great friends of Venice themselves – and in this sense Gifford's decision to take one of his prizes to Tunis was typical of such expeditions.[101] The influx of unreformed English privateers into the North African Barbary States had a

[95] Jowitt, 'Piracy and Politics', 218–219.
[96] Pagano De Divitiis, *English Merchants*, 29. Concerns about 'pirates', and the negative effect they could have on legitimate trade, were still present in the early 1620s: see the Court Books of the Levant Company, in TNA, *SP* 105/148, 22v–25r and *passim*.
[97] Andrews, 'Sir Robert Cecil', 519–523.
[98] Andrews, 'Sir Robert Cecil', 513: Cecil writing in January 1603 to Sir Walter Raleigh.
[99] Tenenti, 'Aspetti della vita Mediterranea', 4.
[100] Tenenti, *Piracy and the Decline*, 73–74.
[101] Andrews, 'Sir Robert Cecil', 591; see also Tenenti, *Piracy and the Decline*, 62.

devastating effect in increasing their military and naval prowess, and Venice was – again – the hardest hit. The capture of the *Reniera e Soderina* in 1607, with her extremely valuable cargo conservatively estimated at £100,000, was just the most sensational of their exploits, but many similar cases further damaged Venetian commercial navigation, and drove insurance costs even higher.[102]

The connection between 'England' and 'piracy' remained strong in the Mediterranean, and would colour the perception of Englishmen – not just seamen – for a long time. In response to a letter from Antonio Possevino in 1605, lamenting the widespread ill behaviour of English sailors – this time concerning the abuse of wine and violence – Sir Henry Wotton, the English ambassador in Venice, wrote that he wished it would not damage the relationship between the two countries:

I am rather surprised to see in your letter (as you are a man of maturity and erudition) that you so quickly connect these incidents with the person of the Most Serene Majesty of the King of Great Britain, as if the holy person of the Prince should be charged with each action or vain word of each of their subjects.[103]

In truth, such thoughts were widely shared in Italy and the Mediterranean, and contemporary foreigners shared the perspective that that the 'intimate connection between Protestantism, patriotism and plunder [had] become a distinctive and formative part of the English national myth'.[104]

[102] Tenenti, *Piracy and the Decline*, 77–78, 61–85.
[103] TNA, *SP* 99/2, 243r (1-3-1605).
[104] N. A. M. Rodger, 'Queen Elizabeth and the Myth of Sea-Power in English History', *Transactions of the Royal Historical Society*, 14 (2004): 153–174, 156.

6   Diplomacy, trade and religion

Notwithstanding universal agreement of how intertwined politics and trade were in Anglo-Venetian relations, no one has hitherto investigated their direct economic relation, as scholars preferred instead to focus on their indirect interactions, especially on their competition regarding their share of the Ottoman textile market.[1]

In the eyes of the English government, the Republic of Venice played a double role: it was a potential ally and, at the same time, it was a very privileged observatory from which to keep a close watch on political and religious developments in Italy.[2] This helps to explain why scholars have studied the relationship between the English ambassadors in Venice – and their entourage – and various sectors of the Venetian ruling class. Attention has been drawn to the attitude of the English with regard to the Interdict crisis of 1606–1607 and the conflict between Venice and the Papal Curia.[3] The correspondence between Paolo Sarpi and Fulgenzio Micanzio (the Republic's legal and theological advisors at the time) and their English correspondents, such as Dudley Carleton (English ambassador in Venice), William Bedell (Carleton's chaplain) and Lord William Cavendish, has been meticulously examined, from both a political and religious perspective.[4] But there has been no comparable effort towards

---

[1] Brulez, 'Les routes commerciales d'Angleterre'; Davis, 'Influences de l'Angleterre'; Davis, 'England and the Mediterranean'; Jeannin, 'The Sea-Borne and the Overland'; Rapp, 'The Unmaking of the Mediterranean'; Sella, *Commerci e industrie a Venezia*, 'Crisis and Transformation' and 'The Rise and Fall'; Tenenti, *Piracy and the Decline*; B. Tenenti, 'Venezia ed il commercio raguseo delle carisee (1550c.–1620c.)', *Studi Veneziani*, 17–18 (1975–76): 235–247.

[2] Pearsall-Smith, *The Life and Letters*, i: 65, 69.

[3] E. De Mas, *Sovranità politica e unità cristiana nel Seicento anglo-veneto*, Ravenna, 1975 and his *L'attesa del secolo aureo, 1603–1625*, Florence, 1982.

[4] P. Sarpi, *Opere*, G. and L. Cozzi eds., Milan and Naples, 1969; see especially the introductory notes to chapters 2, 3 and 4, at 113–128, 221–246, 635–642; G. Cozzi, *Paolo Sarpi tra Venezia e l'Europa*, Turin, 1979; Cozzi, 'Fra Paolo Sarpi, l'anglicanesimo e la "Historia del Concilio Tridentino"', *Rivista Storica Italiana*, 68 (1956): 559–593; F. A. Yates, 'Paolo Sarpi's "History of the Council of Trent"', *The Journal of the Warburg and Courtauld Institutes*, 7 (1944): 123–142; V. Gabrieli, 'Bacone, la Riforma e Roma nella versione hobbesiana di un carteggio di Fulgenzio Micanzio', *English*

investigating the direct commercial links between the two countries, and the English mercantile community based between Venice and the Ionian islands – probably because the focus of Anglo-Venetian scholarship has primarily been political, and English merchants based in Venice and in the *Stato da Mar* always endeavoured to distance themselves from the political sphere.

Navigating between commercial, political and religious interests was never an easy task for English ambassadors and consuls abroad. A classic example of this is the problems encountered in the 1570s by the English mercantile community in Spain.[5] The particularly delicate state of Anglo-Spanish relations, with the tensions that preceded open (albeit undeclared) war, made it difficult to protect merchants and their interests whilst transmitting news and advice back home. Even after peace was signed in 1604, and Sir Charles Cornwallis was sent as ambassador to Madrid, his job of protecting merchants from the Inquisition, and making sure that the provisions of the treaty which allowed the English to practise their religion in private were enforced, proved a very delicate task.[6]

The two communities

An interesting peculiarity of Anglo-Venetian trade was the voluntary detachment of the mercantile community from the political one, something rather uncommon in this – or any other – phase or area of English commercial expansion. Unlike the ambassador in Constantinople, whose salary was paid by the Levant Company[7] and who was therefore extremely attentive to the needs of trade, the ambassador in Venice was a straight 'political' appointee. Yet in 1603 one of the strongest arguments in favour of restoring diplomatic relations between Venice and England had been the need to take care of trade requirements, as this was considered a solution to the customs war that since 1575 had raged over the currant trade and its impositions.[8] However, the scarcity of direct contacts between the embassy and English merchants resident in the city emerges clearly from the primary evidence.

Miscellany, 8 (1957): 195–250; M. P. Terzi, *Una vicenda della Venezia seicentesca: l'amicizia e la corrispondenza tra Fulgenzio Micanzio e Sir Dudley Carleton, ambasciatore d'Inghilterra*, tesi di laurea, University of Venice, 1979.

[5] P. Croft ed., *The Spanish Company*, London, 1972, xiii–xxi.

[6] P. Croft, 'Englishmen and the Spanish Inquisition, 1558–1625', *English Historical Review*, 87 (1972): 249–268; see also *DNB*, s.v.; on English representatives abroad in this period see also Games, *Web of Empire*, 147–179, contrary to what she argues (147) though, English ambassadors were not always paid by trading companies.

[7] Epstein, *The Early History*, 74; Wood, *A History*, 12–13.

[8] Fusaro, *Uva passa*, 12, 34–44, 67.

Religious affiliation certainly played an important role in this detach-ment, as there was a certain ambiguity amongst English merchants active in Venetians lands. Therefore a healthy distance from the embassy and its circle – a beacon of Protestantism – could be seen as a smart strategy to preserve business whatever the vagaries of religious policy. The Republic's attitude towards other faiths was, in general, fairly tolerant, given that the paramount concern of Venice's government had always been to ensure that trade ran smoothly. This had became particularly evident by the sixteenth century, when the economic crisis made the Republic especially sensitive to the preservation of commercial interests, something incompatible with enforcing tight controls against heretics and Protestants, much to the chagrin of the Holy See. In the words of John Martin, 'if the Venetian government were to clamp down too harshly on members of a particular community, the city risked losing their participa-tion in the Venetian economy'.[9] The sixteenth century saw the Venetian government recognise the importance of German and Italian Jews in lending money to poor Christians and acknowledge the role of Levantine Jews in reviving trade with the Eastern Mediterranean. Jews were granted permanent residence in town in 1509, and the Ghetto was established in 1516.[10] The Venetian government was keen to preserve its powerful position within the large German market, historically probably the most important European one for the Republic; given the strong presence of Germans in the city itself, it is understandable, in those years of violent religious confrontation throughout Europe, that a tacit tolerance was observed towards Protestants.[11]

The modalities of the earlier phases of the English presence in the Mediterranean gave the English relative familiarity with the Venetian commercial environment, thanks to the strong alliance between English merchants and the Greek subjects of the Republic involved in the produc-tion and sale of currants and wine – the staples of trade.[12] As protection-ism reduced the possibilities of getting trading privileges, keeping a low profile, getting on with business and taking advantage of the cracks emerging within the Venetian world proved to be the way to secure a solid commercial foothold.

---

[9] J. Martin, *Venice's Hidden Enemies: Italian Heretics in a Renaissance City*, London, 1993, 189.
[10] B. Ravid, *Studies on the Jews of Venice, 1382–1797*, Aldershot, 2003; Cozzi ed., *Gli ebrei a Venezia*.
[11] A useful and up-to-date survey of ethnic and religious minorities in Venice can be found in B. Ravid, 'Venice and its Minorities', in Dursteler ed., *A Companion to Venetian History*, 449–485.
[12] More details in Fusaro, 'Les Anglais et les Grecs'.

The strongest reason for the re-establishment of diplomatic links had been the violence at sea and the consequent deterioration of trading conditions, and English ambassadors throughout the century directly intervened regarding those issues. However, contacts between the embassy circle and merchants seem to have been purely operational, and diplomatic pressure over the everyday running of trade appears to have been rather unproductive in improving conditions on the ground. Evidence of this is provided by the fact that the effective breakdown of English political representation in town during the civil wars did not seem to adversely affect trade then, or later during the Protectorate.

Another factor which certainly played an important role in the distance between English diplomatic and mercantile circles was the relatively low social profile of merchants compared with the aristocratic milieu converging around the embassy. The popularity of Venice as a destination since the early stages of the Grand Tour, and the long-standing attraction of the University of Padua for English students, put the English ambassador in Venice in close contact with middle to high echelons of English society, which although well represented amongst the merchants active in the Ottoman empire were less so in Venetian territories.[13]

It is my contention that this detachment was a deliberate strategy by the English, and that this schizophrenia at the root of Anglo-Venetian relations resulted from the fact that Venice was both England's potential political ally on the European stage and, at the same time, its strongest commercial competitor in the Mediterranean. The underlying assumptions of the Walsingham *Memorandum* regarding England's ambition to supplant Venice as intermediary between Europe and the East openly clashed with the desire to maintain an amicable understanding with the Republic. This internal tension remained the defining cipher of Anglo-Venetian relations throughout the seventeenth century, though shared distrust of Spanish intentions provided a resilient political link.

A similarly ambivalent attitude characterised the Venetian government, on the one hand fully aware of the growing dangers posed by England, on the other growing increasingly dependent on the support that England provided in case of military need, something which happened with painful regularity over that century. If English soldiers were considered not very effective, given their dependency on the three

[13] On Wotton's role as a host in Venice, and educator of English travellers see D. Howarth, *Images of Rule. Art and Politics in the English Renaissance, 1485–1649*, Berkeley, 1997, 235; E. Chaney, *The Evolution of the Grand Tour: Anglo-Italian Cultural Relations since the Renaissance*, London and Portland, 1998, 205–206.

Bs – 'beer, beef and bed'[14] – a far higher opinion was held of their strength at sea, a fruitful corollary to their well-established reputation as sea marauders. Thus ambassador Henry Wotton found himself mediating to hire English troops and ships for the war against the Uskoks.[15] Commenting on that particular conflict, Logan Pearsall Smith argued that 'although Sir Henry Peyton's ships were merchantmen in the pay of the Venetian government, they nevertheless were really part of the navy in England, which at this time was largely composed of armed merchant ships; and in sanctioning their employment, James I was deliberately parting with a portion of his maritime force in order to protect an ally, and preserve the balance of force in the Mediterranean'.[16] Through the employment of English and Dutch ships and soldiers Venice managed to show Spain that the Republic had powerful allies. This pattern continued up until the War of Candia (1646–1669) during which, rather cunningly, private English ships were regularly employed by both sides to provide logistical support. This cautious, and in practice only operational, political alliance between Venice and England was just one side of the relationship, as the underlying commercial rivalry did not cease. Still in 1651, when assessing Levantine trade on the eve of the Anglo-Dutch war, Thomas Bendish – then English ambassador in Constantinople – commented that the Venetians '*privately*, as the French openly, have endeavoured for a long time to destroy our trade'.[17] Certainly the Venetian government could not afford to *publicly* attack England whilst English vessels provided essential support in its war with the Ottoman empire.

A window into Italian – and papal – affairs

Paolo Sarpi and his friend and collaborator Fulgenzio Micanzio, and the complex story of their links with England, where Sarpi's *Historia del Concilio di Trento* was published, splendidly exemplify the central political interest that England had in the Republic of Venice.[18] Venice's

---

[14] Pearsall Smith, *The Life and Letters*, i: 153; also *CSPVe*, vol. x, n. 739, 523: see www.british-history.ac.uk/report.aspx?compid=9565 (date accessed: 17 February 2014).

[15] Pearsall Smith, *The Life and Letters*, i: 152–153.

[16] Pearsall Smith, *The Life and Letters*, i: 154, see also 163. On Sir Henry Peyton's military activities in service of the Republic of Venice see *DNB*, s.v.

[17] Thomas Bendish to the council of State (1-3-1651) quoted by S. Pincus, *Protestantism and Patriotism: Ideologies and the Making of English Foreign Policy, 1650–1668*, Cambridge, 1996, 42. The emphasis is mine.

[18] Pietro Soave Polano [Paolo Sarpi], *Historia del Concilio Tridentino*, London (ed. Marco Antonio de Dominis), 1619; the following year it was translated into English by Nathanael Brent: *The Historie of the Councel of Trent*, London, 1620.

proud defence of its jurisdictional prerogatives, by both the Republic's government and the local Catholic Church, had given hopes to Protestants (Anglicans in particular) that Venice might abandon Catholicism and join Protestant Europe. The well-earned reputation of Venice as a centre of global news gathering, and the presence of many foreign ambassadors there, made Venice the perfect place to gather political and financial news from all of Italy, and from Rome in particular, which would then be sent back to London.[19] As Wotton wrote to Secretary of State Sir Ralph Winwood at the beginning of his second mission, 'the two Fountaines of my charge (as I conceive it) are Venice and Rome'.[20]

As the only official English diplomatic representative in the Italian peninsula, Wotton during his first embassy in Venice had 'charge of all matters of trade in Italian ports'.[21] At the beginning of his mission he was kept busy trying to rebuild some modicum of trust with Italian states, especially given the ghastly reputation that years of piracy had attached onto the English nation. At the moment of his appointment, Cecil had written to English merchants based in Pisa and Livorno telling them to report to Wotton about any 'wrecks, piracies, attempts, sale of ships etc', and Wotton immediately negotiated with the Grand Duke of Tuscany about English vessels captured by the Tuscan fleet, at the same time sending one of his secretaries to Naples to arrange for the establishment of an English consulate in that port. Most interestingly, Wotton was also originally 'commissioned to act as superior to the English ambassador at Constantinople, who was ordered to take his policy from him'.[22] This might point to the fact that James' policy at this stage was to try to contain the autonomy of the ambassador at the Porte nominated by the Levant Company, a move that can be seen both as an act of foreign policy and a message to the Company that the crown was keeping a closer eye on its dealings in the area, so as to re-establish the pre-eminence of the political element over the commercial one.

The issue of piracy was the most urgent one at Wotton's arrival in Venice, and he personally commented to Lord Salisbury that English

[19] F. de Vivo, *Information and Communication in Venice: Rethinking Early Modern Politics*, Oxford, 2007, 81–82.
[20] TNA, *SP* 99/21, 162r–163r (26-8-1616).
[21] Pearsall Smith, *The Life and Letters*, i: 328. Sir Henry Wotton was resident ambassador to the Republic of Venice from 1603 to 1610, he was then ambassador ordinary from 1615 to 1619, and again resident ambassador from 1620 to 1623: see Bell, *A Handlist*, 289, 290–291; see also 'Accredited Diplomatic Agents in Venice', *CSPVe*, vol. i: www.british-history.ac.uk/report.aspx?compid=94083 (date accessed: 17 February 2014).
[22] Pearsall Smith, *The Life and Letters*, i: 69.

sailors were 'many times not very innocent in these matters'.[23] After long negotiations, English ships were forced to comply with the 'right of search claimed by the Venetians in the Adriatic'.[24] However important, these commercial concerns were only part of his instructions and did not reflect his real interests. Piracy and trade were indeed the urgent topics, but religion too was important, and far closer to his own personal concerns. Consequently a large part of Wotton's business in Venice was to collect information on Rome and the pope from spies and forward it to London.[25]

By the beginning of the seventeenth century, the pope and his entourage had grown increasingly suspicious of the Venetian attitude towards Protestant countries. Especially dangerous was the re-establishment of diplomatic links with England and the fact that King James openly took the Venetian side during the Interdict affair.[26] The circle surrounding Wotton was correctly perceived to be close to Sarpi and therefore came under close scrutiny, with the nuncio himself openly expressing his concern.[27] During the Interdict crisis, Wotton followed all the developments in Venice, Italy and Europe with extreme attention, and his papers to the secretary of state and his private correspondence provide a running commentary on almost a daily basis.[28]

Venetian patricians were forbidden to have any dealings with foreign ambassadors or their employees. Similar rules governed the behaviour of *cittadini originari* (the upper echelons of Venetian non-patrician citizens, in charge of the state bureaucracy). Although it is probably an exaggeration to claim that 'their fear of the arbitrary powers of the Council of Ten meant that they [the patricians] not only extended this prohibition to the extent of avoiding all contacts with foreigners, but they went continuously in fear of each other',[29] it is indeed true that, with such limitations, most political information circulated informally through the wide use of informants.

Venetians were masters of this. Their impressive network of ambassadors and diplomatic agents – an essential tool in their political and commercial structure – always relied upon a wide web of professional

[23] Pearsall Smith, *The Life and Letters*, i: 73.
[24] Pearsall Smith, *The Life and Letters*, i: 74.
[25] Pearsall Smith, *The Life and Letters*, i: 65; 149 for the same activities during his second embassy.
[26] Sarpi, *Opere*, 114–116.
[27] De Vivo, *Information and Communication*, 74.
[28] *CSPVe*, vol. x, *passim.*; on his understanding – and misunderstanding – of the Republic's strategy see de Vivo, *Information and Communication*, 168–170, 183 footnote.
[29] Wootton, 'Ulysses Bound?', 357–368.

and informal informants. It comes therefore as no surprise that foreigners had learned this lesson, and a vast network of spies supported the work of all ambassadors in Venice. Since the 1580s, the English secretary of state regularly received letters from spies reporting relevant political and economic news.[30] Governments spied, and so did ambassadors, and both were of course also spied upon. Informers were regularly posted around embassies in Venice, and the documentary material produced by them is especially rich for the beginning of the seventeenth century, mostly due to the delicate international situation and the dangers (real and perceived) to the Venetian state.[31]

Though commercial relations could exist without the support of political ones, political and diplomatic relations frequently relied upon ties to merchants. Some of these men played an important role as brokers, and it is worth noting that the most important link between the English embassy and the Venetian intelligentsia at the beginning of the seventeenth century was, indeed, a merchant, but from the Netherlands, not England. Daniel Nijs, a long-time resident of Venice, played a pivotal role in facilitating Carleton's correspondence with Sarpi and Micanzio, since Carleton was in The Hague as ambassador to the United Provinces.[32] Wotton had been in close contact with Sarpi and Micanzio already during his first embassy (1603–1610), and especially close to them had been his chaplain, William Bedell. The relationship was not interrupted at Wotton's departure, but continued under his successor, Carleton. Behind this close connection was King James' desire to become the flag bearer of Protestantism. When, in 1616, Carleton moved to The Hague and Wotton returned for his second mission as ambassador in Venice, the relationship was not only renewed but strenghtened, now with the practical objective of secretly transferring Sarpi's manuscript to London, where arrangements had been made for its publication. Nijs was the chosen man for this delicate task, which he successfully completed. Nijs' finest hour, though, was still to come: in 1627 he brokered the sale of the Gonzaga art collection to King Charles I, which in a single stroke created the basis of the English royal art collection. However, it also proved his financial undoing when the king refused to pay for the second tranche of the collection, which Nijs had hastily bought (without previous royal authorisation) in 1627 whilst Mantua was being overrun by French and Spanish troops. Nijs declared bankruptcy in 1631 and spent the rest of his life trying to get the king to

[30] TNA, *SP* 99/1 and 2, *passim*.
[31] De Vivo, *Information and Communication*, 11.
[32] Cozzi, 'Fra Paolo Sarpi'.

pay. He died in poverty in London in 1647, still trying to recover his money.[33]

English ambassadors in Venice

A closer analysis of Wotton's first embassy in Venice is important, as it set a blueprint for all his successors, whose patterns of engagement with both Venetian society and English merchants mirrored his. If anything, Wotton's personal contacts with English merchants resident in Venice were more frequent than was to be the case with some of his successors, such as Carleton.[34]

Wotton's career was built on his travels in the continent during the 1590s, when he acquired a wide network of informants. Later he became one of the secretaries of the earl of Essex, who came to greatly value the access Wotton could provide him to European political circles through his contacts in Siena, Florence, Geneva, Heidelberg, Basel, Vienna, Prague, Utrecht and The Hague.[35] He subsequently had the good political sense to detach himself from Essex, and his European links proved essential once again when he acted on the the prompting of Ferdinand, Grand Duke of Tuscany, to warn James of a plot against him in 1600. In this way he became instrumental in Anglo-Tuscan diplomacy and furthered his own career by providing valuable support to James VI of Scotland well before the latter's ascension to the English throne.[36] Despite these auspicious beginnings, however, his political career was rather chequered and never lived up to its earlier promise. Where Wotton truly excelled was in sending (mostly, but not exclusively Italian) art to the king and to Robert Cecil, Earl of Salisbury.[37] He also had a good relationship with

---

[33] On Nijs' involvement with the arts and with this sale see M. van Gelder, 'Acquiring Artistic Expertise: The Agent Daniel Nijs and His Contacts with Artists in Venice', in M. Keblusek and B. Noldus eds., *Double Agents: Cultural and Political Brokerage in Early Modern Europe*, Leiden and Boston, 2010, 111–124. See also C. Anderson, *Art Dealing and Collecting in Venice: The Multi-Faceted Career of Daniel Nijs (1572–1647), Broker of the Gonzaga Sale*, DPhil thesis, University of Oxford, 2010; F. Haskell, N. Penny and K. Serres, *The King's Pictures: The Formation and Dispersal of the Collections of Charles I and His Courtiers*, New Haven, 2013.

[34] Sir Dudley Carleton was resident ambassador to Venice from 1610 to 1615; he spent approximately the last year of his mission in Turin, Duchy of Savoy, although he formally remained the English Ambassador to Venice: see Bell, *A Handlist*, 290; also *CSPVe*, 'Accredited Diplomatic Agents in Venice'. On his stay in Venice see also M. Lee Jr, *Dudley Carleton to John Chamberlain, 1603–1624: Jacobean Letters*, New Brunswick, 1972.

[35] *DNB*, s.v. Wotton.

[36] Contini, 'Aspects of Mediceans Diplomacy', 92. See also *DNB*, s.v. Wotton.

[37] R. Hill, *Art and Patronage: Sir Henry Wotton and the Venetian Embassy 1604–1624*, in Keblusek and Noldus eds., *Double Agents*, 27–58. For his patronage of Italian artists see L. M. Walters, *Odoardo Faletti (1573–ca1638): The Interrelation of Venetian Art and*

Prince Henry, to whom he sent Venetian art, and influenced his adopting Italian fashion in dress. Henry's premature death in 1612 deprived Wotton of a crucial patron and certainly did not help his career.[38] His most trusted agent in these dealings was, once again, Daniel Nijs, who did the same for two of his successors: Carleton and Isaac Wake, thus securing his reputation as the perfect example of those multifaceted merchants who also dealt in sensitive political information.[39]

Before being appointed as ambassador to Venice, Wotton had already been in contact with merchants there. In 1589, preparing to travel to Europe for the first time, he got in touch with Henry Parvis (or Parvish) about financial matters relating to his trip.[40] Whilst living in Florence in 1592, though his travels had no official sanction, he sent political analyses to Lord Zouche in England using the services of Paul Pindar, one of the most prominent English merchants in Venice, who acted as an agent of Henry and Jacob Parvis, 'currant merchants'.[41] Wotton's general attitude towards English merchants in Venice was non-interventionist, and he got actively involved only in times of real crisis, such as when the commercial position of English merchants became untenable, or when some crime was committed against them, like the killing in 1605 of the English merchant Nicholas Pert by the Venetian aristocrat Nicolò Balbi.[42] Few names of merchants appear in Wotton's papers. Through these we learn that one of the merchants based in Venice – Jeffrey Luther – was in charge of conveying to London the correspondence of Thomas Glover, ambassador in Constantinople.[43] In fact, throughout the seventeenth century, diplomatic mail from Constantinople to London appears to have been regularly routed via Venice, evidence of the city's continuing role as a centre of information exchange and of the superiority of its mail system.[44]

Anatomy, and His Importance in England, PhD thesis, University of St Andrews, 2009, especially 152–197.

[38] Hill, *Art and Patronage: Sir Henry Wotton*, 35.

[39] Pearsall Smith, *The Life and Letters*, ii: 209–210; van Gelder, 'Acquiring Artistic Expertise', 115.

[40] Pearsall Smith, *The Life and Letters*, i: 228, 237.

[41] Pearsall Smith, *The Life and Letters*, i: 288–289. Henry Parvis at that time was probably still in England; the first trace of him in Venetian documentation dates to 1604. No evidence has surfaced of his brother's activities there, so he was probably based in London.

[42] Wotton would not spare any attempt to see Balbi condemned for the killing of Pert; on how Balbi managed to get away with it, and on the wider implications for Venetian justice's attitude to the patriciate, see Pearsall Smith, *The Life and Letters*, i: 323–325; on this episode see also J. Walker, *Honour and the Culture of Male Venetian Nobles, c.1500–1650*, PhD thesis, Cambridge University, 1998, 90–91.

[43] TNA, *SP* 99/5, 8r–9r (5/15-1-1608) Wotton to Salisbury.

[44] References to this in TNA, *SP* 99 *passim*. On these issues see M. Infelise, 'From Merchants' Letters to Handwritten Political *Avvisi*: Notes on the Origins of Public

As regards accommodation and the provision of services, Wotton and his successors took advantage almost exclusively of local providers. After occupying temporary lodgings, he settled into a palace in Cannaregio, which Pearsall Smith referred to as 'Palazzo Silvia at the Ponte degli Ormesani'.[45] During his first mission Wotton rented furniture and linens from Isaac Luzzati, and Carleton did the same.[46] The house appears to have been relatively sumptuously furnished; in the words of Pearsall Smith, 'the walls were hung with arras and gilded leather, and adorned with pictures and armour; there were green velvet armchairs, great andirons and lanterns, tables with their "carpets" (as table-covers were called); and a "ground carpet" is mentioned in the dining room. There was a billiard table in the house, and in Wotton's parlour hung a portrait of the young Prince Henry. Many of the large pieces of furniture Wotton hired from the Jews, and apparently on exorbitant terms; for after his departure they boasted that they had "a fleece of him"'.[47] In effect, Carleton appears to have paid less money for the very same items.[48] All these were necessary expenditures; the house of the ambassador performed a crucial political role, as there were no embassies where work could be done: 'provision of lavish hospitality would also reflect positively on the honour of the ambassador's prince'.[49] Therefore, there was money to be made in providing all the ceremonial trappings necessary to the practice of diplomacy and of representing one's sovereign. English ambassadors resorted to local suppliers for these needs and do not appear to have used the mediation of their co-national merchants. It was certainly the large availability which pushed their choice in this direction.[50] Only in his third

---

Information', in F. Bethencourt and F. Egmond eds., *Cultural Exchange in Early Modern Europe*, vol. iii: *Correspondence and Cultural Exchange in Europe, 1400–1700*, Cambridge, 2007, 33–52.

[45] Pearsall Smith, *The Life and Letters*, i: 57.

[46] TNA, *SP* 99/6, 158r, 211r, 213r, 215r–216v; by the end of his first stay Wotton owed Luzzatti 1,220 ducats; Carleton was to pay Luzzatti off in June 1611: see *SP* 99/7, c. 389v. On the Jews being licensed, from the early sixteenth century, to trade (and loan) second-hand furnishings see T. A. Allerston, *The Market in Second-Hand Clothes and Furnishings in Venice (ca.1500-ca.1650)*, PhD thesis, European University Institute, Florence, 1996.

[47] Pearsall Smith, *The Life and Letters*, i: 57.

[48] TNA, *SP* 99/6, 209r.

[49] C. Fletcher, '"Furnished with Gentlemen": The Ambassador's House in Sixteenth-Century Italy', *Renaissance Studies*, 24 (2009): 518–535, 518; on diplomats' role in fostering the taste for Italian art see H. Jacobsen, *Luxury and Power: The Material World of the Stuart Diplomat, 1660–1714*, Oxford, 2011.

[50] *Mutatis mutandis*, a similar interdependence is visible in London in the relationship between the court and its providers, which were not necessarily Englishmen: on this see I. W. Archer, 'City and Court Connected: The Material Dimensions of Royal Ceremonial, ca. 1480–1625', *Huntington Library Quarterly*, 71 (2008): 157–179.

mission, in 1620, did Wotton resort again to the mediation services of an English merchant, this time Randolph Simes, whom he used as guarantor for the rent of a fully furnished villa in Ponte di Brenta.[51] Wotton's financial means seemed to have been fairly diminished since his previous tenures, and this time his choices of residences were more restrained; in 1616 he had rented from the Gussoni family a palace on the Grand Canal and a villa in Noventa for the total of 460 ducats.[52]

If selecting local vendors was a fairly logical and, in a sense, obligatory choice, slightly more puzzling appears the reluctance of English diplomats to make use of the services of their co-nationals for their own financial needs, an area in which Wotton's involvement with Englishmen was minimal. The financial guarantee asked of Randolph Simes for the rental of the Ponte di Brenta villa appears to be the only exception, and it can be argued that this particular choice might have been governed by Wotton's desire to use an alternative credit network to help finance what was just a personal luxury, which he could hardly afford, given his diminished liquidity, and which was unrelated to his professional concern as ambassador. During his first mission to Venice Wotton gave power of attorney to James Higgons in 1606, at that time acting both as consul in Venice for the Levant Company and as agent for Thomas Garway and Edward Holmden.[53] Contacts between Wotton and Higgons dated to 1604 when, on his way to Venice, Wotton mentioned to Ralph Winwood (the English agent at The Hague) that Higgons would handle his correspondence there.[54] However, only two months later, Wotton nominated a member of his household as procurator for his affairs in Venice.[55] Again in August he used Higgons' services; in a letter to Salisbury he mentioned receipts of money, through the help of

---

[51] ASV, *Notarile Atti*, reg. 12558 (Gio Battista Tomasi), cc.n.n. (25-5-1621); the first instalment was paid by Randolph Simes to the owner of the villa (Pietro Morosini *quondam* Michele) on the following day; it was equivalent to one full year of rent for the sum of 100 ducats (side notation to the above-mentioned contract). The inventory of the villa, is in ASV, *Notarile Atti*, reg. 12558 (Gio Battista Tomasi), cc.n.n. (11-6-1621).

[52] 'There were at this date two Gussoni palaces on the Grand Canal, the Cavalli Palace (now Palazzo Franchetti) at St Vitale, and the present Grimani della Vida Palace, above the Rialto, opposite St Staë. This latter was Wotton's residence, as Asselinau (a French doctor in Venice) writes on 3 June 1616 that Wotton's secretary had taken a palace on the Gran Canal opposite St Staë, and adjoining the Traghetto della Maddalena. The Grimani, formerly Gussoni, Palace is near this *traghetto*, and must be the one Wotton occupied: in Pearsall Smith, *The Life and Letters*, ii: 101–102 and footnote.

[53] ASV, *Notarile Atti*, reg. 11927 (Andrea Spinelli), cc.229r/v (7-4-1606); see also ASV, *Notarile Atti*, reg. 11919 (Andrea Spinelli), cc.466r/v (14-10-1598); Pearsall Smith, *The Life and Letters*, i: 320, 374.

[54] Pearsall Smith, *The Life and Letters*, i: 319–320.

[55] He gave power of attorney to Giorgio Boes *quondam* Gerolamo 'suo familiar di casa', in ASV, *Notarile Atti*, reg. 11927 (Andrea Spinelli), c.493r (27-7-1606); cc.620r/v (9-10-1606).

Higgons, who wrote bills payable to Garway.[56] From that date onwards all remittances of money from the secretary of state in London to ambassadors in Venice seem to have been handled by the banking firm of Burlamachi and Calandrini, Italian Protestant émigrés and naturalised English subjects.[57] Philip Burlamachi was one of the major financiers of the Stuart dynasty, acting as a sort of unofficial paymaster for English and English-financed expeditions abroad and for the diplomatic service at large, regularly extending lines of credits in the tens of thousands of pounds.[58] This was not always an easy relationship, and in fact Burlamachi seems to have created problems when Carleton asked for another extension of credit in 1613, but the relationship was clearly mutually convenient as, notwithstanding Carleton's threats to get better conditions from other 'Italian and English merchants',[59] he continued to make extensive use of their services until the end of his mission.[60] Given the high level of liquidity available to English merchants active in Venice, not making regular use of their services to finance the embassy is an interesting choice, which once more points to a deliberate desire by the English government to keep the commercial and diplomatic spheres separate in the Venetian case. Indirectly, this is also evidence of the absence of Venetian bankers in London, as they would have been a logical choice if available, especially given that in the times of Henry VIII it had been Venetian bankers who dealt with these kinds of transactions for English ambassadors.[61]

Religion and trade

Though Italian culture was popular in Renaissance England, there was ambiguity regarding mutual perception and image. For a long time

[56] TNA, *SP* 99/5, 294r/v (28-8-1609); also Pearsall Smith, *The Life and Letters*, i: 470, letter of 28-8-1609.
[57] See for example TNA, *SP* 99/7, 114r (s.d. [23-2-1611]); *SP* 99/11, 193 (24-12-1612); and *SP* 99/12, 166r (19-3-1613). On their activities in Italy see R. De Roover, 'Thomas Mun in Italy', *Historical Research*, 30 (1957): 80–85, 84. The Calandrini brothers – Italian Protestant exiles who had left Lucca for London in the late 1560s – were also involved in supporting the epistolary exchange between Sarpi, Carleton and Micanzio mentioned above: see Cozzi, 'Fra Paolo Sarpi'.
[58] Ultimately he declared bankruptcy in 1633, due to the crown's inability to fulfil its obligations: see *DNB*, s.v.
[59] TNA, *SP* 99/12, 230r/v (26-4-1613); no further evidence of these dealings, nor individual names of such merchants, has surfaced from the archives.
[60] See TNA, *SP* 99/12, 269r (April 1613), 332r (20-5-1613), 340 (21-5-1613), 359r–360v (28-5-1613); also *SP* 99/13, 94r (8-7-1613), 204r/v (27-8-1613); *SP* 99/14, 40 r (14-10-1613); *SP* 99/15, 32r (11-1-1613), 137r (28-2-1613); *SP* 99/17, 25r (10-8-1614); *SP* 99/18, 207r (12-1-1614), 251 (21-1-1614), 259 (26-1-1614); *SP* 99/19, 47 (17-2-1615), 56 (25-2-1615), 176r/v (15-5-1615).
[61] Fletcher, *Our Man in Rome*, 73.

Italians in all their varieties – Tuscans, Florentines, Genoese, Venetians – had been wealthier than the English and ready to flaunt their supposedly superior culture and sophistication, and the English had replied with understandable jibes and criticism of Italians' morality and honesty. By the sixteenth century, even when Italian economic superiority was fast receding and the English were on the advance, these old images continued to be employed as powerful tools of propaganda.[62]

In the words of Patrick Collinson, 'mistrust and fear of the Catholic powers, the pope and those rulers deemed to be his agents, fuelled the most powerful of political motives and emotions'.[63] With the Grand Tour starting to become a fixture of gentlemanly education, Italy was the most popular destination, but it was considered, overall, a dangerous place; 'the rapidly growing English enthusiasm for the literature of voyages and ventures was accompanied by a steady undertow of scepticism about the benefits of travel'.[64] Journeying there was considered morally risky, and there was fear 'that the qualities of the moral, Protestant and well-educated Englishman will be turned into their "natural" opposites upon indiscriminate and unsuspecting contact with contemporary Italy and its products'.[65]

Amongst Italian cities, Venice was granted a particularly ambiguous status. Though the capital of a Catholic state, it was also famed for its religious tolerance and fierce opposition to the intrusion of papal authority, two factors that helped mitigate the general contempt in which Italian mores and corruption were held in England.[66] Still, Venice was also exotic and different, and though a young Englishman travelling there might avoid the 'pernicious lure of Catholicism', more difficult would it be to avoid the dangers associated with the 'social sophistication of Venetian courtesans'.[67] In short, the negative judgement was more moral than religious.[68] Notwithstanding all these dangers, Venice – also thanks to the University of Padua's long tradition of hosting English

---

[62] Bovilsky, *Barbarous Play*, 103–133.

[63] P. Collinson, 'The Politics of Religion and the Religion of Politics in Elizabethan England', *Historical Research*, 82 (2009): 74–92, 79.

[64] W. H. Sherman, 'Bringing the World to England: The Politics of Translation in the Age of Hakluyt', *Transactions of the Royal Historical Society*, 14 (2004): 199–207, 201.

[65] M. Ord, 'Classical and Contemporary Italy in Roger Ascham's *The Scholemaster* (1570)', *Renaissance Studies*, 16 (2002): 202–216, 209; see also Chaney, *The Evolution of the Grand Tour*; R. Sweet, *Cities and the Grand Tour: The British in Italy ca. 1690–1820*, Cambridge, 2012.

[66] M. J. Redmond, *Shakespeare, Politics, and Italy: Intertextuality on the Jacobean Stage*, Farnham, 2009, 100.

[67] Ord, *Classical and Contemporary Italy*, 213.

[68] L. Kooijmans, 'Risk and Reputation: On the Mentality of Merchants in the Early Modern Period', in Lesger and Noordegraaf eds., *Entrepreneurs and Entrepreneurship*, 25–34, 32.

students – was the English travellers' gateway to the peninsula, both physically and intellectually.[69] In other Italian places where the English had mercantile communities, religious allegiance was a more delicate subject. Even in Livorno, a city rightly famed for its tolerance of many faiths, where English Catholics represented the majority of the expatriate group and Protestants were a rarity until the middle of the seventeenth century, it was still considered prudent to avoid proclaiming too openly one's Protestantism.[70]

Wotton's embassy became a centre of Protestantism in Venice, and practical problems connected with religious affiliations were amongst his daily concerns. In spite of the pope's protests, he had been allowed to celebrate religious services in his private chapel. This was indeed a privilege, which the Venetian government probably had granted with an eye to reasserting its independence from Rome. Religious services were supposed to be held in English, and attendance should have been limited to the ambassador and his household, although it appears that a few of his compatriots were quietly admitted.[71]

Very little is known about the religious affiliation of English merchants in Venice. Wotton's Sunday religious gatherings should have been a meeting point for merchants in town.[72] But, with the exception of Francis Lowe, who will be discussed below, this does not seem to have been the case, at least for those settled in the city for extended periods of time. Henry Parvis was another merchant who had some connection with the embassy circle, most likely due to his status as a 'gentleman'. Parvis in fact is one of the two merchants of aristocratic birth active in Venice. He appears based there from at least 1604,[73] and he was clearly quite successful, enjoying business connections in Zante, Ragusa and at the fairs of 'Bisenzone'.[74] He married Cecilia, the illegitimate daughter of the patrician Vincenzo Gritti, and thanks to the fact that after his death she was thoroughly examined by the *Avogadori di Comun* in conjunction with her plans to marry the patrician Lorenzo Contarini, we have many

[69] K. R. Bartlett, 'Dangers and Delights: English Protestants in Italy in the Sixteenth Century', in *Forestieri e stranieri nelle città basso-medievali*, Florence, 1988, 215–222, 216.

[70] P. Castignoli, 'Aspetti istituzionali della nazione inglese a Livorno', in *Atti del Convegno: 'Gli inglesi a Livorno e nell'Isola d'Elba' (sec. XVII–XIX)*, Livorno, 1980, 102–115, 103–106.

[71] Pearsall Smith, *The Life and Letters*, i: 77.

[72] P. Mathias, 'Strategies for Reducing Risk by Entrepreneurs in the Early Modern Period', in Lesger and Noordegraaf eds., *Entrepreneurs and Entrepreneurship*, 5–24, 16.

[73] ASV, *Notarile Atti*, reg. 11925 (Andrea Spinelli), cc.499r/v (8-7-1604).

[74] ASV, *Notarile Atti*, reg. 11938 (Andrea Spinelli), cc.571r/v (21-7-1616); reg. 11944 (Andrea Spinelli), cc.135v–136r (12-7-1618); and reg. 11937 (Andrea Spinelli), cc.573r/v (20-7-1615).

testimonies of Parvis' aristocratic status amongst the witnesses summoned to testify regarding her suitability to marry a member of the Major Council.[75] He therefore enjoyed substantially better social connections than his countrymen, and his familiarity with the embassy and its social circle was well known.[76] He was not only a trusted member of the English mercantile community, but also loaned money to travellers and stored and shipped goods for them and fellow merchants.[77]

It has frequently been argued that militant Protestantism was common amongst Levant Company members in London, but the evidence surrounding their agents in Venice and its territory is more complex in this regard.[78] Parvis is an interesting example of ambiguity in his religious affiliation. To his mother, Lady Hicks, he endeavoured to appear as a devout Protestant. However, he married a Catholic, and in the first will he wrote in Venice he asked to be buried wearing the habit of a Capuchin monk – 'da capucino' – hardly the choice of a devout Protestant.[79] His cousin Francis Lowe praised him to Lady Hicks, who was reassured about his religious behaviour:

Yet above all thinges his cheaffest care is (and for which I am most bound to him) to have me confirmed in that faith and sencerity of religion which first received in my fathers house. [...] not one Sonday passeth but I am present at my lord imbassadors [sic] and pertaker of those godly exercises which are there.[80]

Parvis' true religious affiliation remains a mystery, especially as a request to be buried in Capuchin habit is a rather strong statement of Catholic piety which went well beyond even a supposed strategy of religious dissimulation.[81]

---

[75] ASV, *Avogaria di Comun, Processi di Nobiltà*, b. 324, fasc. 5. Although illegitimate, Cecilia had been born of a reputable woman from the *Terraferma*, and brought up in the paternal home. The 'trial of nobility' (*processo di nobiltà*) was a standard procedure when a non-patrician woman wished to marry a patrician, and the scope of it was to ascertain the absence of practitioners of mechanical arts amongst her direct close ancestors; this was necessary so that the eventual offspring of this marriage would have had access to the Major Council. On these issues see A. Cowan, *Marriage, Manners and Mobility in Early Modern Venice*, Farnham, 2007.

[76] ASV, *Avogaria di Comun, Processi di Nobiltà*, b. 324, fasc. 5, cc.n.n. (25-6-1620), testimony of Trifon Fortezza.

[77] Lee Jr ed., *Dudley Carleton to John Chamberlain*, 163.

[78] P. Croft, 'Fresh Light on Bate's Case', *Historical Journal*, 30 (1987): 523–539, 527.

[79] ASV, *Notarile testamenti*, bb. 402–406 (Giulio Figolin), n.68 (unpublished will, dated 2-4-1607).

[80] BL, *Lansdowne* 93, n.24, cc.46r/v (11-7-1613); n.25, c.48r (12-7-1613); J. W. Stoye, (*English Travellers Abroad 1604–1667: Their Influence in English Society and Politics*, London, 1989, 75) is certain of his Protestantism.

[81] On English merchants' practice of dissimulation in the Mediterranean, see Games, *Web of Empire*, 74–79.

Eleazar Hickman appears as one of the few merchants resident in Venice for whom there seems to be proof of religious persuasion: he was defined as a person of 'excellent commercial reputation' and 'a good catholic' in an official declaration signed by several of his business associates.[82] His brother Matthew had been procurator for Parvis.[83] But despite the formality of a notarised statement, there are solid reasons to believe that Hickman was a textbook example of Nicodemism.[84] Eleazar's mother was the famed Rose Throckmorton (*née* Locke) and his father was her first husband, Anthony Hickman.[85] Rose's short memoir, written in 1613 when she was 85 years of age, and preserved in the family Bible, has been defined as being written 'to cement her family members' status as Protestant heroes'.[86] Sir William Locke, Eleazar's grandfather, ennobled by Henry VIII for service to the Protestant cause, had been involved in the import of religious books from the continent. Eleazar's father financed and sheltered Protestant preachers during the Marian period and for this had been imprisoned in the Fleet in the spring of 1554 before moving to Antwerp, where Rose and the children later joined him. Eleazar's Catholicism would indeed sit rather badly with such a militant family pedigree. The explanation for his behaviour probably lies in his mother's memoir, where she details several episodes when she outwardly conformed to Catholic practices to protect her family whilst inwardly dissenting, a true definition of Nicodemism. It is plausible that Eleazar was following his mother's lead as a successful merchant in Venice, especially, as it has been noted 'how often the concerns of business seem to take precedence over spiritual aims' in Rose's story.[87]

It is both difficult and dangerous to deduce general rules of behaviour from such scarce evidence, especially as the surviving documentation does not lend itself to considerations about their spiritual lives. Whilst a proper analysis of such issues is beyond the scope of this volume, the

---

[82] ASV, *Notarile Atti*, reg. 11918 (Andrea Spinelli), c.78r (7-2-1597); also in Brulez and Devos, *Marchands Flamands*, i: n.712, 239.

[83] ASV, *Notarile Atti*, reg. 11919 (Andrea Spinelli), cc.399r/v (3-9-1598). We shall encounter the brothers again in Chapter 8.

[84] On this term, crucial remains the seminal D. Cantimori, *Eretici italiani del Cinquecento*, Turin, 1992 (1939), esp. 447–455; on its practice in Venice, J. Martin, 'Marranos and Nicodemites in Sixteenth-Century Venice', *Journal of Medieval and Early Modern Studies*, 41 (2011): 577–599, 589–599.

[85] The complete family genealogy is in J. Goodwin Locke, *Book of the Lockes: A Genealogical and Historical Record of the Descendants of William Locke of Woburn*, Boston, 1853, 358–359.

[86] J. Heller, *The Mother's Legacy in Early Modern England*, Farnham, 2011, 97.

[87] Heller, *The Mother's Legacy*, 95, and generally 97–104; on Rose see also M. Dowling and J. Shakespeare, 'Religion and Politics in Mid-Tudor England through the Eyes of an English Protestant Woman: The Recollections of Rose Hickman', *Historical Research*, 55 (1982): 94–102; *DNB*, s.v.

overriding impression is that, for these men, when business was at stake, religious affiliation was quietly put aside and business interests took precedence.

Between king and commonwealth

The missions of Wotton's successors undoubtedly had a lower profile than his first one, or indeed his own subsequent two. Carleton's appointment boosted his career but was uncongenial: in short, 'he was a Protestant in a Catholic state, his Italian was imperfect, and he was often bored'.[88] He collected Italian and classical art and used Venice mostly as a base whilst mediating the peace between Spain and Savoy, afterwards reaping the benefits of such a high-profile role by becoming ambassador to the United Provinces. He kept very little contact with the mercantile community, although, back in London in 1630, he married the widow of Paul Bayning, one of the very few merchants who capitalised on his Venetian experience to build himself a fortune and a political career.[89]

Three secretaries followed Wotton's third and last mission: Sir Isaac Wake, Thomas Rowlandson and Gilbert Talbot. Basil Feilding was ambassador extraordinary in the late 1630s, but the importance of the Venice embassy for England was by then diminished. Reading the papers of the secretary of state one gets the distinct impression that the Italian peninsula as a whole was receding from the English political horizon, and this was reflected also in the worsening knowledge of the Italian languages on the part of diplomatic envoys. Italian was still, up to the eighteenth century, the lingua franca of Mediterranean merchants, as witnessed by the fact that English merchants in the Ottoman empire tended to hire an Italian clerk to help them run their business, but its status in international politics was waning.[90] If we take language to be one of the critical constitutive elements of politics,[91] the shift to English (or even French) as a mode of communication by English ambassadors in Venice clearly defines an epochal change from the prevailing Italophonia that characterised the Tudor and early Stuart diplomats, with Carleton being a

[88] *DNB*, s.v.
[89] *DNB*, s.v.
[90] Davis, *Aleppo and Devonshire Square*, 86; Grassby, *The Business Community*, 181; G. D. Ramsay, *The City of London in International Politics at the Accession of Elizabeth Tudor*, Manchester, 1975, 217; Games, *Web of Empire*, 113. For a general overview of the importance of the Italian language in the early modern period see E. R. Dursteler, 'Speaking in Tongues: Language and Communication in the Early Modern Mediterranean', *Past and Present*, 217 (2012): 47–77, and bibliography quoted therein.
[91] Wyatt, *The Italian Encounter with Tudor England*, 204.

notable exception. Whilst Wake mastered Latin and French, and his Italian was good, and both Rowlandson and Talbot seem to have been proficient, the arrival of Jerome Weston as ambassador extraordinary in 1632 marked the first case of a non-Italian-speaking diplomat sent to Venice, the *Collegio*'s clerk duly noting that he spoke French and arrived at his audiences with an interpreter.[92] All subsequent English ambassadors, up to the end of the century, would make excuses for their poor knowledge of the Italian language.

The beginning of the English civil war occasioned another period of disruptions in direct diplomatic relations between Venice and England. In 1642 the Republic suspended the commission of Vincenzo Contarini, who had been elected to succeed Giovanni Giustinian. For the following decade, Venice kept abreast of English political and military developments through secretaries and secret agents, sometimes relying on other residents to forward newsletters to Venice, frequently via the ambassador in France.[93] The Venetian government did not particularly trust Oliver Cromwell, and sent an official representative only when the naval needs of the Candia war (1646–1669) forced the *Senato* to dispatch Lorenzo Paoluzzi (then secretary to the ambassador in Paris) to open direct negotiations in 1652 aiming at obtaining English naval support to fight the Ottomans.[94] The same complaints about the absence of diplomatic links that had been expressed by Queen Elizabeth were replicated by Cromwell in his dealings with Giovanni Sagredo di Agostino, the patrician who had been sent as extraordinary ambassador to England to complete Paoluzzi's mission seeking help against the Ottomans. His negotiating position was not particularly strong, especially as Levant Company members were opposing his mission in every possible way and applying strong pressure to the Lord Protector, arguing that their working capital in the Ottoman empire would have been put at risk if there was suspicion that Venice was being helped.[95] This issue dominated not only his embassy, but also the mission of Francesco Giavarina, the secretary he left behind to continue negotiations.[96] We see again a divergence between the position of the London-based Levant Company members, concerned with possible Ottoman retaliation against their commerce, and that of their agents

---

[92] ASV, *Esposizioni Principi*, reg. 41, cc.121r–122v (11-11-1632).
[93] H. F. Brown, *Studies in the History of Venice*, 2 vols, London, 1907, i: 323–324.
[94] Brown, *Studies in the History*, ii: 296–321.
[95] Brown, *Studies in the History*, ii: 298–299.
[96] Giovanni Sagredo, 'Relazione d'Inghilterra (1656)', in Firpo ed., *Relazioni di ambasciatori veneti*, 851–874; his analysis was focused on England's military strength, and he reported also on the attention lavished by the Levant Company on his mission; see also ASV, *Senato, Dispacci, Inghilterra*, ff. 47–51, *passim*.

active on the ground, who did not hesitate to loan their ships to both sides during the conflict in exchange for ready cash or customs rebates.[97] Cromwell's delicate balancing game was a true success in appeasing both the Porte and the Republic about English neutrality, whilst English vessels were happily employed by both sides.[98]

Writing from Madrid on 21 June 1651, Pietro Basadonna, the Venetian ambassador to the Spanish court, reported on the expediency of establishing proper diplomatic relations with the English government. He was sceptical of the durability of the Parliamentary regime, but also aware that

Owing to the care of Parliament they have 80 men of war, which are certainly the finest now afloat, whether for construction, armament or crews. They can increase these numbers with incredible facility to 150, 200 or more sail. The revenue, which is the basis of all the rest, is now augmented by saving the cost of the royal family, by the spoliation of church property and by the confiscation of the estates of royalists. It is reasonable to infer that with good management, upon which there is some doubt, the English might at this moment maintain double the force they now have and at the same time accumulate immense treasure. In addition there is the facility with which the English increase their fortunes by trade, which has made great strides for some time past, and is now improved by the protection it receives from Parliament, the government of the commonwealth and that of its trade being exercised by the same individuals. The advantage of this was formerly recognised by other nations, who are now impoverishing themselves because in our time the source of our greatness is considered dishonourable.[99]

Bernard Capp synthesised well Basadonna's opinion of Parliament: 'the Rumpers were ignorant mechanics but possessed the finest navy in the world'.[100] For a republic which had been engulfed in a lonely fight with the Ottomans for more than fifteen years this alone would be a good incentive for re-establishing diplomatic links. Two things emerge powerfully from Basadonna's text: a certain wistfulness regarding not so much England's naval strength but rather its policy of supporting trade, so clearly reminiscent of Venetian past glories, and the absence of that undertone of social disdain which had plagued Venetian patricians whose claim to 'nobility' had always been questioned.[101] The argument is not further developed, but its implications must have been clear to the

---

[97] On these issues see Goffman, *Britons in the Ottoman Empire*.

[98] On this see the analytical synthesis in T. Venning, *Cromwellian Foreign Policy*, Basingstoke, 1995, 230–237 and bibliography quoted therein.

[99] Letter to the Doge and Senate dated 21 June 1651, in CSPVe, vol. xxviii (1647–1652), 182–189: see www.british-history.ac.uk/report.aspx?compid=89705 (date accessed: 28 October 2011).

[100] B. Capp, *Cromwell's Navy: The Fleet and the English Revolution, 1648–1660*, Oxford, 1989, 72.

[101] On this issue see the masterful analysis in C. Donati, *L'idea di nobiltà in Italia: secoli XIV–XVIII*, Rome and Bari, 1988.

Doge and *Senato*, as the 'government of the commonwealth and that of its trade being exercised by the same individuals' had been the load-bearing pillar of Venice's past glories.

In these same years Thomas Killigrew, Charles II's representative, was languishing in Venice. He had arrived in Italy in 1649 as the king's special envoy with the task of gaining recognition and funding for his cause. After a tour to gauge support, and with little to show for his efforts, given the noncommittal way in which Italian states were reacting to the events in England, Killigrew settled in Venice in 1650. There he kept a low profile, mostly due to a lack of cash with which to support himself. With indirect talks with Parliament cautiously advancing, in 1652 he was dismissed by the Venetian *Senato* on the pretext of having set up an illegal butcher shop in his own home.[102] Tax rebates on meat were indeed granted to foreign diplomats in Venice, and he was accused of abusing this privilege to earn some money on the side.[103] His dismissal was most likely the result of political expediency, given Venice's tentative efforts to please Cromwell. The secretary Alessandro Businello recounts that he brought him the news 'with as much sweetness as possible', and when he bade him goodbye Killigrew lamented his destiny of being 'the servant of an unlucky king'.[104] Reading through the papers of his embassy, it is difficult not to feel sorry for his real poverty and for the clear sense of isolation he seems to have suffered. Setting up an illegal butcher shop to ease his financial ruin does not sound that far-fetched.

Consuls and controversies

Consuls are only Merchants, who notwithstanding their Office of Judge in the Controversies that may arise among those of their own Nation, carry on at the same time their own Traffick, and are liable to the Justice of the Place where they

---

[102] He is not included in Bell, *A Handlist*. He was also a playwright, and his woes are recounted in *DNB*, s.v.: 'Killigrew reached Venice on 14 February 1650 and remained there as Charles's resident for more than two years. During his Italian stay, he found the time to write two lengthy dramatic romances, *Cecilia and Clorinda*, its first part composed in Turin, its second in Florence, and *Bellamira her Dream*, entirely written in Venice. As of June 1651 Killigrew began to experience difficulties in his relationship with the Venetian senate over his alleged involvement in illegal slaughtering and smuggling practices. The senate's request in June 1652 that the English resident be dismissed was largely inspired by political expediency, as the Venetian Republic did not wish to antagonize Cromwell's government.' On his period in Venice see also Brown, *Studies in the History*, i: 324.

[103] Brown, *Studies in the History*, i: 333.

[104] ASV, *Esposizioni principi*, reg. 62, cc.73r–75r (20-6-1652); see his subsequent letter to the *Collegio*, protesting his innocence, in ASV, *Esposizioni principi*, reg. 62, c.82r (27-6-1652).

reside, as well in civil as in criminal Matters; which is altogether inconsistent with the Quality of Publick Ministers.[105]

It was with these words that Abraham de Wicquefort described the post of consul in the late seventeenth century. Unfortunately, in the previous period the matter was substantially more confused. During the Middle Ages the role of consul was conceived as a somewhat elective duty, whose principal role was mediation between foreign merchants and local authorities. Frequently – in this earlier phase – the consul was a citizen of the host-town and not a member of the foreign nation, chosen presumably for his superior ability to network in a familiar environment. The figure of the ambassador, on the other hand, was one of full 'representativity' in connection with the principle of sovereignty. The political asymmetry of this instance seems to be the relevant point in its definition. The consul did not normally have immunity because, as a merchant or merchant representative, he subscribed to various contracts and was therefore subject to local jurisdiction. On the other hand, the ambassador, or the envoy, could refer only to the authority which was the direct source of his position – that is to say, his king or ruler. As a result, some sort of immunity protected his person, his house, his 'family' (in the larger sense), and sometimes this allowed him to enjoy some other prerogatives, such as a customs exemption (like the just mentioned one on meat duties) or the right to practise his own religion in his house.

As far as Venice was concerned, the confusion between the political and commercial functions of consuls was solved at the beginning of the sixteenth century with the creation of the *Cinque Savi alla Mercanzia*, which resulted in a clear division: diplomatic representatives were elected by the *Senato*, consuls by the *Cinque Savi*.[106] Foreign consuls in Venice were never granted any jurisdictional power to solve controversies amongst their countrymen. When they performed such a role, this was done in a totally informal manner. In Venice and her empire foreign merchants were obliged to resort to local courts to resolve their controversies.[107]

In England, it was only in the seventeenth century, 'from having been chiefly an agency of trading companies or of groups of influential London merchants', that the institute of 'consul' took on 'quite imperfectly, a

---

[105] Monsieur de Wicquefort, *The Rights Privileges and Office of Embassadors and Publick Ministers. Illustrated with Historical Narrations of the most important Affairs that have been transacted by them through all the Courts of Europe* . . . , London, 1740 (1682), 40.

[106] A. Trampus, 'La formazione del diritto consolare moderno a Venezia e nelle Province Unite tra Seicento e Settecento', *Rivista di Storia del Diritto Italiano*, 67 (1994): 283–319, 284–285.

[107] On these issues see Fusaro, 'Politics of Justice'.

national and a public character'.[108] A classic example was the English consul in Livorno, who had been elected locally by English merchants since the end of the sixteenth century; it was not until 1634 that the English government formally appointed Morgan Read.[109] Read's appointment had been approved four years earlier by the 'Master, Wardens and Assistant of the Trinity House',[110] so the government's involvement was just a confirmation of a *de facto* situation. In the Ottoman empire, English consuls were employed by the Levant Company and reported to its board of directors. They were responsible for making sure that only Company members and their agents traded in the area, in practice to enforce the Company's trading monopoly with England. They also collected consular dues from their countrymen and others seeking the protection of the English flag.[111]

The nationality of a consul was another complex issue: the mercantile community could either choose a local or a fellow national. A good example of medieval practice is Genoa, whose consular network developed quite early and provided a sort of blueprint. Within the large network of Genoese mercantile communities, merchants tended to choose a national in places considered especially strategic and to leave matters to a local notable in places of secondary importance.[112] But the nationality of consuls also depended on the interaction between the community and the host country; consuls seem always to have belonged to the country that had the superior position in the bilateral commercial relationship.

By the seventeenth century more strictly 'political' considerations played an increasingly important role in the choice of consuls. When Morgan Read died in 1665, the local mercantile community pushed for the position to be given to his widow and her brothers, all Italians. However, the English resident in the Grand Duchy – Sir John Finch – refused, because he believed that the position should remain in the hands of English nationals, who could be punished by English authorities for

[108] V. Barbour, 'Consular Service in the Reign of Charles II', *American Historical Review*, 33 (1927–28): 553–578, 553.
[109] Engels, *Merchants, Interlopers*, 126.
[110] *LMA*, CLC/526/MS30337/003, 837 (7-4-1630); *LMA*, CLC/526/MS30045/002, c.43v (7-4-1630) Read is proposed; c.46r (21-4-1630) he is confirmed by the king. Read was still asking Trinity House in 1660 for a certificate to confirm his appointment, in *LMA*, CLC/526/MS30337/003, 838 (10-11-1660). See also G. G. Harris, *Trinity House of Deptford: Transactions 1609–36*, London, 1983.
[111] Masters, *The Origin of Western Economic Dominance*, 78. See also Steensgaard, 'Consuls and Nations'.
[112] Petti Balbi, *Mercanti e nationes nelle Fiandre*, 75; Abulafia, 'Cittadino e "denizen"', 282; Pagano De Divitiis, *English Merchants*, 72.

negligence or betrayal. He also 'thought it unadvisable that Italians should receive information on the cargoes, weapons, routes and departure times of the English ships which called at Livorno'. A few years later he maintained the same opinion when Alvise Morelli was proposed as the English consul in Venice. Morelli had the added disadvantage of having a Dutch wife, which, given the political sensitivity at that juncture, posed an undeniable barrier.[113]

In the first half of the seventeenth century the Trinity House of Deptford still had influence in maritime affairs of the whole country.[114] Historically, there was friction between Trinity House, which acted as a sort of guild for shipmasters, and merchants. This centred around the fact that 'although some mariners were formally apprenticed, it was also possible to just join a ship, rise to mate and master and act as supercargo and agent for merchants in the international and coasting trades', which was seen by the trading companies as contravening the legislation on apprentices.[115] Another area in which Trinity House claimed a role, and which could lead to clashes especially with the great trading companies, was the appointment of consuls, particularly in the Mediterranean. Genoa[116] and Livorno were 'instances particularly in point', as Charles Barrett claimed,[117] but we shall see how Trinity House also tried to claim the right to appoint a consul in Venice. The underlying issue was, again, jurisdiction. Even contemporary authorities seem to have expressed their opinion in the vaguest of terms, probably a deliberate strategy when different institutions were trying to expand their jurisdiction without strong precedents. Correspondence was frantically exchanged between all interested parties whenever an election was contested for whatever reason.

---

[113] Pagano De Divitiis, *English Merchants*, 72–73.

[114] R. W. K. Hinton, 'The Mercantile System in the Time of Thomas Mun', *Economic History Review*, 2nd series, 7 (1955): 277–290, 279.

[115] Grassby, *The Business Community*, 53.

[116] On the appointment of consuls in Genoa, see *LMA*, CLC/526/MS30045/002, 400, cc.53v–54r (7-12-1631). The supplication of merchants active in Genoa is in *LMA*, CLC/526/MS30045/002, 401, c.54 (26-3-1631) and 402, 54v (10-12-1631). The request to the king for the confirmation of the election is in *LMA*, CLC/526/MS30045/002, 405, c.57r (25-8-1632). On subsequent elections in Genoa, see also 441, c.72v (s.d.) and 442, cc.72v–73r (23-4-1634).

[117] Barbour, 'Consular Service', 556. C. R. B. Barrett, *The Trinity House of Deptford*, London, 1893, 54; Harris, *The Trinity House of Deptford, 1514–1660*, 241 claimed the same thing; unfortunately they all neglected to reference those claims. Trapani was also included in this list: *LMA*, CLC/526/MS30337/003, 838 (4-6-1634) for Henry Dick 'settled Consull at Trappany'; on the appointment of consuls in Trapani, see also *LMA*, CLC/526/MS30045/002, 450, c.75v (4-6-1634).

The experience of the English consulate in Venice highlights particularly well some of the peculiarities of the English presence in the Venetian territories. The English mercantile community's detachment from the political sphere emerges even when an apparently exquisitely political controversy brought total confusion to the role of the consul and the question of who had the right to appoint him. However, the fluid behaviour by all parties (merchants, aspiring consuls, the *Cinque Savi*) is key to an understanding of the internal dynamics of the community and of the Republic's attitude towards external political events.

The list of English consuls appended to the *Calendar of State Papers Venetian* is not complete and shows that the appointment of English consuls was made by different authorities until the Restoration, when it appears to have passed to the crown.[118] The first consul for whom there is evidence is James Higgons, active in Venice from at least 1595,[119] then briefly in London in 1600;[120] at his return he resumed his commercial activities, and in 1605 he received commissions from the Levant Company to be its consul in Venice.[121] In 1610 he returned to London.[122] The next consul to appear in the documentation is Thomas Guther in 1620, whose appointment was made by Wotton in conjunction with Trinity House;[123] many years afterwards, trying to reconstruct the list of English consuls in town, the *Cinque Savi* were still unsure from which agency Guther had derived his authority.[124] Wood, in his history of the Levant Company, confidently wrote that 'there was evidently a regular succession of consuls for a time, for in 1618 Henry Parvis was appointed to succeed a Mr. Hassal in the office';[125] no claim to this title has been found for either of them in the documentation examined. Between 1631 and 1633 Ottavio Robazzi appears to have acted as

---

[118] And indeed in some cases the archival references provided there do not seem to correspond to the extant material.

[119] ASV, *Notarile Atti*, reg. 3366 (G.Andrea Catti), cc.208r–209r (18-5-1595). As agent of Holmden: reg. 11919 (Andrea Spinelli), cc.466r/v (14-10-1598); reg. 11920 (Andrea Spinelli), cc.204v–205v (8-4-1599).

[120] He gave power of attorney for his business to Thomas Vaters, and was himself the recipient of many powers of attorney for dealing with business in London: see ASV, *Notarile Atti*, reg. 11921 (Andrea Spinelli), cc.198r–199r; reg. 3372 (G. Andrea Catti), cc.381v–382r (9-8-1600) and cc.384v–385r (11-8-1600).

[121] The commission is in TNA, *SP* 105/143, 2 (1605): for his activities see: TNA, *SP* 105/110, cc.n.n. (1606).

[122] ASV, *Notarile Atti*, reg. 11936 (Andrea Spinelli), c.500r (3-7-1614).

[123] Pearsall Smith, *The Life and Letters*, i: 163 footnote.

[124] ASV, *Cinque Savi alla Mercanzia, Risposte*, reg. 154, cc.96v–97r; copy in ASV, *Cinque Savi alla Mercanzia*, b. 23 n.s., fasc. iii, cc.n.n. (10-6-1648). With this exception, other documents about Guther's presence or commercial activity in Venice have not emerged so far from the Venetian archives.

[125] Wood, *A History*, 65.

English consul.[126] Throughout this period, the Republic's policy in this regard appears to have been to stay out of all issues concerning foreign consuls and their appointment, as long as the merchants recognised their authority. Government intervened only when it was felt that the appointment contravened long-standing usage. For example, Andrea Pelegrini in 1638 presented to the *Cinque Savi* some 'universal patents granted by the Majesty of Great Britain [...] to act as consul in Italy for his Nation', but he was turned down because the Republic did not accept 'universal patents'.[127] The following year Paul Ramacks presented two supplications to the *Collegio* on behalf of English captains of ships serving in the Venetian *Armata*; interestingly, he defined himself as 'consul substitute', but once again the authority behind his claim remained a mystery.[128]

John Hobson Sr, one of the leading merchants in Venice, in 1645 was an 'agent' of the Levant Company, but the title of 'consul' appeared to elude him.[129] There is little doubt about his capacities, being the most influential English merchant in Venice for the longest period of time. We shall see in a later chapter what a pivotal role he played in saving English merchants' goods during the *Popolari* revolt in Zante in 1628, and on the same occasion he was the crucial mediator between the rebellious islanders and the Venetian authorities.[130] Active as a merchant, shipowner and agent of the Levant Company, well settled in town and quite wealthy, he would have seemed the obvious choice for this charge.

The 'consular controversy' started in mid-May 1648 when Hobson wrote to the *Collegio* asking to be confirmed as English consul in Venice. He presented a patent

drawn in London by the Governor and Assistants of Trinity House, to whom this election corresponds according to ancient prerogative granted by Kings and Parliaments of England.

In his petition he explained that he already had been elected in 1646 but, because he had had to go to the islands 'for the important business of

---

[126] Robazzi was formerly a servant of Antonio Foscarini, and was married to a Protestant woman. See *CSPVe*, 'Appendix: Miscellaneous 1616', vol. xiv (1615–1617), 592–600, see: www.british-history.ac.uk/report.aspx?compid=95975 (date accessed: 1 January 2014). We shall see him, as consul, involved in the problems that arose from the death of Randolph Simes in chapter 10.

[127] ASV, *Cinque Savi alla Mercanzia, Risposte*, reg. 151, cc.189 r/v; another copy in ASV, *Cinque Savi alla Mercanzia*, b. 23 n.s., fasc. vi, cc.n.n. (30-12-1638).

[128] He also appears as 'Ramacher'; the only trace of his passage in Venice is represented by these two petitions: ASV, *Collegio, Rdd*, f. 30, cc.n.n. (31-3-1639) and (23-5-1639).

[129] TNA, *SP* 105/111, cc.n.n. (16-1-1644/5) and Wood, *A History*, 65.

[130] This episode will be examined at length in chapter 11.

currants', with the help of the English Resident he had found a substitute in the person of Michael Francis. Now that Francis had left 'to take care of his own business, and [myself] not being able to abandon the Consulate for the duty I owe to the King my Master', he was asking to be officially recognised.[131] During his brief office, Francis had actively represented ship-captains trading in the Levant;[132] the business that had forced him to leave Venice and to which Hobson was referring was, in fact, the aftermath of his massive bankruptcy.[133] When Hobson asked to be officially recognised, the *Cinque Savi* gave a positive answer.[134] They had absolutely no reason to doubt the validity of his patent, but still they were bemused by the fact that each time English aspiring consuls asked for recognition, they seemed to present accreditations from a different agency. For this reason they wrote a more detailed answer the following month. They confirmed their approval of Hobson and also tried to provide a short history of the English consular presence in Venice.[135]

The following September, Joseph Kent burst onto the scene, claiming his right to be recognised as consul. After Francis had left, he claimed, the Resident Gilbert Talbot[136] had appointed him:

I understand that a certain Mr. John Hobson, on the basis of some fraudulent Commission obtained from the Governor of Trinity House in London, incompetent in such matters, and composed of a small number of Sailors, with authority to decide only on minor navigational matters, and now rebellious

---

[131] ASV, *Collegio, Rdd*, f. 39, cc.n.n. (14-5-1648). The letter was indeed dated 4 November 1646.
[132] ASV, *Collegio, Rdd*, f. 38, cc.n.n. (15-10-1647).
[133] He would be condemned by the *Quarantia* in 1649, and when he requested a safe conduct to settle his affairs in 1653, his creditors supported his request to the *Collegio*: see ASV, *Collegio, Rdd*, f. 44, cc.n.n. (28-11-1653).
[134] ASV, *Cinque Savi alla Mercanzia, Risposte*, reg. 154, c.88r; copy in ASV, *Cinque Savi alla Mercanzia*, b. 23 n.s., fasc. iii, cc.n.n. (19-5-1648).
[135] They acknowledged the existence of an English consul in town for the previous forty years. Amongst the consul they mentioned Guther, the 'Venetian Thomaso Lorenzoni' – who must be the Englishman Thomas Rowlandson, and does not actually appear anywhere else in the documentation as consul, but as the resident between the ambassadorships of Wake and Feilding. Rowlandson received a salary from the Secretary of State until 1635, in 1637 came back to Venice as a private citizen (Stoye, *English Travellers*, 107–108). 'Then the [extraordinary] ambassador Lord Feilding nominated someone from his household, leaving the business related to ships to Ottavio Robazzi, who exercised it until recently': in ASV, *Cinque Savi alla Mercanzia, Risposte*, reg. 154, cc.96v–97r; another copy in ASV, *Cinque Savi alla Mercanzia*, b. 23 n.s., fasc.vi, cc.n.n. (10-6-1648).
[136] Talbot came to Venice as secretary of the Ambassador Extraordinary Viscount Feilding in 1634, assumed the residency whilst Feilding was in Savoy, and became a permanent *chargé d'affaires* after Feilding's departure in April 1639 until June 1644. He then returned to Venice as a fully accredited Ambassador in 1645. See Bell, *A Handlist*, 292–293; 'Accredited Diplomatic Agents', cxliii–cl.

against His Majesty, dared in a supplication presented to the Most Excellent Collegio the 14th of May passed, to claim that of his pretended and temerary election, had been not only aware, and approving, but also executor the Most Illustrious [English] Resident. This assertion will be proved wrong by this letter written by the Resident to Your Serenity, that I humbly present.[137]

Talbot's letter – written from London the previous July – after some excuses about his absence from Venice, which he attributed to the king's difficulties, stated that Hobson's claims were unsubstantiated. His supposed patent had been issued by Trinity House in November 1646, but Talbot himself had left Venice in May 1645, and therefore could not have approved it. Furthermore:

Never have English Kings or Parliaments granted authority to that Company of Merchants [sic] to nominate the Consul in Venice, but this has always been the prerogative of His Majesty's Public Ministers or Residents in Venice.[138]

Interestingly, the Levant Company – which had appointed Higgons as consul at the beginning of the century – was not mentioned in this letter. Asking the Republic to confirm Kent as consul, Talbot added a copy of a letter of the king's councillor George Digby,[139] written to him in March 1643 from Oxford. In it, Hobson was mentioned for the consulate, but it was also said that before formalising any appointment the king wanted to hear Talbot's opinion on the matter.[140]

Hobson did not waste any time in replying. In his letter to the *Collegio* at the end of September, he questioned Talbot's authority to interfere with issues regarding Venice, 'as Sir Talbot is not resident there [. . .] having left more than four years ago for England'. Moreover, he pointed out how Talbot never had any authority to nominate consuls, and that all he could have done was to confirm Hobson's appointment, which he claimed the king had signed in Oxford on 13 March 1643. He went on:

However, the Resident did not give due obedience to the orders of the King. Rather, for his own personal interest, and on his own authority he gave the charge of consul to Michiel Francis, who is young and inexperienced, and he concealed His Majesty's commission, which I personally had delivered into his hands.

His letter was accompanied by another letter from Digby, dated 29 August 1648 from Paris, once again supporting Hobson's claim.[141]

---

[137] ASV, *Collegio, Rdd*, f. 39, cc.n.n. (17-9-1648).
[138] ASV, *Collegio, Rdd*, f. 39, cc.n.n. (17-9-1648).
[139] George Digby in 1643 was with the king, and was appointed as one of the principal Secretaries of State, see *DNB*, s.v.
[140] Both letters are enclosed with ASV, *Collegio, Rdd*, f. 39, cc.n.n. (17-9-1648).
[141] ASV, *Collegio, Rdd*, f. 39, cc.n.n. (24-9-1648).

The situation appears therefore to have been far more complex than a simple division between a 'parlamentarian' and a 'royal' consul, which would have been expected given the events in London. In England, the period from 1646 to 1648 saw growing dissatisfaction with the parliamentary regime, which in 1648 led to a series of uprisings and the invasion of England by a royalist Scottish army.[142] The spring and summer of 1648 – exactly when the consular controversy exploded in Venice – were particularly difficult for the maritime community. Richard Blakemore argues that, by the summer of 1648, Trinity House, 'a local institution with a specific function – to deal with issues of pilotage and shipping on the Thames – had become the conduit for the expression of opinions relating to national concerns and attempting to influence the government's policy'.[143] With the military and political situation in flux, whilst beforehand the maritime community and navy had leaned towards the Parliamentary side, at this point there was disagreement on Parliament's more radical policies. In the spring of 1648 Trinity House's allegiance split, with a majority of its members supporting peace and settlement with the king.[144]

Both Kent and Hobson claimed to have been appointed by royal authority, but Hobson had the additional weight of a patent from Trinity House – which must have been extremely happy to provide it, considering it gave them an excellent opportunity to enlarge their claim to nominate consuls in the Mediterranean. The most likely explanation is therefore that Kent was supported by Talbot on behalf of the king, whilst Hobson was supported by the 'royalist' faction of Trinity House. The confusion in England due to the civil wars played a role in this dispute, but disagreements within the English mercantile community in Venice, more than events in England, were most likely the key to events.[145]

The following June, Kent presented the *Collegio* with a patent dated August 1648 'from the navy at sea' in which Prince Charles supported his claim. The patent was carefully worded:

we are informed at present there is no one with authority from His Majesty who can perform the Office and Charge of Consul, resident in the lands of the Republic of Venice, which is a matter of concern for the interests of merchant subjects of His Majesty.

---

[142] See R. Ashton, *Counter-Revolution: The Second Civil War and Its Origins, 1646–1648*, New Haven, 1994, 412–414.

[143] R. J. Blakemore, *The London & Thames Maritime Community during the British Civil Wars, 1640–1649*, PhD thesis, University of Cambridge, 2013, 279; for an analysis of these events see 255–299.

[144] Capp, *Cromwell's Navy*, 30, 49–40, 51; Blakemore, *The London & Thames*, 286.

[145] I wish to thank Richard Blakemore for our conversations on this topic.

No reference was made at any point of a competing candidate in the person of Hobson or of the claim of Trinity House.[146] In the meantime total silence was the reply of choice of the Venetian government. The Republic clearly wished to avoid involvement in what it perceived to be an internal English political squabble. Any statement by a Venetian magistracy could be taken as a political endorsement regarding the English civil wars, which was to be avoided at all costs.

The Venetian *Senato* would vote for formal recognition of Cromwell's regime only in 1651, when the implications of the Rump's expansion in the Mediterranean became impossible to ignore.[147] Hobson did not insist further, since at that time he was still enveloped in a long and messy commercial controversy with the Greek merchant Anzolo Bonisello, and probably he did not want to push the consular matter at a moment of personal and financial weakness.[148] Kent remained in Venice for the next few years,[149] but he also kept a low profile. In the autumn of 1652 he appears as creditor of Gualtier Woolf,[150] then disappears from the Venetian documentation.[151]

---

[146] ASV, *Collegio, Rdd*, f. 40, cc.n.n. (7-6-1649); the certified translation dates from 5 October 1648, and the handwriting of Prince Charles is certified by Henry Wood and Gualtier Woolf in presence of the notary Gabriel Gabrieli. The patent itself is dated 13 August 1648; the royalist and parliamentarian fleets faced off in the Thames on 25 August 1648: see Blakemore, *The London & Thames*, 292–296.

[147] Capp, *Cromwell's Navy*, 72.

[148] John Hobson Sr with Randolph Simes, John Eglesfield and Samuel Vassal had made a deal with the Greek merchants Anzolo and Dimitri Bonisello. It concerned investment in currant production in Morea; the Englishmen contributed 20,000 *reali*, and an equivalent sum was invested by the Greeks. The deal had not been respected – allegedly by the Greeks – and a massive controversy had started. After a failed attempt at a compromise in 1638 (ASV, *GdF*, 468 (*Risposte*, f. 2), c.389 (19-2-1637mv)), the issue was still unresolved in the early 1650s. Repercussions were so great in England that some merchants asked for letters of marque to recuperate the losses. On this issue see: *CSPVe*, vol. xxv (1640–1642) and vol. xxvi (1642–1643), *passim*. Also ASV, *Collegio, Notatorio*, b. 67, fasc. ii, c.76r (4-9-1641); ASV, *GdF*, 478 (*Multorum*, f. 3), c.34 (19-10-1641); ASV, *Collegio, Rdd*, f. 40, cc.n.n. (12-5-1649).

[149] Defined as the 'Royalist resident in Venice' in Pincus, *Protestantism and Patriotism*, 109.

[150] Creditor of Samuel Luce in ASV, *GdF*, 494 (*Domande in causa*, f. 7), c.307 (24-10-1651). Controversy on silk customs in ASV, *Collegio, Rdd*, f. 42, cc.n.n. (1-12-1651). Creditor of Gualtier Woolf in ASV, *GdF*, 495 (*Domande in causa*, f. 8), c.222 (11-9-1652). He lent some money to his cousin Richard Symonds, a royalist officer travelling through Italy in 1651: see BL, *Harleian* 943, cc.119r/v (7-9-1651). He acted as guarantor for the rent of the house of the royalist resident Killigrew at San Cassan, see ASV, *GdF*, 494 (*Domande in causa*), f. 7, c.431 (19-2-1651mv).

[151] In the following years he appeared in Livorno where he was consul during the 1660s. He seems to have been rather itinerant, though because in 1666 he was substituted by Charles Chellingsworth, whilst he was travelling around Italy: see Pagano De Divitiis, *English Merchants*, 72n, 78, 102, 114.

On his departure from Venice in May 1652, Kent left his charge to Woolf. It proved a very unpopular choice. Woolf had been active in Venice since 1640, mostly dealing with ship-captains and occasionally acting as their translator,[152] but also providing lodgings.[153] Still, his appointment was not accepted by the English merchants in Venice, and many challenges to his right to exact consulage rights followed.[154] We can easily understand why the captain of the *Northumberland* – of which Hobson was the principal owner – refused to pay consulage rights to Woolf,[155] but many others took a similar stance. This was unique: it had never happened before, and it was never to happen again. At the end of 1652 English merchants and captains wrote to the *Cinque Savi* lamenting Woolf's impositions and asked 'how did he come to interfere with this charge, with what authority and patents?'[156] The *Savi* were confused. They knew that Kent had left his charge to Woolf, and that the Resident Killigrew had approved it, but they also admitted that the *Senato* had never formally confirmed his appointment. The lack of official approval by the *Senato* is perfectly in line with the policy of silent neutrality which Venice was then practising towards the English civil wars. The *Savi* were also puzzled that English merchants should ask the Venetian government who had provided authority to their own supposed consul. More confusion was to follow when the *Savi* tried, once more, to reconstruct the list of English consuls in Venice. The fact that this list was even patchier than the one five years before testifies to both the confusion of England and the lamentable state of the archives of Venetian magistrates. Ultimately the *Savi* all agreed that this issue was political and swiftly delegated it to the 'singular prudence' of the *Senato*.[157]

Woolf died in summer 1653 without his position having been clarified. The following September, Hobson came forward again with his claims. He rounded up support from resident merchants and from 'many English ship-captains, as testified by a notarised declaration'. Kent and Woolf

[152] ASV, *Notarile Atti*, reg. 8449 (Alberto Mastaleo), cc.123v–124v (31-8-1640) and cc.152v–153r (16-10-1640); ASV, *Notarile Atti*, reg. 8450 (Alberto Mastaleo), cc.173v–174v (31-8-1641) and cc.232r/v (28-9-1641); ASV, *Notarile Atti*, reg. 6668 (Gabriel Gabrieli), cc.177r/v (2-8-1646); ASV, *Notarile Atti*, reg. 8456 (Alberto Mastaleo), cc.112v–113r (20-8-1647).

[153] ASV, *AdC, Penale*, b. 353, fasc. 21, cc.n.n. (10-6-1646).

[154] ASV, *GdF*, 495 (*Domande in causa*, f. 8), c.186 (22-8-1652); there were also some posthumous complaints: see ASV, *GdF*, 495 (*Domande in causa*, f. 8) c.288 (25-9-1653), and 478 (*Multorum*, f. 3), c.98 (3-10-1655).

[155] ASV, *GdF*, 496 (*Domande in causa*, f. 9), c.108 (6-5-1653).

[156] ASV, *Cinque Savi alla Mercanzia, Risposte*, reg. 155, cc.12r–13r; another copy is in ASV, *Cinque Savi alla Mercanzia*, b. 23 n.s., fasc. vi, cc.n.n. (22-1-1652mv).

[157] ASV, *Cinque Savi alla Mercanzia, Risposte*, reg. 155, cc 12r–13r; another copy is in ASV, *Cinque Savi alla Mercanzia*, b.23 n.s., fasc. vi, cc.n.n. (22-1-1652mv).

were dead, and their 'machinations' had gone with them.[158] Hobson
sought endorsement for his appointment from the Levant Company
itself, which in the confusion of the civil wars had remained quiet.[159]
But unfortunately for him, though he was already an agent of the
Company, the answer was not quite what he expected:

as for the name of Consul, which you conceive might enable you the better to
perform the service, we are not willing to renew a title which hath been so long
discontinued.[160]

The Company was quite happy for him *to act* in the capacity of consul,
and even to provide him with an allowance, but not to grant him the
formal title. If nothing else, this document confirms that the Levant
Company had stayed well out of the dispute. It is hardly surprising that
the Company was not willing to bestow such a title upon a member of
the Bristol lobby. Bristol merchants had a special dispensation that
allowed them to import currants outside of the Levant's privilege, but
giving one of them an official role was clearly deemed inappropriate.[161]
Even so, things seemed to be looking better for Hobson this time
around. Whilst he was still waiting for the *Savi*'s response to his
September supplication, the strength of his candidature increased in
November 1653 when Michael Filippi died in Venice at the house of
Paolo Rodomonte. Filippi was the bearer of a letter from Parliament that
nominated him as consul in Venice, and on his deathbed he entrusted it
with his credentials to Hobson.[162]

The *Savi* finally answered his petition the following March; they were
wary:

---

[158] ASV, *Collegio, Rdd*, f. 44, cc.n.n. (24-9-1653).

[159] Wood, *A History*, 56.

[160] TNA, *SP* 105/112, cc.n.n. (10-9-1652); on this see also *CSPVe*, vol. xxix (1653–1654),
n.14, 11: see www.british-history.ac.uk/report.aspx?compid=89752 (date accessed:
4 March 2014). Also Wood, *A History*, 65–66.

[161] On the Bristol privilege, see Fusaro, *Uva passa*, 153–154; D. H. Sacks, *The Widening
Gate: Bristol and the Atlantic Economy 1450–1700*, Berkeley, Los Angeles and Oxford,
1991, 48.

[162] ASV, *Notarile Testamenti*, b. 65 (Andrea Bronzini), n.220 (30-11-1653). Filippi died
the following day. In the will the date of the Parliament letter is not given, nor has the
letter itself emerged from the archives. Given the tumultuous times in England there
might have been some problems with its validity: if the letter was dated before April
1653 it would have been issued by the Rump Parliament, and therefore might not have
been valid in November. If dated after July, the letter would have been issued by the
Barebones Parliament, and would have therefore been valid until the following
December. As both the Rump and the Barebones were part of the commonwealth,
the appointment should have been legitimate across both parliaments, but the matter
could have been contentious. I wish to thank Richard Blakemore for these
clarifications.

Given the well-known turbulence of England, [we are concerned about] what declarations could be made using the decrees of Your Serenity by those involved in the affairs of that Kingdom. We leave this to public reflection.[163]

Once again the *Savi* demurred when faced with a decision which could have international political implications. Finally, the following February, Hobson managed to acquire a patent from Cromwell himself, and this paved the way for his formal recognition by the Republic.[164] By that time, the Republic and the Protectorate were exchanging pleasantries and commercial goodwill at every opportunity.[165]

In 1660 Giles Jones was appointed consul by the Secretary of England after the Restoration, and the *Savi* accepted his appointment.[166] Hobson's situation is not clear: he certainly remained an agent of the Levant Company until his death in 1661, when his charge and salary passed to his nephew, John Hobson Jr.[167] The elder Hobson in the last years of his life was less active, but there is no documentary trace of him relinquishing the consular charge. The Levant Company did not seem to be involved in trying to appoint a consul even after his death; otherwise there would have been no point in paying his nephew to act as an agent.

Jones was rich and not afraid to show it. He was a splendid host, and he certainly had the opportunity to entertain well in his prestigious Venetian residence, welcoming influential travellers as well as English ship-captains at his home.[168] He also was the only English merchant who rented a villa

---

[163] ASV, *Cinque Savi alla Mercanzia, Risposte*, reg. 155, c.36v; another copy in ASV, *Cinque Savi alla Mercanzia*, b. 23 n.s., cc.n.n. (30-3-1654).

[164] ASV, *Cinque Savi alla Mercanzia, Risposte*, reg. 155, c.36v. A side note to the above-mentioned *risposta*, dated 2-6-1654, confirmed the arrival of Cromwell's letter (dated 18-2-1654), and the positive opinion of the *Savi* about his election. See also *CSPVe*, vol. xxix (1653–1654), n.234, 195: see www.british-history.ac.uk/report.aspx?compid=89766 (date accessed: 17 February 2014).

[165] See for example the letter of the Senate to the extraordinary ambassador in England, in ASV, *Senato secreta, Corti*, reg. 32, cc.144v–146r (13-11-1655). On the diplomatic relations between Venice and the commonwealth, see Brown, *Studies in the History*, ii: 296–321.

[166] ASV, *Cinque Savi alla Mercanzia, Risposte*, reg. 155, cc.179r/v; another copy in ASV, *Cinque Savi alla Mercanzia*, b. 23 n.s., cc.n.n. (4-12-1660). See also *CSPVe*, vol. xxxii (1659–1661), n.251, 227, see: www.british-history.ac.uk/report.aspx?compid=90063 (date accessed: 17 February 2014). Steve Pincus calls him 'the English resident in Venice' (*Protestantism and Patriotism*, 310), which is a position he never enjoyed, although on occasion he did send 'political reports' to the Secretary of State.

[167] 'In 1689 it was discussed whether "as very few letters pass through the hands of Mr. Hobson" the Company might ease itself of its stipend, but it was eventually resolved to continue it. There was an English consulate in Venice after the Restoration, but it was maintained by the crown; the Company had no connection with it, though its members were certainly trading there in Charles II's reign': Wood, *A History*, 66.

[168] ASV, *Cinque Savi alla Mercanzia*, b. 23 n.s., cc.n.n. (6-3-1673).

outside town. In 1662, however, an episode tainted his reputation. John and Francis Ravenscroft, brothers of the glass merchant George, wounded him in a fight and consequently were condemned by the *Quarantia* and banned from the territories of the Republic. The Duchess of Modena intervened on their behalf and pleaded with the Republic to lift the ban.[169] Letters were sent to London to solict the king's opinion on the matter. The Venetian resident in London Giavarina reported that the king 'expressed his pleasure at the communication and his regret for the ill behaviour of his subjects, whilst blaming the procedure of the consul, of whom all the merchants complain bitterly, and these propose, I fancy, to remove him'.[170] He was also very happy for the Ravenscrofts to be pardoned, mostly on account of their old father, who, being a royalist, had suffered. No other complaints about Jones have been found in the Venetian documentation, and he appears to have kept his position until 1668, when George Hayles was appointed with royal patents.[171] Jones lived in largesse but died almost broke. His three wills show a dwindling fortune, and after his death his remaining possessions and home furnishings turned out to have been pawned, mostly to friends and business associates.[172]

A few final considerations are due on the consular controversy. Confusion of competencies was to be expected in a period in which the jurisdiction was developing, and the turmoil of the civil wars did not help the matter. What is particularly interesting is the attitude of the protagonists. No other merchant intervened in the controversy between Hobson and Kent. When Kent claimed the mantle of royalist consul, Hobson – with royalist credentials himself – did not challenge him. Political controversies within the English community seem to have been avoided at all costs, and allegiances used only when necessary to suit one's interests.

Kent in his petition of September 1648 accused Trinity House of rebelling against the king, which as we have seen was not exactly the case. With

---

[169] ASV, *AdC, Penale*, b. 378, fasc. 4. See also *CSPVe*, vol. xxxiii, n.127, 104–105: see www.british-history.ac.uk/report.aspx?compid=90101 (date accessed: 17 February 2014).

[170] *CSPVe*, vol xxxiii (1661–1664), n.150, 119–121: see www.british-history.ac.uk/report. aspx?compid=90102 (date accessed: 17 February 2014).

[171] ASV, *Cinque Savi alla Mercanzia*, b. 23 n.s., cc.n.n. (14-5-1668).

[172] His wills are in ASV, *Notarile Testamenti*, bb. 186–188 (Pietro Antonio Bozini), n.94 (2-11-1653) [unpublished will] and n.138 (18-11-1658) [unpublished will]; ASV, *Notarile Testamenti*, b.904 (Francesco Simbeni), n.135. The inventory is in ASV, *Giudici del Petizion, Inventari*, b. 374/39, n.61. Jones' is the only surviving inventory for an Englishman before the eighteenth century. On inventories as evidence for standard of living, consumption and economic activities in regard to Venice, see F. Zanatta, 'L'inventario come fonte per lo studio della storia della ricchezza privata: Venezia nel 1661', *Studi veneziani*, 34 (1997): 199–223.

its loyalty divided, in the summer of that year Trinity House, 'the corporation of shippers, had taken part in the movement to bring back the King and supported the navy's revolt against Parliament',[173] and for this it would undergo a purge the following February. If anything, Kent's credentials seem to have been more tainted than Hobson's, Digby being clearly more influential than Talbot. So why did Hobson abandon the fight, and how did Kent manage to acquire a letter of support from the royal prince? Probably at that point the situation in the royalist camp was so confused that a double endorsement was possible. The endorsement of Hobson by Digby, which even Talbot somewhat acknowledged, and the fact that there was no mention of him in the prince's patent could be seen as evidence of this. What appears to have been a political controversy was most likely a simple private feud. Even the fact that Hobson would finally receive endorsement by the Protector himself is proof that the interests of trade came before anything else; for if Hobson had been proven to be a royalist, why would the Protector endorse him? Recent historiography has confirmed that allegiances during the civil wars were more fluid than previously acknowledged; Hobson was most probably simply a moderate trying to pursue his business interests whilst navigating a confused political situation.

The Levant Company's behaviour is interesting in this instance as well. It was not involved in the election of any consul in Venice after the 1610s, though it always kept a close eye on the situation in the Ionian islands. Although sources are sketchy, its involvement with consular elections in the islands was substantially more active than in Venice,[174] further evidence of the centrality of the islands and of the secondary status of Venice in the Company's eyes.

A company's consul was very different from a government's consul. And the English government's attitude towards Venice changed with the passing of time. Up until the point when Venice was central enough to England's foreign policy to warrant the presence of an ambassador – or a diplomatic resident – interest in consular affairs was limited. Afterwards, however, they became central. The last resident ambassador, John Dodington, left Venice in 1673, and the last extraordinary envoy was Thomas Higgons in 1679. From that moment until the end of the Republic, there were no more permanent English ambassadors in Venice, just consular envoys, and all of these had the government's endorsement.[175]

---

[173] Brenner, *Merchants and Revolution*, 554.

[174] See ASV, *Cinque Savi alla Mercanzia*, b. 23, *passim*.

[175] Bell, *A Handlist*, 294; see also *CSPVe*, 'Attested Diplomatic Agents in Venice', vol. i (1202–1509), 151–152: see www.british-history.ac.uk/report.aspx?compid=94084 (date accessed: 1 December 2014).

7   The Venetian peculiarities

In the popular imagination, as well as in scholarship, the connection between the history of Venice and long-distance trade is immediate. From the adventures of Marco Polo to the epic journeys of galleys full of spices from the East, Venice's role as 'the' European medieval commercial powerhouse has always been well known, its golden age analysed by the giants of twentieth-century classic economic history, from Frederic Lane to Fernand Braudel. Scholarship tends to focus mostly on the city, as the quality and consistency of the urban data sets are far greater than for the rest of the state. Because of archival losses, complete state budgets are available only for the eighteenth century.[1] Since the mid-1990s this gap has partially been filled, and we now have a more rounded analysis of the Venetian state's public finances from the fourteenth to the eighteenth centuries.[2] There are other solid reasons for this historiographical bias; first, the political nature of Venice as a city-state cast a wide shadow, leading to the neglect of its other incarnations: regional state and imperial power. Its long-term survival as a city-state and the debate on crisis vs. relative resilience of its economy during the early modern period became central to the narrative of Italian economic and social decline. At the same time, the economic relationship between cities – to be precise, metropolises – and their states is not a simple and linear one, and many European capitals played a crucial role as engines of economic growth during the early modern period.[3] The history of Anglo-Venetian relations is also the history of two metropolises: great commercial centres highly dependent on maritime trade, with

---

[1] L. Luzzati, F. Besta and A. Ventura eds., *Bilanci generali dello stato*, 4 vols, Venice, 1902–1972.

[2] L. Pezzolo, *Il fisco dei veneziani: finanza pubblica ed economia tra XV e XVII secolo*, Verona, 2003; *Una finanza d'Ancien Régime: la repubblica veneta tra XV e XVIII secolo*, Naples, 2006; for a recent synthesis see his 'The Venetian Economy', in Dursteler ed., *A Companion to Venetian History*, 255–290.

[3] D. Keene, 'Cities and Empires', *Journal of Urban History*, 32 (2005): 8–21 and bibliography quoted therein.

174

similarities also at the level of urban administration.[4] Both London and
Venice dominated the states of which they were capitals, and this lack of
real urban competition set them apart from most of their European
counterparts, most notably the Netherlands, whose strong internal
urban competition has recently been given pride of place by Oscar
Gelderblom as crucial for both economic growth and state-building.[5]
Compared to other European capitals, in Venice the urban element was
more all-encompassing, but comparisons are still possible. The most
visible aspect of the predominance of the 'city' over the 'state' – in other
words of the city-state nature of Venice – was the web of privileges which
supported urban manufacture in the city to the detriment of those in the
rest of the state. This policy guaranteed the loyalty of the Venetian urban
populace to the aristocratic Republic, but for centuries it was a source of
friction between Venice and its subject populations both in the *Dominio
da Mar* and in the *Terraferma* as, especially in the latter, manufactures
were strong and successful and greatly contributed to the economy of
the state.[6] From the economic perspective, this was a multifaceted
relationship, but its essence can be defined as a centre–periphery
conflict, and this element played a crucial role in the way in which the
Venetian political system intervened in economic issues throughout the
territories it controlled.[7] Having said this, it is also important to highlight that the power of economic interest groups was very strong in all
major European metropolises, and the tension between London-based
and country-based merchants also played a crucial role in the development of English economic policy during the early modern period.[8]
Steven Epstein well summarised these issues when he wrote
that 'Italian city-states were highly efficient modes of economic organisation in societies with highly fragmented jurisdictions, but were less
effective than monarchies in coordinating markets over larger and
politically more complex territories; their smaller scale may also have
made it easier for vested economic interests to capture the political
agenda'.[9] During the medieval centuries of economic growth this

[4] R. MacKenney, *Tradesmen and Traders: The World of the Guilds in Venice and Europe,
c.1250–c.1650*, London, 1987, 155–160.
[5] O. Gelderblom, *Cities of Commerce: The Institutional Foundations of International Trade in
the Low Countries, 1250–1650*, Princeton, 2013.
[6] Literature on these issues is fairly large. For recent syntheses see the contributions to
Lanaro ed., *At the Centre of the Old World*, and bibliography quoted therein.
[7] Knapton, 'The *Terraferma* State', 98–99, 103, 114–115.
[8] F. J. Fisher, 'London as an "Engine of Economic Growth"', in J. S. Bromley and
E. H. Kossmann eds., *Britain and the Netherlands*, 4 vols., The Hague, 1971, iv: 3–16.
[9] S. R. Epstein, *Freedom and Growth: The Rise of States and Markets in Europe 1300–1750*,
London, 2000, 171.

overlap of the political and commercial elites had created a virtuous circle, but with the sixteenth-century restructuring of the European economy it became a hindrance. The strong connection between the Venetian ruling elite and trade loosened, a development that worried some contemporaries.

Leonardo Donà commented in 1610 that in Venice there was no shortage of capital to invest, but the patriciate – including his own family – preferred to invest it in real estate and landed properties, thereby withdrawing capital from maritime trade.[10] The temptation to turn to land was not a new concern for the Venetian government; already in 1274 Venetian patricians were prohibited from acquiring possessions on the Italian mainland, a measure designed to stimulate their engagement with the sea.[11] Patricians started to invest in land in the fourteenth century, during the initial phase of expansion on the mainland, and this process accelerated dramatically in the decades following the recovery of the Italian territories lost at Agnadello (1509), as a necessary political way to secure the Republic's position on the *Terraferma*.

The sixteenth-century turn to land was a European-wide phenomenon, which also has been labelled the 'betrayal of the bourgeoisie'.[12] Within the Italian historiographical context, this was considered to be one of the primary causes for the economic stagnation of the peninsula in the centuries that followed. However, even without taking into consideration the ideological implications of such a label, the hard economic facts point to a growing profitability of land throughout the century, fuelled by the general continental increase of food prices, which made it a relatively simple and profitable investment.[13] In the same period Mediterranean maritime trade was becoming more expensive and dangerous, and

---

[10] Quoted in Romanin, *Storia documentata di Venezia*, vii: 532–533. On Leonardo Donà, in the words of Gaetano Cozzi, 'one of the last great voices of Venetian renaissance', and Doge during the 1606 Interdict controversy, see *DBI*, s.v.

[11] P. Morosini, *Historia della città e Republica di Venetia*, Venice, 1637, libro VIII, 193 quoted in A. Tenenti, 'Il senso del mare', in A. Tenenti and U. Tucci eds., *Storia di Venezia*, vol. xii: *Il mare*, Rome, 1991, 7–76, 7.

[12] Braudel, *The Mediterranean*, ii: 725–734. Later he slightly revised his position, see *Civilization and Capitalism, 15th–18th Century*, vol. ii: *The Wheels of Commerce*, Berkeley, 1992, 594–595. H. Soly, 'The "Betrayal" of the Sixteenth-Century Bourgeoisie: A Myth? Some Considerations of the Behaviour Pattern of the Merchants of Antwerp in the Sixteenth Century', *Acta Historiae Neerlandicae*, 8 (1975): 31–49.

[13] For the Venetian angle on this phenomenon: G. M. Varanini, 'Proprietà fondiaria e agricoltura', in A. Tenenti and U. Tucci eds., *Storia di Venezia*, vol. v: *Il Rinascimento: società ed economia*, Rome, 1985, 807–879; R. T. Rapp, 'Real Estate and Rational Investment in Early Modern Venice', *Journal of European Economic History*, 8 (1979): 269–290; S. Ciriacono, 'The Venetian Economy and the World Economy of the 17th and

competition was growing. Therefore, turning to agriculture was probably the most efficient and safe choice for investors at the time. The progressive detachment of the Venetian aristocracy from trading created a space which was filled by citizens and subjects, prepared to take more risks to improve their economic condition. This phenomenon was particularly evident in the Levant trade, and accelerated throughout the course of the seventeenth century.[14]

Doing business in an oligarchic republic

Venice has always been described as a 'mercantilist' state *ante litteram*. It is not my intention here to enter into the debate over what has become a rather controversial category, but there is a general consensus about Venice being a precursor of 'mercantilist policies'. It was the first European state to consistently pursue the economic interest of the state through specifically targeted legislation aimed at protecting local manufactures and shipping from foreign competition through an interventionist strategy of economic management and regulation. What, towards the end of the sixteenth century, became a general European approach to the state management of the economy had been the norm in the Republic for centuries.[15] In fact Venetian economic success in the Middle Ages was based precisely on the creation of a tight state-controlled structure which maximised the incentives for citizens to play an active role in commercial and financial activities, providing them with a stable currency, an efficient (relative to the times) judicial system, and effective naval protection for maritime routes. In short, it was a pioneer of capitalism, as argued by Frederic Lane when the word had a less contested identity.[16] 'Citizens' were the core of this structure. The Venetian patriciate, in actual practice, was simply the highest level of citizenship and enjoyed full political and

---

18th Centuries', in H.-J. Nitz ed., *The Early Modern World System in Geographical Perspective*, Stuttgart, 1993, 120–135.

[14] Tucci, *Mercanti, navi e monete*, 43; Fusaro, 'Cooperating Mercantile Networks'; Knapton, 'Tra Dominante e Dominio', 251; Dursteler, *Venetians in Constantinople*, 48–52. On these issues see also Isabella Cecchini's forthcoming book: *Mercanti a Venezia in età moderna: pratiche e istituzioni*.

[15] Lane, *Andrea Barbarigo, Merchant of Venice*, 48; Israel, *European Jewry*, 2; Landes, *The Wealth and Poverty*, 443.

[16] F. C. Lane, *Profits from Power. Readings in Protection Rent and Violence Controlling Enterprise*, Albany, 1979. Also M. M. Bullard, S. R. Epstein, B. G. Kohl and S. M. Stuard, 'Where History and Theory Interact: Frederic C. Lane on the Emergence of Capitalism', *Speculum*, 79 (2004): 88–119, and bibliography quoted therein. An analytical synthesis of these issues can be found in I. Cecchini and L. Pezzolo, 'Merchants and Institutions in Early Modern Venice', *Journal of European Economic History*, 41 (2012): 87–114.

economic rights. Its membership was defined by inclusion in the Major Council, the primary governmental body, whose access was regulated in 1297. The second level was that of *cittadini originari*, who by the early modern period effectively monopolised state bureaucracy. Then came two lower levels of citizenship: *de intus et de extra* and finally just *de intus*. The level of citizenship had important consequences for economic activities, especially trade. This was highly regulated, and participation in its most lucrative branch – the Levant – was allowed on the basis of citizenship. The status of subjects was defined along the same lines: those coming from the Levant dominions were *de facto* granted the trading privileges associated with *de intus et extra* citizenship, allowing them to trade between Venice and the Levant. Beginning in 1406, subjects coming from the Italian mainland and Dalmatia were granted the privileges associated with *de intus* citizenship, allowing them to trade within a smaller geographic area.[17] It is clear even from such a brief sketch that access to commerce was clearly perceived to be a central manifestation of Venetian identity and was thus enshrined in legislation. Even though Levantine trade was also open to 'lower' citizens and subjects of the Republic, in actual practice the closed and complex nature of the Venetian political and economic systems limited their active participation. During the medieval centuries, when the economic conjuncture favoured Venice and there was an almost perfect overlap between political and economic elites, this was not a problem, but in the sixteenth century, when the ruling elite started to detach itself from trade, this system entered into a systemic crisis which dragged on until the very end of the Republic in 1797.

Given that the economic system relied heavily upon state protection and organisation, when the political elite no longer corresponded to the ruling class, a fissure developed within the state. The new economic elite did not have direct access to the centres of power, as only patricians could be elected to any council of state or executive position. The only avenues for influencing political action were lobbying and petitioning the government. Both strategies had long played an important role in Venetian statecraft, and grew exponentially during the sixteenth and seventeenth centuries. However, the absence of the new mercantile elite from the

---

[17] There is a short and analytical description of the issue of citizenship in A. Bellavitis, '"Per cittadini metterete ... ": la stratificazione della società veneziana cinquecentesca tra norma giuridica e riconoscimento sociale', *Quaderni Storici*, 89 (1995): 359–383. A comprehensive overview is in A. Zannini, *Burocrazia e burocrati a Venezia in età moderna: i cittadini originari (sec. XVI–XVIII)*, Venice, 1993; on the role of women in the transmission of citizenship and its privileges see A. Bellavitis, *Identité, mariage, mobilité sociale: citoyennes et citoyens à Venise au XVIe siècle*, Rome, 2001.

upper echelons of government had another consequence which proved equally important: if citizens and subjects were excluded from government they also were cut off from the information exchange at the heart of the Republic's politics and policy, which had been a crucial component of its success. Even the fabled Venetian diplomatic system was originally developed to support trade, and in the seventeenth century Venice still kept thirteen stable legations, which provided a constant flow of information to government.[18] Thus governing meant having access to a massive network, and the very republican structure of the Venetian state meant that information was more widely spread across the political elite than in monarchical states. At the same time, within Venetian political discourse there was constant tension over the tendency for leaks and the need for secrecy. Information did indeed flow across the political elite and governmental agencies, but it should not have moved beyond these.[19] In practice it most certainly did, a development that fostered professional spycraft and two long-standing industries: printing and newswriting.[20]

These internal social developments, along with the profound restructuring of European trade routes, resulted in a substantial hardening of the conditions underpinning Levantine trade. Profits were still possible, but opportunities to really succeed were limited to those who could successfully mobilise alternative networks to support their commercial activities, Greeks and Jewish merchants being classic examples.[21] Under these new rules of the game, the new protagonists of Venetian trade no longer enjoyed the comparative advantage.

The *Cinque Savi alla Mercanzia* – the Venetian board of trade

Patricians could occupy the higher offices of the state through their membership on the Major Council. Most of what we would now define as the executive power of the state was the remit of the *Senato* – which Marin Sanudo described as the 'council which governs the state' – and the *Collegio*.[22] The latter played a crucial role as, in the words of Paul Grendler, it had 'the tremendous advantage of initial, and sometimes

---

[18] 'Six were located in the peninsula (Florence, Mantua, Milan, Naples, Rome Turin) and seven outside of Italy (Constantinople, London, Madrid, Paris, as well as the various seats of the imperial court, of the Republic of the United Provinces and of the Swiss Confederation)', in Zannini, *Economic and Social Aspects*, 111–112.

[19] De Vivo, *Information and Communication*, 46–70.

[20] De Vivo, *Information and Communication*, 74–85.

[21] Fusaro, 'Cooperating Mercantile Networks'.

[22] M. Sanudo, *De origine, situ et magistratibus urbis veneta ovvero la Città di Venetia (1493–1530)*, A. Caracciolo Aricò ed., Milan, 1980, 100. See also E. Besta, *Il Senato veneziano*

exclusive, access to information, especially in foreign policy' and also of setting the agenda for the *Senato*.[23]

Many different governmental bodies had come to share responsibility for overseeing the economy over the course of the centuries, with a consequent crossing and overlapping of jurisdictions. This pattern was most evident in all matters relating to the sea, where the overlap is itself evidence of how much 'trade' and 'sea' were load-bearing elements of Venetian identity. By the beginning of the sixteenth century, in the wake of the multifaceted crisis engulfing the Republic, it became evident that there was a real need to rationalise the economic sector. The response was the creation of a new magistracy with clear and sweeping powers to oversee, revitalise and organise economic activities across the state.

The *Cinque Savi alla Mercanzia* were established in 1507, and became a permanent body ten years later. Their area of competence underwent massive expansion until the middle of the eighteenth century, ending up encompassing all matters with any economic relevance. They were responsible for trade in all its incarnations, shipping (including shipwrecks and insurance), manufactures in the city and state, all types of customs and taxation of goods, the regulation of middlemen (*sensali*), the fight against contraband, commercial treaties, consuls (both Venetians abroad and foreigners in Venice), foreign merchants throughout the state and even agriculture.[24] Election to the *Cinque Savi* brought a relatively prestigious position, mid-way through the *cursus honorum* of a Venetian patrician; members were chosen from amongst the senators with previous experience in commercial matters, and the workload was rather heavy.[25] Most of their work was consultative, as on the instructions of the *Signoria* and *Collegio* they collected data, expert opinions and testimonies. On the basis of this research they provided analyses and policy proposals to the *Collegio* or *Senato* for approval, thus contributing to the legislative process.[26] The *Cinque Savi* acted also as a

---

(*origine, costituzione, attribuzioni e riti*), Venice, 1899, especially ch. 3; Lane, *Venice: A Maritime Republic*, 254–256.

[23] P. F. Grendler, 'The Leaders of the Venetian State, 1540–1609: A Prosopographical Analysis', *Studi Veneziani*, 19 (1990): 35–86, 37–38. This article provides a very clear synthesis of the Venetian government structure. On the relationship between *Senato* and *Collegio*, see de Vivo, *Information and Communication*, 37–39.

[24] For a comprehensive description of its areas of jurisdiction see M. F. Tiepolo *et al.* eds., *Archivio di Stato di Venezia: estratto dal vol. IV della Guida Generale degli Archivi di Stato Italiani*, Rome, 1994, 980–982. Also Borgherini-Scarabellin, *Il Magistrato dei Cinque Savi*. I am working on a comprehensive monograph about this magistrate.

[25] Borgherini-Scarabellin, *Il Magistrato dei Cinque Savi*, 16, 20.

[26] On the flow of information between different governmental bodies see de Vivo, *Information and Communication*, 32–40.

civil tribunal for commercial matters, and increasingly as a first instance civil tribunal for foreigners who were granted the privilege of trading in the city and state.[27] From 1551 the *Cinque Savi* also worked in conjunction with the *Provveditori di Comun* to evaluate controversies surrounding the granting of citizenship, more proof – if needed – of the tight link between citizenship and trade.[28]

The *Cinque Savi* were also asked to provide their opinion regarding petitions sent to the *Signoria* on economic matters; the increased number of these mostly ended up in the *Savi*'s archive, providing the historian with a veritable treasure trove. On the one hand it shows the active engagement of non-patricians and subjects in maritime trade and their constant attempts to provide the government with suggestions and solutions. On the other, the trail of the *Cinque Savi*'s responses allows us to follow in extreme detail how much disagreement there was amongst the patriciate itself. The usual praxis was for all five members of the magistracy to sign every *risposta*, thereby providing a unanimous answer. However, from the beginning of the seventeenth century an interesting phenomenon emerges; when the topic was maritime trade in all its facets – especially the currant trade – opinions frequently differed, and a single query might generate up to five different *risposte*, individually signed by each of them. The *Cinque Savi* are therefore a clear exception to the desire for unanimity which traditionally surrounded the legislative process of the Republic. Filippo de Vivo argued in this regard that 'the rationale of these arrangements was essentially political, to preserve a consistent image of unity in the ruling class'.[29] But this image of unity is shattered by this documentary evidence, which shows how central maritime trade was to the Republic's political economy and to the internal reflections – and ultimately self-perception – of its ruling class. Whatever the *risposte* discussed, there was one consensus: trade was crucial to the Republic, it was in crisis, and something had to be done to address this.

English trading companies

The sixteenth-century reorganisation of the institutions behind economic management and trade was a pan-European phenomenon. Whilst Venice was in crisis, England was rising, and the protagonists of this phase were

---

[27] Borgherini-Scarabellin, *Il Magistrato dei Cinque Savi*, 13; on the civil jurisdiction of the *Cinque Savi*, especially in relation to foreigners, see Fusaro, 'Politics of Justice/Politics of Trade'.

[28] Borgherini-Scarabellin, *Il Magistrato dei Cinque Savi*.

[29] De Vivo, *Information and Communication*, 18.

the chartered trading companies. The first of these was the Merchant Adventurers, founded in 1407 to join English wool exporters. But it was only in the following two centuries that other companies followed. Their history, organisation and development were the subject of a long and intense debate in the central decades of the twentieth century, when different (and sometimes diverging) interpretations were put forward regarding their role in economic growth.[30] It can be argued that this historiographical debate was nothing more than the reincarnation of the heated confrontation which characterised the beginning of the Stuart era, which witnessed a tense debate between crown and parliament, and between London and other urban centres, on the value and limitations of trading companies. To put it simply, the debate hinged on whether companies were the best method to advance trade and safeguard English interests, or whether they were just crown-supported monopolies which favoured the existing commercial elite, thus stifling opportunities for all other potential players.[31] In an earlier chapter I have briefly discussed these issues in relation to the different ways in which European states organised their trade with the Levant; here I want to briefly take up these issues again to connect some of the major features of trading companies with the peculiarities of trading with the Venetian state, as the interplay between these two elements played an important role in the development of Anglo-Venetian commercial and political relations.

All English trading companies were privileged, corporate organisations that, in the words of David Ormrod, 'depended upon the royal prerogative rather than parliamentary sanction'.[32] In his analysis, 'the regulated model was especially suited to a monarchical system in a commercial world dominated by bilateral trading relations'.[33] The debate on trading companies has mostly focused on the East India Company and on those engaged in inter-oceanic trades, in line with the traditional argument

---

[30] Synthetic summaries of this in Chaudhuri, *The English East India Company*, 24; Davis, *Aleppo and Devonshire Square*, 43. There are some words of caution about overestimating their role thanks to the strength of companies' records in W. E. Minchinton, 'Introduction', in W. E. Minchinton ed., *The Growth of the English Overseas Trade in the Seventeenth and Eighteenth Centuries*, London, 1969, 1–63, 3. Analytical overviews can be found in A. M. Carlos and S. Nicholas, '"Giants of an Earlier Capitalism": The Chartered Trading Companies as Modern Multinationals', *The Business History Review*, 62 (1988): 398–419; N. Steensgaard, 'The Companies as a Specific Institution in the History of European Expansion', in Blussé and Gaastra eds., *Companies and Trade*, 245–264.

[31] A lively and critical appraisal of these issues in J. O. Appleby, *Economic Thought and Ideology in Seventeenth Century England*, Princeton, 1978.

[32] Ormrod, *The Rise of Commercial Empires*, 31.

[33] Ormrod, *The Rise of Commercial Empires*, 32.

that 'the only big monopoly companies to have a long life were those overseas trading companies dealing with trade outside of Europe'.[34] The Levant Company has received comparatively less attention. However, entrance into the Levant market, and therefore into intra-Mediterranean trade, was as important as the developments in Asia for enlarging the scope of English commercial activities beyond simply provisioning the domestic market, as had been done by previous companies.[35] The organisation of complex trades, both in the Indian Ocean and in the Mediterranean, was the first phase in the evolution of a maritime commercial system which was both proto-global and multi-lateral. No single area covered by this phenomenon can claim an exclusive on these developments, and lessons can be learned through the analysis of the different operational strategies which characterised this period of English commercial expansion. Oftentimes when the Levant Company is discussed, little mention is made of its activities in Venice and its territories; by the Restoration, the main source of income for the Company was indeed the Ottoman empire, but in the earlier phase this was not the case. Indeed, until the civil wars the most lucrative branch of the Levant Company's trade was the importation of currants from Venice and its dependencies, Zante and Cephalonia. In addition to the relative importance of the currant trade, given that the Venetian branch of the Levant Company operated rather differently from the Ottoman one, the comparative analysis of these two branches of the same company could provide an excellent case study of business administration.

The Levant Company was not unique in organising its trade into inter-related sections. Kirti Chaudhuri argued that the East India Company in its first phase of operations 'was composed of three interrelated sections. In the first place, there was the purely bilateral trade between England and the Indies. Secondly the Company developed an intra-European trade in the form of re-exports of East India goods to the Continent, and conversely, the provision here of naval stores, silver and other exports commodities. Finally there was the Company's local port to port trade in Asia, the so-called "country trade"'.[36] The Levant Company's situation was slightly different, in that at this stage it operated as a regulated company, not as joint stock, so the operations of its members' agents were more loosely connected. But I would argue that the major structural

---

[34] S. E. Åstrom, *From Cloth to Iron: The Anglo-Baltic Trade in the Late Seventeenth Century*, Helsinki, 1963, 199.
[35] On these issues Games, *Web of Empire*, especially ch. 2: 'The Mediterranean Origin of the British Empire', 47–79, although she ignores the Anglo-Venetian interaction, concentrating almost exclusively on the Ottoman empire.
[36] Chaudhuri, *The English East India Company*, 4.

difference in its operations – especially compared to the East India Company – was due to the stark contrast between the countries that hosted its trade. This forced Company members and their agents to develop substantially different trading structures at the Ottoman and Venetian ends.

Trade within the area of the Levant Company monopoly lay somewhat at the frontier between short- and long-distance trades, and it shared aspects of both. Although London-based like all major companies, the Levant also had a small provincial presence, thanks to the privilege we have seen granted to Bristol merchants. Because of the central position of the Mediterranean, Levant members enjoyed close links with the East India Company and with merchants active on the Spanish market. The connection was not really based on geographic proximity, but more on financial convenience; the central feature of the Levant Company's trade in its first few decades – the purchase of currants from Zante and Cephalonia – greatly benefitted from Spanish trade, as currants were 'largely financed by the dollars and pieces of eight picked up en route at ports such as Lisbon, Cadiz, Malaga and Alicante'.[37]

One of the underlying questions is whether trade with Venice and its dominions really needed a specific trading company. The case for its existence in Ottoman lands was fairly straightforward, as the complexity and alien nature of the empire meant foreign merchants needed institutional support allowing them to operate effectively. But Venice was not really alien, and trade between England and the Italian peninsula had been active for centuries, albeit controlled by the Italians, not the English. Venice and the Ionian islands were indeed distant from London, but this does not seem a strong enough reason for the creation of a company. More important was the capital necessary for these trades, which acted as a barrier for the kind of 'casual' trade common between England and Spanish, French and Baltic coasts. The capital required for trading in Venice and its territories was comparable to that required in Ottoman lands, as cash was necessary to purchase currants. Another reason for the existence of a Company is probably to be found not in London, but in Venice itself, where the Company's support could help merchants combat Venice's fierce protectionism. English merchants active in Venice and in its empire also took a leaf out of Venetian subjects' practices, and skilfully lobbied the Republic, individually or as a group, depending on the circumstances, in this way trying to maximise their chances of success.

---

[37] Croft ed., *The Spanish Company*, xlix. The very short-lived Spanish Company (1605–1606) succumbed to the hostility of the out-ports merchants, traditionally very active in this area, but excluded from its membership.

Taxation and financial revenue were at the forefront of political economy during the Stuart era, raising fundamental constitutional questions which inevitably drew merchants into the debate. Trading companies and individual merchants all actively contributed and lobbied on these issues, and the issue of 'free trade' – which in this period meant 'not under the monopoly of a company' – was particularly hotly debated.[38] The trade in currants, and the profits the crown derived from it, were a central issue in the so-called 'Bate's case' in 1606. This famous legal case, filed by the Levant Company merchant John Bate against the crown's imposition on currants, in the words of Robert Ashton, 'afforded some scope for the alignment of the interests of the Levant merchants – of whom the celebrated John Bate was one – with those of the Parliamentary opposition'.[39] The judge Sir Thomas Fleming supported – with some qualifications – the prerogative of the crown to impose customs, and the result of this was that Robert Cecil used this verdict as the precedent to impose additional charges on the importation of a wide range of luxury commodities.[40] In the following years, these new impositions generated additional revenue of around £70,000 yearly, a sum comparable with a parliamentary subsidy and capable of increasing as trade increased.[41] The London mercantile community was divided over Bate's case, probably as it sensed the potential trouble of raising such issues and losing privileges.[42]

However, the most serious challenge to the Levant Company's activities came from other chartered companies. Its charter clearly excluded non-members from trading *to* and *from* the area of their privileges, but this rule 'strictly interpreted, did not exclude non-members from trading in goods *of* the Levant'. In 1617 a member of the Merchant Adventurers was challenged about his import of currants, which precipitated a confrontation between the two companies on the proper definition of their respective monopolies, the Merchant Adventurers arguing that it was their right to import currants from Germany.[43] The Privy Council got involved, and the two companies came to a somewhat amicable settlement.[44]

---

[38] P. Croft, 'Free Trade and the House of Commons 1605–6', *The Economic History Review*, 28 (1975): 17–27, and bibliography quoted therein. Also R. Ashton, *The City and the Court, 1603–1643*, Cambridge, 1979; Appleby, *Economic Thought and Ideology*; T. Leng, 'Commercial Conflict and Regulation in the Discourse of Trade in Seventeenth Century England', *The Historical Journal*, 48 (2005): 933–954, 941.

[39] Ashton, *The City and the Court*, 92.

[40] *DNB*, Sir Thomas Fleming, s.v.

[41] *DNB*, Robert Cecil, s.v.

[42] Grassby, *The Business Community*, 208; Croft, 'Fresh Light on Bate's Case', 537–538.

[43] I. W. Archer, *The Pursuit of Stability: Social Relations in Elizabethan London*, Cambridge, 1991, 48.

[44] R. W. K. Hinton, *The Eastland Trade and the Common Weal in the Seventeenth Century*, Cambridge, 1959, 25.

I have argued earlier on in Chapter 3 that one of the main differences between the two branches of the Levant Company's trade was the difference in the social profile of merchants active in the two areas. Family links within the Levant Company's membership have been a classic concern of its historians, as it has been argued that its 'regulated' nature made it a favourite outlet of the more established London merchants, who enjoyed the freedom to exercise their own initiative and employ their own capital.[45] The favour shown to the Levant Company by offspring of the gentry remained constant throughout the century; summarising the situation at the eve of the Restoration, Richard Grassby commented how

> the Levant Company had glamour, prestige, and a reputation for profitability. It offered both the institutionalized structure of a regulated Company, and a measure of independence for young men who were not salaried but acted as self-employed commission agents for London principals. It had always been popular with, and welcomed, the gentry, whose expatriate younger sons crowded into the factories in Turkey.[46]

Serving one's apprenticeship as a means to gain entrance in a Company was a practice that survived longer in the Levant Company than in any other, and still happened in the eighteenth century when apprenticeship was in decline throughout England.[47] When not formally apprenticed, young men could still serve in Ottoman lands as factors for Levant Company members, and 'any Levant factor who did not succumb to disease or forfeit his commercial reputation during his stay in the Levant could be certain of admission to the Company when he returned to England'.[48] An additional reason which made the Company a coveted place for young merchants was that the Company allowed apprentices, with their master's permission, to trade on their own account.[49] These opportunities appear to have been enjoyed also by factors working in Venice, even given their lower social profile, and this gave them wider latitude in managing their masters' and their own affairs, much to the detriment of the Republic.

During the seventeenth century, companies evolved and slowly loosened their connections to the crown.[50] The Levant Company was

[45] N. Steensgaard, *The Asian Trade Revolution in the Seventeenth Century*, London, 1973, 56–58; Willan, 'Some Aspects', 406.

[46] Grassby, *The English Gentleman*, 23 and bibliography cited therein.

[47] Davis, *Aleppo and Devonshire Square*, 64–67.

[48] Davis, *Aleppo and Devonshire Square*, 67.

[49] Grassby, *The English Gentleman*, 23 and bibliography quoted therein. Grassby underlines that many members still neglected to take their freedom of the City, once abroad.

[50] These developments are traced in Brenner, *Merchants and Revolution*.

one of those which maintained its privileges after the civil wars and Restoration, as its members in London successfully managed to acquire parliamentary support. Its factors in the field appear to have had a more ambiguous attitude towards politics and to have taken advantage of the disturbances at home to pursue their own business interests. Most trading companies, the Levant amongst them, suffered considerable losses during the Anglo-Dutch wars,[51] and it is important to keep in mind that from 1646 to 1669 the Cretan war disrupted maritime trade in the Eastern Mediterranean. However, even given the scarcity of reliable data, the surviving Venetian evidence appears to show an actual increase of the activities of English operators during all these conflicts, and it is possible to hypothesise that the total volume of trade in the area did not diminish, and possibly actually increased. What most probably happened is that formal institutions such as trading companies suffered losses, especially as political uncertainties at home further weakened their formal mechanisms of control over commercial operations and operators in the Mediterranean. However, the primary evidence on the ground instead shows that these 'state crises', whilst weakening institutions, provided individual traders with plenty of economic opportunities in the Mediterranean, which was certainly not in their interest to advertise to their company, and thus these profits do not appear in national data sets.[52] Such a state of affairs would support the fact that by the early 1660s Mediterranean trade was judged to have the best potential for growth. David Ormrod has posited a new phase of commercial growth starting in that same decade, fuelled by rising demand for colonial and exotic goods and for the more traditional European luxury products.[53]

The evident success of English trading companies attracted the attention of Venetians, and diplomats frequently commented on their activities. Marcantonio Correr and Pietro Contarini, ambassadors in London in the 1610s, were especially impressed by the East India Company's organisation. The same admiration was also bestowed on the Dutch East India Company (*Vereenigde Oost-Indische Compagnie* – VOC) on whose activities Correr became knowledgeable in the Netherlands on his return

---

[51] R. Harris, *Industrializing English Law: Entrepreneurship and Business Organization, 1720–1844*, Cambridge, 2000, 47.

[52] I am currently collecting data on this issue as part of the ERC-funded project 'Sailing into Modernity: Comparative Perspectives on the Sixteenth and Seventeenth Century European Economic Transition'.

[53] Grassby, *The English Gentleman*, 23 and bibliography cited therein; Ormrod, *The Rise of Commercial Empires*, 181.

journey to Venice. There is a distinctly wistful tone behind the latter's matter of fact description of these companies' trade with Asia:

They bring from the Indies pepper, cloves, indigo and mostly silks; all things that in other times came to this city [Venice] and from here were redistributed throughout Germany, France and even England; now with these new maritime routes, and the ease of movement in Europe, the English and Dutch have absorbed all this traffic.[54]

Correr and Contarini's tone of admiration for those two countries – 'valiant and strong at sea' – vividly emerges from their reports. Twenty years later, Vincenzo Gussoni di Andrea again praised the East India Company, and the focus of his commentary was the strength of its fleet which supported and defended its maritime routes and trade. The attention bestowed by the English government on maintaining naval superiority on its neighbours also attracted his praise.[55] All these narratives are suffused with a mixture of sadness and admiration, and from them transpire a clear awareness that the strategies behind England's success were very similar to those which had supported Venetian exploits in the past: the presence of merchants in the most important commercial nodes, and efficient shipping backed by naval strength.

Marinarezza – a shared concern

At the height of their success, the famous political testament of Doge Tommaso Mocenigo (1423) had powerfully restated the need for Venetians, if they were to retain their might, to seek their destiny on the sea.[56] In the early sixteenth century Girolamo Priuli argued in his *Diaries* that trade profits had enabled the military activities which led to the conquest of the Italian mainland. His argument was that Levant possessions were crucial for Venice, and their loss – were it ever to happen – would have been swiftly followed by that of its Italian territories.[57] The centrality of the sea as the most appropriate arena for Venice continued to be expressed in the following centuries, until the end of the Republic in 1797.

There is a tendency to assume that a strong concept and awareness of the sea – socially, economically and politically – has always been an

---

[54] Correr, 'Relazione d'Inghilterra', 611–612; Pietro Contarini, 'Relazione d'Inghilterra (1617–18)', in Firpo ed., *Relazioni di ambasciatori veneti al Senato*, 671–684, 673–674.

[55] Vincenzo Gussoni, 'Relazione d'Inghilterra (1635)', in Firpo ed., *Relazioni di ambasciatori veneti al Senato*, 775–790, 780–782.

[56] Luzzati, Besta and Ventura eds., *Bilanci generali*, i: 94–97; see also Lane, *Venetian Ships and Shipbuilders*, 102–106.

[57] Girolamo Priuli quoted by Alberto Tenenti in 'Il senso dello spazio e del tempo', 85.

essential part of English (later British) politics, and that what contemporary political and military analysts call 'sea-blindness' is a phenomenon which dates from the period after the Second World War.[58] In fact, as Nicholas Rodger has magisterially shown, it took several centuries – and a long process of ebbing and flowing – for the British to fully appreciate the crucial importance of the sea to their safety and economy.[59] At the beginning of the early modern period England was a profoundly rural and agrarian society, which 'transformed its government in a mercantile and maritime direction under the extreme pressure of war'.[60] The Anglo-Spanish conflict was the moment which sealed for England the crucial importance of sea power. Within the same decades a new political and economic appreciation of the sea was quickly developing, and England's maritime exploits (both military and commercial) were loudly advertised by Richard Hakluyt's magnum opus and by the crystallisation of the image of Queen Elizabeth as the handmaiden of England's sea triumphs.[61]

The reliance on a sea-oriented economy, and the need for naval power to support and defend it, thus connected the history of Venice and that of England, and throughout the seventeenth century there are frequent references to how this common maritime destiny should be a reason for strengthening links between the two countries.[62]

Within a culture apparently not given to self-reflection, and where public debate was not traditionally supported by the production of pamphlets and treatises, it is in the folds of the massive state-generated documentation that we need to turn our gaze to see how Venetians reflected and conceptualised their past eminence and present state of crisis. Pride and self-consciousness regarding Venice's maritime history and exploits emerge vividly from the dispatches of ambassadors, especially those returning from England. From the second half of the seventeenth century to the end of the Republic, ambassadors' narratives of the ascent of England and its growing commercial fortunes are tinged with pride for Venice's past and regret for its present less exalted state. In fact

---

[58] Sea-blindness is 'the inability to connect with maritime issues at either an individual or political level'; in D. Redford, 'The Royal Navy, Sea Blindness and British National Identity', in D. Redford ed., *Maritime History and Identity: The Sea and Culture in the Modern World*, London, 2013, 61–78, 62.

[59] Rodger, *The Safeguard of the Sea*.

[60] Scott, *When the Waves Ruled Britannia*, xiii, 36.

[61] Hakluyt, *The Principall Navigations*; see also Andrews, *Trade, Plunder*; and D. Loades, *England's Maritime Power: Seapower, Commerce and Policy, 1490–1690*, London, 2000.

[62] See, amongst many, the considerations of Vincenzo Gussoni, 'Relazione d'Inghilterra', 787.

English success was frequently utilised to incite fellow Venetians to claw back their past glories.[63]

A strong awareness of these matters emerges also from the English side of the story. Problems connected with navigation and trade had been the reason for re-establishing diplomatic contacts at the end of Elizabeth's reign, and the shared concern for these issues peppers both diplomatic activities and correspondence. Henry Wotton, appearing in late October 1607 in front of the *Collegio* to complain about the purported malicious attempts by Venetians to thwart English trade in Constantinople, opened his speech thus:

This morning I shall discuss with Your Serenity issues concerning the Sea, grave and important matters that belong to my own Prince's Majesty and to this Most Serene Republic more than to any other Prince, as on the Sea is built their Power.[64]

It was clear to him that 'sea power' was tightly linked to commercial matters for both states, as he reiterated a decade later in another audience with the *Collegio*, when he declared how matters of state and matters of trade were one.[65] Even assuming that the rhetoric of diplomatic exchange required a certain element of *captatio benevolentiae*, the assured pairing of the Republic's traditional concern for sea matters with that of England was a loud and clear political statement which would not have been lost on his audience. 'Matters of the sea' had indeed been a constant concern of the Venetian government, but in those years the matter had acquired a new gravity and urgency.[66]

Lazarini's memorandum (1578) – which in Chapter 2 was discussed as the basis of the establishment of the *Nuova Imposta* – directly linked the problems surrounding the English penetration of the currant trade in the Ionian islands with the ongoing shipbuilding crisis in Venice, and with the challenge of keeping up the 'seaworthiness' (*marinarezza*) of the Venetian population.[67] I have argued elsewhere how the crisis of the Venetian mercantile fleet went hand in hand with the crisis of Venetian shipbuilding, and that acquiring ships abroad had become a cheap way for shipowners and merchants to short-circuit this problem. Once purchased – usually in Northern Europe, Danzig and England being favourite shopping

[63] Tenenti, 'Il senso del mare', 70.

[64] Hatfield House, *Cecil Papers*, 125/112 (5–11/26-10-1607).

[65] ASV, *Collegio, Esposizioni Principi*, reg. 29, cc.108r–111v (22-11-1618).

[66] A. Tenenti, *Venezia e il senso del mare: storia di un prisma culturale dal XIII al XVIII secolo*, Milan, 1999, 11–19.

[67] ASV, *Cinque Savi alla Mercanzia*, b. 836b, I fasc., doc n. 1.

destinations – ships were then naturalised so they could take full advantage of the benefits in place for Venetian ships, even though frequently these vessels were manned with foreign crews.[68] As discussed earlier, this policy did not help to overcome the crisis, and the *Senato* was still trying to regulate the issues by the early seventeenth century.[69] A policy of providing financial incentives to stimulate shipbuilding was also implemented in Crete, a rare example of a policy directly targeted at stimulating subjects' entrepreneurial activities.[70] It was a relatively successful experiment, but the island was lost to the Ottomans in 1646, although the capital city of Candia withstood the siege until 1669, dragging out the conflict for twenty-five years.

The Venetian fleet was the oldest permanent navy in Europe, and since the early fourteenth century it had played an essential role in the defence of the empire and of the Republic's maritime trade.[71] Since the Cyprus War (1570–1573), when the hollow European victory at Lepanto had not saved the prized Venetian possession of Cyprus, there had been low-level tensions in the Eastern Mediterranean characterised by frequent minor naval engagements. After a short phase of retrenchment, the Venetian navy entered a phase of growth throughout the seventeenth century. The growing organisational complexity of the navy fostered an increase in the needs for officers, and a number of patricians specialised in naval careers, even though, in Guido Candiani's recent analysis, Venice did not manage to create a 'modern' and well-organised real 'naval service'.[72] Notwithstanding this, by the end of the Candia war – when, interestingly, Venetian naval superiority remained strong – the navy was substantially improved in its structure and organisation and was armed comparably to other European states.[73] The shipbuilding crisis had two facets – mercantile and naval – and the parallel growth of England played a decisive role in both. As much as it is important to make a distinction

---

[68] Maria Fusaro, 'Coping with Transition: Greek Merchants and Shipowners between Venice and England in the Late Sixteenth Century', in G. Harlaftis, I. Baghdiantz-McCabe and I. Pepelasis-Minoglou eds., *Diaspora Entrepreneurial Networks: Four Centuries of History*, London, 2005, 95–123.

[69] ASV, *Senato Mar*, reg. 44, cc.149 r/v (23-8-1579); see also f. 260, cc.n.n. (22-12-1627); for these issues Fusaro, 'Coping with Transition', and her 'The Invasion of Northern Litigants: English and Dutch Seamen in Mediterranean Courts of Law', in Fusaro, Allaire, Blakemore, Vanneste eds., *Law, Labour and Empire*, 21–42.

[70] Fusaro, 'Coping with Transition'. See also Costantini, *Una repubblica nata sul mare*, 41–65; and Baroutsos, 'Sovention per fabricar galeoni'.

[71] J. Glete, *Warfare at Sea, 1500–1650: Maritime Conflicts and the Transformation of Europe*, London, 2000; also Doumerc, 'An Exemplary Maritime Republic', 151–165.

[72] Tenenti, 'Il senso del mare', 72–76; G. Candiani, *Dalla galea alla nave di linea: le trasformazioni della marina veneziana (1572–1699)*, Novi Ligure, 2012, 261–317.

[73] Candiani, *I vascelli della Serenissima*, 577–582; Tenenti, 'La navigazione veneziana nel Seicento', 550–555.

between 'maritime' and 'naval' activities – as these are two separate analytical categories and as such should be assessed – it is undeniable that the two were indeed connected, and in some cases intertwined.[74]

The last decades of the sixteenth century were difficult for the Republic on many fronts. Its politics had been transformed by the so-called 'giovani' patricians, an informal group that pushed for a stronger engagement of Venice with European politics, which was an expensive strategy.[75] The cost of supporting the fleet continued to grow throughout the following century, and defence of the Levant took up a growing proportion of state income, including some of the profits of the *Nuova Imposta*. At the beginning of the seventeenth century, military costs were around 60 per cent of the total expenditure of the Republic; in 1618 – a tough year in the confrontation with the Habsburgs – these reached 75 per cent of the total.[76] Despite the heroic efforts of the Venetian *Arsenale* to keep up the numbers of galleys in the fleet, it had neither the expertise nor the personnel to build the kind of sailing vessels which were becoming essential to naval warfare.[77] Notwithstanding a period of peace with the Ottomans, the international situation was not easy, and the disruptions to maritime trade caused by Uskok pirates in the Adriatic greatly contributed to the souring of relations with the Habsburgs, which led to open war in 1615.[78] This came to be known as the War of Gradisca (1615–1618), and for the first time the Venetian government resorted to hiring English and Dutch vessels, mostly privately owned mercantile vessels with military capability, to add sailing power to its galley-based navy.[79] This pattern continued on the occasion of the naval build-up surrounding the famed 'Bedmar conspiracy' (1618);[80] and it boomed during the Candia war, when northern ships played an essential supporting role in just about all naval campaigns.

---

[74] Tenenti, 'La navigazione veneziana nel Seicento', 533.
[75] Bouwsma, *Venice and the Defense*, 232–292, and the bibliography referred to in Chapter 5, footnote 25.
[76] Fusaro, 'Cooperating Mercantile Networks', 709, and bibliography quoted therein.
[77] A synthesis can be found in L. Sicking, 'Naval Warfare in Europe c.1330–c.1680', in F. Tallett and D. J. B. Trim eds., *European Warfare, 1350–1750*, Cambridge, 2010, 236–263.
[78] G. Cozzi, 'La politica della Repubblica dopo l'Interdetto (1607–1619)', in G. Cozzi, M. Knapton and G. Scarabello, *La Repubblica di Venezia nell'età moderna*, 2 vols., Turin, 1986–92, ii: 92–102, 99–102; R. Cessi, *La Repubblica di Venezia e il problema Adriatico*, Naples, 1953, 182–270; M. E. Mallett and J. R. Hale, *Military Organisation of a Renaissance State: Venice*, Cambridge, 1984, 242–247; Bracewell, *The Uskoks of Senj*.
[79] Candiani, *Dalla galea alla nave*, 208–232; and his *I vascelli della Serenissima*. On English ships and troops see Pearsall Smith, *The Life and Letters*, i: 154. On the Uskoks' damages also in relation to further developing Spalato as the Venetian gateway to the Balkans see Paci, *La 'Scala' di Spalato*, 69.
[80] G. Coniglio, 'Il Duca di Ossuna e Venezia dal 1616 and 1620', *Archivio Veneto*, 54–55 (1955): 42–70; a stimulating interpretation, with particular attention to its historiography

In 1618 the need of the Republic for naval support was real, and important political considerations were also at play, with the Venetian anti-Spanish stance being followed with interest both in the United Provinces and in England. Both these governments were keen to provide support to a state pursuing an anti-Spanish policy in the Mediterranean, and political domestic issues spurred English and Dutch private shipping entrepreneurs to take full advantage of the opportunities available in the area.[81]

Throughout the seventeenth century Venetian diplomats kept an eye on the fast-growing naval strength of England. Already in 1618 Pietro Contarini commented on how this might come in useful for Venice in the future, and he argued that for this reason alone it was essential to maintain a good relationship with England.[82] Later on, especially during the late 1640s and early 1650s, England experienced an extraordinary build-up and projection of naval power, which did not go unnoticed in Venice.[83] From the Venetian perspective the fortunes of the new regime in England were frequently directly connected with its strength on sea. A good example of this attitude is Pietro Basadonna, who was ambassador at the Spanish court in 1651, and who used his position to report back to the Doge and *Senato* in Venice any intelligence which reached him about 'the constitution, durability and strength of the English government'. The importance of the military to the fortunes of Parliament was clear to him, and amongst the forces, pride of place was given to the navy.[84] When the war for Candia stretched the Republic's naval forces, England became the obvious place to look for naval support. A considerable number of foreign vessels – Dutch and English – were hired by the Venetian government to support the war effort. These were involved especially in the massive provisioning and victualling operation that supported the twenty-five-year siege of the town of Candia, and the long blockades of the Dardanelles put in place by the Venetians. Analysing the *Senato* registers, Alberto Tenenti calculated that eighteen armed merchantmen sailed for Candia in 1654, thirty-five in 1655, twenty-two in 1656, fifteen in 1657 and twenty-eight in 1658. He also argued that it is not always easy to determine the 'real' nationality of these

---

is in R. MacKenney, "'A plot Discover'd?" Myth, Legend, and the "Spanish Conspiracy" against Venice in 1618', in Martin and Romano eds., *Venice Reconsidered*, 185–216.

[81] Fusaro, 'The Invasion of Northern Litigants'; and 'Public Service and Private Trade: Northern Seamen in Seventeenth Century Venetian Courts of Justice', *The International Journal of Maritime History*, 27 (2015): 3–25.

[82] Contarini, 'Relazione d'Inghilterra', 682–683.

[83] Scott, *When the Waves Ruled Britannia*, 75.

[84] *CSPVe*, vol. xxviii (1647–1652), n. 498, 187–188: see www.british-history.ac.uk/report.aspx?compid=89705 (date accessed: 18 February 2014).

vessels, although – on the basis of the particularly detailed figures for 1655 – it can be argued that only one-quarter were really 'Venetian'.[85] Some were also used for proper military operations, in which case the *Senato* preferred to hire them from foreign merchants active in Venice, either with cash or in exchange for commercial privileges, and very frequent amongst these were rebates of duties on currants.[86]

Some of these contracts were rather substantial, such as the 1655 contract between the *Senato* and the Fleming Giovanni van Alst which involved ten men-of-war, and the one with the Englishman James Stricher.[87] The Venetians did not hide the foreign contribution to their military efforts; the English ships *Maria Isabetta*, *Tomaso Francesco* and *Profeta Samuel* are duly listed amongst the Venetian fleet at the end of the pamphlet celebrating the famed naval victory of Mocenigo against the Turks in 1651.[88]

Given the former dominance of the Venetian navy, the presence of foreign vessels to support the fleet was an open and evident declaration of crisis, and as such was rightly interpreted by contemporaries and commentators. In the following century Adam Anderson – the author of the most comprehensive history of English early modern trade – was scathing in describing the use of foreign ships as 'a sure Mark [...] of the Feebleness of Venice's naval Power'.[89] However, as is frequently the case when English political economists discussed Venice, some level of ambiguity was present. A few pages after these comments, Anderson highlighted the naval superiority of Venice over the Turks in the conflict (interestingly failing to mention the English contribution to these successes), and then rounded off his argument by complaining of the Dutch lower tariffs which 'cut us out of that Employment also, by serving them cheaper'.[90]

For Venice the real problem was not so much that it needed foreign military support to withstand its military effort against the Ottomans. There was no shame inherent in needing support to fight against an adversary whose resources were of such scale. A certain element of crusading rhetoric always emerged during direct confrontation between

[85] Tenenti, 'La navigazione veneziana nel Seicento', 551–552.
[86] Some examples: ASV, *Collegio Rdd*, f. 37 (6-4-1646); f. 39, cc.n.n. (16-3-1648); f. 41, cc.n. n. (28-8-1650); f. 41, cc.n.n. (6-2-1650mv); f. 43, cc.n.n. (18-11-1652). Lists of hired foreign ships in ASV, *PTM*, b. 1080, *passim*; ASV, *Collegio, Rdd*, f. 44, cc.n.n. (s.d. [1653]).
[87] Tenenti, 'La navigazione veneziana nel Seicento', 554.
[88] *Lettera di Ragguaglio Della Vittoria Navale conseguita dall'Armata della Serenissima Repubblica di Venezia Sotto il Comando del Procurator Capitan General da Mar Mocenigo Contro Turchi nell'Arcipelago*, Venice, 1651; also Fusaro, 'Public Service'.
[89] Anderson, *An Historical and Chronological Deduction*, ii: 90. On Anderson's importance see Ormrod, *The Rise of Commercial Empires*, 1 and bibliography quoted therein.
[90] Anderson, *An Historical and Chronological Deduction*, ii: 94 and 103.

Venice and the Ottomans, which was skilfully employed to justify and explain the support provided by other European countries to the Republic. Even with all these caveats, the connection between naval power and the capacity to control maritime trade was clear to everyone, and the War of Candia proved that Venice was no longer capable of defending its colonial possessions overseas. The real problem was that support could be asked only from its fiercest economic competitors in that region, and the logistical aid provided by the English ended up further enhancing and strengthening their presence in the area.

After the diplomatic silence caused by the English civil wars and the interruption of direct diplomatic relations between the two countries, the situation did not change with the Restoration or the end of the Candia war. The running commentary on England's strength at sea continued to be part of the analysis of Venetian diplomatic narratives. In 1671 Pietro Mocenigo started his final relation about England with a passage that in other times could have been applied to Venice:

I shall therefore consider how, since strength on the seas is most important for a state, consequently England is one of the major powers, as its strength is rooted in its naval power. The territory of that kingdom is the Ocean, where practising navigational lore it trades with the whole world and establishes its dominion with its ships – mobile fortresses – which, having both strength and speed and confidence in their courage, extend their trade to the ends of the world carrying its virtue and glory. England is indeed formidable and does not fear its enemies as its safety is in the nature of its site and in the dominion of the seas.[91]

Venetian trade and foreign merchants

The traditional organisation of Venetian traffic pivoted on the central role of Venice as an entrepôt for goods imported from the Levant or produced in its dominions.[92] To support this policy, throughout the centuries the government had put into place an extremely complex system of customs legislation, whose aim was to guarantee that trade remained in the hands of Venetian citizens. From the sixteenth century this system was constantly thwarted, and the legislative response was an effort to fill the loopholes.

Every port city is characterised by the presence of foreigners, and the great number and variety of these was always one of the defining factors of

[91] Pietro Mocenigo, 'Relazione d'Inghilterra (1671)', in Firpo ed., *Relazioni di ambasciatori veneti*, 913–941, 913–914.
[92] On complaints from the *Terraferma* on these issues see: P. Lanaro, *I mercanti nella Repubblica veneta: economie cittadine e stato territoriale (sec. XV–XVIII)*, Venice, 1999, esp. 86–89.

Venice, as Philippe de Commynes famously noted.[93] However, it is important to distinguish between various levels of presence – both in terms of function and duration of residence – and to be especially attentive to the intersections. The presence of foreign commercial operators needs to be always analysed within the specific economic conjuncture. It is usually a good sign in times of expansion of the host economy, as foreigners' activities can facilitate access into new markets, and provide expertise.[94] For example when in 1596 the *Senato* was evaluating the expedience of establishing a new state bank, it called on the expertise of several foreigners active in financial operations, most prominently Florentines, Genoese, Germans and Flemings.[95]

During the sixteenth century Venetian authorities showed a growing concern towards the presence of all foreigners in the city, resulting in laws to control their presence, which in practice did not work. Originally this was connected with religious issues, such as managing the presence of Protestants, but by the end of the century there was fear that foreigners were involved in financial speculation and in the spread of political rumours.[96]

We have seen how in Venice only citizens had full autonomy and full rights in taking care of their business, whilst limitations were imposed upon the scope and the geographical areas in which non-citizens could operate. During the Middle Ages the Venetian government was able to effectively implement this legislation, and many foreigners – after living in Venice for the prescribed number of years and paying all their dues – successfully obtained citizenship.[97] From the sixteenth century onwards fewer and fewer foreign merchants applied for citizenship, even though the relevant policies and limitations on their activities had not changed. The number of applications decreased because the

[93] De Commynes, *Mémoires*, 557.

[94] Fusaro, 'Gli uomini d'affari stranieri'.

[95] M. van Gelder, 'Supplying the *Serenissima*', 55–56; see also I. Cecchini, 'Piacenza a Venezia: la ricezione delle fiere di cambio di Bisenzone a fine Cinquecento nel mercato del credito lagunare', *Note di lavoro del Dipartimento di scienze economiche, Università Ca' Foscari di Venezia*, 18 (2006): see www.unive.it/media/allegato/DIP/Economia/ Note_di_lavoro_sc_economiche/NL2006/NL_DSE_Cecchini_18_06.pdf (date accessed: 20 December 2013).

[96] G. Cozzi, 'Religione, moralità e giustizia a Venezia: vicende della magistratura degli esecutori contro la bestemmia', *Ateneo Veneto*, n.s. 29 (1991): 7–95, esp. 44–49. On these issues see de Vivo, *Information and Communication*.

[97] R. C. Mueller and L. Molà, 'Essere straniero a Venezia nel tardo Medioevo: accoglienza e rifiuto nei privilegi di cittadinanza e nelle sentenze criminali', in S. Cavaciocchi ed., *Le migrazioni in Europa*, Florence, 1994, 839–851, 842; R. C. Mueller, '"Veneti facti privilegio": stranieri naturalizzati a Venezia tra XIV e XVI secolo', in D. Calabi and P. Lanaro eds., *La città italiana e i luoghi degli stranieri, XIV–XVIII secolo*, Bari and Rome, 1998, 41–51, 45.

legislation that limited trade had become practically unenforceable within the Republic's territories, making it easier and more convenient to simply ignore the laws rather than going through the lengthy and expensive process of acquiring citizenship.[98] There were many ways to circumvent laws which restricted commercial activities for non-citizens, the easiest being for a citizen to act as a front-man, stating that certain goods were his when they were not. These abuses became so frequent that from 1552 citizens had to swear on the Gospels that the goods were really their own before they could take advantage of the privileges they were entitled to.[99] English merchants frequently made use of this *escamotage* to trade with the Levant. A classic example is the activities of Eleazar Hickman and Paul Pinder, who traded illegally into Alexandria with the collusion and under the name of Giovanni Peverello, 'mercator venetus', having set up with him a partnership in violation of the 1524 *parte* which forbade such ventures; for this they were condemned by the *Avogaria*.[100] Their activities came to the attention of the authorities thanks to an anonymous denunciation, which was encouraged in such circumstances, but this kind of illegal partnership was absolutely common, and only a very small percentage were uncovered. There was simply too much to gain by all parties in flouting the law.

Foreigners could and did trade in Venice since the Middle Ages; they were allowed to do so provided they respected the limits enforced by the Republic and, crucially, did not attempt to trade directly with the Levant. The most famous and well-known example of foreign merchants active in Venice is that of the Germans. Since the peace of Venice (1177), when the Republic successfully blocked their presence in the Levant, they had always been welcomed in the city, and it can be argued that the economic and fiscal interest of the Republic towards trade with Germany is exemplified by the tight set of normative strictures that controlled the presence of German merchants in the city: Germans were welcome to trade with Venetian citizens and subjects in the city itself, under strict regulation by local authorities, but were forbidden to trade with non-Venetians or

---

[98] Fusaro, 'Gli uomini d'affari stranieri'.

[99] Bellavitis, 'Per cittadini metterete', 361. On the seriousness of the problem see ASV, *Cinque Savi alla Mercanzia*, b. 103 n.s., fasc. iv, cc.n.n. (4-9-1546).

[100] ASV, *AdC*, *raspe*, reg. 3689, cc.29v–30r (14-7-1593); we have encountered Eleazar in Chapter 6, and will do so again in Chapter 8. The *parte* which forbade commercial partnerships between Venetian citizens and subjects and foreigners was dated 19 April 1524: see ASV, *Senato Mar*, reg. 20, cc.97v–98r; another copy is in ASV, *Compilazione Leggi*, b. 278, cc.452r–458v.

participate in maritime trade.[101] German merchants were forced to reside in the *Fondaco*, whose activities were controlled by a specific Venetian magistracy, the *Visdomini*.[102] The German market remained the most important one for Venetians throughout the early modern period, so much so that income from the *Fondaco* customs can be used as a reliable barometer of the economic health of Venice.[103]

Whilst restrictions on non-citizens were partially repealed only at the very end of the seventeenth century, with some earlier exceptions exclusively for some individuals on very specific occasions, from the sixteenth century there was a distinct change of strategy, and the Republic started to encourage specific groups of foreign merchants to come to the city. This began after the end of the Venetian–Ottoman war of 1537–1540 when the *Senato*, in an attempt to recover lost trade, passed legislation to attract Levantine Jews.[104] They were put under the jurisdiction of the *Cinque Savi*, where they would enjoy the privilege of resolving all their commercial controversies in a cheap and speedy way through summary procedure. Nearly one century later, in 1625, the *Senato* decided that all commercial controversies involving 'Turkish merchants and subjects, Levantine and Ponentine Jews, who trade in Venice' should also enjoy the privileges associated with the jurisdiction of the *Cinque Savi*.[105] Eight years afterwards (1633) Persians, Bosnians and Wallachians followed suit.[106] But the Republic's attitude towards English merchants was completely different, as their presence was immediately perceived as dangerous for the core Venetian commercial interests. Whilst not

---

[101] P. Braunstein, 'Venezia e la Germania nel medioevo', in G. Cozzi ed., *Venezia e la Germania: arte, politica, commercio, due civiltà a confronto*, Milan, 1986, 35–49, 49. Also K.-E. Lupprian, *Il fondaco dei tedeschi e la sua funzione di controllo del commercio tedesco a Venezia*, Venice, 1978; see also H. Kellenbenz, 'Relazioni commerciali tra il Levante ed i paesi d'oltralpe', in R. Ragosta ed., *Navigazioni mediterranee e connessioni continentali (secoli XI–XVI)*, Naples, 1982, 301–314.

[102] On the *Visdomini* see V. Sandi, *Principi di storia civile della Repubblica di Venezia dalla sua fondazione fino all'anno di n.s. 1700*, parte I, vol. ii, Venice, 1755: 768–70; A. da Mosto, *L'archivio di Stato di Venezia*, vol. 1: *Archivi dell'amministrazione centrale della Repubblica veneta e archivi notarili*, Rome, 1937, 189; G. M. Thomas, *Capitolare dei Visdomini del Fontego dei Todeschi in Venezia*, Berlin, 1874; H. Simonsfeld, *Der Fondaco dei Tedeschi in Venedig und die deutschvenetianischen Handelsbeziehungen*, 2 vols., Stuttgart, 1887.

[103] Sella, *Commerci e industrie a Venezia*, 11.

[104] Ravid, 'A Tale of Three Cities', 142.

[105] ASV, *Cinque Savi alla Mercanzia*, b. 75 n.s., fasc. i, cc.n.n. (16-1-1625mv). See also Sandi, *Principi di storia civile*, part III, vol. i, 94.

[106] ASV, *Cinque Savi alla Mercanzia*, b. 75 n.s., fasc. i, cc.n.n. (12-9-1633). Finally in 1676 also the Armenians fall under the *Cinque Savi* jurisdiction: see ASV, *Cinque Savi alla Mercanzia*, b. 75 n.s., fasc. i, cc.n.n. (9-5-1676), copy of the Senate's *parte*. See also the copy in ASV, *Maggior Consiglio, Indice e repertorio generale delle leggi statutarie del Serenissimo Maggior Consiglio . . .*, reg. ii, c.353v. All these issues are followed in detail in Fusaro, 'Politics of Justice/Politics of Trade'.

welcomed as merchants, however, the English were needed for their naval power, and the role they played within the Venetian maritime world was one of the main reasons for the swiftness of their penetration within its commercial system. This ambiguity in Anglo-Venetian relations will remain the cipher of their bilateral relations throughout the seventeenth century.

The *Senato* allowed the purchase and naturalisation of foreign ships, but at the same time had put into place measures to protect the seaworthiness of its own citizens and subjects. Already in 1597 it decreed that all 'officers' of the ships built abroad and then naturalised as Venetian should be of the *Natione Veneta* – that is to say, citizens or subjects of the Republic:

The owners of these [vessels] shall be obliged to bring with them during navigation the principal officers of the vessels – that is to say, the master, the pilot, the coxwain, the scribe and others, who need to be seamen of this place.[107]

In 1602 the Republic further expanded this legislation and declared that at least two-thirds of the crewmen on *all* mercantile vessels of the Republic (not only those bought abroad and naturalised) should be Venetian citizens or subjects. On this occasion the Greeks were singled out amongst the latter as being particularly praiseworthy for their contribution.[108] These rules were further confirmed in 1682 when the entire legislation on the manning of ships was reorganised.[109] All these regulations were implemented more than fifty years before the Navigation Laws established similar rules for England, and it can be argued that the entire legislative corpus produced by the Republic to redirect the currant trade to Venice was a clear precursor – a direct example? – of the 1651 English Navigation Laws. The 1580 *Nuova Imposta* had at its core the effort to prohibit foreign vessels from trading in the Venetian colonies, and to divert this 'colonial' trade back onto Venetian ships. The *Nuova Imposta* itself was to be paid only by foreign vessels not prepared to sail to Venice and purchase currants there.

---

[107] 'dovendo li portionevoli di essi esser obligati condur seco nella navigatione li principali ministri del vassello, cioè patron, peota, paron, scrivan et altri che siano marineri di questa piazza', in ASV, *Cinque Savi alla Mercanzia*, prima serie, b. 26, c.192v (27-9-1597). I thank Mauro Bondioli for bringing this document to my attention. All these issues are further analysed in Fusaro, 'The Invasion of Northern Litigants'.

[108] ASV, *Compilazione delle leggi*, 2nd series, b. 23, *Codici* 241–242, cc.33r–34r (31-8-1602).

[109] Copies of the 1682 *parti* are in ASV, *Cinque Savi alla Mercanzia*, b. 91 n.s., cc.n.n. (9-5-1682) and (8-8-1682).

At the end of July 1602 the *Cinque Savi* produced a long *scrittura* that, starting with a discussion of the income generated by the *Nuova Imposta*, analysed the many damages that the English presence in the Ionian islands inflicted upon the whole Venetian maritime sector. This long and detailed document was signed by all five *Savi*, and must have made for very painful listening for the *Collegio*. None of the concerns raised in the late 1570s, and which had been behind the 1580 *parte*, had been solved. In the last twenty years the English presence had been steadily increasing, both in Venice and in the Ionian islands, and their lobbying for repeal of the *Nuova Imposta* continued relentlessly. Now they were threatening to move all their currant operations to the Ottoman Morea if their demands were not met. The *Savi* (rightly) deemed this an empty threat, given the low quantity and bad quality of the Morea production, but at the same time they suggested implementation of even stronger measures to again try to make English trade in the islands unviable.[110] The *Senato* responded quickly and in mid-August forbade all exports of currants from the Ionian islands for all destinations but Venice and on Venetian bottoms.[111] The first consideration to make is that the promulgation of the 1602 legislation was followed by a flurry of petitions by Greek Ionian subjects, all lamenting their demise and utter financial ruin as a direct consequence of this new regulation. On the other hand, quite unlike what had happened in 1580, the English were completely silent: no petitions, no diplomatic interventions, no letter exchanges, just total silence. A letter written by Henry Wotton to Salisbury in 1608 sheds some light on why there had never been any need to intervene for the repeal of the 1602 *parte*; he breezily explained that, thanks to the 'nimblenesse' of the Greeks, in the previous year alone eighteen English ships had been fully loaded with currants at Zante and then sailed directly for England.[112] Smuggling on a grandiose scale had won the day.[113]

Two weeks after the publication of the *parte* forcing all currants to come to Venice on Venetian ships, at the end of August 1602, the *Senato* published another decree which further tightened the rules regarding nationality of all shipping between Venice and the Levant. The *parte* contained several provisions: all Venetian ships (and those belonging to subjects) would have precedence in being loaded not only in Venice and throughout the Venetian maritime empire but also in Alexandria, Syria,

[110] ASV, *Cinque Savi alla Mercanzia, Risposte*, reg. 141, cc.2r–8r (25-7-1602).
[111] ASV, *Senato Mar*, reg. 62, cc.79v–80r (16-8-1602).
[112] TNA, *SP* 99/5, 194r–195v.
[113] Fusaro, *Uva passa*, 117–123.

Constantinople and in any other place where there was an official Venetian representative. Regarding foreign ships arriving in Venice, only if two-thirds of their original cargo had been unloaded in Venice were they allowed to reload, and only if they then sailed directly back to their home country.[114] Domenico Sella defined this decree 'a navigation act' and attributed to it a short-lived increase in the number of ships registered as 'Venetian'.[115] This experiment did not really work, and seven years afterwards the 1602 legislation was repealed, and the original 1580 regulations re-established.[116]

Taken together, those two *parti* of August 1602 clearly aimed to dissuade foreign merchants and ships from interfering within the traditional Venetian economic space. Alas, it proved to be just a temporary blip. However, the existence in Venice of such policies designed to support local shipping was well known in England. Marchamont Nedham in 1652 criticised the 'failure of the Stuart government to imitate the Dutch and "Venetian State's Care for their Navigation" by forbidding the "transportacon [sic] of English goods in forraine Bottomes"'.[117]

Venice had indeed pioneered this kind of legislation; the problem was that the prerequisite for its success was to have available capital to invest, and a thriving shipbuilding industry capable of providing the necessary vessels.[118] Neither condition existed. Therefore the principal result of trying to cut out English ships from trade in the Eastern Mediterranean – something Venetian subjects had grown increasingly dependent upon – had been to boost contraband, with the corollary damage to state income due to customs and tax evasion. When the Navigation Laws were enacted in 1651, the English had a booming shipbuilding industry and the capital to support it, and therefore the promulgation of these laws had the desired effect of dealing a powerful blow to their Dutch rival, whose success was based on the carrying trades on a global scale. David Ormrod has defined the English Navigation Laws as the expression of a 'staggeringly ambitious' strategy for the creation of an 'overarching national monopoly within which English shipping and long-distance trade could develop'.[119] The new 'mistress of the sea' was clearly emulating the old one.

[114] ASV, *Senato Mar*, reg. 62, cc.91r/v (31-8-1602).
[115] Sella, *Commerci e industrie a Venezia*, 34–40.
[116] ASV, *Senato Mar*, reg. 68, cc.138v–139r (9-5-1609).
[117] M. Nedham, *The Case Stated Between England and the United Provinces*, London, 1652, 13 quoted in Scott, *When the Waves*, 65.
[118] As observed by English pamphleteers when discussing the reasons behind the Dutch success in the carrying trade, which was reliant on a strong shipbuilding industry: see Leng, 'Commercial Conflict', 948 and bibliography quoted therein.
[119] Davis, *The Rise of the English Shipping Industry*; Ormrod, *The Rise of Commercial Empires*, 32–33.

8   The English mercantile community in Venice

Before describing the behaviour and characteristics of the English mercantile community in Venice, it is important to define the meaning of the word 'community', as employed in the following pages.[1] Rather than signifying a completely homogeneous group with rigidly defined social and cultural characteristics, what will be analysed is the network created by the personal and commercial relationships of English merchants based in Venice and her colonies.[2] Where there is a foreign mercantile community, it is always possible to divide its members into two groups: the permanent residents and the temporary ones, counting amongst the latter seamen and travellers, who do not properly belong to the community but can take advantage of its existence and privileges, for example if they find themselves in trouble or need credit whilst passing through. Indeed, English merchants and seamen frequently interacted both in Venice and in the *Dominio da Mar*, which is unsurprising given their role in maritime trade and transport and in supporting the Venetian navy.

The English mercantile community was rather close-knit: everyone knew everyone else, everyone did business with everyone else, and everyone was ready to vouch for everyone else. Slightly more than 50 per cent of the notarial deeds preserved in the Venetian archives involving Englishmen concern acts in which both parties were English. The majority of these are deeds granting powers of attorney, normally using the most extended of the legal *formulae* available in Venice. In these cases, the proxy could act for the principal on all occasions, in front of all magistracies and agencies of the Republic and for all the affairs of the principal. Although the formulaic nature of these deeds tells us little about the specific instances in which they were drawn up, and thus lends

---

[1] On the various meanings of the word 'community', and concepts associated with it, see R. Esposito, *Communitas. Origine e destino della comunità*, Turin, 1998.

[2] A short and sharp analytical survey of the strengths and pitfalls of defining 'mercantile communities' can be found in S. Subrahmanyam, 'Introduction', in S. Subrahmanyam ed., *Merchants Networks in the Early Modern World*, Aldershot, 1996, xii–xvi.

them little value for narrative purposes, the vagueness and vastness of their terms demonstrate the solid trust between the subscribers and can therefore be taken as a reliable index of intra-national solidarity. Given the frequent mobility of merchants between Venice and the Ionian islands during the whole period analysed, these deeds are a constant reminder of the links binding this network together both in the city of Venice and in its empire.

If interactions were strong within the community, they were also strong with the outside world, with most English merchants actively engaged with their host society: they frequently married women who were Venetian subjects, and a large proportion of their personal and commercial relationships were with Venetians citizens and subjects.[3] More evidence of the frequent contacts between the English and other commercial operators can be drawn from their choice of arbitrators. Still extremely common today for disputes arising out of international commercial contracts, in the early modern period arbitration was a popular extrajudicial solution throughout Europe.[4] This was freely available to everyone in Venice, and documentary evidence indicates its popularity amongst foreigners.[5] Resorting to court was a long and expensive process, particularly for foreigners embroiled in civil litigation. As the English were not granted access to the *Cinque Savi* court until 1698,[6] with its low cost and summary procedure, they made frequent use of arbitration.[7] Unlike other foreigners, who tended to be endogamous in their choice of arbitrators, the English did not necessarily favour their own countrymen.[8] Both in Venice and in the Ionian

---

[3] On the relevance of the issues of 'loss' v 'conservation' of identity within mercantile communities, see the observations of Abulafia, 'Cittadino e "denizen"', 274.

[4] G. Cordero-Moss ed., *International Commercial Arbitration: Different Forms and their Features*, Cambridge, 2013; for its popularity amongst members of London's livery companies see S. Rappaport, *Worlds within Worlds: Structures of Life in Sixteenth-Century London*, Cambridge, 1989, 383; for Rome, see Ago, *Economia barocca*, 128.

[5] F. Marrella and A. Mozzato, *Alle origini dell'arbitrato commerciale internazionale: l'arbitrato a Venezia tra medioevo ed età moderna*, Padua, 2001, 20, 34. An example of English merchants, in the eventuality of a controversy arising between the parties, expressly forbidding the two counterparts to 'litigate in the Palace' (*Corti di Palazzo*), and instead resorting to 'common friends', can be seen in ASV, *Notarile Atti*, reg. 6699 (Gabriel Gabrieli), cc.87r–88v (18-9-1659).

[6] ASV, *Cinque Savi alla Mercanzia*, b. 81 n.s., fasc. vi, cc.n.n. (24-3-1698). For the reasoning behind this decision, see also fasc. iv, cc. n.n. (18-3-1698); on granting justice to foreigners, see Fusaro, 'Politics of Justice/Politics of Trade'.

[7] M. Roberti, *Le magistrature giudiziarie veneziane e i loro capitolari fino al 1600*, 3 vols, Padua, 1906, i: 103–105.

[8] The Lucchese mercantile community is a classic example of this behaviour, see Molà, *La comunità dei lucchesi*, 126; and this happened also amongst the Netherlandish merchants: see van Gelder, *Trading Places*, 99, 117.

islands, they were just as likely to choose Venetian citizens or subjects or even other foreigners as adjudicators.[9]

A striking peculiarity of the English presence in Venice was the almost complete absence of non-merchants. Usually, artisans and craftsmen were a presence in foreign mercantile communities, in Venice and elsewhere. In both Livorno and Genoa, English artisans were active alongside merchants, but in Venice the situation was very different: excluding travellers and aristocrats, whose presence in town will not be analysed here and who, in any case, had very scarce contact with English merchants, the only British non-merchant emerging from the documents was a Scottish tailor who had a shop in Campo San Luca in the 1640s.[10] This dearth of artisans and craftsmen is mirrored in the patents issued by the Venetian government to foreign inventors. Compared to the forty-six patents given to Frenchmen, thirty-three to Germans and twenty-five to *Fiamenghi*, only two patents were issued to Englishmen for the entire period between 1474 and 1788: one for a loom to make stockings, and another for a machine to stop fires.[11] It is true that from the sixteenth century onwards patents were regularly issued in England,[12] but Venice had been the first to regularise patents to attract skilled artisans and provide them with financial advantages, so it was common for inventors from other countries to come to Venice and register their inventions.

Not all merchants were 'real' merchants. The aristocrat-adventurer Sir Anthony Sherley tried to pass himself off as a merchant – without too much success – during his stay in Venice.[13] His threats to a Persian

---

[9] For a sample of such arbitrations, see ASV, *Notarile Atti*, reg. 3366 (Gio Andrea Catti), cc.212r/v (20-5-1595) and c.267r (21-6-1595); ASV, *Notarile Atti*, reg. 11927 (Andrea Spinelli), c.632r (1-12-1606); ΓAK-ANK, *Notarial Archive*, b. 61 (Dimo Ardavani), fasc. iv, c.2v (9-1-1638); ASV, *Notarile Atti*, reg. 6698 (Gabriel Gabrieli), cc.44v–46r (28-2-1658) and c.65r (11-3-1659); ASV, *Notarile Atti*, reg. 1176 (Cristoforo Brombilla), cc.61v–65v (4-4-1674).

[10] ASV, *Notarile Atti*, reg. 657 (Andrea Bronzino), *primus*, cc.3v–4v (3-3-1643).

[11] R. Berveglieri, *Inventori stranieri a Venezia (1474–1788). Importazione di tecnologia e circolazione di tecnici artigiani inventori. Repertorio*, Venice, 1995, 90–92: patent to Sauthcot Vaijmont (22-5-1616); and 179–180: patent to Gasparo Brand and Archibaldo Glover (1686).

[12] C. MacLeod, *Inventing the Industrial Revolution: The English Patent System, 1660–1800*, Cambridge, 1988, Introduction.

[13] Connected by family links to Sir Henry Wotton, he travelled with him to Rome in 1601. He was considered potentially dangerous enough that Cecil had him watched during his stay in Venice from 1601 by at least two spies: see A. Haynes, *Invisible Power: The Elizabethan Secret Services, 1570–1603*, Bath, 1992, 151; on Anthony and Robert Sherley see also N. Steensgaard, *Carracks, Caravans and Companies: The Structural Crisis in the European-Asian Trade in the Early Seventeenth Century*, Copenhagen, 1973, 212–224, 258–262.

merchant, and the shady deals that he was probably transacting, got him into trouble with the *Quarantia*. In the words of Kenneth Andrews, 'wherever he went he left behind him a trail of unpaid debts and worthless promissory notes'.[14] Indeed, he was imprisoned in Venice for debt and remained there until the death of Queen Elizabeth.[15] Notwithstanding his attempts at passing for a wealthy merchant, with some diplomatic endorsement to match, the only contact he appears to have had with English merchants in Venice was a meeting he arranged with James Higgons and Jeffrey Luther to enquire if his brother Thomas had actually arrived in Livorno.[16]

The major figures of the Venice Company – Edward Holmeden, Paul Bayning,[17] Thomas Cordell and William Garraway (who built their fortunes with the trade in Ionian currants and Cretan wines) – further raised their profiles to become important shipowners and promoters of privateering and oceanic enterprise.[18] Bayning's career exemplifies the multifariousness of this generation of English merchants. In the 1570s he traded illegally with Spain and got into trouble with Spanish authorities, but the links he forged then provided him with a privileged position when trade was resumed between the two countries. He was one of the early investors in trade with Venice, and one of the founders of the East India Company.[19] Cordell had a similar profile; like Bayning, he was closely associated with the Mercers' Company. His business partner, Garraway, was also involved in trade with Spain and was one of the early investors in the Venice Company. His main area of interest was sugar, but he was also

---

[14] K. R. Andrews, *Elizabethan Privateering: English Privateering during the Spanish War, 1585–1603*, Cambridge, 1964, 65.

[15] Pearsall Smith, *The Life and Letters*, i: 38. On his incarceration and release: *CSPVe*, vol. x (1603–1607), 'May 1603', 16–28: see www.british-history.ac.uk/report.aspx?compid=95600 (date accessed: 29 July 2012). His clumsy attempt at facilitating an alliance between European powers and Shah Abbas of Persia caused panic amongst Levant Company's merchants in London: L. Publicover, 'Strangers at Home: The Sherley Brothers and Dramatic Romance', *Renaissance Studies*, 24 (2010): 694–709, 696–697.

[16] ASV, *Quarantia Criminale*, b. 114, fasc. 142, cc.n.n. (5-5-1603): he declared this during one of his interrogations during the trial. The story of his life is told in D. W. Davies, *Elizabethans Errant: The Strange Fortunes of Sir Thomas Sherley and His Three Sons, As Well in the Dutch Wars as in Muscovy, Morocco, Persia, Spain and the Indies*, New York, 1967; his Venetian adventures are recounted at 141–160.

[17] On Paul Bayning, his family wealth and his connections with the Grocers' Company see also Lang, 'Social Origins and Social Aspirations', 35–36, 38; G. Ungerer, *The Mediterranean Apprenticeship of British Slavery*, Madrid, 2008, 90 and bibliography cited therein.

[18] Andrews, *Trade, Plunder*, 98; on Cordell see also V. Pearl, *London and the Outbreak of the Puritan Revolution: City, Government and National Politics, 1625–1643*, Oxford, 1961, 297–298.

[19] Andrews, *Elizabethan Privateering*, 109–111.

an important shipowner and was involved with some of the biggest ships in Mediterranean trading.[20]

Moving down one level from the Company members to their principal factors and agents in Venice, all were shipowners; the most important amongst them were Paul Pindar,[21] Henry Parvis,[22] John Hobson, Sr[23] and Giles Jones.[24] Their vessels were engaged in direct traffic with England and in inter-Mediterranean trade, and frequently were employed by the Venetian *Armata* during the War of Candia. A successful mercantile career in the Ottoman territories seems often to have resulted in a homecoming with social distinction, but in Venice a very different picture emerges. With a few exceptions, mostly in the first generation (like Pindar, James Higgons, Michael Locke and his nephews Eleazar and Matthew Hickman, and, at a later time, George Ravenscroft), the majority of merchants never seemed to have made it back to England, or, if they did, they did not enjoy a visible social or political ascent back home. There was a tendency to remain marooned abroad, as their lower social rank probably provided less incentive to return.[25] Still, their English identity was preserved and carefully nurtured, even by families successfully integrated within Venetian society for more than one generation, like the Hobsons of Bristol. This is evident by the bequests made in their wills, which show a remarkable loyalty to their home country and an active concern for English affairs and contacts. Around sixty English merchants and ship-captains died in Venice between 1570 and 1700, and twenty-seven of them have surviving wills.[26] Twenty-four of them left legacies or nominated heirs in England, and only three did not mention England in their will and left their estates entirely to their wives, who appear to

---

[20] Andrews, *Elizabethan Privateering*, 111–112. Amongst the ships he owned (or co-owned) were the *Merchant Royal*, *Edward Bonaventure*, *George Bonaventure*, *Centurion* and the *Royal Exchange*.

[21] ASV, *Notarile Atti*, reg. 3372 (G. Andrea Catti), cc.610v–611r (24-3-1600).

[22] ASV, *Notarile Atti*, reg. 11937 (Andrea Spinelli), cc.753r–755r (8-10-1615) and enclosed papers.

[23] He had financial interests in various ships, and he owned the *Northumberland*.

[24] He owned the *Orsola Bonaventura* and the *Profeta Samuel*: see ASV, *Collegio, Rdd*, f. 43, cc.n.n. (20-12-1652); f. 45, cc.n.n. (24-11-1654); f. 45, cc.n.n. (8-7-1654).

[25] On higher social standing as an incentive for return home, see M. E. Bratchel, 'Alien Merchant Colonies in Sixteenth-Century England: Community Organisation and Social Mores', *Journal of Medieval and Renaissance Studies*, 14 (1984): 39–62, 55.

[26] Thanks to the kindness of Franco Rossi of the Venetian state archive, I was able to examine not only the card indexes to the *Notarile testamenti* series, but also the complete series of the *Alfabeti*, folio volumes that record all wills deposited in the *Cancelleria*. Because of the completeness of this source, it is fair to say that the wills examined should represent the entirety of wills made in Venice by English merchants between 1570 and 1700.

be Venetian subjects.[27] This pattern of legacies, with a strong preference for their home (as opposed to their host) country, was the norm amongst mercantile communities abroad. Some were to spend their entire lives abroad, but none of them left England with the intention of staying away forever; a useful contemporary parallel is found in today's financial bankers. The essence of their being foreigners was drastically different from what would have been experienced by silk-weavers from Lucca, refugees who were victims of political upheavals, or members of diasporic communities such as the Sephardic Jews who in those years were settling all around the Mediterranean and who were free agents with no state to back them.[28] English merchants taking root in the host countries – whether in Venice, Constantinople or Surat – with their frequent movements from place to place, were not running away from their homeland, nor they were emigrating for reasons of economic betterment; rather, they were expanding with their economy.[29]

The English mercantile community was peculiar for several reasons. No artisans appear to have followed them, which can be explained only partially by Venice's protectionist measures, as substantial incentives were in place for qualified foreign artisans willing to move there. More likely the reason was that English artisans did not have expertise in luxury trades, which is where German and Flemish artisans were employed, and where there were still plenty of opportunities in Venice.[30] The major English industry was textile manufactures, which at that time were expanding fast and absorbing all available expertise. Amongst the German artisans settled in Venice, in the Middle Ages the traditional profession was that of baker, an occupation where German dominance was never challenged; in the early modern period there was more diversification and many were employed in the trades connected with the printing industry.[31] Flemish artisans – especially jewellers, leather sellers, bookbinders and printers – generally were fairly affluent and well

[27] Those are: Jeffrey Luther in ASV, NT 1047 (Francesco Zordan), n.141 (4-11-1607); Giles Jones in ASV, NT 904 (Francesco Simbeni), n.135 (14-12-1667); Roberto Brune in ASV, NT 470 (Marco Generini), n.501 (28-12-1682).

[28] Molà, La comunità dei lucchesi, 23–30.

[29] G. Pinto, 'Gli stranieri nelle realtà locali dell'Italia basso-medievale: alcuni percorsi tematici', in Rossetti ed., Dentro la città, 23–32, 30; for the English case Games, Web of Empire.

[30] Especially prominent were also jewellers, metal workers, leather sellers, bookbinders and printers: see C. Hollberg, Deutsche in Venedig im späten Mittelalter: Eine Untersuchung von Testamenten aus dem 15. Jahrhundert, Göttingen, 2005.

[31] To give an example of the scale of this dominance, amongst the thirty-nine maestri pistori active in 1471, thirty-two were Germans: in P. Braunstein, 'Appunti per la storia di una minoranza: la popolazione tedesca di Venezia nel medioevo', in R. Comba, G. Piccinni and G. Pinto eds., Strutture familiari, epidemie e emigrazioni nell'Italia medievale, Naples, 1984, 511–517, 512.

integrated both with Flemish merchants and Venetian society.[32] In contrast, the English community was fairly homogeneous, and seems to have been made up of middle to low social levels, with the exception of the very beginning, when a few people of high social profile were active.

English trading and living in Venice

Venice was the only European metropolis in which the English had a strong mercantile representation. Throughout the period under investigation, there were around twenty English merchants settled in the town in a semi-permanent manner at any given time. Amongst the other Italian mercantile centres, as we have seen before, Livorno was booming, but certainly was not comparable to Venice, whilst Genoa was more of a financial centre and until the Restoration the English presence there was slight. In the rest of continental Europe, by the end of the seventeenth century many English mercantile communities of differing sizes existed: we find them in Dutch and north German ports, in seaports in Norway, Sweden and elsewhere in the Baltic, and in a number of centres in Spain and Portugal.[33] Most of the communities were small, like the ones in Naples and Messina, which were nothing more than stopovers in the inter-Mediterranean trade between the Levant and Italy.[34] Another community, quite large, albeit very isolated, was resident in the Canary island of Tenerife, where there was a thriving market due to the English demand for the locally produced wine.[35] Other English mercantile communities found themselves either in dangerous places[36] or in remote corners of the world with little to do except trade. In Venice, by contrast, they were settled in what was still one of the most exciting and stimulating places in Europe. Venice's influence may have been dwindling, but this did not affect everyday life, and even merchants living on the colonial outposts of Zante and Cephalonia enjoyed a relatively comfortable existence. Unlike the predicament of English merchants in the Spanish Caribbean colonies,

[32] Van Gelder, *Trading Places*, 105.
[33] H. E. S. Fisher, 'Lisbon, its English Merchant Community and the Mediterranean in the Eighteenth Century', in P. L. Cottrell and D. H. Aldcroft eds., *Shipping, Trade and Commerce. Essays in Memory of Ralph Davis*, Leicester, 1981, 23–44, 23.
[34] H. Koenigsberger, 'English Merchants in Naples and Sicily in the Seventeenth Century', *English Historical Review*, 62 (1947): 304–326.
[35] G. F. Steckley, 'The Wine Economy of Tenerife in the Seventeenth Century: Anglo-Spanish Partnership in a Luxury Trade', *Economic History Review*, 33 (1980): 335–350.
[36] The commercial and military garrison of Tangier comes to mind, just to mention one example: on their everyday life, see E. M. G. Routh, 'The English at Tangier', *English Historical Review*, 26 (1911): 469–481.

the English were not enemies of Venice nor was their presence in Venetian colonies illegal, as it was in the Spanish ones.

Trading circumstances were strikingly different on the other side of the Levant traffic, in the Ottoman territories. There, especially in land-locked settlements, European merchants led a hard, monotonous life in a situation which could well be defined as self-imposed exile.[37] Everyday life in port cities, like Izmir, was indeed easier, with more opportunities for exchange and contacts, but it remained almost impossible to reach some degree of integration with the local population.[38] The English in Constantinople have been described by Daniel Goffman as being a 'community of expatriate eccentrics', and there were certainly enough colourful characters to justify the sobriquet but, as his narrative clearly shows, the connection between diplomatic and commercial presence was paramount there, in contrast with the situation in Venice.[39] The largest group of English merchants in Ottoman territories was based in Aleppo, where foreign merchants lived in *khans*, institutions that provided them with a perfect organisation to deal effectively with many issues at the same time: safety, the operational needs of trade, and obligations to the Ottoman government. The *khan* could be defined as a sort of fortified settlement, as its physical structure was very similar to that of a *fondaco*: a square building around a central courtyard. There the foreign merchants lived together and kept their goods. Their local organisation was a reproduction in miniature of their parent company back in London.[40] They were not living amongst a poor and backward people whilst exploiting them; rather, they were tolerated foreigners living in a highly civilised community and dealing with local merchants who were as rich, well informed and sharp as themselves.[41] Moving eastwards we see the same in India, with the factory in Surat appearing to a contemporary writer 'more like a College, a Monastery, or a House under Religious Orders than any other'. Here the factors, as at an Oxbridge college, dined together in Hall, and attended daily prayers in Chapel. Discipline in these settlements was, and had to be, strict.[42] However, in all these cases, foreign

---

[37] A. Brett-James, 'The Levant Company's Factory in Aleppo', *History Today*, 12 (1962): 793–798, 794; Goffman, *Britons in the Ottoman Empire*, 29–43.

[38] Brett-James, 'The Levant Company's Factory', 795; Goffman, *Britons in the Ottoman Empire*, 41–42.

[39] Goffman, *Britons in the Ottoman Empire*, 5.

[40] P. R. Harris, 'An Aleppo Merchant's Letter-Book', *British Museum Quarterly*, 22 (1960): 64–69, 66; see also G. P. Ambrose, 'English Traders at Aleppo, 1658–1756', *Economic History Review*, 3 (1931–1932): 246–267.

[41] Davis, *Aleppo and Devonshire Square*, 146.

[42] H. G. Rawlinson, 'Life in an English Factory in the Seventeenth Century', *Proceedings of the Indian Historical Record Commission*, 3 (1921): 24–35, 26.

mercantile communities never integrated with the locals, and social life was mostly restricted to contacts with other Europeans.[43]

Venice was a completely different environment. It was a highly civilised place, with plenty of opportunities not only to deal with locals and several different mercantile communities but also to enjoy free time from work, and the English were certainly not left to their own devices to provide entertainment for themselves. If diplomats were active members of the local art market, as we have seen with both Wotton and Carleton, music seems to have been the favourite diversion of merchants.[44] Robert Bargrave leads the way in this area, and Beth Glixon has recently uncovered his activities as a composer and impresario of opera.[45] Bargrave's contribution to music was unusual, but it is worth noting that musical instruments are frequently mentioned amongst the bequests in the wills of English merchants.[46]

There was no need for the English to organise and finance a 'protection system' in Venice itself or in her empire. When the need arose – for example to fight highwaymen in Cefalonia – they simply had to address the Venetian *Rettore* and lobby the *Senato*.[47] This allowed them and their Company to save substantial amounts of money, since defence was the major expenditure in some areas of trade, affecting the profits of every company in the Mediterranean as well as in more distant lands.[48] Within Mediterranean waters the English had a substantial comparative advantage in the strength of their own ships, better armed to deal with pirates – when they were not pirates themselves – and this was an important factor in their success in penetrating the Mediterranean.[49] Later, in the second

---

[43] Goffman, *Britons in the Ottoman Empire*, 13–28.

[44] Jacobsen, *Luxury and Power*, 164.

[45] Beth Glixon, 'Cavalli, Robert Bargrave and the English *Erismena*', unpublished paper: I thank Beth Glixon for generously sharing her material with me; see also R. Bargrave, *The Travel Diary of Robert Bargrave: Levant Merchant (1647–1656)*, M. G. Brennan ed., London, 1999, 34, 37–38: it is worth noting that this edition contains several inaccuracies in its critical apparatus, especially regarding the identification of toponyms. See also M. Tilmouth, 'Music on the Travels of an English Merchant: Robert Bargrave (1628–61)', *Music and Letters*, 53 (1972): 143–159.

[46] Lawrence Hider learnt to play the lute in Venice: see ASV, *AdC, Penale*, b. 285, fasc. 26, cc.n.n., testimonies were D. Todorin Sagomalà *quondam* D. Tomaso, merchant from Morea; Piero Zagia of Francesco *barber*, and his assistant Paulo Marchesini of Mattio (cc.n.n., 3-11-1628). For Henry Parvis at the theatre see TNA, *SP* 99/19, 150 (1615): I wish to thank Filippo de Vivo for bringing this to my attention. Michiel Filippi left in his will a viola and a violin to his friend Thomaso Arnegi, English merchant based in Genoa (ASV, *NT*, b. 65 (Andrea Bronzini), n.220 (30-11-1653)).

[47] TNA, *SP* 99/38, 42r–43v; ASV, *SDR*, Cefalonia, *passim*.

[48] I. B. Watson, 'Fortifications and the "Idea" of Force in Early English East India Company Relations with India', *Past and Present*, 88 (1980): 70–87, 74–81.

[49] A recapitulation of the role of English privateering in the decline of the Venetian commercial fleet is in Fusaro, *Uva passa*, 65–78, and bibliography quoted therein.

half of the seventeenth century, when trade was well established, their good relationship with the Barbary states favoured them against their competitors. Even taking these factors into account, being able to take also advantage of the defence structure of the Venetians – especially in the *Dominio da Mar* – and their control over the indigenous population in the Greek islands not only saved the English money but allowed them to concentrate on naval supremacy in the Mediterranean, in itself a means of defence.[50]

All these factors resulted in a series of peculiar ways to transact business in the early stages of Mediterranean trade. It is difficult to separate conscious strategies from simple responses to local circumstances, or just chance. However, it is clear that commercial and political tactics were tailored to the differing areas where trade was conducted, and the Levant Company adjusted its behaviour according to the social and political contexts, exercising flexibility in every situation. Levant Company merchants traded as independent merchants and, as argued in Chapter 3, this allowed them more freedom and flexibility in handling their own affairs. Conversely, it could also be argued that this flexibility derived from the fact that the English were latecomers and needed to adjust not only to the requirements of the host countries but also to the ways of doing business which other foreign mercantile communities had developed there. In this way, the English quickly established themselves in the region, helped by the Venetian shipping crisis and by the Ottoman need for strategic goods and allies in Europe.

Within this wider context, Venice represents a magnificent case study of English merchants abroad, as the attitude and behaviour of the mercantile community in Venice and its dependencies sheds light on a specific phase of English trade expansion. During this first phase a highly structured organisation would adopt a very informal approach and a deceptively informal structure to penetrate deeply into the logic and the expertise of the host country. This allowed them to undermine quickly, from within, the formalised ways through which trade had traditionally been carried out. This behaviour proved to be the most effective way to trade with a sophisticated commercial culture like the Venetian one and was crucial to the reversal of fortunes between the two countries. This was

---

[50] Frederic Lane has pointed up some economic functions of protection and 'protection payments' in an important series of articles, based on the experience of the medieval Mediterranean, but with a much wider relevance: Lane, *Venice and History*, especially 373–428. For the issue of protection costs, see also Curtin, *Cross-Cultural Trade*, 41–42; G. M. Anderson and R. D. Tollison, 'Adam Smith's Analysis of Joint-Stock Companies', *Journal of Political Economy*, 90 (1982): 1237–1256; and their 'Apologiae for Chartered Monopolies in Foreign Trade, 1600–1800', *History of Political Economy*, 15 (1983): 549–566.

achieved through the efforts of merchants who, within the same company, came from a lower social rank than their colleagues in the Ottoman territories.

Lack of formal organisation

Whilst it appears that almost no documentation produced by English merchants has survived in Turkish archives, there is plenty in Venice. My focus here will be the community in its totality, as a working group, and in this regard the first set of questions regards the status of the community vis-à-vis Venetian authorities and how its informal organisation and the pattern of English merchant settlements contributed to its success. These issues are at the centre of the study of mercantile communities in general: why and how were some communities formally represented whilst others were not? How did their official status and structure influence the ways in which they dealt with their host country and how they conducted their business? How did some manage to be successful without formal representation? And, between host and guest country, which was more influential in determining the ways and means of formal representation?

In sixteenth-century London, French merchants were not organised under their own consul; neither were high Germans, nor the merchants from the Low Countries,[51] Spain or Portugal. Some of these communities were of considerable size and importance. According to Michael Bratchel, their failure to become organised was that they 'developed alternative mechanisms for their protection and representation'.[52] What does this mean exactly? He continues:

Obviously one might invoke the force of numbers. The high Germans, Spaniards, and Portuguese in England were perhaps never sufficiently numerous to make organization worthwhile. Patterns of residence and of trade might be significant. It has been argued that Spanish and Portuguese consulates in England were rendered unnecessary by the dominant role played by the Government of the much larger Iberian communities in the Low Countries. French, historians, characteristically, have approached the problem through geography. Ingenuity suggests a host of ways in which geographical proximity might weaken the urge towards a statutory self-discipline.[53]

More than ingenuity, it seems common sense to infer that traffic which involved a large number of merchants from outports as well as from

---

[51] A situation that did not change even in the following century: see Barbour, 'Consular Service', 574–575.

[52] Bratchel, 'Alien Merchant Colonies', 47.

[53] Bratchel, 'Alien Merchant Colonies', 48.

London was bound to be carried out in a dispersed and informal manner, because of the wider distribution of the merchants involved. Numbers are not a very good reason either: there were only ten French merchants in London in the 1540s, but to infer from this fact alone that they did not need representation seems unsubstantiated. Thirty years later, the remains of the Venetian community in London – consisting of fewer than ten people – ignored directions from the *Senato* and proceeded to elect their own consul, without any official backing from the Venetian government, because they felt the need for one.[54] Numerical considerations are only one factor in such decisions.

The secondary literature tends to define a 'non-organised community' as one lacking formal consular authority. Under this definition every mercantile community in Venice was organised, but there are substantial structural differences amongst them. In Venice there were foreign mercantile communities with a *fondaco*, like the Germans and the Turks, and then there were those which had only the consul to represent them, like the English, the Dutch and the Genoese. No mercantile community was completely free from some form of control, but there was a great difference between having to run one's business transactions through a *fondaco* and not having to do so. Another frequent assumption is that each community was the emanation of the home society; I would rather propose that each community – and its behaviour – was the result of the mediation between the needs and traditions of host and guest societies. A community is not simply a fragment of its homeland, but an active entity in its own right that sometimes develops ways of operating quite differently from their mother-culture.

If we consider only the community itself, regardless of the host country's attitude towards it, it is possible to argue that the complexity of its internal structure is also a function of the status and social standing of its members. In other words, the higher the social level of the members, the higher the level of formalisation within the community itself. A highly formalised structure – like the one in the Ottoman territories – has the advantage that everyone knows their place within it, and this makes it easier to exercise some degree of social control over internal questions of precedence and commercial disputes in a foreign environment where it is always wiser to control aggression. On the other hand, it is also possible to argue that a lower social standing of the merchant members of the community makes it easier to settle internal squabbles within a more

---

[54] On the election of Placido Ragazzoni, see earlier in the book in Chapter 2 and Fusaro, *Uva Passa*, 12, 21.

informal frame. Normally merchants were very mobile during their career: it is quite often the case to find an apprentice somewhere reappearing elsewhere as an authoritative businessman. In the particular case of the English mercantile community in Venice and its empire, there are plenty of factors and agents who did not return to England, or at least they never made enough money to become serious players back home, and so they do not easily resurface in the English side of the documentation, additional proof of their lower social standing. It is also arguable that one of the reasons behind the lack of formal organisation in the English mercantile community in Venice was their late arrival on the Venetian scene. They started to arrive in the second half of the sixteenth century, later than just about all other foreign mercantile communities.[55] The Dutch also arrived around the same time, and their numerical increase followed the same pattern as the English one. Their community also had no formal structure, but they had the advantage of being quickly absorbed by the pre-existing local Flemish community, with which they had a wealth of commercial contacts. This makes it nearly impossible to differentiate between those who came from the northern provinces and those who came from the southern ones, especially because the Venetians did not distinguish between them, but called them all *Fiamenghi*.

The social profile of the Dutch community in Venice was decisively higher than that of the English, and so on average was their personal wealth.[56] It is therefore unsurprising that the Flemish community had frequent social and commercial contacts with the upper echelons of Venetian aristocracy. This also characterised their presence in Livorno, where they enjoyed commercial relationships with some of the major families of the Tuscan aristocracy.[57] English merchants in Venice do not appear to have enjoyed such privileged contacts: their links with Venetians seem to have been limited to *cittadini* or subjects of the Republic. With no internal divisions between the diplomatic and the commercial sides, and with the advantage of pre-existing contacts, the Flemish in Venice appear as a richer, better educated and better integrated group than the English until at least the beginning of the eighteenth century.[58]

---

[55] The first evidence of an English mercantile presence in Venice which had some sort of continuity is to be found in the papers of the notary Luca Gabrieli and dates from the late 1560s: see ASV, *Notarile Atti*, from b. 6515.

[56] A detailed analysis of these issues is in van Gelder, *Trading Places*. To have an idea of the kind of contacts enjoyed by the Dutch it is sufficient to take a look at the notarial deeds in Brulez and Devos, *Marchands Flamands*.

[57] Engels, 'Dutch Traders in Livorno', especially 70–71.

[58] Van Gelder, *Trading Places*.

The Turks were another community that settled very late in Venice, roughly in the second half of the sixteenth century. From the last quarter of that century they lobbied to have 'a place of their own like the Jews',[59] and in 1621 they achieved their goal: their own *fondaco* in town.[60] It is not really appropriate to compare the Turks with either the English or the Dutch, or with any other European presence in town, for that matter. Their otherness – socially, politically, religiously and ethnically – made them distinct from other foreigners, including the Jews who, notwithstanding their physical segregation in the ghetto, were relatively integrated into Venetian society in their professional activities and were considered part of it.[61] The existence of a *Fondaco dei Turchi* in Venice reflects the same cultural logic that lies behind the *khans* of Aleppo, and the Turks themselves lobbied for its establishment.

Trying to give an estimate of the total number of English merchants in Venice and the Ionian islands is not easy.[62] The task is complicated by the fact that the English commercial network was spread between Venice and Zante and Cephalonia. At any given time there were around twenty merchants permanently established in Venice, and fewer than ten based between Zante and Cephalonia. Circulation of men and capital between these three foci was frequent, and one can argue that, notwithstanding this geographical distribution, the mercantile community was in effect one, as the same names keep on appearing in these three centres depending on the needs of trade. This movement was greatly facilitated by the informal structure of the English community in the Venetian territories, as indicated by the wealth of deeds in which power of attorney was bestowed upon fellow merchants.

---

[59] P. Preto, *Venezia e i Turchi*, Florence, 1975; A. Buffardi ed., *Nunziature di Venezia*, 42 vols., Rome, 1958–2008, xi: 283–295. See also ASV, *Cinque Savi alla Mercanzia*, b. 187 n.s., fasc. i–ii (petitions dated 1574, 4-6-1588, 5-12-1618); and also ASV, *Compilazione Leggi*, b. 210 (28-3-1620).

[60] ASV, *Cinque Savi alla Mercanzia*, b. 187 n.s., fasc. i–ii (1621). See also Preto, *Venezia e i Turchi*; E. Burke, 'Francesco di Demetri Litino: The Inquisition and the *Fondaco dei Turchi*', *Thesaurismata*, 36 (2006): 79–96.

[61] On the level of integration of Jews with Venetian society, see S. Schwarzfuchs and A. Toaff eds., *The Mediterranean and the Jews: Banking, Finance and International Trade, XVI–XVIII*, Ramat Gan, 1989; Ravid, 'A Tale of Three Cities'; B. Pullan, *The Jews of Europe and the Inquisition of Venice, 1550–1670*, Oxford, 1983, 145–167; Ruspio, *La nazione portoghese*; a recent synthesis can be found in Ravid, 'Venice and its Minorities'.

[62] Even in the absence of precise figures, it is generally acknowledged that by the seventeenth century the largest English community in Italy was based in Livorno.

Taverne and *osterie*

Given the absence of a formalised settlement, the patterns of habitation of Englishmen in Venice acquire additional importance. Embedded in the fabric of the city, without an institutional structure to control and regulate their actions, English merchants proved very difficult to control. In Venice, as in the Ionian islands, their frequent contacts and business relationship with Greek subjects of the Republic broke a central tenet of any imperial strategy, which is to prevent subjects – especially the entrepreneurs amongst them – from establishing partnerships with competitors.

The receptivity of early modern towns to foreign merchants and sailors is a subject still in need of thorough study.[63] Several attempts to centralise and control structures of reception were implemented by most local governments, but the increase of sanctions for non-compliers is the ultimate proof of their failure. The presence of unruly sailors in port cities additionally created problems of public order, which were almost impossible to solve because of their mobility. Their drinking and the trail of unpaid debts they left behind were two of the reasons behind attempts to keep sailors aboard ship as much as possible.[64] By 1446 English and French sailors had created such troubles in Venice, by drinking too much and lodging with prostitutes, that legislation was passed to punish this behaviour and forbid the sale of alcohol in the vicinity of ships.[65]

In Venice only Venetian ships could moor in the *Bacino* of St Mark; foreigners were forced to stop outside Malamocco, a village on the western side of the Lido, which separates the lagoon from the Adriatic. With an increasing number of foreign ships arriving in Venice, Malamocco underwent a massive transformation towards catering to their needs, and its economy became increasingly dominated by victualling and contraband. In theory only ships' captains and 'officers' could disembark to take care of business, but even a superficial analysis of the papers of the *Podestà* – the local Venetian representative – shows that this was not the case, and that illegal watering holes prospered and contraband flourished.[66] English and Flemish crews seem to have been particularly resistant to local legislation, and throughout the seventeenth century there were frequent episodes when the peace was broken, including the

---

[63] D. Calabi and P. Lanaro, 'Introduzione', in Calabi and Lanaro eds., *La città italiana*, vii–xix, xv.

[64] G. Casarino, 'Stranieri a Genova nel Quattro e Cinquecento: tipologie sociali e nazioni', in Rossetti ed., *Dentro la città*, 137–150, 139–140. On the thorny issue of sailors' behaviour, see Cipolla, *Il burocrate ed il marinaio*, 97–100.

[65] ASV, *Compilazione Leggi*, b. 12, cc.266r/v (1446).

[66] ASV, *Podestà di Malamocco*, bb. 1–50, *passim*.

use of firearms leading to casualties.[67] The *Podestà* regularly issued proclamations such as:

It shall be prohibited to all inhabitants of this place [Malamocco] to host English
and Flemish and people of any other foreign nation, both by day and by night, or
to provide them with food, drink and lodgings in their private homes, which is
damaging to the local *osterie* and goes against the laws of this most Serene
Dominion.[68]

Additional legislation was issued by the *Podestà* to forbid weapons, open
or concealed, but again it appears that as arms were always present
aboard, it was impossible to avoid these coming onto shore.[69]

The city of Venice itself, due to its long history of being a commercial
entrepôt, had more experience and legislation on these issues than most
places, but nonetheless the situation was complex and delicate. At the
top level of the reception system were taverns: between the fourteenth
and the eighteenth centuries their number oscillated between twenty
and twenty-four at any given time. Officially licensed, they paid their
taxes, and were extremely expensive.[70] From 1505 private individuals
were also permitted to rent rooms – called *albergarie* – following payment
of the *dazio del vino a spina*, a customs duty. Foreigners had to register
their presence in town, and legally one was allowed to move into one of
these *albergarie* only after having spent three days in a tavern.[71] But these
regulations were practically unenforceable and mostly disregarded. The
dazio del vino a spina was an important revenue for state coffers, paid by
all establishments granted the right to sell wine – *taverne*, *osterie* and
bastioni – and its payment was a prerequisite for a licence. The astonish-
ing variety of lodgings and eateries presented the Republic with the
constant challenge of checking that each offered only those services for
which they had paid their taxes. *Taverne* could sell hot food and alcohol,
osterie only cold food and alcohol, and *bastioni* were wine warehouses
and, up to the beginning of the eighteenth century, could only sell wine
wholesale (that is, to *osterie* and taverns), not to private individuals.
Locande could host paying guests but could not provide them with
food or drink. These differences implied different types of taxation,
and although rules got looser with time, were still enforced in the

[67] ASV, *Avogaria di Comun, Penale*, b. 353, fasc. 21 (1646); ASV, *Podestà di Malamocco*,
b. 2, *passim*.
[68] ASV, *Podestà di Malamocco*, b. 1, cc.n.n., s.d. (not dated [1654]).
[69] For example, see ASV, *Podestà di Malamocco*, b. 19, cc.n.n. (14-1-1652).
[70] M. Costantini, 'Le strutture dell'ospitalità', in *Storia di Venezia*, vol. v: *Il Rinascimento:
società ed economia*, A. Tenenti and U. Tucci eds., Rome, 1996, 881–911, 891–892.
[71] Costantini, 'Le strutture dell'ospitalità', 893–894.

seventeenth century.[72] Of these establishments, *taverne* and *osterie* could host guests for the night and provide them with food and wine. Needless to say, there were many abuses.

Foreigners were generally perceived as potentially dangerous, and drinking and eating establishments were natural meeting places and therefore possibly centres of dissent, whether religious or political.[73] As the idle chit-chat which flourished in taverns could have dangerous financial or political consequences,[74] the Republic decided early on that aristocrats should not be associated with taverns and lodgings.[75] These concerns, and the rise of vagrancy at the end of the sixteenth century, were at the root of an increase in the powers of the magistracy of the *Esecutori contro la Bestemmia* in 1583. These new dispositions stipulated that every foreigner should register his arrival in Venice, after which he would receive a certificate (*bollettino*) that allowed him to seek lodgings.[76] Needless to say, this measure was also constantly disregarded.

Only three taverns could legally host foreigners and were granted special permission to provide them with hot food and drink: the *Aquila Negra*, *Lion Bianco* and *San Zorzi*. Originally these were established to cater for the overflow of German merchants – the so-called *ultramontani* – who could not find room in the *Fondaco dei Tedeschi*, and with the passing of time they also accommodated other foreigners.[77] However, in practice, the sheer cost of taverns made them a feasible option only for wealthy travellers, and English merchants appear to have frequented them primarily to socialise and conduct business, not so much to lodge. Fynes Moryson at the beginning of the seventeenth century found Venice incredibly expensive, and noted the 'greater price of chambers

---

[72] On these differences see ASV, *Compilazione Leggi*, bb. 12 and 299, *passim*.

[73] Martin, *Venice's Hidden Enemies*, 170–171.

[74] Cozzi, 'Religione, moralità e giustizia', 46; de Vivo, *Information and Communication*, 94–97; see also F. Barbierato, 'Dissenso religioso, discussione politica e mercato dell'informazione a Venezia fra Seicento e Settecento', *Società e Storia*, 24 (2003): 707–757.

[75] ASV, *Compilazione Leggi*, b. 12, cc.220r–224r (25-5-1280). Patrician-owned properties could be rented out and used as *osterie*; in these cases the magistracy of the *Giustizia Nuova* took care of the administration of the building and collected rent from the licensees (Costantini, 'Le strutture dell'ospitalità', 891). Marin Sanudo earned 800 ducats per annum from the rent of an *osteria* (Sanudo, *De origine, situ*, 29).

[76] R. Derosas, 'Moralità e giustizia a Venezia nel '500 e nel '600, gli Esecutori contro la Bestemmia', in Cozzi ed., *Stato, società e giustizia*, i: 431–528, 447, 452. Unfortunately, the surviving archive of this magistracy is so small that no research is really possible on these issues. On this legislation see ASV, *Compilazione Leggi*, b. 12, cc.389r–390v (29-12-1583); and cc.411r–412v (8-5-1619).

[77] Costantini, 'Le strutture dell'ospitalità', 890, 901–904; also P. Braunstein, 'Immagini di una identità collettiva: gli ospiti del Fondaco dei Tedeschi a Venezia (sec. XII–XVII)', in Del Treppo ed., *Sistema di rapporti*, 63–69.

[in comparison to Padua], and extraordinary inticements [sic] to spend'.[78] William Lithgow, who visited Venice in 1609, lodged at the *Capello Rosso*;[79] but the most popular choice amongst Englishmen was to stay 'at honest Signor Paulo Rhodomante's [sic] at the Black Eagle, near the Rialto, one of the best quarters in the towne'.[80] John Evelyn, who in Genoa had stayed at an 'English tavern',[81] was certainly impressed with Rodomonte's hospitality,[82] as was Robert Bargrave ten years afterwards.[83] Paolo Rodomonte was a trusted figure for foreigners in Venice, especially for the English, always hospitable[84] and sometimes even in charge of business on their behalf.[85] During his administration of the *Aquila Negra*, the tavern became a centre for Englishmen in town, and this seems to have had a positive impact on his commercial dealings with English merchants.[86] However, in 1648 he suddenly left for mysterious reasons, and within two years he was begging the *Collegio* for financial help.[87] A possible explanation for his departure could be the crisis that hit the three taverns (*Aquila Nera, Lion Bianco* and *San Zorzi*) that had been specifically set aside for the use of the *oltramontani*, as a result of the collapse in the numbers of German merchants in Venice during the Thirty Years' War.

Albergarie

Some travellers instead took advantage of the hospitality of the English mercantile community. Philip Skippon on his three visits to Venice between 1663 and 1665 was lodged and fed like a king by 'Mr. Jones, consul of the English nation, who kept an entertaining-house'. Also Lord Maynard 'in 1661 lived with our Consul, Gideon [sic] Jones, and enjoyed

[78] F. Moryson, *An itinerary written by Fynes Moryson Gent . . .*, London, 1617, 70.

[79] Interestingly, the *Cappello Rosso* was not one listed amongst those taverns allowed to host foreigners: W. Lithgow, *The Totall Discourse of the Rare Adventures and Painefull Peregrinations of long Nineteene yeares Travayles from Scotland to the most famous Kingdomes in Europe, Asia and Affrica*, Glasgow, 1906 (1632), 34.

[80] H. B. Wheatley ed., *The Diary of John Evelyn*, London, 1906, 235.

[81] E. Grendi, 'Fonti inglesi per la storia genovese', in *Studi e documenti di storia ligure*, Genoa, 1994, 349–374, 350.

[82] Wheatley ed., *The Diary of John Evelyn*, 235; Stoye, *English Travellers*, 131.

[83] Stoye, *English Travellers*, 152–154; Bargrave, *The Travel Diary*, 225.

[84] For example, it was in his own private home that Robert Bargrave settled his accounts with the Jewish merchants Jacob and Josef Aboaf and the German Martin Piers: see ASV, *Notarile atti*, b. 11057 (Andrea Piccini), cc.598r–599v (29-2-1655mv).

[85] For example, acting as procurator for English merchants and captains: see ASV, *GdF*, 490 (*Domande in causa*, f. 3), c.93 (29-7-1643). He also acted as a translator: see ASV, *NT*, b. 756 (Giovanni Piccini), n.73 (29-9-1648).

[86] Stoye, *English Travellers*, 131.

[87] ASV, *Collegio, Rdd*, f. 41, cc.n.n. (19-1-1650mv).

entertainment fit for a king both in Venice and in Jones' country villa outside'.[88] On the same occasion Skippon also sampled the hospitality of 'Mr. Ravenscraft, a Venice merchant, and Dr. Harper, both Papists'.[89] Giles Jones also appears to have hosted captains and passengers of English ships at his own homes, first in San Lio and later in Santa Maria Formosa, and it is worth noting that this happened before the period when he was the official consul for the English (1660–1668), when such hospitality would have been an expected part of his professional duties.[90] John Evelyn was extremely happy to sample the hospitality of John Hobson's household: on the eve of his departure he was pleased to report that 'I was invited to excellent English potted venison at Mr. Hobbson's, a worthy merchant'.[91] The habit of dining with countrymen passing through was common amongst all mercantile communities, whether at home or abroad, and it was especially common amongst the English.[92] Venetian sources are somewhat reticent on this issue, but evidence from Constantinople provides us with a picture of lively sociability, with references to the nefarious effects of 'the hot Greek wine in the evenings', and considerations of the fact that 'it is well known that the merchants abroad are too much given to the bottle'.[93]

Rodomonte, in addition to running the *Aquila Negra*, appears to have rented rooms in his own house (or in his own properties) as *albergarie*; Peter Ireland died in a house of his in San Giovanni Novo in 1638, and still in 1653 Rodomonte was hosting English merchants at his own home in Santa Sofia.[94]

Whilst resident merchants rented homes from Venetians, captains of ships and merchants recently arrived, or staying for a short time, normally rented rooms in the *albergarie*. Authorisation was required to let rooms in

---

[88] Stoye, *English Travellers*, 131. Lord Maynard was on a tour of Italy. Gideon is a misspelling of Giles.

[89] P. Skippon, *An Account of a Journey made thro' part of the Low Countries, Germany, Italy and France*, London, 1752, 520.

[90] We have evidence of this from some wills: Edward Waterman, captain of the *Mercante Venturato*, in ASV, *NT*, bb. 64–65 (Andrea Bronzini), n.100 (26-12-1652); William Robin, passenger on the *Pietro e Giovanni* coming from Lisbon, in ASV, *NT*, b. 65 (Andrea Bronzini), n.122 (24-11-1649); Nicolò Guiscomb, scribe of the *Vero Amor*, in ASV, *NT*, b. 65 (Andrea Bronzini), n.234 (7-12-1651).

[91] Wheatley ed., *The Diary of John Evelyn*, 261.

[92] For example see Routh, 'The English at Tangier', 476–477. On social relationships in economic exchange see Q. van Doosselaere, *Commercial Agreements and Social Dynamics in Medieval Genoa*, Cambridge, 2009.

[93] R. North, *The Lives of the Right Hon. Francis North, Baron Guildford [. . .] the Hon. Sir Dudley North [. . .] And the Hon. and Rev. Dr. John North [. . .]*, 3 vols, London, 1826, ii: 415.

[94] Peter Ireland's will in ASV, *NT*, b. 857 (Gio Batta Profettini), n. 142 (11-9-1638); Michael Filippi left Rodomonte thirty agate to make knife-handles, in ASV, *NT*, b. 65 (Andrea Bronzini), n.220 (30-11-1653).

exchange for money, and from 1502 a licence from the *Collegio* was also necessary, in theory to ensure that in each house there was only one lodger so as to avoid untoward speculation by landlords. The Venetian authorities were especially concerned to prevent private homes from becoming in effect taverns, which would have meant possible problems of both social control and loss of income from the *vino a spina*.[95] In theory it was possible to rent only one room in each home, and this only to one person and any eventual associates. However, the reality was very different, with multiple rooms being routinely rented out, and co-renters being total strangers. Another problem regarded food: authorisation to rent a room was given on condition that no food was to be served to the renter, because this would have been an infringement of the duty of *vino a spina*. But, once again, this proved to be unenforceable.

In certain cases it is genuinely difficult to ascertain the nature of the hospitality. For example, Hobson appears to have hosted in his own house Timothy Paine, who was captain of Hobson's ship *Northumberland*. Paine was ill, and indeed he died there, leaving in his will 150 ducats to Hobson 'for the inconvenience given him' and some money also for the domestic staff of his household.[96] Was he a paying guest, or just a business partner in need of temporary shelter and care during his illness? This is a classic example of the potentially ambiguous issues behind certification of foreigners based in Venice. The legislation had been designed to deal with vagrancy and immigration, and was not really fit to control the movements of foreign merchants and ship-captains, extremely mobile individuals by nature. Merchants who came with the intention of residing should have been certified by the *Esecutori* like every other foreigner arriving in Venice, and until 1610 their identity would also have to be certified in front of a notary, through the testimony of fellow countrymen already resident there. From 1610 onwards, however, they had to register instead with the *Cinque Savi alla Mercanzia* if they intended to do business in town, so these rich notarial registrations stopped abruptly.[97] A few examples of the engagements of Englishmen with *albergarie* help to illuminate the complexity of these issues.

Earlier on in the book I argued that English merchants tried to distance themselves from political and religious activities so as to be better able to take care of their business undisturbed. Indirect evidence of this

---

[95] ASV, *Compilazione Leggi*, b. 12, cc.264r–265r (24-3-1411); ASV, *Compilazione Leggi*, b. 12, cc.309r–311r (17-9-1502).

[96] ASV, *NT*, b. 65 (Andrea Bronzini), n. 273 (16-5-1657).

[97] Copy of the *parte* of the *Senato* is in ASV, *Compilazione Leggi*, b. 210, cc.780r–782v (6-8-1610). There are no surviving registers of the *Cinque Savi* on this subject.

behaviour is provided by their absence from the archive of the *Inquisitori di Stato*, the Venetian magistracy in charge of controlling 'any instance of political communication outside the government'.[98] English political and religious refugees and many travellers became objects of their investigations, and, even if merchants are not directly present, something about them can be obliquely gleaned from those papers.

In the last weeks of 1618 – as we have seen, a rather difficult year for the Republic – the *Inquisitori* interrogated Diana Palermitana, widow of an Englishman called John Bartlett, who lived in San Giovanni in Bragora, an area of high density of foreigners, where she made her living selling tobacco.[99] The scope of the *Inquisitori* enquiry was to clarify the background of events in the previous months, at the height of the conflict with the Habsburgs and at the time of the Bedmar conspiracy. Her testimony shed some light on how things really were in the *albergarie* business. She defined her late husband as a heretic and a 'bad person', who used to lodge up to twenty Englishmen at the same time, all without permission. She claimed that she was not doing it any more, as it was a very expensive business and lodgers always created trouble in the house. Furthermore, she said that many Englishmen lodged with John Holland in a large house which Gio Batta Bragadin rented to him at a high price. Holland had already been to prison twice for improperly lodging guests, but he was clearly undeterred. He had completely transformed the interior of the house: walls had been demolished in order to make larger rooms, and several secret doors had been inserted so that people could run away unnoticed. Palermitana also advised the *Inquisitori* to keep an eye on Henry Parvis, because many Englishmen were always around his place, and he too might be illegally lodging some of them.[100] It is difficult to evaluate her credibility and the reasons for her statement. No other evidence has surfaced about her. Venice during 1618 was particularly fraught, with many foreign soldiers looking for employment,[101] and therefore the situation she described – even if not an exaggeration – was probably not representative of the 'normal' state of affairs.

---

[98] De Vivo, *Information and Communication*, 34.

[99] Tobacco does not appear at this time in the import cargoes, but was widely used by English sailors, see ASV, *Collegio, Rdd*, f. 47, cc.n.n. (15-1-1656mv); f. 54, cc.n.n. (16-12-1659).

[100] ASV, *Inquisitori di Stato*, b. 1046, fasc. 49. This episode also in *CSPVe*, vol. xv (1617–1619), n. 677 (31-12-1618): see www.british-history.ac.uk/report.aspx?compid=88693 (date accessed: 21 February 2014); and n. 750 (19-2-1619): see www.british-history.ac.uk/report.aspx?compid=88698 (date accessed: 21 February 2014).

[101] Amongst them Henry de Vere, eighteenth earl of Oxford (1593–1625), who, with the king's approval, offered to raise 6,000 men for the Republic's service – an offer the *Senato* declined, see *DNB*, s.v.

There is more evidence on the presence of English seamen in *albergarie*, and it is not surprising that officers and sailors made use of them. In 1626 foreign ship-captains were forbidden from being hosted in private residences during their stay in Venice, and they were forced to stay in inns and register their presence with the relevant authorities. If there were no rooms available, they could remain in the private residence of the consul of their nation, but this had to be a temporary measure.[102] But ship-captains' intrinsic transience made them almost impossible to track, whilst the nature of their profession frequently gave their wives a high profile and got them involved in *albergarie* themselves. Nicholas Colvell was captain of the *Orsola Bonaventura*, and by 1653 he had already served for seven years in the Venetian *Armata*.[103] His wife Caterina, most likely an Englishwoman, was having serious problems making ends meet, so she presented a petition to the *Collegio* asking to 'be granted licence to freely host in her home people of her own English nation'. In her petition she recounted how even her previous husband, 'Tomaso de Marchi Inglese', had served the Republic, and how all these factors should be considered in her favour.[104] The following year Colvell died in one of the battles of the Dardanelles.[105] Caterina wrote once again to the *Collegio*, this time asking for financial help, because:

[Colvell] left behind him myself, Catarina, his bereft wife and our son Guglielmo in a most dire state, as with the death of my husband we have lost all our sustenance, which was on that vessel, and [I] have also lost my son from my first husband, who served as coxswain on that same ship and was burned with her.[106]

Her petition was successful and she was granted a subsidy of 10 ducats per year for ten years. In 1670, when her only surviving son came back from having served seven years in the navy as a simple sailor, he found her destitute once again and was forced to petition for a renewal of the subsidy.[107] We have no proof whether Caterina's request to lodge Englishmen was approved in 1653. But we can reasonably suppose it was, because otherwise she would surely have presented another petition, or would have mentioned the previous negative answer when she pleaded for financial help after her husband's death, particularly considering the

---

[102] Trampus, 'La formazione del diritto consolare', 310.
[103] ASV, *Collegio, Rdd*, f. 43, cc.n.n. (20-12-1652); and f. 44, cc.n.n. (not dated [1653]).
[104] ASV, *Collegio, Rdd*, f. 44, cc.n.n. (27-6-1653).
[105] ASV, *Collegio, Rdd*, f. 45, cc.n.n. (not dated [November 1654?]) and cc.n.n. (8-7-1654). On 16 and 17 May 1654, a great battle was fought in the Dardanelles area between the Venetian and the Ottoman fleet; the result of this one was slightly in favour of the Venetians: see G. Benzoni, 'Morire per Creta', in Ortalli ed., *Venezia e Creta*, 151–173.
[106] ASV, *Collegio, Rdd*, f. 45, cc.n.n. (28-9-1654).
[107] ASV, *Collegio, Rdd*, f. 74, cc.n.n. (10-5-1670).

loss of her husband's estate in the burning of his ship whilst fighting for the Republic.

Even taking into account the traditional rhetoric on 'need' which characterised petitions, where the insistence on the petitioners' poverty and need should not be taken at face value, we can infer from Palermitana's interrogation that renting a room did not necessarily guarantee a living income. Keeping an *albergaria* was probably profitable only for an active merchant, not so much from the rent itself but more because of the collateral income that could be generated by doing business with (or through) the lodger. Money earned by acting as a translator or as a middleman with local traders was probably the real perk of having lodgers.[108] This may explain why John Hobson, Jr (nephew of John Hobson, Sr, at that time consul of the *Natione Inglese*) wrote a petition himself to the *Collegio* asking for a licence to lodge Englishmen in his home. He argued that after fourteen years in town, 'having in this time established many business links with England and with my co-nationals in other parts of the world', being granted such a licence would allow him to 'accommodate in my house some people of my own Nation, who come to Venice and are recommended to me personally, and take care both of their lodging and all their other needs'. He particularly stressed the fact that most of them did not speak the language and needed his help for this very reason.[109] The last comment is worthy of some consideration, as knowledge of Italian was commonplace amongst merchants earlier in the century, and this remained the case until the eighteenth century.[110] Evidence from other sources in Venice, such as trial testimony, shows little evidence of the need for translators, and in the vast majority of dealings everything was perfectly handled in Italian.[111] Even from a cursory glance of the extant documentation it is clear that in Genoa the situation was different, and that recourse to interpreters – frequently, but not always, the consuls – was relatively frequent, especially amongst the Flemish, less so amongst the English.[112] This can be explained by the differences in trade and cargoes. In Genoa (as in Livorno) foreign ships were heavily involved in the grain trade, from the North of Europe, of course, but also from other Mediterranean places – mostly Sicily and

---

[108] For such a case see the activities of the Greek Francesco di Demetri Litino, in Burke, 'Francesco di Demetri'.

[109] ASV, *Collegio, Rdd*, f. 51, cc.n.n. (29-1-1658mv).

[110] On English merchants and foreign languages see Ramsay, *The City of London*, 217; Grassby, *The Business Community*, 181; Games, *Web of Empire*, 113, 136–137.

[111] See ASV, *GdF, Sentenze, passim*.

[112] ASG, *Conservatori del Mare, Atti civili, passim*.

Puglia. Genoa, thanks to its relative proximity to the North of Europe, and the strength of its grain *portofranco*, was more open to occasional trade, and thus crews arriving there were not necessarily Mediterranean specialists. Venice was different: it was more distant, and there were no special customs facilitations to attract casual trade, so it was frequented mostly by Mediterranean specialists – and that is even before one takes into account the English Levant Company monopoly of its trade. All these factors, from the linguistic point of view, resulted in a far stronger knowledge of Italian amongst seamen on the Eastern Mediterranean routes. Hobson's remark therefore was probably a rhetorical one to give strength to his request, rather than an assessment of the situation on the ground.

Renting

If ship-captains rented rooms, resident merchants tended to rent houses. In Venice foreigners were forbidden to own real estate, but there was a common practice to live in rented accommodation at all levels of Venetian society, even amongst the aristocracy.[113]

For a foreigner the choice of where to live was the result of various considerations; most important amongst these were the distribution of foreigners in town and the legal restrictions. Foreign communities tended to settle in specific areas, and, once there, newcomers would congregate around them.[114] The Greeks tended to settle in Castello, particularly in the relatively small area between San Giorgio dei Greci and San Giovanni in Bragora.[115] The Germans were concentrated around the *Fondaco* in the fifteenth century, but later spread around Venice, favouring the area at the edge of Cannaregio and Castello.[116] As a general rule it can be said that Cannaregio was a transit area, mostly for newcomers, and Castello was an area of settlement for immigrants.[117]

---

[113] L. Megna, 'Comportamenti abitativi del patriziato veneziano (1582–1740)', *Studi Veneziani*, 22 (1991): 253–323, 272.

[114] J. F. Chauvard, 'Scale di osservazione e inserimento degli stranieri nello spazio veneziano tra XVII e XVIII secolo', in Calabi and Lanaro eds., *La città italiana*, 85–105, 85; D. Calabi, 'Gli stranieri e la città', in A. Tenenti and U. Tucci eds., *Storia di Venezia*, vol. v: *Il Rinascimento: società ed economia*, Rome, 1996, 913–946, 914–915.

[115] F. Thiriet, 'Sur les communautés grecque et albanaise à Venise', in Beck, Manoussacas and Pertusi eds., *Venezia centro di mediazione*, i: 217–231, 219; B. Imhaus, *Le minoranze orientali a Venezia, 1300–1510*, Rome, 1997, 219.

[116] P. Braunstein, 'Remarques sur la population allemande de Venise à la fin du Moyen Age', in Beck, Manoussacas and Pertusi eds., *Venezia centro di mediazione*, i: 233–243, 238; Hollberg, *Deutsche in Venedig*.

[117] Calabi and Lanaro, 'Introduzione'; P. Braunstein, 'Cannaregio, zona di transito?', in Calabi and Lanaro eds., *La città italiana*, 52–62. Calabi, 'Gli stranieri e la città', 919.

The majority of English merchants lived in rented properties in the area of Castello (Map 2), but rather than renting directly from the owners, most seem to have sublet from another tenant. Since the 1460s Venice had produced *estimi*, fiscal surveys listing the tax liability of individuals on the basis of their landed income. Cross-referencing these with the records of the *decima*, a self-declaration of real-estate ownership, it is possible to get a pretty accurate idea of the real-estate situation in Venice.[118] In the *redecima* of 1582 no English were officially registered as living in town.[119] At the time of the *catastico* of 1661 only six Englishmen appear.[120] As only the principal tenant appears in these records, we have to assume that all the others were subletting properties. Given the scarcity of information on rent paid by English merchants in Venice, only the most general conclusions can be drawn. We have rental figures for only ten merchants, and these oscillate widely between 33 and 200 ducats per year. On average, during the period examined 70 per cent of the rents in town were below the sum of 30 ducats,[121] so all the figures we have for the English were above average. Randolph Simes and Giles Jones stand out, paying rents of 200 ducats. Simes rented his house in San Lio from the Gussoni family, whilst Jones rented a house from Giovanni Sagredo in Santa Maria Formosa.[122] Judging from their high rents, these must have been very large and prestigious residences; interestingly, in Simes' contract it was stated that he was allowed to sublet the property during his lease.[123] Amongst the other English merchants for whom we have data, four paid rent varying between 100 and 200 ducats;[124] to put these figures in perspective, only 20 per cent of Venetian aristocrats rented houses in this price bracket.[125] The last four

[118] Issues analysed in J.-F. Chauvard, *La circulation des biens à Venise: stratégies patrimoniales et marché immobilier (1600–1750)*, Rome, 2005.

[119] I owe this information to Jean-François Chauvard and I thank him for his generosity in sharing his data.

[120] They were as follows. In San Marco: Giovanni Pricco, who rented a house for 46 ducats in the *sestiere* (ASV, *Savi alle Decime, Catastico di San Marco*, b. 419, house n.724). In Castello: Zuanne Rafael paid 48 ducats, Giorgio Nailes [Hailes?] paid 180 ducats and Raffael Inglese paid 38 ducats (ASV, *Savi alle Decime, Catastico di Castello*, b. 420, houses n.109, n.223, n.673.) In Cannaregio: John Hobson paid 145 ducats and Francesco Salvini – 'e compagni, mercanti inglesi' – paid 190 ducats (ASV, *Savi alle Decime, Catastico di Cannaregio*, b. 421, houses n.109 and n.20). There were no Englishmen in Santa Croce.

[121] I wish to thank Jean-François Chauvard for providing me with this information.

[122] ASV, *Dieci Savi alle Decime*, reg. 420, *Castello, Santa Maria Formosa*, n.480.

[123] ASV, *Notarile Atti*, reg. 3399 (Gio Andrea Catti), cc.10r/v (16-1-1620).

[124] They were: Francesco Salvini, who paid 190 ducats; Giorgio Nailes, who paid 180 ducats; John Hobson, who paid 145 ducats; Matthew Hicman, who paid 110 ducats. See also ASV, *Notarile Atti*, reg. 4882 (Nicolò Doglioni), cc.26r–27r (26-1-1601).

[125] Forty per cent of aristocratic rents fell between 50 and 100 ducats: see Megna, 'Comportamenti abitativi', 279–280.

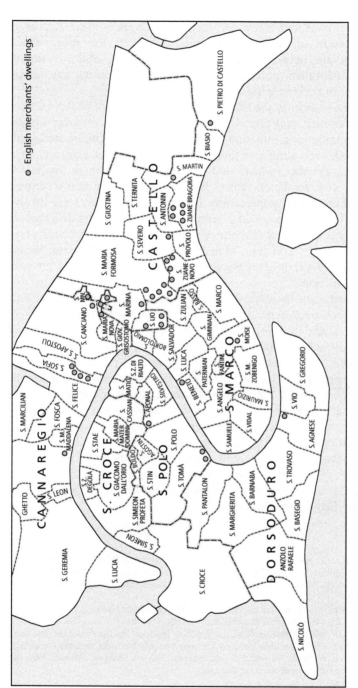

○ English merchants' dwellings

Map 2. English merchants' dwellings in Venice

Englishmen paid rent below 50 ducats.[126] Overall, these figures give an impression of relative affluence. However, the more affluent merchants are over-represented in this sample, and for the vast majority of English merchants based in Venice nothing has emerged in relation to their lodgings.

Given the scarcity of the English presence in all the official documentation on Venetian real estate, it is not surprising to discover a similar situation concerning litigation on the same issue. Englishmen, unlike the Flemish, are almost entirely absent from rental litigation in the *Giudici del Forestier*, which had jurisdiction over these matters for Venetians and foreigners alike. For the entirety of the seventeenth century, there are only three cases in which Englishmen were involved: Giacomo Corner summoned Joseph Kent for 500 ducats that Kent had guaranteed for one year of advance rent for the English resident's house in San Cassan,[127] and John Hobson Sr sued Baldin Franzon for back payments on the rent of his house in Padua that Hobson had previously bought at auction.[128]

The third case involves the heirs of Thomaso Rowlandson and a dispute over back rent due for a vineyard in Malamocco.[129] The material is scant and the controversy is complex; it is worth mentioning it here, though, as the property whose rent is questioned is in Malamocco, which as we have seen was the place where English ships stopped in Venice. It is unlikely that Rowlandson got involved in this vineyard as an investment, as properties in Malamocco were all rather small. On the other hand, vineyards were coveted by local inhabitants as even the small quantities of wine they produced were sellable (illegally) to English ships, and there is ample evidence of contact between English crews and owners of such properties.[130] According to the suit, the property was given to Rowlandson in payment for a debt, which hints at possible credit links between the locals and English crews.

---

[126] They were: Zuanne Rafael, who paid 48 ducats; Giovanni Pricco, who paid 46 ducats; Raffael Inglese, who paid 38 ducats; Roberto Assal, who paid 33 ducats (100 for three years) (ASV, *Notarile Atti*, reg. 6550 (Luca and Giulio Gabrieli), cc.229v–230r (19-7-1603)).

[127] ASV, *GdF*, 494 (*Domande in causa*, f. 7), c.431 (19-2-1651mv).

[128] ASV, *GdF*, 489 (*Domande in causa*, f. 2), c.168 (4-9-1637).

[129] ASV, *GdF*, 478 (*Multorum*, f. 3), c.136 (26-1-1650mv). In the document the name is spelled as Thomaso Rolenzon, which was one of the most common spellings of 'Rowlandson' in the Venetian documentation, but his identity, although very likely, cannot be fully corroborated in this case.

[130] ASV, *Podestà di Malamocco, passim*.

The Hickman–Locke affair

Family partnership, factors' relationship with the Levant Company and the cost of living in Venice all emerge vividly from the analysis of the sorry – long and unpleasant – tale of the litigation between Michael Locke and his nephew Matthew Hickman in 1600.

Locke was an Elizabethan adventurer of good Protestant stock, brother of Rose Throckmorton and therefore uncle of those two Hickman brothers we have already encountered: the 'Nicodemite' Eleazar and Matthew. All the protagonists were part of that first generation of English merchants based in Venice who had a relatively high social profile in England. Locke had been involved in several trading and exploration ventures since the 1550s, and had 'collected a significant library of travel literature, charts, and other cosmographical data, to a value of some £500, which he later put at the disposal of Richard Hakluyt the younger during the preparation of his *Divers Voyages* (1582)'. In 1574 he helped Martin Frobisher set up an expedition to discover a sea route to Cathay via the northwest. This was his financial undoing, as he lost his own large investment and Frobisher denounced him for financial improprieties (probably wrongly). Once out of prison, in 1591 he managed to become the Levant Company consul in Aleppo, where he hoped to recover his fortune. Instead he apparently argued with the Company's merchants and, 'on the initiative of the company's governor, Sir John Spencer (a distant relative)', was dismissed without compensation. James McDermott says Locke 'fled to Venice and initiated a suit in the courts there for compensation',[131] but the suit in Venice appears to be only marginally connected with what had happened in Ottoman lands.

His nephew Eleazar Hickman appears active in Venice from at least 1593, when he was convicted by the *Avogaria* for the illegal partnership he had set up with Giovanni Peverello to trade with Alexandria under the Venetian's name in order to enjoy the customs and tariff privileges reserved there for Venetian merchants.[132] In 1595 Locke arrived in Venice from Aleppo, and from the end of that June to the end of September 1597 he lodged (with a servant) in Eleazar's house, helping him to run his affairs. In November 1597 Eleazar returned to London and left his brother Matthew to take care of his business in Venice in

---

[131] He also argued that this 'effectively paralysed the company's trade in the Levant' in *DNB*, s.v. Michael Locke. I have not found evidence to support this claim.

[132] As discussed in Chapters 6 (155) and 7 (197).

conjunction with Locke and Locke's son Benjamin, who appears in the documentation as Matthew's 'servant'.[133]

By the autumn of 1599 the relationship between Locke and Matthew was irretrievably broken, and Benjamin was trying to mediate, writing from Zante to Eleazar in London asking him to stop his brother Matthew from mistreating Locke in Venice.[134] Michael Locke's situation was rather difficult (and confused) as he was playing on many tables to recoup his old losses: trading in Venice both independently and as an associate of the Hickmans, whilst at the same time fighting in London Spencer's decision to dismiss him without pay from the consulate at Aleppo. Realising he needed to be in London to attend in person to the suit with the Company, he tried to compromise with his nephew and get an additional loan which would have allowed him to travel back home. Matthew had apparently agreed to this, but reneged at the last minute and instead had his uncle's goods impounded by the *Giudici dell'Esaminador*, which effectively trapped Michael in Venice.[135] But there was a lot more to it.

In November 1599 the *Giudici del Forestier* issued a judgment in favour of Matthew regarding another loan he had made to Michael Locke.[136] Michael was undeterred, and declared that the judgment had not taken into account the full complexity of the business transactions between him and his nephews, first Eleazar and later Matthew. An arbitration process was therefore started, and three judges were appointed: two English merchants, Jeffrey Luther and James Higgons, and the Venetian Battista Albinoni.[137] A few days afterwards, Michael deposited with the Venetian notary Antonio Callegarini a lengthy and extremely detailed memorandum, with additional copies of letters and accounts to be used as evidence for the arbitration procedure.[138] Intriguingly, no documents appear to have been produced by Matthew, which would allow us to have both sides of the story. Matthew must have given the relevant paperwork directly to the arbiters, without depositing it first with the notary, as his uncle did. Within the prescribed time of a month the three arbiters gave their

---

[133] ASV, *Notarile Atti*, reg. 3148 (Antonio Callegarini), cc.380v–404r (14-7-1600), 386v. I thank Vittorio Mandelli for bringing this act to my attention.

[134] ASV, *Notarile Atti*, reg. 3148 (Antonio Callegarini), 393v–395r.

[135] The *Esaminador* dealt with the admission of witnesses in civil trials, the publicity of real estate contracts, and the seizures of goods, properties and revenues of debtors, but also started the procedure for the recognition of 'testamenti per breviario' – that is to say, to legally recognise wills that had been expressed orally on the deathbed: see Tiepolo *et al.* eds., *Archivio di Stato di Venezia*, 989.

[136] ASV, *GdF*, 227 (*Sentenze*, reg. 23), cc.3r–5v (13-11-1599).

[137] ASV, *Notarile Atti*, reg. 3147 (Antonio Callegarini), cc.221–222r (20-6-1600); six days later Higgons was substituted by Eduardo Colinx.

[138] ASV, *Notarile Atti*, reg. 3148 (Antonio Callegarini), cc.380v–404r (14-7-1600).

judgment, and their solution shows that overall they supported Michael's interpretation of events. There was no doubting he owed Matthew money, but far less than Matthew claimed; there were some basic mistakes in the accounts, and Matthew appeared to have accounted for certain sums twice without including the reimbursements which in the meantime he had received from Michael.[139] The arbiters were all high-profile merchants and had no obvious reason to favour Michael over Matthew; if anything, the reverse could be true, as Michael was an old man with a chequered past and a somewhat tainted reputation in England, whilst Matthew and especially Eleazar (who clearly had the more senior role in the partnership) were young and successful merchants.

At the end of August Matthew was still holding nine boxes of Michael's, and the latter asked the notary to issue an injunction to release the property and get it independently assessed. Matthew was on his way to England by then, and Michael, who wanted also to leave as soon as possible, was worried that in Matthew's absence he would be unable to recover his goods. Matthew replied immediately that he was holding the boxes as security for the 100 ducats which the arbiters had decreed he should lend to Michael to allow him to travel to London.[140] Michael here was right, as the arbiters had decreed that Matthew needed to honour his promise of a loan, but, at the same time, the value of Michael's goods should have been decided by independent evaluators, and this had not been done. Michael then voluntarily renounced the loan in exchange for his boxes.[141] As is frequently the case, we do not know the end of the story. What we know is that Michael Locke made it back to London at some point in late 1600, where, at the Privy Council's urging, he accepted a compromise settlement from the Levant Company of £300 in 1601.[142]

This dispute illustrates many of the peculiarities of English commercial and social activities in Venice. The overlap of family and business appears to be typical of the Levant Company milieu. Many factors active in Venice combined the duties of agents for their principals with their own independent trading activities, a situation which was less frequent in other areas of trade.[143] Benjamin Locke was exactly in this position. By the time

---

[139] ASV, *Notarile Atti*, reg. 3148 (Antonio Callegarini), cc.357r–359v (20-7-1600).

[140] ASV, *Notarile Atti*, reg. 3148 (Antonio Callegarini), cc.434v–436v (30-8-1600).

[141] ASV, *Notarile Atti*, reg. 3148 (Antonio Callegarini), cc.486r–487v (28-9-1600).

[142] *DNB*, s.v.

[143] Chaudhuri (*The English East India Company*, 75–76) argues that this flexibility in the relationship between 'the factor and the merchant operating in Europe' made the task of exercising control over factors a lot easier. He juxtaposed this with the East India Company's attitude in Asia, which considered factors as 'salaried agents' who should owe their loyalty exclusively to the Company. T. S. Willan (*Studies in Elizabethan Foreign Trade*, Manchester, 1959, 1–33, 11) argued instead that Levant Company's

of the dispute he was thirty years old, and had agreed to work for Eleazar in Venice in exchange for his expenses – including food – and with the agreement that he also would invest with him once his father had recovered the money he was owed from the Levant Company, thus providing Benjamin with capital to invest personally. In his memorandum Michael Locke clearly states that his son Benjamin 'was free to serve whom he liked, being a man of thirty years of age, and with good experience of both Western and Eastern trades'.[144] Given this statement and his age, it seems unlikely that he was formally apprenticed to the Hickmans; most probably he was just a junior partner.

Kinship was the basis of this partnership. Sons and nephews served as factors for their fathers and uncles all over the world, often linking different areas of trade.[145] Benjamin had started working for Eleazar following the flight from Venice of Robert Assal, who had worked as Eleazar's 'cashier' and left Venice without settling his accounts. Michael elaborated at length on how Eleazar had recovered large sums of money and resolved many problems in his business both locally and in London thanks to the help provided by him and Benjamin. When Eleazar left for London, he asked Benjamin to work for his brother, apparently also asking him to train Matthew 'until [he] reaches a good level of understanding of the practice of trade, and of [Eleazar's] business'.[146] Benjamin agreed, and for a few months he had been showing the ropes to Matthew, before departing for the Ionian islands in September 1598 to accompany Henry Garway.[147] The arbitrators were clearly convinced of the positive contribution of Locke father and son to the Hickmans' business, and for this reason they discounted a lot of Michael's expenses. They also argued that it had been rather improper for Matthew to involve Benjamin's accounts in his litigation with Michael, and that sorting out the financial dealings between the Hickmans and Benjamin should be done separately from sorting out Michael's.

Michael might have been embroiled in litigation with the Levant Company about his salary as consul in Aleppo, but he appears to have

factors were not allowed to trade for themselves. Factors active in the Baltic were frequently agents for more than one merchant: see Åstrom, *From Cloth to Iron*, 122–124.

[144] ASV, *Notarile Atti*, reg. 3148 (Antonio Callegarini), c.383v.
[145] Grassby, *The Business Community*, 90, 82–83. See also S. Anderson, *An English Consul in Turkey: Paul Rycaut at Smyrna, 1667–1678*, Oxford, 1989, 99; BL *Stowe* MS 219, c.220. In the Levant Company, the active traders of the 1630s were grandsons of the founders: Brenner, *Merchants and Revolution*, 72.
[146] ASV, *Notarile Atti*, reg. 3148 (Antonio Callegarini), c.394v.
[147] ASV, *Notarile Atti*, reg. 3148 (Antonio Callegarini), c.394r.

been very loyal towards the Company. One of the major reasons for contention between him and Matthew was the cost of food which Matthew (in lieu of Eleazar, who had left Venice) was supposed to have paid for Michael and Benjamin, and was now instead billing them for. From the rather confused documentation, it appears that the Levant Company was prepared to pay 15 ducats a month to feed 'its servants', and Michael hints that Matthew was trying to defraud the Company by claiming more.[148] The cost of food and the expenses of entertaining were also part of the dispute; Michael on the one hand argued forcefully that these expenses were to be paid by the Hickmans in exchange for the services he provided them. On the other hand, he was at pains to underline how, due to his advanced age (he was nearly seventy), he ate very frugally and simply and did not partake in the constant feasting at the Hickmans' house in Venice. He states that only during the three months of Garway's visit in Venice (June–August 1598) had he joined Matthew at his dining table, and then only because Garway was keen to hear his opinions on trade in the Levant. Michael provides a long list of people who daily ate and drank freely at Matthew's house 'in the way and custom of England'.[149] Other English merchants based in Venice or passing by – such as Richard Eldred, Thomas Mun and Alessandro Fryche – and also captains and seamen of English ships and other business associates were regularly entertained. Some of these were also hosted in the Hickmans' house for months at a time, and there is reason to believe this was in violation of the law.[150]

Michael was scathing about Matthew's competence to properly follow and administer his brother's business, and the mistakes spotted by the arbiters in his accounts appear to support these accusations. Michael claims to have tried to be his mentor, and further

> to have been the sole reason of your departure from Bristol (where you dealt with fishermen), and come to Venice, where you're now dealing with merchants.[151]

And he ends his memorandum attributing to his incompetence the troubles which Eleazar was having with his company's associates in the Levant and in London, and which Michael had helped him to resolve. Now Matthew's reputation was tainted, and as much as he liked to

[148] ASV, *Notarile Atti*, reg. 3148 (Antonio Callegarini), c. 384v.
[149] On English merchants' hospitality see F. Heal, *Hospitality in Early Modern England*, Oxford, 1990, 192–222, 301.
[150] ASV, *Notarile Atti*, reg. 3148 (Antonio Callegarini), c.393r.
[151] ASV, *Notarile Atti*, reg. 3148 (Antonio Callegarini), cc.389r/v.

entertain in style, 'he should go back to Bristol to fetch pilchards as he did before'.[152]

The Hickman–Locke controversy provides us with a good sample of the kind of troubles affecting early modern trading. Even taking into account all the limits traditionally associated with litigation, the wealth of information opens a window onto the social and commercial practices of the English mercantile community in Venice which would have otherwise remained shut due to the absence of commercial correspondence.

The members of this particular family had a long history of strong religious belief and business success to bind them, but this did not protect them from serious internal disagreements and litigation. The English mercantile community in Venice certainly enjoyed a high level of internal cohesion and trust, but this – again – was not enough to avoid such episodes. 'Trust' is a most slippery analytical category, frequently used in tautological terms, and even trickier to use when family and business links are intertwined.[153] All those examples of cooperation mentioned at the beginning of this chapter – power of attorney, acting as guarantors or witnesses – had been commonplace for centuries, and crucially involved a legal contract rather than a relationship of pure trust. Legally binding agreements were paramount even within a family environment and a tight mercantile community. Michael's Venetian experience might have been made possible by his nephew Eleazar in the way a young and successful family member decides to help an elderly relative down on his luck. The relationship between them, and with Matthew at a later stage, might have been originally based on family links – and therefore trust.[154] However, ultimately all their important dealings were also supported by an abundance of written evidence which the parties could deposit – and have notarised – and use as evidence in court when need arose. When troubles emerged, all parties were happy to subject themselves to their peers' judgement through arbitration. Kin and social ties were clearly crucial elements within this community, but this should not lead to an underestimation of the importance of the institutional and legal infrastructure which the Venetian system provided to solve intra-community controversies such as this one.

For a long time a natural tendency to cooperate was assumed within members of homogeneous ethnic and religious groups. I have argued

---

[152] ASV, *Notarile Atti*, reg. 3148 (Antonio Callegarini), cc.389v–390r.
[153] D. Gambetta ed., *Trust: Making and Breaking Cooperative Relations*, Oxford, 1988.
[154] Y. Ben-Porath, 'The F-Connection: Families, Friends, and Firms and the Organization of Exchange', *Population and Development Review*, 6 (1980): 1–30.

elsewhere how I support Francesca Trivellato's view that equating kinship and ethno-business ties with trust in business creates a fallacious
boundary between a pre-modern world of trust and a modern world of
impersonal institutions.[155] Throughout the period under investigation,
the ability of English merchants to make use of Venetian institutions, its
legal framework and commercial infrastructure provided them with some
of the necessary tools to succeed, and therefore to undermine the very
same Venetian system from within. In the short term, this provided
welcome savings in transaction costs; in the long term, it was a blueprint
for handling the challenges of long-distance trade and for administering
their own colonial possessions.[156]

---

[155] Fusaro, 'Cooperating Mercantile Networks', and bibliography quoted therein.
[156] Fusaro, 'Representation in Practice'.

9   The English and other mercantile communities

Quite a lot of attention has been given to intercultural trade in the early modern period, especially since the seminal work of Philip Curtin opened new avenues of investigation and interpretation.[1] Since then, analysis has concentrated on encounters which were both geographically and culturally 'long distance', bridging backgrounds which were radically different from previous European experiences.[2]

Intra-European commercial contacts were usually less culturally traumatic for both parties, being that within Europe all parties were, in some way, offspring of Roman law and of European commercial usage – even given all the local variances, which in some cases have been underestimated.[3] Their common legal background allowed merchants to build relations through notarised contracts, creating evidence they could present to courts either in Mediterranean countries or at home. However, a relevant percentage of these contracts – especially partnerships – were in flagrant breach of local legislation and would not have been admissible in court. Still, their very existence shows that trust might have existed; however, producing written evidence was an excellent insurance for all parties.

English penetration of Venetian commercial space benefitted tremendously from the close networks of economic cooperation which English merchants had built – in Venice and in the Levant – with two other mercantile communities: the Greeks and the Flemish, as this allowed them to quickly penetrate the Venetian commercial system and take advantage of its weaknesses. For different reasons, which will be analysed in the following pages, the English shared substantive interests with both groups: something that fostered their mutual collaboration. Especially in the case of the Greeks, these links developed into an interdependent relationship which was mutually beneficial for both parties

[1] Curtin, *Cross-Cultural Trade*.
[2] An excellent example of these analyses is Trivellato, *The Familiarity of Strangers*.
[3] On these issues see Fusaro, 'The Invasion of Northern Litigants', and bibliography quoted therein.

involved. In the case of the Greeks, Venice provided a useful common 'enemy', as its customs and duties seriously impinged on profits. In the case of the Flemish, common concerns in facing Venetian bureaucracy and local lobbying provided the necessary incentive to cooperate. This chapter will focus on these relationships in Venice; later the focus will shift to developments in the Venetian Levant.

Greeks in Venice: 'loyal subjects'

The foundation of the relationship between the English and the Greeks was currants. And the roots of the Anglo-Greek alliance are to be found in the web of contacts established with English merchants by Greek traders who sent their ships to England in the last quarter of the sixteenth century, analysed in Chapter 3. These early contacts were reinforced when the English started to penetrate the Mediterranean themselves.[4] Therefore, especially in the earlier phase of their direct presence in Venice, English merchants favoured commercial partners who were Greeks and Venetian *cittadini,* and a handful of other Italian and Ragusean merchants complete the picture. Extremely few patricians were involved in this trade, the biggest exception being the Corner family, which was extremely active due to their large Cretan possessions.[5] Later on there will be occasion to discuss the implications that this had within the Ionian islands and in the Eastern Mediterranean at large; here we will try to exemplify Anglo-Greek interactions in Venice itself.

The Greek community in Venice was unique in many ways. The majority of its members came from Venetian possessions in the Levant, and this put them in the category of subjects, rather than foreigners.[6] The common heritage of Byzantium allowed them to claim a shared past with the Venetians, thereby facilitating both their settlement in town and their integration within the Venetian economic and cultural world,[7] although the level of their 'assimilation' in Venice is still a somewhat contentious issue.[8] Jonathan Harris has argued that for Greek intellectuals the move

---

[4] All these issues are analysed at length in Fusaro, 'Coping with Transition' and 'Les Anglais et les Grecs'.

[5] ASV, *Notarile Atti,* reg. 7850–7868 (Gerolamo Luran), *passim.*

[6] G. Plumidis, 'Considerazioni sulla popolazione greca a Venezia nella seconda metà del '500', *Studi Veneziani,* 14 (1972): 219–226, 223.

[7] G. Fedalto, 'Le minoranze straniere a Venezia tra politica e legislazione', in Beck, Manoussacas and Pertusi eds., *Venezia, centro di mediazione,* i: 143–162, 145.

[8] A recent assessment of these issues, especially in regard to the lower socio-economic groups, with a state-of-the-art bibliography, can be found in S. McKee, 'Sailing from Byzantium: Byzantines and Greeks in the Venetian World', in J. Herrin and G. Saint Guillain eds., *Identities and Allegiances in the Eastern Mediterranean after 1204,* Farnham, 2010, 291–300.

to Venice did not result in their rejection of Byzantine culture in exchange for assimilation,[9] but for the lower social strata of Greek emigrants the situation was different; the strongest link with Venice was most probably their sharing of the Ottoman threat, but the possibility of economic betterment which Venice afforded them was also important. Many had arrived in Venice fleeing the Turks, and the generosity with which the Republic had welcomed them in those difficult times resulted generally in a feeling of loyalty and gratitude. Greeks in Venice were permitted to freely practise their Orthodox faith, and from 1498 were also granted their own confraternity, thereby achieving an important mark of assimilation within Venetian society.[10]

Merchants constituted the backbone of the Greek presence in Venice, immediately followed by sailors and skilled artisans, several of whom worked in the *Arsenale*. Ersie Burke estimates merchants and shopkeepers as constituting 30 per cent of the community, 'maritime occupations' (in which she includes captains and crews) as 24 per cent, and artisans as 14 per cent.[11] Other well-represented occupations were oarsmen (*galeotti*) and soldiers (*stradioti*).[12] Most Greek merchants kept in contact with their birthplace and frequently acted as middlemen for trade in the Eastern Mediterranean. This two-pronged strategy contributed to a dual identity: on the one hand they were loyal subjects increasingly integrated into Venetian society; on the other they were intermediaries with the Eastern Mediterranean, nurturing the social and commercial networks connected to their places of origin.

Additional indirect evidence of the integration of Greeks in Venice can be found in their frequent petitions to the government. These were always presented by private individuals, following exactly the same pattern of those of *cittadini*, highlighting instances of loyal service the

---

[9] J. Harris, 'Common Language and the Common Good: Aspects of Identity among the Byzantine Emigres in Renaissance Italy', in McKee ed., *Crossing Boundaries*, 189–202.

[10] On these issues of assimilation and identity, see: Thiriet, 'Sur les communautés grecque', 217; J. G. Ball, 'Poverty, Charity and the Greek Community', *Studi Veneziani*, 6 (1982): 129–145; and also his *The Greek Community in Venice 1470–1620*, Ph.D. thesis, University of London, 1985, 36.

[11] I wish to thank her for providing me these details, further developed in E. Burke, *The Greek Neighbourhoods of Sixteenth Century Venice 1498–1600: Daily Life of an Immigrant Community*, Ph.D. thesis, University of Monash, 2004. On the Greeks working in the *Arsenale* see R. C. Davis, *Shipbuilders of the Venetian Arsenal: Workers and Workplace in the Preindustrial City*, Baltimore and London, 1991; I. Iordanou, *Maritime Communities in Late Renaissance Venice: The Arsenalotti and the Greeks*, Ph.D. thesis, University of Warwick, 2008.

[12] Thiriet, 'Sur les communautés grecque', 220; Plumidis, 'Considerazioni sulla popolazione greca', 224; D. J. Geanakoplos, *Interaction of the 'Sibling' Byzantine and Western Cultures in the Middle Ages and Italian Renaissance, 330–1600*, New Haven and London, 1976, 176–186.

individual – and his family – had performed for the Republic as a necessary rhetorical preamble for the request.[13] In contrast, petitions from Greek residents in the *Stato da Mar* were frequently expressions of a collective instance; the same rhetoric of loyal service is employed, but their status as colonial subjects who were part of a separate community is very evident, and frequently directly claimed in the petitions themselves.[14] The frequency with which Venice answered favourably to petitions and demands by Greeks clearly represents open recognition of the role they played within the Venetian state and public acknowledgement of the Republic's protective role towards them.[15] Exceptions to this rule are those petitions which went against the Republic's political economy strategy, such as those requesting the abolition of the *Nuova Imposta*, which have been sketched in Chapter 2.

From the early sixteenth century, Greeks' participation in the Venetian commercial system grew rapidly, as they took advantage of its growing weakness vis-à-vis the Ottomans to increase their role in the region and beyond. Their commercial networks benefitted from their institutional connection with Venice, and this helped them to trade with the major Western European states, where their status as Venetian subjects provided them with a considerable amount of protection. At the same time, Venetian Greeks were able to make use of their kinship with Ottoman Greeks to extend their commercial activities throughout the Eastern Mediterranean and the Balkans. For their most prominent merchants and shipowners, there were certainly good rewards to be reaped by being part of the Venetian commercial system. However, if Greek entrepreneurs' sense of belonging to the Republic was sincere, and effectively reflected loyalty towards Venice, at the same time they were drawn towards the English, with whom they shared interests in the same commodities and in the same areas of trade in the Eastern Mediterranean. In addition, both groups specialised in trading bulk commodities and non-luxury items, and were frequently and consistently involved in transporting goods for third parties on their own ships.

I have shown elsewhere that Greek and English merchants in Venice appear to have kept a low profile in the speculative game of financial exchange, whilst, at the same time, both groups frequently used bills of

---

[13] On Venetian petitioning practices see Davis, *Shipbuilders*, 183–197; on *arsenalotti*'s collective petitions, 186.

[14] ASV, *Collegio, Rdd* and *Rdf, passim.*

[15] The increased integration of the Greeks into Venetian society is extensively argued in E. Burke, '"Your Humble and Devoted Servants": Greco-Venetian Views of the *Serenissima*', available at: www.academia.edu/4022010/_Your_Humble_and_Devoted_Servants_Greco-Venetian_Views_of_the_Serenissima (date accessed: 7 January 2014).

exchange as a convenient mechanism for transferring money between Venice and the Levant. Through these operations the Republic showed its continued ability to harness mercantile capital – both Venetian and foreign – to support its own state infrastructure in the years running up to the War of Candia, and the documentary evidence shows how different networks cooperated amongst themselves and with the authorities, each in pursuit of its own economic interests.[16] These kinds of operations benefitted the Venetian state and, as such, were welcomed. However, documents in Venice, as in the Ionian islands, provide incontrovertible proof that many of the Anglo-Greek commercial operations were designed to damage Venetian economic interests by allowing partners to take advantage of the cheapest and most convenient tariffs at both ends of the transaction.

It can certainly be argued that their close commercial interaction laid the groundwork for the establishment of a British protectorate on the Ionian islands after the fall of the Venetian Republic.[17] However, this does not mean that their relationship remained always smooth, as at many junctures it was tested by private and public disagreements. The major problems arose between the English and the Greek population in Zante and Cephalonia, peaking during the 1630s, a very trying decade for the alliance. In Venice the English dealt mostly with Greek merchants and shipowners with whom there was a consistent convergence of interests; but in the islands they interacted with a wider socio-economic spectrum of the local population, and this complicated things, especially as the English presence profoundly changed the structure of local credit at all levels of Ionian society. But whether active in Venice or in the islands, for both groups Venice remained central as the seat of government, and ultimately all important decisions were taken there, be they political, economic or judicial. Venice was indeed the centre of the empire.

A case in point is the reaction of English and Greeks to the promulgation of the *Nuova Imposta* in 1580, and to the 1602 Navigation Act. Greek merchants and shipowners based in Venice in both cases did not respond, most likely because their own interests could be furthered by legislation which favoured subjects and reoriented maritime trade to the *Dominante*. They might have originally come from the Ionian islands, and most of them had close family and business links there, but their ships were naturalised Venetian and automatically stood to benefit from legislation which favoured Venetian shipping. The Seguro and Sumacchi, for

---

[16] Fusaro, 'Commercial Networks of Cooperation'.
[17] Fusaro, 'Representation in Practice'.

example, amongst the principal Greek shipowners in Venice, greatly profited from the 1580 legislation, and they made their fortune legally – and illegally – precisely by trading with England.[18] To the illegal partnership of Marco Seguro with some English merchants we owe the only surviving trial for smuggling currants in the islands. This was a complex deal between Greek and English merchants involving the delivery of currants in Venice – free of customs – in exchange for textiles – also free of customs – to be delivered 'at sea' so the Greeks could sell them in the Ottoman Morea.[19] No wonder this 'interest group' did not object to the *Nuova Imposta*; conversely, the Greeks based in the Ionian islands were vociferously opposed to this legislation. Given their differing economic interests, it is no surprise that the same pattern was repeated in 1602; whilst the islanders lamented the negative consequences to their income of the navigation laws, the Greek shipowners' silence was matched by that of the English merchants based in Venice.

Even given the well-known complexity associated with defining Greek identity, it is undeniable that some form of Greek collective identity within the Venetian state was strong. But it is important not to assume that the simple fact of being Greek was the main determinant of their behaviour. This collective identity – based on values, norms and in most cases religion[20] – could and did fragment in the face of diverging economic and social interests. Individual strategies, business interests and social ambitions remained essential in determining behaviour. In the analysis of the Anglo-Greek interactions it is difficult to avoid concluding that socio-economic considerations were better determinants than ethnicity. The following episode elucidates some of these issues.

Lawrence Hider and Elia Vignari

On a balmy September evening in 1628, Lawrence Hider was walking alone behind St Mark's Square making his way towards the Rialto when Elia Vignari ambushed him and repeatedly hit him over the head with a large stick. Hider had the presence of mind to run into a nearby shop to get shelter, and thus saved his own life. The trial that followed in the

---

[18] Fusaro, 'Coping with Transition'.

[19] ASV, *Quarantia Criminale*, b. 193, fasc. 73. Several of these deals, forbidden by reiterated Venetian legislation, characterised the currant trade, few were discovered, and even fewer were prosecuted successfully. The trial is recounted in detail in Fusaro, *Uva passa*, 108–115; more details are given in this volume in Chapter 11.

[20] P. Prodi, 'Introduzione: evoluzione e metamorfosi delle identità collettive', in P. Prodi and W. Reinhard eds., *Identità collettive fra Medioevo ed Età Moderna*, Bologna, 2002, 9–27, 11.

Avogaria well illustrates the idiosyncrasies and peculiarities of the Anglo-Greek relationship.[21]

Elia Vignari, originally from Cephalonia, was in Venice to deal with a controversy in the *Quarantia*. According to Hider's description, Vignari was a man who lost his temper easily and frequently got involved in fights. Moreover, he reported, Vignari 'was reputed to be a *bravo*' in Giacomo Metaxà's service.[22] To support these accusations Hider presented a list of witnesses. None of them, however, supported his claims, especially that Vignari was a *bravo*. Vignari was instead described as a respectable gentleman from Cephalonia and captain of the *stradioti*.[23] Two of the witnesses presented by Hider were women who made their living running an *albergaria* which served the Greek community, and the others were guests in that same establishment, where Vignari and Metaxà had been lodging. So it was in no one's interest to support accusations about their clients and associates. What is surprising, however, is that Hider called them at all to support his claims; he had recently arrived in town and did not seem to be aware of the political subtleties of the situation. Nevertheless, Hider had certainly been attacked, there were abundant witnesses and the identity of his attacker was certain; in fact the whole *piazza* was commenting and gossiping. Therefore the *Avogadore* decided to press on with the case and to hear Metaxà and Vignari themselves.[24] The latter was nowhere to be found. Metaxà, a rich gentleman of Cephalonia, was accused by Hider of being the instigator of the beating; he strongly denied any involvement, and particularly any connection between the beating and a debt which Hider had very recently repaid him, and about which there had been some disagreement. Metaxà maintained that the debt had been paid and that all disputes had been solved 'in a mercantile manner', which in this context I take to mean 'in a civil manner'. During his interrogation Metaxà maintained that his contacts with Vignari were of a polite nature: yes, they had dined together, and sometimes strolled, but this was the norm amongst 'compatriots, as we do with all members of our nation'.[25] All witnesses supported his testimony by concurring that conviviality was at the basis of Greek sociability in town. Metaxà vehemently denied every accusation, and more witnesses were called in by the *Avogaria* to fathom the episode. During their examinations, the name of

[21] The trial is in ASV, *AdC, Penale*, b. 285, fasc. 26.
[22] J. Walker, '*Bravi* and Venetian Nobles, c.1550–1650', *Studi Veneziani*, n.s. 36 (1998): 85–113, gives an outline of *bravi* presence in Venice.
[23] ASV, *AdC, Penale*, b. 285, fasc. 26, cc.n.n., depositions of the 11th, 12th and 14th of October 1628.
[24] ASV, *AdC, Penale*, b. 285, fasc. 26, cc.n.n. (14-10-1628).
[25] ASV, *AdC, Penale*, b. 285, fasc. 26, cc.n.n. (16-10-1628).

Vignari was mentioned only by non-Greeks – and this once again makes perfect sense. No one denied having heard of the attack, which would have been impossible, given that it had been the talk of the town for the past month, but every Greek called to testify appeared to have extremely hazy recollections of how the event was discussed, and no recollection at all about how, when or from whom they had learned about it. At the same time, when directly asked, they all acknowledged they personally knew both Vignari and Metaxà.[26]

Slowly a different story started to emerge: one evening in St Mark's Square, Hider had rudely denigrated the ability of the Venetian navy, in the presence of many witnesses who had been quite upset by the incident. Vignari had openly confronted Hider and accused him of speaking under the influence of alcohol, to which Hider had replied even more rudely. Beneath the argument lay a skirmish between Venetian and English ships in June 1628 in the bay of Iskenderun, where Sir Kenelm Digby – armed with letters of marque against French ships – had attacked some of these ships. Venetian galeasses in the harbour had intervened to try to stop him. Sharp action ensued but without any decisive result, although the Venetian ships appear to have suffered more than the English ones.[27] The background to the assault then became even more complicated when it emerged that two of the three witnesses called by Hider to support the fact that Metaxà had been behind the beating had just left Venice and were thus unavailable to give testimony. In addition to this they were also discovered to have been involved with the previous administration in Cephalonia, where they had been convicted for financial wrongdoing. The third witness was a dependant of Hider, and his impartiality therefore was compromised.[28]

So what had originally appeared to be a pretty straightforward fight ended up proving to be a case of collateral revenge. Most probably Hider had been beaten up by Vignari to defend not Venice's honour, but his own

[26] ASV, *AdC, Penale*, b. 285, fasc. 26.
[27] On Digby, courtier and eclectic intellectual see *DNB*, s.v., and bibliography quoted therein. The Iskenderun episode is reported in: *CSPVe*, vol. xxi (1628–1629), xliii–xlvi: see www.british-history.ac.uk/report.aspx?compid=89175 (date accessed: 22 February 2014), and *passim*. within that volume.
[28] He was Zuane Antonio Brilli *quondam* Domenego, *senser ordinario*. ASV, *AdC, Penale*, b. 285, fasc. 26, cc.n.n. (29-10-1628). He was still living in Hider's household in 1630 and acting as his factor: see ASV, *AdC, Civile*, b. 27, fasc. 20, c. 32r. For merchants and *senseri* to live together was quite uncommon. Turkish merchants were the only ones for whom it was fairly common to lodge in *senseri*'s houses in Venice, but this was due to the needs of the translation of the language and the regulations of the trade of Turkish merchants in town: see G. Vercellin, 'Mercanti turchi e sensali a Venezia', *Studi Veneziani*, n.s. 4 (1980): 45–78, 53. On these issues also Rothman, *Brokering Empire*.

244 The English and other mercantile communities

after having been publicly insulted in St Mark's Square. The involvement of many protagonists of the trial with the currant business, the coyness of Ionian witnesses, the negative role attributed to Metaxà, paired with the absence of the only two supporting witnesses, who also happened to have serious grudges against Metaxà, all point towards more than simply a defence of Venetian seaworthiness by a 'devoted subject'. However, seaworthiness was an important element of Greek identity in Venice, and the role played by Greek subjects of the Republic in the maritime and naval sectors was well known and discussed. It also was common knowledge that the English held a very poor opinion of Greeks' navigational skills. A few years before, Fynes Moryson had commented that the Greeks were incapable of navigating without seeing the shore, 'are often in doubt, sometimes ignorant where they are, and the least storme arrising, make such a noise and confusion, as they bewray [sic] their ignorance and want of courage'.[29] In his second round of questioning, Metaxà claimed to have gathered further information and to have understood that Vignari's actions had been aimed at defending Venice's reputation:

He came to a fight with the said Englishman for a matter of honour between the English and Venetian nations. The Englishman had spoken ill of the vessels of this Most Serene Republic, and therefore [Vignari] had been forced to take offence, as he did.[30]

The second batch of witnesses summoned by the *Avogaria* all concurred that Hider was clearly drunk and had openly insulted the Republic and its naval forces, stating that 'the Venetians could not resist the English [in direct combat]'.[31] In the space of a fortnight Vignari had morphed from *bravo* to patriot. How could the loyal subject Elia Vignari not react when faced with insults to the Republic's reputation? Francesco Rali *quondam* D. Nicolò from Candia not only supported Metaxà's version of events, but added:

[Vignari], after having with patience suffered the temerity and impudence of the Englishman, who talked the worst kind of nonsense, told him that he [Hider] had had too much to drink, and the Englishman replied, 'you are lying, ignorant beast'.[32]

---

[29] Moryson, *An itinerary*, iii: 112.
[30] ASV, *AdC, Penale*, b. 285, fasc. 26, cc.n.n. (2-11-1628).
[31] ASV, *AdC, Penale*, b. 285, fasc. 26, cc.n.n., declaration of Giacomo Metaxà (3-11-1628).
[32] ASV, *AdC, Penale*, b. 285, fasc. 26, cc.n.n., declaration of Francesco Rali *quondam* D. Nicolò from Canea (cc.n.n, 3-11-1628); confirmed also by D. Livio Boneme of D. Demetrio 'Venetian citizen', D. Zambatta Specchieretto of D. Arigo, all in *ibidem* (cc.n.n, 3-11-1628). Also by D. Domenego Girardi of D. Gabriel of Cologna, captain destined for the Zante garrison, D. Giulio Soderini *quondam* D. Zuan Antonio, merchant (cc.n.n, 4-11-1628).

Hider had certainly been beaten very badly, and his status as a victim of assault was never questioned. The motives for this though could be seen as an extenuating circumstance. At the end of the trial Vignari was banned from Venice and Cephalonia for six years, and Metaxà was let go.[33]

The assault did not dissuade Hider from conducting further business with Greek merchants. The following year he got into trouble with another Cephaloniote, Theodoro Abbati, over shipment of textiles and cash in exchange for currants.[34] Hider certainly seems to have been a man courting controversy. Amongst the English merchants in Venice, he holds the dubious distinction of being the only one to have left documentary traces which are entirely concerned with litigation. But it was not only with Greeks that he quarrelled, for he had serious problems with fellow Englishmen as well. Randolph Simes, for example, accused him of hiring assassins to kill him. Whilst awaiting the decision of the *Quarantia* about this accusation, of which he would ultimately be acquitted, Hider had to remain in town at the disposal of the judiciary. Having inadvertently stepped out of the Isle of St Mark – where he was supposed to be confined – he was fined 1,500 ducats; in total he claimed that the episode had cost him some 20,000 ducats, taking both expenses and lost business into account. Simes died shortly afterwards, so Hider could not reclaim any money.[35] At this point he claimed that he wanted to go back to England, and pleaded through the ambassador for his business to be resolved so he could leave the country.[36] But two years later he was still in Venice, embroiled in another controversy, this time with Zuanne Opa;[37] at the same time, the arbitration[38] to resolve some of the outstanding business in the Abbati controversy had failed, and Hider was also involved in a trial against John Hobson Sr in the Court of the *Forestier*.[39] Four years later we know that Hider was still in town because James Hall, captain of the ship *Sol*, nominated a procurator to recover money from Hider.[40] He also got into serious trouble with the *commissaria* of the deceased Bernardin Damiani, over payment for a consignment of caviar that Damiani had paid to Hider's brother Valentin. Lawrence Hider had refused to recognise this payment because his brother did not

[33] ASV, *AdC, Penale*, b. 285, fasc. 26, cc.n.n. (5-11-1628).
[34] ASV, *GdF*, 749 (*Mandati*, reg. 10), cc.69v–72r.
[35] ASV, *Collegio, Rdd*, f. 20, cc.n.n. (26-1-1629mv).
[36] ASV, *Esposizioni Principi*, f. 43, cc.n.n. (2-8-1635).
[37] ASV, *GdF*, 489 (*Domande in causa*, f. 2), c.272 (14-12-1637).
[38] ASV, *Notarile Atti*, reg. 643 (Francesco Beazian), cc.504r/v (12-6-1637).
[39] ASV, *GdF*, 468 (*Risposte*, f. 2), c.378 (28-1-1637mv).
[40] ASV, *Notarile Atti*, reg. 654 (Francesco Beazian and Andrea Bronzini), *sextus*, cc.269v–270v (17-12-1641).

have power of attorney to receive payments on his behalf.[41] But in this final case in which we find him in a Venetian court, all his legal experience was helping him: Hider's defence is dotted with the sentence 'I fully trust the written evidence', and ended on a rather ironic note: 'my lawyers have been dealing with these things, as I do not have any experience of matters concerning litigation'.[42]

The relationship between English and Greek merchants was based on mutual commercial interests. In the Ionian islands, English and Greek interests partly coincided and partly were mutually compatible; however, things were not quite so clear cut as the close links within both communities – both in Venice and in the islands – further complicated matters, because events in Venice had repercussions in the islands and vice versa. As we will see in later chapters, these elements helped to single out Venice as the common commercial adversary. When such an adversary was not there to provide focus, or when the Greek interests were aligned with Venetian ones, the Anglo-Greek partnership weakened substantially.

The 'Flemish'

The Flemish were the other important foreign community with which the English maintained sustained contacts throughout the seventeenth century, even when their mother countries were engaged in war.

In Venice 'Flemish' was a generic name used to indicate people from both the northern and the southern provinces; the impossibility in most cases of distinguishing their true origin is the reason why they are referred to here as Flemish, which is the way they appear in the documents.[43] Flemish merchants themselves were frequently ambiguous about their exact provenance, aiming to evade the Spanish embargoes; another consequence of this is the difficulty in using these documents to try to assess the Dutch – as opposed to the Flemish – presence in the Mediterranean.[44] As if this was not confusing enough, another crucial ambiguity existed in contemporary terminology: English and Flemish were jointly referred to

---

[41] ASV, AdC, Civile, b. 27, fasc. 20.

[42] ASV, AdC, Civile, b. 27, fasc. 20, cc.34v–38v (9-1-1641mv).

[43] Maartje van Gelder chose instead the term 'Netherlandish' as a solution to overcome the same problem (Trading places, 1).

[44] On the challenges of the quantitative evaluation of the 'Dutch' presence, see P. C. van Royen, 'The First Phase', 99; and his 'The Maritime Relations between the Dutch Republic and Italy, 1590–1605', in R. Mazzei and T. Fanfani eds., Lucca e l'Europa degli affari, Lucca, 1990, 243–272; E. O. G. Haitsma Mulier, 'Genova e l'Olanda nel Seicento: contatti mercantili ed ispirazione politica', in R. Belvederi ed., Atti del Congresso Internazionale di Studi Storici 'Rapporti Genova-Mediterraneo-Atlantico nell'età moderna', Genoa, 1983, 431–444.

as *Ponentini* – Westerners. Unfortunately, *Ponentini* and *Fiamenghi* seemed to have been considered almost synonymous, and consequently it is not uncommon to find Englishmen referred to as ... *Fiamenghi!* This usage was so common as to be taken for granted by contemporaries and it appears even in notarial deeds, where the legal value of the document should have ensured extra care in defining provenance.[45] An interesting example of this is given by one Gasparo Berton, called as a witness in the trial involving Lawrence Hider analysed in the previous pages. Hider and Berton did business together on a regular basis; he was a glassmaker in Murano at the sign of the *Lionfante* and was perfectly aware that Hider was an Englishman.[46] Still, when reporting what a Venetian crowd was talking about when he passed close by, Gasparo declared that 'a Greek had beaten up Signor Lorenzo Hider, *Flemish* merchant'.[47] It is easy to see how this can create problems of identification.

Contacts between Venice and the Low Countries dated from the Middle Ages, and Flemish merchants had been resident in Venice for centuries, operating mostly within the orbit of the *Fondaco dei Tedeschi*. Until the mid-sixteenth century, Flemish merchants in Venice traded mostly as 'Germans', with Antwerp being their most frequent place of origin. Later on in that century, links started to develop also with Amsterdam, and a few merchants also traded under Hansa flags, although several ships which were registered as Hanseatic in the 1590s Mediterranean were actually from the Low Countries and used Hansa flags only to avoid troubles with the Spanish.[48] From early on the Flemish were active in finance and maritime trade, far less in land-based trade.[49] The secular association with the Germans in Venice supported the creation of long-term business

---

[45] Some examples: 'Giorgio Opto de Londino, partibus Anwerpiae' in ASV, *Notarile Atti*, reg. 6530 (Luca e Giulio Gabrieli), c.393r (9-11-1583); 'Rodolfo Simes mercante fiamengo' in ASV, *Notarile Atti*, reg. 11940 (Andrea Spinelli), c.193r (13-3-1618). Even the authority on the Flemish presence in Venice, Wilfrid Brulez, fell victim to some of these misinterpretations: see Brulez and Devos, *Marchands Flamands*, i, n.183, 66 (16-7-1587) when Tomaso Ciolo is defined as 'fiamengo', n.709, 238 (5-2-1597) for James Higgons and n.3667, 627 (13-3-1618) for Randolph Simes. A similar problem exists also in Genoese sources: see E. Grendi, *La repubblica aristocratica dei genovesi: politica, carità e commercio fra Cinque e Seicento*, Bologna, 1987, 343.

[46] 'Berton al Lionfante' was a glassmaking firm active in Murano in the seventeenth and eighteenth centuries; on their banner was an Elephant (*Lionfante*). Gasparo appears active up to the early 1660s. I thank Francesca Trivellato for providing me with this information.

[47] The italics are mine. The testimony is in ASV, *AdC, Penale*, b. 285, fasc. 26, cc.n.n. (17-10-1628). On this issue see also van Gelder, *Trading Places*, 106–110.

[48] Israel, 'The Phases of the Dutch *Straatvaart*', 136; Israel based this statement on Dutch notarial deeds and the general state of Hansa shipping in this period. See also van Royen, 'The Maritime Relations', 252.

[49] Brulez and Devos, *Marchands Flamands*, i: xxv–xxvii.

relations, which helped to make this community particularly wealthy and socially diverse, and also fostered strong connections with the Venetian patriciate.[50] A corollary of this proximity was that some Flemish families made the transition and became part of the patriciate itself.[51] Still, it is important not to assume that integration was a universal aspiration for foreign merchants, especially in Venice, being that from the sixteenth century it was frequently easier (and cheaper) to trade as a foreigner than to comply with all the requirements of acquiring citizenship.[52]

The maritime presence of the Flemish in the Mediterranean was limited until the great famine of 1590, when poor harvests throughout the basin created almost overnight a large market for Northern European grain.[53] The Flemish were quick in taking advantage of this opportunity, and the Venetian government sent diplomatic missions to Northern Europe, first to Danzig and then to Amsterdam, to make sure the city was well provisioned. Maartje van Gelder has convincingly argued that these early contacts were actively supported by Flemish merchants already established in Venice and frequently were financed by those Italian firms still active in the Low Countries.[54] The Flemish participation in the grain trade was indeed an important first step, but their position in the Mediterranean remained fragile, subject to the ebbing and flowing of the fight between the rebellious northern provinces and the Spanish crown. Only with the 1609 truce did the Flemish – from both the northern and southern provinces – manage to strengthen their presence in the region, and over the next decade they consolidated their positions. Up to that point their maritime trade, especially in the Eastern Mediterranean, had mostly consisted of transport for third parties. Fernand Braudel argued that the grain trade was the engine behind the Dutch expansion in both Northern and Southern Europe.[55] Jonathan Israel revised this interpretation, arguing instead that in Italy the fight for supremacy centred on the so-called luxury trades – spices and silver in

---

[50] Particularly the Morosini family enjoyed very close contacts with the Amsterdam mercantile elite: see A. Bicci, '"Sotto il segno dell'avventura, della cultura e del denaro" capitale e know-how italiano ad Amsterdam nel Seicento', in Mazzei and Fanfani eds., *Lucca e l'Europa*, 258–280, 277.

[51] M. van Gelder, 'Gaining Entrance to the Venetian Patriciate in the Seventeenth Century: The van Axel and Ghelthof Families from the Low Countries', *Mélanges de l'École française de Rome: Italie et Méditerranée modernes et contemporaines*, 125–1 (2013) (online): see http://mefrim.revues.org/1201 (date accessed: 7 October 2013).

[52] These issues are analysed in depth in Fusaro, 'Gli uomini d'affari stranieri'.

[53] M. Aymard, *Venise, Raguse et le commerce du blé pendant la seconde moitié du XVIe siècle*, Paris, 1966, 110–111, especially 'Graphique II – Moyennes annuelles des prix par année-récolte [1565–1600]'.

[54] Van Gelder, 'Supplying the *Serenissima*'.

[55] Braudel, *The Mediterranean*, i: 634.

exchange for Italian silks and other products, and also northern textiles.[56] Moreover, Baltic grain never really entered the game in Ottoman lands. Diversification came in a second phase, and from the beginning of the seventeenth century chartering contracts show that trade to Italy comprised 'grain, rye, wheat, lead and fish'.[57]

Like all other mercantile communities in Venice, but unlike the English, there were Flemings who were not merchants but had close ties with them: tailors, jewellers, painters and sculptors. During this period, Flemish merchants were relatively affluent, to judge from the inventories they left behind and the locations of their homes. The majority had varied business interests (dried fish, hemp, canvas and woollens were the staples), and all of them appear to have been involved in the grain trade. Some specialised in precious stones (for example the Helman family),[58] and some in art, like the great art merchant Daniel Nijs, whom we have seen employed by Wotton, Carleton and Sir Isaac Wake to collect pictures for them and other English collectors.[59] This preference of the Flemish for luxury trade was somewhat mirrored by the quasi-monopoly that Italian merchants based in Amsterdam had in the same goods for Central and Eastern European markets.[60]

Competitors or partners?

Venice was one of the first places where the United Provinces established diplomatic relations in the early seventeenth century,[61] but Flemish merchants based in Venice made little use of the Provinces' diplomatic representative when negotiating with the Republic's government.[62]

---

[56] Israel, 'The Phases of the Dutch *Straatvaart*'; van Gelder, 'Supplying the *Serenissima*'.

[57] Van Royen, *The Maritime Relations*, 252.

[58] M. van Gelder, *De Vlaamse natie te Venetië, 1590–1620*, MA dissertation, University of Amsterdam, 1999. For the period 1590–1620 there are a dozen inventories of Flemish households in the notarial archives, and one with a monetary estimate in the *Giudici del Petizion*. No such documentation exists for the English.

[59] Pearsall Smith, *The Life and Letters*, ii: 210. Sir Isaac Wake briefly substituted Carleton during his embassy in 1614, and then came back as ordinary ambassador to Venice from 1624 to 1631. During this period his accreditation shifted between Venice and Savoy, but he kept on being paid under the privy seal warrant for Venice, in Bell, *A Handlist*, 290–291.

[60] A. Bicci, 'Italiani ad Amsterdam nel Seicento', *Rivista Storica Italiana*, 102 (1990): 899–934, 900; also her 'Sotto il segno dell'avventura'; R. Mazzei, *Itinera mercatorum: circolazione di uomini e beni nell'Europa centro-orientale, 1550–1650*, Lucca, 1999.

[61] P. Stabel, 'Venice and the Low Countries: Commercial Contacts and Intellectual Inspirations', in *Renaissance in Venice and in the North: Crosscurrents in the time of Dürer, Bellini and Titian*, London, 1999, 31–43.

[62] M. van Gelder, 'Favouring Foreign Traders? The Venetian Republic and the Accommodation of Netherlandish Merchants in the Late Sixteenth and Seventeenth

The comparison with the English strategy is enlightening; the English frequently resorted to diplomatic pressure to defend their commercial interests, even though we have seen how merchants were more detached from embassy circles than were the Flemish. Why these differences, or, more to the point, what do these differences tell us about the Flemish and English networks? Maartje van Gelder has argued in this regard about the supranational nature of the Flemish network, which, starting with the early grain trade, remained a central characteristic of the community throughout the seventeenth century. Flemish merchants in Venice never used ambassadors or consuls from the United Provinces to intercede with the Venetian authorities on commercial matters. Although members of the mercantile community were actively engaged in the reception of Dutch diplomats and frequently socialised with them, discussions about – or indeed requests for – commercial privileges were always brought by the merchants themselves without diplomatic endorsement.[63] In van Gelder's analysis, petitioning the Republic directly was clearly considered the most efficient way forward, as

delegating the negotiation of their business interests to foreign envoys would not only have meant relinquishing control, but inevitably would have triggered reactions from representatives of the enemies of the Dutch Republic, such as Spain and the pope. Also, in their dealings with the Venetian state the traders may have wanted to avoid being associated too closely with a foreign state, which would only have put more emphasis on their position as outsiders. Instead they opted to keep matters in their own hands.[64]

Certainly before 1648 the somewhat fragile state of the United Provinces, and the fact that there was no universal recognition of their status as an independent state, was an element of the equation which suggested caution. However, I believe it is essential to add two further reasons for such a different attitude towards active diplomatic involvement with the Venetian government. Both had to do with the relative positions of the English and the Flemish, as regards both their social composition and the ambitions of the states behind them.

Regarding social composition, for a mercantile community which was already well settled and connected within the city, and with access to the highest level of the Venetian ruling class, reliance on personal networks was the smarter strategy. Their constant rhetorical formulation of petitions in terms of 'service' and 'loyalty' underlines how they were better

Centuries', in U. Bosma, G. Kessler and L. Lucassen eds., *Migration and Membership Regimes in Global and Historical Perspective*, Leiden and Boston, 2013, 141–166.
[63] Van Gelder, *Trading Places*, 158–165.
[64] Van Gelder, 'Favouring Foreign Traders?'

embedded in Venetian society, their rhetoric sounding rather similar to that employed by *cittadini* and subjects of the Republic. The supranational nature of their networks, the diversification of their trades, and the focus of their shipping on transport as well as on trade, all facilitated such an approach.

The English situation was substantially different, and this is where the different ambitions of England played an important role. English merchants generally had a lower social status but, crucially, they also had a stronger state supporting them, and by the beginning of the seventeenth century they also just about fully controlled the economy of the Ionian islands. So it benefitted them better to play tough, as their bargaining position was substantially stronger than that of the Flemish. The Flemish were (rightly) perceived by Venice as useful and long-standing commercial partners who provided goods and services, and as such were welcome contributors to the Venetian economic system. The English were (rightly again) perceived as a threat to that very same system. Quite apart from the long history of commercial disputes between the two states, the fact that the English established a solid foothold in the Venetian *Stato da Mar* was alone reason for Venice to mistrust them and their intentions.

Crucially the United Provinces' political economy gravitated towards the North of Europe and Asia. They never shared the kind of ambitions which England openly had towards Mediterranean commercial space, as exemplified in the Walsingham memorandum. The Flemish, in short, never showed the aggressiveness and ambition that characterised the English. David Ormrod commented how 'England's maritime imperial policy in the century after 1650 was also based on the drive to expand trade rather than to acquire territory, but she was a much less reluctant colonizing nation than the [Dutch] republic'.[65] However, I would argue that evidence from the Venetian sources shows clearly that this attitude started far earlier, from the last quarter of the sixteenth century.

Seen in this light, the commercial network of the Flemish was a more traditional one in which a supranational network had its strength in personal and kinship contacts above and beyond state allegiances. Given the heavy involvement of the Flemish in the game of high finance, it becomes almost natural to see them as members of the late stages of that 'international republic of money' which covered Europe and financed its global expansion.[66] The English were a different kettle of fish; family links were indeed strong and frequently the basis of commercial partnerships, but theirs was a national community and, as much as individual

---

[65] Ormrod, *The Rise of Commercial Empires*, 339.
[66] De Maddalena and Kellenbenz eds., *La repubblica internazionale*.

merchants might not always comply with English political economy, their government's ambitions made the option of taking advantage of diplomatic channels tempting indeed.

In short, the Flemish were never a threat to Venetian ambitions; the English always were.[67]

The financial connection

England and the United Provinces both expanded their commercial reach in the last quarter of the sixteenth century. For both countries, customs duties were a major source of income, and both chartered trade companies granting them monopolies. There were also important differences though, especially in the financial sector, which was substantially more sophisticated in the United Provinces.[68] It is not surprising, therefore, to discover that Flemish merchants in Venice were extremely active in local and international financial markets.[69] This made them ideal correspondents for the cashing-in of letters of exchange and for operations that involved deposits in Venetian banks. And it was to their expertise that the English would turn very frequently for operations at international fairs.[70]

Not only English merchants, but also travellers found these kinds of services extremely useful, and they frequently resorted to them rather than to their countrymen. Sometime the Flemings' role as financial correspondents included more mundane tasks. Fynes Moryson, for example, left part of his luggage with a Flemish merchant before embarking for the Holy Land: 'Our swords, daggers and European garments we left in our chests with a Flemmish Merchant lying at Venice, to be kept against our returne; and howsoever he, falling banckerout, left the City before that time, yet our goods were be the publicke officer laid apart and readily delivered to us at our returne'.[71]

In the 1640s, most of the purely financial transactions of the English merchants in Venice were handled by the brothers Gualtier and Isaac van der Voort, defined by the *Cinque Savi* as the firm 'which in this city

[67] On these issues see Fusaro, 'Gli uomini d'affari stranieri', specifically on the Flemish 386–388.
[68] O. Gelderblom ed., *The Political Economy of the Dutch Republic*, Farnham, 2009. See also O. Gelderblom and J. Jonker, 'Public Finance and Economic Growth: The Case of Holland in the Seventeenth Century', *The Journal of Economic History*, 71 (2011): 1–39 and bibliography quoted therein.
[69] Cecchini, 'Piacenza a Venezia'.
[70] Two typical examples: ASV, *Notarile Atti*, reg. 11920 (Andrea Spinelli), cc.622r/v (14-5-1599); ASV, *Notarile Atti*, reg. 11929 (Andrea Spinelli), cc.622r/v (23-10-1608).
[71] F. Moryson, *Shakespeare's Europe*, C. Hughes ed., London, 1902, xvi, 165.

supports the business of the English'.[72] In 1648 the Bristol merchant Henry Goughe died whilst staying as a guest in their home after having appointed them his executors, and it is clear from his will that the van der Voorts were his financial agents, not his trading partners.[73] The van der Voort firm was indeed powerful, and Gualtier and Isaac also inherited important commercial interests from previous Flemish firms active in Venice during the first decades of the seventeenth century.[74] In 1651 the van der Voorts were the protagonists of a massive bankruptcy, whose fallout left traces in many sources and dominates the papers of the *Giudici del Forestier* for that year.[75] Their undoing had been their pivotal role in procuring Flemish ships for the Venetian *Armata*, and advancing money for this purpose. At the time of the bankruptcy, the Republic owed them the staggering sum of 480,000 ducats.[76]

Interestingly, amongst the dozens of claims made against their estate by all sorts of merchants – Venetians and foreigners alike – few Englishmen appear actively involved. Gualtier and Isaac demanded that Gio Friedrich and Thomas Rune – 'our friends in London' – pay them restitution for guarantees they had provided them.[77] Thomas Lawrence declared ownership of some thirty-five barrels of salted beef intestines which had been confiscated as belonging to the van der Voorts.[78] This could be seen as the sign of frosty reciprocal relations due to the Navigation Act, but in the light of the long and intense contacts they had with the English, I think it should be seen instead as proof that most probably their business partners were prepared to grant them the time to sort out their business and rebuild their creditworthiness. This is supported by the fact that English dependence on them for handling financial transactions was a phenomenon that did not end with their bankruptcy, nor with the beginning of Anglo-Dutch hostilities. Once he had settled his affairs, Gualtier van der Voort started again to operate on the Venetian financial market, and the English started again to made frequent use of his services.[79] In the 1660s and 1670s the Druijvensteins would be very active handling financial

---

[72] ASV, *Cinque Savi alla Mercanzia*, b. 23 n.s., cc.n.n. (10-1-1649mv). On their role as financiers for the English see ASV, *Notarile Atti*, reg. 6669 (Gabriel Gabrieli), *passim*. They also acted as John Evelyn's bankers: 'received of Vandervoort my merchant, my bills of exchange of 300 ducats for my journey', in Wheatley ed., *The Diary of John Evelyn*, 61.

[73] ASV, *NT*, b. 756 (Giovanni Piccini), n.73 (29-9-1648).

[74] Van Gelder, *Trading Places*, 110–112.

[75] ASV, *GdF*, 494 (*Domande in causa*, f. 7), *passim*.

[76] ASV, *Collegio, Rdd*, f. 42, cc.n.n. (19-6-1651) and (4-11-1652).

[77] ASV, *GdF*, 494 (*Domande in causa*, f. 7), c.40 (23-3-1651).

[78] ASV, *GdF*, 494 (*Domande in causa*, f. 7), c.201 (28-6-1651).

[79] For example, in 1653 Michael Filippi had letters of exchange payable by him, see ASV, *NT*, reg. 65 (Andrea Bronzini), n.220 (30-11-1653).

transactions for English merchants.[80] Indeed, this phenomenon was not limited to Venice: in 1665 Sir John Finch, the English resident in Tuscany, commented about the level of Dutch involvement in English affairs in Livorno as well.[81]

Northern European politics and Mediterranean trade

English and Flemish merchants active in Venice and its dominions enjoyed an excellent commercial relationship, their cooperation extending to every level of business practice.

Although the Flemish were the second-largest exporters of currants from Zante and Cephalonia, there does not seem to have been a permanent Flemish settlement in the islands in this period; they preferred instead to keep just one or two men during the harvest season and otherwise relied heavily on the English to acquire their currants.[82] In the next two chapters we shall see how their joint action led to the liberalisation of the trade in dried fish and we shall discuss their cooperation in the currant trade in the Ionian islands.[83] These are just two examples of a consistent pattern of collaboration; simply enumerating the number of times that English merchants gave power of attorney to Flemish ones, and vice versa, would fill several pages alone. Moreover, we also have instances where English merchants trying to resolve a mutual controversy through arbitration would resort to a Flemish arbiter.[84] In Wilfrid Brulez's book on Flemish merchants in Venice, the reference book on the subject, there are more than 200 contracts that show Anglo-Flemish cooperation between 1568 and 1621. What emerges from his work is how ties between the two communities were extremely strong in all aspects of commercial and financial deals. The English and Flemish undertook joint business ventures in relation to the big financial

---

[80] Roseveare ed., *Markets and Merchants*, xvi, 112. On the activities of Jan Druijvenstein see van Gelder, *Trading Places*, 103, 106–107, 116.

[81] Sir John Finch was minister to the Duke of Tuscany from 1665 to 1672, when he took up the place of ambassador at Constantinople: see *DNB*, s.v., also Barbour, 'Consular Service'.

[82] The first consul for the 'Flemish' in Zante and Cephalonia seems to have been Zorzi Balsamo: see ASV, *Cinque Savi alla Mercanzia*, b. 24 n.s., fasc. ix, cc.n.n. (7-7-1617).

[83] Cooperation in the Islands started early: see ASV, *Collegio, Rdd*, f. 11, cc.n.n. (27-9-1602). They jointly petitioned the *Collegio* also on subjects of apparently less importance, such as the problems of victualling in Malamocco, where they supported the application of Odoardo Lizza for the place of victualler because of his honesty, see ASV, *Collegio, Rdd*, f. 55, cc.n.n. (17-2-1660mv).

[84] For example, in the case of Randolph Simes and Henry Parvis, Parvis chose Robert Assal, an Englishman, but Simes chose a Flemish, Giovanni de Wale: in ASV, *Notarile Atti*, reg. 11943 (Andrea Spinelli), cc.431v–432v (11-4-1617).

centres of Europe;[85] they regularly rented each other's ships for inter-
Mediterranean traffic, as well as for trips to England or the Low
Countries.[86] This was a cooperation that worked even at the height of
English piracy in the Mediterranean, when several Flemish ships were
captured, and English merchants back at home had to lobby for their
release.[87]

With the advancing of the century, strong concerns were increasingly
voiced in England about the Dutch, and their perceived growing
dominance of trade and shipping. The latter was particularly resented,
as, in the middle decades of the seventeenth century, an awareness started
to emerge in England in regard to the importance of shipping profits
derived from transport (as opposed to trade), which gave also a positive
contribution to the navy, and therefore to the defence of the realm.[88]
Complaints about the role of the Dutch as an adversary in the
Mediterranean trade started to appear in Levant Company papers. In
1615 it complained to the crown that, in breach of their monopoly, Dutch
merchants were importing Mediterranean goods into England at a
competitive rate due to their cheaper freights. As a consequence of this
the 'Crown gave the Levant Company a proclamation which had the

---

[85] Brulez and Devos, *Marchands Flamands*, i: n.67, 24 (20-7-1583); n.85, 32 (5-5-1584);
n.134, 50 (12-3-1586); n.167, 61 (6-3-1587); n.869, 290 (9-12-1598); n.1193, 395 (25-
9-1601); ii: n.2444, 237 (10-7-1609); n.2488, 252 (26-9-1609). On this see also ASV,
Notarile Atti, reg. 6698 (Gabriel Gabrieli), cc.102r–103r (19-4-1659).

[86] Brulez and Devos, *Marchands Flamands*, i: n.86, 32 (1-5-1584); n.168, 61 (7-3-1587);
n.169, 62 (7-3-1587); n.170, 62 (14-3-1587); n.183, 66 (16-7-1587); n.187, 99 (16-3-
1591); n.333, 117 (14-5-1592); n.339, 118 (16-6-1592); n.637, 213 (28-3-1596);
n.665, 221 (13-9-1596); n.756, 253 (12-5-1597); n.1005, 334 (17-4-1600); n.1058,
351 (6-9-1600); n.1104, 366 (19-1-1601); n.1563, 508–9 (25-6-1604); n.1564, 509
(25-6-1604); n.1647, 532–523 (23-2-1605); n.1702, 550 (6-6-1605); ii: n.2147, 124
(3-1-1608); n.2166, 133 (13-2-1608); n.2231, 157 (14-5-1608); n.2326 and 2327, 196
(12-12-1608); n.2573, 277–278 (12-3-1610); n.2998, 416 (7-11-1613); n.3013, 421
(3-12-1613); n.3031, 426 (4-2-1614); n.3150, 466 (14-1-1615); n.3153, 467 (19-1-
1615); n.3204, 481 (16-5-1615); n.3213, 483 (5-6-1615); n.3718 and 3719, 644 (9-5-
1618); n.3734, 650 (2-6-1618); n.4096, 772 (9-12-1620). See also ASV, *Notarile Atti*,
reg. 6699 (Gabriel Gabrieli), cc.172v–174r (5-12-1659); reg. 11918 (Andrea Spinelli),
cc.74v–75r (5-2-1597); reg. 11921 (Andrea Spinelli), cc.62r/v (21-2-1600). On this see
also ASV, *Notarile Atti*, reg. 11918 (Andrea Spinelli), cc.74v–75r (5-2-1597); and for a
later period see M. P. Ashley, *Financial and Commercial Policy under the Cromwellian
Protectorate*, London, 1962 (2nd edn), *passim*.

[87] Brulez and Devos, *Marchands Flamands*, i: n.503, 173 (17-6-1594); n.856, 287 (17-10-
1598); n.917, 304–305 (11-5-1599); n.1347, 440 (10-12-1602); n.1355, 442 (20-12-
1602); n.1389, 451–452 (8-4-1603); n.1390, 452 (8-4-1603); n.1419, 460–461 (18-7-
1603). The Dutch reciprocated by vouching for the good behaviour of English ships
when mistakenly taken for pirate ships: for example see Brulez and Devos, *Marchands
Flamands*, i: n.1473, 479 (12-12-1603).

[88] Leng, 'Commercial Conflict', 941.

effect of making them sole importers of Mediterranean goods. Hitherto the Levant Company had controlled trade *in* the Mediterranean, but it was lawful to import Mediterranean goods from elsewhere. The proclamation, by placing imports of Mediterranean goods solely in the hands of the Levant Company, ensured that in future they would be imported only from the Mediterranean'.[89] In 1617 another proclamation was made to place the imports of Mediterranean goods solely in the hands of the Company. Originally devised to stop Merchant Adventurers who imported Mediterranean goods from the Low Countries, this measure also hit Dutch traders, and could be considered a precursor to the Navigation Act of 1651.[90] The situation on the ground was different, but the multiplicity of areas in which English and Dutch merchants interacted around the world makes it very difficult to arrive at any general conclusions about their mutual relationship; however, cooperation appears to have been common and normal in the Mediterranean.

The English civil wars and their Mediterranean repercussions created more grumblings in London about the role of the Dutch, accused of taking advantage of English weakness to gain commercial advantages particularly in Ottoman territories.[91] But the same advantages had been enjoyed by the English in the active phases of the Hispano-Dutch conflict.[92] Seen from the Mediterranean perspective, the situation corresponded more to Israel's description of Anglo-Dutch trade in the area as 'a division of labour [...] the Dutch sold the fine cloth, linens, camlets, and most of the spices; the English sold the lower-grade cloth. Both nations bought raw silks in Italy and Turkey'.[93] Their cooperation went through some sensitive patches during the times of the direct Anglo-Dutch conflicts. Specifically, the already small Flemish presence in the Ionian islands indeed decreased as a consequence of the Anglo-Dutch wars,[94] and this conflict certainly damaged the Levant Company shipping,[95] although probably did not diminish English participation – and profits – from intra-Mediterranean

---

[89] Hinton, *The Eastland Trade*, 10, the text of the proclamation itself at 175–176; see also Davis, *The Rise of the English Shipping Industry*, 242.

[90] On the issue of the origin of goods imported into England, see Hinton, *The Eastland Trade*, 10, 25; Brenner, *Merchants and Revolution*, 209; Israel, *Dutch Primacy*, 208.

[91] Brenner, *Merchants and Revolution*, 600; Wood, *A History*, 54–55. In the middle of the 1640s a relative diminution of English presence was also noted in Cephalonia: see ASV, *Collegio, Rdd*, f. 35, cc.n.n. (16-9-1644).

[92] ASV, *Cinque Savi alla Mercanzia, Risposte*, reg. 146, cc.104r–110r (27-4-1624).

[93] Israel, *Dutch Primacy*, 226–227.

[94] And this was used by Marco Nomicò, administrator of the *Nuova Imposta*, to justify his delays in paying his instalments: ASV, *Collegio, Rdd*, f. 47, cc.n.n. (7-8-1656).

[95] Pincus, *Protestantism and Patriotism*, 173–174.

trade overall. But, as in other areas of the Mediterranean, contacts were never interrupted, and frequently cooperation continued on the ground even during the conflict.[96]

Seen from the Venetian vantage point, for the English the dangers of the Dutch rise in Mediterranean trade were evident, and it is therefore no surprise that diplomats there were aware of the need to protect the interests of the English state. Dudley Carleton, as early as 1618, advised that the Dutch 'must be roundly dealt with, and rather by way of intimidation than persuasion or inducement'.[97] A couple of years afterwards, such feelings were aired in London, where Thomas Mun said the Dutch 'in the guise of friends, were eating away the very foundations of English prosperity'.[98] Steve Pincus, analysing Anglo-Dutch economic interaction from the perspective of London politics, observed that 'the records of the two great trading companies – the Levant Company and the East India Company – reveal that the war was certainly not fought on their behalf'. And he attributed the damage to Company's interests in the 1640s to the English state's lack of interest in the Levant trade during the war:

the Company sent letter after letter to the Council of State begging for a convoy to allow them to maintain a presence in the Mediterranean. These complaints fell on deaf ears; the Council of State was concerned to humble the Dutch, not to seize their trade. Soon the Company gave up all pretences of maintaining its economic activities, and signed over its remaining ships for state service.[99]

In this case the 'Company's interests do not seem to be aligned with those of its factors in the Mediterranean, as there is little evidence of a diminution in either English trade or shipping locally, and in fact it is possible to argue that opportunities for both English and Dutch shipping entrepreneurs remained available, even though the standard interpretation is that the first Anglo-Dutch conflict had been particularly damaging for Dutch trade in the Mediterranean.[100] In a situation echoing the consular controversy described in an earlier chapter, what appears to have happened is that various elements contributed to a growing fissure between the Company in London and its factors on the ground. In the central decades of the seventeenth century the involvement of English merchants and

[96] Pincus, *Protestantism and Patriotism*, 240; Roseveare, *Markets and Merchants*, 140.
[97] Quoted by J. R. Jones, 'English Attitudes to Europe in the Seventeenth Century', in J. S. Bromley and E. H. Krossman eds., *Britain and the Netherlands in Europe and Asia*, London, 1968, 37–55, 42.
[98] Thomas Mun's *England's Treasure by Forraign Trade* as quoted by Brenner, *Merchants and Revolution*, 272.
[99] Pincus, *Protestantism and Patriotism*, 98.
[100] Israel, *Dutch Primacy*, 211. I am working on these issues as part of the 'Sailing into Modernity' ERC project.

shipowners in the Mediterranean appears to have grown more independent from London.

The internal division between the two branches of the English Levant trade also contributed to this state of affairs. The difficulties of managing the currant trade in the Ionian islands were lamented in both London and in Venice around the 1630s; however, the Flemish were never active on this front.[101] On the Ottoman side, which by then was the most important, both quantitatively and qualitatively, state support was increasingly required in the form of naval escorts. According to Pincus, in January 1665, on the eve of the second Dutch war, 'England's naval experts unanimously agreed that the navy could not spare men-of-war to convoy Levant Company's ships, establishing the principle that commercial interests needed to be sacrificed to military ones'.[102] I agree with Pincus that, regarding the Mediterranean, the Anglo-Dutch confrontation was primarily a political issue,[103] not truly shared by their merchants on the ground.

Trade and transport

There was one area of Mediterranean commercial activities where competition between the English and Dutch was strong: intra-Mediterranean carrying trade. Concern about the Dutch role in the carrying trade was shared by both London merchants and their factors starting from the late 1610s.[104] But even in this case it is possible to find examples of Anglo-Dutch partnerships.[105] Southern Europe was an important outlet for inter-Mediterranean trade, whilst North Africa and the Levant had more to offer

[101] Pincus, *Protestantism and Patriotism*, 240. On English complaints about the currant trade conditions in the islands, presented to the *Collegio* by Ambassadors between 1628 and 1651, it is worth noting that the Dutch are never mentioned: ASV, *Esposizioni principi*, reg. 40, cc.245v–246r (23-1-1628mv); reg. 41, cc.132r/v (24-11-1632); reg. 42, cc.274r–275r (20-1-1633mv); reg. 43, cc.101r–103r (1-9-1634); reg. 44, cc.186v–187r (11-8-1635), cc.253v–254v (15-9-1635), cc.261v–262r (18-9-1635), cc.270r/v (2-10-1635), cc.368r–369r (21-2-1635mv), cc.371v–372r (28-2-1635mv); reg. 45, cc.76r–77r (29-7-1636), cc.88r/v (19-8-1636), cc.89r–90r (21-8-1636); reg. 46, cc.112r–114r (26-6-1637), cc.122r–123r (3-7-1637); reg. 47, c.7r (8-3-1639 [error, as is 1638]), cc.234r–235r (18-9-1638); reg. 48, cc.40r–41r (7-4-1639), cc.57v–64r (18-4-1639); reg. 50, cc.70v–71r (31-5-1641), cc.75r/v (5-6-1641), cc.97r/v (29-7-1641); reg. 69, cc.13r–14r (24-3-1651).
[102] Pincus, *Protestantism and Patriotism*, 319.
[103] Pincus, *Protestantism and Patriotism*, 243.
[104] David Ormrod agues instead that this attitude of the Levant Company started in the early 1650s, in *The Rise of Commercial Empires*, 35, 310.
[105] Typical examples: ASV, *Notarile Atti*, reg. 11918 (Andrea Spinelli), cc.74v–75r (5-2-1597); ASV, *Notarile Atti*, reg. 11921 (Andrea Spinelli), cc.351r–352r (6-9-1600); ASV, *Notarile Atti*, reg. 6699 (Gabriel Gabrieli), cc.22r–24v (31-7-1659).

on the supply side. In England in previous centuries, this traffic was conducted by merchants trading with Spain, and in an earlier chapter we discussed the links between Ionian currants and pieces of eight.[106] Another important transport trade was between the Mediterranean and the Baltic. Because these transactions did not touch England, there is no trace of them in the official English statistics, which leaves us with the problem of how to evaluate these invisible earnings. Although they are impossible to assess with traditional trade statistics, an idea of the pervasiveness of such deals emerges from the analysis of notarial deeds.[107]

It is therefore important to distinguish between trade and transport. Many English and Flemish ships spent several seasons in the Mediterranean before sailing back home, playing a significant role in inter-Mediterranean trade independently from the trade with England and the Low Countries. Comparing documentary evidence in Genoa and Venice shows that, although ships of both countries were active throughout the internal sea, there was also a division: the Dutch were more active in the western side, and the English in the Levant.[108] The Mediterranean was a dangerous sea, teeming with corsairs and pirates, and English ships were generally better armed and safer and, consequently, cheaper to insure. After 1604 England was also neutral in Mediterranean wars and, again, this contributed to safety and economic convenience, whilst the presence of Dutch ships oscillated according to the events of the Dutch–Spanish conflict up to the middle of the century. After 1655 the English were also relatively protected from Barbary corsairing by treaties, which was not the case for the Dutch.[109] Having said that, it is also important to keep in mind that from the 1650s until the end of the eighteenth century it is relatively easy to overestimate England's role in inter-Mediterranean trade: 'this overstatement [comes] from the practice of foreign vessels, and particularly Genoese, in the Mediterranean and related trades of fraudulently sailing under British colours by means of falsely obtained Admiralty Mediterranean passes, the practice arising from the relative immunity such passes granted from the Barbary privateers, and the corruption of some of those issuing passes in Mediterranean ports as well as the holders of passes'.[110] In the earlier period, between 1570

---

[106] Croft, *The Spanish Company*, xlix.
[107] Engels, *Merchants, Interlopers*, 64–65; Grendi, 'Gli inglesi a Genova', 23–24.
[108] ASV, *GdF, Sentenze, passim* and ASG, *Conservatori del Mare, atti civili, passim*.
[109] Davis, *The Rise of the English Shipping Industry*, 247. The dangers of Barbary corsairs are frequently factored in the agreements of Dutch crews sailing in the Mediterranean: see ASG, *Conservatori del Mare, passim*.
[110] Fisher, 'Lisbon', 23–44, 30.

and 1650, this was not the case; as newcomers in the area, the English were not in a position to offer any official diplomatic protection such as passes. But they could offer competitive freight tariffs, designed to be lower than the competition, and heavily armed ships which benefitted from lower insurance rates.[111] All in all, English bottoms provided an excellent deal for the transport needs of inter-Mediterranean trade and this helped the English no end in penetrating this complex new market.

The Jews and the Balkan connection

In the eyes of the English, Venice represented an excellent observatory from which to study the Italian situation, both politically and financially. This was why a sizeable percentage of the contracts finalised in the town itself were connected to deals to be performed in other places, places not even necessarily part of the Venetian dominions, like Ragusa and the Balkans. This was also true for purely financial operations, a sizeable majority of which (admittedly few) dealt with business relevant to other localities.[112] This reinforces the idea that Venice was considered by English merchants as a sort of intermediate location where it was possible not only to trade directly in local commodities, but also to establish commercial contacts and complete financial deals that could prove very useful in other regions which, unlike Venice and its territories, were not under the monopoly of the Levant Company. Precisely for these reasons the number of English merchants in Venice was larger than needed for the volume of direct trade alone.

The arrival of the English in the Mediterranean coincided with a period of general rearrangement in Balkan trade. In the central decades of the sixteenth century the so-called Levantine Jews – which meant Ottoman subjects – had been allowed into Venice in recognition of their activities in long-distance trade.[113] Their role as intermediaries grew apace in the following decades, especially after the 1570s Ottoman–Venetian war. The general economic conjuncture in Venice was complex, and change was fast-paced. The loss of Cyprus forced an overhaul of the whole strategy – logistical and financial – of trading in the Levant, and we have seen earlier the role played by the *Cinque Savi alla Mercanzia* in

---

[111] Tenenti, *Naufrages, corsaires*; A. Tenenti and B. Tenenti, *Il prezzo del rischio: l'assicurazione mediterranea vista da Ragusa (1563–1591)*, Rome, 1985.

[112] For some examples see ASV, *Miscellanea Gregolin*, f. 42, *passim*; ASV, *Notarile Atti*, b. 11937 (Andrea Spinelli), cc.573r/v; b. 11940 (Andrea Spinelli), cc.291r–292r. One of the rare letters of exchange to be paid in Venice is in ASV, *Notarile Atti*, b. 11927 (Andrea Spinelli), cc.333v–334v.

[113] ASV, *Senato Mar*, reg. 26, cc.44v–46r (2-6-1541).

rationalising trade organisation and economic strategy. In this general reorganisation, Jewish merchants were perceived by most governments as essential, and we have seen how settlement, especially of members of the Sephardi diaspora, was encouraged. Benjamin Arbel argued that Venetian and Jewish merchants shared a business language, and for this reason they were welcome and successful.[114] Equally important for Venice was the growing importance of Sephardic commercial networks in the Ottoman empire.[115] Towards the end of the sixteenth century the so-called Portuguese Jews also came to play an important role within the Venetian economy, and their commercial activities – such as trade in Spanish wool and Spanish American dyestuff – were vital for the manufacture of fine quality woollen cloth.[116] The English took advantage of Jewish Mediterranean trade networks extremely rarely, a partial exception to this being trade between Venice and the Balkans, where both Greek and Jewish intermediaries were used; as every player had correspondents in Venice, deals were frequently finalised there.[117]

A large part of the English trade with Ragusa was also controlled from Venice.[118] These activities were in breach of the Venetian aspiration at controlling Adriatic trade, embodied by the prohibition, for all foreign ships reaching Venice, to load (and unload) at other ports in the Adriatic. Amongst the Englishmen active there three merchants stand out from the rest.

Tomaso Ciolo arrived in Venice in 1580, and shortly afterwards became factor for the Levant Company merchants Henry Ferenton, William Garway and Harry Anderson. In his contract it was specified

---

[114] B. Arbel, *Trading Nations: Jews and Venetians in the Early Modern Eastern Mediterranean*, Leiden and New York, 1995, 191.

[115] B. Arbel, 'Jews in International Trade: The Emergence of the Levantine and Ponentines', in R. C. Davis and B. Ravid eds., *The Jews of Early Modern Venice*, Baltimore and London, 2001, 73–96, 83.

[116] Israel, *European Jewry*, 61. On the Portuguese Jews in Venice see Ruspio, *La nazione portoghese*. For an assessment of the woollen industry see Panciera, *L'arte matrice*.

[117] A very complex and typical contract of this kind, with precise details of the quality of the goods, times and mode of payments, can be found in ASV, *Notarile Atti*, reg. 8319 (Francesco Mondo), cc.365v–367r (20-8-1582). I wish to thank Luca Molà for bringing this contract to my attention. Other examples: ASV, *Notarile Atti*, reg. 11892 (Gerolamo Savina), cc.70v–71v (1-3-1582); ASV, *Notarile Atti*, reg. 11921 (Andrea Spinelli), c.124r (26-4-1600).

[118] Two typical deals in: ASV, *Notarile Atti*, reg. 11925 (Andrea Spinelli), cc.177r–178r (20-3-1604); reg. 8422 (Francesco Mastaleo and Pietro Partenio), cc.282r–283r (23-9-1616).

that he had to exclusively work for his principals and that any other personal deals had to be approved by them, but it was also made equally clear that all the limiting clauses in his position as factor applied 'exclusively to the parts of Italy, and not for other places'.[119] This clause left him free to trade personally outside of Italy, which he did extensively and successfully. Very soon he was actively dealing with Ragusa and the Balkan region in general. Only two years afterwards, in 1583, Ciolo became the executor and administrator of the extremely rich and complex inheritance of one of the most important Ragusan merchants, Zuanne Lughini, for whom he had worked previously as agent in Venice.[120] Within a few years, by wisely reinvesting the gains of his Balkan trading ventures, Ciolo appears as an important player in the insurance business, both personally and for his principals.[121] He was also in a position to lend money to fellow countrymen.[122] By the time of his death in July 1591, he was managing capital and deals for many other Levant Company merchants who were active in the Venetian market from their London base, Edward Holmden and Paul Bayning amongst others.[123] He left a rather large and unsorted inheritance, which was hotly contested by his associates and partners both in the *Giudici del Forestier* and in the *Avogaria*.[124] There were still pending issues in 1597, so much so that his widow resorted to arbitration to sort out the remaining issues with the English Thomaso Fernelle, a former business partner of her husband.[125]

[119] ASV, *Notarile Atti*, reg. 7848 (Gerolamo Luran), cc.411r/v (26-9-1581).

[120] ASV, *Notarile Atti*, reg. 6529 (Luca e Giulio Gabrieli), cc.42r–44r (26-1-1583); cc.85v–86r (25-3-1583); cc.111v–112r (1-4-1583); cc.190r/v (3-5-1583); cc.249v–251v (3-6-1583); reg. 6530 (Luca and Giulio Gabrieli), cc.274r–275r (11-7-1583); cc.275r–276r (12-7-1583).

[121] ASV, *Notarile Atti*, reg. 6531 (Luca and Giulio Gabrieli), cc.69v–70r (21-2-1584); reg. 6534 (Luca and Giulio Gabrieli), cc.198v–199r (2-6-1587); cc.407 r/v (26-10-1587); reg. 6536 (Luca and Giulio Gabrieli), cc.280v–281r (7-9-1589); cc.319v–320v (23-10-1589); reg. 6537 (Luca and Giulio Gabrieli), cc.292v–293r (4-11-1590); reg. 3568 (Luca and Giulio Gabrieli), cc.70v–71r (23-3-1591). On the insurance business as an investment, see Tucci, *Navi, mercanti e monete*, 146–148, 159. Amongst foreign merchants the Portuguese Jews were also extremely active in this sector: see Ruspio, *La nazione portoghese*.

[122] Interestingly without charging interest, at least officially the loan was made 'gratis et amore Dei'. Beneficiaries were Lancillotto Rolanzon and his wife, Bianca Campanata; they were paying back through some income that she derived from the soap customs, see ASV, *Notarile Atti*, reg. 6531 (Luca and Giulio Gabrieli), c.367r (31-12-1584).

[123] ASV, *Collegio, Rdd*, f. 9, cc.n.n. (8-7-1591); ASV, *AdC, Raspe*, reg. 3690, cc.35r/v (1596–1598).

[124] ASV, *GdF*, 217 (*Sentenze*, reg. 13), c.160v (9-7-1591); c.177v (14-8-1591); c.197v (11-9-1591).

[125] ASV, *AdC, Raspe*, reg. 3690, cc.35r/v (21-5-1596); ASV, *GdF*, 221 (*Sentenze*, reg. 17), cc.24v–25r (20-9-1597).

It is worth noting that the arbiters were both Venetian merchants: Jacopo Ragazzoni and Sebastiano Balbiani.

William Holovais was another merchant who divided his interests between Venice and the Balkans. He was based in Ragusa, but also kept a house in Fiume (present-day Rijeka) and was frequently in Venice to pursue his interests there.[126] It was on one of those occasions, whilst 'in Venice for the occasion of litigation', that he died of malignant fever, aged 28. He was hosted by one of his business associates, the mercer Francesco Ferro – whom he appointed executor for his estate.[127] His sole heir was his brother Thomas, a ship-captain (and probably also shipowner) active in intra-Mediterranean trades.[128]

Ferro was Holovais' agent in the construction of the ship *Madonna dei Carmini*, which had been built at Curzola in partnership with the Ragusan merchant and shipmaster Giacomo Strinich and whose effective ownership was a matter of contention between them, being brought before the *Forestier* in the summer of 1641.[129] Two months after Holovais' death, Ferro sued Strinich in that court. In his suit he requested that Strinich present legal, full and proper accounts ('conto giuridico e legale, distinto e particolare') of all the expenses, including chartering the ship, for a trip to Curzola and Lissa the previous year.[130] Strinich counter-sued, accusing the former ship-captain of having colluded with Ferro to commit fraud at his expense. Not only was he still owed money by Ferro, but he was also unable to produce the ship's account books because the former master of the ship, Lorenzo Forner, had given them to Ferro.[131] This could have had serious consequences for the outcome of the trial, given that there were strict requirements regarding which merchants' books could be presented as evidence in a trial. The claim of their theft, if proven true, would have been a very serious offence indeed.[132] The controversy was still not solved the following January, when Ferro – both personally and as executor of Holovais' will, which shows he was actually a partner,

[126] Some scant information on his trades in Ragusa can be acquired from J. Luetić, 'English Mariners and Ships in Seventeenth-Century Dubrovnik', *The Mariner's Mirror*, 64 (1978): 276–284, 280.
[127] ASV, *NT*, b. 94 (Francesco Balanzan), n.15 (23-7-1641), Ferro was mercer at the sign of the *Volpe d'oro*; Holovais died in his home two days after writing his will.
[128] For his trips to Venice, see ASV, *Notarile Atti*, reg. 1176 (Cristoforo Brombilla), cc.133r/v (31-5-1674), and cc.133v–134r (31-5-1674).
[129] ASV, *GdF*, 277 (*Sentenze*, reg. 73), cc.49v–50r (13-9-1640), and cc.166v–170v (5-7-1641).
[130] ASV, *GdF*, 490 (*Dimande*, f. 3), c.24 (28-9-1641).
[131] ASV, *GdF*, 490 (*Dimande*, f. 3), c.42 (27-6-1642).
[132] K. W. Nörr, 'Procedure in Mercantile Matters: Some Comparative Aspects', in *Iudicium est actus trium personarum*, Goldbach, 1993, 195–201, 199.

notwithstanding all the legislation forbidding this – was still trying to acquire the necessary documentation from Strinich.[133] Holovais spent his last few months in Venice trying to sort out another, far more complex, controversy with Priamo Suriati that, after several appeals, had finally ended up in the *Avogaria*. Suriati had been banned from town, and some goods that Holovais claimed were his had been confiscated as part of Suriati's estate. Because Suriati's original trial had been before the *Quarantia Criminal*, Holovais was pleading that the same magistrate should take care of this final act and release his goods.[134]

Samuel Vassal, 'one of the greatest figures in the colonial trades during the pre-civil wars period',[135] apparently never personally set foot in Venice, but he was one of the most important traders of English textile products with Ragusa and its hinterland in the first half of the seventeenth century.[136] He used Venice as a remote base for his business operations, and some of the most important English merchants resident in Venice were his partners, including Randolph Simes and John Hobson Sr, the latter frequently acting as Vassal's procurator. Vassal's activities were well known to the Venetian authorities; he was admired for his entrepreneurial skills, especially his experiments 'in the Levant market with high quality fringed cloth which he was selling at a time when trade was at a low ebb'.[137] He also had a high profile in England and acquired some notoriety when he was imprisoned by the Court of Aldermen for refusal to pay their assessment towards royal loans in 1628.[138]

In late 1636 the *Collegio* was warned that some English merchants active in Ragusa were discussing moving to Spalato – where (as mentioned in Chapter 3) the Venetian Republic had set up a competing trade centre which was enjoying a discreet success, revitalising trade between Venice and the Ottoman lands. That December the Ragusan merchant Francesco Marino de Giorgi – difficult not to see him as a straw man for the English – submitted a memorandum encouraging the Republic to allow English merchants to settle in Spalato and move their commercial operations there. The *Cinque Savi* appeared wary of this proposal in their *risposta*. Notwithstanding that 'the intention of Your Excellencies has

[133] ASV, *GdF*, 278 (*Sentenze*, reg. 74), c.16v (4-1-1641mv).
[134] ASV, *Collegio Notatorio*, reg. 97, part i, c.25r (19-4-1641).
[135] He was very active in Virginia and the West Indies, in Brenner, *Merchants and Revolution*, 135 and *passim*.
[136] On his ships reaching Ragusa see Tenenti, 'Venezia ed il commercio raguseo'; information on the width of his trades can also be acquired from V. Kostić, *Dubrovnik i Engleska, 1300–1650*, Belgrade, 1975.
[137] Pearl, *London and the Outbreak*, 190–191.
[138] Grassby, *The Business Community*, 207.

always been to weaken the trade of Ragusa', they advised extreme caution in granting the English access to Spalato, as this would have allowed them full use of the infrastructure built by Venetians to support their own trade. The experiment was working, and Spalato had become the privileged door to the Balkans for Venetian textiles. Formally allowing the English to bring their own textiles there could only bring ruin to Venice.[139]

The Venetian government found itself in a difficult situation regarding the *Scala di Spalato*. On the one hand they were extremely keen to foster its growth and make it into the main trading port for the Balkans, thus increasing the return on their investment and damaging Ragusa. On the other hand it was also important for Venice to maintain its upper hand in Spalato, and not to allow competitors to gain privileges there, and this ambivalent approach helps to explain the Republic's attitude towards Samuel Vassal in those years.

In December 1637 Francesco Zonca, at the time the Venetian secretary in London, learned from his informants that Vassal was growing rather displeased with the Ragusan authorities, who were no longer allowing him to directly export his textiles from Ragusa to Hungary, his preferred market, and instead were now forcing him to sell to local traders. Zonca thought this a good opportunity to convince Vassal to move his business to Spalato, and approached him about this directly. From Zonca's report to the Doge and Senate it is clear that he had acted on his own initiative, with the aim of fostering trade through Spalato, and to stop ships going to Venice to unload in Ragusa part of their cargo 'contrary to the ordinances of your Excellencies and to the rights of your dominion over the Gulf'. Taking advantage of his knowledge about Vassal's recent displeasure with the authorities in Ragusa, Zonca

pointed out in a friendly way the risks he ran, since the goods do not pay the duties owed to your Excellencies. I expressed my belief that if his ship met with the fleet in the Gulf, it would get into trouble, as the places are prohibited, and he may not trade in those ports without paying the ordinary gabelles. I expressed astonishment at his preferring to trade with so much risk with a poor and small city like Ragusa, rather than in safety at Venice, a great place, rich in gold and trade.

Vassal listened attentively and asked a few technical questions: for example, whether the Spalato harbour could accommodate large ships, to which Zonca replied it could not, but Liesena could, and the two places

[139] ASV, *Cinque Savi alla Mercanzia, Risposte*, reg. 151, cc.50r–51v (28-1-1636mv). On the 'scala' of Spalato see Paci, *La 'Scala' di Spalato*; and his 'La scala di Spalato e la politica veneziana in Adriatico', *Quaderni Storici*, 13 (1970): 48–105; Ravid, 'A Tale of Three Cities'.

were well connected.[140] Vassal looked interested, and shortly afterwards wrote directly to the *Collegio* petitioning to be personally granted trading privileges in Spalato, and stating his willingness to move the core of his trade interests there, in exchange for substantial privileges. For the Venetians the most appealing part of his proposal was his stated intention to redirect through Venice the entirety of English trade in the Balkans; at present English merchants based in Livorno used also Ancona for these transactions, and Vassal was known to reinvest his profits there. The problems was that, in exchange for this, and unable to provide any assurance about it to the Republic, Vassal was asking to be granted rather substantial privileges: he wanted to pay half the customs duties in Venice, Spalato and Liesena for ten years; he wanted the right to choose the English consuls in both Spalato and Liesena; and, finally, he wished to be able to resort to summary justice for all his commercial disputes.[141] The Republic demurred, frightened of granting such massive privileges to an already successful English merchant.

This episode is most indicative of many of the central issues that Venice faced in establishing Spalato as its Balkan hub. The recent example of Livorno's *portofranco* and its success was clear to all parties, but equally clear was that these kinds of provisions for non-Venetian merchants should and could not have been available in Spalato. The *Scala* had been conceived to counteract Ragusa's success as a gateway to the Balkans, and had been set up as a place where Venetian and Jewish Levantine merchants could easily interact to take back parts of that market. Other merchants were welcome there too, especially if they severed their Ragusan links. However, giving them further privileged treatment would have undermined the local Veneto-Jewish strength, behind which there was substantial financial investment. Welcomed yes, privileged no: the underlying political economy of the Republic had not changed that much.

From the documentary trail left by the sudden death of Holovais we also learn that, in 1639, Vassal was still active in the trade in kerseys between England and Ragusa, where Holovais acted as his agent.[142] Vassal had entrusted a large consignment to Holovais and sought compensation in the local courts. At the beginning of 1642, he sued Holovais' estate in the Venetian courts as he believed there was sufficient capital to recover the

[140] *CSPVe*, vol. xxiv (1636–1639), 328–342: see www.british-history.ac.uk/report.aspx?compid=89426 (date accessed: 24 January 2013).
[141] ASV, *Collegio, Rdd*, f. 29, cc.n.n. (6-5-1638).
[142] ASV, *GdF*, 278 (*Sentenze*, reg. 74), cc.40r/v (12-2-1641mv).

4,000 *reali* which Vassal argued were still owed him.[143] Two years earlier Vassal took some sort of late revenge on the Republic: 'in 1640 after the calling of the Long Parliament, [he] became the spokesman of the City merchants in the House of Commons. He was elected to the Committee for Trade, and played the leading part in presenting Levant Company petitions and securing the prohibition of the import of currants from Venetian territories'.[144]

In Venice, English merchants wove an extremely effective web of alliances, particularly with Greek subjects of the Republic and with Flemish merchants. The alliance with the Greeks – both in Venice and in the Ionian islands – was essential to the English for procuring what was the staple of the Anglo-Venetian trade: the currants of Zante and Cephalonia. But even beyond currants, Greeks represented the connecting link between English merchants and Balkan markets. The English relied heavily on the Greeks as middlemen, to penetrate this market with their textiles. The Flemish were the other foreign community with which the English kept strong and regular commercial and financial ties. Together they dominated the trade in dried fish to the territories of the Republic, and thanks to the united front by English and Flemish merchants we shall see in the next chapter how the Venetian *Arte dei Salumieri* (preserved beef and fish sellers) were slowly but steadily made to relinquish a considerable part of their privileges. The Flemish frequently acted as financial agents for the English for letters of exchange, contacts with international financial fairs, and the handling of international transactions. Most interestingly, these contacts seem to have existed even when the two countries were not exactly in the warmest of diplomatic relations.

The English never sought official recognition of their status as a foreign community. This is consistent with their behaviour whenever and wherever they had a chance to avoid regimentation. From the very beginning of their active trading in the Venetian territories they realised that their best chance of success rested on an alliance with the local population of the Ionian islands, and with the international mercantile network in Venice itself. For their part the Venetians never pushed for – or indeed offered – any formal recognition. The Dutch sneaked in almost unnoticed, not only because they had previous contacts that facilitated their establishment, but because their presence was never considered a threat

---

[143] Interesting to note that he asked the heir to repay his debt directly to the English resident in Venice, William Talbot, who would have then transferred the sum to England: see ASV, *GdF*, 278 (*Sentenze*, reg. 74), c.40r.

[144] Pearl, *London and the Outbreak*, 191. For the consequences of this temporary prohibition, see Fusaro, *Uva passa*, 172–173.

to the Venetian economy. Indeed, on the contrary, their usefulness in providing help in times of grain shortage was widely recognised and appreciated. In contrast, the English presence was considered a threat from the very beginning, and the Venetian tactic was to ignore them overtly whilst trying to make their lives as difficult as possible.[145] Until the second decade of the seventeenth century, the Venetians refused to accept the English presence in the Mediterranean, and all their legislation was designed to discourage them from staying. They seem to have been considered transitory interlopers. They were not.

[145] Amongst the innumerable documents on this subject, see Contarini, *Historiae*, ii, book vi, cc.368–373, in Cozzi, *Il Doge Nicolò Contarini*, 363. A vast selection of opinions on this subject is in ASV, *Cinque Savi alla Mercanzia*, b. 836b, fasc. i.

10   The goods of the trade

The most important commodities of the Anglo-Venetian trade were currants, grains, oil, fish, textiles and glass. English merchants traded oil and currants mostly in conjunction with Greek merchants, and they traded fish with the Flemish. The other goods were traded by everyone, the only exception being glass which, in the second half of the seventeenth century, came to be dominated by two individuals in frequent partnership: the Venetian Alvise Morelli and the Englishman George Ravenscroft.

It is almost impossible to overestimate the importance of currants as the foundation of the trade between England and the Venetian Mediterranean. Currants were discussed at the beginning of the book, and the last chapter will focus again on this trade, analysing in some detail the English presence in the Ionian islands. Venice remained somewhat peripheral to currants, and only when English merchants first penetrated the market were deals mostly finalised there. From the beginning of the seventeenth century, when the English had firmly established themselves in the islands, currants deals were usually made there. Currants remained the single most important commodity exported out of Venetian territories into England throughout the early modern period, and they certainly represented the staple of the trade. Their importance was such that Robert Brenner used imports – broken down by Levant Company member – as the benchmark for judging their relative weight within the Company.[1]

Since the 1970s there has been a growing consensus that whilst in the sixteenth century the growth of English foreign trade was export-led, in the following century it shifted to import-led. Several phenomena were behind this shift, with demographic growth and the increase in the standard of living in England playing a major role in fostering demand for foreign goods. Particularly impressive was the growth of demand for fruits, cheap silks and spices, sugar and new commodities such as tobacco and

---

[1] Brenner, *Merchants and Revolution*, 375 and *passim*.

calicoes.[2] By the early seventeenth century, many of these goods were procured directly at source by English merchants, and Venice's role of middleman suffered from these developments. In addition, between the last quarter of the sixteenth century and the 1620s, several of those 'foreign fripperies' whose import previously had been criticised started being produced in England and, in many cases, in quantities such as to also become export items. Silk knitted stockings are a good example; their production started in England as copies of products previously imported from the Italian peninsula.[3] These developments were a further blow for Venice, as small luxuries were one of the specialities of its manufactures.

Starting in the mid-sixteenth century, wine and foodstuff imports into England increased so much that Craig Muldrew has argued that the onset of the English consumer revolution should be moved forward to this period.[4] Currants and, to a lesser extent, olive oil were the long-term protagonists of Anglo-Venetian trade and remained so until the end of the eighteenth century.[5] In fact, the types of goods exchanged between England and Venice, as well as between England and the rest of Italy, remained pretty stable from the late sixteenth to the end of the eighteenth century. Edoardo Grendi lamented the fact that although English figures on imports from the peninsula in the eighteenth century are clearly divided between those from 'Venice' and those from 'Italy', in the documentation there was no clear trace of the aggregative process at the basis of this dichotomy.[6] But the division was based on the fact that traffic with Venice remained under the monopoly of the Levant Company, whilst trade with the rest of Italy was open to all merchants. Although formally clear, this was not always clear in practice, even to contemporary Venetians; in 1607 Nicolò Molin, at that time ambassador in London, was still under the impression that the Levant Company monopoly covered

---

[2] Fisher, 'London as an "Engine"', 7. Brenner (*Merchants and Revolution*, 3–50, esp. 11) also supports the argument for an import-led growth in foreign trade.

[3] Thirsk, *Economic Policy and Projects*, v, 45–47.

[4] C. Muldrew, *The Economy of Obligation: The Culture of Credit and Social Relations in Early Modern England*, Basingstoke, 1998, 20. 'In 1559 groceries constituted less than 10 per cent of the value of all imports. Pepper was the major mass-consumed grocery. The value of imported dried fruits far exceeded that for sugar': C. Shammas, 'Changes in English and Anglo-American Consumption from 1550–1800', in J. Brewer and R. Porter eds., *Consumption and the World of Goods*, London and New York, 1993, 177–205, 179; see also Thirsk, *Economic Policy and Projects*, Appendix I, 181–185.

[5] E. Grendi, 'Sul commercio anglo-italiano del Settecento: le statistiche dei customs', *Quaderni Storici*, 79 (1992): 263–275, 266.

[6] Grendi, 'Sul commercio anglo-italiano', 271. On the commercial realities behind the 'labels invented by the Inspector General of Imports and Exports in 1696', see Ormrod, *The Rise of Commercial Empires*, 334.

the whole of the Italian peninsula, not just Venice and its dominions.[7] The main reason for this confusion is to be found in the growing role of Livorno as a redistribution hub during the seventeenth century. It attracted many English merchants and ships with wide-ranging economic interests, which somewhat blurred the borders between the area of the Levant Company monopoly and that of general Mediterranean English 'free trade'. A consequence of this was that Levant Company factors frequently moved across monopoly lines, and Company agents concluded deals in Livorno and sometimes even traded from there. The best known of these was Thomas Mun, who was in Livorno at the beginning of the seventeenth century as factor for the Levant Company's powerful founding members Thomas Cordell and William Garway.[8] There he traded also under his own name and admired the Grand Duke's policies, of which he took personal advantage.[9] In contrast, there is scarce documentary evidence of his presence in Venice, where he appears to have mostly dealt with and through James Higgons.[10]

Precious cargoes

Venetian fears about Livorno taking over as a redistribution centre were well founded. Cargoes arriving in Venice from England were roughly divisible into two categories: they either comprised mostly dried fish, together with large consignments of lead and tin,[11] or were extremely varied. A typical mixed shipment at the beginning of the seventeenth century would consist of lead, iron, tin, pitch, kerseys, stockings, wax, India gum, veal skins, wool and felt.[12] An English memorandum of the 1620s gives a very similar picture:

Commodities to and from Venice: the best commoditie for Venice, wooll, leade and carsies. From Venice Currans of Zante, [. . .] for which the New Impost is not

---

[7] Nicolò Molin, 'Relazione d'Inghilterra (1607)', in Firpo ed., *Relazioni di ambasciatori veneti*, 499–556, 502.

[8] J. C. Appleby, 'Thomas Mun's West Indies Venture, 1602–1605', *Historical Research*, 67 (1994): 101–110; Andrews, 'Sir Robert Cecil', 521. Worth noting that Cordell was also Mun's stepfather, *DNB*, s.v.

[9] De Roover, 'Thomas Mun in Italy'. The passage discussing the Grand Duke's financial support is in: T. Mun, *England's Treasure by Foreign Trade: or, the Balance of our Foreign Trade is the Rule of our Treasure*, London, 1698, 36–38.

[10] For an example of such deals, see: ASV, *Notarile Atti*, reg. 11928 (Andrea Spinelli), cc.838r–844r (13-11-1607), see also de Roover, 'Thomas Mun in Italy', 85.

[11] ASV, *Notarile Atti*, reg. 11920 (Andrea Spinelli), cc.42r/v (16-1-1599); reg. 11919 (Andrea Spinelli), cc.154r/v (8-4-1598); reg. 11924 (Andrea Spinelli), cc.137r/v (11-3-1603); reg. 3371 (G. Andrea Catti), cc.121r/v (29-3-1600).

[12] ASV, *Notarile Atti*, reg. 11921 (Andrea Spinelli), cc.351r–352r (6-9-1600) from the *libretto di carico* of the ship *Salamandra*, captain Gugliemo Brun from London.

payd in Venice. Which is more cleane than the Currans of Patrasso, though is thought fattest and best. Silkes, ardasa, ardafbetta, strugi, sowyng oilk, silke grogranes, carpole, light of glabres, nutmeg, Turkey clones fish, ryce, Light of glasses, the Currans of Patrasso are best cheque.[13]

Increasingly throughout the seventeenth century, English goods reached Italian markets (and, even more worrying, the Venetian mainland) not via Venice, but from Livorno, and sometimes even Genoa. In 1670, Lord Fauconberg, ambassador extraordinary to Venice, Savoy and Florence, could so comment on England's trade with Genoa:

The Trade and Commerce stands thus, they [the Genoese] furnish England with Argal, Soape, Hemps, Rice, Oyle, Oranges, Leamons, Paper, Corall, Silkes of all sorts, & Marble, They receive from us all sorts of Woollen Manufactures, Lead, Tynn, Hydes, Tobacco, Sugars, Fish, all sorts of Indian Commoditys, Linnings, Spice, dying wares, Druggs &C: *most of which they transport over Land by Mules, & Waggons into Lombardy, and up to Venice itself.*[14]

Cargoes of precious goods were few and far between, unlike shipments of bullion that were fairly regular, though mostly directed to the Ionian islands and not to Venice.

The trade in precious stones, thriving amongst Flemish merchants, does not seem to have been pursued by the English in Venice, who preferred Livorno for this kind of merchandise. Consignments of precious stones, or jewellery, are almost completely absent on the direct route between Venice and England.[15] Apparently Paul Pindar brought back to England from Venice diamonds allegedly worth £35,000, which he later sold to the crown, but no evidence of this operation has emerged from the local archives.[16]

A 'packet of pearls' landed Henry Parvis into a lot of troubles and nearly created a diplomatic incident in 1608, even though, from the extant documentation, Parvis appears to have been innocent and probably was not involved at all. The son of the Venetian jeweller Lorenzo Pencini was in

[13] TNA, *SP* 99/30, 325r (not dated, but from the end of the 1620s, beginning of 1630s).
[14] The italics are mine, in BL, *Sloane* 2752, cc.1–28, c.13r: 'Report presented to the King of England, of observations made by Thomas Belasyse. Earl of Fauconberg, ambassador extraordinary to divers Princes of Italy ... '. His mission was between November 1669 and November 1670; see also Bell, *A Handlist*, 293.
[15] Some examples: ASV, *Notarile Atti*, reg. 11924 (Andrea Spinelli), cc.554r/v (17-9-1603); reg. 6668 (Gabriel Gabrieli), cc.129r/v (2-6-1646); cc.156v–157v (9-6-1646). Germans and Flemish controlled the trade in precious stones and jewels between the East and the North of Europe: see Kellenbenz, 'Relazioni commerciali'. From the documentation only one shipment of 'ori filati' was encountered on its way to London directly from Venice: see ASV, *GdF*, 516 (*Dimande, Scritture, Risposte delle parti*, f. 61), fasc. v, cc.n.n. (20-4-1643).
[16] Grassby, *The English Gentleman*, 52.

Constantinople at the time, and wanted to send some pearls to his father in Venice. Enclosing jewellery and precious stones in regular correspondence had been expressly forbidden by the *Bailo* in Constantinople, as it was deemed a sure way to endanger all correspondence (commercial and diplomatic) and encourage theft along the way. Pencini Jr did not want to pay for and insure a proper shipment, so he approached Sir Thomas Glover, the English ambassador in Constantinople, and asked him to include the pearls in his next packet of diplomatic mail. We have seen earlier in the book how English diplomatic correspondence was regularly routed to London via Venice, and Parvis was in charge of this at the time. Having been alerted by his son in a letter that the package had been sent with the same ship, Pencini Sr approached Parvis, who denied the existence of any package addressed to him in the bundle he had just received from Constantinople. Pencini Sr did not believe him and promptly sued Parvis for theft. Given the content of Pencini Jr's letter which gave assurances to his father about the package containing pearls, Parvis was swiftly convicted. In the meantime Parvis made his enquiries and discovered that Glover had indeed accepted the package, but this had not left Constantinople, having been intercepted and confiscated by one the *Bailo*'s men. Glover was rather embarrassed about the events; he wrote to Parvis' uncle in England narrating this episode, and enclosed a copy of the letter he had sent Parvis to explain what had happened.[17] Ottaviano Bon, on the eve of his return to Venice after the end of his long period as *Bailo*,[18] assured Glover that he would clarify the case with the Venetian authorities.

Amongst expensive merchandise, even the famous *triaca*, 'medicament extraordinnaire' of the period, thought to cure even the plague, was found only in two instances, and in one of them it was sent as a present by Wotton to a friend in England.[19]

Just as rare were slaves. A single shipment has been found arriving in Venice on board an English ship in 1594.[20] A few years later, the wife and daughter of the *kadi* of Mecca arrived as captives, having been taken prisoner by an English ship, and they were redeemed in a complex operation that involved the English, Venetians and Armenians.[21]

---

[17] ASV, *Esposizioni principi*, reg. 20, cc.130r–134r (16-12-1608), cc.140v–144r (13-1-1608mv); reg. 21, cc.75v–79v (7-7-1609). See also Glover's letters on these events in BL, *Landsdowne* 91, n. 30.

[18] He had been there since 1604: see *DBI*, s.v.

[19] Sir Henry Wotton sent it to Sir David Murray, in BL, *Landsdowne* 90, n.67 (non dated [1608?]). Martin Piers sent it to Roger Clarke, in ASV, *Notarile Atti*, reg. 6698 (Gabriel Gabrieli), cc.186v–188r (4-7-1659).

[20] ASV, *Notarile Atti*, reg. 11915 (Andrea Spinelli), cc.333v–334r, cc.334r–335r, cc.365r–366r.

[21] ASV, *Notarile Atti*, reg. 5912 (Giulio Figolin), cc.365r–366r (4-8-1608).

If rare on the direct Venice–England route, luxury goods were frequently transported on English bottoms in inter-Mediterranean trade. During the 1621–1647 Spanish embargo on Dutch shipping and goods, the English took over their share of shipping to the Iberian peninsula on behalf of Venetian, German and Dutch merchants. In these cases rich cargoes were the norm. Typical merchandise sent to Spain included silk and wool rugs, paintings, medicinal products, colour pigments, mirrors, ivory combs and miscellaneous ivory decorative objects.[22]

The grain trade

We have already briefly discussed how the 1590s were years of famine throughout the Mediterranean and how this facilitated Flemish commercial penetration.[23] This situation was made all the worse in Venice because of the recent loss of Cyprus, which had been the granary of the Republic, and the concomitant diminished production of wheat in the Ionian islands, where its production was being replaced by currants. As the famine affected the whole Mediterranean basin, exports from the Ottoman territories were also prohibited. European ambassadors at the Porte tried during the 1590s to negotiate exceptions to the restrictions, but this was always denied.[24] Most probably the reason was the growing population pressure in the empire, which probably also was the explanation behind the general drop in grain exports from Ottoman Anatolia starting roughly from the 1560s.[25]

Although smuggling grains out of the Ottoman territories was rife, it was insufficient to satisfy growing demand in Venice and the islands.[26] The Flemish role is well known, but the English also took advantage of this to strengthen their position, trying to make themselves indispensable both in Venice and in the Ionian islands.[27] This approach was then

---

[22] ASV, *Notarile Atti*, reg. 6669 (Gabriel Gabrieli), cc.107r/v (31-1-1646) Simon Borlon; cc.114v–115r (8-2-1646) Simon della Santa; cc.131v–132r (25-2-1646) Alessandro Tasca; cc.148v–149r (7-3-1647) Martin Piers. All the merchants freighting the ship had to sign declarations about the 'non-Dutch' origin of their goods. On the Spanish embargo: Israel, *Dutch Primacy*, 125–136.

[23] On this see also J. K. Fedorowicz, *England's Baltic Trade in the Early Seventeenth Century: A Study in Anglo-Polish Commercial Diplomacy*, Cambridge, 1980, 111.

[24] Goffman, *Izmir*, 37.

[25] Braudel, *The Mediterranean*, i: 593–594; for the consequences of this in the Ottoman lands see H. İnalcik, 'Impact of the *Annales* School on Ottoman Studies and New Findings', in his *Studies in Ottoman Social and Economic History*, London, 1985, IV: 69–96, 80–83.

[26] İnalcik, 'Impact of the *Annales*', 81–83; Goffman, *Izmir*, 36.

[27] Braudel and Romano, *Navires et marchandises*, 51. On the relative role of Dutch and English shipping on this occasion, see Israel, 'The Phases of the Dutch *Straatvaart*'.

applied to achieve favourable terms in the currant trade. It met with great success in Venice during the crisis of the 1590s,[28] and in the Ionian islands it became a standard procedure.

A notable exception to this strategy was Paul Pindar, one of those first-generation English merchants active in Venice at the end of the sixteenth century. We encountered him in an earlier chapter helping Wotton send political reports back to England, and he was well known to Venetian authorities as a merchant of substance.[29] Pindar was one of the few who managed to use his Venetian experience and capital to build a successful career in England.[30] He apparently arrived in Venice as an apprentice to Henry Parvis in 1594–1595, although just a single trace has emerged of their link: Pindar giving Parvis power of attorney upon his departure from Venice in 1611.[31] From 1609 Pindar was consul at Aleppo, and two years later became the English ambassador at the Porte.[32] In the early 1620s he moved back to England, where he employed his capital in the alum trade and invested also in jewels. He built himself a very large mansion at Bishopsgate, famed for its 'marble portico, ornate facade and ornamental gate'. The house was demolished at the end of the nineteenth century, but its impressive façade is preserved at the Victoria and Albert Museum. Pindar paid a high personal and financial price for his royalist beliefs, as he died almost bankrupt in 1650 at the age of 84.[33]

Pindar was the largest single importer of grain to Venice at the height of the crisis (1590–1592), and the only Englishman involved directly with the *Provveditori alle Biave* (Grain Office).[34] His credibility was greatly enhanced in the eyes of the Republic by the fact that he never asked for rebates in the currant customs in exchange for grain provisions, preferring instead to concentrate on trading in high-quality silks.[35] In 1591 Pindar persuaded the *Senato* to grant him a massive loan, 52,200 ducats, to buy

---

[28] *LMA*, CLC/B/062/MS22274, n.1195 (31-8-1590); ASV, *Notarile Atti*, b. 3638 (Luca e Giulio Gabrieli), cc.70v–71r (23-3-1591).

[29] Giovan Carlo Scaramelli reported to the Senate that he was 'an intimate of Cecil': *CSPVe*, vol. ix (1592–1603), 'Venice: February 1603, 16–28': see www.british-history.ac.uk/report.aspx?compid=95575%26str (date accessed: 12 December 2014).

[30] *DNB*, s.v.; C. W. F. Goss, 'Sir Paul Pindar', *Transactions of the London & Middlesex Archeological Society*, n.s. 6 (1933): 219–256.

[31] ASV, *Notarile Atti*, reg. 11921 (Andrea Spinelli), cc.101v–102v (25-11-1611); he also appears to have helped with forwarding Wotton's correspondence to London for a time, but Wotton was not really happy with his services: on this see Pearsall Smith, *The Life and Letters*, i: 228, 288, 293.

[32] Epstein, *The Early History*, 78.

[33] And his executor committed suicide trying to handle his complex and debt ridden estate: see Goss, 'Sir Paul Pindar', 255; Grassby, *The Business Community*, 335, 252.

[34] Van Gelder, *Trading Places*, 62. See also Aymard, *Venice, Raguse*, 158–159 (where he appears as Paulo Finder); Braudel and Romano, *Navires et merchandises*, 53.

[35] ASV, *Collegio, Rdd*, f. 9 cc.n.n. (2-5-1591).

grain in the Baltic region and import it to Venice. His guarantors were the elite of the Venetian mercantile and banking world and of the Tuscan banking circles in Venice: Giacomo and Placido Ragazzoni, Lorenzo, Roberto and Alessandro Strozzi, Donato and Camillo Baglioni, Francesco and Nicolò Capponi and Agostin da Ponte.[36] This impressive, and unique, list of players is completely different from the social circles of most English merchants in Venice. Part of the explanation is Pindar's high profile, the sheer volume of his transactions in Venice acting in itself as a guarantee of this trustworthiness. However, I would argue that the crucial strategic importance of this transaction was such that the *Senato* itself probably provided him with an impressive line-up of guarantors. Indeed, these names do not appear in association with Pindar on any other occasion, and in his everyday affairs Pindar's closest business associate in Venice seems to have been the Venetian merchant Gasparo Cerchieri, whom he nominated his procurator during a brief trip to England in 1597.[37]

Part of the deal between Pindar and the *Senato* to provision Venice was that grain ships would pay just half the customs duties in the Venetian Levant as a goodwill sign of recognition for their help.[38] Even if Pindar did not trade in currants, once again the interaction between Venice and England pivoted on Venetian colonial possessions, and to properly evaluate how disruptive the English were to the Venetian commercial system it is important to briefly sketch their activities in the grain trade to Venice and the Ionian islands. The Mediterranean grain crisis of the 1590s was a short-term crisis, which was resolved by the beginning of the seventeenth century. This was not the case in the Ionian islands, where grain famine turned from a conjunctural problem into a permanent one. In fact the Ionian islands' demand for grain persisted throughout the seventeenth and well into the eighteenth century, in contrast with the Southern European trend of rising grain production which, paired with local demographic stagnation, generally led to a decline of grain shipments.

From the 1550s, the growth of currant cultivation in Zante and Cephalonia was directly tied to a decline in grain. The impact of this close connection was keenly felt in Venice. Ionian grain production was essential for the local population, but its most important outlet was the

---

[36] ASV, *Senato Zecca*, b. 1, c.86v (16-6-1591). More details on how this transaction was organised in: *Museo Correr, Manoscritti Donà delle Rose*, b. 218, c.306 (12-6-1591).

[37] ASV, *Collegio, Rdd*, f. 10, cc.n.n. (31-5-1598). Another large contract for the delivery of miscellaneous goods in which Pindar and Cerchieri were partners is in ASV, *Notarile Atti*, reg. 12534 (Giovanni Battista Tomasi), cc.n.n. (16-1-1597).

[38] ASV, *Collegio, Rdd*, f. 9, cc.n.n (28-4-1592).

Venetian navy, particularly the fleet which patrolled the Ionian Sea and defended the entry into the Adriatic – the Gulf of Venice.[39] Therefore, from the very onset, the diminution of the islands' grain output created problems for the defence strategy of the Republic, and England's grip on a classic colonial good such as currants ended up damaging the whole naval defence structure of the Republic. Ionian Greeks themselves had few problems in provisioning themselves on the Ottoman Morea, where they enjoyed close family and commercial links, which fostered a disregard for Ottoman legislation forbidding such traffic. But for the Venetian authorities who needed to victual the navy, large-scale provisioning on the Ottoman shores was clearly not an option, and what little could be obtained from local contraband was prohibitively expensive.[40]

Though in Venice the English were not major players in the grain trade, in the islands they absolutely dominated it, and by the end of the sixteenth century they were already in a position to control the local market. As the local population was converting all good land in Zante and Cephalonia to the production of currants at the expense of grain, the English quickly realised that importing grain was a most efficient (and cheap) way to pay at least partially for their currants.[41] In addition, the English also attempted to obtain rebates on the *Nuova Imposta* by offering the local *Rettori* to import grain to satisfy the needs of the fleet. In response, the *Cinque Savi alla Mercanzia* developed a siege mentality in regard to the application of the *Nuova Imposta* in the islands, and suspected English foul play whenever rebates were requested. Indirect evidence of Venetian fears is provided by the *Savi* attitude towards emissaries of the town of Danzig who had come to Venice offering a deal for providing grain. As part of the negotiation they asked to be exempt from paying the *Nuova Imposta* on currants: the request was not granted because the *Savi* suspected that English merchants were behind the offer.[42] The Flemish role in the Ionian grain trade was more limited, though they were involved in the trade between Italy and the Levant, and from the 1620s they provided a steady flow of grain from Palestine and Syria into Tuscany.[43] Genoa benefitted as well, as the low

---

[39] On the importance of Ionian grain production, and its customs income, for the needs of the *Armata* see ASV, *Compilazione Leggi*, 1st series, b. 30, cc.n.n. (31-12-1555).

[40] All these issues are discussed in detail in Fusaro, *Uva passa*, 79–106.

[41] For an example of this see: ASV, *Cinque Savi alla Mercanzia, Risposte*, reg. 138, c.148v (8-7-1591).

[42] ASV, *Cinque Savi alla Mercanzia, Risposte*, reg. 139, cc.148v–152r (23-6-1597); cc.154r–155v and cc.156r–158r (9-7-1597); see also ASV, *Cinque Savi alla Mercanzia*, b. 188 n.s., fasc. iii, cc.n.n. (22-9-1600). On grain exported from Danzig to Venice, see Jeannin, 'The Sea-Borne and the Overland', 38–39.

[43] Engels, 'Dutch Traders in Livorno', 73.

customs tariffs available there for grain imports increased the potential profits for Dutch ships prepared to run the risks associated with this kind of contraband.[44] Profits were further increased as these dangers, including that of the crew being taken captive, allowed them to charge double freight and still profit from the transaction.[45]

Olive oil

Olive oil was essential for the Venetian economy, not only as a food item but as a necessary ingredient for the soap industry – which had a strong stake in the higher-quality segment of the European market – and in the woollen industry during the carding process, where lower-quality olive oil was utilised. The oil from Apulian olives was the most desirable, and Venice managed for centuries to acquire a majority share of its production. Only by the eighteenth century did England, the United Provinces and France manage to become serious players in that market.[46]

From the last quarter of the seventeenth century, when their predominance on the Apulian market started to be challenged, Venetian authorities tried to stimulate the cultivation of olive trees in the Ionian islands. The first priority was to provide for the consumption needs in Venice and the *Terraferma*, but this strategy also had another important aim: whilst olive oil was as much a colonial crop as currants, it had the advantage of a far larger market throughout Europe, unlike currants, where England dominated demand. Thus, encouraging oil production should have freed the islands from the grip of English merchants. This policy was extremely successful in Corfu, although it needs to be stressed that the currant production of this island was always very small, but substantially less so in Zante and Cephalonia, whose economic fortunes remained involved mostly with currants.[47]

Olive oil was one of the Italian products most coveted by the English for their return cargoes. By the 1630s imports of Italian oil were meeting practically the entirety of English demand, and providing – with currants – the bulk of return cargoes to England.[48] The trade of oil in Venice was

---

[44] Kirk, *Genoa and the Sea*.

[45] ASG, *Conservatori del Mare, Atti civili, passim*; on the repercussions in Venice: ASV, *Collegio, Esposizioni Principi*, reg. 35, cc.9v–10v (19-4-1625).

[46] S. Ciriacono, 'L'olio a Venezia in età moderna. I consumi alimentari e gli altri usi', in S. Cavaciocchi ed., *Alimentazione e nutrizione*, Florence, 1997, 301–311.

[47] M. Couroucli, *Les oliviers du lignage : une Grèce de tradition vénitienne*, Paris, 1985; a sketch of oil's impact on the colonial economy can be found in Arbel, 'Venice's Maritime Empire', 231–233.

[48] Davis, 'Influences de l'Angleterre', 219, 226–227; also his *The Rise of the English Shipping Industry*, 244.

subject to limitations and constraints. The needs of the town were paramount, and every precaution was taken to avoid any cornering of the market, particularly by foreign merchants.[49]

Oil produced in the Ionian islands could be shipped exclusively to Venice, where it satisfied around 50 per cent of its needs, and this trade was firmly in the hands of Greek Jewish traders.[50] The English tried on several occasions to obtain permission to export oil from Zante and Cephalonia, but they never managed more than the occasional small personal allowance. So concerned was the Republic with preventing export of oil from the islands that it forbade even the export of empty barrels:

Strict Orders are come from Venice forbidding their Subjects to be any way assistinge unto us either in buying Oyle and, in Turky upon sever penalties, and prohibiting the exportation of any Oyle Caske, or Coops to fill them, into any of the Grand Signor dominions contrary to the Common and continued Custome, thereby to prevent the ladyng Oyles for the Western parts.[51]

In 1639 Marco Nomicò, member of a powerful Zantiote merchant family, and later the administrator of the *Nuova Imposta* farm in Zante, formally petitioned the *Collegio* that English ships be allowed to load small quantities of oil, up to twenty *miara* a year.[52] To counterbalance this, he offered to personally import forty *miara* from the Morea into the islands. His argument was that allowing them to load some oil would have a positive effect on currant customs: providing the English legally with some quantity of oil would encourage them to stay away from the Ottoman Morea, where they also loaded currants to the detriment of the Republic.[53] The *Senato* accepted this proposal.[54] Emboldened by this success, a few months afterwards he proposed new customs directly based on oil exports from the islands. His argument was again built around satisfying the demand of the northerners for 'oil, which is to the taste of the English and Flemish nations, who appreciate Zante oil with their food more than any other kind'.

---

[49] S. Ciriacono, *Olio ed Ebrei nella Repubblica Veneta del Settecento*, Venice, 1975, 10; Knapton, 'Tra Dominante e Dominio', 297.

[50] Israel, *European Jewry*, 93, 144.

[51] TNA, *SP* 99/28, 114r (14-10-1627), summary of a letter from Zante.

[52] *Miaro*: 'an oil measure of 40 *mirri* (in Venice). 1 Venetian *mirro* = 30 heavy lbs, 3 oz.': F. Edler De Roover, *Glossary of Medieval Terms of Business: Italian Series 1200–1600*, Cambridge (Mass.), 1934, 184.

[53] ASV, *Collegio, Rdd*, f. 30, cc.n.n. (17-10-1639).

[54] Nomicò, and his heirs, would benefit from this for thirty years, receiving 3 per cent of the income generated by the export of these 20 *miara*. In ASV, *Senato Mar*, reg. 97, cc.294v–295r (4-2-1639mv).

He said the strength of demand was one of the reasons behind smuggling, and legalising this trade would help the fight against contraband whilst providing income for the state coffers:

Your Serenity should not worry that such a measure will be detrimental to this city [Venice]; as at present large quantities of oil are illegally extracted directly to the West through fraud, collusion, and [secret] agreements without any benefit for Your Serenity.

He argued that even the English would prefer to pay customs and be allowed to export legally, as at present they were at the mercy of greedy traders who, taking advantage of the need for secrecy, cheated them in both quality and quantity. A regulated market was in everyone's interest, he said, and this way the better quality Apulian oil would be back in Venetian hands.[55]

Although exporting oil outside Venice was forbidden, several English merchants were involved. These transactions were mostly centred on the traffic of Morea oil to Venice, where it was then sold to Venetian buyers. Henry Hider and Randolph Simes were amongst the largest operators in the field who particularly specialised in the importation of *olio mosto* from the Peloponnese, an inferior quality of oil used in wool manufacturing and for mid-quality soap-making.[56] The fate of a large consignment of olive oil was at the centre of a controversy concerning Simes' inheritance, through which we can glimpse the web of commercial interests and the scale of English financial engagement with the Venetian Levant. Simes died of plague in Venice in 1631 'without any order in his affairs'. Ottavio Robazzi, at the time acting as consul of the English nation, and Antonio Retano, one of the principal Flemish merchants in Venice,[57] pleaded to the *Collegio* to intervene so that his affairs and papers could be frozen for six months whilst they enquired in England about the heirs to his estate. They claimed that his business interests were so relevant that great damage would follow unless this was granted.[58] Indeed, Simes' mercantile activities in Venice were multifaceted; active from around 1608 in Venice as an agent for James Higgons,[59]

[55] ASV, *Collegio, Rdd*, f. 30, cc.n.n. (20-2-1639mv). Since the beginning of the sixteenth century, olive oil had been popular as a condiment for salad, and this was fairly widespread amongst the nobility and gentry, see J. Thirsk, *Food in Early Modern England: Phases, Fads, Fashions 1500–1760*, London, 2007, 31, 42, 81.

[56] On *ogli mosti*, see Ciriacono, *Olio ed Ebrei*, 96 footnote.

[57] Antonio Retano had requested, and obtained, Venetian citizenship in 1627, see van Gelder, *Trading Places*, 137 footnote 21.

[58] ASV, *Collegio, Rdd*, f. 22, cc.n.n. (31-7-1631).

[59] ASV, *Notarile Atti*, reg. 11929 (Andrea Spinelli), cc.99r/v (3-3-1608); reg. 11936 (Andrea Spinelli), c.500r (3-7-1614); reg. 11939 (Andrea Spinelli), c.122r (27-7-1617).

within the next decade he had become a prominent member of the English mercantile community. In 1619 he had managed to obtain an exception to the rules prohibiting the export of currency and had bought currants in Zante and Cephalonia for the value of 100,000 Spanish *reali* in cash.[60] He was active in the trade of cloth and dyes, especially 'endeghi e Giurini',[61] and frequently acted as a procurator for captains of English ships.[62] He was also an important player in the maritime insurance market[63] and maintained important business contacts with Ragusa[64] and Florence.[65] During a controversy with the powerful Cephalonian merchant Marin Migliaressi,[66] Simes specifically requested that the case be tried in the *Forestier*, and not in the court where Migliaressi had sued him. The *Forestier* judges had been happy to comply with this request and summoned Migliaressi:

if he [Migliaressi] has any claim with Signor Redolfo he needs to appear in front of our Court, as we have jurisdiction over such matters, and it is not possible to remove the alleged offender from the Court where he belongs.[67]

It is rather surprising that a man with so many and varied commercial interests should die intestate, particularly as before dying he had spent a couple of days confined to his house, as the plague was ravaging Venice and had already struck his own household.[68] But, for whatever reason,

---

[60] ASV, *Cinque Savi alla Mercanzia, Risposte*, reg. 145, cc.27v–28r (12-7-1619).

[61] And in this business he had got into trouble with the *Governatori delle Intrade*: see ASV, *Cinque Savi alla Mercanzia, Risposte*, reg. 147, cc.60–63v (11-12-1626). *Endeghi* means indigo, a blue dye obtained from plants of the genus *Indigofera*. *Giurini* was the term used in Venice for a type of fabric used to line and reinforce clothes: see A. Vitali, *La moda a Venezia attraverso i secoli: lessico ragionato*, Venice, 1992, 206.

[62] ASV, *Notarile Atti*, reg. 11936 (Andrea Spinelli), c.373r (15-5-1614); reg. 11937 (Andrea Spinelli), c.279r (18-4-1615); reg. 11938 (Andrea Spinelli), cc.571r/v (21-7-1616); reg. 11944 (Andrea Spinelli), cc.16v–17r (9-5-1618) and cc.289r–290r (17-10-1618).

[63] ASV, *Notarile Atti*, reg. 3400 (G.Andrea Catti), enclosed after c.4r (8-2-1624); reg. 3399 (G.Andrea Catti), cc.319v–320r (24-12-1620) and c.56r (2-3-1620) and cc.298v–299r (9-12-1620); reg. 11937 (Andrea Spinelli) c.469r (13-6-1615).

[64] ASV, *Notarile Atti*, reg. 11939 (Andrea Spinelli), cc.258r–259r (9-9-1617); reg. 11940, c.193r (13-3-1618); reg. 11944, cc.135v–136r (12-7-1618).

[65] ASV, *Notarile Atti*, reg. 11944 (Andrea Spinelli), cc.284v–285v (12-10-1618).

[66] Migliaressi was a very prominent Greek merchant active between Cephalonia and Venice. He had been administrator of the *Nuova Imposta* in 1624 (ASV, *Cinque Savi alla Mercanzia*, b. 188 n.s., cc.n.n. (15-7-1624)); ambassador of the *Comunità* to the *Signoria* in regard to the *Novissima* in 1629 (ASV, *Collegio, Rdd*, f. 20, cc.n.n. (11-7-1629)); and again administrator of the *Nuova Imposta* in 1631 (ASV, *Collegio, Rdd*, f. 24, cc.n.n. (29-7-1633)).

[67] ASV, *GdF*, 661 (*Lettere missive*, reg. 25), c.64r (23-6-1629); more details on the jurisdiction of the *Forestier* in Fusaro, 'Politics of Justice/Politics of Trade'.

[68] From evidence produced in the trial of Giovanni Peterlin vs. Henry Hyde, in ASV, *AdC, Civile*, b. 245, fasc. 7. In December of that year the *Cinque Savi* decreed the sale of part of the goods belonging to Simes' estate to pay the wages of his household domestic staff. Because the estate was still frozen, and trying to protect its interests, they decided that the

no will was found,[69] and the after-effects of his death left a long trail in various Venetian magistracies.[70] To begin with, his apprentice - John Petersen – was accused of having connived with the Venetian merchant Lorenzo Minelli to transfer to his name a large consignment of olive oil, which was in fact the property of Henry Hyde, another prominent English merchant. A long trial followed in the *Avogaria* against the middleman (*sensale*) who had helped with this fraud, which also involved some forgery regarding the effective price of the oil, which had been undervalued for purposes of customs evasion.[71] Antonio Rettano wrote a very angry letter to the *Forestier* denying any involvement with Petersen with regard to the *Avogaria* trial, and interestingly Petersen wrote a similar document that very same day. For procedural purposes this trial represented a classic case of competing competencies: the main suit itself had been delegated to the higher tribunal of the *Avogaria*, but a collateral citation to a foreigner was still sent to the *Forestier*.[72] And indeed a substantial portion of the trial is to be found in the papers of the *Forestier*. The 155 barrels of oil at the centre of the controversy came in part from Modon and in part from 'Zante and the Morea',[73] in itself an interesting detail, as oil coming from those places should have been taxed differently and therefore should not have been mixed. The issue, though, was never raised in the relevant papers, indirect evidence that there was a certain amount of forbearance regarding transactions lying at the border between legal and illegal trade. An additional procedural complication was that the controversy was embedded in international inheritance procedure. If someone died

---

goods to be sold should be the ones most at risk of perishing, in this case a consignment of leathers: see ASV, *Cinque Savi alla Mercanzia*, b. 81 n.s., fasc. vii, cc.n.n. (12-12-1631).

[69] Given the circumstances of his death, and the interests at play, it's difficult not to harbour the thought that maybe the will existed and was made to disappear.

[70] ASV, *GdF*, 269 (*Sentenze*, reg. 65), cc.86v–94r, 87r (19-11-1633); 272 (*Sentenze*, reg. 68), cc.17v–19r (8-10-1634); 270 (*Sentenze*, reg. 66), cc.127r–128r (27-6-1636); from this can be seen how the aftermath was still felt five years after his death.

[71] ASV, *AdC*, *Civile*, b. 245, fasc. 7.

[72] ASV, *GdF*, 468 (*Risposte*, f. 2), c.87 and c.89 (7-9-1633). There is an interesting puzzle behind these two declarations: Petersen's declaration makes perfect sense, and his appeal to the *Forestier* is logical given his foreign nationality. The Rettano of the declaration is here named Anzolo (and not Antonio); this could be a mistake of the scribe (there are frequent other cases and as no trace of any Anzolo Rettano has emerged from the archives) but in this case his writing to the *Forestier* is procedurally odd as he had acquired Venetian citizenship by 1627. This 'Anzolo' could be another – unrelated – individual, but this hypothesis seems far-fetched. Most likely, given that both declarations are in same hand and follow immediately one after the other under the same date, Rettano was supporting Petersen's declaration and therefore did this in the same court.

[73] ASV, *GdF*, 269 (*Sentenze*, reg. 65), cc.86v–94r, 87r (19-11-1633).

intestate in Venice and without a direct heir,[74] once the potential heir/s had been found, a complete inventory of the estate should have been deposited in one of the *Corti di Palazzo*, most commonly the *Petizion*.[75] Since no trace of Simes' inventory is to be found in the splendidly indexed inventory series of the *Petizion* or in the *Proprio*,[76] we can assume that a direct heir must have been found in England.[77] What we do know is that John Hobson, Sr became the procurator for Simes' estate, and in this capacity he was sued in the *Forestier* by Anzolo Bonisello, who had been Simes' partner in deals between the Morea and Ragusa.[78]

In 1626, for the first time, some allowances were made permitting oil to be exported out of Venice, as part of the concessions granted that year to foreign merchants by the *Senato* to redirect trade through Venice.[79] Ten years later, in appreciation of the fact that the needs of the city were being met more than sufficiently, and bowing to *Ponentini* pressure, the Venetian authorities relented and allowed oil from Puglia to be exempt from exit customs if exported from Venice directly to either England or the Netherlands.[80] Throughout this time Flemish merchants were not directly involved in the oil trade, preferring instead to take advantage of English ships and shipments for their needs;[81] in any case they normally favoured Apulian oil.[82] In 1672 Alvise Morelli, whom we shall soon encounter as one of the largest exporters of Venetian glass to England, was granted some

[74] In this particular instance the case instead passed to the *Giudici del Proprio*, which had jurisdiction over these cases. Attempts to find Simes in the *Proprio* have brought no results so far.

[75] An identical procedure was used also in the circumstance when the heir was uncertain about whether to accept the inheritance or not, and a complete inventory had to be deposited with the *Petizion*. This is the procedure still known in contemporary Italian law as 'beneficio d'inventario'.

[76] The only inventory regarding an Englishman in the period analysed is that of Giles Jones' estate.

[77] Although attempts at finding his will in England have borne no fruit so far.

[78] ASV, *GdF*, 468 (*Risposte*, f. 2), c.389 (19-2-1637). In this transaction was also involved Samuel Vassal, whom we met in the previous chapter, of whom Hobson was also procurator. On Hobson having power of attorney for the Simes' estate, see ASV, *Notarile Atti*, reg. 658 (Francesco Beazian and Andrea Bronzini), *sextus*, cc.252v–253r (2-9-1643). In the latter there is direct reference of the election of Hobson Sr as procurator for Simes' estate in the acts of the London notary Gio Emans under the date of 14 July 1637.

[79] ASV, *Senato Mar*, reg. 84, cc.177v–182v (25-7-1626).

[80] This was a temporary measure, valid for two years: in ASV, *Senato Mar*, reg. 94, cc.148r–149r (2-8-1636).

[81] On the relatively minor importance of oil in the Venetian–Flemish trade see van Gelder, *Trading Places*, 84.

[82] For a typical contract of this kind, see ASV, *Notarile Atti*, reg. 6669 (Gabriel Gabrieli), cc.46v–48r (27-11-1646).

personal privileges towards the export of oil for England. Several Venetian merchants followed suit and asked for the same benefits, promising in return to import oil from Puglia.[83] Once again the *Senato* replied favourably to their demands.[84] In the meantime, though, English merchants had turned their interest to the producers, and during the last quarter of the seventeenth century they started to regularly obtain their supplies directly from Liguria and Puglia.[85] Ligurian oil enjoyed particular success because it provided a much-needed return cargo from Livorno, which had been a long-term concern for all foreign merchants based there.[86] Trade with Puglia intensified as well, and in the harbour town of Gallipoli a consulate was established to take specific care of the olive oil trade.[87]

Dried fish – *salumi*

Traditionally, dried fish (*salumi*) had been supplied to the Republic from the Aegean Sea and the Dalmatian coast, whose waters were rich in pilchards.[88] Unfortunately, those fisheries were drying up exactly at the same time that demand was rising thanks to the Council of Trent's reinforcement of the religious precept to avoid meat during Lent.[89] Since the beginning of the seventeenth century, Venice experienced serious problems in ensuring that supply kept up with demand,[90] notwithstanding the fact that, from 1591, English and Flemish ships loaded with *salumi* had been regularly reaching Venice.[91] The Flemish had long-standing expertise in the international trade in dried fish, which had been regulated in 1519 by Charles V with precise instructions to guarantee the quality of the product.[92] English fish ships

[83] The *parte* of the *Senato* granting Morelli these facilitations is dated 14-5-1672; the petitions of the other merchants are in ASV, *Collegio, Rdd*, f. 78, cc.n.n. (24-5-1672).
[84] Ciriacono, *Olio ed Ebrei*, 21.
[85] Ciriacono, *Olio ed Ebrei*, 32–34.
[86] Davis, *The Rise of the English Shipping Industry*, 244.
[87] Pagano De Divitiis, *English Merchants*, 71–72.
[88] ASV, *Cinque Savi alla Mercanzia*, b. 134 n.s., fasc. ii, iii, vi, vii, *passim*.
[89] M. Montanari, *The Culture of Food*, New York, 2003, 78–82, 114–115.
[90] ASV, *Giustizia Vecchia*, b. 23, cc.n.n. (28-2-1601). I wish to thank James Shaw for this reference.
[91] Worth noting that whilst in modern Italian this word related to preserved meats, in the early modern period John Florio defined *salame* or *salume* as 'any kinde of salt, pickled or poudred meats [...] both fish and flesh' (J. Florio, *A Worlde of Wordes, or most copious and exact Dictionarie in Italian and English*, London, 1598, 340) and in Venice it was used almost exclusively for fish.
[92] D. Kirby and M. L. Hinkkanen, *The Baltic and the North Sea*, London and New York, 2000, 168 and bibliography therein. On the technology behind Dutch superiority in the northern markets see R. Unger, 'Dutch Herring, Technology and International Trade in the Seventeenth Century', *Journal of Economic History*, 40 (1980): 253–280.

reached Venice mostly from English provincial ports,[93] where they stopped to load on their way to the Mediterranean. The importance of the fish trade to the Mediterranean was fully appreciated in England; one of the early proclamations of Elizabeth's reign was the confirmation of the prohibition to eat meat during Lent, and the Venetian ambassador in Spain at the time commented that this was due more to economic reasons – to support fisheries – than as a show of religious piety at a time when her religious stance was still unclear.[94] Throughout her reign, Elizabeth supported English fisheries, developing a strategy that saw them as essential 'nurseries for seamen', thus bolstering both local industry and the navy. In 1580 imports of foreign cured fish was forbidden so as to support local production.[95] Interestingly this trade was considered so important that export of dried fish was allowed in foreign bottoms.[96] A good example is the case of Yarmouth, which during the first decades of the seventeenth century, and until the beginning of the Anglo-Dutch war, was permitted to export its red herring on foreign ships, notwithstanding the constant protestation of the shipping lobby.[97]

As the seventeenth century advanced, so did the importance of Italy as a market for English dried fish, until the peninsula alone would absorb half total production of red herrings.[98] During the first half of the century, out of an annual production of around 70,000 barrels, 38,000 were absorbed by Italian ports: Livorno imported 13,000, Naples 7,500, Venice 5,700, Genoa 5,500 and Ancona 4,500.[99] It was a delicate trade, which needed to be handled carefully due to the perishable nature of the produce and the ease with which the market became glutted, which frequently happened in Livorno, where most of the English fish ships arrived.[100]

---

[93] Davis, *The Rise of the English Shipping Industry*, 244.

[94] The ambassador was Paolo Tiepolo: *CSPVe*, vol. vii (1558–1580): see http://www.british-history.ac.uk/report.aspx?compid=94938 (date accessed: 5 August 2012).

[95] This measure lasted until 1597, when the act was repealed as production could not keep up with demand: see J. Dyson, *Business in Great Waters: The Story of British Fishermen*, London, 1977, 41.

[96] *Transactions of Trinity House*, 509, c.81v (c.1631); and 511, cc.82v–83r (28-10-1631 and 4-11-1631).

[97] Davis, *The Rise of the English Shipping Industry*, 4.

[98] A synthesis of the English fish trade to Italy is in Pagano De Divitiis, *English Merchants*, 157–166.

[99] Sella, *Commerci e industrie a Venezia*, 75–79.

[100] A. R. Mitchell, 'The European Fisheries in Early Modern History', in E. E. Rich and C. H. Wilson eds., *The Cambridge Economic History of Europe*, vol. v: *The Economic Organization of Early Modern Europe*, Cambridge, 1977, 133–184, 178; Pagano De Divitiis, *English Merchants*, 162.

On the Venetian market, four varieties of northern fish were particularly popular: *renghe fumade* (smoked herring), *cospettoni* (salted/brined herring), *salamoni* (salted salmon) and *bacaladi* (salted cod).[101] Trade in dried fish since the beginning of the seventeenth century was controlled by of the *Arte dei Salumieri*, which felt threatened by the English. Concerns to keep the market well supplied, and especially protect popular items such as dried fish, led to consistent state intervention in managing *salumi* availability and controlling their price. At the end of the sixteenth century an attempt at liberalising the trade in fresh fish failed after a few years, and the reinstitution of the Fishmongers' Guild in 1605 followed the realisation that this was still the best way to manage the market and guarantee provisions at a controlled price.[102] There were substantial differences between fresh and preserved fish; the former arrived daily and was sold through wholesale auction to the retailers, whilst *salumi* arrived in large quantities on a more irregular basis, and, thanks to their longer shelf life, there was no urgency to sell. The solution to control *salumi*'s distribution, making sure that both the market was provisioned and that prices were controlled, had been to organise a 'guild-based system of *divisioni* (shares), where stocks were divided up evenly amongst retailers in order to prevent any one of them from cornering the market'.[103]

All English merchants in Venice were involved in the *salumi* trade, and unlike with other goods, no single merchant emerged as dominant. The fish trade was a truly communal enterprise throughout the seventeenth century, and only in the 1730s did a single firm appear to have dominated this market.[104]

In 1618 the English ambassador presented a petition to the *Collegio*, lamenting the frauds and irregularities committed by the *salumieri* against English merchants. The *Arte* was quick to reply that the fault lay with the Republic, for as soon as the market had started to expand with the arrival of the northerners, the state had increased the contributions of the *Arte*, forcing them, in turn, to charge more and to be tougher with importers.[105] This was the last petition concerning fish to be presented by English merchants alone: henceforth all petitions regarding *salumi* would be

---

[101] G. Marangoni, *Le associazioni di mestiere nella Repubblica Veneta (vittuaria, farmacia, medicina)*, Venice, 1974, 106–109.

[102] J. E. Shaw, 'Retail, Monopoly and Privilege: The Dissolution of the Fishmongers' Guild of Venice, 1599', *Journal of Early Modern History*, 6 (2002): 396–427.

[103] I am thankful to James Shaw for providing me with these details, and for the generosity with which he shared with me documentary evidence on this topic.

[104] It was the firm of William Smith and Co.: see ASV, *Arti*, b. 494, fasc. 17.

[105] ASV, *Giustizia Vecchia*, b. 25, cc.n.n. (the petition is dated 1618).

presented jointly by the English and the Flemish, and this trade became the great hinge of the Anglo-Flemish commercial alliance. In Venice the Flemish appeared involved on a slightly lesser scale than the English, but they had higher stakes in a little corner of the fish trade, the import of caviar, which had its largest market in Italy.[106]

This operational alliance is a most interesting example of the differences between the relationship of the two countries and that of their merchants in the Mediterranean. From the perspective of state political economy, the fishing trade was a major bone of contention between the two states, and Dutch predominance, especially their very efficient fishing fleet, was for the English a constant thorn in the side.[107] In Venetian territories the fish trade was instead a bedrock of the Anglo-Flemish alliance.

A breakthrough came in 1626, when the Republic relented under the pressure of the northerners and implemented a series of temporary measures to facilitate imports. Customs duties were halved and the sale of fish was partially freed from the constraints of the *Arte*, to whom English and Flemish merchants had been forced to leave half of their fish cargoes; now instead they had the freedom to sell their fish to whomever they wanted. Re-export of unsold fish was also allowed for the first time.[108] The Republic, growingly aware of the dangers presented by the rise of Livorno, and painfully conscious of its slipping forces in the Eastern Mediterranean, during 1626 implemented a long series of measures designed to increase the presence of foreign shipping in its harbour. The *Novissima Imposta* on currants, an additional tax on currants exported directly from the Ionian islands; an exemption of entrance duties for 'western wool'; and the halving of the anchorage duty for foreign ships were all new developments welcomed by English and Flemish merchants

---

[106] It is worth noting that caviar was then not a luxury produce as today, but it was affordable by the 'middling sort'. Italy alone consumed 97 per cent of Russian production. On the role played by the Muscovy Company in this trade, and on its commercial route via Livorno, see Pagano De Divitiis, *English Merchants*, 12, 27–28; and her 'Il Mediterraneo nel XVII secolo', 121. On the Flemish claim to be the most important importers of caviar, see ASV, *Collegio, Rdd,* f. 10, cc.n.n. (21-1-1597mv). On the Netherlandish dried fish trade see also van Gelder, *Trading Places*, 72, 74, 148–149.

[107] On this the literature is massive: for some classic examples see J. Keymors, *Observations made upon the Dutch Fishing about the year 1601*, London, 1664; H. Grotius, *The Works of Hugo Grotius on Fisheries in his controversy with William Welwod* [chapter 5 of *Mare Liberum*], Leiden, 1928; G. Malynes, *An Essay on the Fishing Trade*, Edinburgh, 1720 [chapter 47 of *Lex Mercatoria*].

[108] ASV, *Senato Mar*, reg. 84, cc.262v–263v (25-9-1626); another copy is in ASV, *Cinque Savi alla Mercanzia*, b. 134 n.s., fasc. viii, cc.n.n. (25-9-1626).

based in Venice.[109] They decided to take advantage of this change of
attitude to press home some other points and immediately petitioned the
Senato asking for further concessions. Their principal request was to be
able to sell fish without the obligatory presence of a representative of the
Arte. It was a sign of the Venetian awareness of the crisis that all their
demands were met and no opposition was raised by the *Cinque Savi*.[110]
These decisions were certainly successful in increasing the presence of
foreign traders in Venice. The scale of success is debatable, but the fact
that the situation improved is demonstrated by the repeated extensions
granted to these measures notwithstanding the repeated protests of the
Arte.[111] Every time they were close to expiring, the debate between the
Arte dei Salumieri and the English and Flemish merchants raged again,
and every time, the threat of moving all traffic to Livorno was used and
abused as a bargaining tool. But the measures were renewed, although the
Arte sometimes managed to recover some ground in regard to its position
as privileged buyer.[112] This tension between Northern merchants and the
salumieri guild persisted until the end of the seventeenth century.
Notwithstanding the grumbling about the 'state of the trade', and the
repeated threats to stop sending *salumi* to Venice, the English clearly
profited from the Venetian market. In the 1670s the volume of English
direct shipping to Venice was estimated at around seventeen to twenty
ships per annum, exporting English goods to the value of about £25,000–
30,000. The dried fish trade played a crucial role in terms of value: 'Five
or six fish ships, arriving in time for Lent with Yarmouth herrings and

[109] ASV, *Senato Mar*, reg. 84, cc.177v–182v (25-7-1626) on facilitating foreign ships;
cc.206v–207v (25-8-1626) on the *Nuovissima Imposta*; cc.223r/v (9-9-1626) on lowering anchorage duties for foreign ships; cc.326v (30-1-1626mv) on 'lane di Ponente'
exempt from entrance duties.

[110] The Anglo-Flemish petition is in ASV, *Collegio, Rdd*, f. 17, c.350 (5-10-1626); the
Cinque Savi opinion on the matter is in ASV, *Cinque Savi alla Mercanzia, Risposte*, reg.
147, cc.51r–53r; another copy is in ASV, *Cinque Savi alla Mercanzia*, b. 134 n.s., fasc.
viii, cc.n.n. (16-11-1626); the decision of the *Senato* to grant them their requests is in
ASV, *Senato Mar*, reg. 84, cc.304v–305v (21-11-1626).

[111] An extension of the *parte* regulating fish trade was asked for by English and Flemish
merchants: ASV, *Collegio, Rdd*, f. 19, cc.n.n. (24-10-1628). The *Salumieri* opposed
their petition, and the answer of the *Cinque Savi* to their counter-petition is in ASV,
Cinque Savi alla Mercanzia, Risposte, reg. 148, cc.94r–95v, another copy in ASV, *Cinque
Savi alla Mercanzia*, b. 134 n.s., fasc. viii, cc.n.n. (20-2-1629mv). The facilitations were
then extended for another five years: a copy is in ASV, *Cinque Savi alla Mercanzia*, b.
134 n.s., fasc. viii, cc.n.n. (16-1-1630mv).

[112] On these issues see ASV, *Collegio, Rdd*, f. 25, cc.n.n. (13-11-1634); ASV, *Cinque Savi
alla Mercanzia*, b. 134 n.s., fasc. viii, cc.n.n. (8-5-1637); ASV, *Collegio, Rdd*, f. 30, cc.n.
n. (9-8-1639); ASV, *Cinque Savi alla Mercanzia*, b. 134 n.s., fasc. viii, cc.n.n. (24-9-
1639); ASV, *Collegio, Rdd*, f. 47, cc.n.n. (25-10-1656); ASV, *Collegio, Rdd*, f. 59, cc.n.n.
(18-9-1662); ASV, *Cinque Savi alla Mercanzia*, b. 134 n.s., fasc. viii, cc.n.n. (30-8-
1670).

Cornish pilchards, accounted for over half the value. The rest, worth some £12,000, was made up of lead, sugar, pepper, woollen cloth and stockings'.[113]

Pietro Mocenigo, returning from his ambassadorship in England in 1671, did not mince words about the state of trade between the two countries. *Salumi* and currants were indeed the staples, but the former was hindered by high tariffs and restrictive legislation, to the point that the English sent to Venice only what could be consumed in the town itself. The *Terraferma*, like the whole of Lombardy, was by then provisioned directly from Livorno, where tariffs were substantially lower, and he argued that much needed to be done to counteract this situation. The trade of currants, thriving as it was, he also considered in danger, as he believed that local populations – and frequently also Venetian officials – did not apply the law, and he reckoned that merchants' patience would not last forever.[114] By the end of that century, the *salumi* trade in Venice was completely free from constraints by the *Arte dei Salumieri*, and the English had even won the privilege of loading their ships in Puglia.[115] The liberalisation of the dried fish trade was a true collective victory of English and Flemish merchants against the regulations of the Venetian market and its guilds.

Textiles

In an earlier chapter we sketched the damage inflicted on the Venetian textile industry by English competition, and even in the absence of any 'sustained and detailed body of inside information on the Levant trade in the seventeenth century',[116] and the scarcity of reliable and comparable quantitative sources, there is no doubt that English merchants played a crucial role in the decline of the woollen industry in Venice.[117] Compared to the Ottoman section of this trade, the volume and value of direct

---

[113] Roseveare ed., *Markets and Merchants*, 108.

[114] Mocenigo, 'Relazione d'Inghilterra (1671)', 939–940.

[115] These new concessions were specifically aimed at the English merchants: see ASV, *Cinque Savi alla Mercanzia*, b. 81 n.s., fasc. vi, cc.n.n. (20-2-1697). Two memorandums that recount the events of the dried fish trade, over the period of more than a century are in ASV, *Cinque Savi alla Mercanzia*, b. 81 n.s., fasc. v, memorandum of 1706 (particularly concerned with the connection between currants and fish as the staples of Anglo-Venetian trade); and ASV, *Cinque Savi alla Mercanzia*, b. 134 n.s., fasc. iv, cc.n.n. (3-9-1714).

[116] Davis, *Aleppo and Devonshire Square*, 241.

[117] Sella, 'The Rise and Fall of the Venetian Woollen Industry', 106–126; Panciera, *L'arte matrice*. What quantitative data exists has been published by Sella; see also his *Commercio e industrie a Venezia*.

exchange between Venice and England in this period is small, which is hardly surprising given that both countries were strong producers in this field. English textiles had almost no market in Venice, a very small one in the Ionian islands, and a potentially very large one in the Ottoman Morea. Their presence in the archives mirrors exactly these patterns of distribution. In the late sixteenth century large consignments of Morea currants exchanged for textiles, for example, were easier to organise from Venice than from the Ionian islands. Currants from the Greek mainland were inferior in quality to the Ionian ones, but they could be paid for with textiles, as opposed to the bullion that the islanders demanded for their higher-quality crops.[118] Throughout the period under investigation, English merchants tried repeatedly to pay for currants with textiles also in the islands, since this would have ended up being cheaper and would have silenced critics at home who complained about the bullion spent to acquire currants. They managed to do so only on very few occasions, especially in the early phase of their presence, when extremely large consignments of goods were arranged well in advance. Those deals normally involved a second phase in which their Greek counterparts would dispose of the textiles in the Ottoman territories, normally with help from Greek Jewish traders who controlled these markets.[119] Once the English presence was solidly established in the Ottoman empire and in Ragusa, these deals disappear from the documentation, and the currant trade in Zante and Cephalonia was paid for in bullion or with grain.

Examples of English textiles sold in Venice are few and far between.[120] There are more frequent examples of luxury Venetian textiles being sold to English merchants. The Hickman brothers seemed to be the only English merchants who regularly bought high-quality Venetian textiles, even establishing direct relationships with cloth-makers.[121] All other purchases, at both ends of the chronological spectrum, seem to have

[118] Issues discussed in Fusaro, *Uva passa*.
[119] For some typical deals, see: ASV, *Notarile Atti*, reg. 11982 (Gerolamo Savina), cc.70v–71v (1-3-1582); reg. 8319 (Francesco Mondo), cc.365v–367r (20-8-1582); reg. 7852 (Gerolamo Luran), cc.535r–536v (23-9-1583); reg. 6531 (Luca and Giulio Gabrieli), cc.181r/v (28-5-1584). An analysis of the role played by Jewish merchants in these trades between the islands and the Ottoman Morea is in ASV, *Cinque Savi alla Mercanzia, Risposte*, reg. 150, cc.186r–189r (10-9-1636).
[120] The largest consignment of English textiles to Venice was that at the root of the trial between the English merchant Francesco Lantburiò and Gasparo De' Cerchieri. Cerchieri had not paid the 839 ducats due for the English textiles that Lantburiò had sold him. They were 'pezze 5 di panni di Londra et 29 di carisee ordinarie e 10 carisee fine bianche e 1 carisea fine nera'. The trial took place in 1582 and is in ASV, *AdC, Civile*, b. 273, fasc. 9.
[121] ASV, *Notarile Atti*, reg. 11919 (Andrea Spinelli), cc.338v–339r (28-5-1598).

been of an occasional nature, and none developed into long-term business relationships. Paul Pindar, for example, commissioned the production of some high-quality black silks, a fabric particularly coveted due to the quality and steadfastness of its colour,[122] whilst Joseph Kent ordered a consignment of extremely expensive 'Crimson velvets with green and white ribbons'.[123] Meanwhile, George Hayles and John Ravenscroft were instructed to procure in Venice some gold brocade as a special gift for the sultan.[124] Unlike the Flemish and Germans,[125] the English were not involved in the trade of Syrian silks in Venice, since their supply went straight from Syria to England.

There are traces of consignments of silks from Vicenza being sent to England by an English–Flemish consortium. This trade used land routes through Germany until the Thirty Years' War blocked them.[126] Some of these silks were also purchased by English merchants through their Italian associates active at the Bolzano fairs at the beginning of the seventeenth century.[127]

Glass

From the fifteenth century England had produced its own basic window glass and green drinking glasses. They initially were of poor quality, though they had slowly started to improve during the sixteenth century when immigrants from the Low Countries and Venice brought improved techniques.[128] The first patent to produce glass in England had been granted in 1552 to Henry Smyth, and in 1567 the making of window glass was also patented.[129] The English glass industry may have been growing, but the undisputed centre of European high-quality glassmaking was the island of Murano, in the Venetian lagoon. During the sixteenth century, Venetian glass enjoyed great success; new techniques were developed, new markets opened, and the production of mirrors greatly increased, especially after a patent for their production had been

---

[122] ASV, *Notarile Atti*, reg. 12534 (Giovanni Battista Tomasi), cc.n.n. (16-1-1597). On the superior quality of Venetian 'black', see R. Berveglieri, 'Cosmo Scatini e il nero di Venezia', *Quaderni Storici*, 52 (1983): 167–179.

[123] ASV, *Collegio, Rdd*, f. 42, cc.n.n. (1-12-1651).

[124] Pagano De Divitiis, 'Il porto di Livorno', 53, 81 footnote 67.

[125] ASV, *Collegio, Rdd*, f. 79, cc.n.n. (22-11-1672).

[126] ASV, *Collegio, Rdd*, f. 18, cc.n.n. (16-2-1627mv).

[127] See F. M. Vianello, *Seta fine e panni grossi: manifatture e commerci nel Vicentino, 1570–1700*, Milan, 2004.

[128] W. H. Price, *The English Patents of Monopoly*, Boston and New York, 1906, 67; I. Scouloudi, 'Alien Immigration into and Alien Communities in London, 1558–1640', *Proceedings of the Huguenot Society of London*, 16 (1937–1941): 27–49, 39.

[129] Thirsk, *Economic Policy and Projects*, 33–34, 56, 52.

granted in 1507.[130] Murano was a virtual fortress, isolated in the lagoon to avoid the spread of fires, which had been the primary reason for moving glass production there. Though emigration of its specialised workforce was strictly forbidden and harshly punished, it was a favourite option in moments of crisis and contributed to the spread of technical knowledge throughout Europe. The policy of the Republic included an odd mix of punishment for people leaving, and incentives to entice glassmakers back to Murano; this mix, of course, did nothing to stop emigration, as run-away glass workers knew very well that coming back was always an option.[131]

In England amongst the most coveted glass products were drinking glasses known as *façon de Venise*. In 1549 eight Murano glassmakers had come to London to set up a drinking-glass factory specialising in their production, but this experiment lasted only two years. Towards the end of the century another Muranese glassmaker, the Protestant émigré Jacopo Verzelini, managed to obtain a monopoly for the production of drinking glasses;[132] this enterprise was more successful, and from 1574 to 1592 entries for drinking glasses in the London port books almost disappear. Due to his monopoly, only a few noblemen and other persons of importance were allowed by special licence to bring back glasses for their own households.[133] Since Verzelini's patent there had been a succession of monopolies in glass production, but no technical improvement to the industry had resulted from them for two main reasons: there were problems in procuring quality raw materials, and the local production never reached the volume necessary to achieve better results.[134] Thus top-quality glass continued to be imported from Venice, and its superior quality continued to be widely recognised. Even when, in the first quarter of the seventeenth century, Robert Mansell was granted a monopoly on the production of drinking glasses – which amongst its privileges included the prohibition of imports of drinking glasses – Venetian products were still allowed in the country.[135] Until the middle of the seventeenth

---

[130] Knapton, 'Tra Dominante e Dominio', 305; also Sella, *Commerci e industrie a Venezia*, 84.

[131] Trivellato, *Fondamenta dei vetrai*, 36–37.

[132] See *DNB*, s.v. Jacopo Verzelini.

[133] E. S. Godfrey, *The Development of English Glassmaking, 1560–1640*, Oxford, 1976, 8, 16, 29–31. The habit of diplomats and nobles to send Venetian glasses to England would continue into the next century: see Pearsall Smith, *The Life and Letters*, ii: 119.

[134] Price, *The English Patents*, 74; D. W. Crossley, 'The Performance of the Glass-Industry in Sixteenth Century England', *Economic History Review*, 25 (1972): 421–433, 432.

[135] Price, *The English Patents*, 77; D. Howarth, 'Merchants and Diplomats: New Patrons of the Decorative Arts in Seventeenth Century England', *Furniture History*, 20 (1984): 10–17, 11.

century, glasses were imported into England erratically and in small quantities. On the other hand, trade in mirrors was brisk, but this is more difficult to follow because it was dispersed within larger cargoes.[136] Most English merchants trading in Venice ended up sending small consignments of glasses and mirrors home, but no one was specialised in this particular trade.[137] A completely different situation emerged in the second half of the seventeenth century when the Anglo-Venetian glass trade was dominated by Alvise Morelli and George Ravenscroft, two figures frequently working in partnership.

Morelli built his family's fortune on trading with England. In 1662 he left Murano, where his family owned a glass furnace, and moved to Venice. There he married the daughter of a prominent Flemish merchant and started to devote himself full-time to commerce, also investing in ships.[138] Morelli built strong contacts with English merchants resident in Zante from 1659, and from this basis he expanded his vast network.[139] He owned four ships, which he used to trade with the Ionian islands, sometimes in partnership with English merchants. He ended up establishing his own agency in Zante, which was run by Guglielmo Wolffenden, the only example of a young English merchant formally apprenticed to a Venetian that has emerged from the Venetian archives.[140] Zante became crucial to Morelli's commercial interests, and his dealings there further fostered his alliance with the local English mercantile community until the beginning of the eighteenth century.[141] From 1662 until 1686 his business expanded in such a way that in 1686 he could afford to pay the

---

[136] An exception to this pattern seemed to be captain Thomas Day of the *Leone*: see ASV, *Notarile Atti*, reg. 6698 (Gabriel Gabrieli), cc.184r–186v, cc.186v–188r and cc.188v–192r (4-7-1659). The trade in mirror plates would dwindle in the 1670s, when a diminution in the English and French demand of Venetian mirrors led also to a stop in the admission of apprentices to this particular form of glassmaking: see Trivellato, *Fondamenta dei vetrai*, 164. By this time the quality of English mirror plate had also improved: MacLeod, *Inventing the Industrial Revolution*, 26.

[137] For example, William Garway and Thomas Cordel received consignments of mirrors from Venice: see Brulez and Devos, *Marchands Flamands*, i: n.687, 228–229 (14-10-1596). Lawrence Hider also traded frequently with the glassmaker Gasparo Berton, owner of the 'Lionfante' furnace: in ASV, *AdC, Penale*, b. 285, fasc. 26, cc.n.n. (17-10-1628).

[138] 'Susana daughter of Tomaso Piscilla of the parish of Santa Maria Nova': L. Zecchin, *Vetro e vetrai di Murano*, 3 vols, Venice, 1990, iii: 67–71.

[139] ASV, *Notarile Atti*, reg. 6699 (Gabriel Gabrieli), cc.39r–40v (9-8-1659).

[140] In 1689 the young English merchant Guglielmo Wolffenden was sent there for five years to complete his apprenticeship: see ASV, *Notarile Atti*, reg. 7043 (Carlo Gabrieli and Andrea Piccini), cc.273v–275r (12-8-1687).

[141] The Morelli's commercial house in Zante is also mentioned in the will of Clemente Harby, consul for Zante and the Morea at the end of the 1680s: see ASV, *NT*, b. 92 (Valerio Bonis), n.66 (28-10-1689).

prescribed sum of 100,000 ducats and buy his way into the Venetian patriciate, the only glassmaker to ever achieve this.[142] This change of status did not end Morelli's active participation in business: at the beginning of the eighteenth century he was the only Venetian amongst the English subscribers of a petition to the *Collegio* demanding greater freedom of trade.[143]

Throughout the 1660s and the 1670s Morelli was an important liaison between Venetian and English merchants in Venice, frequently representing English interests in front of the Venetian magistrates. In 1672, for example, he mediated between the *Collegio* and a group of ship-captains over pilotage duties in the Lagoon, an issue which had been festering for a long time.[144] So crucial was his role within the English mercantile community that in 1668 his name was put forward as a possible consul for the English nation. The project was never realised, as having a Dutch wife proved to be a political hindrance, but he continued to enjoy a high level of trust.[145] Throughout this period Morelli had been dealing with the London glass merchant John Greene,[146] and with the Worshipful Company of Glass Sellers in London. Their partnership left a trail of extremely helpful documents for understanding English taste in glassware at the end of the seventeenth century. Greene sent Morelli several detailed drawings of glasses with his commissions so that the Venetian imports would be more suited to English tastes whilst maintaining that distinct stylistic flair which would make them easily recognisable and marketable as 'Venetian'.[147]

This attention to 'branding' was becoming increasingly important. In those years English glass production was on the rise, meaning that imported goods faced stiffer competition and therefore needed to develop a distinct identity to remain in demand. The style of these commissioned glasses was therefore quite relevant. Venetian glasses had strong social and performative value as aspirational objects which conferred on the

---

[142] E. Cicogna, *Delle iscrizioni veneziane*, 7 vols, Bologna, 1969–1970 (1824–1853), vi: 464. Alvise and his brother Bartolomeo had been certified *cittadini originari* only fifteen years before, in 1671: Zannini, *Burocrazia e burocrati*, 288 footnote. On the Morelli being the only family of glass-makers to be elevated to patriciate see Trivellato, *Fondamenta dei vetrai*, 94, 97–100.

[143] ASV, *Cinque Savi alla Mercanzia*, b. 81 n.s., fasc. viii, cc.n.n. (not dated, the *fascicolo* contains material from 1702–1705).

[144] ASV, *Collegio, Rdd*, f. 78, cc.n.n. (29-3-1672).

[145] Pagano De Divitiis, *English Merchants*, 72–73.

[146] For a typical consignment, see *LMA*, CLC/270/MS00366/008 (1677): this one was for five chests of drinking glasses.

[147] These drawings are in BL, *Sloane 857, passim*.

owner both taste and discernment.[148] However, the models most sought after by the English market would have been considered antiquated by contemporary Venetian and continental taste, and this created some problems in finding the right furnace to manufacture them in Murano.[149] This was one of the reasons behind the slow decrease in the trade volume. Venetian glasses, when produced exclusively for export into England, ended up being too expensive, and this coupled with the growing technical development of local glassmakers slowly priced the Venetians out of the expanding English middling market.

George Ravenscroft was the second son of a Hertfordshire Catholic gentleman whose fortunes had been severely damaged in the civil wars due to his royalist sympathies.[150] From the mid-1650s Ravenscroft was in Venice trading in partnership with his brothers John and Francis,[151] and specialising in the export of mirror plates to England.[152] However, his trade interests were by no means limited to glass, and we find him involved in all the traditional merchandise of the Anglo-Venetian trade: currants[153] woollens,[154] lead,[155] textiles[156] and dried fish.[157] He was also an investor in the *Banco Giro*, and with some German and Flemish

---

[148] W. Harrison, *The Description of England: The Classic Contemporary Account of Tudor Social Life by WH*, G. Edelen ed., Mineola, 1994, 127–128.

[149] On the issue of English taste in drinking glasses, see W. Ramsey, *The Worshipful Company of Glass-Sellers of London*, London, 1898, 59–77; Trivellato, *Fondamenta dei vetrai*, 237; H. Tait, *The Golden Age of Venetian Glass*, London, 1979, 96; A. Gasparetto, 'Le relazioni fra Venezia e l'Inghilterra nei secoli XVI e XVII e la loro influenza sulle forme vetrarie inglesi', *Vetro e silicati*, 16 (1970): 16–20.

[150] On George Ravenscroft's life see: R. Rendel, 'Who was George Ravenscroft?', *The Glass Circle*, 2 (1975): 65–70; and her 'The True Identity of George Ravenscroft, Glassman', *Recusant History*, 13 (1975): 101–105, 102; C. MacLeod, 'Accident or Design? George Ravenscroft's Patent and the Invention of Lead-Crystal Glass', *Technology and Culture*, 28 (1987): 776–803.

[151] ASV, *Notarile Atti*, reg. 6698 (Gabriel Gabrieli), cc.95r–96r (8-4-1659); cc.192r–193r (10-7-1659); reg. 6699 (Gabriel Gabrieli), cc.28v–30r (1-8-1659). It is worth noting that in Venetian documentation he appears as 'Ravenscraft'.

[152] Grassby, *The Business Community*, 160.

[153] ASV, *GdF*, 508 (*Domande in causa*, f. 21), c.40 (23-3-1665) and c.304 (31-8-1665).

[154] ASV, *GdF*, 507 (*Domande in causa*, f. 20), c.83 (8-7-1664).

[155] ASV, *GdF*, 478 (*Multorum*, f. 3), c.446 (22-2-1669).

[156] He was involved in a long dispute with the Venetian trader Gio Bovis over large consignments of *zambellotti*: in ASV, *GdF*, 473 (*Risposte*, f. 7), c.349 (28-7-1661); ASV, *GdF*, 504 (*Domande in causa*, f. 17), c.305 (23-7-1661), c.358 (13-8-1661) and c.434 (13-9-1661). *Zambellotti* originally were Anatolian woollen textiles made of camel or goat hair; by this period the term had also come to describe textiles of silk and wool: see Vitali, *La moda a Venezia*, 109–111.

[157] ASV, *GdF*, 498 (*Domande in causa*, f. 11), c.479 (17-2-1655mv); f. 12, c.528 (12-1-1656mv) and c.532 (14-1-1656). ASV, *GdF*, 472 (*Risposte*, f. 6), c.104 (10-1-1656mv). See also ASV, *Notarile Atti*, reg. 6698 (Gabriel Gabrieli), cc.28r/v (7-2-1658).

merchants he suffered heavy losses at the hands of two disgraced officers of the *Banco*.[158] He was also a long-standing business associate of the French merchant Giustino Dorat, whose bankruptcy in 1668 was a hard blow for many foreign merchants active in Venice.[159] Furthermore Ravenscroft kept close business contracts with Livorno,[160] where – jointly with Morelli – he frequently dealt with the glassmaker Domenico Cittadini. The latter was a runaway glassmaker from Murano who, between 1657 and 1660, kept a very profitable production of mirrors and *conterie* in Livorno, doing brisk trade with local English and Flemish merchants, always keen for return cargoes. Cittadini was a classic case of the return immigration to Murano, as in 1660 he went back and opened a furnace in partnership with another glassmaker for the production of the same kind of products he had perfected in Tuscany.[161]

Ravenscroft's name is mostly connected with his having patented lead crystal on his return to England in 1674, a real turning point for English glassmaking. The traditional version of the story is that, after several attempts at producing 'crystalline'[162] glasses very similar to those produced in Venice, all his attempts – and therefore his reputation – were being damaged by crizzling, which meant that the glasses did not remain transparent but, with time, became opaque due to tiny cracks. After several experiments in 1676, lead was added to the mixture and the result was lead crystal (also referred to as flint glass).[163] It has since been proved that this story is apocryphal. Since Ravenscroft was not a glassmaker himself, he probably simply used recipes he had gathered in Italy, which his workmen adapted to local materials, achieving a new result.[164] Still, this patent was a breakthrough, and back in England he used his monopoly to set up two furnaces that supplied the Worshipful Company of Glass Sellers with 'fine christaline glasses in resemblance of Cristoll for

[158] ASV, *Collegio, Rdd*, f. 62, cc.n.n. (11-6-1664); and f. 65, cc.n.n. (28-9-1665).
[159] ASV, *GdF*, 501 (*Domande in causa*, f. 14), c.239 (1-8-1668). This *filza* is dominated by the aftermath of Dorat's bankruptcy. On Ravenscroft's business with Dorat, see also ASV, *GdF*, 473 (*Risposte*, f. 7), c.52 (12-8-1659) and c.78 (28-7-1661).
[160] ASV, *Notarile Atti*, reg. 1176 (Cristoforo Brombilla), cc.216v–217v (13-7-1674).
[161] Trivellato, *Fondamenta dei vetrai*, 38. See also ASV, *Notarile Atti*, reg. 6698 (Gabriel Gabrieli), cc.65v–66v (12-3-1659). I wish to thank Francesca Trivellato for providing me with further biographical information on Cittadini.
[162] 'Such glass was historically known as "crystal" from its similarity to natural quartz crystal, and so was called, whatever its chemical composition, as opposed to the modern use of the word to apply to high-quality glass with a certain lead-content.' The most coveted of these semi-transparent products were produced in Venice, which being very thin and ductile allowed for very elaborate shapes. See Godfrey, *The Development of English Glassmaking*, 3, 7.
[163] R. C. Allen, *The British Industrial Revolution in Global Perspective*, Cambridge, 2009, 253.
[164] On the technical side of the patent on lead crystal, see MacLeod, 'Accident or Design?', 776–803; and Trivellato, *Fondamenta dei vetrai*, 196.

Figure 4. Ravenscroft's bowl *façon de Venise* (© Trustees of the Victoria and Albert Museum)

beere [and] wines'.[165] Many examples have survived of this new and improved product (Figure 4), which is easy to recognise as part of his own output; Ravenscroft, to distinguish this new glass from his previous production, developed a signature comparable with modern branding: a seal with a raven's head.[166]

Ravenscroft was unique amongst his generation of English merchants active in Venice not only in being a successful entrepreneur but also in putting his Italian experience – manufacturing know-how and capital acquired – to excellent use on his return home.

The market of another Venetian glass product – *conterie* – was cornered by a business associate of Ravenscroft's, who deserves mention here as the only German who had consistent business links with the English: Martin Piers, the largest importer of glass beads into England and the Levant.[167]

---

[165] *LMA*, CLC/L/GC/E/001/MS05556/1, cc.n.n. (5-9-1674) and (29-5-1677).

[166] R. Liefkes, *Glass*, London, 1997, 88; R. Dodsworth, *Glass and Glassmaking*, Haverfordwest, 1982, 10.

[167] ASV, *Notarile Atti*, reg. 6699 (Gabriel Gabrieli), cc.22v–24r (31-7-1659). ASV, *AdC, Penale*, b. 146, fasc. 5 (1665).

The fortunes of Venetian glass in England well embody the relative destiny of the two places. Murano glass was initially a coveted and desirable luxury import to satisfy the sophisticated tastes of the nobility. William Harrison, in the 1580s, could write that amongst the English upper classes 'only the clearest glass is most esteemed'.[168] But he also expressed that traditional condemnation of the wastefulness of spending money on an expensive foreign object whose intrinsic nature was utterly fragile and ephemeral; another foreign frippery along the lines of those silks and marmusets discussed in the *Libelle* a century and a half earlier. Still, through emulation – and possibly industrial espionage – crystal glass started being produced in England, adding to the woes of Venetian manufacture. By the 1670s, the English glass industry, stimulated also by the Venetian ban on the export of unfinished glass plates, was producing glass which was starting to be comparable (at least in appearance if not in actual quality) to Venetian products, and this worried the Venetian ambassador in London.[169] Around the end of the seventeenth century, potash crystal of high quality was also beginning to be produced in Bohemia, and this put the Venetian glass industry in a critical situation which for a few decades depressed its international demand. However, glass proved a lot more resilient than other sectors of Venetian manufacture. Technological development never stopped in Murano, and by the 1730s the new variety of crystal glass developed by Giuseppe Briati allowed for new styles, re-establishing the primacy of Venetian glass at least in the upper echelons of the European market.[170] Inferior products catering for the lower market sector survived the crisis too; there was, additionally, some reconversion from the production of large mirrors, where French competition was proving hard to beat, to that of medium- to small-sized plates, where Venetian production proved rather successful. And then there was the eighteenth-century boom of *conterie* – those small glass beads which were the currency of the slave trade.[171]

The most important goods exchanged between Venice and England can thus be divided into three categories. Currants and olive oil were colonial goods, classic examples of raw materials exported out of the Mediterranean in exchange for finished goods, thus exemplifying well that commercial revolution which Thomas Mun argued happened between the sixteenth

[168] Harrison, *The Description of England*, 199.
[169] MacLeod, *Inventing the Industrial Revolution*, 26.
[170] Tait, *The Golden Age*, 96.
[171] Trivellato, 'Murano Glass'; and her 'Guilds, Technology and Economic Change in Early Modern Venice', in S. R. Epstein and M. Prak eds., *Guilds, Innovation, and the European Economy, 1400–1800*, Cambridge, 2008, 199–231.

and the seventeenth centuries, inverting the roles of Northern and Southern European countries: Mediterranean economies went from being sellers of Asian products and their own manufactures to being raw-material producers for Northern European markets.[172] Currants and olive oil were mostly produced for export, and the relative size (and variety) of their markets had an important weight in the different ways in which these contributed to the local economies of their places of production.

Grain and dried fish were traditional European staples: grain from time immemorial; dried and preserved fish increasingly in these centuries. Their market was regulated by governments throughout Europe, given their role as staple of early modern diet and governmental concerns with keeping markets well supplied, always a good insurance against social disturbances.

Textiles and glass stand somewhat apart, presenting interesting parallels in their structural challenges, including market distribution, taste and fashion, and resistance to foreign competition. Technological innovation played a crucial role in the resilience of Venetian glass production, and specialisation in the top layer of the market was the necessary choice for survival. The Venetian textile industry tried the same solution, with less success, but it certainly laid the basis of its nineteenth- and twentieth-century descendant, which transformed the Veneto into a powerhouse of high-quality textile production.

---

[172] T. Mun, *A Discourse of Trade, from England unto the East-Indies*, London, 1621, 39–40.

11 Empires and governance in the Mediterranean

Analysing the early modern economic and social structure of the *Dominio da Mar* allows us to deal with two separate but inter-related issues: the beginning of the crisis of Venice and the modalities of the English penetration in the Mediterranean. Developments in the Levant (such as the Ottoman advance) or connected with it (such as the reorientation of the spice trade in the central decades of the sixteenth century) were crucial elements in the onset of the crisis which enveloped Venice and its economy in this period. The arrival of the English in the Ionian islands might have been just a commercial move for the Levant Company, the most efficient way to organise the currant trade to satisfy the insatiable demand of the English market. However, this had profound consequences for all involved. For the local population it was a catalyst for economic and social change, setting into motion a series of events which contributed to the financial difficulties of Venice. It was also the real beginning of an active British presence in the Eastern Mediterranean, which was to have important long-term repercussions for European and world history.

Histories of the British empire in the Mediterranean usually start with the late eighteenth century, but it is my contention that investigating the earlier phase of the English presence is essential for correctly analysing the roots of the complex relationship between Britain and the Greeks.[1] In this pre-colonialist phase the position of the English in the Ionian islands shifted from a purely commercial presence in the late sixteenth century, to their becoming informal political players in the islands – exemplified by their role in the 1628 revolt in Zante. The islands' growing economic dependence from the English market and commercial system is what ultimately led to the self-devolution of Zante and Cephalonia to England in 1809. For these reasons the interaction between Venice, England and the Ionian islands went far beyond the immediate effects

---

[1] P. J. Marshall ed., *The Oxford History of the British Empire*, vol. ii: *The Eighteenth Century*, Oxford, 1998.

on local trade networks, Venetian colonial administration and the socio-economic development of the local population. Studying this triple inter-action is essential if we want to arrive at a proper understanding of the more recent history of the Eastern Mediterranean.

As frequently happens in these cases, currants were both the wealth and the curse of Zante and Cephalonia and became the major determinants of their history. Few products better embody all the issues central to the political economy of empires: it was a cash crop and the growing English demand transformed the islands into a quasi-monoculture. Land owner-ship was fragmented, so at the beginning the profits were relatively well spread out amongst the population. However, the increase in the volume of trade required the growth of credit structures to support production, and this benefitted a restricted group of people to the detriment of all others, making small landowners dependent on the local elite who could provide credit.[2] All these issues are so tightly intertwined that it is difficult to deal with one without addressing the others; all played a crucial role in the administration of these territories, and the Venetian government, notwithstanding its efforts, never managed to solve them. There was the problem of territorial control, made difficult by the geographical structure of the islands, with rough mountainous terrain and few inland roads, and many coves and caves on the coast. And there were the financial interests of the local population, which increasingly became opposed to those of the Venetian administration, creating a deadly mix that hampered the activities of the local *Rettori*. The revenue from the cultivation of currants required personnel to keep the books in order and money coming in, but it became almost impossible to find capable and honest bookkeepers. Instead, the injection of cash in the local economy fostered a culture of greed that proved extremely detrimental to a proper administration. Widespread dishonesty would increasingly characterise the local financial administration until the fall of the Republic. Antonio da Ponte, *Provveditore Generale Inquisitore delle Tre Isole del Levante*, said this quite clearly when he commented on Zante's situation in 1623:

this Island needs restraint, as here the only thing that rules is self-interest and greed; public representatives are not respected, public money is seized for private profit and these subjects know neither charity nor justice.[3]

---

[2] On *prosticchi*, the local credit mechanism, see Fusaro, *Uva passa*, 59–60, 91–93 and bibliography quoted therein.

[3] ASV, *PTM*, b. 1151, cc.n.n. (18-6-1623). On the temporary successes obtained by the Republic by sending extraordinary magistrates like da Ponte to supervise things, see Knapton, 'Tra Dominante e Dominio', 340, 376. On the same issues see also the considerations of the *Inquisitore e Commissario in Levante* Antonio Civran in ASV, *PTM*,

The quantity of currant production itself remained a mystery to the Venetian government, as it proved impossible to survey the land devoted to its production.[4] Determined to continue growing currants against the wishes of their Venetian overlords, the locals effectively sabotaged any survey attempts. The difficulties of the Venetian government to control these territories ultimately made it really hard to administer them effectively. Governing would have been made easier by cooperating with the local inhabitants, especially taking into account their economic interests. However, Venice remained blind to their needs, and because of this the economies of Zante and Cephalonia grew dependent on the English market. And this happened despite the strong political, cultural and moral presence of Venice in the islands over the *longue durée*, something to which we shall have occasion to return.

To understand the importance of the *Dominio da Mar* at this particular juncture it helps to invert the traditional point of view which sees Venice as the centre of all events and decisions. Most of the deliberations taken in Venice in the early modern period concerning trade and economic policy were reactions to events in the Eastern Mediterranean. Much has been said about the inability of the Venetian ruling class to go beyond an image, and therefore a policy, of Venice as an entrepôt whose success was based on the redistribution of goods and products, either produced in its empire or traded by the Venetian mercantile network. Seen from the viewpoint of the history of the Ionian islands, and from English and Greek documentary sources, what is most striking is neither the policy itself, nor the determination with which it was pursued by the Venetian government despite continuous setbacks. What catches the attention is instead the purely reactive attitude of Venice in regard to her maritime empire and the events unfolding therein. Venetian administrative bodies had always been extremely sensitive to external economic stimuli, especially when they came from the Levant territories, as Venice was militarily and financially dependent upon them. But, whilst in earlier periods there had been serious attempts to define policies before crises struck, during the sixteenth and seventeenth centuries all the decisions were taken on a reactive basis, as if there were no real strategy. Conversely, the Greek subjects of Venice were always proactive in finding ways to cope with incoming crises, but their proposals were nearly always dismissed by the Senate even when they had the support of other

b. 863bis, cc.n.n. (28-5-1628). On problems with the personnel of the local exchequers, see Fusaro, *Uva passa*, 142–144.

[4] ASV, *Cinque Savi alla Mercanzia, Risposte*, reg. 146, cc.121r–123r; Fusaro, *Uva passa*, for the 'currant census' see 130–138 and the table at page 104.

governmental agencies like the *Cinque Savi alla Mercanzia* or the *Rettori* of the islands. After the fall of Cyprus, it would appear, the issue of defence left no room for any other consideration in Venice's policy towards her Levant dominions.[5]

The Ionian islands represent an ideal case study regarding the administration and financial policy of Venice with respect to its empire because of their long mutual association with the Republic until its collapse in 1797. It is true that the only extant complete budget for the islands is the one of 1756,[6] but even from the scattered information for the previous centuries it is possible to draw some conclusions about the relative importance of the islands in the general economy of the Republic. The islands continued to make a substantial financial contribution even after the fall of Cyprus, certainly until the end of the war of Candia, which completely changed the role of Venice in the Eastern Mediterranean and definitively shrank the Republic's horizons.[7]

From the last quarter of the sixteenth century the real centres of the English presence in the Venetian territories were Zante and Cephalonia. Mercantile colonies normally situated themselves at the centre of the system they were trying to penetrate – that is to say, in the major city.[8] In this case, however, we are faced with a different situation: the English presence was crucial at the periphery – in the islands – and less important at the centre – in Venice. We have seen that Venice maintained an important role for English merchants and also for trade with Ragusa and the Balkans. The reason why the islands were the real focus of interest for English merchants was currants – by far the most important commodity of the bilateral trade. Venice played a role in the currant trade because the islands were ruled by the Republic, and from the *Dominante* it was possible to effectively provide the financial and political support needed

---

[5] On this in reference to Candia see: A. Papadia-Lala, 'Soldati mercenari stranieri e vita urbana nella città di Candia veneziana (secoli XVI–XVII)', *Thesaurismata*, 29 (1999): 273–285, 284; on defending the maritime empire see also Arbel, 'Venice's Maritime Empire', 198–213.

[6] A. M. Andréadès, 'L'administration financière et économique de Venise dans ses possessions du Levant', *L'Acropole*, 1 (1926): 13–25, 14. See also his Οἰκονομικαι μελεται περι Ἑπτανησου: Περι της οἰκονομικης διοικησεως της Ἑπτανησου ἐπι Βενετοκρατιας *(Studies on the Economy of the Eptanese: On the Financial Administration of the Ionian Islands under Venetian Domination)*, 2 vols., Athens, 1914.

[7] For figures on the relative importance of currants for the income of the Republic (1580–1645) see Fusaro, *Uva passa*, Venice, 132, 135. Benjamin Arbel wrote that once Cyprus was lost the *Stato da Mar* became 'marginal' ('Colonie d'Oltremare', 980); recently he revised his opinion and now argues that even after 1571 Levantine possessions played a positive role in the Republic's economy ('Venice's Maritime Empire', 217–220).

[8] Curtin, *Cross-Cultural Trade*, 2–3.

by the English for their operations. English merchants frequently moved between Venice and the islands, and a stream of legal deeds and ships English, Venetian and Greek – connected Venice with Zante and Cephalonia. Only by understanding the centrality of the islands for the English can we fully appreciate how closely intertwined the social and economic developments of the islands were with their presence. The history of the English presence in Zante and Cephalonia is the history of a lost opportunity for Venetian economic growth and financial improvement. The Republic failed to properly incorporate the islands into its own economic system, whilst it attempted this in the *Terraferma* with some success. In the Levant, instead, it proved impossible for Venice to coordinate a prolonged defensive effort in these strategically essential territories whilst, at the same time, investing and operating directly for the benefit of the local population by increasing the productivity of the area, integrating it fully into the economic system of the state. As a result, the economies of Zante and Cephalonia developed autonomously to fulfil the demands of the English market, setting in motion a profound transformation in their social fabric that made them substantially different even from the other Ionian islands such as Corfu.

The English managed to maintain a good working relationship with all strata of the Greek population they came in contact with. This is illustrated well by the *Popolari* rebellion of 1628, during which the English merchants in Zante managed to extricate themselves from the conflict between the *Popolari* and *Cittadini* factions with amazing dexterity and political acumen, and in so doing they reinforced their essential role in the history of the islands. Once established, this pattern of mutually beneficial cooperation between the population of Zante and Cephalonia and English merchants continued until the end of the eighteenth century. In the second half of the seventeenth century there was a brief period of tension, and the English tried to free themselves from their dependence on the currant crop of the islands by investing in the Ottoman Morea. Still, the superior quality of the production of Zante and Cephalonia in effect protected the islands from this competition. In earlier chapters it has been discussed how from the 1640s until the end of the century the civil wars in England and the Candia war in the Mediterranean affected Anglo-Venetian trade, but, at the same time, these events also calmed the tensions in the islands, and re-established commercial cooperation between Greeks and English. The long-term strength of this special relation thus proved pivotal in understanding the political behaviour of the populations of Zante and Cephalonia in the volatile decades following 1797.

Structuring dominion

Zante and Cephalonia were peculiar because they were almost deserted when they became part of the Venetian empire; there were no feudal structures or jurisdictions on either island. Of the Ionian islands, only Corfu had some true feudal jurisdictions, albeit of late creation, not being 'properly divided into fiefs until it was added to the dominions of Charles of Anjou, King of Naples, in 1267'.[9] Scholars have frequently missed this crucial aspect, instead assuming that all islands had the same social and economic makeup.[10]

When Zante in 1485, and Cephalonia in 1500, became part of Venice's dominions, the main concern of the Senate was to repopulate them and to stimulate their production of grain. Venice put a great deal of effort into repopulation, favouring the immigration of people from territories under Ottoman control, and large numbers came from the outposts of Modon and Coron, which had just been lost by the Venetians to the Ottomans. To entice these immigrants, the Republic granted ownership of parcels of land and advantageous long-term fiscal privileges. A sizeable percentage of these settlers were *stradioti*, members of a light cavalry corps mostly composed of Morean Greeks, which had been organised by the Venetians in their Levant territories since the Middle Ages.[11] Throughout the sixteenth and seventeenth century the islands were also the destination of a small but steady stream of immigrants and refugees from nearby territories under Ottoman control. All these factors created a very peculiar property situation, characterised by a large number of small and free landowners, and this would be dramatically affected by the currant boom.

The uniqueness of this property structure was often cited by the locals as a propaganda weapon to defend their interests, first when the Venetian

---

[9] M. Pratt, *Britain's Greek Empire: Reflections on the History of the Ionian Islands from the fall of Byzantium*, London, 1978, 3. A proof of this is the fact the *Assisi di Romania*, the feudal legal code used by Latins in the Levant after the Fourth Crusade, in the Ionian islands was introduced by the Venetians and applied only in Corfu and not in the other islands: see D. Jacoby, *Le féodalité en Grèce médiévale: les 'Assises de Romanie' sources, application, diffusion*, Paris, 1971, 311; and his 'Les "Assises de Romanie" et le droit vénitien dans les colonies vénitiennes', in *Recherches sur la Méditerranée orientale du XIIe au XVe siècle*, London, 1970, IV: 356–359.

[10] See, for example, G. Yannoupoulos, 'State and Society in the Ionian Islands, 1800–1830', in G. Clogg ed., *Balkan Society in the Age of Greek Independence*, London, 1981, 43–45; T. W. Gallant, *Experiencing Dominion: Culture, Identity and Power in the British Mediterranean*, Notre Dame, 2002, 4. Some 'fiefs' in Zante and Cephalonia were created from the period of the War of Candia onwards, and sold to local landowners as a way to raise income: see Lunzi, *Della condizione politica*, 469.

[11] D. Vlassi, 'La politica annonaria di Venezia a Cefalonia: il fondaco delle biade (sec. XVI–XVIII)', *Thesaurismata*, 25 (1995): 274–318, 274–275.

government attempted to redirect the currant trade through Venice and later, when that failed, when the Venetian government tried to curtail their production. In full compliance with the traditional rhetoric at the basis of Venetian dominion, the dialogue between the inhabitants of Zante and Cephalonia and the Republic was articulated around the concept of the peculiarity of the two islands and around the mutual ties of loyalty and obligation this had created. All the petitions from Zante and Cephalonia to the Senate recounted the difficult beginnings and the achievements by their ancestors, and emphasised the traditional freedom granted – and defended – by the Republic:

> From little or nothing this small rock was made into a famous island, [. . .] our Ancestors abandoned their very own and natural homes and transported here all their possessions and industries, some from the Morea, some from Modon and Coron, some from Patrasso and Lepanto, some from Napoli of Romania and Malvasia, some from Puglia and other places, [to enjoy] the freedom promised, preserved and exercised in all the lands and places of this Most Serene Dominion.[12]

In the decades immediately following the re-establishment of settlements in Zante and Cephalonia, the main export had been grain, mostly sent to Venice and used for the needs of the fleet. This crop was strongly favoured by the Venetian government for obvious strategic reasons and because of the chronic grain shortages characteristic of that period. But from the middle of the sixteenth century currants became instead the dominant agricultural product of both islands, in the face of strong opposition by the Venetian government. Within a few years the production of currants spiralled out of control. Already by the early 1580s they had gone from being self-sufficient in grain to having enough only for three months of local consumption. Even thinking about grain exports became nonsensical, and this remained a characteristic of the islands' economy well into the nineteenth century.[13] The *Rettori* did their best by investing in *Fondaci* of grains, and tried to satisfy the needs of the military (fleet and garrisons) and of the poor as best they could – mostly with loans and imports from the Ottoman territories, well aware that this would not be a viable option in case of war with the Porte.[14] The rest of the population was not unduly upset by the lack of grain, as the huge amounts of

---

[12] ASV, *Cinque Savi alla Mercanzia*, b. 836b, fasc. i, n. 14 (3-10-1602); also document out of the index (follows the one dated 13 February 1608mv).

[13] The problems of currant overproduction are analysed extensively in Fusaro, *Uva passa*, 79–106. For the nineteenth-century situation see S. Gekas, *Business Culture and Entrepreneurship in the Ionian Islands Under British Rule, 1815–1864*, LSE Working Paper n. 89/05, 24.

[14] Vlassi, 'La politica annonaria di Venezia'.

ready money with which the English paid for their currants allowed them to buy grain from Ottoman territories. As discussed in the previous chapter, it was also quite common for the English to purchase grain themselves and to use it to pay for their currants.[15] Notwithstanding legislation prohibiting any increase in the land dedicated to currants and constant efforts to favour wheat, the idea of cultivating grain instead of currants became unthinkable for the locals. Their attitude is self-explanatory given the fact that a field of currants yielded up to 60 ducats of profit, whilst a field of grain yielded around 6.[16]

In an earlier chapter we mentioned that Greek shipowners based in Venice did not react to the establishment of the *Nuova Imposta*. For the Greeks in the islands the situation was completely different, and vociferous protestations followed its promulgation. Petition after petition arrived in Venice in the early 1580s, each more dramatic in tone, lamenting the utter financial ruin befalling them as a consequence of the new legislation. The rhetoric in these texts insists on the islands inhabitants' long service to the Republic and on the privileges granted to them on the occasion of their repopulation in 1485.[17] The Greek islanders lamented the pernicious effects of the English near-monopoly of currant exports (and little did they know how much worse things would get in the following decades), and saw no benefit in the new law.[18] The very same file in the *Cinque Savi* archive contains English petitions on the same topic, also lamenting – from the other perspective – the negative results of the lack of free trade.[19]

Whilst Greek maritime entrepreneurs were reaping the benefits, Greeks in the islands tried to take matters into their own hands, and in 1587 the *Comunità* of Zante after a heated debate, which ended in a very close vote (63 in favour and 57 against), decided to bypass Venice and send a local 'ambassador' directly to London. The mission was to plead directly with Queen Elizabeth to reopen negotiations with the Republic

---

[15] Something which was noted also by travellers to the islands: for example, see Sandys, *A Relation of a Journey began AD 1610*, 5.

[16] ASV, *Collegio, Relazioni*, b. 62, cc.84r–86r, report of Alvise Minotto, after his term as *Rettore* in Zante in 1678.

[17] ASV, *Senato Mar*, reg. 12, c.35v (1485).

[18] As a classic example of such supplications, see ASV, *Cinque Savi alla Mercanzia*, b. 836b, fasc. ii, cc.n.n. (5-8-1584); see also the related *scrittura* of the *Provveditore* Zuanne Venier and his Councillors Scipion Minio and Antonio Trevisan, which was requested by the *Cinque Savi* around the same date: ASV, *Cinque Savi alla Mercanzia*, b. 836b, fasc. ii, cc. n.n. (17-8-1584).

[19] ASV, *Cinque Savi alla Mercanzia*, b. 836b, fasc. ii, cc.n.n. (17-10-1584); (25-10-1584).

with the goal of repealing all reciprocal customs duties.[20] Nothing came
of this, but it is most interesting to note how this horrified the *Senato* in
Venice. In October 1586, the *Senato* had already decreed that strict
instructions were to be sent to the islands' *Rettori* to avoid similar
missions:

This might rightly appear to be a very extraordinary and unusual attempt, that of
sending a [local] ambassador to a foreign prince, as it is the duty and right of Our
Serenity to deal with such matters and other necessary business, and [this does]
not belong to subjects, who for all their needs should defer to their own Prince's
will.[21]

There was no mincing of words in the reaction to the possibility of
an independent embassy which would have put Venetian subjects and a
foreign power in direct contact. It is difficult not to agree with this analysis.
That the local *Comunità* of a subject island such as Zante could propose the
dispatch of a local diplomatic mission to a foreign prince is in itself an
extraordinary thing, and should be considered evidence that the rhetoric
of 'freedom' which Venice employed in its colonial administration was
finding eager and willing ears in the colonies themselves. It also shows
that the power of commercial interests was pushing subjects dangerously
close to insubordination.

Controlling dominion

What did not help the Venetian government in Zante and Cephalonia was
the very thing that made the islands so important: their strategic position
and their role as maritime frontier of the Adriatic.[22] They were at the
centre of the great majority of sea routes to the Eastern Mediterranean.
Situated as they are in the middle of the Ionian Sea, close to the entrance
of the Adriatic, from classical times they represented the perfect place for
victualling.[23] This was particularly true for Zante, at the crossroads of the

---

[20] ASV, *Cinque Savi alla Mercanzia*, b.836b, fasc. ii, cc.n.n. (20-3-1587) includes further
details about how to run negotiations, both in Venice and London, and expenses are
listed in the *scrittura* which follows, cc.n.n (22-3-1587).

[21] '[P]otrebbe giustamente parer tentativo molto estraordinario et insolito il procurar
licenza di mandar un ambasciator ad un principe esterno, col quale tocca alla Serenità
Nostra di trattar questo, et altri negotij che occorrono, et non a sudditi che per ogni
ragione debbono rimettersi al beneplacito del Principe loro', in ASV, *Senato Mar*, reg. 47,
cc.216v–217v (11-10-1586).

[22] A. Tenenti, 'Le isole Ionie: un area di frontiera', in Costantini ed., *Il Mediterraneo centro-
orientale*, 11–18.

[23] Just about all ships on their way to, or from, the Eastern Mediterranean stopped at one of
the two, most frequently at Zante; see Sanderson, *The Travels of John Sanderson*, London,
1931; Constantine, *Early Greek Travellers*, *passim*.

Adriatic and Aegean sailing routes, thereby making it an excellent rendezvous for convoys.[24] At the time of the war with Spain in the last quarter of the sixteenth century, English ships used to gather there before crossing the Mediterranean towards Gibraltar. In the words of Richard Hakluyt:

the generall agreement was to meete at Zante, an Island neere the maine continent of the West part of Morea, well knowen of all the Pilots, & thought to be the fittest place of their Rendezvous.[25]

Zante and Cephalonia also had excellent natural ports, offering refuge in case of storms but also providing even more excellent protection for illegal cargoes and pirates. Their position also made them perfect places from which to gather intelligence. The whole of the Eastern Mediterranean was covered by a network of spies, controlled on the one hand by the Venetian *Bailo* in Costantinople, and on the other by the *Rettori* of the Ionian islands and the *Provveditore Generale da Mar* based in Corfu. Merchants and travellers were also widely used for espionage.[26] The proximity of Zante to the Ottoman Morea, however dangerous in times of war, was also useful for gathering information about the Porte's intentions and military movements. Greek merchants and sailors, captains of ships sailing in the area, and even the English consuls in Patrasso – masters at balancing opposing powers – all provided information to the *Rettori*.[27]

Each of the major Ionian islands was governed by a *Rettore* and by two councillors, elected from amongst the members of the Venetian Major Council and remaining in office for twenty-four months. In their everyday activities they collaborated with the local councils, made up of the *Cittadini* of the islands. This structure of government – extremely stream-lined and heavily dependent on local personnel, with limited financial means at its disposal – meant that it was impossible for the Venetian *Rettori* to ever achieve any real control of the territory. In the plain words of Zuan Marco da Molin, then *Rettore* of Zante:

The location of this place, open on all sides, makes it difficult to ward off smuggling, and a single mounted officer with a few inept and useless underlings cannot

---

[24] Convoys start to appear regularly from the 1650s: see ASV, *SDR*, Zante, from b. 20, *passim*.
[25] Hakluyt, *The Principall Navigations*, 47.
[26] Knapton, 'Tra Dominante e Dominio', 203–524. See also ASV, *Collegio, Rdd*, f. 21, cc.n.n. (14-9-1630).
[27] See ASV, *SDR*, Zante, b. 17, *passim*; b. 19, cc.n.n. (15-3-1650); b. 20, cc.n.n. (8-6-1651) and (11-9-1650); b. 21, cc.n.n. (enclosed in the dispatch of 21-6-1655).

fight it, especially as local villagers frequently have interests [in smuggling]. I suspect, in fact I am certain, that they do not properly perform their duties.[28]

This was a problem that went far beyond skirmishes with highwaymen and difficulties in collecting the tithe, which were universal problems in that period. Control would have necessitated properly patrolling towns and harbours to discourage illegal activities, something which was difficult because of the scarcity of troops and the boom in illegal building, discussed in an earlier chapter.

There are innumerable references to smuggling throughout the documentation, but only one trial has survived. It took place in Zante in 1589 against Ottaviano Volterra, the administrator of the *Nuova Imposta*. I have recounted the story in detail elsewhere,[29] but it is important to refer to it again because it reveals many illegal everyday practices. Almost all the protagonists have appeared in earlier pages: Giovanni da Riviera was the Greeks' agent in London and Marco Seguro a prominent merchant and shipowner. The other Greek involved was Volterra, one of the richest merchants of Zante. The illegal contract that formed the basis of the trial had been signed in London in 1584 and involved a large-scale smuggling operation: currants in exchange for tin and textiles. Seguro was to provide a ship to carry currants to the harbour of Cephalonia, where they would have been delivered to Thomas Daelnes free of customs.[30] Only a small percentage of the *Nuova Imposta*, on that portion of the goods used by the English to pay for currants, would have been paid.[31] The cost of the entry–exit duty was to have been divided between Greeks and English. The goods would then be sold around the Morea and in the Archipelago for the sole profit of the Greeks. It was a fairly straightforward operation with substantial savings for the English partners. However, in the meantime, Seguro had died, and the contract had not been completed because his associates had not managed to acquire all the currants required. To this end they asked Daelnes for a loan, which he had provided to avoid having troubles with his principals in London; although no figures are mentioned this confirms the ready availability of cash for English merchants in the islands. Volterra admitted the existence of a previous

---

[28] ASV, *Cinque Savi alla Mercanzia*, b. 836b, fasc. i, document not indexed (dated 14-10-1608), following n.64.

[29] Fusaro, *Uva Passa*, 108–115.

[30] Daelnes arrived in Zante in 1579, working in the service of Andrew Bayning until the latter left at the end of 1583. At the same time he was agent for Thomas Baxter. Between 1584 and 1586 he had been in the service of Thomas Cordell, and was now working for Edward Holmden – all prominent Levant Company founding members.

[31] Amongst the ships that carried English textiles, and paid regular customs, was the *Santa Maria di Scoppo*; property of Marco Seguro, her captain was 'Gioan Botteler Inglese'.

contract with the English, but denied this one.[32] This was a peculiar defence tactic, considering we have seen how Venetian subjects were not allowed to establish partnerships with foreigners. Additionally, as administrator of the *Nuova Imposta* he was forbidden to reach this kind of agreement with merchants.[33] Now that Seguro was dead, Volterra could blame everything on him, but at the same time he kept on repeating and emphasising how common these kinds of contracts were.[34] His defence was messy and repetitive, and he never really answered the points made against him by the prosecution, preferring instead to point the finger to others. The fact that he should have administered the customs to the benefit of the state coffers does not seem to have occurred to him.[35] He was sentenced to repay the state the value of half the smuggled currants in the year of the deal, up to a total of 4,000 ducats.

It is clear from the trial papers that the practices therein described represented the normal way of conducting business in the islands. Not all contracts involved such large amounts of merchandise, and most contracts involved cash rather than goods. But everyone made contracts of partnership with foreigners, and administrators were both meddling with producers and smuggling themselves. Illegality was the basis of these deals, and legislation promulgated in Venice was consistently disregarded. It is relevant that the accusations were brought by an Englishman, not by a Greek. The English were still trying to find a secure footing in the islands, particularly in adjusting to the practicalities of a trade whose volume was growing quickly. The breaking of this contract by the Greeks had surprised the English, and they were looking for redress. The islanders themselves were also at a moment of transition, and a new balance of internal power was still in the making. Volterra would never have made such loud accusations a few years later, by which time both Greeks and English had realised that it was better to take care of their common business quietly and discreetly. The conspiracy of silence that characterises the next phase of trade reflects a shared awareness that it was better to avoid the involvement of the Venetian government. This tacit

---

[32] ASV, *Quarantia Criminale*, b. 193, fasc. 73, c.41r.

[33] ASV, *Quarantia Criminale*, b. 193, fasc. 73, cc.5r/v (10-8-1584).

[34] Not scared of 'naming names' about these contracts, he declared: 'Che et sotto li suoi Chiarissimi Precessori e sotto il Reggimento di Vostra Chiarissima Signoria molti mercati et in Venetia et qui sono stati fatti da questi dell'Isola con essi Inglesi di uve passe à barato di carisee. [...] il sopradetto Leo Nomicò, Anzolo Foscardi, Michiel Sumachi, Giacomo Frangopulo per li mercati da Venetia', in ASV, *Quarantia Criminale*, b. 193, fasc. 73, cc.45r–49r.

[35] '[...] mentre voglio giustificar che anco altri et qui et a Venetia hanno fatto li istessi mercati con li Inglesi, et altre nationi forestieri, come ho fatto io [...]': in ASV, *Quarantia Criminale*, b. 193, fasc. 73, cc.58v–62r.

agreement eventually broke down during the 1630s, but for forty years before then the Greeks and English kept to themselves as much as possible. This was the period of their closest alliance.

In 1592 the ambassador of the *Comunità* of Zante proposed farming out the *Nuova Imposta* to the islanders, the idea being that this would help them deal with the newly reinforced Levant Company currant monopoly as well as to fight smuggling.[36] The experience garnered in a decade of administering the customs though a local administrator with a fixed salary had shown this was not a solution conducive to honesty. It was argued that farming the tax would make the Greeks stakeholders in the enterprise, as the farmer would have an interest in recouping his original investment. The custom was duly farmed out, but unfortunately for Venice this did not achieve the desired results, as farming became involved in the factionary fights that characterised the islands.[37] Moreover, trying to keep commercial activities separate from administering the custom was simply impossible.[38] The potential gains of smuggling were such that the islands' population was always willing to accept some degree of risk. Filippo Pasqualigo, *Provveditore Generale da Mar*, stated it very clearly in 1607 during a period which we have already seen it was forbidden to export from the islands directly:

The profit of smugglers is so high as to persuade and seduce them to act in this way, and to direct to this all [available] capital . . . provided that just one deal is successful.[39]

Banishing convicted smugglers was not a solution either. Once ensconced on the Ottoman mainland, they were an even worse threat to legal trade, as there they could use their personal connections to make a living as intermediaries for English ships.[40]

Anglo-Greek shipping cooperation on the long-distance routes of international trade has already been discussed, but this was just one side

---

[36] ASV, *Collegio, Rdf,* f. 343, cc.n.n (16-6-1592).
[37] On the administration of the *Nuova Imposta,* see Fusaro, *Uva passa,* 107–146. Detailed instructions on how to administer the custom were reissued with each new administration: see ASV, *Cinque Savi alla Mercanzia,* b. 188 n.s., *passim.*
[38] ASV, *Compilazione Leggi,* b. 378, cc.111–113v (31-3-1606). The problem persisted and more severe penalties were decided for non compliers (fines of up to 500 ducats): in ASV, *Senato, Secreta, Ordini di Cefalonia,* cc.n.n. (10-11-1623); also ASV, *Sindici Inquisitori in Terra Ferma e Levante,* b. 67, lxxiv, cc.4r–5v.
[39] ASV, *PTM,* b. 862, cc.n.n. (15-10-1607).
[40] ASV, *Senato Mar,* reg. 86, cc.229v–230r (25-9-1628); a worsening of penalties for these crimes can be seen in reg. 86, cc.239r (2-12-1628).

of the story. Equally, if not more, important were their partnerships in local shipping and trade, and much can be learned about the role that the English merchants played in the Venetian Mediterranean at large by concentrating on the flow of traffic between Venice and the islands.

On the Venetian side, the protagonists of maritime trade in the Adriatic and up to the Ionian islands were those small, unarmed ships called *marciliane*. Throughout the second half of the sixteenth century the Venetian shipbuilding industry built many of these, which were very efficient on short-distance trips thanks to their small crew; for this reason Jean-Claude Hocquet has compared them with Dutch *fluyts*. However, we have also seen how the Venetian government increasingly wanted to encourage the construction of large, armed ships such as galleons, and therefore financial incentives were put in place for their production. The market, though, continued to respond well to *marciliane*, and indeed experimented also with their size, resulting in serious problems for their safety and seaworthiness.[41] Another favourite, and dangerous, trick was to refit *marciliane* and then call them 'round ships' to get around the limits to their navigational range.[42] In 1602 the *Senato* decided to take matters into its own hands by limiting their navigational range to Corfu. As a result, whilst in 1602 there appear to have been seventy-eight *marciliane* in service, by 1619 only thirty-eight were still active.[43] Still, until the 1620s *marciliane* dominated maritime trade between the Ionian islands and Venice. The seascape quickly changed in the following decades, though, as the diminution of their numbers further facilitated English penetration in intra-Mediterranean trade.

English merchants in the islands often acquired small ships and boats for inter-island trade in partnership with Greek merchants. This kind of joint property was beneficial to everyone involved. For the English it avoided the need to rent boats for short-distance transport;[44] for factors it was an easy way to increase one's income by renting out the boat when

---

[41] Lane, *Venetian Ships and Shipbuilders*, 53. As late as the 1620s three merchants presented individual requests to lengthen *marciliane* to increase their cargo capacity; the *Savi* were rather worried about the safety implications of such modifications, but also tempted to allow these to counteract the low number of Venetian ships active in the Levant: see their arguments in ASV, *Cinque Savi alla Mercanzia, Risposte*, reg. 145, c.156r (26-4-1622), and cc.156v–157r (4-5-1622).

[42] Tenenti, *Piracy and the Decline*, 104–105.

[43] Hocquet, *Le sel et la fortune*, 512–516, 514.

[44] In the contract between Simon Waite and the brothers Procopio and Antonio Vergotis, there was a special clause that allowed Waite to use the ship for his own businesses, simply by paying the crew personally. For all other business, the gain was to be divided in half. See ΓΑΚ-ΑΝΚ, *Notarial Archive*, b. 74a (Pietro Sarlo), vol. i, c.68r (10-1-1633). In this particular instance, the fact that Vergotis did not appear anywhere as a merchant supports the fact that the brothers were just seamen.

not needed; and having Greeks as co-owners could be a most convenient cover to avoid the payment of duties.[45] For the Greeks it meant a larger cash flow and the certainty of employment. Because this trade was considered as smuggling by the Venetian authorities, it left rather scant documentary traces. The most frequent use of these small ships was in fact to move goods from the islands to the Morea, where the goods were then loaded onto English ships, thereby avoiding the payment of customs duties.[46] This trade constituted the backbone of local small-scale trading, and northerners played a crucial role.[47]

A commercial dispute between two merchants from Zante – Nicolò Toma and Demetrio Cutrica – gives us a snapshot of the trade connecting the island with Venice between 1635 and 1646. The protagonists were merchants of quite small calibre; however, exactly for this reason their activities are particularly representative. Amongst the papers of their dispute are the bills of freight of the ships on which they loaded their merchandise. And it is striking to note their nationality: out of twenty-three ships on the Zante–Venice route: ten were English, seven Flemish and six either Venetian or Greek; on the opposite leg of the journey (Venice–Zante) amongst ten ships, five were English, two Flemish and three Venetian or Greek. This means that trade with Venice was carried out mostly on northerners' ships, English in more than 50 per cent of the cases.[48] From Zante to Venice the goods were knives, velvets, hats, coloured satin, *grana* and silks. On the opposite leg they were coloured satins and Venetian woollens (especially *panni alti*).[49] The middleman for the chartering of English ships appeared always to be Simon di Moisè Copio, the principal Jewish merchant in Zante, and all ships also appear to be carrying merchandise belonging to Agesilao Seguro, scion of that local mercantile dynasty we have already encountered. It is rather risky to draw conclusions from just one partnership; however, this small but extremely detailed dataset confirms the general impression given by the rest of the documentation. Whilst in the last quarter of the sixteenth century the Greek subjects of the Republic were heavily engaged in shipowning and trade on the routes to northern Europe, by the central

---

[45] ΓΑΚ-ΑΝΚ, *Notarial Archive*, b. 91 (Rafael Pignatore), vol. i, c.35v (25-2-1636); I wish to thank Stamatoula Zapandi for bringing this contract to my attention. See also ASV, *Notarile Atti*, b. 8449 (Alberto Mastaleo), cc.141r/v (21-9-1640).

[46] See, for example, ASV, *Senato Mar*, reg. 97, cc.144r, 177r (1639). The *Rettore* of Cephalonia started a trial against two *fregate* that brought currants to the English ship *Leon dorato*, avoiding the payment of customs.

[47] Knapton, 'Tra Dominante e Dominio', 269.

[48] ASV, *AdC, Civile*, b. 152, fasc. 91; and b. 48, fasc. 13.

[49] These were woollen textiles of mid to high quality.

decades of the seventeenth century the English had established a strong-hold on medium-distance maritime trade. And this was happening even before the beginning of the War of Candia (1646–1669), during which the engagement of English ships within Venetian Levantine trade increased, as Ottoman ports were formally closed to Venetian ships.[50] The extant documentation of this trial does not discuss the reasons behind the choice of carriers, and were these limited to the business of Toma and Cutrica it could be argued that the small scale of their operations, or pre-existing personal links with English merchants, justified the choice of foreign carriers. The worrying sign is that even a Seguro, part of that family which a generation before was at the forefront of shipowning, was now resorting to English carriers: control over a primary maritime route, directly connecting the metropolis with a colony, appears to have been just about lost. The major Greek merchants of the islands also appear as losers. Whilst in the previous generation they had taken advantage of the arrival of the northerners to enlarge the scope of their operations, and to strengthen their own shipping networks thanks to the general increase in trade, they clearly had not been able to sustain this effort. Conversely the picture was more positive for smaller players such as Toma and Cutrica, who had much to gain from the presence of foreign merchants; they could more easily move their goods to Venice and increase their chances of income, taking advantage of the presence of foreign ships as carriers.

Contesting dominion? The *Popolari* revolt in Zante

The 1628 revolt of Zante represents a *unicum* in the Venetian territories.[51] In a century characterised by social revolts throughout Europe, the *Serenissima* managed to emerge almost unscathed except for this incident.[52] The question is almost banal: why here? My argument is that the foreign presence in Zante was at the root of the social changes that led to the rebellion. The English presence brought to light and to

---

[50] Fusaro, 'The Invasion of Northern Litigants'.

[51] On the *Popolari* revolt, I am greatly indebted to the analysis of Dimitris Arvanitakis (*Το ρεμπελιό των ποπολάρων (1628)*). I wish to thank him here for the material he generously shared with me, and the most stimulating conversations we had on these issues over the years. The trial about the insurrection itself is in ASV, *AdC, Penale*, b. 427, fasc. i. A related trial against some of the 'agitators' is in ASV, *AdC, Penale*, b. 340, fasc. 13.

[52] A smaller revolt also took place in the *Terraferma*: see A. Tagliaferri, *Per una storia sociale della Repubblica Veneta: la rivolta di Arzignano del 1665*, Udine, 1978. Small, but significant episodes of disrespect towards Venetian authorities also did take place there: on these see G. Corazzol, *Cineografo di banditi su sfondo di monti (Feltre, 1634–1642)*, Milan, 2006. A compact analysis of seventeenth-century revolts in Europe is H. Kamen, *The Iron Century: Social Change in Europe 1550–1660*, London, 1971, 365–426.

maturation a series of social issues latent in its social fabric. In this regard Michael Knapton has already stressed the centrality of the 'relation between patrimony and status' for the ruling class of the Levant colonies. He has underlined how the 'riotous meetings of the Cephalonia council' at the beginning of the seventeenth century worried the *Rettori*.[53] The social and political tensions of these two Ionian islands in those years cannot be fully attributed either to the diverging interests between Venice and the islands over foreign trade, or to the way power was administered locally by the Venetian authorities: the central issue was the growing gap between money and status on the island.

The rebellion of 1628 has been mythologised by traditional Greek historiography as the first bourgeois revolution of the Mediterranean. As Zante had no feudal nobility, at the top of the social pyramid were the *Cittadini*, members of the local council. They had political rights and participated in local administration alongside the Venetian *Reggimento*. Everyone else living in towns was considered part of the *Popolari*, whilst inhabitants of the countryside were referred to as *Villani*. From the beginning of the seventeenth century the council underwent a progressive aristocratisation – a situation common to the whole of Europe.[54] Until then it had been relatively easy for 'new money' to become part of the council, but new legislation made this increasingly difficult, and only at the end of the seventeenth century were detailed rules put into place to establish how new families could acquire this status through registration in the *Libro d'oro*.[55] During the first decades of that century the situation was different, and the large influx of cash – earned through the currant trade – became a catalyst that heightened discontent. The most active *Popolari* amongst the 'new moneyed' became *Caporioni del popolo* and aroused the lower strata of the population to rebellion, something which was not particularly difficult in a society traditionally as violent as the Ionian one and where factions were a normal part of socio-political life.

A decision by the *Inquisitore* Antonio da Ponte in 1623 was the spark; it dealt with changing the rosters for night wardens of the town, extending these to all *Popolari*. Widely interpreted as an abuse of power pushed through by the *Cittadini*, it was also considered a formal codification of the *Popolari*'s inferiority. The *Cittadini* could easily manipulate the warden-ships, and one thing that provoked particular objections was that the

---

[53] Knapton, 'Tra Dominante e Dominio', 374, 385; see also Arbel, 'Venice's Maritime Empire', 184–188.

[54] And that in the Venetian territories on the Italian mainland had started in the previous century: see Ventura, *Nobiltà e popolo*.

[55] E. Rizo-Rangabè, *Livre d'or del noblesse ionienne*, Athens, 1927, 7–9; Lunzi, *Della condizione politica*, 324–325.

Cittadini extorted money from the *Popolari* in exchange for leaves of absence. The situation remained at a stalemate until May 1628, when the *Popolari* decided to solve these problems by electing four *Procuratori*[56] as their representatives and one *Avvocato* of the people – an 'abominable novelty' – and they also elected four ambassadors to go to Venice to plead directly to the Senate. To maintain the peace, the *Rettore* accepted these elections, which were technically illegal. The following August, the *Capitano dell'Armata*, Antonio Civran, demanded that everyone sign up on the new rosters, but no one did, and therefore he arrested the four *Procuratori*. The population rose up in arms, the flag of St Mark was insulted, *Cittadini* homes were threatened with fire, the galley of the *Capitano* was shot at, and it appears that someone even threatened to call the Viceroy of Naples for help. Just when the situation was spiralling out of control, the day was saved by the mediation of English merchants, high-level Venetian officers and members of the Orthodox clergy, and the *Commessi* were freed. For the next three years the *Procuratori* were made part of the council, but in June 1631 the *Inquisitore* Antonio Pisani arrived and started a trial that lasted until February 1632. The sentences for the rebels were extremely severe, but a few years afterwards there was a general pardon.

These sorts of problems were not exclusive to this territory or to Venice's dominions. What made the situation in Zante extraordinary was the speed with which they manifested themselves, due to the wide availability of cash. With such swift social transformation in progress, the difficulties in entering the council became an unacceptable denial of opportunity. The problem was general and European: what to do with rich *Popolari*? Venice had always been very attentive to this issue and had favoured a policy of slow assimilation, and this is the reason why ultimately the Republic was lenient with the leaders of the revolt. The rich *Popolari* did not want to get rid of Venice, nor did they want the abolition of the social hierarchy (*società degli ordini*); they simply wanted to be able to rise within it. They manipulated the populace not to destroy the establishment, but to scare it into admitting them. Since 1542 there had been a mutual agreement between the Venetian authorities and the local council concerning the division of the island's population into three classes, and the responsibility for military defence, organisationally and financially, had been squarely put onto the *Cittadini* in exchange for their privileges. So when the *Cittadini* tried to involve the *Popolari*, the latter felt they were being oppressed as if they were peasants, who had always provided the

---

[56] Also referred to as *Commessi*.

manpower. *Popolari* rhetoric in defending their stance is most telling; they underlined their status as 'free subjects' of the Republic who had *voluntarily* chosen to settle in the island and were *voluntarily* prepared to defend it against all enemies, but they also declared that they were neither mercenary troops nor peasants living under the power of the landowners.[57] The traditional discourse about voluntary subjection and self-devolution, and about the freedom traditionally enjoyed under the Republic, was smartly employed to defend their actions.

The other issue which emerges powerfully from the documentary evidence is that of the *Popolari's* public service and contribution to the islands' and the Republic's welfare. In the interrogations during the trial, references are frequently made to the 'more than comfortable' economic situation of the wealthy *Popolari* and to their active and positive contribution to the social and economic life of Zante. In their defence, and to assuage the Venetian authorities, they claimed the *Cittadini* had tried to humiliate them and wanted to exclude them from the Council in revenge for having proved better at managing the customs of the island. Christodulo Cimi, one of the leaders of the *Popolari*, 'lived comfortably from his own income' and farmed both the wine and the 'entry–exit' customs in the period between the rebellion and the trial. During the trial he argued that the *Cittadini* wanted to monopolise customs to rob the Republic; in contrast, he argued forcefully, he was loyal and 'promptly paid his own Prince'.[58] This, by the way, was indeed the case, as customs' income had been rising and would continue to do so in the years following the revolt under *Popolari* management, something which was noted by the Venetian authorities.[59]

Under such circumstances, the role of the English merchants in the trial becomes a litmus test. The delicate diplomacy shown by all of them was essential for a group that needed as much support as possible from all strata of the population. All Englishmen living in the islands at the time of the trial were called to give testimony. All other witnesses, regardless of whether they were Venetians or *Cittadini* or *Popolari*, stressed their role as

---

[57] L. Augliera, *Libri, politica, religione nel Levante del Seicento: la tipografia di Nicodemo Metaxas, primo editore di testi greci nell'Oriente ortodosso*, Venice, 1996, 129–131.

[58] ASV, *AdC, Penale*, b. 427, fasc. i, c.92r (19-8-1631), interrogation of Christodulo Cimi *quondam* Giorgio; c.111r (19-9-1631), interrogation of Marc'Antonio Boldù *quondam* Francesco: he supported Cimi's arguments and claims against the *Cittadini*. ASV, *AdC, Penale*, b. 340, fasc. 13, cc.148v–149r, interrogation of Antonio Monemvasioti: he also agreed with the above-mentioned interpretation of the *Cittadini* behaviour.

[59] The figures are in Fusaro, *Uva passa*, 132–137; see also Augliera, *Libri, politica, religione*, 133–134.

mediators.[60] The slight presence of the local clergy during the revolt might come as a surprise, given the essential place of the Orthodox hierarchy amongst the Greek population in the Ottoman Empire. However, things were very different in the *Stato da Mar*, and Venetian authorities never granted the Orthodox clergy any intermediary or representative role with regard to the local population. Fully aware of the importance of the Orthodox Church for the islands' population, Venice had approached these issues with its customary political finesse, for example by obtaining from the papacy two bulls delineating the spaces of autonomy regarding baptism, marriage and religious rites. But, following the Venetian tradition of separation between church and state, governance always remained in secular hands.[61] During the revolt itself, the local Orthodox clergy was divided, and Venice therefore watched them carefully, especially as the new archbishop was rumoured to support the *Popolari*.[62] The English merchants managed not only to mediate to end the revolt, but also to navigate the trial by giving testimony that simultaneously underlined their role as collaborators with the Venetian authorities whilst not betraying the *Popolari* or upsetting the *Cittadini*. Some Englishmen simply denied having recognised any particular individual in the fracas, and they stuck to this line even after persistent questioning by the Venetian authorities.

At the time of the trial, Giovanni Mun had lived in Zante for four years.[63] During the rebellion the English merchants had been greatly concerned that one of them, John Hobson Sr, was renting a house belonging to Piero Martelao, a *Cittadino* whose own house the *Popolari* were threatening to burn down, and the two houses adjoined each other.[64] The season for currants was just about to begin and Hobson kept 'a large quantity of cash' at home. Therefore they decided to transfer the cash to an English

---

[60] For example Stathi Manessi *quondam* Fabricio – a *Cittadino* – who did not know any of the English directly, not being involved in trade, declared that when the *Popolari* were threatening the houses of *Cittadini* with fire, the English merchants put themselves forward as mediators: in ASV, *AdC, Penale*, b. 427, fasc. i, c.20r (15-6-1631). The *Popolari* also stressed the mediation role played by the English: ASV, *AdC, Penale*, b. 427, fasc. i, c.92r (19-8-1631) evidence given by Christodulo Cimi *quondam* Giorgio; c.102r (21-8-1631), evidence given by Andrea Monemvasioti *quondam* Giorgo.

[61] On the complex, and ambiguous relations between Venetian government and Orthodox clergy, with a focus on the Ionian islands, see A. Viggiano, *Lo specchio della repubblica: Venezia e il governo delle isole Ionie nel '700*, Sommacampagna, 1998, 197–249; Tenenti, 'Le isole Ionie'; Arbel, 'Venice's Maritime Empire', 164–182.

[62] Augliera, *Libri, politica, religione*, 137–138.

[63] Interrogation of Giovanni Mun *quondam* Guglielmo in ASV, *AdC, Penale*, b. 427, fasc. i, cc.48v–51r (17-6-1631).

[64] Probably the same houses that Martelao had asked permission to build at the *Marina* in 1593: see ASV, *Collegio, Rdf*, f. 346, cc.n.n. (18-1-1593mv).

vessel in the harbour, and on the same vessel they also allowed some *Cittadini* to take refuge.[65] Since Martelao's house was still threatened, Hobson tried to mediate. The *Popolari* had assured him that 'they would have left his own house intact, but wanted to burn that of Martelao'. Hobson managed to avoid this by interceding for the release of the *Commessi*. Mun did not recognise any of the *Popolari* involved in the violence; he declared that he travelled a lot and had just returned, was very busy and therefore did not know many people.

The second Englishman to be interrogated – Guglielmo Gievan – confirmed Mun's version of events, and was equally unable to provide names, notwithstanding the fact that he had been there considerably longer: 'it's been seven years since I arrived in this town; I know many people, but I would not be able to say with certainty "so and so was there"'.[66] The same line was taken by Giovanni Bromhall: 'I know many people, and many Zantiots, as I have been living and working here for four or five years, but I am not in a position to give you the names of who I saw then'.[67] Samuel Whitehead chose a slightly different tactic being that, having traded in the area for some eighteen years, lived in Zante for six, and being one of the few Englishmen who actually spoke Greek, he could hardly claim not to know the *caporioni*. Therefore he declared how, being very scared, he 'ordered all the balconies of the house to be shut', and therefore had not seen a thing.[68]

The last one to be interrogated was John Hobson, Sr, probably the most important English merchant in town. Having mediated between the authorities and the *Popolari* during the actual revolt, he could not deny knowing them, and so he instead resorted to giving a couple of names of people who had already been recognised as *caporioni*, though he stressed that they were 'the most gentlemanly amongst the *Popolari*' ('popolari de più garbo'). Like all other English merchants, Hobson also flatly denied that they were angry with the Republic – 'they were angry only with the [local] Gentlemen' – and thus consistently downplayed their rebelliousness towards Venice, something that considerably facilitated the later quick dispensation of pardons.[69] Whilst not betraying the

---

[65] This was confirmed by all witnesses. See, for example, ASV, *AdC, Penale*, b. 427, fasc. i, c.39v, evidence given by Candiano Roma *quondam* Curtio of Venice (16–6–1631).

[66] Guglielmo Gievan/Gierart [?] *quondam* Thomaso, in ASV, *AdC, Penale*, b. 427, fasc. i, cc.51r–53v (18–6–1631).

[67] Giovanni Bromhall *quondam* Riccardo, in ASV, *AdC, Penale*, b. 427, fasc. i, cc.53v–55v (18–6–1631).

[68] Samuel Whitehead *quondam* Tomaso, in ASV, *AdC, Penale*, b. 427, fasc. i, cc.75r–77v (13–7–1631).

[69] John Hobson *quondam* Milles, in ASV, *AdC, Penale*, b. 427, fasc. i, cc.79v–82r (13–7–1631).

Popolari, in fact Hobson Sr personally interceded successfully for the liberation of their *Commessi*;[70] he also took care of the safety of the *Cittadini* by allowing some of them to take refuge on the English ship in the harbour.[71]

Throughout these events the English merchants managed to stay out of any trouble whilst at the same time offering support to all factions involved. They provided shelter to the threatened *Cittadini* and also managed to convince the crowd not to burn their homes. At the same time, they refused to disclose the names of *Popolari* – unless it was manifestly impossible not to do so – and they underplayed the violence of the *Caporioni*, even coming to their aid as character witnesses.[72] They managed to stay on the right side of the Venetian authorities. This was an extraordinary feat that was made possible by the essential nature of the presence of English merchants; both the *Cittadini* and the rich *Popolari* depended upon the income of the currant trade.

Administering dominion: wealth

As currant cultivation could not be curtailed, the Venetian government raised taxes so at least it received income from it. The 1580 *Nuova Imposta* had quickly become the principal source of revenue from the islands, and one of the most important customs duties for the whole Republic. In 1626 the *Nuovissima* was put in place, adding another 5 ducats per *miaro* of currants.[73] Neither stopped the English, and by the 1670s England absorbed nearly 85 per cent of Zante's currants.[74]

The most visible effect of the currant boom was the conspicuous consumption that swept Zante and Cephalonia. This was a phenomenon that all travellers noted and that maddened the Venetians because it proved the existence of money and underlined their incapacity to control it. Spyros Asdrachas has highlighted how in Zante and Cephalonia it was common for peasants to pay their dues to the landlords in cash, evidence of the monetisation of the local economy, which belied the complaints of

---

[70] Stated also in the interrogation of Giovanni Mun *quondam* Guglielmo in ASV, *AdC*, *Penale*, b. 427, fasc. i, cc.48v–51r (17-6-1631).

[71] This was confirmed by all witnesses. See, for example, ASV, *AdC*, *Penale*, b. 427, fasc. i, c.39v, evidence given by Candiano Roma *quondam* Curtio of Venice; *ibidem*, c.20r evidence given by Stathi Manessi, *Cittadino* of Zante.

[72] See the evidence given by Antonio Monemvasioti, in ASV, *AdC*, *Penale*, b.340, fasc. 13, c.148v.

[73] ASV, *Senato Mar*, reg. 84, cc.206v–207v (25-8-1626). On the *Nuovissima* see Fusaro, *Uva passa*, 138–142.

[74] Roseveare ed., *Markets and Merchants*, 51.

Rettori about the inability of the Venetian administration to make the population pay their dues promptly with cash.[75]

Everyone involved in the currant trade enjoyed a windfall, which may not have lasted, but for a long time currants were synonymous with becoming rich quickly. When Volterra was convicted at the end of the smuggling trial, his estate was conservatively estimated by the authorities at more than 10,000 ducats, 9,000 of which were in real estate, and this did not take into account all he had managed to hide, steal and embezzle before and during the trial itself.[76] His influence in the islands was so strong that when his real-estate properties were put up for auction to reimburse the *Camera Fiscale*, the auction drew no bidders. The same happened on the second attempt, and only at the third attempt did two 'non-islanders' acquire two small properties. The *Rettore* gave up on the auctions and decided the properties would be administered directly by the *Reggimento* so their income would directly go into the state coffers.[77]

Francesco Foscardi's postmortem inventory is a showpiece of luxury textiles from the Low Countries and Venice, furs from England and silverware. Some items were so luxurious that his wife gave them to local monasteries to be used during liturgy. And, though he was part of a family seriously involved in the currant trade, he was by no means one of the major merchants of Cephalonia.[78] Dowries also provide evidence of conspicuous consumption, but it is important to emphasise that I have examined only dowry instruments written in Italian, which do not represent a real sampling of the population of Cephalonia, as people writing in Italian were mostly likely to belong to the upper class. Nevertheless, it is still possible to make some claims. The average figure of 3,000 ducats is high for a colonial backwater and is comparable with dowries of Venetian citizens.[79] None of these documents is related to the major mercantile families of Cephalonia, with the exception of that of Marietta Diorzi, who married a Metaxà. There is also one marriage into the Venetian patriciate, as Giulia Cimmera 'of Giovanni, Cephalonian nobleman', married 'Christofforo da Canal of Francesco Nobile Veneto', an exceptionally good marriage for someone of her standing and which cost her father the

---

[75] S. Asdrachas, 'Agricoltura e rapporti di proprietà', in Costantini ed., *Il Mediterraneo centro-orientale*, 127–132.

[76] ASV, *Quarantia Criminale*, b. 103, fasc. 73, cc.86r–95v.

[77] ASV, *Quarantia Criminale*, b. 103, fasc. 73, c.97v (6 and 7-6-1588): both auctions were deserted. The third one is at cc.105r–106r (10-6-1588).

[78] ΓΑΚ-ΑΝΚ, *Notarial Archive*, b. 117 (Teodoro Peccator), vol. iii, cc.65v–68r (14-11-1663 and following dates).

[79] On *cittadine* dowries in seventeenth century Venice see F. Medioli, 'Arcangela Tarabotti: una famiglia non detta ed un segreto indicibile in famiglia', *Archivio Veneto*, 144 (2013): 105–144.

princely sum of 14,000 ducats of dowry 'in so much gold and silver as per contract'.[80] When an inventory of goods is included, Dutch fine textiles, English woollens, and Venetian laces and brocades are always present in abundance.[81] In general, the extant evidence in Cephalonia shows that the quality and quantity of the clothes is again comparable with those of wealthy Venetians.[82] This corroborates the impressions of travellers such as Thomas Dallam, who, passing through a remote mountain village in Zante in 1599, encountered women 'very rychly apparled, som in red satten, som whyte, and som in watchell Damaske, their heads verrie finly attiered, cheanes of pearle and juels in there eares'.[83] The islanders certainly gave the impression of having a flair for luxury clothes and the finer things of life.

In 1639 English merchants based in the islands delivered to the ambassador in Venice a memorandum on their grievances so that he could present the matter to the *Collegio* and solve the problems. What matters here are not so much the specific grievances (which shall be discussed later), but that a direct connection was being made between the currant trade and the wealth of the islands' inhabitants.

[Whilst beforehand the islands] were in most miserable state [...] by reason of which scarcity, those people were forced to live very sparingly; the Habitts of the better sorte being of Sheepeskinns, and amongst those, the choifest of them were knowne by wearing a Hatt of woole and leather shoes, all of them wearing Schiavonian or Marriners Capps, of the value of a quarter of a piece of eight at the most, and for Shoes they served themselves of a peece of an Ox hide, tyed together with Pachthred, which att this day the Countrie prople continue to wear . . .

The situation had now dramatically changed thanks to the currant trade and the money brought by the English merchants, so much that:

---

[80] ΓΑΚ-ΑΝΚ, *Notarial Archive*, b. 91 (Rafael Pignatore), reg. α, cc.1r/v (1-9-1635). Cristoforo did not appear to have had an important career within the patriciate: on his entry into the Major Council through the *Balla d'oro*, see Biblioteca Museo Correr, *Ms. Provenienze Diverse, Venier*, cod. 69, 'Consegi dal 1606 fino 1610', c. 338r (4-12-1610). 'Giulia Cimera of Giovanni married Cristofor Canal fu Francesco in Cefalonia on 15 April 1610 [sic]; the marriage was notified to the *Avogaria* on 29 November 1633 [sic]': see ASV, *AdC, Libro d'Oro Matrimoni*, IV, c. 66v. They had at least one son – Francesco – whose trial for admission in the Major Council is in ASV, *AdC, Processi di nobiltà*, b. 20/13. I wish to thank Vittorio Mandelli and Antonio Mazzucco for providing me with these details.

[81] On dowries see ΓΑΚ-ΑΝΚ, *Notarial Archive*, b. 143 (Nicolò Andronà), vol. i, c.113r (25-10-1669); b. 143 (Nicolò Andronà), vol. ii, cc.7v–13r (12-11-1674); b. 104 (Sotirio Stravaletrà), cc.22r/v (26-4-1643), c.23r (12-5-1643), c.168r (23-2-1646); b. 117 (Teodoro Peccator), vol. i, cc.181v–183r (6-12-1656), cc.232v–234r (19-5-1660).

[82] Zanatta, 'L'inventario come fonte'.

[83] J. T. Bent ed., *Early Voyages and Travel in the Levant: The Diary of Master Thomas Dallam 1599–1600*, London, 1893, 23.

the people are become so rich by meanes of the English Trafique, that they have made greate & noble buildings, like the forms used in Venice particularly in Ceffalonia, in the principall Port wherof called Argostoli, they have spent in building, within few yeares, more than halfe a Million of Gold besides the Pallaces in the cheife Citty and in other villages. The Gentrie at present are cloathed equall to the cheifest gent in Italy, with silke upon silke, and Cloaks lyned with plush having converted their woollen Hatts [...] into Beavers, as disdayning to weare any inferior.[84]

The economy and the social fabric of Zante and Cephalonia were thus dramatically transformed by the presence of English merchants. Tensions deriving from the quick enrichment of a relatively large part of the population brought to the surface tensions which had been simmering for some time and, as a result, Zante became the only subject territory of the Republic of Venice to witness a proper revolt. The English presence was behind all of these developments. Quietly and swiftly, within a few years after their arrival, they effectively controlled the islands' economy and changed them forever, and their position was strong enough to be able to effectively mediate during the rebellion. It should have been an ideal position from which to continue a fruitful alliance with the local population, but problems were emerging.

Administering dominion: tensions

Throughout the 1620s, the declining price of currants was a concern both in England and in the islands. Prices had been falling mostly because of overproduction, but a substantial role had been also played by English merchants' attempts to pay as little as possible.[85] In 1623, major producers had managed to fix quantities and prices in accordance with the English merchants,[86] but this success was not repeated, and in a market with many sellers and a single buyer, the tendency of prices to fall seemed unstoppable. The English had perfected their bargaining techniques such as making their ships wait, anchored away from the islands, and even sending ships away to lower prices even further.[87] Only when the Greeks

---

[84] TNA, *SP* 99/44, 180r–191v (13/23-9-1638). There is another copy (in TNA, *SP* 99/39, 146r–151v), titled: 'An information of the state, in which was found some years since the Islands of Ceffalonia and Zant; their augmentation, by meanes of the English, and the many extortions and oppressions, there used against Diverse matters of that Nation'.

[85] Ducal letter of the Senate to the *Provveditore* of Cephalonia, in answer to a supplication of the *Comunità* about the constant lowering of prices of currants and the role played by the English: see ASV, *Compilazione leggi*, b. 126, cc.118r–126r (11-5-1627).

[86] ASV, *SDR*, Zante, b. 7, cc.n.n. (20-3-1623).

[87] This was a tactic employed by Simon Whitcombe: ASV, *SDR*, Cefalonia, b. 5, cc.n.n. (12-12-1632).

were scared into accepting lower prices would pacts be underwritten and ships called in to load.[88] These deals were damaging for local producers and for the principal merchants in London, who were fixing prices for higher sums than the currants effectively ended up costing in the islands. The factors there simply pocketed the difference. Besides, overproduction did not help local producers or the Venetian administration. As soon as a producer broke ranks and started to sell currants, all the others followed quickly, terrified of not being able to sell if they waited too long.

Another way to lower prices was for English merchants to buy currants far in advance at a lower price, and to sell later to fellow countrymen at a higher price, pocketing the difference.[89] It was only in 1637 in Zante that Zuanne Cappello, *Inquisitore in Levante*,[90] published strict pricing rules. He prohibited advance payments from foreigners if these came with instructions to hoard currants for the buyer; he also forbade gifts which were given with the same purpose, and the storage of currants which did not belong to the warehouse owner.[91] These regulations (especially the latter) were almost impossible to implement, but they showed that the government was at least aware of what was happening. A few months afterwards, he also prescribed that all ships trading in the islands should have a dedicated booklet – to be kept in the island's local exchequer – wherein should be detailed all cargo movements and their situation with regard to customs payments. The aim was for the Venetian authorities to have available at a glance the history of each ship, so as to be able to act quickly and effectively when necessary. Cappello additionally made tenure of the *Nuova Imposta* incompatible with tenure of the entry–exit customs, a hitherto common situation that had facilitated all sorts of improprieties.[92] In 1627 a secret pact between English and Flemish merchants had been discovered. Signed the year before, it arranged for the English to hoard currants at a low price on behalf of the Flemish.[93] The existence of these kinds of pacts had been suspected for a long time, but the discovery of certain proof caused great uproar in the *Reggimento*.

[88] ASV, *SDR*, Cefalonia, b. 5, cc.n.n. (12-9-1632).
[89] ASV, *SDR*, Zante, b. 8, cc.n.n (2-7-1624); on attempts to solve the problem, see also ASV, *PTM*, b. 1191, cc.n.n. (22-1-1637).
[90] (*Sindici ed*) *Inquisitori* were itinerant magistrates who oversaw governmental activities, and acted as appeal judges around the *Stato da Mar*: see Knapton, 'Tra Dominante e Dominio', 376.
[91] ASV, *PTM*, b. 1191, cc.n.n. (22-6-1637).
[92] ASV, *PTM*, b. 1191, cc.n.n. (27-1-1637mv).
[93] ASV, *SDR*, Zante, b. 8, cc.n.n (enclosed with the dispatch of 8-11-1626), signed by 'Gio Plumonton, Ricardo Gresuel, Gio Obson, Humfredo Beniton' for the English, and Daniel Heel – also for the names of 'Giacomo Frets, Arnoldo Clocher e Gio Martin Agazzi' for the Flemish.

The merchants, convicted jointly by the *Reggimenti* of Zante and Cephalonia,[94] immediately contested the judgment in Venice and were granted an appeal on the grounds that their trade was essential to the local population and to the customs' income.[95]

The English also tried to influence prices through traditional local loans, called the *prosticchi*. The *prosticchio* was – to put it simply – an advance payment made on a future crop. On the islands there were no official Jewish pawnbrokers and moneylenders (as there were in Venice and the *Terraferma*), and no pawnshops, so the way to obtain credit was through *prosticchi*. It was easy to speculate on the needs of cultivators or the market, and Venetian authorities tried unsuccessfully to oppose this practice.[96] The major concern was that the prices paid in advance were in fact substantially lower than those obtainable by waiting for the right season. Another problem caused by the *prosticchi* was that the loan usually had as collateral the borrower's real estate. Lenders preferred not to exercise their right of repossession, preferring instead to bind the borrower by granting further loans. In a territory rife with factional conflict, this was an easy way to create networks of dependency which could be later cashed in on non-monetary terms.[97] This had long-term implications particularly for small landholders: incapable of taking care of the commercialisation of their own crop, they relied on major producers or middlemen, and in so doing they became increasingly indebted to them. By the end of the seventeenth century, the *prosticchi* had made property in Zante and Cephalonia far less fragmented, and this offered great opportunities to English merchants to make money on the side by arranging

---

[94] The sentence was published in Cephalonia on 21 April 1627, in ASV, *SDR*, Cefalonia, b. 4, cc.n.n (enclosed with the dispatch of 2-5-1627).

[95] The original supplication is in ASV, *Collegio, Rdd*, f. 18, cc.n.n. (27-8-1627). The supplicants were 'Zuanne Plomenton, Zuanne Obson, Riccardo Gresuel, et Anfredo Boniton Mercanti Inglesi'. The reply of the *Cinque Savi* is in ASV, *Cinque Savi alla Mercanzia, Risposte*, reg. 147, cc.135v–137r. It allowed them to remain and trade in the islands until the trial was finished. The merchants had also appealed to ambassador Wake to defend them: see TNA, *SP* 99/28, 303r (not dated [1627]). In 1634 the abovementioned were still waiting for the restitution of the money they had deposited, as a warranty that they would not leave town before the trial: see ASV, *Collegio, Rdd*, f. 25, cc.n.n. (6-5-1634).

[96] ASV, *SDR*, Zante, b. 8, cc.n.n (2-7-1624).

[97] Fusaro, *L'uva passa*, 59–60, 91–93; also M. Michelon, 'La peste dei prosticchi: travagli legislativi di un contratto agrario nelle Isole Ionie (secoli XVI–XIX)', *Atti dell'Istituto veneto di scienze, lettere ed arti*, 110 (1991–1992): 365–398. This situation is similar to the one studied by Campbell in the case of the Sarakatsani of Northern Epirus, 'by the extension of interest-free credits, which in fact are seldom entirely repaid, he [the rich man] binds the interests of the shepherd to his own and assists him to maintain his way of life in the face of increasing difficulties': see J. K. Campbell, *Honour, Family and Patronage: A Study of Institutions and Moral Values in a Greek Mountain Community*, Oxford, 1964, 247–256, particularly 250.

loans. A complex web of transactions was woven daily in the islands, intertwining the English and Greek merchants.[98]

On 2 September 1629, Zante woke up to some interesting news: in three conspicuous places in town a pasquinade against the *Rettore* had appeared during the night (Figure 5).

> Ò povera cità che tutti esclama
> Di te Proveditor non pensi à niente
> Se non di tuor in gola allegramente
> Sin nella Sanità che tutti l'ama
> Non Pater Zacÿnthi
> Sed Pater Angliæ

> (Oh poor city! Everyone cries out against you, Provveditore
> you think of nothing save cheerfully gobbling
> even the beloved Sanità
> Non Pater Zacÿnthi
> Sed Pater Angliae)

Giacomo Bembo, the *Rettore* at the time, did not like this at all, and immediately wrote a heated letter of justification to the *Consiglio dei Dieci*. He had not favoured anyone in his year of tenure, quite the opposite, in fact, given his handling of the recent revolt in the island which had avoided further violence. Both the *Consiglio* of the *Cittadini* and the *Popolari* – at that time still involved in the local government – rallied to his defence with letters of support, which were duly included with the dispatch.[99]

Pasquinades (or *cartelli*) were a common mode of political communication in Venice, and very rarely did authorities manage to discover their authors. They were almost always concerned with political criticism, and their effectiveness lay in their capacity to reach a very wide audience.[100] Nothing in the documentary evidence hints at the previous existence of such problems in Zante. Customs income had risen considerably during Bembo's first year of tenure, with an increase of 30 per cent over the previous year, gained mainly in the highly sensitive customs of entry–exit (now in the hands of the *Popolari*) and in the tax on new currant plantations. On the other hand, the figures for the *lazaretto* customs, to which

---

[98] For example see: ΓAK-ANK, *Notarial Archive*, b. 92 (Fabio Stravaletrà), vol. i, cc.202v–203r (25-2-1639); b. 104 (Sotirio Stravaletrà), cc.46r/v (18–11-1643); b. 17 (Giacomo Suriano), c.87v (1-4-1651); b. 117 (Teodoro Peccator), vol. i, c.180v (17-11-1656).

[99] ASV, *Capi del Consiglio dei X, Lettere di Rettori e altre Cariche*, b. 296 (Zante 1506–1749), fasc. iv, n.167 (10-9-1629).

[100] On pasquinades in Venice see de Vivo, *Information and Communication*, 136–141, 194–197, 203. Rather wide-ranging collections can be found in ASV, *Inquisitori di Stato*, b. 920, fasc. ii; ASV, *Atti Diversi Manoscritti*, b. 91.

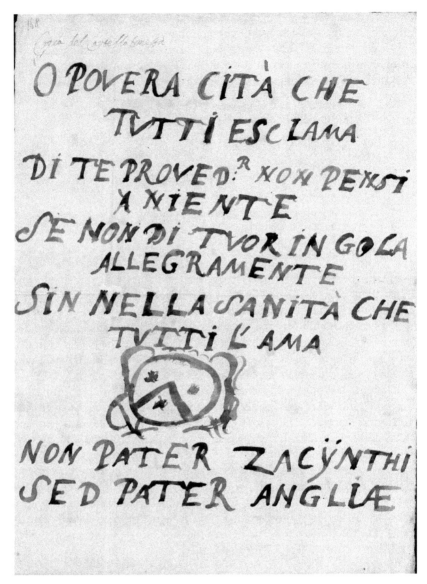

Figure 5. Pasquinade in Zante © Archivio di Stato di Venezia

the pasquinade clearly referred, had remained almost stationary.[101] What we have is tantalising, but, as frequently happens, we have no evidence on

[101] ASV, *SDR*, Zante, b. 9, cc.n.n. (enclosed in the dispatch of 24-11-1629).

how this incident developed nor what results the investigation brought. But we can make an educated guess.

The English were notorious throughout the Mediterranean for their disregard of common safety measures (*regole di Sanità*) to avoid the plague.[102] Although there was no specific reference that year in Zante about ships suspected of being contaminated with the plague, these were relatively frequent events, and ships often were quarantined as a precaution. Local authorities always experienced difficulties in making the English respect the quarantine rules, though the Greeks were equally problematic and frequently also had to be forced to comply.[103] So the notion of the local Greek population complaining about the English disregard of *Sanità* rules is quite ludicrous – unless we look at it from the financial point of view. A 30 per cent increase in the entry–exit customs without a similar increase in the *lazaretto* customs could be the sign of something irregular. Was Bembo pocketing the difference? We do not know, but it certainly is a possibility. For an impoverished Venetian patrician, becoming *Rettore* could also represent the chance to earn some money illegally on the side.[104]

We have no proof that this was the case with Bembo, but we know his predecessor, Piero Malipiero, had been accused by the *Inquisitore e Commissario in Levante*, Antonio Civran, of irregularities during his tenure at Zante. Amongst the charges were: helping the English evade customs, pocketing customs revenues, and tampering with the procedure for farming customs (traditionally done through a formal auction in the Market Square whilst he was accused of doing it privately at home 'at the burnt hour, immediately after lunch').[105]

By the end of the 1620s cracks were beginning to appear in the relationship between local and English merchants. Samuel Whitehead made a

---

[102] On this see Cipolla, *Il burocrate e il marinaio*. Many years afterwards in a memorandum by Giavarina on the behaviour of English ships, he reported that English trade was not stopped by the plague: in TNA, *SP* 99/45, 148r (1/11-8-1660).

[103] ASV, *Cinque Savi alla Mercanzia*, b. 836b, fasc. i, n.22 (20-11-1602); the issue is extensively dealt in Konstantinidou, *Το κακό οδεύει έρποντας ... (The disaster creeps crawling)*.

[104] Knapton, 'Tra Dominante e Dominio', 373–374.

[105] ASV, *PTM*, b. 836bis, cc.n.n. (9-8-1628). Malipiero had denied all the accusations and in the end was tried 'only' for embezzlement, see ASV, *AdC, Penale*, b. 215, fasc. iv. Murky deals were frequent in the financial administration of the islands, and Civran had been sent there to deal with the recent troubles caused by the embezzlement by Basilio Gaurilopulo, one of the local officers of the local exchequer, see ASV, *AdC, Penale*, b. 169, fasc. 17, and M. Koliva-Karaleka, 'Il "Memorial di tuti libri della Camera di Zante" (1498–1628): problematica sulla ricostruzione dell' "Arkeiophylakeion" di Zante', *Studi Veneziani*, 13 (1987): 301–337.

330 Empires and governance in the Mediterranean

deal in Cephalonia in 1629 with local merchants for a conspicuous
quantity of currants that, whilst waiting to be loaded on an English ship,
were in the warehouse of Nicolò Cochino, one of the most powerful local
merchants. Once the currants had left, Cochino rounded up some fake
witnesses and claimed that the currants were his property and had not
been paid for. After he was ordered by the *Reggimento* of Cephalonia to
indemnify Cochino, Whitehead appealed to the *Provveditor General*,
Antonio Pisani. When the latter left the islands, delegating the case to
the *Reggimento* of Zante, Whitehead was worried that Cochino's allies
were going to interfere again, so he asked for the trial to be moved to
Venice, as he believed this was his only chance of a proper judgment.[106]
Richard Griswold found himself in a similar position shortly afterwards.
The new currant crop of 1631 was due very soon, and some damaged
remains of the previous year's crop still remained to be sold. Concerned
that this was going to adversely influence prices, Marin Migliaressi,
farmer of the *Nuova Imposta*, obtained special permission from the
Rettore of Cephalonia to export the old crop under his own name; as a
subject, he was not supposed to pay the *Nuova Imposta*. Not having the
means of transportation himself, he asked Griswold to carry the currants
on his own ship. Griswold accepted and was then accused by Migliaressi
of not having paid customs. A small ship of Griswold's was confiscated
and sold to compensate for the loss.[107] Griswold asked the *Collegio* that
his case be heard in Venice because he did not trust the *Reggimento*. The
Cinque Savi alla Mercanzia granted the request.[108] The Migliaressi family
was obviously fond of this trick, because another member of the family
did it again in 1633, this time with a ship belonging to John Hobson Sr.
The same deal, followed by the same method of anonymous denunciation
which led to its discovery. Hobson ended up in prison and, once there,
was told that by paying 2,000 *reali* in cash to the *Rettore*, Gasparo
Querini – instead of the 6,400 *reali* he had been ordered to pay to the
local exchequer – and by promising that he would not appeal in Venice,
the matter would be closed.[109] Hobson promptly paid and then went to

---

[106] ASV, *Collegio, Rdd*, f. 24, cc.n.n. (6-3-1633). His case was one of those specifically
highlighted in the 1638 memorandum mentioned earlier in the chapter (TNA, *SP* 99/
44, 180r–191v (13/23-9-1638)).

[107] For the price of 700 *reali*. This should have been a larger vessel than the kind described
earlier on in the chapter.

[108] ASV, *Collegio, Rdd*, f. 24, cc.n.n. (29-7-1633). The answer is in ASV, *Cinque Savi alla
Mercanzia, Risposte*, reg. 149, cc.81r–82v. On Griswold case see also: TNA, *SP* 99/34,
143r–144r (10-2-1633); 171r (s.d. [February 1633]); 292r/v (13-10-1634); ASV,
Esposizioni principi, reg. 44 (1635), cc.371v–372r (28-2-1635mv).

[109] ASV, *Senato, Rettori*, f. 5, cc.n.n. (23-11-1633 enclosed with the document dated 31-1-
1633mv).

Venice where, with the support of the English Resident, he appealed against the *Reggimento*.[110]

Trust was becoming quite scarce in the islands. The Greeks, displeased at the decrease in the price of currants and the consequent diminishing returns, were trying anything to recover their losses at the expense of the English. The latter were finding out that appealing to the local *Reggimento* was not necessarily a guarantee of redress and were therefore appealing directly to the *Collegio* in Venice. In those cases where the ambassador got involved, the language employed is quite interesting as there was a constant effort to shift the blame from the Republic's patrician officers in the islands to the local ministers. The English – merchants as well as diplomats – were always at pains to stress their loyalty to the Republic and hinted in their petitions that the provincial government and administration were not up to their tasks. Part of this was simply the usual rhetoric of diplomacy, but the colonial relationship further complicated the political relationship.

Finally in 1636 the English ambassador in Venice presented the *Collegio* with a memorandum that summed up all the problems encountered by the merchants in the islands. It was a long list of accusations against the customs farmers and their ways of abusing their position, and it represented a serious fissure in the alliance between English and Greeks. It recounted in detail all the irregularities in weighing goods, all the problems with loading ships, and all the deliberate and continual delays aimed at obtaining bribes. In a sign of the change in the reciprocal positions of Venetians and English, this memorandum was welcomed by the *Senato* and practical measures were taken to help English

---

[110] Documents relating to this case are to be found in *CSPVe*, vol. xxiii (1632–6), n.241, n.247: see www.british-history.ac.uk/report.aspx?compid=89342; n.335: see www. british-history.ac.uk/report.aspx?compid=89349; n.346: see www.british-history.ac. uk/report.aspx?compid=89350; n.362: see www.british-history.ac.uk/report.aspx? compid=89351; n.413 and n.415: see www.british-history.ac.uk/report.aspx? compid=89354; n.520: see www.british-history.ac.uk/report.aspx?compid=89363; n.605 and n.611: see www.british-history.ac.uk/report.aspx?compid=89369 (date accessed: 26 February 2014). Also in ASV, *Cinque Savi alla Mercanzia*, b. 23 n.s., fasc. iii, cc.n.n. (15-1-1634 and 25-8-1635). Unfortunately, although we know that the *Cinque Savi* took up the appeal, we do not know its final outcome. See also: TNA, *SP* 99/34, 141r–142v (10-2-1634); cc.286r–287r (10-10-1634) the latter is a copy of the *parte* of the *Senato* which delegates his case to the *Cinque Savi*; cc.292r/v (13-10-1634); also ASV, *Esposizioni principi*, reg. 42 (1633), cc.274–275r (20-1-1633mv); reg. 43, cc.77v–78r (11-8-1634); cc.101r–103r (1-9-1634); reg. 44, cc.371v–372r (28-2-1635mv); reg. 45, cc.76r–77r (29-7-1636); cc.88r/v (19-8-1636); reg. 46, cc.112r–114r (26-6-1637); cc.122r–123r (3-7-1637); reg. 49, cc.159v–160r (23-8-1640); reg. 50, cc.75r/v (5-6-1641), and c.79r (11-6-1641). This was another one of the cases also highlighted in the 1638 memorandum (TNA, *SP* 99/44, 180r–191v (13/23-9-1638)).

commerce.[111] Long gone were the times when the Venetians wanted the English to abandon Zante and Cephalonia; now they were terrified that the currant trade might move to the Morea, leaving the islands completely destitute. Morean currants were of worse quality, though, and that was the ultimate reason behind the English reluctance to move their operations and invest there. Increasingly, the favoured tactic was to mix Ionian and Morean currants to improve the overall quality of shipments.[112]

Up to this point crimes against Englishmen had been against property,[113] something to be expected considering that they were always laden with bullion. But from the 1630s, such crimes were overshadowed by the rise in the number of violent crimes. There were increasingly frequent outbursts of violence amongst the islanders themselves – Dimitri Rucani had obtained permission to carry weapons to protect himself whilst farming the customs of the *Nuova Imposta*, and had ended up using them to punish his factional adversaries – but until now these tendencies had not been directed towards foreigners.[114] In 1631 Andrew Weston, 'for not consenting unto certayne unlawfull pretences of some Islanders' – we know no more details – was murdered in his house in Zante, and all his money and jewels were stolen. All these were lost because the authorities did not move quickly enough, and the involvement of Cristoforo da Canal – a 'gentleman of Venice' – on whose person some of the jewels were found, probably did not help to bring about a quick solution.[115] A nasty fate also awaited the pilot of the ship *Abigail*, who in 1632

was by night slaine in the village of Argostoli, and robbed of his money and Cloathes, some daies after his bodie was found in the sea with a stone tied about his neck, and his Cloathes being knowne upon the bach [sic] of one of the Murtherers ...

---

[111] On the memorandum, see ASV, *Cinque Savi alla Mercanzia*, b. 81 n.s., fasc. vi, cc.n.n. (16-8-1636); the consequent decisions of the Senate are in ASV, *Senato Mar*, reg. 94, cc.180v–181v (10-9-1636).

[112] On the threat of the move to the Morea, where taxation was extremely light in comparison with the Ionian islands, see ASV, *Collegio, Rdd*, f. 11, cc.n.n. (31-8-1603); and ASV, *Cinque Savi alla Mercanzia, passim* in the series. See also Fusaro, *Uva passa*, 166–173.

[113] For example, see ASV, *SDR*, Zante, b. 5, cc.n.n. (8-1-1614).

[114] ASV, *SDR*, Zante, b. 6, *passim*. When he wrote to the Senate to obtain the licence to carry weapons, he also accused his enemies of wanting to prepare ships to carry currants to England directly, thereby ruining the *Nuova Imposta* custom and therefore Rucani himself. He was believed and his request accepted. See ASV, *Cinque Savi alla Mercanzia, Risposte*, reg. 144, cc.48v–50r.

[115] Probably the husband of Giulia Cimmera: see p. 322 above.

He was detained on the English merchants' instance, but then:

being favoured by certaine Gent in that place, he was by their helpe sent to the
Gallies, in execution of a former condemnation, which they founde in the
Chancery, whereby the justice was deluded, and the more haynous crime passed
over, and not punished.[116]

The situation worsened throughout the 1630s; in the spring of 1638, an
attack against William Bordet, English consul in Zante, provoked English
merchants to write a petition to the *Rettore* which included a long list of
recent violent episodes against English merchants.[117] Shortly afterwards,
a long memorandum was handed to the Resident in Venice with the usual
complaints about the behaviour of officers and their venality, especially
their demands for bribes.[118] It contained an even longer list of recent
episodes of violence against Englishmen.[119] The appeasing answers of the
Venetian government did not seem to make a difference on the ground.
Another memorandum the following year aimed even higher, for the first
time directly accusing the local *Reggimento* of not applying the law
because it had business interests in the currant trade.[120]

Co-administering dominion?

This period of tension ended with the appointment of Henry Hyde as
farmer of the *Nuova Imposta*. A man of great personality and entrepreneurial flair, he had been active in Cephalonia since the early 1630s and
had quickly become one of the principal merchants there.[121] In 1635, he
personally lent to the Cephalonia exchequer the considerable sum of
12,000 *reali*, giving genuine assistance to the beleaguered *Rettore* during

---

[116] TNA, *SP* 99/44, 180r–191v (not dated [23-9-1639]).
[117] ASV, *SDR*, Zante, b. 12, cc.n.n. (10-5-1638 enclosed in the dispatch of 18-5-1638).
[118] On the venality of officers, and the fact that, to have currants weighed, it was necessary
to pay a bribe to the officers, see also TNA, *SP* 105/143, 62r (not dated [1638?]).
[119] TNA, *SP* 99/42, 25r (29–6/9-7-1638).
[120] TNA, *SP* 99/44, 180r–191v, discussed before at p. 324. There is a direct reference to Paolo
Malipiero, son of that Piero who was the *Rettore* of Cefalonia during the revolt, accusing
him to have frequently taken advantage of his father's position. Already in 1630 the then
Rettore of Cefalonia, Gerolamo Lippomano, cautiously suggested that the young man had
not acted properly: see ASV, *SDR*, Cefalonia, b. 5, cc.n.n. (14-3-1630).
[121] In 1632 he was caught not paying the 'transit custom' for five boxes of silks and one of
gold buttons, also involved in the deal were Giovanni Marchetti, a Venetian living in
Zante, and Costantino Lazzari: see ASV, *Cinque Savi alla Mercanzia, Risposte*, reg. 149,
cc.28v–29v (10-1-1632mv). The English had always been particularly intolerant of the
transit custom, and in 1627 they had presented a memorandum complaining of the way it
was enforced in the islands. See TNA, *SP* 99/28, 114r (14-10-1627). For his activities see
also ASV, *SDR*, Cefalonia, b. 6, cc.n.n. (12-1-1634); ASV, *Cinque Savi alla Mercanzia,
Risposte*, reg. 150, cc.172r–173v (2-4-1636); ASV, *SDR*, Cefalonia, b. 6, cc.n.n. (29-6-
1635).

a year of grain famine.[122] The following year, with the famine still ravaging the Morea, he sent a ship to load grain in Candia, once again giving essential assistance in a period of terrible grain crops, earthquakes and unseasonable rains.[123] As a consequence, and at the request of the English ambassador in Venice, Hyde was granted the privilege of speeding up his litigation by dealing in the first instance not with the islands' *Rettori* but directly with the *Sindici Inquisitori ed Avogadori in Levante*. This was rarely granted, and it was a measure of Hyde's status and of the Republic's fears that such a privilege was bestowed on him.[124]

In 1636, with the support of the extraordinary ambassador Basil Feilding in Venice, he proposed farming the *Nuova Imposta* himself.[125] The *Savi*, initially taken aback, in the end responded positively, because there was no law 'that forbids foreigners to farm your [Serenity's] customs, although he should choose local islanders to manage it and provide financial guarantees'.[126] Hyde then took the fatal step of choosing as his administrator Marc'Antonio Boldù, stepson of Pietro Aquila, who was the Minister (*Fiscale*) of the local exchequer.[127] The situation quickly collapsed as Boldù and Aquila connived behind his back, and Hyde ended up accused of embezzlement on a massive scale.[128] Frightened for his life, he fled to the Morea, whence he tried to defend his position and asked for his case to be tried on appeal at Zante and not at Cephalonia, where Aquila and Boldù were very powerful. The *Savi* agreed.[129] Biasio Vondagni, a merchant of Cephalonia who had been convicted alongside him,[130] came to Hyde's help with a long memorandum in which he explained how Aquila had abused his position for his own personal gain and how he meddled in the affairs of Cephalonia: most of the signatures of

---

[122] ASV, *SDR*, Zante, b. 10, cc.n.n (18-8-1635).

[123] ASV, *SDR*, Zante, b. 11, cc.n.n (4-4-1636).

[124] ASV, *Senato Mar*, reg. 93, cc.85v–86r (29-6-1635); for the implementation, see ASV, *Sindici Inquisitori in Terra Ferma e Levante*, b. 67, lxxvi, c.31v (24-5-1636).

[125] TNA, *SP* 99/38, 126r–127v (31–8/10-9-1636).

[126] ASV, *Cinque Savi alla Mercanzia, Risposte*, reg. 150, cc.189v–193v (2-9-1636).

[127] Aquila will be accused by the English merchants of being one of the men behind the attack on Bordet. He had also had a previous brush with justice in 1628 when he was first nominated *Fiscale*: on that occasion he had neglected his charges so much that the nomination had been annulled. See ASV, *PTM*, b. 836bis, cc.n.n. (7-7-1628sn): 'a man intent on private interests, and stimulated by the greed of profit'.

[128] ASV, *SDR*, Cefalonia, b. 7, cc.n.n. (20-12-1638sn). His debts were apparently to the sum of 15,468 ducats. From the account that should have proved his debts in the exchequer, we gather that on average he loaded six ships each year from 1630 to 1637. In ASV, *PTM*, b. 1191, cc.n.n. (enclosed to the dispatch of 8-3-1638).

[129] ASV, *Cinque Savi alla Mercanzia, Risposte*, reg. 151, cc.183r–185v (2-9-1638). For diplomatic support of Hyde's plight see ASV, *Esposizioni Principi*, reg. 47, cc.234r–235r (18-9-1638).

[130] ASV, *Senato Mar*, reg. 96, c.184v (11-10-1638).

warranties for his customs farming were fake.[131] He also denounced how Aquila's associates were administering most of the other customs, thereby creating a web of support for smuggling and other wrongdoing. In the meantime, the books had been better examined, and Hyde appeared to be in the black.[132] His case was sent to a specially convened committee of the *Senato*.[133]

Hyde had made himself very comfortable in the Morea. Long-standing Venetian fears about traffic moving to the Morea appeared to finally materialise, as spies of Antonio Molino, the Zante *Rettore*, reported that Hyde 'is loved and esteemed by the Turks'.[134] The *Inquisitore in Levante*, Zuanne Cappello, tried to counteract. A preliminary move was to stop barrel-makers travelling to the Morea, as their skills were essential to the long-distance trade of currants.[135] But a steady trickle of people experienced in currant cultivation appeared to be moving there, and evidence surfaced of English investment in plantations. General trade with the Morea was growing, particularly English textiles that the islands had never been able to absorb and which found an excellent market there. An alarmed Cappello said this newly revitalised Morea trade could even damage Venetian trade with Spalato, becoming an alternative gateway to Ottoman territory which was not controlled by Venice.[136]

Worse was to come as, in the middle of the Hyde controversy, the Secretary of England asked for patents for Thomas Simonds to go to the islands as 'factor general' to 'resolve some grievances' – the merchants' strong complaints from the previous years. The *Cinque Savi alla Mercanzia* answered positively, stressing that although this was a novelty, it could be conceded in order to keep English merchants

---

[131] ASV, *Collegio, Rdd*, f. 34, *passim*.
[132] ASV, *SDR*, Zante, b. 12, cc.n.n (30-3-1639); also ASV, *Cinque Savi alla Mercanzia, Risposte*, reg. 152, cc.66r–69r (1-2-1639mv); cc.88v–89r (14-5-1640), shows the positive opinion about the customs' profits being divided amongst the *caratadori*.
[133] ASV, *Cinque Savi alla Mercanzia, Risposte*, reg. 152, cc.16r/v (14-5-1639).
[134] ASV, *SDR*, Zante, b. 13, cc.n.n. (29-1-1642). Further evidence of this is in ASV, *SDR*, Cefalonia, b. 7, cc.n.n. (16-11-1641), and (26-5-1642). 'Henry Hyde the consul of the Morea in the late 1630s and early 1640s, took full advantage of his position not only to live well but also to carve out a base of considerable influence in both the English and Ottoman spheres [and in the Greek, I would add]. Currants provided the fiscal underpinning for this political and social leverage, [...]', in Goffman, *Britons in the Ottoman Empire*, 52–53.
[135] ASV, *PTM*, b. 1191, cc.n.n. (11-6-1637). Barrels were preferred for two different reasons: they preserved the fruit better, and they were less easy to smuggle. On this see ASV, *Compilazione leggi, Cefalonia*, b. 126, cc.91r–92v (22-11-1605). On commissioning the making of barrels, see, ГАК-ANK, *Notarial Archive*, b. 91b (Rafael Pignatore), cc.22r/v (23-9-1645).
[136] ASV, *PTM*, reg. 1191, cc.n.n. (5-1-1637); ASV, *SDR*, Zante, b. 14, cc.n.n. (18-9-1643), but references to his successes in the Morea are spread throughout the *busta*.

happy.[137] Simonds was in fact already in the islands, experimenting with a
currant joint-stock company, and a furious *Senato* recalled him to Venice
and only then allowed him to go back to the islands with the proviso that
he could not act as the sole buyer.[138]

The English were finally reacting to the deterioration of relations with
the locals by making full use of their unity – under the Levant Company's
organisation – to force a settlement to their own benefit. It proved impossible for the Greeks and Venetians to act in a similarly unified manner.
Simonds was playing with a marked deck of cards. Although his official
title was that of 'Consull and General Factor' of the Levant Company, it
was clear from his 'Commissions, Articles of Agreement and Instructions'
that his role was to buy all currants:

in our name and behalfe to buy and take up the whole quantity of Currans that
shalbe yearely laden for the Englise Nation from those places,

and that the traditional chores of a consul, mostly related to ship business,
were left to 'Mr Bordet'.[139] Another of his duties was to oversee factors'
behaviour, a matter that was creating some concern at the General Court of
the Company. A distinct feeling had been growing in London that factors
were not always keeping in mind the best interests of the Company and
were instead favouring their own,[140] and even those of their Greek partners. To this end, Simonds had a 'dormant commission' amongst his
papers, which in case of his death would have automatically settled the
succession without waiting for instructions from London. The pseudo-
secrecy around it was designed to create fear amongst both the English
merchants and their Greek counterparts regarding which of the English
was going to become the next 'Company man'.[141]

Simonds' arrival also exacerbated the Greeks' fears about the English
being the masters of the trade. His activities were no different from the
tactics used by other merchants to push down prices, but the fact that he
had a precise mandate to do so scared the islanders. The *Sindici* of the
Comunità in Cephalonia immediately petitioned the *Reggimento* and
Senato to expel him.[142] For once there was total agreement between the
Senato and the local population, and Simonds' behaviour was to be tightly

[137] ASV, *Cinque Savi alla Mercanzia, Risposte*, reg. 152, cc.10r–13v (10-5-1639), see also
cc.30v–31r (17-8-1639).
[138] ASV, *Senato Mar*, reg. 97, cc.188v (1-9-1639).
[139] TNA, *SP* 105/143, 59r, 59v–60r, 60v–61v (May 1638).
[140] References are dotted throughout the documentation; see particularly TNA, *SP* 105/
148, 30v–31r, 31v–32r, 163r.
[141] TNA, *SP* 105/143, 60v–61v 'Instructions from the Governor and Company [...] unto
Thomas Simonds Merchant [...]'; on this see also Epstein, *The Early History*, 98–99.
[142] ASV, *SDR*, Cefalonia, b. 7, cc.n.n. (26-12-1639 enclosed in dispatch 7-1-1639mv).

controlled.[143] Simonds was clearly acting as sole buyer; a contract emerged in which all the English had agreed to pay a fixed price, lower than the one decided by the Company, and to pocket the difference. Trade was at a standstill.[144] There were several voices wishing for the return of Henry Hyde, but he never came back. He remained consul in Morea until he was dismissed in 1643, and later lost his head in London for supporting the crown.[145]

Currants and empire

With the advancing of the 1640s an eerie calm set in on the currant trade, both in the islands and in Venice. Bigger concerns occupied the Venetians – from 1646 they were engaged in a long war with the Ottomans – and the English kept a low profile locally, whilst at home the civil wars raged. English diplomatic intervention at the *Collegio* was whittled down and then stopped with the suspension of diplomatic relations.[146]

When some normality returned in the 1660s the currant trade had found a new arrangement which was to last until the end of the Republic. On the one hand little seemed to have changed, and merchants' (very few) petitions were similar to those of thirty years earlier – albeit with a substantially more subdued tone.[147] Traffic had diminished from its peak of the 1630s, but the English were still very active, and the threat of abandoning the islands was ultimately not put into practice.[148] The recent uncertainties of the trade resulted in becoming impossible to find local people willing to farm out the *Nuova Imposta*, or financially able to support the costs associated with it, so it had to be administered by petty officials on behalf of the *Serenissima Signoria*.[149] This was by no means a guarantee of efficiency. Currant production had finally been brought under some sort of control and, though this had created social

---

[143] Memorandum of the ambassador of the *Comunità* of Zante in ASV, *Collegio, Rdd*, f. 30, cc.n.n. (2-10-1639); instructions to the *Rettore* of Cephalonia about Simonds in ASV, *Senato Mar*, reg. 97, c.294v (4-2-1639mv).
[144] ASV, *SDR*, Zante, b. 12, cc.n.n (15-1-1639mv), (28-2-1639mv); ASV, *SDR*, Cefalonia, b. 7, cc.n.n. (8-8-1641).
[145] TNA, *SP* 105/144, 2v–3r. On his operations in Ottoman territories and on the last years of his life see Goffman, *Britons in the Ottoman*, and M. C. Fissel and D. Goffman, 'Viewing the Scaffold from Istanbul: The Bendysh–Hyde Affair, 1647–1651', *Albion*, 22 (1990): 421–448.
[146] A few references still in ASV, *Esposizioni Principi*, reg. 50, cc.70v–71r (31-5-1641), cc.75r/v (5-6-1641), cc.79r (11-6-1641); cc.97r/v (29-7-1641).
[147] TNA, *SP* 99/46, 89r-90r (8-1-1666).
[148] ASV, *SDR*, Cefalonia, b. 12, cc.n.n. (20-1-1659mv) and (22-4-1660).
[149] ASV, *Collegio, Rdd*, f. 72, *passim*.

disturbances, it also had a positive effect on prices. From the 11 million *libbre* of 1639, production in Cephalonia was down to 4.5 million in the mid-1660s. Grain production was also slowly picking up.[150]

During the 1650s and 1660s the feeling of life in the islands can be compared to waking up after a massive binge. Things fell slowly back into place and traffic quietly resumed a more regular pace. No more memorandums were sent to Venice on commercial issues, these having been sidelined first by the needs of war, and then by the plight of the administration of justice. The English presence had shrunk somewhat, and merchants kept a lower profile than in previous times.[151] During the 1650s Venetians' concerns about the Morea trade subsided. Hyde had certainly developed that side of the traffic, but his successors lacked his flair for keeping the Ottomans happy, and with the settling down of the situation in the islands, most of the traffic returned there. Everyone was on the lookout for a 'new Hyde', someone who would be able to keep both the Venetian government and the Greek traders happy. Indeed, the Senate even promised Cromwell to give special treatment 'to the Ministers and individual merchants whom you shall judge to be the most worthy'.[152] But no one appeared to take up Hyde's mantle. Daniel Goffman is mesmerised by Hyde's ability in 'cross-cultural and even multicultural discourse', but this was something he shared with all of his colleagues.[153] The English would have not survived in the Levant – be it Ottoman or Venetian – without it. Hyde was exceptional insofar as he had a great gift for communication, and, judging by the extant documentation, he was a most charismatic individual. But he could not be the solution to a structural problem, which is precisely what the Ionian situation was.

It is difficult to say what conclusions to draw from the 'currant century' in Zante and Cephalonia. The English presence changed their history and had an important influence in their development. Like all intense relationships, its balance was mixed. There had been a long convergence of interests, and for a few decades the English were strong allies of the locals against the centralising aspirations of the Republic. Even when the relationship turned sour, this period was not forgotten. The large space dedicated in this text to confrontations between English and Greeks

[150] ASV, *SDR*, Cefalonia, b. 13, cc.n.n. (1-3-1664mv); ASV, *Senato, Deliberazioni, Rettori*, f. 64. Report of Christoforo Gabriel on Cephalonia (9-11-1665 enclosed with the dispatch of 11-11-1665).
[151] ASV, *Cinque Savi alla Mercanzia*, b. 81 n.s., cc.n.n. (12-9-1670).
[152] ASV, *Senato Secreta, Corti*, reg. 32, cc.144v–146r (13-11-1655).
[153] Goffman, *Britons in the Ottoman*, 221.

should not give the impression that there was more disagreement than agreement. The opposite is true, but it should not be forgotten that documentary sources are far quieter when things are running smoothly, and even more so when silence helps business.

The quick enrichment enjoyed by the local population during the first phase of the currant trade did not last, and nor did the exploits of Greek shipowners. The crisis of the Venetian commercial fleet had given them the chance to appear on the international stage, but after the first generation's successes, the second one did not continue in its wake, at least not on the same scale. The massive increase in the English maritime presence in the Mediterranean, with safer ships and lower insurance rates, hurt both Venetians and Greeks, pushing them out of the market. Ultimately, both were downsized to being purely regional in scope. Their unmaking was their inability to capitalise on their prior success. The islanders never acquired sufficient unity to be able to deal simultaneously with the Venetian authorities and the English mercantile organisation. They tried on several occasions to deal directly with England, attempting to send to London ambassadors of the *Comunità*, but each time the Venetians quashed the attempt, managing to keep at least the formal diplomatic side of things under their control.[154]

With the currant trade stabilised, during the eighteenth century Venice decided to change its policy and at last endeavoured to integrate the islands into the state's economy. The establishment of state-subsidised olive oil production, to satisfy demand from the textile and soap industries in Venice and the Italian mainland, was a partial success.[155] In Corfu the already strong production of olive oil became even more central to the local economy, though in Zante and Cephalonia reconversion had only limited success, as currants remained the staple. Unlike oil, currant production was *never* stimulated, encouraged or imposed by Venice; contrary to what has been written, Venice always opposed it.[156]

The currant tale highlights Venice's major problem in its imperial policy: privileging defence over development created a gulf between rulers and ruled. A fissure developed which allowed commercial competitors to penetrate, exploit and ultimately dominate the colonial economy. Within this volatile environment, the injection of cash which entered

[154] See for example ASV, *Senato Mar*, reg. 93, cc.92r/v (10-7-1635).
[155] Ciriacono, *Olio ed ebrei*, 97–98, 129–134.
[156] This is another example of the interpretative problems caused by assuming the situation in all the islands was the same: see Dudan, *Il dominio veneziano di Levante*, 243; Yannoupoulos, 'State and Society', 40; Gekas, *Business Culture*, 24.

the system thanks to the currant trade had a profoundly destabilising effect: economically, socially and politically.

Defence was, once again, the guiding light of the *Senato*. In line with the traditional discourse of benign protection, and stimulated by the presence of a powerful enemy such as the Ottoman empire, when troubles arose throughout the seventeenth and eighteenth century the *Senato* tended to side with the local population – especially the indigenous ruling classes – to maintain their support and therefore their dominions. Over the *longue durée* this kind of policy substantially weakened the effective governance by Venetian officers in the islands, as it became common for locals to appeal directly to Venice and to sideline local representatives.[157] Historians have long criticised the Venetian administration for not reining in the local ruling classes, whose autonomy was growing unchecked by the executive power of the Venetian metropolis. The reason for this inaction has been too simplistically attributed to the mediocre quality of the Venetian representatives in the islands – the expression of a decadent and increasingly poor ruling class, far too willing to take advantage of the opportunities for corruption which were afforded them in the Ionian environment. Similarly, the local populations themselves often are tarnished as being innately 'violent' and 'corrupt'. However, no one seriously considered the magnitude of the economic and social transformations set into motion by the arrival of the northerners.

It is not my intention to enter into the long-standing debate on the moral and intellectual qualities of the patricians sent to govern the islands. Undoubtedly, some of them proved not to be up to the challenges they encountered, and certainly some tried to take private advantage of the economic opportunities available, and privileged this over public service. However, even the best amongst them – Maffio Michiel, to name just one – had to bow to the economic impact of the currant trade and the lack of a clear strategy by the *Senato* to attend to the economic and social interests of their subjects. These circumstances made the positions of *Rettore* in Zante and Cephalonia thankless and undesirable charges, which increasingly the most able and ambitious patricians tried to avoid. At the same time the possibility of illicit enrichment made these posts desirable to the poorest – and thus considered weakest – members of the patriciate. Contemporaries were fully aware of these problems, and it was exactly the experience of governing those islands which was the basis of some of the most stimulating reflections and writings of Venetian Enlightenment reformers.[158]

[157] Viggiano, *Lo specchio della repubblica*.
[158] F. M. Paladini, 'Né uomini né strutture: ultimi anni del dominio veneto nelle Isole Jonie attraverso i dispacci dell'ultimo Provveditore Generale da Mar Aurelio

Sir Thomas Roe, one of the most vociferous critics in London of the money which the English spent on currants, passing through Zante and Cephalonia in 1621 on his way to be ambassador in Constantinople, wrote:

here is a little barren island or two, that devours more money, returns nothing but a trash berry, takes none of our native merchandize, and in conclusion laughs at us.[159]

The Greeks did not laugh for long afterwards, but their feeling of having been in control was not forgotten. What lingered was the sense of having been through exceptional times of wealth and opportunity, and that the English had been part of it. This memory would play a crucial role at the beginning of the nineteenth century.

Widmann', *Atti dell'istituto veneto di scienze, lettere ed arti*, 152 (1993–94): 183–222. G. Nani, *Divisamenti e confronti per il governo delle provincie d'oltremare* (1780), on which see the analysis in Viggiano, *Lo specchio della repubblica*; on Giacomo Nani and his work see P. Del Negro, 'Giacomo Nani. Appunti biografici', *Bollettino del Museo Civico di Padova*, lx (1971): 115–147; and *DBI*, s.v. Giacomo Nani, and bibliography quoted therein.
[159] M. Strachan, *Sir Thomas Roe, 1581–1644: A Life*, Salisbury, 1989, 140.

12   Coda and conclusions

The Venetian Major Council voted itself out of existence on 12 May 1797; French troops landed in Corfu at the end of June, and by mid-August all Ionian islands seemed securely in French hands. Napoleon wrote to Talleyrand that controlling Corfu and Zante 'makes us masters of the Adriatic and the Levant' and that possession of these strategic locations would allow the French to play their part at the forthcoming collapse of the Ottoman empire.[1] The French played the role of 'liberators' not 'conquerors' to the Ionians, the same strategy they had used with northern Italians. To this end they made full use of republican propaganda, peppering all their actions and proclamations with references to the antiquity of the republican ideals of Greece. Napoleon himself recommended this strategy to Anselmo Gentili, commander of the Division of the Levant, though in reality he viewed the islands in very practical terms as the key to the Adriatic and a bridgehead from which to control the Mediterranean and oppose British interests.[2]

At the treaty of Campoformio (17 October 1797) – which formally sanctioned the end of the Republic of Venice – Napoleon ceded the town of Venice and the whole of the *Terraferma* to Austria, but kept for France the Ionian islands. Interestingly enough, he used the same arguments that the Republic had used for so many centuries.[3] He wrote to the Directory:

The islands of Corfu, Zante and Cephalonia are more interesting for us than the whole of Italy [...] The Ottoman Empire crumbles more every day and the

---

[1] P. Pisani, *L'expédition Russo-Turque aux Îles Ioniennes en 1798–1799*, n.p., n.d., [*Revue d'histoire diplomatique*, undated reprint], 8–12.

[2] N. G. Moschonas, 'L'idéologie politique dans les Îles Ioniennes pendant la période républicaine (1797–1799)', in *La révolution française et l'hellénisme moderne*, Athens, 1989, 123–136, 123–124.

[3] On Napoleon's plans for the islands, see E. Rodocanachi, *Bonaparte et les Îles Ioniennes: un épisode des Conquêtes de la République et du Premier Empire (1797–1816)*, Paris, 1899, especially 33.

342

possession of these islands will allow us to support it as much as will be possible, or to take our part.[4]

Time was to prove him wrong in his prediction for Ottoman collapse, but the strategic importance of the islands was quite clear to all the other European powers of the day. Shortly afterwards, in March 1799, a Russo-Turkish coalition conquered them, and in order to achieve a balance between the two allied empires, the islands were turned into an independent state. In 1800 the Convention of Constantinople created the Septinsular Republic under Russo-Turkish sovereignty. In a convention between the sultan and the tsar, in which Great Britain also participated, it was decided that because the islands were particularly close to the Peloponnese and to the Albanian coast, and therefore 'very dear to the tranquility and safety of the Sublime Porte', they would form a republic similar to the one of Ragusa – that is to say, dependent from and protected by the Ottoman Porte.[5] However, the islands fell quickly into a state of anarchy.

After Venice

On 20 February 1801 Zante proclaimed its independence from the rest of the Ionian islands, and the leaders of the rebellion, calling themselves the Noble Presidency of the Island of Zante, raised the British flag on the fort declaring their will to become a protectorate of the British crown.[6] On 23 March the Presidency wrote to Lord Grenville, the minister of foreign affairs, explaining the reasons behind such a move, affirming that, even when they were subjects of the former Republic of Venice,

thanks to the trade of its most important commodity, currants, [Zante] started to adopt and sustained unfailingly a passionate genius towards the Illustrious British Nation to which it owned its sustenance through the yearly sale of the abovementioned commodity.

Not liking the 'abhorred French yoke' they had hoisted the English flag,

convinced by inveterate experience of the great good obtained through the currants trade [...] Your Excellency would allow us to remind him the peculiar situation of the island that always traded with England, and whose trade could flourish even more, to others' envy, if it was to be under your high Protection.

---

[4] G. Pauthier, *Les Îles Ioniennes pendant l'occupation française et le protectorat anglais*, Paris, 1863, 1.

[5] E. Lunzi, *Della repubblica settinsulare libri due*, Bologna, 1863, 37.

[6] Lunzi, *Della repubblica settinsulare*, 66; Kirkwall ed., *Four Years in the Ionian Islands*, 61.

They proceeded to describe the wealth of the island and the currant trade in detail, highlighting how advantageous its income would be for Britain. They ended their letter by underlining how bad it would be for English trade and the safety of its navigation if the island were under the French.[7] Interestingly the argument was made against the French, even though Russo-Turkish troops had been occupying the islands since 1799. The situation in the other islands was chaotic, but only Zante made moves towards Britain. The Senate of the Septinsular Republic did not recognise the rebels but was not in a position to send troops to stop them. The British government was not at all happy at this turn of events, and the ambassador at the Porte 'speedily expressed through Mr. Forest, Consul at Corfu, the disgust of the king of England at the unauthorised use of his flag by parties in Zante hostile to the Porte'.[8] The British diplomatic machine engaged at full speed, assuring all the powers that Britain was committed to the unity of the Ionian islands and not only did not support the actions at Zante but was outraged at the injury done to the British flag. Only in September did the situation return to normality, when Russian ships arrived in Zante and peacefully retook it.[9] The island remained fairly unstable throughout the Russo-Turkish occupation, and also after the Treaty of Tilsit (1807), which gave all the Ionian islands back to France.[10]

Whilst Zante was making a beeline for Britain, the other islands were hardly tranquil, prompting the Russians in 1802 to send the Zante-born Count Mocenigo as a plenipotentiary. Thanks to his intimate knowledge of the local situation, Mocenigo organised a temporary regency government on each island under a foreign regent (i.e. not involved with local interests) to oversee the creation of a constitution. However, all this work came to an abrupt end in 1807 when the islands returned to French rule. The French implemented a policy of relative independence from Paris, their only concern being the creation of the post of imperial commissioner to supervise the local Senate and approve its deliberations.[11] The economy slumped and trade was slow. French attempts at redirecting trade towards Marseilles were only partially successful, and Venice and Trieste remained the favourite destinations

---

[7] *Gennadius Library, American School of Classical Studies at Athens*, Mss 103, cc.n.n, letter of the Presidency to Lord Grenville, dated 23 March 1801; this is followed by a petition to the king, using the same arguments.
[8] Kirkwall ed., *Four Years in the Ionian Islands*, 62.
[9] Lunzi, *Della repubblica settinsulare*, 73; W. D. Wrigley, *The Diplomatic Significance of Ionian Neutrality, 1821–31*, New York, 1988, 47–48.
[10] Lunzi, *Della repubblica settinsulare*, 105, 132–133, 139–140, 144–146.
[11] Lunzi, *Della repubblica settinsulare*, 238.

of Ionian shipping.[12] The main problem was that trade with Britain, understandably, slowed considerably.

In 1809 the Zantiots were again seriously restless, and Cephalonia, Ithaca and Cerigo this time were happy to join in. But the British attitude had substantially changed, and this time they sent Admiral Lord Collingwood from Malta to take over the islands.[13] The balance of European powers and alliances had shifted between 1801 and 1809, making the Ionian islands very appealing for Britain, but also allowing the British to pursue their interests in the area without fear of upsetting their allies.

Initially the population of all the Ionian Islands had been enthusiastic in celebrating the collapse of the Venetian Republic and the arrival of the French, with all their promises of a future of freedom and wealth. With the passing of time, the attitude changed. Specifically the economies of Zante and Cephalonia, dependent on trade with England, had started to suffer because of the French presence and its strong anti-British policies. It was for this reason that their inhabitants had been so keen to put themselves under British protection, and for the same reason the dominant political faction on both islands was the so-called 'English party'. The French had been concerned about the strength of the English party since the beginning of their occupation, especially since the events of 1801. Therefore they employed spies on both islands to discover who the supporters of the English party were so as to contain their influence. The results of these investigations must have made painful reading for French authorities. From the spies' reports it became obvious that, in Zante and Cephalonia, both the local landowning aristocracy and the merchants of the middling sort might have been divided politically on the precise makeup of the local assemblies and on matters of representation, but they agreed wholeheartedly in championing the British presence.[14] A report listed those Zante inhabitants who, in case the French returned to the island, should be either deported or closely watched, as they were

[12] H. Yannacopoulou, 'Français, républicains et impériaux, aux sept Iles Ioniennes: quelques aspects de leur présence', in *La révolution française et l'hellenisme moderne*, 137–154, 149.

[13] Zante on 2 October 1809, Cephalonia and Ithaca three days later, and Cerigo on 12 October: Viscount Kirkwall ed., *Four Years in the Ionian Islands*, 71; Lunzi, *Della repubblica settinsulare*, 239; Wrigley, *The Diplomatic Significance*, 53–55.

[14] *Gennadius Library, American School of Classical Studies at Athens*, Mss 102, fasc. iv undated [1809] (Cephalonia); *Gennadius Library, American School of Classical Studies at Athens*, Mss 103, cc.n.n.: on Zante there are two undated reports, one clearly done after the events of 1801 and one after the self-devolution of 1809. On this see also G. Lévy, *De la condition internationale des Îles Ioniennes depuis le Congrès de Vienne jusq'à nos jours*, Paris, 1901, 28.

strong supporters of Britain. From this report it is clear that the French could not trust any of the local notables, who were all leaning towards Britain. The spies reported that the only advocates of the French in Zante and Cephalonia were all poor and wielded no influence whatsoever.[15] Why was that? Once again, it was currants, as it had been for the previous three hundred years.

Corfu was happy to remain under the French. Its economy did not suffer, as it was rather diversified, and its trade remained stable; its own cash crop – olive oil – enjoyed a healthy market in France and Italy. Still, when Paris ordered General Berthier to confiscate all British goods and property in Corfu, he had to employ all his diplomatic skills not to unduly upset the locals, and he dedicated time and energy to make sure that the many Corfiotes doing business with the British were properly reimbursed.[16] For Zante and Cephalonia the situation was substantially different: their own cash crop – currants – had Britain as its major market, and local shipowners were keenly interested in the advantages that British protection could grant them for enlarging their already expanding tramp-shipping operations. The pervasiveness of currants in Zante and Cephalonia's economies fostered, as it had three centuries earlier, an alliance between notables and the middle classes that strengthened the English party. Conversely in Corfu, whose economy was more diversified, this was not the case. More research needs to be done on these issues, but it is evident that their respective cash crops and their relative economic diversification played a crucial role in determining the different political paths taken after the fall of the Republic.[17] Ermanno Lunzi, the most prominent Ionian historian in the early nineteenth century, commented on how the population of Zante and Cephalonia 'were becoming very unhappy because of the terrible damage that trade was suffering due to the continuous presence of enemy ships in the area, and this enlarged the "English faction"'.[18] With most of the Islands' trade directed towards Britain, the losses of currant growers and traders during French rule were substantial. The French commented positively on this:

---

[15] *Gennadius Library, American School of Classical Studies at Athens*, Mss 103, cc.n.n, undated French spy report.

[16] *Gennadius Library, American School of Classical Studies at Athens*, Mss 102, fasc. i, c.5.

[17] On the role of merchants in the political development of the Eastern Mediterranean in the nineteenth century see: A. Gekas, 'Class and Cosmopolitanism: The Historiographical Fortunes of Merchants in Eastern Mediterranean Ports', *Mediterranean Historical Review*, 24 (2009): 95–113.

[18] Lunzi, *Della repubblica settinsulare*, 239; Rodocanachi, *Bonaparte et les Îles Ioniennes*, 213.

The audacity of our corsairs, the activities of our trade officers brought good results: English trade was severely hit in the Mediterranean.[19]

But the inhabitants of Zante and Cephalonia were obviously much less happy, as they perceived the British as the ideal guarantors of their commercial interests.

After the collapse of the Napoleonic empire and the Treaty of Paris (1814) – which pushed the French back to their 1792 borders – the islands were declared a British protectorate. For Zante and Cephalonia this was simply the recognition of the *de facto* situation. Paradoxically, of all the Ionian islands, Corfu – which lacked an English presence in the early modern period and had been substantially less enthusiastic than Zante and Cephalonia towards the British – became particularly dear to Britain.[20] This was due to its powerful military and naval infrastructure inherited from the Venetians, who had considered it, since its acquisition in 1386, the keystone of its maritime defence system.[21] The island maintained this role under Britain, a role which Malta inherited after Corfu's cession to the Greek kingdom.[22]

During the Protectorate the convergence of economic interests that had been so crucial for the relationship between Britain and the islanders for such a long time became secondary. What mattered to the British now was strategic location, which was crucial in their plans for Mediterranean supremacy, in the same way as it had been in the past for all the previous overlords of the Ionian islands.[23] The British Protectorate over the 'Free and Independent Septinsular Republic' turned out to be a failure. The local ruling classes, which in the last two centuries of the Republic's life had become increasingly involved in local government, were shunned by the British authorities. The formal independence of the islands was not respected, and it is most telling that the islands' Lord High Commissioner

[19] G. Douin, *La Méditerranée de 1803 à 1805: pirates et corsaires aux Îles Ioniennes*, Paris, 1917, 179.

[20] The only Venetian harbours mentioned in the charter of the Levant Company were Venice, Zante, Cephalonia and Candia: Epstein, *The Early History*, 230.

[21] D. Calabi, 'Le basi ultramarine', in Tenenti and Tucci eds., *Storia di Venezia*, vol. xii: *Il mare*, 861–878; E. Concina, 'Città e fortezze nelle "tre isole nostre del Levante"', in *Venezia e la difesa*, 184–194.

[22] Tenenti in 'Il senso dello spazio e del tempo', 88–89; G. Zucconi, 'Corcira Britannica: Urban Architecture and Strategies in the Capital of the Ionian Islands', in E. Concina and A. Nikiforou-Testone eds., *Corfu: History, Urban Space and Architecture, 14th–19th centuries*, Corfu, 1994, 95–103, 98–100; G. Panagopoulos, 'The Urban Transformation of Corfu during the Protectorate: The Role of the Esplanade', in J. R. Melville-Jones ed., *Studies in the Architecture of Dalmatia and Corfu*, Venice, 2001, 53–64.

[23] C. A. Bayly, *Imperial Meridian: The British Empire and the World: 1780–1830*, London, 1989, 104.

348   Coda and conclusions

answered to the colonial secretary, not the foreign secretary.[24] Autocratic
British rule worsened the Anglo-Greek relationship, and a long series of
political, economic and cultural misunderstandings ensued.

By the middle of the nineteenth century, the shifting scenario of
Mediterranean politics made the islands' position less relevant for
British interests. The creation of the Greek state, achieved with the backing of British philhellenes, put Britain in a very ambiguous situation,
which was not made any easier by its support towards the movement for
Italian independence. Starting in the 1840s, sympathies grew in the
islands for reunification with the independent Greek state. The 1862
royal crisis in Greece gave Britain the perfect excuse to make use of the
islands as a political bargaining tool whilst, at the same time, having an
important say in the choice of a candidate for the Greek throne. The
British abandoned the Protectorate in 1864. The practical challenges
encountered by the British during their administration were exactly the
same as those encountered by the Venetian *Rettori* and *Senato* in the
previous centuries: difficulty in controlling the territory, widespread
smuggling, problems in collecting local revenue from taxes and customs.
For the British, being overlord proved to be a very different experience
from being business partner in the previous centuries. Anglo-Greek relations deteriorated rapidly under the strains of governance, and Britain did
not even benefit from currant income.[25]

The structure of the currant trade, once established at the end of the
sixteenth century, remained fundamentally the same for three hundred
years.[26] Grain production in the islands never really recovered, and the
local population continued to acquire wheat from the Turkish Morea until
the end of the eighteenth century. The treaty of Kutchuk-Kainardji (1774),
after the Russian victory against the Ottoman empire, opened the Black
Sea to international navigation and provided a massive boost for the
activities of Ionian shipowners, who quickly cornered the market in
wheat distribution. Ever since the fall of Venice, full freedom to navigate
in the Black Sea had been granted to vessels with the flag of the Septinsular
Republic, which made the Black Sea the cradle of Greek tramp shipping.[27]

[24] B. Knox, 'British Policy and the Ionian Islands, 1847–1864: Nationalism and Imperial
Administration', *The English Historical Review*, 99 (1984): 503–529, 505.
[25] All these issues are analysed in depth in Fusaro, 'Representation in Practice' and bibliography quoted therein.
[26] Paladini, 'Né uomini né strutture', 208–213.
[27] *Regolamento della Marina della Repubblica Ionica*, Corfu, 1805, 3; G. Harlaftis, *A History of
Greek-Owned Shipping: The Making of an International Tramp Fleet, 1830 to the Present Day*,
London and New York, 1996, 29; S. Gekas, 'The Merchants of the Ionian Islands between
East and West: Forming International and Local Networks', in M. Schulte Beerbühl and

Currant production in Zante and Cephalonia experienced a boom during the war for Greek independence, which halted production on the mainland, substantially raising the prices of the Ionian crop. The situation did not change with the annexation of the islands to the Kingdom of Greece. In fact currants remained the major growth sector of Greek agriculture throughout the second half of the nineteenth century, with production and acreage increasing more than threefold between 1860 and 1890. Between 1886 and 1890 currants alone made up more than 55 per cent of the value of all Greek exports. Exactly as had happened during the Venetian domination, the problem remained that producing exclusively for export did not allow the government to implement protectionist measures and left producers at the mercy of foreign buyers and economic conjuncture.[28] It was a dangerous strategy:

The abolition of the tithe in 1880, and with it the extortions of its collection which we have described, encouraged farmers to increase their production. But Greece continued to depend heavily on the importation of grain partly paid for with the earnings of exported currants. The danger of this reliance on one predominant export crop were distressingly exposed in 1892 when France introduced a high tariff against Greek currants, the price of which fell overnight by 70 per cent.[29]

Obviously the lesson regarding the need to diversify production had not been learned.[30]

Commercial empire?

The reversal of the balance between Venetian and northern merchants in the Mediterranean was a feat achieved by a relatively small number of merchants who managed to infiltrate and establish themselves in the sophisticated Venetian commercial system. Why did Venice fail, and how did England succeed during the long seventeenth century?

J. Vögele eds., *Spinning the Commercial Web: International Trade, Merchants and Commercial Cities, c.1640–1939*, Frankfurt, 2004, 43–63, 52–55.

[28] J. Morilla Critz, A. L. Olmstead, P. W. Rhode, 'International Competition and the Development of the Dried Fruit Industry, 1880–1930', in S. Pamuk and J. G. Williamson eds., *The Mediterranean Response to Globalization Before 1950*, London and New York, 2000, 199–232, 221–226.

[29] J. K. Campbell, *Modern Greece*, London, 1968, 97.

[30] Throughout these centuries the English market played a crucial role in stimulating Greek production: S. Petmezas, 'El comercio de la pasa de Corinto y su influencia sobre la economía griega del siglo XIX (1840–1914)', in J. Morilla, J. Gómez-Pantoja and P. Cressier eds., *Impactos exteriores sobre la agricultura mediterranea*, Madrid 1997, 523–562; and his 'L'économie agricole grecque pendant la Grande Dépression': see www.ims.forth.gr/ims/history_studies/agrotiki_oikonomia/CrisedellaGlobalisation.pdf (date accessed: 30 June 2012).

Adam Smith's famed definition of political economy provides a good starting point:

political œconomy, considered as a branch of the science of statesman or legislator, proposes two distinct objects: first, to provide a plentiful revenue or subsistence for the people, or more properly to enable them to provide such a revenue or subsistence for themselves; and secondly, to supply the state or commonwealth with a revenue sufficient for the public services. It proposes to enrich *both the people and the sovereign*.[31]

It is undisputable that – in theory – support for maritime trade remained a constant of Venetian political economy and legislation throughout its long history.[32] However, at the same time, the Republic's government remained paralysed by its vision of Venice as an emporium whose role was that of middleman and whose revenue was derived mainly from customs and taxation on imports, exports and re-exports. The institution of the *Nuova* and the *Novissima Imposta*, taxes payable by foreigners who exported currants directly out of Zante and Cephalonia bypassing Venice, are paradigmatic examples of this policy, and therein lies the problem. The economic interest of subjects was ignored, and policy continued to be based on an old, primarily ideological vision which saw Venice as the centre of all commercial activity, not as the hub coordinating a growingly multifaceted imperial economic strategy.

There is nothing inherently new in the core of this interpretation, but I want to posit a new explanation for its causes: at the root of this policy were misjudged imperial preoccupations. Throughout the early modern period the perpetual concern of the Republic was the conservation and even the expansion of its empire, as shown by the territorial gains in Dalmatia and Albania during the last century and a half of the Republic's life, and the conquest of the Peloponnese and Athens (1685–1718). Imperial conservation *and* the opportunity for new acquisitions – *pace* Machiavelli – meant that naval power and defence acquired and maintained paramount importance. The Ionian islands are an excellent case study in this regard, as their strategic position was placed above any other interest: no money was spared for their fortification, and no words were spared in trying to convince their inhabitants of the islands' importance as granaries for the fleet. Unfortunately, though, Venice as an imperial overlord conceived the islands primarily as a military outpost of empire, thus weakening the opportunities for its economic improvement. That, plus the alliance

---

[31] A. Smith, 'Introduction, Book IV', *An Inquiry into the Nature and Causes of the Wealth of Nations*, London, 1799, 428. Emphasis mine.

[32] Tenenti, 'La navigazione veneziana nel Seicento'; Costantini, *Una repubblica nata sul mare*.

between the English – with their (almost) insatiable demand for currants – and a local population which craved cash, proved to be an unbeatable enemy for the Republic.

In short, whilst talking like a commercial empire, Venice was acting like a territorial empire. Trade and the Levant possessions might have remained matters of interest to the legislative machine, but for years little attention was paid to the *economic* concerns of the empire's populations, and the partial success of the eighteenth-century policy of incentives for olive oil production is just a tantalising glimpse of what might have been achieved if such policies had been implemented earlier for a wider variety of goods. The political and defence aspects of empire became the overarching determinant also in Veneto-Ottoman relations, where appeasement was frequently preferred to more aggressive commercialism. Thus towards both its own imperial subjects, as towards its strongest military adversary, Venice favoured an imperial 'political' approach instead of an 'economic' one. This attitude was the expression of the desire to maintain and expand territorial holdings, as Venice confronted the Ottomans, with access to resources of a scale incomparably larger to those available to Venice.

Venice spent an inordinate amount of human, political and financial energies in defending its empire in the Levant, whilst it conspicuously failed to make its own subjects stakeholders in this project. The primacy of the political and commercial economy of the metropolis remained supreme, and even the *Terraferma*'s economy became increasingly geared towards bankrolling the *Stato da Mar*.[33] On a purely economic level, it is difficult not to agree with the analysis by Michael Mallett and John Hale of the cost-effectiveness of defending the *Dominio da Mar*:

empire was assumed to be needed to preserve Venice's still active function as an entrepôt between east and west, and to give credibility to its claim that the Adriatic was mare nostrum which alien vessels should only enter were their cargoes destined for Venice, with its harbour dues and customs charges. But the balance between defence cost and commercial profit was not worked out.[34]

But empires – and indeed states – rarely think in terms of cost-effectiveness when protecting their own possessions or – even more crucially – defending their own self-representation.

[33] Knapton, 'Tra Dominante e Dominio', 262; Pezzolo, 'La finanza pubblica', 713–716.
[34] Mallett and Hale, *Military Organisation*, 460.

... and mercantile communities

The peculiar way in which English merchants did business in the Venetian territories proved to be an essential ingredient of their ultimate triumph. Their superior commercial organisation, and the broad freedom that the Levant Company merchants allowed their factors, provided an extremely flexible structure that proved effective in penetrating the Venetian market and successfully challenging Venice's dominance of trade in the eastern Mediterranean. Thanks to this flexibility, which allowed them to adjust their behaviour according to the social and political context in which they operated, the English managed to overcome the disadvantages which followed from not having been granted any commercial privileges in Venice. At the same time, their operating system was unique amongst English mercantile communities abroad, characterised by close interaction with their fellow countrymen and, just as importantly, openness towards the host country and the other mercantile communities. In Venice, and in the Ionian islands, English merchants wove a web of fruitful alliances with the rising Venetian *cittadini* merchants and the established Flemish merchants in Venice, but they mostly dealt with the Republic's subjects. With the Greeks – with whom they shared goals and interests – they enjoyed a long, mutually beneficial relationship that ended up undermining the commercial and financial interests of the Republic.

The traditional interpretation of the development of modern capitalism in Europe gives pride of place to the role played by institutional innovations such as trading companies, whose activities allowed for a superior rationality in the organisation of business and for better mechanisms of capital accumulation and investment.[35] The impact of these developments, though, is more evident in Atlantic and Asian long-distance trade than in the Mediterranean, where there was a wealth of pre-existing intra-European trading structures and commercial networks active within a thick jurisdictional jungle, where many institutions jostled for primacy.

When analysing the behaviour of pre-modern mercantile communities, it is important not to fall into the trap of anachronism, such as thinking of their operations solely in terms of nation-states. However, Anglo-Venetian Mediterranean interaction during the early modern

---

[35] An analytical synthesis can be seen in O. Gelderblom and J. Jonker, 'Completing a Financial Revolution: The Finance of The Dutch East India Trade and the Rise of the Amsterdam Capital Market, 1595–1612', *The Journal of Economic History*, 64/3 (2004): 641–672.

period points clearly to the importance of state support in both English and Venetian commercial activities. Each of these networks was confronted with centrally directed economic policies, and the key to understanding their development is to see how these policies were interpreted and implemented locally by the individual operator on the ground. The chartered companies such as the Levant rationalised pre-existing networks, adding a managerial layer which could more efficiently lobby governments and mobilise financial resources. Within Venice and its empire, these networks were interdependent for their individual pursuit of profits, and it is probably not a coincidence that the strongest of these relationships was that between two upstarts – Greeks and English – versus the established powers in the region – Venetian and Ottoman.

Many commercial communities active in Venice and the Levant operated within supranational webs, the classic example being the Jews, who could count on tight networks which were dispersed geographically. Similar considerations can be made for members of the other classic diasporas, such as Greeks and Armenians.[36] Within the Venetian state the position of Greeks is particularly interesting due to their peculiar status, which gave them some advantages. Those coming from the *Stato da Mar* were fully fledged subjects of the Venetian state, so from the operative point of view their diasporic status was mitigated, and whilst they could (and did) take advantage of Venetian institutional support, they could also benefit from the Greek diaspora to further their links in Ottoman lands.[37] Even the Flemish showed many characteristics of this structure, particularly evident amongst the Antwerpians – effectively transformed into a diaspora by the 1585 sack of the city – whose presence covered a wide geographical area, but had a clear internal structure of collaboration.[38] Venice benefitted greatly from their activities, which supported and enhanced its commercial reach and played an important part in fostering the resilience of the Republic's economy.[39] The English arrival in the Mediterranean proved nefarious for Venice precisely because it operated along very different lines, arguably rather

---

[36] The Armenians played a crucial role in the Persian silk trade. For two different interpretations of their activities see R. Matthee, *The Politics of Trade in Safavid Iran: Silk for Silver, 1600–1730*, Cambridge, 1999, and I. Baghdiantz-McCabe, *The Shah's Silk for Europe's Silver: The Eurasian Trade of the Julfa Armenians in Safavid Iran and India (1530–1750)*, Philadelphia, 1999.

[37] Fusaro, 'Les Anglais et les Grecs'.

[38] Van Gelder, 'Supplying the *Serenissima*'.

[39] Fusaro, 'Gli uomini d'affari stranieri', and bibliography quoted therein.

similar to those employed by Venetians themselves. Like Venice had done since the Middle Ages, the English built a commercial network which, although they did not miss any opportunity to collaborate when convenient, was clearly constructed along 'national' lines, and used governmental lobbying at home and diplomatic intervention abroad to further their economic interest. Like the Venetians in their medieval heyday, when state-coordinated institutional support had provided the fundamental mainframe where private entrepreneurship could flourish – *mutatis mutandis* – English trading ventures were equally supported by their own state and, fundamentally, increasingly by the military support of their navy. Edward Gibbon argued that Venice did not 'often forget that if armed galleys were the effect and safeguard, merchant vessels were the cause and supply, of her greatness'.[40] Gibbon was wrong about this; under the pressure of the sixteenth-century perfect storm – created by oceanic discoveries, reorientation of proto-global trade and the Ottoman military advance – Venice did indeed forget this maxim, and in supporting naval expansion at the cost of the merchant marine, although it managed to maintain parts of its empire in the Levant, lost its fight for commercial primacy in the region. Not properly supporting its own *cittadini* and subjects with the kind of strong financial and logistic institutional support, and continuing to insist on the utter centrality of the city at the expense of a more organic policy of integration of its empire into the economy of the state, opened fissures in its economic structure which were quickly filled by its major competitor.

The English were quick to graft their activities onto those private and supranational trade networks which still dominated international trade, and this allowed them to thrive even during times of internal turmoil. Interdependence is the crucial reason for their success; trade depended on everyone behaving well towards everyone else, and Venice provided a useful common enemy, as its customs and duties seriously impinged on the profits of both sides of the transaction.

The flexibility of English merchants, a tight community with strong informal connections to other networks, would probably not have been enough to conquer the Mediterranean without the institutional support of the Levant Company – facilitating capital accumulation – and of the English state, keen to foster commercial expansion through diplomatic efforts. And it was precisely this connection between trade and state support which contemporary Venetians wistfully admired during the seventeenth century as they recognised this to have been at the root of their past golden age.

---

[40] As quoted by Reinert, 'Lessons on the Rise and Fall', 1412.

Naval and maritime empires

The conjunctural situation greatly facilitated English success. The grain famine in the Mediterranean basin in the last quarter of the sixteenth century made the presence of northern ships necessary exactly when they should have been fought and repelled. By the time that crisis had receded, the weakness of the Venetian navy made English help crucial in the fight against the Uskoks. The impending crisis of the Venetian fleet – both commercial and military – played a crucial role in paving the way for English dominance. Starting in the mid-sixteenth century Venice had favoured investment in the navy over investment in commercial shipping, and legislation to preserve wood for the needs of the Arsenal penalised local commercial shipbuilding.[41] This policy broke the vital link between maritime and naval strength, and further investment in naval forces was hindered by the absence of a healthy shipping industry. Venice had indeed become, by the end of the sixteenth century, a 'protection-producing enterprise' – in the sharp words of Frederic Lane. The problem is that it was protecting its territorial empire in the Levant, not the commercial activities of its own merchants, as had been the case in previous centuries.[42]

The English Navigation Acts – remarkably similar to previous Venetian legislation – were implemented at a time of growth of the English shipping industry, and this set into motion a virtuous circle in the English shipping sector that broke only in the twentieth century. In seventeenth-century Venice the opposite happened, and it was a vicious circle that was set into motion. The military effort of the Candia war would have been unsustainable for Venice without foreign vessels, those same vessels that were challenging her maritime supremacy. For the English, playing an active role in the Republic's naval campaigns was also the best way to gain credit in the eyes of the Venetian government, and thus reinforce their commercial position. Proof of how important trade with Venice was for the English is that they never withheld logistic and naval support to Venice, even when the Ottomans threatened to retaliate commercially. It could be that an ulterior reason behind keeping separate the diplomatic and commercial sides of the English presence in Venice was exactly to solve the delicate balance between political alliance and commercial competition on the European stage, by creating the conditions for deniability, and in this way silence possible Ottoman criticism of English military support to Venice.

[41] Fusaro, 'The Invasion of Northern Litigants'.
[42] Lane, *Profits from Power*, 3, 53.

One of the founding elements of the myth of Venice was its absence of walls – the waters were its defence – and a few centuries later this attitude was further developed in Britain: the only wall it needed being not so much 'sea', as 'sea power'.[43] It would be difficult to overestimate the role of Richard Hakluyt as a protomaster of English political spin. He was the most influential individual in the long term to put forward an image of the Elizabethan sea dog as a successful conqueror of commercial and political spaces. Fernand Braudel's reliance on him to chronicle the English role in the 'invasion of the northerners' helped to refresh and cement the renown of the Elizabethan merchant adventurers along lines that the queen certainly would have approved of. Still, *pace* Hakluyt, by the end of Elizabeth's reign, 'the English reputation abroad was more for insularity and piracy than for global mastery'.[44] But the seeds sown by the Tudors were quick to bloom during the reigns of the Stuarts and to bear fruit during the Protectorate.

Jonathan Scott's analysis of the role played by the sea in British policy and identity clearly shows it was a central element of British identity from the end of the sixteenth century to the early twentieth century. The similarity between the language of early modern Venetians and that of the Victorians is striking and well worthy of future investigation.[45] Adopting geographical and historical arguments to justify one's unique destiny was a Venetian lesson well learned by the British.

Still, on 3 February 1902 the *Times*' main editorial could declare that:

England is mistress of the seas, not by virtue of any arrogant or aggressive pretensions, but by virtue of her history, of her geographical situation, of her economic antecedents and conditions, of her Imperial position and expansion. These conditions have given the dominion of the seas to her, not by any prescriptive right, but by a normal and almost natural process of evolution; and, so long as they subsist and she is true to herself, they will retain it for her.[46]

And this attitude was not limited to high culture, but also pervaded popular British culture. Jonathan Scott quotes an Erskine Childers character saying, in 1903, 'we're a maritime nation, we've grown by the sea and live by it ... we're unique in that way, just as our huge empire, only linked by the sea, is unique'.[47] Sea-blindness was indeed far away in Britain's past as in its future.

[43] Scott, *When the Waves Ruled Britannia*, 48.
[44] Sherman, 'Bringing the World to England', 200.
[45] A British naval-centred start is Lambert, 'Now is come'.
[46] *The Times*, 3 February 1902 as quoted by Kennedy, *The Rise and Fall*, 149.
[47] Scott, *When the Waves Ruled Britannia*, 6.

Seventeenth-century Venice instead experienced partial sea-blindness: it concentrated so much on the naval side, where its efforts were also hindered by the increasing technological gap between its own and northern shipping, that it did not manage to elaborate an appropriate strategy to counteract maritime commercial decline. The sea remained at the centre of Venetian legislation and preoccupations, but this was increasingly a wistful activity, in some cases bordering on wishful thinking. In the words of Alberto Tenenti, one of the major twentieth-century historians of the Republic and of its engagement with the sea, 'it seems as if the Venetian community remained pervaded – even beyond the fall of the Republic and in a permanent manner – with a pronounced nostalgia towards maritime supremacy, and with a not quite hidden sense of regret regarding what might have been done to preserve it or to defend it'.[48]

Identities, though, are not always rational, and they have a strong basis in sentiment.

What is clearly perceivable is a sort of schizophrenia in the English attitude towards Venice. Even after the Restoration, when the anti-myth started to gain momentum, the opinion of political economists about Venice never turned fully negative, as if there were a clear division between literary authors and social commentators (not necessarily only moralists), who embraced the anti-myth, and the economic literature, which instead remained fairly positive. During the eighteenth century, when the causes of decline represented a favourite topic of discussion amongst political economists throughout Europe, it is not surprising that Venice's medieval heyday – so similar to that of contemporary Britain – would be discussed.[49] Venetians themselves, always proudly aware of their uniqueness, were equally painfully aware of their own economic decline. On these issues, the most eloquent late eighteenth-century patrician was Andrea Tron, a member of the European Republic of Letters and an active politician during the last decades of the Republic.[50] Tron transformed the plaintive tone of his ancestors' narratives on the decline of Venice and the rise of England into a proud analysis which saw the roots of decline not in mismanagement, but in international emulation. For him 'the northern princes are nothing but copies of ancient Venetian maxims', as Venice was 'the first to be their model and example'.[51]

---

[48] Tenenti, 'Il senso del mare', 8.
[49] For two classic examples see: Anderson, An Historical and Chronological Deduction; Macpherson, Annals of Commerce.
[50] On Tron, see G. Tabacco, Andrea Tron e la crisi dell'aristocrazia senatoria a Venezia, Udine, 1980.
[51] As argued by Sophus Reinert, 'Blaming the Medici', 440.

Within the genealogy of maritime empires, by the end of the Republic it was generally acknowledged that England had somehow inherited its mantle from Venice. By Victorian times the central question had become how to avoid following Venice in its decline. The anti-myth provided a good moral argument: Venice declined and fell as the state had become tyrannical and, more importantly, immoral. The nineteenth-century historiography of the Republic, especially after the publication in 1819 of Pierre Daru's *Histoire de la République de Venise*, had fostered this interpretative line with damning narratives of aristocratic abuse and the *Consiglio dei Dieci* ruling a city replete with courtesans celebrating carnival.[52] However, other strands of interpretation were emerging which tried to foster a comparative dialogue between Venice's glorious naval past and Britain's contemporary global naval and maritime hegemony. Andrew Lambert, tracing the evolution of British politicians' perception of Venice, clearly shows how different interpretations ultimately merged, establishing Venice loud and clear as a historical example with strong contemporary relevance. 'Did the Victorians use Venice as a morality tale replete with lessons, or an educational tool to tease out insight and ideas? The answer is both, a fact made manifest in the shape and structure of the empire Victoria bequeathed'.[53]

Ruskin said there were three maritime empires in the history of mankind: 'the thrones of Tyre, Venice, and England'.[54] Venice's Mediterranean-centred empire passed its mantle to Victorian England's global hegemony of 'blue waters'. The dedicatory poem to John Selden's *Dominion or Ownership of the Sea* had presciently declared:

> If little Venice bring's alone
> Such waves to her subjection
>   As in the Gulf do stir
> What then should great Britannia pleas,
> But rule as Ladie o're all seas
>   And thou as Queen of her
> For Sea-Dominion may as well be gain'd
> By new acquests, as by descent maintain'd.[55]

---

[52] For a nuanced analysis of these issues, and their long-term impact, see C. Povolo, 'The Creation of Venetian Historiography', in Martin and Romano eds., *Venice Reconsidered*, 491–519.
[53] Lambert, 'Now is come', 38.
[54] Ruskin, *Stones of Venice*, 1.
[55] Frontispiece in J. Selden, *The Dominion or Ownership of the Sea: Two Books Translated by Marchmont Needham*, London, 1652.

Printed primary sources and bibliography

Abulafia D., 'Cittadino e "denizen": mercanti mediterranei a Southampton e a Londra', in M. Del Treppo ed., *Sistema di rapporti ed elites economiche in Europa (sec. XII–XVII)*, Naples, 1994, 271–291.

Ago R., *Economia barocca: mercato e istituzioni nella Roma del Seicento*, Rome, 1998.

Albèri E. ed., *Relazioni degli ambasciatori veneti al senato*, series 1, vol. ii, Florence, 1840.

Allen R. C., *The British Industrial Revolution in Global Perspective*, Cambridge, 2009.

Álvarez Nogal C., L. Lo Basso and C. Marsilio, 'La rete finanziaria della famiglia Spinola: Spagna, Genova e le fiere dei cambi (1610–1656)', *Quaderni Storici*, 124 (2007): 97–110.

Ambrose G. P., 'English Traders at Aleppo, 1658–1756', *Economic History Review*, 3 (1931–1932): 246–267.

Amelotti M. and G. Costamagna, *Alle origini del notariato italiano*, Rome, 1975.

Anderson A., *An Historical and Chronological Deduction of the Origin of Commerce From the Earliest Accounts to the Present Time containing An History of the great Commercial Interests of the British Empire . . .*, 2 vols., London, 1764.

Anderson G. M. and R. D. Tollison, 'Adam Smith's Analysis of Joint-Stock Companies', *Journal of Political Economy*, 90 (1982): 1237–1256.

Anderson G. M. and R. D. Tollison, 'Apologiae for Chartered Monopolies in Foreign Trade, 1600–1800', *History of Political Economy*, 15 (1983): 549–566.

Anderson S., *An English Consul in Turkey: Paul Rycaut at Smyrna, 1667–1678*, Oxford, 1989.

Andréadès A. M., 'L'administration financière et économique de Venise dans ses possessions du Levant', *L'Acropole*, 1 (1926): 13–25.

Andréadès A. M., Οἰκονομικαι μελεται περι Ἑπτανησου: Περι της οἰκονομικης διοικησεως της Ἑπτανησου ἐπι Βενετοκρατιας (*Studies on the Economy of the Eptanese: On the Financial Administration of the Ionian Islands under Venetian Domination*), 2 vols., Athens, 1914.

Andrews K. R., *Elizabethan Privateering: English Privateering during the Spanish War, 1585–1603*, Cambridge, 1964.

Andrews K. R., 'Sir Robert Cecil and Mediterranean Plunder', *English Historical Review*, 87 (1972): 513–532.

Andrews K. R., *Trade, Plunder and Settlement: Maritime Enterprise and the Genesis of the British Empire, 1480–1630*, Cambridge, 1984.

Angold M., 'The Anglo-Saxon Historiography of the Fourth Crusade: A Crime against Humanity or just an Accident?', in G. Ortalli, G. Ravegnani and P. Schreiner eds., *Quarta Crociata: Venezia, Bisanzio, Impero Latino*, Venice, 2006, 301–316.

Anselmi S., *Venezia, Ragusa, Ancona tra Cinque e Seicento*, Ancona, 1969.

Appleby J. C., 'Thomas Mun's West Indies Venture, 1602–1605', *Historical Research*, 67 (1994): 101–110.

Appleby J. O., *Economic Thought and Ideology in Seventeenth Century England*, Princeton, 1978.

Appuhn K., *A Forest on the Sea: Environmental Expertise in Renaissance Venice*, Baltimore, 2009.

Arbel B., 'Colonie d'oltremare', in A. Tenenti and U. Tucci eds., *Storia di Venezia*, vol. v: *Il Rinascimento: società ed economia*, Rome, 1996, 947–985.

Arbel B., 'Jews in International Trade: The Emergence of the Levantine and Ponentines', in R. C. Davis and B. Ravid eds., *The Jews of Early Modern Venice*, Baltimore and London, 2001, 73–96.

Arbel B., 'Maritime Trade and International Relations in the Sixteenth Century Mediterranean: The Case of the Ship *Girarda* (1575–1581)', in V. Costantini and M. Koller eds., *Living in the Ottoman Ecumenical Community: Essays in Honour of Suraiya Faroqhi*, Leiden, 2008, 391–408.

Arbel B., *Trading Nations: Jews and Venetians in the Early Modern Eastern Mediterranean*, Leiden and New York, 1995.

Arbel B., 'Venice's Maritime Empire in the Early Modern Period', in E. Dursteler ed., *A Companion to Venetian History, 1400–1797*, Leiden and Boston, 2013, 125–253.

Archer I. W., 'City and Court Connected: The Material Dimensions of Royal Ceremonial, ca. 1480–1625', *Huntington Library Quarterly*, 71 (2008): 157–179.

Archer I. W., *The Pursuit of Stability: Social Relations in Elizabethan London*, Cambridge, 1991.

Armitage D., *The Ideological Origins of the British Empire*, Cambridge, 2000.

Arnoux M. and J. Bottin, 'La Manche: frontière, marché ou espace de production? Fonctions économiques et évolution d'un espace maritime (XIVe–XVIIe siècles)', in S. Cavaciocchi ed., *Ricchezza del mare, ricchezza dal mare, secc. XIII–XVIII*, 2 vols, Florence, 2006, ii: 875–906.

Arvanitakis D., *Το ρεμπελιό των ποπολάρων (1628): κοινωνικές αντιθέσεις στην πόλη της Ζακύνθου (The Revolt of the Popolari (1628): Social Contrasts in the City of Zante)*, Athens, 2001.

Asdrachas S., 'Agricoltura e rapporti di proprietà', in M. Costantini ed., *Il Mediterraneo centro–orientale tra vecchie e nuove egemonie: trasformazioni economiche, sociale ed istituzionali nelle Isole Ionie dal declino della Serenissima all'avvento delle potenze atlantiche (sec. XVII–XVIII)*, Rome, 1998, 127–132.

Ashley M. P., *Financial and Commercial Policy under the Cromwellian Protectorate*, London, 1962 (2nd edn).

Ashton R., *The City and the Court, 1603–1643*, Cambridge, 1979.

Ashton R., *Counter-Revolution: The Second Civil War and Its Origins, 1646–1648*, New Haven, 1994.

Ashtor E., *Levant Trade in the Later Middle Ages*, Princeton, 1983.
Ashtor E., 'Levantine Sugar Industry in the Late Middle Ages: A Case of Technological Decline', in A. L. Udovitch ed., *The Islamic Middle East, 700–1900: Studies in Economic and Social History*, Princeton, 1981, 91–132.
Ashtor E., 'Profits from Trade with the Levant in the Fifteenth Century', *Bulletin of the School of Oriental and African Studies*, 38 (1975): 250–275.
Ashtor E., 'The Venetian Supremacy in Levantine Trade: Monopoly or Pre-Colonialism?', *Journal of European Economic History*, 3 (1974): 5–53.
Aspetti e cause della decadenza economica veneziana nel secolo XVII, Atti del Convegno, Venice and Rome, 1961.
Åström S. E., *From Cloth to Iron: The Anglo-Baltic Trade in the Late Seventeenth Century*, Helsinki, 1963.
Atti del Convegno: 'Gli inglesi a Livorno e nell'Isola d'Elba' (sec. XVII–XIX), Livorno, 1980.
Atti del Convegno 'Livorno ed il Mediterraneo nell'età Medicea', Livorno, 1978.
Augliera L., *Libri, politica, religione nel Levante del Seicento: la tipografia di Nicodemo Metaxas, primo editore di testi greci nell'Oriente ortodosso*, Venice, 1996.
Aymard M., 'L'Europe, Venise et la Méditerranée', in G. Franchini, G. Ortalli and G. Toscano eds., *Venise et la Méditerranée*, Venice, 2011, 3–11.
Aymard M., *Venise, Raguse et le commerce du blé pendant la seconde moitié du XVIe siècle*, Paris, 1966.
Baghdiantz-McCabe I., *The Shah's Silk for Europe's Silver: The Eurasian Trade of the Julfa Armenians in Safavid Iran and India (1530–1750)*, Philadelphia, 1999.
Balard M., *Les Latins en Orient, XIe–XVe siècle*, Paris, 2006.
Balbi de Caro S. ed., *Merci e monete a Livorno in età granducale*, Milan, 1997.
Ball J. G., 'Poverty, Charity and the Greek Community', *Studi Veneziani*, 6 (1982): 129–145.
Barbierato F., 'Dissenso religioso, discussione politica e mercato dell'informazione a Venezia fra Seicento e Settecento', *Società e Storia*, 24 (2003): 707–757.
Barbour V., 'Consular Service in the Reign of Charles II', *American Historical Review*, 33 (1927–28): 553–578.
Bargrave R., *The Travel Diary of Robert Bargrave: Levant Merchant (1647–1656)*, M. G. Brennan ed., London, 1999.
Baroutsos F., 'Sovention per fabricar galeoni: Ο Βενετικός μερκαντιλισμός και οι αντανακλάσεις του στην Κρητική κοινωνία του υστέρου 16ου αιώνα' ('Financing Galleons: Venetian Mercantilism and Its Consequences on Late Sixteenth Century Cretan Society'), *Thesaurismata*, 29 (1999): 187–223.
Barozzi N. and Berchet G. eds., *Le relazioni degli stati europei lette al Senato dagli ambasciatori veneziani nel secolo decimosettimo*, 9 vols., Venice, 1863.
Barrett C. R. B., *The Trinity House of Deptford*, London, 1893.
Bartlett K. R., 'Dangers and Delights: English Protestants in Italy in the Sixteenth and Seventeenth Century', in *Forestieri e stranieri nelle città basso-medievali*, Florence, 1988, 215–222.
Bartlett K. R., 'The English Exile Community in Italy and the Political Opposition to Queen Mary I', *Albion: A Quarterly Journal Concerned with British Studies*, 13 (1981): 223–241.

Bartlett K. R., *The English in Italy, 1525–1558: A Study in Culture and Politics*, Geneva, 1991.

Bartlett R., *The Making of Europe: Conquest, Colonization and Cultural Change, 950–1350*, Princeton, 1993.

Basso E. and P. F. Simbula, 'Il commercio del vino nelle pratiche di mercatura italiane del basso medioevo', in *I Symposion de la Associación Internacional de Historia de la Civilización de la Vid y del Vino* (18–20 March 1999), Cadiz, 2002, 393–402.

Bayly C. A., *Imperial Meridian: The British Empire and the World: 1780–1830*, London, 1989.

Beardwood A., 'Alien Merchants and the English Crown in the Later Fourteenth Century', *The Economic History Review*, 2 (1930): 229–260.

Beck H. G., M. Manoussacas and A. Pertusi eds., *Venezia, centro di mediazione tra Oriente e Occidente (secoli XV–XVI): aspetti e problemi*, 2 vols., Florence, 1977.

Bell J. M., *A Handlist of British Diplomatic Representatives, 1509–1688*, London, 1990.

Bellavitis A., *Identité, mariage, mobilité sociale: citoyennes et citoyens à Venise au XVIe siècle*, Rome, 2001.

Bellavitis A., '"Per cittadini metterete . . . ": la stratificazione della società veneziana cinquecentesca tra norma giuridica e riconoscimento sociale', *Quaderni Storici*, 89 (1995): 359–383.

Bennassar B. and L. Bennassar, *Les chrétiens d'Allah: l'histoire extraordinaire des renégats XVIe–XVIIe siècles*, Paris, 1989.

Ben-Porath Y., 'The F-Connection: Families, Friends, and Firms and the Organization of Exchange', *Population and Development Review*, 6 (1980): 1–30.

Bent J. T. ed., *Early Voyages and Travel in the Levant: The Diary of Master Thomas Dallam 1599–1600*, London, 1893.

Benzoni G., 'Morire per Creta', in G. Ortalli ed., *Venezia e Creta*, Venice, 1998, 151–173.

Berveglieri R., 'Cosmo Scatini e il nero di Venezia', *Quaderni Storici*, 52 (1983): 167–179.

Berveglieri R., *Inventori stranieri a Venezia (1474–1788): importazione di tecnologia e circolazione di tecnici, artigiani, inventori. Repertorio*, Venice, 1995.

Besta E., *Il Senato veneziano (origine, costituzione, attribuzioni e riti)*, Venice, 1899.

Beutin L., 'La décadence économique de Venise considérée du point de vue nord-européen', in *Aspetti e cause della decadenza economica veneziana nel secolo XVII*, Atti del Convegno, Venice and Rome, 1961, 87–108.

Biagi M. G., 'Da Ferdinando I a Ferdinando II: congiunture internazionali e "politica corsara"', *Bollettino Storico Pisano*, 62 (1993): 1–23.

Bicci A., 'Italiani ad Amsterdam nel Seicento', *Rivista Storica Italiana*, 102 (1990): 899–934.

Bicci A., '"Sotto il segno dell'avventura, della cultura e del denaro": capitale e know-how italiano ad Amsterdam nel Seicento', in R. Mazzei and T. Fanfani eds., *Lucca e l'Europa degli affari*, Lucca, 1990, 258–280.

Bindoff S. T., 'Clement Armstrong and His Treatises of the Commonweal', *Economic History Review*, 14 (1944): 64–73.

Biscaro G., 'Il banco Filippo Borromei e compagni di Londra (1436–1439)', *Archivio Storico Lombardo*, series iv, 19 (1913): 37–126, 283–386.

Biscaro G., 'Mercanti inglesi a Milano nella seconda metà del secolo XV', *Archivio Storico Lombardo*, series iv, 45 (1918): 476–479.

Block J. S., 'Political Corruption in Henrician England', in C. Carlton *et al.* eds., *States, Sovereigns and Society in Early Modern England: Essays in Honour of A. J. Slavin*, New York, 1998, 45–57.

Blussè L. and F. Gaastra eds., *Companies and Trade*, Leiden, 1981.

Boerio G., *Dizionario del dialetto veneziano*, Venice, 1856.

Bono S., *I corsari barbareschi*, Turin, 1964.

Bono S., *Corsari nel Mediterraneo: cristiani e musulmani fra guerra, schiavitú e commercio*, Milan, 1993.

Borgherini-Scarabellin M., *Il Magistrato dei Cinque Savi alla Mercanzia dalla istituzione alla caduta della Repubblica*, Venice, 1925.

Bouwsma W. J., *Venice and the Defense of Republican Liberty: Renaissance Values in the Age of the Counter Reformation*, Berkeley and Los Angeles, 1968.

Bovilsky L., *Barbarous Play: Race on the English Renaissance Stage*, Minneapolis, 2008.

Bracewell W. C., *The Uskoks of Senj: Piracy, Banditry and Holy War in the Sixteenth-Century Adriatic*, Ithaca and London, 1992.

Bratchel M. E., 'Alien Merchant Colonies in Sixteenth-Century England: Community Organisation and Social Mores', *Journal of Medieval and Renaissance Studies*, 14 (1984): 39–62.

Bratchel M. E., 'Italian Merchant Organization and Business Relationships in Early Tudor London', *Journal of European Economic History*, 7 (1978): 5–32.

Bratchel M. E., 'Regulation and Group Consciousness in the Later History of London's Italian Merchant Colonies', *Journal of European Economic History*, 9 (1980): 585–610.

Braude B., 'International Competition and Domestic Cloth in the Ottoman Empire, 1500–1650: A Study in Underdevelopment', *Review*, 2 (1979): 437–451.

Braudel F., *Civilization and Capitalism: 1400–1700*, vol. ii: *The Wheels of Commerce*, London, 1982; vol. iii: *The Perspective of the World*, Berkeley, 1992.

Braudel F., 'L'Italia fuori d'Italia: due secoli tre Italie', in *Storia d'Italia: dalla caduta dell'Impero romano al secolo XVIII*, ii, Turin, 1974, 2092–2247.

Braudel F., *The Mediterranean and the Mediterranean World in the Age of Philip II*, 2 vols., London, 1972.

Braudel F., P. Jeannin, J. Meuvret and R. Romano, 'Le déclin de Venise au XVIIe siècle', in *Aspetti e cause della decadenza economica veneziana nel secolo XVII*, Atti del Convegno, Venice and Rome, 1961, 23–86.

Braudel F. and R. Romano, *Navires et marchandises à l'entrée du port de Livourne (1547–1611)*, Paris, 1951.

Braunstein P., 'Appunti per la storia di una minoranza: la popolazione tedesca di Venezia nel medioevo', in R. Comba, G. Piccinni and G. Pinto eds., *Strutture familiari, epidemie e emigrazioni nell'Italia medievale*, Naples, 1984, 511–517.

Braunstein P., 'Cannaregio, zona di transito?', in D. Calabi and P. Lanaro eds., *La città italiana e i luoghi degli stranieri, XIV–XVIII secolo*, Bari and Rome, 1998, 52–62.

Braunstein P., 'Immagini di una identità collettiva: gli ospiti del Fondaco dei Tedeschi a Venezia (sec. XII–XVII)', in M. Del Treppo ed., *Sistema di rapporti ed elites economiche in Europa (sec. XII–XVII)*, Naples, 1994, 63–69.

Braunstein P., 'Remarques sur la population allemande de Venise à la fin du Moyen Age', in H. G. Beck, M. Manoussacas and A. Pertusi eds., *Venezia, centro di mediazione tra Oriente e Occidente (secoli XV–XVI): aspetti e problemi*, 2 vols., Florence, 1977, i: 233–243.

Braunstein P., 'Venezia e la Germania nel medioevo', in G. Cozzi ed., *Venezia e la Germania: arte, politica, commercio, due civiltà a confronto*, Milan, 1986, 35–49.

Brenner R., *Merchants and Revolution: Commercial Change, Political Conflicts, and London's Overseas Traders, 1550–1653*, Cambridge, 1993.

Brenner R., 'The Social Basis of English Commercial Expansion, 1550–1660', *Journal of Economic History*, 32 (1972): 361–384.

Brett-James A., 'The Levant Company's Factory in Aleppo', *History Today*, 12 (1962): 793–798.

Britnell R. H., 'England and Northern Italy in the Early Fourteenth Century: The Economic Contrasts', *Transactions of the Royal Historical Society*, 39 (1989): 167–183.

Britnell R. H., 'The Towns of England and Northern Italy in the Early Fourteenth Century', *Economic History Review*, 44 (1991): 21–35.

Bromley J. S. and E. H. Krossman eds., *Britain and the Netherlands in Europe and Asia*, London, 1968.

Brown H. F., 'The Marriage Contract, Inventory, and Funeral Expenses of Edmund Harvel', *English Historical Review*, 20 (1905): 70–77.

Brown H. F., *Studies in the History of Venice*, 2 vols, London, 1907.

Brulez W., 'L'exportation des Pays-Bas vers l'Italie par voie de terre au milieu du XVIe siècle', *Annales*, 14 (1959): 461–491.

Brulez W., 'Les routes commerciales d'Angleterre en Italie au XVIe siècle', in *Studi in onore di Amintore Fanfani*, 6 vols, Milan, 1962, iv: 123–184.

Brulez W. and G. Devos, *Marchands flamands à Venise 1568–1621*, 2 vols, Brussels and Rome, 1965–1986.

Brummett P., *Ottoman Seapower and Levantine Diplomacy in the Age of Discovery*, New York, 1994.

Buffardi A., *Nunziature di Venezia*, 42 vols., Rome, 1958–2008.

Bullard M. M., S. R. Epstein, B. G. Kohl and S. M. Stuard, 'Where History and Theory Interact: Frederic C. Lane on the Emergence of Capitalism', *Speculum*, 79 (2004): 88–119.

Burke E., 'Francesco di Demetri Litino: The Inquisition and the Fondaco dei Turchi', *Thesaurismata*, 36 (2006): 79–96.

Buzzati J. C., 'Relations diplomatiques entre l'Angleterre et Venise au XIV siecle', *Revue de droit international et de legislation comparée*, 16 (1884): 589–597.

Calabi D., 'Le basi ultramarine', in A. Tenenti and U. Tucci eds., *Storia di Venezia*, vol. xii: *Il mare*, Rome, 1996, 861–878.

Calabi D., 'Gli stranieri e la città', in A. Tenenti and U. Tucci eds., *Storia di Venezia*, vol. v: *Il Rinascimento: società ed economia*, Rome, 1996, 913–946.

Calabi D. and P. Lanaro eds., *La città italiana ed i luoghi degli stranieri, XIV–XVIII secolo*, Bari and Rome, 1998.

Calendar of State Papers and Manuscripts, Relating to English Affairs, Existing in the Archives and Collections of Venice, 38 vols., London, 1864–1947.

Campbell J. K., *Honour, Family and Patronage: A Study of Institutions and Moral Values in a Greek Mountain Community*, Oxford, 1964.

Campbell J. K., *Modern Greece*, London, 1968.

Candiani G., *Dalla galea alla nave di linea: le trasformazioni della marina veneziana (1572–1699)*, Novi Ligure, 2012.

Candiani G., *I vascelli della Serenissima: guerra, politica e costruzioni navali a Venezia in età moderna, 1650–1720*, Venice, 2009.

Cantimori D., *Eretici italiani del Cinquecento*, Turin, 1992 (1939).

Capp B., *Cromwell's Navy: The Fleet and the English Revolution, 1648–1660*, Oxford, 1989.

Carile A., 'Partitio terrarum imperii Romanie', *Studi Veneziani*, 7 (1965–1966): 125–305.

Carlos A. M. and S. Nicholas, 'Agency Problems in the Early Chartered Companies: The Case of the Hudson's Bay Company', *Journal of Economic History*, 50 (1990): 853–875.

Carlos A. M. and S. Nicholas, '"Giants of an Earlier Capitalism": The Chartered Trading Companies as Modern Multinationals', *The Business History Review*, 62 (1988): 398–419.

Carson E., *The Ancient and Rightful Custom: A History of the English Custom System*, London, 1972.

Carus-Wilson E. M., *Medieval Merchant Venturers*, London, 1954.

Casarino G., 'Stranieri a Genova nel Quattro e Cinquecento: tipologie sociali e nazioni', in G. Rossetti ed., *Dentro la città: stranieri e realtà urbane nell'Europa dei secoli XII–XVI*, Naples, 1989, 137–150.

Casini M., 'Fra città-stato e Stato regionale: riflessioni politiche sulla Repubblica di Venezia in età moderna', *Studi veneziani*, 44 (2002): 15–36.

Castignoli P., 'Aspetti istituzionali della nazione inglese a Livorno', in *Atti del Convegno: 'Gli inglesi a Livorno e nell'Isola d'Elba' (sec. XVII–XIX)*, Livorno, 1980, 102–115.

Castignoli P., 'Il governo', in *Livorno: progetto e storia di una città tra il 1500 e il 1600*, Pisa, 1980, 217–218.

Castignoli P., 'La nazione inglese', in *Livorno: progetto e storia di una città tra il 1500 e il 1600*, Pisa, 1980, 231.

Cecchini I., 'Piacenza a Venezia: la ricezione delle fiere di cambio di Bisenzone a fine Cinquecento nel mercato del credito lagunare', *Note di lavoro del Dipartimento di scienze economiche, Università Ca' Foscari di Venezia*, 18 (2006); www.unive.it/media/allegato/DIP/Economia/Note_di_lavoro_sc_econ omiche/NL2006/NL_DSE_Cecchini_18_06.pdf.

Cecchini I. and L. Pezzolo, 'Merchants and Institutions in Early Modern Venice', *Journal of European Economic History*, 41 (2012): 87–114.

Cessi R., 'La "Curia Forinsecorum" e la sua prima costituzione', *Nuovo Archivio Veneto*, 28 (1914): 202–207.

Cessi R., 'Un patto fra Venezia e Padova e la Curia "Forinsecorum" al principio del secolo XIII', *Atti e memorie della Regia Accademia di scienze, lettere ed arti di Padova*, 30 (1914): 263–275.

Cessi R., *La Repubblica di Venezia e il problema Adriatico*, Naples, 1953.

Chambers D., *The Imperial Age of Venice, 1380–1580*, London, 1970,

Chaney E., *The Evolution of the Grand Tour: Anglo-Italian Cultural Relations since the Renaissance*, London and Portland, 1998.

Chaudhuri K. N., *The English East India Company: The Study of an Early Joint-Stock Company, 1600–1640*, London, 1965.

Chauvard J.-F., *La circulation des biens à Venise: stratégies patrimoniales et marché immobilier (1600–1750)*, Rome, 2005.

Chauvard J. F., 'Scale di osservazione e inserimento degli stranieri nello spazio veneziano tra XVII e XVIII secolo', in D. Calabi and P. Lanaro eds., *La città italiana e i luoghi degli stranieri, XIV–XVIII secolo*, Bari and Rome, 1998, 85–105.

Cheney P. B., *Revolutionary Commerce: Globalization and the French Monarchy*, Cambridge (Mass.), 2010.

Ciano C., 'Corsari inglesi a servizio di Ferdinando I', in *Atti del Convegno di Studi 'Gli inglesi a Livorno e all'isola d'Elba (sec. XVII–XIX)'*, Livorno, 1980, 77–82.

Ciano C., *Navi, mercanti e marina nella vita Mediterranea del Cinque Seicento*, Livorno, 1991.

Ciano C., *La Sanità marittima nell'età Medicea*, Pisa, 1976.

Ciano C., 'Uno sguardo al traffico fra Livorno e l'Europa del Nord verso la metà dei Seicento', in *Atti del Convegno Livorno e il Mediterraneo nell'età Medicea*, Livorno, 1978, 149–168.

Cipolla C. M., *Il burocrate ed il marinaio: la 'Sanità' toscana e le tribolazioni degli Inglesi a Livorno nel XVII secolo*, Bologna, 1992.

Cipolla C. M., 'The Decline of Italy: The Case of a Fully Matured Economy', *Economic History Review*, 5 (1952): 178–187.

Ciriacono S., *Olio ed Ebrei nella Repubblica Veneta del Settecento*, Venice, 1975.

Ciriacono S., 'L'olio a Venezia in età moderna: i consumi alimentari e gli altri usi', in S. Cavaciocchi ed., *Alimentazione e nutrizione*, Florence, 1997, 301–311.

Ciriacono S., 'The Venetian Economy and the World Economy of the 17th and 18th Centuries', in H.-J. Nitz ed., *The Early Modern World System in Geographical Perspective*, Stuttgart, 1993, 120–135.

Çizakça M., 'The Ottoman Government and Economic Life: Taxation, Public Finance and Trade Controls', in S. Faroqhi ed., *The Cambridge History of Turkey*, 4 vols., Cambridge, 2013, ii: 241–275.

Clark G. N., *Guide to English Commercial Statistics 1696–1782*, London, 1938.

Clay C. G. A., *Economic Expansion and Social Change: England 1500–1700*, 2 vols, Cambridge, 1984.

Cochrane E., *Florence in the Forgotten Centuries, 1527–1800: A History of Florence and the Florentines in the Age of the Grand Dukes*, Chicago, 1973.

Collinson P., 'The Politics of Religion and the Religion of Politics in Elizabethan England', *Historical Research*, 82 (2009): 74–92.

Comba R., G. Piccinni, and G. Pinto eds., *Strutture familiari, epidemie, migrazioni nell'Italia medievale*, Naples, 1984.

Concina E., 'Città e fortezze nelle "tre isole nostre del Levante"', in *Venezia e la difesa del Levante da Lepanto a Candia (1570–1670)*, Venice, 1986, 184–194.

Coniglio G., 'Il Duca di Ossuna e Venezia dal 1616 and 1620', *Archivio Veneto*, 54–55 (1955): 42–70.

Constantine D., *Early Greek Travellers and the Hellenic Ideal*, Cambridge, 1984.

Contarini G., *The Commonwealth and Government of Venice*, trans. Lewes Lewkenor, London, 1599 (1543).

Contarini P., 'Relazione d'Inghilterra (1617–18)', in L. Firpo ed., *Relazioni di ambasciatori veneti al Senato*, vol. i: *Inghilterra*, Turin, 1965, 671–684.

Contini A., 'Aspects of Medicean Diplomacy in the Sixteenth Century', in D. Frigo ed., *Politics and Diplomacy in Early Modern Italy: The Structures of Diplomatic Practice, 1450–1800*, Cambridge, 2000, 49–94.

Cooper J., *The Queen's Agent: Francis Walsingham at the Court of Elizabeth I*, London, 2011.

Corazzol G., *Cineografo di banditi su sfondo di monti (Feltre, 1634–1642)*, Milan, 2006.

Cordero-Moss G. ed., *International Commercial Arbitration: Different Forms and their Features*, Cambridge, 2013.

Correr M., 'Relazione d'Inghilterra (1611)', in L. Firpo ed., *Relazioni di ambasciatori veneti al Senato*, vol. i: *Inghilterra*, Turin, 1965, 565–617.

Cortesão A. ed., *The Suma Oriental of Tomè Pires*, 2 vols, London, 1944.

Costantini M., 'I galeoni di Candia nella congiuntura marittima veneziana cinque-seicentesca', in G. Ortalli ed., *Venezia e Creta*, Venice, 1998, 207–231.

Costantini M. ed., *Il Mediterraneo centro-orientale tra vecchie e nuove egemonie: trasformazioni economiche, sociale ed istituzionali nelle Isole Ionie dal declino della Serenissima all'avvento delle potenze atlantiche (sec. XVII–XVIII)*, Rome, 1998.

Costantini M., *Una repubblica nata sul mare: navigazione e commercio a Venezia*, Venice, 2006.

Costantini M., 'Le strutture dell'ospitalità', in A. Tenenti and U. Tucci eds., *Storia di Venezia*, vol. v: *Il Rinascimento: società ed economia*, Rome, 1996, 881–911.

Costantini V., *Il sultano e l'isola contes: Cipro tra eredità veneziana e potere ottomano*, Turin, 2009.

Couroucli M., *Les oliviers du lignage: une Grèce de tradition vénitienne*, Paris, 1985.

Cowan A., *Marriage, Manners and Mobility in Early Modern Venice*, Farnham, 2007.

Cozzi G., *Il Doge Nicolò Contarini*, Venice, 1958.

Cozzi G. ed., *Gli ebrei a Venezia*, Milan, 1987.

Cozzi G., 'Fra Paolo Sarpi, l'anglicanesimo e la "Historia del Concilio Tridentino"', *Rivista Storica Italiana*, 68 (1956): 559–593.

Cozzi G., *Paolo Sarpi tra Venezia e l'Europa*, Turin, 1979.

Cozzi G., 'La politica del diritto nella Repubblica di Venezia', in Cozzi ed., *Stato, società e giustizia nella Repubblica Veneta (sec. XV–XVIII)*, Rome, 1980, 15–152.

Cozzi G., 'La politica della Repubblica dopo l'Interdetto (1607–1619)', in G. Cozzi, M. Knapton and G. Scarabello, *La Repubblica di Venezia nell'età moderna*, 2 vols., Turin, 1986–92, ii: 92–102.

Cozzi G., 'Religione, moralità e giustizia a Venezia: vicende della magistratura degli esecutori contro la bestemmia', *Ateneo Veneto*, n.s. 29 (1991): 7–95.

Cozzi G., *Repubblica di Venezia e stati italiani: politica e giustizia dal secolo XVI al secolo XVIII*, Turin, 1982.

Cozzi G., 'La Spagna, la Francia e la Repubblica di Venezia (1573–1598)', in G. Cozzi, M. Knapton and G. Scarabello, *La Repubblica di Venezia nell'età moderna*, 2 vols., Turin, 1986–92, ii: 60–67.

Cozzi G., 'Venezia Regina', *Studi Veneziani*, 17 (1989): 15–25.

Cozzi G., 'Venezia nello scenario europeo', in G. Cozzi, M. Knapton and G. Scarabello, *La Repubblica di Venezia nell'età moderna*, 2 vols., Turin, 1986–92, ii: 5–183.

Cozzi G., M. Knapton and G. Scarabello, *La Repubblica di Venezia nell'età moderna*, 2 vols., Turin, 1986–92.

Croft P., 'Englishmen and the Spanish Inquisition, 1558–1625', *English Historical Review*, 87 (1972): 249–268.

Croft P., 'Free Trade and the House of Commons, 1605–6', *The Economic History Review*, 28 (1975): 17–27.

Croft P., 'Fresh Light on Bate's Case', *Historical Journal*, 30 (1987): 523–539.

Croft P., 'Rex Pacificus, Robert Cecil, and the 1604 Peace with Spain', in G. Burgess, R. Wymer and J. Lawrence eds., *The Accession of James I: Historical and Cultural Consequences*, Basingstoke, 2006, 140–154.

Croft P. ed., *The Spanish Company*, London, 1972.

Crossley D. W., 'The Performance of the Glass-Industry in Sixteenth Century England', *Economic History Review*, 25 (1972): 421–433.

Crouzet-Pavan E., *Sopra le acque salse: espaces, pouvoirs et société à Venise à la fin du Moyen Âge*, Rome, 1992.

Crouzet-Pavan E., *Venice Triumphant: The Horizons of a Myth*, Baltimore and London, 2002.

Currin J. M., 'England's International Relations 1485–1509: Continuities amidst Change', in S. Doran and G. Richardson eds., *Tudor England and Its Neighbours*, Basingstoke, 2005, 14–43.

Currin J. M., 'Henry VII, France and the Holy League of Venice: The Diplomacy of Balance', *Historical Research*, 82 (2009): 526–546.

Curtin P. D., *Cross-Cultural Trade in World History*, Cambridge, 1984.

Damerini G., *Le isole Ionie nel sistema Adriatico dal dominio veneziano a Buonaparte*, Milan, 1943.

da Mosto A., *L'archivio di Stato di Venezia*, vol. i: *Archivi dell'amministrazione centrale della Repubblica veneta e archivi notarili*, Rome, 1937.

Davies D. W., *Elizabethans Errant: The Strange Fortunes of Sir Thomas Sherley and His Three Sons, As Well in the Dutch Wars as in Muscovy, Morocco, Persia, Spain and the Indies*, New York, 1967.

Davis R., *Aleppo and Devonshire Square: English Traders in the Levant in the Eighteenth Century*, London, 1967.

Davis R., 'England and the Mediterranean', in F. J. Fisher ed., *Essays in the Economic and Social History of Tudor and Stuart England*, Cambridge, 1961, 117–137.

Davis R., 'Influences de l'Angleterre sur le déclin de Venise au XVIIème siècle', in *Aspetti e cause della decadenza economica veneziana nel secolo XVII*, Atti del Convegno, Venice and Rome, 1961, 185–235.

Davis R., *The Rise of the English Shipping Industry in the Seventeenth and Eighteenth Centuries*, London, 1972 (2nd edn).

Davis R. C., *Shipbuilders of the Venetian Arsenal: Workers and Workplace in the Preindustrial City*, Baltimore and London, 1991.

de Commynes P., *Mémoires*, J. Blanchard ed., Paris, 2001.

De Groot A. H., 'The Organization of Western European Trade in the Levant 1500–1800', in L. Blussè and F. Gaastra eds., *Companies and Trade*, Leiden, 1981, 231–241.

Del Treppo M. ed., *Sistema di rapporti ed élites economiche in Europa (sec. XII–XVII)*, Naples, 1994.

Delumeau J., *L'Alun de Rome XVe–XIXe siècles*, Paris, 1962.

De Maddalena A. and H. Kellenbenz eds., *La repubblica internazionale del denaro tra XV e XVII secolo*, Bologna, 1986.

De Maria B., *Becoming Venetians: Immigrants and the Arts in Early Modern Venice*, Princeton, 2010.

De Mas E., *Sovranità politica e unità cristiana nel Seicento anglo-veneto*, Ravenna, 1975.

De Mas E., *L'attesa del secolo aureo, 1603–1625*, Florence, 1982.

De Mordo D., *Saggio di una descrizione geografico-statistica delle isole Ionie (Eptanesia) proposto ad uso della gioventù studiosa*, Corfu, 1865.

Denores G., *A Discourse on the Island of Cyprus and on the Reasons for the True Succession in that Kingdom*, P. Kitromilides ed., Venice, 2006.

de Roover R., *The Rise and Decline of the Medici Bank 1397–1494*, Cambridge (Mass.), 1963.

de Roover R., 'Thomas Mun in Italy', *Historical Research*, 30 (1957): 80–85.

Derosas R., 'Moralità e giustizia a Venezia nel '500 e nel '600, gli Esecutori contro la Bestemmia', in G. Cozzi ed., *Stato, società e giustizia nella Repubblica Veneta (sec. XV–XVIII)*, 2 vols., Rome, 1980, i: 431–528.

de Vivo F., 'The Diversity of Venice and Her Myths in Recent Historiography', *The Historical Journal*, 47 (2004): 169–177.

de Vivo F., 'Historical Justifications of Venetian Power in the Adriatic', *Journal of the History of Ideas*, 64 (2003): 159–176.

de Vivo F., *Information and Communication in Venice: Rethinking Early Modern Politics*, Oxford, 2007.

Del Negro P., 'Giacomo Nani: appunti biografici', *Bollettino del Museo Civico di Padova*, lx (1971): 115–147.

Dini B., 'Produzioni e mercati nell'occidente europeo', in S. Gensini ed., *Europa e Mediterraneo tra medioevo e prima età moderna: l'osservatorio italiano*, Pisa, 1992, 99–124.

d'Istria D., 'Les Îles-Ioniennes sous la Domination de Venise et le protectorat britannique: origines et tendances actuelles des partis indigènes', *Revue des deux mondes*, 16 (1858): 381–422.

Dodsworth R., *Glass and Glassmaking*, Haverfordwest, 1982.

Donati C., *L'idea di nobiltà in Italia: secoli XIV–XVIII*, Rome and Bari, 1988.

Doria G., 'Conoscenza del mercato e sistema informativo: il know-how dei mercanti-finanzieri genovesi nei secoli XVI e XVII', in A. De Maddalena and H. Kellenbenz eds., *La repubblica internazionale del denaro*, Bologna, 1982, 57–122.

Douin G., *La Méditerranée de 1803 à 1805: pirates et corsaires aux Îles Ioniennes*, Paris, 1917.

Doumerc B., 'An Exemplary Maritime Republic: Venice at the End of the Middle Ages', in J. Hattendorf and R. W. Unger eds., *War at Sea in the Middle Ages and in the Renaissance*, Woodbridge, 2003, 151–165.

Dowling M. and J. Shakespeare, 'Religion and Politics in Mid-Tudor England through the Eyes of an English Protestant Woman: The Recollections of Rose Hickman', *Historical Research*, 55 (1982): 94–102.

Dudan B., *Il dominio veneziano di Levante*, Bologna, 1938.

Dursteler E. R. ed., *A Companion to Venetian History: 1400–1797*, Leiden, 2013.

Dursteler E. R., 'Speaking in Tongues: Language and Communication in the Early Modern Mediterranean', *Past and Present*, 217 (2012): 47–77.

Dursteler E. R., *Venetians in Constantinople: Nation, Identity and Coexistence in the Early Modern Mediterranean*, Baltimore, 2006.

Dyer C., *An Age of Transition? Economy and Society in England in the later Middle Ages*, Oxford, 2005.

Dyson J., *Business in Great Waters: The Story of British Fishermen*, London, 1977.

Edler De Roover F., *Glossary of Medieval Terms of Business: Italian Series 1200–1600*, Cambridge (Mass.), 1934.

Eglin J., *Venice Transfigured: The Myth of Venice in British Culture, 1660–1797*, New York, 2001.

Eldem E., 'Capitulations and Western Trade', in S. Faroqhi ed., *The Cambridge History of Turkey*, 4 vols., Cambridge, 2013, iii: 283–335.

Elliott J. H., 'A Europe of Composite Monarchies', *Past and Present*, 137 (1992): 48–71.

Engels M. C., 'Dutch Traders in Livorno at the Beginning of the Seventeenth Century: The Company of Joris Jansen and Bernard van den Broecke', in C. Lesger and L. Noordegraaf eds., *Entrepreneurs and Entrepreneurship in Early Modern Times. Merchants and Industrialists within the Orbit of the Dutch Staple Market*, The Hague, 1995, 63–75.

Engels M. C., *Merchants, Interlopers, Seamen and Corsairs: The 'Flemish' Community in Livorno and Genoa (1615–1635)*, Leiden, 1997.

Epstein M., *The Early History of the Levant Company*, London, 1908.

Epstein S. R., *Freedom and Growth: The Rise of States and Markets in Europe 1300–1750*, London, 2000.

Esposito R., *Communitas: origine e destino della comunità*, Turin, 1998.

Faroqhi S. ed., *The Cambridge History of Turkey*, 4 vols., Cambridge, 2013.

Faroqhi S., 'Crisis and Change, 1590–1699', in H. İnalcik, S. Faroqhi, B. MacGowan, D. Quataert and S. Pamuk, *An Economic and Social History of the Ottoman Empire*, 2 vols., Cambridge, 1997, ii: 413–636.

Fedalto G., 'Le minoranze straniere a Venezia tra politica e legislazione', in H. G. Beck, M. Manoussacas and A. Pertusi eds., *Venezia, centro di mediazione tra Oriente e Occidente (secoli XV–XVI): aspetti e problemi*, 2 vols., Florence, 1977, i: 143–162.

Fedorowicz J. K., *England's Baltic Trade in the Early Seventeenth Century: A Study in Anglo-Polish Commercial Diplomacy*, Cambridge, 1980.

Filippini J. P., *Il porto di Livorno e la Toscana*, 3 vols, Naples, 1988.

Firpo L. ed., *Relazioni di ambasciatori veneti al Senato*, vol. i: *Inghilterra*, Turin, 1965.

Fisher F. J., 'London as an "Engine of Economic Growth"', in J. S. Bromley and E. H. Kossmann eds, *Britain and the Netherlands*, 4 vols., The Hague, 1971, iv: 3–16.

Fisher H. E. S., 'Lisbon, its English Merchant Community and the Mediterranean in the Eighteenth Century', in P. L. Cottrell and D. H. Aldcroft eds., *Shipping Trade and Commerce: Essays in Memory of Ralph Davis*, Leicester, 1981, 23–44.

Fissel M. C. and D. Goffman, 'Viewing the Scaffold from Istanbul: The Bendysh–Hyde Affair, 1647–1651', *Albion*, 22 (1990): 421–448.

Fletcher C., '"Furnished with Gentlemen": The Ambassador's House in Sixteenth-Century Italy', *Renaissance Studies*, 24 (2009): 518–535.

Fletcher C., *Our Man in Rome: Henry VIII and His Italian Ambassador*, London, 2012.

Fletcher C., 'War, Diplomacy and Social Mobility: The Casali Family in the Service of Henry VIII', *Journal of Early Modern History*, 14 (2010): 559–578.

Florio J., *A Worlde of Wordes, or most copious and exact Dictionarie in Italian and English*, London, 1598.

Folin M., 'Spunti per una ricerca su amministrazione veneziana e società ionia nella seconda metà del Settecento', in *Studi veneti offerti a Gaetano Cozzi*, Venice, 1992, 333–347.

Forestieri e stranieri nelle città basso-medievali, Atti del Convegno Internazionale di Studio (Bagno and Ripoli, Florence, 4–8 June 1984), Florence, 1988.

Fortini-Brown P., *Venice and Antiquity: The Venetian Sense of the Past*, New Haven and London, 1996.

Franchini S. G., G. Ortalli and G. Toscano eds., *Venise et la Méditerranée*, Venice, 2011.

Frankopan P., 'Byzantine Trade Privileges to Venice in the Eleventh Century: The Chrysobull of 1092', *Journal of Medieval History*, 30 (2004): 135–160.

Frattarelli-Fischer L., 'Livorno città nuova 1574–1609', *Società e storia*, 46 (1989): 872–893.

Frattarelli-Fischer L., 'Merci e mercanti nella Livorno secentesca', in S. Balbi de Caro ed., *Merci e monete, a Livorno in età granducale*, Milan, 1997, 65–104.

Frigo D. ed., *Politics and Diplomacy in Early Modern Italy: The Structures of Diplomatic Practice, 1450–1800*, Cambridge, 2000.

Fryde E. B., 'Italian Merchants in Medieval England, c.1270–c.1500', in *Aspetti della vita economica medievale*, Florence, 1985, 215–242.

Fryde E. B., *Studies in Medieval Trade and Finance*, London, 1983.

Fusaro M., 'After Braudel: A Reassessment of Mediterranean History Between the Northern Invasion and the Caravane Maritime', in M. Fusaro, C. J. Heywood and M.-S. Omri eds., *Trade and Cultural Exchange in the Early Modern Mediterranean: Braudel's Maritime Legacy*, London, 2010, 1–22.

Fusaro M., 'Les Anglais et les Grecs: un réseau de coopération commerciale en Méditerranée vénitienne', *Annales. Histoire, Sciences Sociales*, 58 (2003): 605–625.

Fusaro M., 'Cooperating Mercantile Networks in the Early Modern Mediterranean', *The Economic History Review*, 65 (2012): 701–718.

Fusaro M., 'Coping with Transition: Greek Merchants and Shipowners between Venice and England in the Late Sixteenth Century', in G. Harlaftis,

I. Baghdiantz-McCabe and I. Pepelasis-Minoglou eds., *Diaspora Entrepreneurial Networks: Four Centuries of History*, London, 2005, 95 123

Fusaro M., 'Politics of Justice/Politics of Trade: Foreign Merchants and the Administration of Justice from the Records of Venice's *Giudici del Forestier*', *Mélanges de l'École française de Rome*, 126/1 (2014).

Fusaro M., 'Public Service and Private Trade: Northern Seamen in Seventeenth Century Venetian Courts of Justice', *International Journal of Maritime History*, 27 (2015): 3–25.

Fusaro M., 'Representation in Practice: The Myth of Venice and the British Protectorate in the Ionian Islands (1801–1864)', in M. Calaresu, F. de Vivo and J.-P. Rubiés eds., *Exploring Cultural History: Essays in Honour of Peter Burke*, Aldershot, 2010, 309–325.

Fusaro M., 'Gli uomini d'affari stranieri in Italia', in *Il Rinascimento Italiano e l'Europa*, 12 vols, vol. iv: *L'Italia e l'economia europea nel Rinascimento*, F. Franceschi, R. A. Goldthwaite and R. C. Mueller eds., Treviso, 2007, 369–395.

Fusaro M., *Uva passa: una guerra commerciale tra Venezia e l'Inghilterra (1540–1640)*, Venice, 1997.

Fusaro, M., B. Allaire, R. Blakemore and T. Vanneste eds., *Law, Labour, and Empire: Comparative Perspectives on Seafarers, c. 1500–1800*, London, 2015.

Fusaro M., C. J. Heywood, and M.-S. Omri eds., *Trade and Cultural Exchange in the Early Modern Mediterranean: Braudel's Maritime Legacy*, London, 2010.

Gabrieli V., 'Bacone, la Riforma e Roma nella versione hobbesiana di un carteggio di Fulgenzio Micanzio', *English Miscellany*, 8 (1957): 195–250.

Gajda A., 'Debating War and Peace in Late Elizabethan England', *Historical Journal*, 52 (2009): 851–878.

Gallant T. W., *Experiencing Dominion: Culture, Identity and Power in the British Mediterranean*, Notre Dame, 2002.

Gambetta D. ed., *Trust: Making and Breaking Cooperative Relations*, Oxford, 1988.

Games A., *The Web of Empire: English Cosmopolitans in an Age of Expansion, 1560–1660*, Oxford, 2008.

Gasparetto A., 'Le relazioni tra Venezia e l'Inghilterra nei secoli XVI e XVII e la loro influenza sulle forme vetrarie inglesi', *Vetro e silicati*, 16 (1970): 16–20.

Geanakoplos D. J., *Greek Scholars in Venice: Studies in the Dissemination of Greek Learning from Byzantium to Western Europe*, Cambridge (Mass.), 1962.

Geanakoplos D. J., *Interaction of the 'Sibling' Byzantine and Western Cultures in the Middle Ages and Italian Renaissance, 330–1600*, New Haven and London, 1976.

Gekas A., *Business Culture and Entrepreneurship in the Ionian Islands Under British Rule, 1815–1864*, LSE Working Paper no. 89/05.

Gekas A., 'Class and Cosmopolitanism: The Historiographical Fortunes of Merchants in Eastern Mediterranean Ports', *Mediterranean Historical Review*, 24 (2009): 95–113.

Gekas A., 'The Merchants of the Ionian Islands between East and West: Forming International and Local Networks', in M. Schulte Beerbühl and J. Vögele eds., *Spinning the Commercial Web: International Trade, Merchants and Commercial Cities, c.1640–1939*, Frankfurt, 2004, 43–63.

Gelderblom O., *Cities of Commerce: The Institutional Foundations of International Trade in the Low Countries, 1250–1650*, Princeton, 2013.

Gelderblom O. ed., *The Political Economy of the Dutch Republic*, Farnham, 2009.

Gelderblom O. and J. Jonker, 'Completing a Financial Revolution: The Finance of The Dutch East India Trade and the Rise of the Amsterdam Capital Market, 1595–1612', *The Journal of Economic History*, 64 (2004): 641–672.

Gelderblom O. and J. Jonker, 'Public Finance and Economic Growth: The Case of Holland in the Seventeenth Century', *The Journal of Economic History*, 71 (2011): 1–39.

Georgopoulou M., *Venice's Mediterranean Colonies: Architecture and Urbanism*, Cambridge, 2001.

Glete J., *Warfare at Sea, 1500–1650: Maritime Conflicts and the Transformation of Europe*, London, 2000.

Godfrey E. S., *The Development of English Glassmaking, 1560–1640*, Oxford, 1976.

Goffman D., *Britons in the Ottoman Empire (1642–1660)*, Washington, 1998.

Goffman D., *Izmir and the Levantine World 1550–1650*, Seattle and London, 1990.

Goldthwaite R., *The Economy of Renaissance Florence*, Baltimore, 2009.

Goodwin Locke J., *Book of the Lockes: A Genealogical and Historical Record of the Descendants of William Locke of Woburn*, Boston, 1853.

Goss C. W. F., 'Sir Paul Pindar', *Transactions of the London & Middlesex Archeological Society*, n.s. 6 (1933): 219–256.

Grassby R., *The Business Community of Seventeenth Century England*, Cambridge, 1995.

Grassby R., *The English Gentleman in Trade: The Life and Works of Sir Dudley North, 1641–1691*, Oxford, 1994.

Greene M., 'Beyond the Northern Invasion: The Mediterranean in the Seventeenth Century', *Past and Present*, 174 (2003): 42–71.

Greene M., *Catholic Pirates and Greek Merchants: A Maritime History of the Mediterranean*, Princeton, 2010.

Greif A., *Institutions and the Path to the Modern Economy: Lessons from Medieval Trade*, Cambridge, 2006.

Grendi E., *I Balbi: una famiglia genovese fra Spagna e Impero*, Turin, 1997.

Grendi E., 'Fonti inglesi per la storia genovese', in *Studi e documenti di storia ligure*, Genoa, 1994, 349–374.

Grendi E., 'Gli inglesi a Genova (sec. XVII–XVIII)', *Quaderni Storici*, 39 (2004): 241–278.

Grendi E., 'I nordici e il traffico del porto di Genova: 1590–1666', *Rivista Storica Italiana*, 83 (1971): 23–63.

Grendi E., *La repubblica aristocratica dei genovesi: politica, carità e commercio tra Cinque e Seicento*, Bologna, 1987.

Grendi E., 'Sul commercio anglo-italiano del Settecento: le statistiche dei customs', *Quaderni Storici*, 79 (1992): 263–275.

Grendler P. F., 'The Leaders of the Venetian State, 1540–1609: A Prosopographical Analysis', *Studi Veneziani*, 19 (1990): 35–86.

Grotius H., *The Works of Hugo Grotius on Fisheries in his controversy with William Welwod*, Leiden, 1928.

Grubb J., 'When Myths Lose Power: Four Decades of Venetian Historiography', *Journal of Modern History*, 58 (1986): 43–94.

Gunn S., 'Politic History, New Monarchy and State Formation: Henry VII in European Perspective', *Historical Research*, 82 (2009): 380–392.

Gussoni, V., 'Relazione d'Inghilterra (1635)', in L. Firpo ed., *Relazioni di ambasciatori veneti al Senato*, vol. i: *Inghilterra*, Turin, 1965, 775–790.

Haitsma Mulier E. O. G., 'Genova e l'Olanda nel Seicento: contatti mercantili ed ispirazione politica', in R. Belvederi ed., *Atti del Congresso Internazionale di Studi Storici 'Rapporti Genova-Mediterraneo-Atlantico nell'età moderna'*, Genoa, 1983, 431–444.

Haitsma Mulier E. O. G., *The Myth of Venice and Dutch Republican Thought in the Seventeenth Century*, Assen, 1980.

Hakluyt R., *The Principall Navigations, Voyages Traffiques & Discoveries of the English Nation. Made by Sea or Over-Land to the Remote and Farthest Distant Quarters of the Earth at any time within the compasse of these 1600 Yeeres*, London, 1589–1600 (reprint Glasgow, 1903–1905).

Hale J. R. ed., *Renaissance Venice*, London, 1973.

Harlaftis G., *A History of Greek-Owned Shipping: The Making of an International Tramp Fleet, 1830 to the Present Day*, London and New York, 1996.

Harris G. G., *Trinity House of Deptford: 1514–1660*, London, 1969.

Harris G. G., *Trinity House of Deptford: Transactions 1609–36*, London, 1983.

Harris J., 'Common Language and the Common Good: Aspects of Identity among the Byzantine Emigres in Renaissance Italy', in S. McKee ed., *Crossing Boundaries: Issues of Cultural and Individual Identity in the Middle Ages and the Renaissance*, Turnhout, 1999, 189–202.

Harris P. R., 'An Aleppo Merchant's Letter-Book', *British Museum Quarterly*, 22 (1960): 64–69.

Harris R., *Industrializing English Law: Entrepreneurship and Business Organization, 1720–1844*, Cambridge, 2000.

Harrison W., *The Description of England: The Classic Contemporary Account of Tudor Social Life by WH*, G. Edelen ed., Mineola, 1994.

Harte N. B. and K. G. Ponting eds., *Textile History and Economic History: Essays in Honour of Miss Julia de Lacy Mann*, Manchester, 1973.

Haskell F., N. Penny and K. Serres, *The King's Pictures: The Formation and Dispersal of the Collections of Charles I and His Courtiers*, New Haven, 2013.

Haynes A., *The Invisible Power: The Elizabethan Secret Services 1570–1603*, Bath, 1992.

Heal F., *Hospitality in Early Modern England*, Oxford, 1990.

Heers J., *Gênes au XVe siècle: civilisation méditerranéenne, grand capitalism, et capitalism populaire*, Paris, 1971.

Heers J., 'Les Génois en Angleterre, la crise de 1458–1466', in *Studi in onore di Armando Sapori*, 2 vols., Milan, 1957, ii: 807–832.

Heller J., *The Mother's Legacy in Early Modern England*, Farnham, 2011.

Heywood C. J., 'The English in the Mediterranean, 1600–1630: A Post-Braudelian Perspective on the "Northern Invasion"', in M. Fusaro, C. J. Heywood and M.-S. Omri eds., *Trade and Cultural Exchange in the Early Modern Mediterranean: Braudel's Maritime Legacy*, London, 2010, 23–44.

Hill R., 'Art and Patronage: Sir Henry Wotton and the Venetian Embassy 1604–1624', in M. Keblusek and B. Noldus eds., *Double Agents: Cultural and Political Brokerage in Early Modern Europe*, Leiden and Boston, 2010, 27–58.

Hillmann H. and C. Gathmann, 'Overseas Trade and the Decline of Privateering', *The Journal of Economic History*, 71 (2011): 730–761.

Hinton R. W. K., *The Eastland Trade and the Common Weal in the Seventeenth Century*, Cambridge, 1959.

Hinton R. W. K., 'The Mercantile System in the Time of Thomas Mun', *Economic History Review*, 2nd series, 7 (1955): 277–290.

Hocquet J.-C., 'L'économie colonial et les sels grecs à la fin du Moyen Âge', in C. Maltezou, A. Tzavara and D. Vlassi eds., *I Greci durante la venetocrazia: uomini, spazio, idee (XIII–XVIII sec.)*, Venice, 2009, 65–81.

Hocquet J.-C., 'Fiscalité et pouvoir colonial: Venise et le sel dalmate aux XVe et XVIe siècles', in M. Balard ed., *État et colonisation au Moyen Âge et à la Renaissance*, Lyon, 1989, 277–315.

Hocquet J.-C., *Le sel et la fortune de Venise*, Lille, 1978.

Hollberg C., *Deutsche in Venedig im späten Mittelalter: Eine Untersuchung von Testamenten aus dem 15. Jahrhundert*, Göttingen, 2005.

Holmes G., 'Anglo-Florentine Trade in 1451', *English Historical Review*, 108 (1993): 371–386.

Holmes G. A., 'Florentine Merchants in England, 1346–1436', *Economic History Review*, 13 (1960): 193–208.

Holmes G. A., 'The *Libel of English Policy*', *The English Historical Review*, 76 (1961): 193–216.

Hont I., *Jealousy of Trade: International Competition and the Nation-State in Historical Perspective*, Cambridge (Mass.), 2005.

Hoshino H., *L'arte della lana in Firenze nel basso medioevo: il commercio della lana ed il mercato dei panni fiorentini nei secoli XIII–XIV*, Florence, 1980.

Howarth D., *Images of Rule: Art and Politics in the English Renaissance, 1485–1649*, Berkeley, 1997.

Howard D., *Venice & the East: The Impact of the Islamic World on Venetian Architecture, 1100–1500*, New Haven and London, 2000.

Howarth D., 'Merchants and Diplomats: New Patrons of the Decorative Arts in Seventeenth Century England', *Furniture History*, 20 (1984): 10–17.

Hunt E. S., *The Medieval Super-Companies: A Study of the Peruzzi Company of Florence*, New York, 1994.

Hunt E. S., 'A New Look at the Dealings of the Bardi and Peruzzi with Edward III', *The Journal of Economic History*, 50 (1990): 149–162.

Hunt Yungblut L., 'Straungers and Aliaunts: The "Un-English" among the English in Elizabethan England', in S. McKee ed., *Crossing Boundaries: Issues of Cultural and Individual Identity in the Middle Ages and the Renaissance*, Turnhout, 1999, 263–276.

Hyde J. K., *Padua in the Age of Dante*, Manchester and New York, 1966.

Imhaus B., *Le minoranze orientali a Venezia, 1300–1510*, Rome, 1997.

İnalcik H., 'Impact of the *Annales* School on Ottoman Studies and New Findings', in his *Studies in Ottoman Social and Economic History*, London, 1985, IV: 69–96.

Infelise M., 'From Merchants' Letters to Handwritten Political *Avvisi*: Notes on the Origins of Public Information', in F. Bethencourt and F. Egmond eds., *Cultural Exchange in Early Modern Europe*, vol. iii: *Correspondence and Cultural Exchange in Europe, 1400–1700*, Cambridge, 2007, 33–52.

Israel J. I., *Diasporas within a Diaspora: Jews, Crypto-Jews and the World Maritime Empires (1540–1740)*, Leiden 2002.

Israel J. I., *Dutch Primacy in World Trade 1585–1740*, Oxford, 1991.

Israel J. I., *Empires and Entrepôts: The Dutch, the Spanish Monarchy and the Jews, 1585–1713*, London, 1990.

Israel J. I., *European Jewry in the Age of Mercantilism 1550–1750*, Oxford, 1985.

Israel J. I., 'The Phases of the Dutch *Straatvaart*, 1590–1713: A Chapter in the Economic History of the Mediterranean', in his *Empires and Entrepôts: The Dutch, the Spanish Monarchy and the Jews, 1585–1713*, London, 1990, 133–162.

Ivetic E., 'Gli uscocchi fra mito e storiografia', in M. Gaddi and A. Zannini eds., *'Venezia non è da guerra': l'isontino, la società friulana e la Serenissima nella guerra di Gradisca (1615–1617)*, Udine, 2008, 389–397.

Jacobsen H., *Luxury and Power: The Material World of the Stuart Diplomat, 1660–1714*, Oxford, 2011.

Jacoby D., 'Les "Assises de Romanie" et le droit vénitien dans les colonies vénitiennes', in his *Recherches sur la Méditerranée orientale du XIIe au XVe siècle*, London, 1970, IV: 356–359.

Jacoby D., 'Creta e Venezia nel contesto economico del Mediterraneo Orientale sino alla metà del Quattrocento', in G. Ortalli ed., *Venezia e Creta*, Venice, 1998, 73–106.

Jacoby D., *La féodalité en Grèce médiévale: les 'Assises de Romanie' sources, application, diffusion*, Paris, 1971.

Jacoby D., *Latins, Greeks and Muslims: Encounters in the Eastern Mediterranean 10th–15th Centuries*, Farnham, 2009.

Jacoby D., 'La production du sucre en Crète vénitienne: L'échec d'une entreprise économique', in *Rodonia: time ston M.I. Manousaka*, Rethimno, 1994, 167–180.

Jacoby D., 'The Venetian Presence in the Latin Empire of Constantinople (1204–1261): The Challenge of Feudalism and the Byzantine Inheritance', in his *Latin Romania and the Mediterranean*, Aldershot, 2001, II: 141–201.

Jardine L., 'Gloriana Rules the Waves: Or, the Advantage of Being Excommunicated (and a Woman)', *Transactions of the Royal Historical Society*, 14 (2004): 209–222.

Jeannin P., 'The Sea–Borne and the Overland Trade Routes of Northern Europe in the XVIth and XVIIth Centuries', *Journal of European Economic History*, 11 (1982): 5–61.

Jenks S., *Robert Sturmy's Commercial Expedition to the Mediterranean (1457/8)*, Bristol, 2006.

Jones J. R., 'English Attitudes to Europe in the Seventeenth Century', in J. S. Bromley and E. H. Krossman eds., *Britain and the Netherlands in Europe and Asia*, London, 1968, 37–55.

Jowitt C., 'Piracy and Politics in Heywood and Rowley's *Fortune by Land and Sea* (1607–9)', *Renaissance Studies*, 16 (2002): 217–233.

Judde de Larivière C., *Naviguer, commercer, gouverner: économie maritime et pouvoirs à Venise (XVe–XVIe siècles)*, Leiden, 2008.

Kamen H., *The Iron Century: Social Change in Europe, 1550–1660*, London, 1971.

Katele I. B., 'Piracy and the Venetian State: The Dilemma of Maritime Defense in the Fourteenth Century', *Speculum*, 63 (1988): 865–889.

Keblusek M. and B. Noldus eds., *Double Agents: Cultural and Political Brokerage in Early Modern Europe*, Leiden and Boston, 2010.

Keene D., 'Cities and Empires', *Journal of Urban History*, 32 (2005): 8–21.

Kellenbenz H., 'Relazioni commerciali tra il Levante e i Paesi d'Oltralpe', in R. Ragosta ed., *Navigazioni mediterranee e connessioni continentali (secoli XI–XVI)*, Naples, 1982, 301–314.

Kennedy P. M., *The Rise and Fall of British Naval Mastery*, London, 2004.

Keymors J., *Observations made upon the Dutch Fishing about the year 1601*, London, 1664.

Kirby D. and M. L. Hinkkanen, *The Baltic and the North Sea*, London and New York, 2000.

Kirk T., 'Genoa and Livorno: Sixteenth- and Seventeenth-Century Commercial Rivalry as a Stimulus to Policy Development', *History*, 86 (2001): 3–17.

Kirk T., *Genoa and the Sea: Policy and Power in an Early Modern Maritime Republic, 1559–1684*, Baltimore and London, 2005.

Kirkwall (Viscount) ed. [George William Hamilton Fitzmaurice, Earl of Orkney, Viscount Kirkwall, Captain 71st Highlanders], *Four Years in the Ionian Islands Their Political and Social Condition. With a History of the British Protectorate*, 2 vols., London, 1864.

Knapton M., 'Lo stato veneziano tra la battaglia di Lepanto e la guerra di Candia 1571–1644', in *Venezia e la difesa del Levante da Lepanto a Candia (1570–1670)*, Venice, 1986, 233–241.

Knapton M., 'The *Terraferma* State', in E. Dursteler ed., *A Companion to Venetian History, 1400–1797*, Leiden and Boston, 2013, 85–124.

Knapton M., 'Tra Dominante e Dominio (1517–1630)', in G. Cozzi, M. Knapton and G. Scarabello, *La Repubblica di Venezia nell'età moderna*, 2 vols., Turin, 1986–1992, ii: 203–325.

Knapton M., 'Venice and the *Terraferma*', in A. Gamberini and I. Lazzarini eds., *The Italian Renaissance State*, Cambridge, 2012, 132–155.

Knapton M. and J. Law, 'Marin Sanudo e la Terraferma', in M. Sanudo, *Itinerario per la Terraferma veneziana*, G. M. Varanini ed., Rome, 2014, 9–80.

Knox B., 'British Policy and the Ionian Islands, 1847–1864: Nationalism and Imperial Administration', *The English Historical Review*, 99 (1984): 503–529.

Koenigsberger H., 'English Merchants in Naples and Sicily in the Seventeenth Century', *English Historical Review*, 62 (1947): 304–326.

Koenigsberger H. G., 'Dominium Regale or Dominium Politicum et Regale', in *Politicians and Virtuosi: Essays in Early Modern History*, London, 1986, 1–26.

Koliva-Karaleka M., 'Il "Memorial di tuti libri della Camera di Zante" (1498–1628): problematica sulla ricostruzione dell' "Arkeiophylakeion" di Zante', *Studi Veneziani*, 13 (1987): 301–337.

Kolyva M., '"Obbedir et esseguir tutti l'infrascritti Capitoli": i Capitoli dell'isola di Zante durante il dominio veneziano (fine XV–fine XII sec.)', in C. Maltezou, A. Tzavara and D. Vlassi eds., *I Greci durante la venetocrazia: uomini, spazio, idee (XIII–XVIII sec.)*, Venice, 2009, 483–495.

Konstantinidou K., *Το κακό οδεύει έρποντας ... Οι λοιμοί της πανώλης στα Ιόνια Νησιά (17ος–18ος αι.)* (*The Disaster Creeps Crawling ... The Plague Epidemics of the Ionian Islands (1th–18th Centuries)*), Venice, 2007.

Kooijmans L., 'Risk and Reputation: On the Mentality of Merchants in the Early Modern Period', in C. Lesger and L. Noordegraaf eds , *Entrepreneurs and Entrepreneurship in Early Modern Times: Merchants and Industrialists within the Orbit of the Dutch Staple Market*, The Hague, 1995, 25–34.

Kostić V., *Dubrovnik i Engleska, 1300–1650*, Belgrade, 1975.

Ladd R. A., *Antimercantilism in Late Medieval English Literature*, New York, 2010.

Laiou A. ed., *Urbs Capta: The Fourth Crusade and its Consequences*, Paris, 2005.

Lambert A., 'Now is come a darker day': Britain, Venice and the Meaning of Sea Power', in M. Taylor ed., *The Victorian Empire and Britain's Maritime World, 1837–1901: The Sea and Global History*, London, 2013, 19–42.

Lanaro P. ed., *At the Centre of the Old World: Trade and Manufacturing in Venice and the Venetian Mainland, 1400–1800*, Toronto, 2006.

Lanaro P., *I mercanti nella Repubblica veneta: economie cittadine e stato territoriale (sec. XV–XVIII)*, Venice, 1999.

Landes D., *The Wealth and Poverty of Nations: Why Some Are so Rich and Some Are so Poor*, London, 1998.

Lane F. C., *Andrea Barbarigo, Merchant of Venice, 1418–1449*, Baltimore, 1944.

Lane F. C., 'The Mediterranean Spice Trade: Further Evidence of its Revival in the Sixteenth Century', *American Historical Review*, 45 (1940): 581–590.

Lane F. C., *Profits from Power: Readings in Protection Rent and Violence Controlling Enterprise*, Albany, 1979.

Lane F. C., *Studies in Venetian Social and Economic History*, B. G. Kohl and R. C. Mueller eds., London, 1987.

Lane F. C., *Venetian Ships and Shipbuilders in the Italian Renaissance*, Baltimore, 1934.

Lane F. C., *Venice and History: The Collected Papers of Frederic C. Lane*, Baltimore, 1966.

Lane F. C., *Venice: A Maritime Republic*, Baltimore, 1973.

Lang R. G., 'Social Origins and Social Aspirations of Jacobean London Merchants', *Economic History Review*, 27 (1974): 28–47.

Larkin J. F. and P. L. Hughes eds., *Stuart Royal Proclamations*, 2 vols., Oxford, 1973.

Latimer J., *The History of the Society of Merchant Venturers of the City of Bristol: With Some Account of the Anterior Merchants' Guilds*, Bristol, 1903.

Lazzarini I., *L'Italia degli Stati territoriali: secoli XIII–XV*, Bari, 2003.

Lee M. Jr, *Dudley Carleton to John Chamberlain 1603–1624: Jacobean Letters*, New Brunswick, 1972.

Leng T., 'Commercial Conflict and Regulation in the Discourse of Trade in Seventeenth Century England', *The Historical Journal*, 48 (2005): 933–954.

Lesger C. and L. Noordegraaf eds., *Entrepreneurs and Entrepreneurship in Early Modern Times: Merchants and Industrialists within the Orbit of the Dutch Staple Market*, The Hague, 1995.

Lettera di Ragguaglio Della Vittoria Navale conseguita dall'Armata della Serenissima Repubblica di Venezia Sotto il Comando del Procurator Capitan General da Mar Mocenigo Contro Turchi nell'Arcipelago, Venice, 1651.

Levi C. A., *Navi venete da codici marini e dipinti*, Venice, 1983 (1892).

Lévy G., *De la condition internationale des Îles Ioniennes depuis le Congrès de Vienne jusq'à nos jours*, Paris, 1901.

The Libelle of Englyshe Policie: a poem on the use of sea power, 1436, D. Warner ed., Oxford, 1926.

Liefkes R., *Glass*, London, 1997.

Lithgow W., *The Totall Discourse of the Rare Adventures and Painefull Peregrinations of long Nineteene yeares Travayles from Scotland to the most famous Kingdomes in Europe, Asia and Affrica*, Glasgow, 1906 (1632).

Livorno: progetto e storia di una città tra il 1500 e il 1600, Pisa, 1980.

Lloyd T. O., *The British Empire, 1558–1995*, Oxford, 1996 (1984).

Loades D., *England's Maritime Power: Seapower, Commerce and Policy, 1490–1690*, London, 2000.

Lopez R. S., *Genova marinara nel Duecento: Benedetto Zaccaria ammiraglio e mercante*, Milan, 1933.

Lopez R. S., 'Majorcans and Genoese on the North Sea Route in the Thirteenth Century', *Revue belge de philologie et d'histoire*, 29 (1951): 1163–1179.

Lowry M., 'The Reform of the Council of X, 1582–3: An Unsettled Problem?', *Studi veneziani*, 13 (1971): 275–310.

Luetić J., 'English Mariners and Ships in Seventeenth-Century Dubrovnik', *The Mariner's Mirror*, 64 (1978): 276–284.

Lunzi E., *Della condizione politica delle Isole Ionie sotto il Dominio Veneto*, Venice, 1858.

Lunzi E., *Della repubblica settinsulare libri due*, Bologna, 1863.

Lupprian K. E., *Il fondaco dei tedeschi e la sua funzione di controllo del commercio tedesco a Venezia*, Venice, 1978.

Luzzati L., F. Besta and A. Ventura eds., *Bilanci generali dello stato*, 4 vols, Venice, 1902–1972.

Luzzatto G., 'La decadenza di Venezia dopo le scoperte geografiche nella tradizione e nella realtà', *Archivio veneto*, 84 (1954): 162–181.

Luzzatto G., 'Introduzione', in *Aspetti e cause della decadenza economica veneziana nel secolo XVII*, Venice and Rome, 1961, 9–20.

Luzzatto G., *Storia economica di Venezia dall'XI al XVI secolo*, Venice, 1961.

Luzzatto G., *Studi di storia economica veneziana*, Padua, 1954.

Machiavelli N., *Discorsi sopra la prima deca di Tito Livio*, F. Bausi ed., Rome, 2001.

MacKenney R., *Tradesmen and Traders: The World of the Guilds in Venice and Europe, c.1250–c.1650*, London, 1987.

MacKenney R., '"A plot Discover'd?" Myth, Legend, and the "Spanish Conspiracy" against Venice in 1618', in J. Martin and D. Romano eds., *Venice Reconsidered: The History and Organization of an Italian City-State, 1297–1797*, Baltimore, 2000, 185–216.

MacLeod C., 'Accident or Design? George Ravenscroft's Patent and the Invention of Lead-Crystal Glass', *Technology and Culture*, 28 (1987): 776–803.

MacLeod C., *Inventing the Industrial Revolution: The English Patent System, 1660–1800*, Cambridge, 1988.

Macpherson D., *Annals of Commerce, manufactures, fisheries, and navigation, with brief notices of the arts and sciences connected with them. Containing the Commercial transactions of the British empire and other countries, from the earliest account to the meeting of the union Parliament in January 1801; and comprehending the most valuable part of the late Mr. Anderson History of commerce, viz. from the year 1492 to the end of the reign of King George II*, 4 vols., London, 1805.

Madden T. F., *Enrico Dandolo and the Rise of Venice*, Baltimore and London, 2003.

Malanima P., *La fine del primato: crisi e riconversione nell'Italia del Seicento*, Milan, 1998.

Mallett M., 'Anglo-Florentine Commercial Relations, 1465–1491', *Economic History Review*, 15 (1962): 250–265.

Mallett M. E., *The Florentine Galleys in the Fifteenth Century: With the Diary of Luca di Maso degli Albizzi. Captain of the Galleys, 1429–30*, Oxford, 1967.

Mallett M. E. and J. R. Hale, *Military Organisation of a Renaissance State: Venice*, Cambridge, 1984.

Maltezou C., 'Dove va la storia della venetocrazia in Grecia? Stato della ricerca e orientamento', in C. Maltezou, A. Tzavara and D. Vlassi eds., *I Greci durante la venetocrazia: uomini, spazio, idee (XIII–XVIII sec.)*, Venice, 2009, 21–38.

Maltezou C., 'The Greek Version of the Fourth Crusade: From Niketas Choniates to the History of the Greek Nation', in A. Laiou ed., *Urbs Capta: The Fourth Crusade and its Consequences*, Paris, 2005, 152–159.

Maltezou C., 'The Historical and Social Context', in D. Holton ed., *Literature and Society in Renaissance Crete*, Cambridge, 1991, 17–47.

Maltezou C., 'La vénétocratie en Méditerranée orientale: tendances historiographiques et état actuel des études', in S. G. Franchini, G. Ortalli and G. Toscano eds., *Venise et la Méditerranée*, Venice, 2011, 161–180.

Malynes G., *An Essay on the Fishing Trade*, Edinburgh, 1720.

Mangiarotti A., 'La politica economica di Ferdinando I de Medici', in S. Balbi de Caro ed., *Merci e monete a Livorno in età granducale*, Milan, 1997, 37–64.

Mangiarotti A., 'Il porto franco, 1565–1676', in S. Balbi de Caro ed., *Merci e monete a Livorno in età granducale*, Milan, 1997, 17–35.

Marangoni G., *Le associazioni di mestiere nella Repubblica Veneta (vittuaria, farmacia, medicina)*, Venice, 1974.

Marrella F. and A. Mozzato, *Alle origini dell'arbitrato commerciale internazionale: l'arbitrato a Venezia tra medioevo ed età moderna*, Padua, 2001.

Marshall P. J., 'The First British Empire', in R. W. Winks ed., *The Oxford History of the British Empire*, vol. v: *Historiography*, Oxford, 1999, 43–53.

Marshall P. J. ed., *The Oxford History of the British Empire*, vol. ii: *The Eighteenth Century*, Oxford, 1998.

Martin J., 'Marranos and Nicodemites in Sixteenth-Century Venice', *Journal of Medieval and Early Modern Studies*, 41 (2011): 577–599.

Martin J., *Venice's Hidden Enemies: Italian Heretics in a Renaissance City*, London, 1993.

Martin J. and D. Romano eds., *Venice Reconsidered: The History and Civilization of an Italian City-State, 1297–1797*, Baltimore, 2000.

Masters B., *The Origins of Western Economic Dominance in the Middle East: Mercantilism and the Islamic Economy in Aleppo, 1600–1750*, New York, 1988.

Mathias P., 'Strategies for Reducing Risk by Entrepreneurs in the Early Modern Period', in C. Lesger and L. Noordegraaf eds., *Entrepreneurs and Entrepreneurship in Early Modern Times: Merchants and Industrialists within the Orbit of the Dutch Staple Market*, The Hague, 1995, 5–24.

Matthee R., *The Politics of Trade in Safavid Iran: Silk for Silver, 1600–1730*, Cambridge, 1999.

Mazzei R., 'L'economia pisana e la dinamica del commercio internazionale dell'età moderna', in M. Tangheroni ed., *Pisa e il Mediterraneo: uomini, merci, idee dagli Etruschi ai Medici*, Milan, 2003, 293–297.

Mazzei R., *Itinera mercatorum: circolazione di uomini e beni nell'Europa centro-orientale, 1550–1650*, Lucca, 1999.

Mazzei R. and T. Fanfani eds., *Lucca e L'Europa degli Affari, secoli XV–XVIII*, Lucca, 1990.

McGrath P., *The Merchant Venturers of Bristol: A History of the Society of Merchant Venturers of Bristol from Its Origin to the Present Day*, Bristol, 1975.

McGrath P. ed., *Records Relating to the Society of Merchant Venturers of the City of Bristol in the Seventeenth Century*, Bristol, 1951.

McKee S. ed., *Crossing Boundaries: Issues of Cultural and Individual Identity in the Middle Ages and the Renaissance*, Turnhout, 1999.

McKee S., 'Sailing from Byzantium: Byzantines and Greeks in the Venetian World', in J. Herrin and G. Saint Guillain eds., *Identities and Allegiances in the Eastern Mediterranean after 1204*, Farnham, 2010, 291–300.

McKee S., *Uncommon Dominion: Venetian Crete and the Myth of Ethnic Purity*, Philadelphia, 2000.

Medioli F., 'Arcangela Tarabotti: una famiglia non detta ed un segreto indicibile in famiglia', *Archivio Veneto*, 144 (2013): 105–144.

Megna L., 'Comportamenti abitativi del patriziato veneziano (1582–1740)', *Studi Veneziani*, 22 (1991): 253–323.

Melis F., 'Sulla "nazionalità" del commercio marittimo Inghilterra-Mediterraneo negli anni intorno al 1400', in his *I trasporti e le comunicazioni nel Medioevo*, Florence, 1984, 81–101.

Micheli [sic] [Michiel] G., 'Relazione d'Inghilterra' (1557), in E. Albèri ed., *Relazioni degli ambasciatori veneti al senato*, series 1, vol. ii, Florence, 1840, 289–381.

Michelon M., ' La peste dei prosticchi: travagli legislativi di un contratto agrario nelle Isole Ionie (secoli XVI–XIX)', *Atti dell'Istituto veneto di scienze, lettere ed arti*, 110 (1991–1992): 365–398.

Millard A. M., *Lists of Goods Imported into the Port of London by English and Alien and Denizens Merchants for Certain Years between 1560 and 1640: Compiled from London Port Books and Other Sources*, typescript, 1955.

Minchinton W. E. ed., *The Growth of Overseas Trade in the Seventeenth and Eighteenth Centuries*, London, 1969.

Mitchell A. R., 'The European Fisheries in Early Modern History', in E. E. Rich and C. H. Wilson eds., *The Cambridge Economic History of Europe*, vol. v: *The Economic Organization of Early Modern Europe*, Cambridge, 1977, 133–184.

Mocenigo P., 'Relazione d'Inghilterra (1671)', in L. Firpo ed., *Relazioni di ambasciatori veneti al Senato*, vol. i: *Inghilterra*, Turin, 1965, 913–941.

Molà L., *La comunità dei lucchesi a Venezia: immigrazione e industria della seta nel tardo medioevo*, Venice, 1994.

Molà L., *The Silk Industry of Renaissance Venice*, Baltimore, 2000.

Molin, N. 'Relazione d'Inghilterra (1607)', in L. Firpo ed., *Relazioni di ambasciatori veneti al Senato*, vol. i: *Inghilterra*, Turin, 1965, 499–556.

Montanari M., *The Culture of Food*, New York, 2003.
Morilla Critz J., A. L. Olmstead and P. W. Rhode, *International Competition and the Development of the Dried Fruit Industry, 1880–1930*, in S. Pamuk and J. G. Williamson eds., *The Mediterranean Response to Globalization Before 1950*, London and New York, 2000, 199–232.
Morris J., *The Venetian Empire: A Sea Voyage*, Harmondsworth, 1980.
Moryson F., *An itinerary vvritten by Fynes Moryson Gent. First in the Latine tongue, and then translated by him into English: containing his ten yeeres trauell through the tvvelue dominions of Germany, Bohmerland, Sweitzerland, Netherland, Denmarke, Poland, Jtaly, Turky, France, England, Scotland, and Ireland. Diuided into III parts. The I. part. Containeth a iournall through all the said twelue dominions: shewing particularly the number of miles, the soyle of the country, the situation of cities, the descriptions of them, with all monuments in each place worth the seeing, as also the rates of hiring coaches or horses from place to place, with each daies expences for diet, horse – meate, and the like. The II. part. Containeth the rebellion of Hugh, Earle of Tyrone, and the appeasing thereof: written also in forme of a iournall. The III. part. Containeth a discourse vpon seuerall heads, through all the said seuerall dominions*, London, 1617.
Moryson F., *Shakespeare's Europe*, C. Hughes ed., London, 1902.
Moschonas N. G., 'L'idéologie politique dans les Îles Ioniennes pendant la période républicaine (1797–1799)', in *La révolution française et l'hellenisme moderne*, Athens, 1989, 123–136.
Mozzato A., 'The Production of Woollens in Fifteenth- and Sixteenth-Century Venice', in P. Lanaro ed., *At the Center of the Old World: Trade and Manufacturing in Venice and the Venetian Mainland, 1400–1800*, Toronto, 2006, 73–107.
Mozzato A., 'Scelte produttive e di mercato di drappieri veneziani in area adriatica e levantina nel XV secolo' in D. Andreozzi, L. Panariti and C. Zaccaria eds., *Acque, terre e spazi dei mercanti. Istituzioni, gerarchie, conflitti e pratiche dello scambio nel Mediterraneo dall' età antica alla modernità*, Trieste, 2009, 303–332.
Mueller R. C., '"Veneti facti privilegio": stranieri naturalizzati a Venezia tra XIV e XVI secolo', in D. Calabi and P. Lanaro eds., *La città italiana e i luoghi degli stranieri, XIC–XVIII secolo*, Bari and Rome, 1998, 41–51.
Mueller R. C., *The Venetian Money Market: Banks, Panics and Public Debt, 1200–1500*, Baltimore, 1997.
Mueller R. C. and L. Molà, 'Essere straniero a Venezia nel tardo Medioevo: accoglienza e rifiuto nei privilegi di cittadinanza e nelle sentenze criminali', in S. Cavaciocchi ed., *Le migrazioni in Europa*, Florence, 1994, 839–851.
Muldrew C., *The Economy of Obligation: The Culture of Credit and Social Relations in Early Modern England*, London, 1998.
Mun T., *A Discourse of Trade, from England unto the East-Indies*, London, 1621.
Mun T., *England's Treasure by Foreign Trade: or, the Balance of our Foreign Trade is the Rule of our Treasure*, London, 1698.
Munro J. H., 'Bullionism and the Bill of Exchange in England 1272–1663: A Study in Monetary Management and Popular Prejudice', in R. S. Lopez and J. Le Goff eds., *The Dawn of Modern Banking*, New Haven, 1979, 169–240.
Munro J. H., 'I panni di lana', in *Il Rinascimento Italiano e l'Europa*, vol. iv: *L'Italia e l'economia europea nel Rinascimento*, F. Franceschi, R. A. Goldthwaite and R. C. Mueller eds., Treviso, 2007, 105–141.

Nani Mocenigo M., *Storia della marina veneta da Lepanto alla caduta della Repubblica*, Rome, 1935.

Nicol D. M., *Byzantium and Venice: A Study in Diplomatic and Cultural Relations*, Cambridge, 1988.

Nörr K. W., 'Procedure in Mercantile Matters: Some Comparative Aspects', in *Iudicium est actus trium personarum*, Goldbach, 1993, 195–201.

North R., *The Lives of the Right Hon. Francis North, Baron Guildford, Lord Keeper of the Great Seal, under king Charles II, and king James II. The Hon. Sir Dudley North, Commissioner of the Customs, and afterwards of the Treasury to king Charles II. And the Hon. and Rev. Dr. John North, Master of Trinity College Cambridge*, and Clerk of the Closet to king Charles II, 3 vols., London, 1826.

O'Brien P., 'Final Considerations', in P. O'Brien and B. Yun Casalilla eds., *European Aristocracies and Colonial Elites: Patrimonial Management Strategies and Economic Development, 15–18 Centuries*, Aldershot, 2005, 247–263.

O'Connell M., *Men of Empire: Power and Negotiation in Venice's Maritime State*, Baltimore, 2009.

Ord M., 'Classical and Contemporary Italy in Roger Ascham's *The Scholemaster* (1570)', *Renaissance Studies*, 16 (2002): 202–216.

Ormrod D., *The Rise of Commercial Empires: England and the Netherlands in the Age of Mercantilism, 1650–1770*, Cambridge, 2003.

Ortalli F. ed., *Lettere di Vincenzo Priuli capitano delle galee di Fiandra, 1521–1523*, Venice, 2005.

Ortalli G. ed., *Venezia e Creta: atti del convegno internazionale di studi* (Iraklio and Chanià, 30 September to 5 October 1997), Venice, 1998.

Paci R., *La 'Scala' di Spalato e il commercio veneziano nei Balcani fra Cinque e Seicento*, Venice, 1971.

Paci R., 'La scala di Spalato e la politica veneziana in Adriatico', *Quaderni Storici*, 13 (1970): 48–105.

Pacini A., 'Genoa and Charles V', in W. Blockmans and N. Mout eds., *The World of Emperor Charles V*, Amsterdam, 2004, 161–199.

Pagano De Divitiis G., *English Merchants in Seventeenth Century Italy*, Cambridge, 1997.

Pagano De Divitiis G., 'Il Mediterraneo nel XVII secolo: l'espansione commerciale inglese e l'Italia', *Studi Storici*, 27 (1986): 109–148.

Pagano De Divitiis G., 'Il porto di Livorno fra l'Inghilterra e l'Oriente', *Nuovi Studi Livornesi*, 1 (1993): 43–87.

Pagratis G. D., Κοινωνία και οικονομία στο βενετικό «Κράτος της Θάλασσας». Οι ναυτιλιακές επιχειρήσεις της Κέρκυρας *(1496–1538) (Society and Economy in the Venetian Stato da Mar: The Maritime Enterprises of Corfu (1496–1538))*, Athens, 2013.

Paladini F. M., *'Un caos che spaventa': poteri, territori e religioni di frontiera nella Dalmazia della tarda età veneta*, Venice, 2002.

Paladini F. M., 'Né uomini né strutture: ultimi anni del dominio veneto nelle Isole Jonie attraverso i dispacci dell'ultimo Provveditore Generale da Mar Aurelio Widmann', *Atti dell'istituto veneto di scienze, lettere ed arti*, 152 (1993–94): 183–222.

Paladini F. M., 'Velleità e capitolazione della propaganda talassocratica veneziana', *Venetica*, 17 (2002): 147–172.

384   Printed primary sources and bibliography

Panagopoulos G., 'The Urban Transformation of Corfu during the Protectorate: The Role of the Esplanade', in J. R. Melville-Jones ed., *Studies in the Architecture of Dalmatia and Corfu*, Venice, 2001, 53–64.

Panayotakis N., 'Premessa', in G. Ortalli ed., *Venezia e Creta*, Venice, 1998, 1 8.

Panciera W., *L'arte matrice: i lanifici della Repubblica di Venezia nei secoli XVII e XVIII*, Treviso, 1996.

Panciera W., '"Tagliare i confini": la linea di frontiera Soranzo-Ferhat in Dalmazia (1576)', in A. Giuffrida, F. D'Avenia and D. Palermo eds., *Studi storici dedicati a Orazio Cancila*, Palermo, 2011, 237–272.

Papadia-Lala A., 'Soldati mercenari stranieri e vita urbana nella città di Candia veneziana (secoli XVI–XVII)', *Thesaurismata*, 29 (1999): 273–285.

Parry J., 'Transport and Trade Routes', in E. E. Rich and C. H. Wilson eds., *The Cambridge Economic History of Europe*, vol. iv: *The Economic of Expanding Europe in the Sixteenth and Seventeenth Century*, Cambridge, 1967, 155–219.

Pauthier G., *Les Îles Ioniennes pendant l'occupation française et le protectorat anglais*, Paris, 1863.

[Paxi B.], *Tariffa de pesi e mesure correspondenti dal Levante al Ponente: da una terra a l'altra: e a tutte le parte del mondo: con la noticia delle robe che se trazeno da una Paese per laltro* [sic], Venice, 1521.

Pearl V., *London and the Outbreak of the Puritan Revolution: City, Government and National Politics, 1625–1643*, Oxford, 1961.

Pearsall Smith L., *The Life and Letters of Sir Henry Wotton*, 2 vols., Oxford, 1907.

Pedani Fabris M. P., *'Veneta Auctoritate Notarius': storia del notariato veneziano (1514–1797)*, Milan, 1996.

Pederzani I., *Venezia e lo 'Stado de Terraferma': il governo delle comunità nel territorio bergamasco (secc- XV–XVIII)*, Milan, 1992.

Peltonen M., *Classical Humanism and Republicanism in English Political Thought, 1570–1640*, Cambridge, 1995.

Persson K. G., 'Was there a Productivity Gap between Fourteenth Century Italy and England?', *Economic History Review*, 46 (1993): 105–114.

Pertusi A., '*Quaedam regalia insignia*: ricerche sulle insegne del potere ducale a Venezia durante il medioevo', *Studi Veneziani*, 7 (1965): 2–124.

Pertusi A. ed., *Venezia e il Levante fino al secolo XV*, Florence, 1973.

Petmezas S., 'El comercio de la pasa de Corinto y su influencia sobre la economía griega del siglo XIX (1840–1914)', in J. Morilla, J. Gómez-Pantoja and P. Cressier eds., *Impactos exteriores sobre la agricultura mediterranea*, Madrid, 1997, 523–562.

Petti Balbi G., *Mercanti e nationes nelle Fiandre: i genovesi in età bassomedievale*, Pisa, 1996.

Petti Balbi G., 'Presenze straniere a Genova nei secoli XII–XIV: letteratura, fonti, temi di ricerca', in G. Rossetti ed., *Dentro la città: stranieri e realtà urbane nell'Europa dei secoli XII–XVI*, Naples, 1989, 121–135.

Pezzolo L., *Una finanza d'Ancien Régime: la repubblica veneta tra XV e XVIII secolo*, Naples, 2006.

Pezzolo L., 'La finanza pubblica', in G. Cozzi and P. Prodi eds., *Storia di Venezia*, vol. iv: *Dal Rinascimento al Barocco*, Rome, 1994, 713–773.

Pezzolo L., *Il fisco dei veneziani: finanza pubblica ed economia tra XV e XVII secolo*, Verona, 2003.

Pezzolo L., *L'oro dello stato: società, finanza e fisco nella Repubblica veneta del secondo '500*, Venice, 1990.

Pezzolo L., 'Sistema di potere e politica finanziaria nella Repubblica di Venezia (secoli XV–XVII)', in G. Chittolini, A. Molho and P. Schiera eds., *Origini dello Stato: processi di formazione statale in Italia fra medioevo ed età moderna*, Bologna, 1994, 303–327.

Pezzolo L., 'Sistema di valori ed attività economica a Venezia, 1530–1630', in S. Cavaciocchi ed., *L'impresa, l'industria, commercio, banca, secoli XII–XVIII*, Florence, 1991, 981–988.

Pezzolo L., 'Stato, guerra e finanza nella Repubblica di Venezia fra medioevo e prima età moderna', in R. Cancila ed., *Mediterraneo in armi (sec. XV–XVIII)*, Palermo, 2007, 67–112.

Pezzolo L., 'The Venetian Economy', in E. Dursteler ed., *A Companion to Venetian History, 1400–1797*, Leiden and Boston, 2013, 255–290.

Pignatorre M. and N. Pignatorre, *Memorie storiche e critiche dell'isola di Cefalonia dai tempi eroici alla caduta della Repubblica veneta*, Corfu, 1887–1889.

Pincus S., *Protestantism and Patriotism: Ideologies and the Making of English Foreign Policy, 1650–1668*, Cambridge, 1996.

Pincus S., 'Rethinking Mercantilism: Political Economy, the British Empire and the Atlantic World in the Seventeenth and Eighteenth Centuries', *William and Mary Quarterly*, 69 (2012): 3–34.

Pinto G., 'Gli stranieri nelle realtà locali dell'Italia basso-medievale: alcuni percorsi tematici', in G. Rossetti ed., *Dentro la città: stranieri e realtà urbane nell'Europa dei secoli XII–XVI*, Naples, 1989, 23–32.

Pisani P., *L'expédition Russo-Turque aux Îles Ioniennes en 1798–1799*, n.p., n.d., [*Revue d'histoire diplomatique*, undated reprint].

Plumidis G., 'Considerazioni sulla popolazione greca a Venezia nella seconda metà del '500', *Studi Veneziani*, 14 (1972): 219–226.

Pocock J. G. A., *The Machiavellian Moment: Florentine Political Thought and the Atlantic Republican Tradition*, Princeton, 1975.

Pomeranz K., 'Social History and World History: From Daily Life to Patterns of Change', *Journal of World History*, 18 (2007): 69–98.

Postan M., *Medieval Trade and Finance*, Cambridge, 2002 (1973).

Povolo C., 'The Creation of Venetian Historiography', in J. Martin and D. Romano eds., *Venice Reconsidered: The History and Civilization of an Italian City-State, 1297–1797*, Baltimore, 2000, 491–519.

Pozza M. and G. Ravegnani, *I trattati con Bisanzio, 992–1285*, 2 vols., Venice, 1993–1996.

Pratt M., *Britain's Greek Empire: Reflections on the History of the Ionian Islands from the Fall of Byzantium*, London, 1978.

Preto P., *Venezia e i Turchi*, Florence, 1975.

Price W. H., *The English Patents of Monopoly*, Boston and New York, 1906.

Prodi P., 'Introduzione: evoluzione e metamorfosi delle identità collettive', in P. Prodi and W. Reinhard eds., *Identità collettive fra Medioevo ed Età Moderna*, Bologna, 2002, 9–27.

Publicover L., 'Strangers at Home: The Sherley Brothers and Dramatic Romance', *Renaissance Studies*, 24 (2010): 694–709.

Pullan B. ed., *Crisis and Change in the Venetian Economy in the Sixteenth and Seventeenth Centuries*, London, 1968.

Pullan B., *The Jews of Europe and the Inquisition of Venice, 1550–1670*, Oxford, 1983.

Querini P. *et al.*, *Il naufragio della Querina*, P. Nelli ed., Venice, 2007.

Raggio O., *Faide e parentele: lo stato genovese visto dalla Fontanabuona*, Turin, 1990.

Ramsay G. D., *The City of London in International Politics at the Accession of Elizabeth Tudor*, Manchester, 1975.

Ramsay G. D., 'The Undoing of the Italian Mercantile Colony in Sixteenth Century London', in N. B. Harte and K. G. Ponting eds., *Textile History and Economic History: Essays in Honour of Miss Julia de Lacy Mann*, Manchester, 1973, 22–49.

Ramsay G., 'Thomas More, Joint Keeper of the Exchange: A Forgotten Episode in the History of Exchange Control in England', *Historical Research*, 84 (2011): 586–600.

Ramsey W., *The Worshipful Company of Glass-Sellers of London*, London, 1898.

Ramusio G. B., *Navigazioni e viaggi*, M. Milanesi ed., 6 vols, Turin, 1978–1980.

Rapp R. T., 'Real Estate and Rational Investment in Early Modern Venice', *Journal of European Economic History*, 8 (1979): 269–290.

Rapp R. T., 'The Unmaking of the Mediterranean Trade Hegemony: International Trade Rivalry and the Commercial Revolution', *Journal of Economic History*, 35 (1975): 499–525.

Rappaport S., *Worlds within Worlds: Structures of Life in Sixteenth-Century London*, Cambridge, 1989.

Ravid B., *Studies on the Jews of Venice, 1382–1797*, Aldershot, 2003.

Ravid B., 'A Tale of Three Cities and their "Raison d'Etat": Ancona, Venice, Livorno and the Competition for Jewish Merchants in the Sixteenth Century', in A. Meyuhas Ginio ed., *Jews, Christians and Muslims in the Mediterranean World after 1492*, London, 1992, 138–161.

Ravid B., 'Venice and its Minorities', in E. Dursteler ed., *A Companion to Venetian History, 1400–1797*, Leiden and Boston, 2013, 449–485.

Rawlinson H. G., 'Life in an English Factory in the Seventeenth Century', *Proceedings of the Indian Historical Record Commission*, 3 (1921): 24–35.

Redford D., 'The Royal Navy, Sea Blindness and British National Identity', in D. Redford ed., *Maritime History and Identity: The Sea and Culture in the Modern World*, London, 2013, 61–78.

Redmond M. J., *Shakespeare, Politics, and Italy: Intertextuality on the Jacobean Stage*, Farnham, 2009.

Reinert S. A., 'Blaming the Medici: Footnotes, Falsification, and the Fate of the "English Model" in Eighteenth-Century Italy', *History of European Ideas*, 32 (2006): 430–455.

Reinert S. A., 'The Empire of Emulation: A Quantitative Analysis of Economic Translations in the European World, 1500–1849', in S. A. Reinert and P. Røge eds., *Political Economy of Empire in the Modern World*, Basingstoke and New York, 2013, 105–128.

Reinert S. A., 'Lessons on the Rise and Fall of Great Powers: Conquest, Commerce, and Decline in Enlightenment Italy', *American Historical Review*, 115 (2010): 1395–1425.

Reinert S. A., *Translating Empire: Emulation and the Origins of Political Economy*, Cambridge (Mass.), 2011.

Rendel R., 'The True Identity of George Ravenscroft, Glassman', *Recusant History*, 13 (1975): 101–105.

Rendel R., 'Who was George Ravenscroft?', *The Glass Circle*, 2 (1975): 65–70.

La révolution française et l'hellenisme moderne, Athens, 1989.

Rich, E. E. and C. H. Wilson eds., *The Cambridge Economic History of Europe*, vol. iv: *The Economy of Expanding Europe in the Sixteenth and Seventeenth Century*, Cambridge, 1967.

Rizo-Rangabè E., *Livre d'or del noblesse ionienne*, Athens, 1927.

Roberti M., *Le magistrature giudiziarie veneziane e i loro capitolari fino al 1600*, 3 vols., Padua, 1906.

Rodger N. A. M., 'Queen Elizabeth and the Myth of Sea-Power in English History', *Transactions of the Royal Historical Society*, 14 (2004): 153–174.

Rodger N. A. M., *The Safeguard of the Sea*, vol. i: *A Naval History of Britain (660–1649)*, London, 1997.

Rodocanachi E., *Bonaparte et les Îles Ioniennes: un épisode des Conquêtes de la République et du Premier Empire (1797–1816)*, Paris, 1899.

Rogers J. E. T. ed., *A History of Agriculture and Prices in England*, 7 vols., Oxford, 1963 (1856–1902).

Romanin S., *Storia documentata di Venezia*, 10 vols, Venice, 1858–1861.

Rosand D., *Myths of Venice: The Figuration of a State*, Chapel Hill, 2001.

Roseveare H. ed., *Markets and Merchants of the Late Seventeenth Century: The Marescoe-David Letters 1668–1680*, Oxford, 1987.

Rossetti G. ed., *Dentro la città: stranieri e realtà urbane nell'Europa dei secoli XII–XVI*, Naples, 1989.

Rothman E. N., *Brokering Empire: Trans-Imperial Subjects between Venice and Istanbul*, Ithaca, 2012.

Routh E. M. G., 'The English at Tangier', *English Historical Review*, 26 (1911): 469–481.

Rublack U., *Dressing Up: Cultural Identity in Renaissance Europe*, Oxford, 2010.

Ruddock A. A., *Italian Merchants and Shipping in Southampton, 1270–1600*, Southampton, 1951.

Ruiz Martín F., 'La banca genovesa en España durante el siglo XVII', in D. Puncuh and G. Felloni eds., *Banchi pubblici, banchi privati e monti di pietà nell'Europa preindustriale: amministrazione, tecniche operative e ruoli economici*, 2 vols., Genoa, 1991, i: 265–274.

Ruskin J., *The Stones of Venice: The Foundations*, London, 1851.

Ruspio F., *La nazione portoghese: ebrei ponentini e nuovi cristiani a Venezia*, Turin, 2007.

Russell E., 'The Societies of the Bardi and the Peruzzi and Their Dealings with Edward III', in G. Unwin ed., *Finance and Trade under Edward III: The London Lay Subsidy of 1332*, London, 1918, 93–135.

Sacks D. H., *The Widening Gate: Bristol and the Atlantic Economy 1450–1700*, Berkeley, Los Angeles and Oxford, 1991.

Sagredo G., 'Relazione d'Inghilterra (1656)', in L. Firpo ed., *Relazioni di ambasciatori veneti al Senato*, vol. i: *Inghilterra*, Turin, 1965, 851–874.

Sanderson J., *The Travels of John Sanderson in the Levant 1584–1602*, Sir W. Foster ed., London, 1931.
Sandi V., *Principi di Storia Civile della Repubblica di Venezia dalla sua fondazione fino all'anno di n.s. 1700*, Venice, 1756.
Sandys G., *A Relation of a Journey began AD 1610. Foure bookes. Containing a description of the Turkish Empire, of Ægypt, of the Holy Land, of the remote parts of Italy, and ilands adioning*, London, 1627.
Sanudo M., *De origine, situ et magistratibus urbis veneta ovvero la Città di Venetia (1493–1530)*, A. Caracciolo Aricò ed., Milan, 1980.
Sanudo M., *I diarii*, R. Fulin ed. *et al.*, 58 vols., Venice 1879–1903.
Sapori A., *La crisi delle compagnie mercantili dei Bardi e dei Peruzzi*, Florence, 1926.
Sarpi P., *The Historie of the Councel of Trent*, London, 1620.
Sarpi P., *Opere*, G. and L. Cozzi eds., Milan and Naples, 1969.
[Sarpi P.] Pietro Soave Polano, *Historia del Concilio Tridentino*, London, 1619.
Scammell G. V., 'Shipowning in the Economy and Politics of Early Modern England', *The Historical Journal*, 15 (1972): 385–407.
Schwarzfuchs S. and A. Toaff eds., *The Mediterranean and the Jews: Banking, Finance and International Trade, XVI–XVIII*, Ramat Gan, 1989.
Scott J., *When the Waves Ruled Britannia: Geography and Political Identities, 1500–1800*, Cambridge, 2011.
Scouloudi I., 'Alien Immigration into and Alien Communities in London, 1558–1640', *Proceedings of the Huguenot Society of London*, 16 (1937–1941): 27–49.
Scouloudi I. ed., *Huguenots in Britain and their French Background, 1550–1800*, London, 1987.
Selden J., *The Dominion or Ownership of the Sea: Two Books Translated by Marchmont Needham*, London, 1652.
Select Cases Concerning the Law Merchant, AD 1270–1638, 3 vols., London, 1908–1932.
Sella D., *Commerci e industrie a Venezia nel secolo XVII*, Venice and Rome, 1961.
Sella D., *Crisis and Continuity: The Economy of Spanish Lombardy in the Seventeenth Century*, Cambridge (Mass.), 1979.
Sella D., 'Crisis and Transformation in Venetian Trade', and 'The Rise and Fall of the Venetian Woollen Industry', both in B. Pullan ed., *Crisis and Change in the Venetian Economy in the Sixteenth and Seventeenth Centuries*, London, 1968, 88–105, and 106–126.
Shammas C., 'Changes in English and Anglo-American Consumption from 1550–1800', in J. Brewer and R. Porter eds., *Consumption and the World of Goods*, London and New York, 1993, 177–205.
Shaw J. E., 'Retail, Monopoly and Privilege: The Dissolution of the Fishmongers' Guild of Venice, 1599', *Journal of Early Modern History*, 6 (2002): 396–427.
Sherman W. H., 'Bringing the World to England: The Politics of Translation in the Age of Hakluyt', *Transactions of the Royal Historical Society*, 14 (2004): 199–207.
Sicca C. M., 'Consumption and Trade of Art between Italy and England in the First Half of the Sixteenth Century: The London House of the Bardi and Cavalcanti Company', *Renaissance Studies*, 16 (2002): 163–201.
Sicca C. M., 'Pawns of International Finance and Politics: Florentine Sculptors at the Court of Henry VIII', *Renaissance Studies*, 20 (2006): 1–34.

Sicking L., 'Naval Warfare in Europe c.1330–c.1680', in F. Tallett and D. J. B. Trim eds., *European Warfare, 1350–1750*, Cambridge, 2010, 236–263.

Simonsfeld H., *Der Fondaco dei Tedeschi in Venedig und die deutschvenetianischen Handelsbeziehungen*, 2 vols., Stuttgart, 1887.

Skilliter S. A., *William Harborne and the Trade with Turkey: A Documentary Study of the First Anglo-Ottoman Relations*, Oxford, 1977.

Skippon P., *An Account of a Journey made thro' part of the Low Countries, Germany, Italy and France*, London, 1752.

Skoufari E., *Cipro veneziana, 1473–1571: istituzioni e culture nel regno della Serenissima*, Rome, 2011.

Smith A., *An Inquiry into the Nature and Causes of the Wealth of Nations*, London, 1799.

[Smith Sir Thomas], *A Discourse of the Common Weal of this Realm of England* [1549], E. Lamond ed., Cambridge, 1929.

Soly H., "The 'Betrayal" of the Sixteenth-Century Bourgeoisie: A Myth? Some Considerations of the Behaviour Pattern of the Merchants of Antwerp in the Sixteenth Century', *Acta Historiae Neerlandicae*, 8 (1975): 31–49.

Stabel P., 'Venice and the Low Countries: Commercial Contacts and Intellectual Inspirations', in *Renaissance in Venice and in the North: Crosscurrents in the time of Dürer, Bellini and Titian*, London, 1999, 31–43.

Steckley G. F., 'The Wine Economy of Tenerife in the Seventeenth Century: Anglo-Spanish Partnership in a Luxury Trade', *Economic History Review*, 33 (1980): 335–350.

Steensgaard N., *The Asian Trade Revolution in the Seventeenth Century*, London, 1973.

Steensgaard N., *Carrack, Caravans and Companies: The Structural Crisis in the European-Asian Trade in the Early Seventeenth Century*, Copenhagen, 1973.

Steensgaard N., 'The Companies as a Specific Institution in the History of European Expansion', in L. Blussé and F. Gaastra eds., *Companies and Trade*, Leiden, 1981, 245–264.

Steensgaard N., 'Consuls and Nations in the Levant from 1570 to 1650', *Scandinavian Economic History Review*, 15 (1967): 13–55.

Stone L., *An Elizabethan: Sir Horatio Pallavicino*, Oxford, 1956.

Storia di Venezia, 12 vols., Rome, 1991–1997.

Stouraiti A., 'Talk, Script and Print: The Making of Island Books in Early Modern Venice', *Historical Research*, 86 (2013): 207–229.

Stouraiti A. and M. Infelise eds., *Venezia e la Guerra di Morea: guerra, politica e cultura alla fine del Seicento*, Milan, 2005.

Stoye J., *English Travellers Abroad, 1604–1667: Their Influence in English Society and Politics*, London, 1989.

Strachan M., *Sir Thomas Roe, 1581–1644: A Life*, Salisbury, 1989.

Stumpo E., 'Livorno in età granducale: la città ideale e la patria di tutti', in S. Balbi de Caro ed., *Merci e monete a Livorno in età granducale*, Milan, 1997, 105–137.

Subacchi P., 'Italians in Antwerp in the Second Half of the Sixteenth Century', in H. Soly and A. K. L. Thijs eds., *Minorities in Western European Cities (Sixteenth-Seventeenth Centuries)*, Brussels, 1995, 73–90.

Subrahmanyam S ed., *Merchants Networks in the Early Modern World*, Aldershot, 1996.

Sullivan V. B., *Machiavelli, Hobbes, and the Formation of a Liberal Republicanism in England*, Cambridge, 2004.

Summit J., *Memory's Library: Medieval Books in Early Modern England*, Chicago, 2008.

Supple B. E., *Commercial Crisis and Change in England 1600–1642*, Cambridge, 1964 (1942).

Sweet R., *Cities and the Grand Tour: The British in Italy ca. 1690–1820*, Cambridge, 2012.

Syros V., 'Between Chimera and Charybdis: Byzantine and Post-Byzantine Views on the Political Organization of the Italian City-States', *Journal of Early Modern History*, 14 (2010): 451–504.

Tabacco G., *Andrea Tron e la crisi dell'aristocrazia senatoria a Venezia*, Udine, 1980.

Tagliaferri A., *Per una storia sociale della Repubblica Veneta: la rivolta di Arzignano del 1665*, Udine, 1978.

Tait H., *The Golden Age of Venetian Glass*, London, 1979.

Tawney R. H., *Business and Politics under James I: Lionel Cranfield as Merchant and Minister*, Cambridge, 1958.

Tawney R. H. and E. E. Power eds., *Tudor Economic Documents*, 3 vols., London, 1924.

Tenenti A., 'Aspetti della vita Mediterranea intorno al '600', *Bollettino dell'Istituto di storia della società e dello stato veneziano*, ii (1960): 3–17.

Tenenti A., 'La congiuntura veneto-ungherese tra la fine del Quattrocento e gli inizi del Cinquecento', in V. Branca ed., *Venezia e Ungheria nel Rinascimento*, Florence, 1973, 135–143.

Tenenti A., 'Le isole Ionie: un'area di frontiera', in M. Costantini ed., *Il Mediterraneo centro-orientale tra vecchie e nuove egemonie: trasformazioni economiche, sociale ed istituzionali nelle Isole Ionie dal declino della Serenissima all'avvento delle potenze atlantiche (sec. XVII–XVIII)*, Rome, 1998, 11–18.

Tenenti A., *Naufrages, corsaires et assurances maritimes à Venise 1592–1609*, Paris, 1959.

Tenenti A., 'La navigazione veneziana nel Seicento', in G. Benzoni and G. Cozzi eds., *Storia di Venezia dalle origini alla caduta della Serenissima*, vol. vii: *La Venezia barocca*, Rome, 1997, 533–567.

Tenenti A., *Piracy and the Decline of Venice*, London, 1967.

Tenenti A., 'La politica veneziana e l'Ungheria all'epoca di Sigismondo', in T. Klaniczay ed., *Rapporti Veneto-ungheresi all'epoca del Rinascimento*, Budapest, 1975, 219–229.

Tenenti A., 'Profilo di un conflitto secolare', in *Venezia e i Turchi: scontri e confronti di due civiltà*, Milan, 1985, 9–37.

Tenenti A., 'Proiezioni patrizie quattrocentesche alle soglie dell'ignoto', in *Studi veneti offerti a Gaetano Cozzi*, Venice, 1992, 109–120.

Tenenti A., 'Il senso del mare', in A. Tenenti and U. Tucci eds., *Storia di Venezia*, vol. xii: *Il mare*, Rome, 1991, 7–76.

Tenenti A., 'Il senso dello spazio e del tempo nel mondo veneziano dei secoli XV e XVI', in *Credenze, ideologie, libertinismi tra Medioevo ed età moderna*, Bologna, 1978, 75–118.

Tenenti A., 'Venezia e la pirateria nel Levante: 1300 circa–1460 circa', in A. Pertusi ed., *Venezia e il Levante fino al secolo XV*, Florence, 1973, 705–771.

Tenenti A., *Venezia e il senso del mare: storia di un prisma culturale dal XIII al XVIII secolo*, Milan, 1999.

Tenenti A. and B. Tenenti, *Il prezzo del rischio: l'assicurazione mediterranea vista da Ragusa (1563–1591)*, Rome, 1985.

Tenenti B., 'Venezia ed il commercio raguseo delle carisee (1550c.–1620c.)', *Studi Veneziani*, 17–18 (1975–76): 235–247.

Thiriet F., *La Romanie vénitienne su moyen âge: le développement et exploitation du domaine colonial vénitienne (XII–XV siècles)*, Paris, 1959.

Thiriet F., 'Sur les communautés grecque et albanaise à Venise', in H. G. Beck, M. Manoussacas and A. Pertusi eds., *Venezia, centro di mediazione tra Oriente e Occidente (secoli XV–XVI): aspetti e problemi*, 2 vols., Florence, 1977, i: 217–231.

Thirsk J., *Economic Policies and Projects: The Development of a Consumer Society in Modern England*, Oxford, 1978.

Thirsk J., *Food in Early Modern England: Phases, Fads, Fashions 1500–1760*, London, 2007.

Thomas G. M., *Capitolare dei Visdomini del Fontego dei Todeschi in Venezia*, Berlin, 1874.

Tiepolo M. F. et al. eds., *Archivio di Stato di Venezia: estratto dal vol. IV della Guida Generale degli Archivi di Stato Italiani*, Rome, 1994.

Tilly C., 'Entanglements of European Cities and States', in C. Tilly and W. P. Blockmans eds., *Cities and the Rise of States in Europe, AD 1000–1800*, Boulder, 1994, 1–27.

Tilmouth M., 'Music on the Travels of an English Merchant: Robert Bargrave (1628–61)', *Music and Letters*, 53 (1972): 143–159.

Toaff R., *La nazione ebrea a Livorno e a Pisa (1591–1700)*, Florence, 1990.

Trampus A., 'La formazione del diritto consolare moderno a Venezia e nelle Province Unite tra Seicento e Settecento', *Rivista di Storia del Diritto Italiano*, 67 (1994): 283–319.

Trivellato F., *The Familiarity of Strangers: The Sephardic Diaspora, Livorno, and Cross-Cultural Trade in the Early Modern Period*, New Haven and London, 2009.

Trivellato F., *Fondamenta dei vetrai: lavoro, tecnologia e mercato a Venezia tra Sei e Settecento*, Rome, 2000.

Trivellato F., 'Guilds, Technology and Economic Change in Early Modern Venice', in S. R. Epstein and M. Prak eds., *Guilds, Innovation, and the European Economy, 1400–1800*, Cambridge, 2008, 199–231.

Trivellato F., 'Murano Glass, Continuity and Transformation (1400–1800)', in P. Lanaro ed., *At the Center of the Old World: Trade and Manufacturing in Venice and the Venetian Mainland, 1400–1800*, Toronto, 2006, 143–184.

A True and Credible Report of a great fight at sea . . ., London, 1600.

Tucci U., 'Le commerce venitien du vin de Crete', in K. Friedland ed., *Maritime Food Transport*, Cologne, 1994, 199–211.

Tucci U., 'Il commercio del vino nell'economia cretese', in G. Ortalli ed., *Venezia e Creta*, Venice, 1998, 183–206.

Tucci U., 'La Grecia e l'economia veneziana', in G. Benzoni ed., *L'eredità greca e l'ellenismo veneziano*, Florence, 2002, 139–156.

Tucci U., *Mercanti, navi e monete nel Cinquecento veneziano*, Bologna, 1981.

Tucci U., 'The Psychology of the Venetian Merchant', in J. R. Hale ed., *Renaissance Venice*, London, 1973, 346–378.

Unger R. W., 'Dutch Herring, Technology and International Trade in the Seventeenth Century', *Journal of Economic History*, 40 (1980): 253–280.

Unger R. W., 'The Technology and Teaching of Shipbuilding 1300–1800', in M. Prak and J. Luiten van Zanden eds., *Technology, Skills and the Pre-Modern Economy in the East and the West*, Leiden, 2013, 161–204.

Ungerer G., *The Mediterranean Apprenticeship of British Slavery*, Madrid, 2008.

van den Boogert M. H., *The Capitulations and the Ottoman Legal System: Qadis, Consuls and Beraths in the 18th Century*, Leiden and Boston, 2005.

van der Wee H., 'Structural Changes in European Long-Distance Trade, and Particularly in the Re-Export Trade from South to North, 1350–1750', in J. D. Tracy ed., *The Rise of Merchant Empires: Long-Distance Trade in the Early Modern World, 1350–1750*, Cambridge, 1990, 14–33.

van Doosselaere Q., *Commercial Agreements and Social Dynamics in Medieval Genoa*, Cambridge, 2009.

Vanes J. ed., *Documents Illustrating the Overseas Trade of Bristol in the Sixteenth Century*, Bristol, 1979.

van Gelder M., 'Acquiring Artistic Expertise: The Agent Daniel Nijs and His Contacts with Artists in Venice', in M. Keblusek and B. Noldus eds., *Double Agents: Cultural and Political Brokerage in Early Modern Europe*, Leiden and Boston, 2010, 111–124.

van Gelder M., 'Favouring Foreign Traders? The Venetian Republic and the Accommodation of Netherlandish Merchants in the Late Sixteenth and Seventeenth Centuries', in U. Bosma, G. Kessler and L. Lucassen eds., *Migration and Membership Regimes in Global and Historical Perspective*, Leiden and Boston, 2013, 141–166.

van Gelder M., 'Gaining Entrance to the Venetian Patriciate in the Seventeenth Century: The van Axel and Ghelthof Families from the Low Countries', *Mélanges de l'École française de Rome: Italie et Méditerranée modernes et contemporaines*, 125/1 (2013).

van Gelder M., 'Supplying the *Serenissima*: The Role of Flemish Merchants in the Venetian Grain Trade during the First Phase of the *Straatvaart*', *International Journal of Maritime History*, 16 (2004): 39–60.

van Gelder M., *Trading Places: The Netherlandish Merchants in Early Modern Venice*, Leiden and Boston, 2009.

van Gelderen M. and Q. Skinner eds., *Republicanism: A Shared European Heritage*, 2 vols., Cambridge, 2005.

van Royen P. C., 'The First Phase of the Dutch *Straatvaart* (1591–1605): Fact and Fiction', *International Journal of Maritime History*, 2 (1990): 69–102.

van Royen P. C., 'The Maritime Relations between the Dutch Republic and Italy, 1590–1605', in R. Mazzei and T. Fanfani eds., *Lucca e L'Europa degli affari*, Lucca, 1990, 243–272.

Varanini G. M., 'Proprietà fondiaria e agricoltura', in A. Tenenti and U. Tucci eds., *Storia di Venezia*, vol. v: *Il Rinascimento: società ed economia*, Rome, 1985, 807–879.

Venezia e la difesa del Levante: da Lepanto a Candia 1570–1670, Venice, 1986.

Venezia ed il Levante fino al secolo XV, 2 vols., Florence, 1973–1974.

Venezia e l'Oriente tra tardo Medioevo e Rinascimento, Florence, 1966.

Venning T., *Cromwellian Foreign Policy*, Basingstoke, 1995.

Ventura A., *Nobiltà e popolo nella società veneta del Quattrocento e Cinquecento*, Milan, 1993 (1964).

Vercellin G., 'Mercanti turchi e sensali a Venezia', *Studi Veneziani*, n.s. 4 (1980): 45–78.

Vianello F. M., *Seta fine e panni grossi: manifatture e commerci nel Vicentino, 1570–1700*, Milan, 2004.

Viggiano A., *Governanti e governati: legittimità del potere ed esercizio dell'autorità nello stato veneto della prima età moderna*, Treviso, 1993.

Viggiano A., *Lo specchio della repubblica: Venezia e il governo delle isole Ionie nel '700*, Sommacampagna, 1998.

Villani S., '"Una piccola epitome di Inghilterra". La comunità inglese di Livorno negli anni di Ferdinando II: questioni religiose e politiche', in S. Villani, S. Tutino and C. Franceschini eds., *Questioni di storia inglese tra Cinque e Seicento: cultura, politica e religione*, Pisa, 2003, 179–208.

Villari L., *The Republic of Ragusa*, London, 1904, 264.

Vitali A., *La moda a Venezia attraverso i secoli: lessico ragionato*, Venice, 1992.

Vlassi D., 'La politica annonaria di Venezia a Cefalonia: il fondaco delle biade (sec. XVI–XVIII)', *Thesaurismata*, 25 (1995): 274–318.

von Wartburg M.-L., 'Production de sucre de canne à Chypre: un chapitre de technologie médiévale', in M. Balard and A. Ducellier eds., *Coloniser au Moyen Âge*, Paris, 1995, 126–131.

Walker J., '*Bravi* and Venetian Nobles, c.1550–1650', *Studi Veneziani*, n.s. 36 (1998): 85–113.

Watson I. B., 'Fortifications and the "Idea" of Force in Early English East India Company Relations with India', *Past and Present*, 88 (1980): 70–87.

Wheatley H. B. ed., *The Diary of John Evelyn*, London, 1906.

Wicquefort [Monsieur de], *The Rights Privileges and Office of Embassadors and Publick Ministers. Illustrated with Historical Narrations of the most important Affairs that have been transacted by them through all the Courts of Europe ...*, London, 1740 (1682).

Willan T. S., 'Some Aspects of English Trade with the Levant in the Sixteenth Century', *English Historical Review*, 70 (1955): 399–410.

Willan T. S., *Studies in Elizabethan Foreign Trade*, Manchester, 1959.

Williamson J. A., *Maritime Enterprise 1485–1558*, Oxford, 1913.

Williamson J. B., *The Foreign Commerce of England under the Tudors*, London, 1883.

Wills G., *Venice, Lion City, the Religion of Empire*, London and New York, 2001.

Wood A. C., *A History of the Levant Company*, Oxford, 1935.

Wootton D., 'Ulysses Bound? Venice and the Idea of Liberty from Howell to Hume', in D. Wootton ed., *Republicanism, Liberty, and Commercial Society, 1649–1776*, Stanford, 1994.

Wrigley W. D., *The Diplomatic Significance of Ionian Neutrality, 1821–31*, New York, 1988.

Wyatt M., *The Italian Encounter with Tudor England: A Cultural Politics of Translation*, Cambridge, 2005.

Yannacopoulou H., 'Français, républicains et impériaux, aux sept Îles Ioniennes: quelques aspects de leur présence', in *La révolution française et l'hellenisme moderne*, Athens, 1989, 137–154.

Yannoupoulos G., 'State and Society in the Ionian Islands, 1800–1830', in G. Clogg ed., *Balkan Society in the Age of Greek Independence*, London, 1981, 43–45.

Yates F. A., 'Paolo Sarpi's "History of the Council of Trent"', *The Journal of the Warburg and Courtauld Institutes*, 7 (1944): 123–142.

Zanatta F., 'L'inventario come fonte per lo studio della storia della ricchezza privata: Venezia nel 1661', *Studi veneziani*, 34 (1997): 199–223.

Zannini A., *Burocrazia e burocrati a Venezia in età moderna: i cittadini originari (sec. XVI–XVIII)*, Venice, 1993.

Zannini A., 'Economic and Social Aspects of the Crisis of Venetian Diplomacy in the Seventeenth and Eighteenth Centuries', in D. Frigo ed., *Politics and Diplomacy in Early Modern Italy: The Structures of Diplomatic Practice, 1450–1800*, Cambridge, 2000, 109–146.

Zecchin L., *Vetro e vetrai di Murano*, 3 vols., Venice, 1987–1989–1990.

Zorzi A., *Una città, una repubblica, un impero, Venezia: 697–1797*, Milan, 1980.

Zucconi G., 'Corcira Britannica: Urban Architecture and Strategies in the Capital of the Ionian Islands', in E. Concina and A. Nikiforou-Testone eds., *Corfu: History, Urban Space and Architecture, 14th–19th centuries*, Corfu, 1994, 95–103.

Dissertations

Allerston P., *The Market in Second Hand Goods in Venice, c.1500–1650*, Ph.D. thesis, European University Institute, Florence, 1996.

Ambrose G. P., *The Levant Company mainly from 1640 to 1753*, B.Litt. thesis, Oxford University, 1933.

Anderson C., *Art Dealing and Collecting in Venice: The Multi-Faceted Career of Daniel Nijs (1572–1647), Broker of the Gonzaga Sale*, University of Oxford, D. Phil. thesis, 2010.

Ball J. G., *The Greek Community in Venice 1470–1620*, Ph.D. thesis, University of London, 1985.

Baroutsos F., *Customs and Fiscal Policies in late Renaissance Crete*, Ph.D. thesis, University of Athens, 2000.

Blakemore R. J., *The London & Thames Maritime Community during the British Civil Wars, 1640–1649*, Ph.D. thesis, University of Cambridge, 2013.

Bradley H., *The Italian Community in London, c.1350–c.1450*, Ph.D. thesis, University of London, 1992.

Bratchel M. E., *Alien Merchant Communities in London, 1500–1550*, Ph.D. thesis, Cambridge University, 1975.

Burke E., *The Greek Neighbourhoods of Sixteenth Century Venice, 1498–1600: Daily Life of an Immigrant Community*, Ph.D. thesis, University of Monash, 2004.

Iordanou I., *Maritime Communities in Late Renaissance Venice: The Arsenalotti and the Greeks*, Ph.D. thesis, University of Warwick, 2008.

Lang R. G., *The Greater Merchants of London in the early Seventeenth Century*, Ph.D. thesis, Oxford University, 1963.

Millard A. M., *The Import Trade of London, 1600–1640*, Ph.D. thesis, University of London, 1956.

Poyser E. R., *Anglo-Italian Trade from the Reign of Elizabeth to the French Revolution with Special Reference to the Port of Leghorn*, M.Litt. thesis, University of Cambridge, 1951.

Roby W., *The History of the Levant Company 1603–1681: A Study in Commercial History*, M.A. thesis, University of Manchester, 1927.

Scaife J., *Venetian Trade and Commercial Relations with England in the Early Tudor Period, 1485–1550*, Ph.D. thesis, University of Kent, 1980.

Terzi M. P., *Una vicenda della Venezia seicentesca: l'amicizia e la corrispondenza tra Fulgenzio Micanzio e Sir Dudley Carleton, ambasciatore d'Inghilterra*, tesi di laurea, University of Venice, 1979.

Tumelty J. J., *The Ionian Islands under British Administration, 1815–1864*, Ph.D. thesis, University of Cambridge, 1952.

van Gelder M., *De Vlaamse natie te Venetië, 1590–1620*, M.A. dissertation, University of Amsterdam, 1999.

Walker J., *Honour and the Culture of the Male Venetian Nobles, c.1500–1650*, Ph.D. thesis, Cambridge University, 1998.

Walters L. M., *Odoardo Faletti (1573–ca1638): The Interrelation of Venetian Art and Fanatomy, and His Importance in England*, Ph.D. thesis, University of St Andrews, 2009.

Index

Page numbers in italics indicate footnotes

Lightning Source UK Ltd.
Milton Keynes UK
UKHW010750291219
355996UK00020B/3899/P